Behavioral Economics

Behavioral Economics: Evidence, Theory, and Welfare provides an engaging and accessible introduction to the motivating questions, real-world evidence, theoretical models, and welfare implications of behavioral economics concepts. Applications and examples — from household decisions, finance, public finance, labor, business, health, development, politics, education, energy, and sports — illustrate the broad relevance of behavioral economics for consumers, firms, markets, and policy makers alike.

This textbook provides readers with both the intuition and analytical tools to apply behavioral economics concepts in understanding the complex social world. Each part of the book covers a key concept, beginning with a range of empirical evidence that is anomalous within the standard economics framework. In light of this evidence, a second chapter introduces and applies a nonstandard behavioral modeling approach. The last chapter of each part explores market and policy responses to individuals behaving in nonstandard ways. Numerous exercises of varying types and levels provide readers the opportunity to check and enrich their understanding.

The book's clear structure orients readers to the many concepts of behavioral economics. It also highlights the process by which economists evaluate evidence and disentangle theories with different social welfare implications. Accessible to students from diverse economic backgrounds, this textbook is an ideal resource for courses on behavioral economics, experimental economics, and related areas. The accompanying Solutions Manual further extends learning and engagement.

Brandon Lehr is Associate Professor of Economics at Occidental College, Los Angeles, USA.

Behavioral Economics

Evidence, Theory, and Welfare

Brandon Lehr

LONDON AND NEW YORK

First published 2022
by Routledge
2 Park Square, Milton Park, Abingdon, Oxon OX14 4RN

and by Routledge
605 Third Avenue, New York, NY 10158

Routledge is an imprint of the Taylor & Francis Group, an informa business

© 2022 Brandon Lehr

British Library Cataloguing-in-Publication Data
A catalogue record for this book is available from the British Library

Library of Congress Cataloging-in-Publication Data
A catalog record has been requested for this book

ISBN: 978-0-367-42646-0 (hbk)
ISBN: 978-0-367-42644-6 (pbk)
ISBN: 978-0-367-85407-2 (ebk)

DOI: 10.4324/9780367854072

Typeset in Bembo
by Apex CoVantage, LLC

Access the Support Material: www.routledge.com/9780367426446

For B.A.

Contents

Empirical Evidence from the Field, by Topic

Household

- Section 4.5.5: Life-Cycle Evidence
- Section 5.4.3: Present-Biased Life-Cycle Evidence
- Section 5.4.4: Credit Card Take-Up
- Exercise 5.6: Credit Card Conundrum
- Section 9.5.3: Life-Cycle Consumption Expectations
- Exercise 9.13: No Place Like Home
- Section 12.3.1: Home Insurance
- Exercise 12.7: Home Security
- Exercise 13.3: Cultural Offerings
- Section 14.5.2: Conspicuous Consumption
- Section 16.3.1: Gambler's Fallacy
- Exercise 16.7: Double Up
- Exercise 16.10: Hot and Cold Numbers
- Section 19.3: Mental Accounting over the Life Cycle
- Exercise 19.7: Drink Up
- Exercise 19.8: Fuel Fungibility
- Exercise 19.9: A Penchant for Savings
- Exercise 19.10: Sweet Variety
- Section 20.2.1: Inattention to Prices in Auctions
- Section 20.2.3: Inattention to Non-leading Digits
- Exercise 20.2: More Shipping Costs

Finance

- Section 6.6.2: Stock Market Fluctuations
- Sections 8.3 and 9.4: Equity Premium Puzzle
- Exercise 8.4: Endowing IPOs in India
- Section 12.3.2: Stocks as Lotteries
- Section 12.6: Personal Finance with Ambiguity Aversion
- Exercise 12.9: Buying Stocks to the Max
- Section 16.3.2: Extrapolative Beliefs
- Section 17.1.3: Investor Trading Volume
- Section 17.3: Extrapolative Beliefs in Financial Markets
- Exercise 17.12: Anomalous Asset Prices

Public Finance

Health

Education

- Section 5.4.2: School Work
- Exercise 5.8: Setting Deadlines
- Exercise 7.7: Dropping the College Dropout Rate
- Section 10.3: Teacher Compensation
- Section 14.5.2: Peer Pressure
- Exercise 20.10: Ranks Rule
- Exercise 21.12: Schooling Limits

Labor

- Exercise 5.7: Targeting Work
- Exercise 5.9: Punctual Proofreading
- Section 9.5.1: Targeting Income
- Section 9.5.2: Job Search Effort
- Exercise 10.4: Group Work Works
- Section 14.4.2: Gift Exchange
- Exercise 14.8: The Thought Counts
- Exercise 14.10: Marriage Matters
- Section 15.1: Employers
- Section 15.2: Unemployment
- Exercise 15.4: Fairly Unequal Pay
- Exercise 15.5: Sticky Salaries
- Section 18.2: Overconfident Employees

Politics & Law

- Section 6.3.1: Voting Habits
- Section 15.4.1: Voting Pressure
- Exercise 15.10: Visible Voters
- Section 16.3.1: Gambler's Fallacy
- Exercise 17.6: Overconfident Voters
- Section 20.3.2: Persuading Voters
- Exercise 20.13: Surprise Endorsements
- Section 21.5: Government Persuasion

Industrial Organization

- Section 7.2.1: Suggested Tips
- Exercise 10.9: Uniform Prices
- Section 13.1.2: Tipping
- Exercise 13.2: Tip Drivers
- Section 14.5.3: Social Norms
- Section 18.3: Overconfident Consumers
- Section 21.3: Shrouding Add-on Prices

Business

- Section 10.4: Worker Bonuses
- Section 17.1.1: Entrepreneurial Entry
- Section 17.1.2: Managerial Mergers
- Exercise 17.2: Management of Overprecision
- Exercise 17.4: Peering into Entrepreneurship
- Exercise 17.5: Equity Financing
- Exercise 18.2: CEO: Chief Executive Overconfidence
- Section 21.1: Mental Accounting: Selling Strategies

Development

- Exercise 3.11: An Education with No Strings Attached
- Section 4.1.3: Poverty and Discounting
- Exercise 6.1: Soap Solution
- Exercise 7.6: Nudging Farmers to Fertilize
- Section 8.1.2: Exposure to Modern Society
- Exercise 9.8: Lost Profits and Loss Aversion
- Section 14.5.3: Social Norms
- Exercise 15.2: Star Sellers
- Exercise 15.12: Adding Value to Tax Payments
- Section 21.2: Mental Accounting: Savings Policy
- Exercise 21.9: Agricultural Attention

Energy and Environment

- Section 3.6: Energy-Efficient Light Bulb Underuse
- Exercise 3.10: Neighbors as Nudges
- Section 10.2: Reusable Bag Use
- Exercise 21.13: A Lack of Energy

Sports

- Section 8.1.2: Sportscard Trading Experience
- Exercise 9.3: March Madness, Indeed
- Exercise 9.14: Bye Bye Birdie
- Exercise 12.10: Horsing around with Probability
- Exercise 14.11: Bending a Soccer Ball Game
- Section 16.3.1: Gambler's Fallacy
- Section 16.3.2: Extrapolative Beliefs
- Exercise 16.9: Courting Randomness

Note to Instructors

My intention in writing this book is to provide an engaging and accessible introduction to the motivating questions, real-world evidence, and policy implications of behavioral economics concepts that hold relevance for a diverse student population. I have endeavored to balance mathematical formalism with informal intuition when presenting theoretical models. The text is consequently an adaptable resource for economics students at both the introductory and more advanced levels. While I defer a discussion of the book's structure and topics to Section 1.3 — as a guide for students and instructors alike — I highlight below several features of relevance for potential adopters:

- **Foundations**   Part I provides a self-contained introduction to the foundational concepts of economic theory and empirical methods that are applied throughout the text.
- **Modular Organization**   Behavioral deviations from the standard model of decision making are organized as six independent parts, allowing instructors to cover the deviations in any order.
- **Learning Objectives**   Each chapter begins with learning objectives that orient students to the topics ahead.
- **Experimental Evidence Boxes**   In-text experimental evidence boxes highlight the methods and results of lab experiments, field experiments, and quasi-experiments that economists use to test competing economic theories.
- **Definitions**   Definitions of key models and terms are located in boxes for ease of reference. Other important terms are boldfaced when accompanied by an in-text definition.
- **Summaries**   Each chapter concludes with an enumerated summary of the key concepts, models, and evidence introduced.
- **Exercises**   End-of-chapter exercises offer students ample opportunity to further develop their understanding by applying concepts to practical settings, interpreting new empirical evidence, and solving math problems. The exercise order aligns with that of the respective chapter's topics — and not necessarily the difficulty level. Particularly challenging questions include hints and those that require calculus are labeled as such.
- **Math Appendices**   Four chapters include math appendices. Two math appendices apply multivariable calculus tools to study the life-cycle model, while the other two cover supplemental concepts related to reference-dependent preferences.

Acknowledgements

I am indebted to my teachers, without whom I would not be an economist and this book would not exist. As an undergraduate at the University of California, Berkeley I was fortunate to first learn economic theory from Raj Chetty, Emmanuel Saez, Shachar Kariv, David Ahn, and Thomas Marschak. I am similarly grateful for my graduate school professors at MIT who introduced me to behavioral economics: Peter Diamond, Ivan Werning, Glenn Ellison, Amy Finkelstein, Jim Poterba, and Haluk Ergin.

This book has its origins in a course I have taught at Occidental College since 2011. The framework for the course — and subsequently this book — was influenced by Stefano DellaVigna's 2009 *Journal of Economic Literature* survey of psychology and economics. In developing the course I benefited from the generosity of Olga Shurchkov, who shared with me her class materials. Over the years I have adapted exercises from many sources and attempt to give credit for all those that appear in this book.

I have learned much from my wonderful Oxy students and colleagues. I am particularly thankful for the advice and encouragement from Woody Studenmund to pursue this book project. And I acknowledge the generous financial support provided by Occidental's Robinson Scholar Grant, Schwartz Scholar Grant, and Faculty Enrichment Grant.

Finally, the excellent team at Routledge, including Andy Humphries, Natalie Tomlinson, Chloe James, Peter Hall, and Emma Morley, have patiently and expertly guided me through the production process from proposal to publication.

Part I

Foundations

1 Introduction

Learning Objectives

★ Be motivated to explore behavioral economics.
★ Reflect on the role of psychological realism in economics, now and in the past.
★ Be aware of the organizing principles for this book.
★ Understand the logic and experimental methods for empirical analysis.

The label "behavioral economics" is not particularly informative. Much of economics, after all, is concerned with understanding behaviors — of consumers, families, firms, countries — and their consequences for society. The distinguishing feature of **behavioral economics** is its focus on integrating insights from psychology into economic settings. As examples, it considers how self-control problems, fairness concerns, overconfidence, and inattention matter for economic outcomes, policy, and welfare. The "behavioral" descriptor acts to underscore the emphasis on actual behaviors, particularly those that are unexpected within the standard economic framework.

This first chapter motivates the study of behavioral economics and introduces the book as a guide to the subject. To begin, I highlight the broad applicability and aims of behavioral economics, followed by a brief intellectual history of psychology's role in economics. I then provide an orientation to the book's structure and topics. The chapter concludes with a discussion of empirical methods that readers will encounter throughout the book.

1.1 Why Study Behavioral Economics?

I might argue that behavioral economics is worth studying because it explores an intrinsically compelling set of questions. But there are surely countless compelling topics to investigate within and outside of economics. I could similarly argue that by studying behavioral economics you will further develop your critical thinking and creative problem-solving skills. Or that you will come to see real-world patterns and behaviors in a new way. Once again, these answers are quite general. They fail to answer a more narrow question: why study behavioral economics instead of a different economics topic?

One answer is that behavioral economics has applications to almost every area of economics. It intersects with household decisions about fertility, education, health, work,

DOI: 10.4324/9780367854072-2

savings, consumption, and retirement. It impacts our understanding of asset prices, corporate finance, business strategies, and sports behaviors. It is relevant for the evaluation of government policies related to taxes, unemployment insurance, environmental regulation, voting, economic growth, and macroeconomic stabilization. In short, behavioral economics provides a lens through which to see all of economics.

A second answer is that relative to the rest of economics, behavioral economics is uniquely concerned with improving the psychological realism of economic analysis. You might be asking, why wouldn't all economists prioritize psychological realism? The challenge is that such realism can at times be in tension with other desirable features of an economic theory. In particular, economic theory often aims to build models of behavior with the following features:[1]

1   *Generality:* the model can be applied across many economic settings.
2   *Tractability:* the model is sufficiently simple in the sense that it can be worked with using standard tools of mathematics and does not rely on large-scale computations to generate insights.
3   *Realism:* the model is grounded in the psychological reality of human behavior.

But a model that is general and tractable tends to be a simple abstraction that ignores certain features of reality. Similarly, a theoretical model that attempts to match the particulars of human psychology in each setting risks becoming overly specific, complex, and intractable (Rabin 2002).

So while economic theory typically prioritizes generality and tractability, we can think of behavioral economics as moving theory closer towards psychological realism. This is not to say that behavioral theory abandons simple models with wide-ranging applicability. In fact, the behavioral models introduced throughout this book are arguably more general and no less tractable than models based on assumptions that neglect psychological realities. The degree to which behavioral theory gives up generality and tractability is a subjective assessment. And in learning behavioral economics, you will be able to make your own judgement about what is gained and what is lost by pushing economic theory in the direction of greater psychological realism.

1.2   Why Behavioral Economics Now? A Brief History

> The process of valuation is distinctly a psychological phenomenon, and the problem of value is the fundamental problem in economic science. It may not be too much to say that the next line of advance in economic theory will be distinctly psychological in character, and that the further progress awaits its new impulse at the hands of the psychologist. (Davenport 1902, 355)

Behavioral economics has emerged as a distinct subfield of economics only in the last few decades. It may therefore be surprising to learn that psychology and economics were once more intertwined. The above 1902 quote from economist Hebert Davenport reveals that insights from psychology were indeed valued by early economists. Behavioral economics is then in some sense, a *return* to psychological concerns that mainstream economists largely ignored for most of the 20th century.

Economics as a distinct field of inquiry developed in the late 18th century with contributions from such well-known figures as Adam Smith, Jeremy Bentham, David

Ricardo, and John Stuart Mill. Karl Marx named this early school of thought classical economics, of which Marx is often considered a member as well. Classical economists conceived of the value of goods as arising from the scarcity of inputs, namely land and labor. In this account, value is determined *objectively* by the total amount of inputs needed to produce a good, and not *subjectively* by how much the user of the good personally values it. The analysis of human psychology was therefore unnecessary for the classical economists. But early economists were not ignorant of psychological considerations. In fact, Adam Smith's *The Theory of Moral Sentiments* (1759) highlights the role of passions and emotions, like hunger, sex, and fear, in driving behavior (Ashraf, Camerer, and Loewenstein 2005).

Psychology later became central to a "new" economic theory of the 1870s, appropriately named neoclassical. In early neoclassical theory, individuals evaluated the impact of consuming a good on their subjective feelings of pleasure gained or pain avoided. This theory was consequently rooted in psychological introspection.

Economics then turned away from psychology in the early 20th century, not necessarily because of differences in philosophical ideology, but for a technical reason (Ross 2014, Ch. 2). Economists realized that consumer choice theory did not require knowledge about the psychic intensity of individuals' preferences, but only that preferences were consistently ordered. Vilfredo Pareto proposed a theory of choice in 1900 that aimed to be entirely separate from psychology (Bruni and Sugden 2007). And in the 1930s John Hicks, Roy Allen, and Paul Samuelson formalized and generalized Pareto's early work. The resulting framework dominates standard microeconomic theory textbooks to the present day.

The foregoing chronology traces psychology out, in, and then out of economics again.[2] The final act in this history, and the subject of this book, is the re-emergence of applying psychological insights to economics. Behavioral economics arguably got its start with a seminal 1979 publication by a psychologist and an economist, Daniel Kahneman and Amos Tversky. The researchers provided evidence that standard consumer theory was not descriptive of actual observed behavior and offered an alternative theory informed by psychology. This publication is now one of the most cited in all of economics.

The behavioral economists of the 1980s and 1990s argued that economics should welcome more psychological realism. They faced substantial skepticism and resistance from mainstream economists who were convinced that the standard assumptions of consumer choice were a sufficiently useful approximation to understanding economic phenomena.[3] In spite of this resistance, the influence of behavioral economics grew. Behavioral economics research began to regularly appear in leading economics journals by the late 1990s. And in 2001 behavioral economist Matthew Rabin received one of the most prestigious awards for a young economist.[4] The Nobel Prize for economics has also recognized the behavioral economics contributions of Herbert A. Simon (in 1978), George Akerlof (in 2001), Daniel Kahneman (in 2002), Robert Shiller (in 2013), and Richard Thaler (in 2017). With behavioral economics now solidly part of the mainstream, the question is how, not if, psychology will influence economics in the years ahead.

1.3   A Roadmap for the Book

This book is designed to provide a clear, consistent framework for navigating the many concepts and applications of behavioral economics.

1.3.1   Structure

The 21 chapters of this book are divided into six parts. Part I motivates behavioral economics and establishes the relevant foundations for its analysis. In particular, the second chapter introduces the standard economic model of decision making, characterized by six key assumptions. And Chapter 3 provides a framework for evaluating welfare. Those new to economics will likely need to progress through these chapters more slowly than intermediate students who are already familiar with concepts like utility functions, discounting, expected utility, and consumer surplus.

Each of the six remaining parts of the book interrogates one of the standard assumptions in the economic model of decision making. Within each part there are (typically) three chapters:

A   *Anomalous Evidence.* The first chapter identifies anomalies — evidence that is inconsistent with the predictions of the standard assumption.
B   *Behavioral Theory.* The second chapter presents alternative behavioral modeling assumptions and supporting evidence.
C   *Welfare.* The third chapter considers market and policy responses to individuals who act in accordance with the new behavioral theory, and the consequences for welfare.

This structure highlights the process by which economists evaluate evidence and disentangle competing theories. Modeling scientific inquiry in this way demonstrates that understanding economic behavior is an active endeavor with important welfare implications, and not simply a set of facts to be memorized.

1.3.2   Topics

In selecting from among the many theoretical models within behavioral economics, my aim is to show how a small number of adjustments to the standard economic model can help to explain a wide range of behaviors. The book therefore guides the reader carefully through relatively few models. The objective is to prioritize the development of analytical thinking skills over specific knowledge accumulation. As a consequence, this book is not a comprehensive reference for all of behavioral economics, let alone all of behavioral science. Notable omissions include happiness economics, level-k and cognitive hierarchy theory, learning, emotions, and neuroeconomics.

The theoretical models are evaluated against empirical evidence from almost every corner of microeconomics: household decisions, finance, public finance, health, education, labor, politics, industrial organization, business, development, energy, the environment, and sports.[5] To facilitate access to the empirical applications, an index immediately following the table of contents sorts them by topic. This index is a useful resource for exploring the relevance of multiple behavioral economics concepts within a single topic.

1.4   Empirical Methods

When describing evidence throughout this book, I often emphasize the empirical method of inquiry. This is to promote quantitative reasoning skills with respect to interpreting data, identifying causal relationships, and assessing the limitations of an empirical finding. No previous knowledge of statistics or econometrics is assumed. The following provides an informal overview of relevant concepts and experimental strategies that readers will encounter.

1.4.1   Testing an Economic Theory

Let's begin with a foundational question: how do we *test* a theoretical model of individual decision making? In other words, how do we know if a hypothesized model does a good job of describing real-world decisions?

The general strategy is to compare *actual* behaviors with the *predicted* behaviors of the model. If there are significant and consistent differences between what the model predicts and how people actually behave, then we should be skeptical of the model. In sum, the logic of **hypothesis testing** follows a sequence of steps:

1   Assume a theoretical model of decision making.
2   Determine what this model predicts for behavior.
3   Evaluate the empirical evidence of actual behavior.
4   Reject the model in Step (1) if the evidence in Step (3) is inconsistent with the theoretical predictions in Step (2).

A perceptive reader might wonder what to conclude if the evidence in Step (3) is consistent with the theoretical predictions in Step (2). Such evidence is certainly suggestive that the assumed model in Step (1) *could* be true. But it is an invalid form of reasoning to conclude that the model *must* be true. This reasoning constitutes a fallacy because multiple models of decision making can each imply the same behavior. So observing that behavior does not tell us which model is correct. But all is not lost. Suppose a model is subjected to numerous tests across many different settings and each time the evidence is consistent with the model's predictions. Even though we would still not have conclusive proof that the model is true, each test that doesn't reject the model builds support and confidence for the model.

The general framework of hypothesis testing is applied throughout the book. Although the logic is relatively straightforward, it requires creativity and hard work to test competing models of behavior. A researcher has to understand the predictions of each model and then find settings in which those predictions can be reliably evaluated with data.

1.4.2   Identifying Causality

A crucial step in the hypothesis testing framework is evaluating empirical evidence. For economists, this typically means determining whether or not one variable has a *causal* effect on another variable. For instance, do higher prices cause consumers to buy less? Or do higher incomes improve health outcomes? Or does more education reduce crime? The challenge is that observational data on prices and consumption, incomes and health, or education and crime, only reveal the extent to which the two variables are associated with each other. That is, the data can show us if any two variables are *correlated*, but not if one *causes* the other.

A correlation between two variables X and Y admits multiple causal interpretations. X could cause Y. Or Y could cause X. Or even if neither causes the other, the variables can be correlated because a third variable Z causes both X and Y. Consider evidence of a positive correlation between income and health (Chetty et al. 2016). This correlation is consistent with higher income individuals investing in and accessing more health care, leading to improved health outcomes. But the causation can run in the opposite direction if healthier individuals are more productive and therefore earn higher incomes than those with worse health. Or it could be that neither income nor health directly impacts the other, but a variable like education increases both incomes and health. For instance, better-educated individuals might earn higher wages, and more effectively navigate the health care system or more consistently adhere to medication regimens.

The problem of identifying which variable is causing another is referred to as the **identification problem** in economics. Solving this problem is important for evaluating whether empirical evidence is inconsistent with the predictions of a model.

The key strategy for solving the identification problem is randomization. In particular, we would like to recruit a large group of volunteers and randomly assign each to either a **treatment group** that is subject to some intervention — the *treatment* — or a **control group** that is not. Because of random assignment, the two groups are close to identical. The only difference between them is that the treatment group receives the treatment. Therefore, any significant difference in behaviors between the groups must be caused by the treatment. Applying this strategy to the health example above, let the treatment be a large cash prize. Suppose that the cash prize recipients exhibit subsequent health improvements relative to those who do not receive the prize. Then we can attribute the difference in health outcomes between the groups to the causal effect of a higher income.

1.4.3 Experimental Data

Economists increasingly make use of evidence from experimental settings in which subjects are randomly assigned to receive a treatment. Among the articles published in the leading economics journals, there were no experimental research papers in 1963, 0.8% in 1983, 3.7% in 2003, and a jump to 8.2% in 2011 (Hamermesh 2013). This section introduces three sources of experimental data: lab experiments, field experiments, and quasi-experiments. The overwhelming majority of evidence in this book is derived from one of these three experimental approaches.

Lab Experiments

One method for generating data is to mimic laboratory experiments in the natural sciences. Instead of mixing chemicals to observe reactions or building particle accelerators to study protons, economists recruit human subjects (often economics college students) to make real decisions or answer hypothetical survey questions in a controlled environment. In such a **lab experiment**, the economist experimenter can *treat* a randomly selected group of subjects with alternative incentives or information about a particular decision or question. Any difference in responses between the treated and control groups can then be credibly interpreted as the causal effect of the treatment. This is an appealing strategy because in the real world outside the lab, there are typically too many factors changing at once to clearly identify which ones matter most for behavior.

Lab experiments are not without their drawbacks. A primary concern is that the results from a controlled laboratory setting may not apply outside the lab context (Levitt and List 2007). In the natural sciences this is generally not a concern — a proton doesn't know whether it is in a lab or not. But research in psychology tells us that individuals act differently when they know they are part of an experiment and their actions are being scrutinized. They may want to behave so as to please the experimenter or appear more ethical than if they were unobserved. Economics lab experiments also often rely on small stakes (e.g., winning at most $50) so as to keep the experiment affordable with many participants, but how people react to small stakes may differ from large-stakes decisions in the real world. And of course, the behavior of college student participants (and economics majors in particular) may not be representative of the average person in society. There is evidence, however, that such concerns may be overstated (Snowberg and Yariv 2021).

Field Experiments

To address the limitations of a lab experiment, an alternative approach is to take the randomization outside the lab — to the *field*. **Field experiments** often take the form of an unobtrusive change in the economic environment for a randomly selected group of people. For example, a field experiment could randomly treat some workers at a large firm with temporarily higher wages. Or a charity could randomly treat some of its recent donors with text message requests to donate again. Comparing the worker efforts and charitable donations between the treated and control groups allows us to identify the causal effect of the respective intervention. Observe that the workers and donors in each example are simply engaging in their everyday lives and are likely unaware that they are part of an experiment. Such field experiments have the advantage of randomization that makes lab experiments appealing, while avoiding the artificial setting and student subject pool. Harrison and List (2004) review field experiments and their distinguishing characteristics.

Although field experiments are used throughout economics, they are limited by financial, legal, and ethical constraints. Treating subjects with higher wages, health insurance coverage, or college grant money could be too expensive for a researcher to implement. Even if an intervention is financially feasible, otherwise similar populations are by design treated differently, inducing inequities that society may find objectionable. And the moral principle of respect for autonomy requires researchers to think carefully about obtaining informed consent from the subjects of a field experiment (Baele 2013).

Quasi-Experiments

A change in the economic environment can also have the effect of treating individuals *as-if* at random, without any intervention by researchers. Such random treatment assignment is referred to as a **quasi-experiment** (or natural experiment). Economists are often on the lookout for events that affect — that is, treat — only some people, leaving the unaffected as a control group. Weather patterns and natural disasters provide one source for generating a quasi-experiment. Economists cannot force randomly selected people from their homes to identify the causal effect of moving to a new neighborhood, but a tornado, fire, or flood may destroy homes in one town, while leaving homes in an otherwise identical neighboring town unaffected. Randomization need not be destructive. Changes in regional policies can also create quasi-experiments. If one region (county, province, state) raises its minimum wage or tobacco taxes, while another similar region does not, the causal effect of the policy can be identified by comparing changes in outcomes across the two regions.

As with the previous experimental methods, there are advantages and disadvantages to quasi-experiments. Like field experiments, they have the advantage that we are observing real-world behavior outside the artifice of a lab populated by college students. This increases confidence in the generalizability of the results. They also do not require the operational work of designing and implementing a legally compliant and ethically responsible field experiment. Instead, the two primary challenges associated with quasi-experiments are finding them and ensuring that the treatment is indeed close to randomly assigned. Economists confront the first challenge by studying the history of environmental, political, and legal events that have created differential environments for otherwise similar groups. But because the world is messy and complex, people rarely fit neatly into control and treatment groups. Addressing the corresponding statistical challenges is the subject of econometrics and beyond the scope of this book (see e.g., Athey and Imbens 2017; Angrist and Pischke 2010). For our purposes, it is sufficient that you recognize the value of randomization — no matter its source — for identifying causality.

1.5   Summary

1   **Behavioral economics** refers to the integration of insights from psychology into economic settings.
2   Economic theory typically aims to be 1) general, 2) tractable, and 3) psychologically realistic. Behavioral economics places greater emphasis on the third aim.
3   The role of psychology within economics has fluctuated since the 18th century.
4   The body of this book is organized into six parts, each of which explores a key assumption in the standard economic model of individual decision making.
5   Each of the book's six parts is (typically) divided into three chapters: 1) anomalous evidence, 2) behavioral theory, and 3) implications for welfare, markets, and policy.
6   Economic theories are evaluated against empirical evidence, using the logic of **hypothesis testing**.
7   The problem of identifying whether a variable is causing, and not simply correlated with, another variable is the **identification problem**.
8   If individuals are randomly assigned to a **treatment group** that receives a treatment and a **control group** that does not, the difference in outcomes between the two groups estimates the causal effect of the treatment.
9   Experimental data is sourced from **lab experiments**, **field experiments**, and **quasi-experiments**.

Notes

1   Rubinstein (2006) offers a compelling perspective on what economic theory is trying to accomplish that is best read *after* this book.
2   Hands (2010) argues for a more nuanced history of psychological concerns in economics.
3   Rabin (2002) and Thaler (2016) provide accounts of skepticism towards behavioral economics.
4   The John Bates Clark Medal is awarded annually by the American Economic Association to an American economist under the age of 40 making significant contributions to economics.
5   Akerlof and Shiller (2009) provide an accessible overview of behavioral economics applications to macroeconomics.

References

Akerlof, George A., and Robert J. Shiller. 2009. *Animal Spirits: How Human Psychology Drives the Economy, and Why It Matters for Global Capitalism*. Princeton: Princeton University Press.

Angrist, Joshua D., and Jörn-Steffen Pischke. 2010. "The Credibility Revolution in Empirical Economics: How Better Research Design Is Taking the Con out of Econometrics." *Journal of Economic Perspectives* 24 (2): 3–30. doi:10.1257/jep.24.2.3.

Ashraf, Nava, Colin F. Camerer, and George Loewenstein. 2005. "Adam Smith, Behavioral Economist." *Journal of Economic Perspectives* 19 (3): 131–145. doi:10.1257/089533005774357897.

Athey, Susan, and Guido W. Imbens. 2017. "The State of Applied Econometrics: Causality and Policy Evaluation." *Journal of Economic Perspectives* 31 (2): 3–32. doi:10.1257/jep.31.2.3.

Baele, Stéphane J. 2013. "The Ethics of New Development Economics: Is the Experimental Approach to Development Economics Morally Wrong?" *The Journal of Philosophical Economics* VII (1): 2–42.

Bruni, Luigino, and Robert Sugden. 2007. "The Road not Taken: How Psychology was Removed from Economics, and How It Might Be Brought Back." *The Economic Journal* 117 (516): 146–173. doi:10.1111/j.1468-0297.2007.02005.x.

Chetty, Raj, Michael Stepner, Sarah Abraham, Shelby Lin, Benjamin Scuderi, Nicholas Turner, Augustin Bergeron, and David Cutler. 2016. "The Association Between Income and Life Expectancy in the United States, 2001–2014." *JAMA* 315 (16): 1750–1766. doi:10.1001/jama.2016.4226.

Davenport, H. J. 1902. "Proposed Modifications in Austrian Theory and Terminology." *The Quarterly Journal of Economics* 16 (3): 355–384.

Hamermesh, Daniel S. 2013. "Six Decades of Top Economics Publishing: Who and How?" *Journal of Economic Literature* 51 (1): 162–172. doi:10.1257/jel.51.1.162.

Hands, D. Wade. 2010. "Economics, Psychology and the History of Consumer Choice Theory." *Cambridge Journal of Economics* 34 (4): 633–648. doi:10.1093/cje/bep045.

Harrison, Glenn W., and John A. List. 2004. "Field Experiments." *Journal of Economic Literature* 42 (4): 1009–1055. doi:10.1257/0022051043004577.

Kahneman, Daniel, and Amos Tversky. 1979. "Prospect Theory: An Analysis of Decision under Risk." *Econometrica* 47 (2): 263–291. doi:10.2307/1914185.

Levitt, Steven D., and John A. List. 2007. "What Do Laboratory Experiments Measuring Social Preferences Reveal about the Real World?" *Journal of Economic Perspectives* 21 (2): 153–174. doi:10.1257/jep.21.2.153.

Rabin, Matthew. 2002. "A Perspective on Psychology and Economics." *European Economic Review* 46 (4-5): 657–685. doi:10.1016/s0014-2921(01)00207-0.

Ross, D. 2014. *Philosophy of Economics*. 1st ed. Palgrave Philosophy Today. London: Palgrave Macmillan UK. https://www.palgrave.com/gp/book/9780230302969.

Rubinstein, Ariel. 2006. "Dilemmas of an Economic Theorist." *Econometrica* 74 (4): 865–883. doi:10.1111/j.1468-0262.2006.00689.x.

Smith, Adam. 1759. *The Theory of Moral Sentiments*. London: printed for Andrew Millar, in the Strand / Alexander Kincaid / J. Bell, in Edinburgh.

Snowberg, Erik, and Leeat Yariv. 2021. "Testing the Waters: Behavior across Participant Pools." *American Economic Review* 111 (2): 687-719. doi:10.1257/aer.20181065.

Thaler, Richard H. 2016. "Behavioral Economics: Past, Present, and Future." *American Economic Review* 106 (7): 1577–1600. doi:10.1257/aer.106.7.1577.

2 Standard Decision Making

Learning Objectives

★ Appreciate the economic methodology of studying social phenomena in terms of individual decisions.
★ Understand the six standard assumptions that economists make to construct a model of individual decision making.
★ Reflect on the meaning of rational behavior.

Economists seek to understand social phenomena, including market prices, unemployment, recessions, crime, discrimination, trade patterns, and health, as the outcomes of many individuals each making their own decisions. Given a model of how individuals make decisions, economists can make theoretical predictions about the impact of changing technology, laws, or government policies on individual behaviors, and subsequently the aggregate impact of those behaviors for society. So although economists are primarily motivated by market-level concerns, since economic analysis begins at the individual level, we need a clear understanding of individual behavior.[1]

This chapter introduces the *standard* model of individual decision making against which behavioral economics is reacting. While there is no official standard model, what I define as standard is consistent with the literature (Rabin 2002; DellaVigna 2009). We will return to the assumptions and implications of this model throughout the remainder of the book. I restrict attention to individual decisions and omit the behavior of firms since much of behavioral economics has traditionally taken firm behavior to align with the standard model of profit maximization.[2]

2.1 The Decision Problem

Consider the multitude of decisions you make in life. These range from the trivial to life-changing. You decided what time to get out of bed this morning, which clothes to wear, and potentially what to post on social media. You have also made decisions about which college to attend and in the future will face decisions about which career to pursue, where to live, and who to marry (if at all).

A decision problem is a problem because there exists a set of alternatives from which to choose. To evaluate these alternatives, economists assume that it is possible for individuals to rank the resulting outcomes from each. Therefore, if you are at a restaurant for dinner and can afford the chicken, beef, and tofu entrees, you should be able to rank the

DOI: 10.4324/9780367854072-3

outcomes of eating each meal. A vegetarian might rank tofu highest, and beef and chicken equally undesirable, while a meat-lover might prefer beef to chicken and chicken to tofu. In sum, an **individual decision problem** consists of alternatives — the **choice set** — together with **preferences** that describe how the individual ranks the outcomes that can result from the alternatives in the choice set.

In many decision problems individuals directly choose outcomes. This is the case in the dinner example, where choosing tofu from the choice set leads to the outcome of eating tofu. But suppose you are uncertain about the quality of the tofu dish on the menu. Then choosing tofu could result in the outcome of a delicious meal or the worse outcome of a mediocre meal. Decision problems with uncertainty are the topic of Section 2.3. It is also possible that outcomes depend on the decisions of others. For example, if you are at dinner with a group of friends and everyone is splitting the bill evenly, then the outcome of your payment is higher when your friends order more. Such *multiperson* decision problems are considered in Part V.

It is standard in economics to narrow the scope of an individual decision problem to one motivated by self-interest. That is, preferences are defined over outcomes that are restricted to an individual's personal consumption, accumulation, or experience. This is in contrast to an individual who also has preferences over the outcomes of others. Do you derive satisfaction or experience frustration from the success of others? If so, then your preferences may not be purely self-interested, but an example of *social* preferences. The traditional focus on self-interested behavior has its roots in the insights of Adam Smith who argued that individuals pursuing their own interest could generate a desirable social outcome (Smith 1776). A century after Smith, Francis Edgeworth declared that "the first principle of Economics is that every agent is actuated only by self-interest" (Edgeworth 1881, 16). While self-interest is a useful benchmark and may be the appropriate assumption for studying many market interactions, it limits the scope of economic analysis. Even Edgeworth considered the role of sympathy for others (Collard 1975). For present purposes, I highlight this first of our standard assumptions:

Standard Assumption 1 Self-Interested Preferences

It is also standard to restrict the domain of the individual decision problem by assuming that preferences are over *final* outcomes. For example, suppose you are fortunate one day and find a $20 bill on the sidewalk. The next week you fortuitously find a $100 bill on the sidewalk, but then moments later discover a $80 parking ticket on your car. In both settings the final outcome is that you have an additional $20 in your pocket. Which of these two outcomes would you prefer? Although many people might prefer the first outcome, the standard assumption in economics is that you are indifferent. More generally, preferences are typically defined over the absolute levels of consumption, wealth, health, etc., and not over gains and losses relative to a point of reference. Such independence of preferences from reference points is our next standard assumption of the individual decision problem.

Standard Assumption 2 Reference-Independent Preferences (i.e., preferences over final outcomes, and not changes)

A challenge with studying the individual decision problem is that preferences are cumbersome to keep track of, especially when there are many (or even an infinite number of) possible outcomes. It is therefore useful to translate preferences to a numerical scale: assign a real number to each possible outcome, with larger numbers corresponding to greater preference. Economists refer to this numerical score as **utility**. By assigning utility to each outcome, we have defined a **utility function** $U(\cdot)$. This is a function because $U(\cdot)$ takes outcomes as its inputs and outputs the corresponding level of utility. We say that a utility function **represents** preferences when for any two outcomes A and B, $U(A) \geq U(B)$ is equivalent to A being (weakly) preferred to B.[3] Returning to the example of a vegetarian at dinner, the choice set is {tofu, chicken, beef} and a possible utility function that represents her preferences is $U(\text{tofu}) = 10$ and $U(\text{chicken}) = U(\text{beef}) = 2$.

Up to this point we have discussed the decision problem, but have not made any assumptions about actual behavior. Perhaps the most significant standard assumption in economics is that an individual, after considering all available information, makes the choice that she most prefers. That is, individuals maximize utility. For instance, the vegetarian would consider her alternatives and then choose tofu for dinner.

Standard Assumption 3 Utility Maximization

Might there be settings in which an individual does not maximize utility? Yes. Some decisions are sufficiently novel or complex that you do not have the experience, ability, or time to actually determine your most preferred outcome. Taking out student loans, choosing a career, getting married, buying a house, and starting retirement each occur so infrequently that you might make a choice you later regret. And trying to choose a health insurance plan or an investment strategy can be overwhelming. To simplify a complex decision process, individuals rely on mental shortcuts or rules of thumb. Or they neglect less obvious, but still relevant information. Choices can also be influenced by the persuasion of others. We return to these issues in Part VII.

Given the assumption of utility maximization, an individual decision is the solution to a math problem of the following form:

$$\max_{x \in X} \quad U(x)$$

where X is the choice set of possible outcomes.

Such a utility-maximization problem is simplified by assuming that individuals are in a *static* environment with *no uncertainty*. But many real-world decisions are made over time with choices today having consequences in an uncertain future. For example, an investment in a college education impacts future earnings and student debt obligations. And future earnings, interest rates, and federal loan forgiveness policies are uncertain. Once we introduce a time dimension and uncertainty, it is standard to assume that the utility function individuals maximize is not any arbitrary function, but one that takes a particular form. Let us build up to this functional form by focusing first on the time dimension and then on uncertainty.

2.2 Decision Making Over Time

2.2.1 Time Discounting

Consider a reward (perhaps a gift card, a computer, or a car) that you can choose to receive today or in the future. Most people prefer the reward sooner than later. Why might that be? One answer is that immediate consumption is simply more exciting than delaying gratification. This idea emerged in the earliest treatments of choice over time. Consider, for example, the following 19th century psychological argument by Scottish economist John Rae:

> such pleasures as may now be enjoyed, generally awaken a passion strongly prompting to the partaking of them. The actual presence of the immediate object of desire in the mind, by exciting the attention, seems to rouse all the faculties, as it were, to fix their view on it, and leads them to a very lively conception of the enjoyments which it offers to their instant possession. The prospects of future good, which future years may hold out to us, seem at such a moment dull and dubious, and are apt to be slighted, for objects on which the daylight is falling strongly, and showing us in all their freshness just within our grasp. (Rae 1834, 54)

Caring less about the future than the present is known as **time discounting**. Another rationale for time discounting (also noted by Rae) is that the future is uncertain and there is always the possibility that you will not be alive or well enough to enjoy future consumption. Early economists argued that factors such as the pain of denying oneself present consumption, the role of fashion, and the difficulty of imagining future desires all influenced the preference for consuming in the present (Loewenstein 1992).

Let us now build a general framework for modeling **intertemporal choice**, or choice across time. Think of time as divided equally into discrete periods (e.g., days or years), numbered sequentially from period 0 to a final period $T > 0$. In each period $k \in \{0, 1, 2, \ldots, T\}$ there is an outcome x_k. The utility obtained in period k is given by $u(x_k)$, where u is the **instantaneous utility function**.

How would a time discounter evaluate the *entire sequence* of outcomes from the present forward? One simple idea is to add up the instantaneous utility that will be realized in each period. But to capture a preference for the present, we can discount each future period's utility with a weight that is smaller for more distant utility realizations. In particular, let $U^t(x_t, x_{t+1}, \ldots, x_T)$ indicate the total discounted utility from the perspective of period $t \in \{0, 1, 2, \ldots, T\}$. Then we have:

$$U^t(x_t, x_{t+1}, ..., x_T) = D(0)u(x_t) + D(1)u(x_{t+1}) + D(2)u(x_{t+2}) + \cdots + D(T-t)u(x_T)$$
$$= \sum_{k=0}^{T-t} D(k)u(x_{t+k}) \tag{2.1}$$

where $D(k)$ is the **discount function** that discounts the utility realized k periods from the present. Assume that individuals do not discount the present, so $D(0) = 1$. In addition, $D(k)$ is decreasing to capture time discounting, but remains nonnegative. There are infinitely many possible discount functions that satisfy these restrictions, each representing a particular time preference. Example 2.1 provides three such examples.

Note that we will often evaluate the sequence of outcomes from the perspective of $t = 0$, in which case expression (2.1) simplifies to:

$$U^0(x_0, x_1, ..., x_T) = D(0)u(x_0) + D(1)u(x_1) + D(2)u(x_2) + \cdots + D(T)u(x_T)$$
$$= \sum_{k=0}^{T} D(k)u(x_k) \tag{2.2}$$

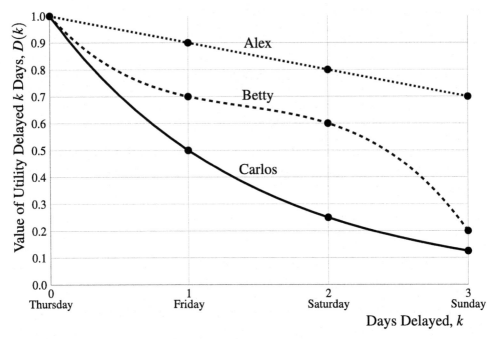

Figure 2.1 Discount Functions, *D*(*k*), in Example 2.1

▪ **Example 2.1 — Discount Functions**. Alex, Betty, and Carlos have different time preferences over consumption this weekend. Let the present period be a Thursday. Then Friday, Saturday, and Sunday are 1, 2, and 3 periods away, respectively. The discount functions are given by:

	$D(k)$	Alex	Betty	Carlos
Thursday	$D(0) =$	1	1	1
Friday	$D(1) =$	0.9	0.7	0.5
Saturday	$D(2) =$	0.8	0.6	0.25
Sunday	$D(3) =$	0.7	0.2	0.125

Figure 2.1 plots these discount functions over time, adding curves for clarity. Alex discounts each day by an additional 10 percentage points; she perceives Friday's utility as worth only 90% of receiving that same utility on Thursday, and Saturday's utility as worth only 80% of receiving it in the present. For Betty, Friday is discounted heavily relative to the present, but she perceives Saturday's utility as discounted only slightly more than Friday's. Carlos' discount function declines rapidly — he perceives Friday's utility as worth 50% of present utility and Saturday's utility as worth 25% of present utility.

To see how these discount functions matter, suppose that Alex, Betty, and Carlos are deciding between two sequences of outcomes that generate instantaneous utility on each day as follows:

Sequences	Thursday $u(x_0)$	Friday $u(x_1)$	Saturday $u(x_2)$	Sunday $u(x_3)$
Smooth (S)	10	10	10	10
Variable (V)	10	14	8	2

The smooth sequence S yields constant utility in each period, while the variable sequence V provides higher utility in period 1 that declines over time. Let's use the expression for total discounted utility in (2.2) to determine which sequence each person prefers from the perspective of Thursday ($t = 0$).

$$U^0_{Alex}(S) = 10 + 0.9 \cdot 10 + 0.8 \cdot 10 + 0.7 \cdot 10 = 34$$
$$U^0_{Alex}(V) = 10 + 0.9 \cdot 14 + 0.8 \cdot 8 + 0.7 \cdot 2 = 30.4$$
$$U^0_{Betty}(S) = 10 + 0.7 \cdot 10 + 0.6 \cdot 10 + 0.2 \cdot 10 = 25$$
$$U^0_{Betty}(V) = 10 + 0.7 \cdot 14 + 0.6 \cdot 8 + 0.2 \cdot 2 = 25$$
$$U^0_{Carlos}(S) = 10 + 0.5 \cdot 10 + 0.25 \cdot 10 + 0.125 \cdot 10 = 18.75$$
$$U^0_{Carlos}(V) = 10 + 0.5 \cdot 14 + 0.25 \cdot 8 + 0.125 \cdot 2 = 19.25$$

Alex prefers S, Betty is indifferent, and Carlos prefers V. Notice that Alex discounts the future the least, so she prefers S, which offers the larger total undiscounted sum of utility. Carlos, on the other hand, heavily discounts the future and therefore prefers V with its higher payoffs in the short term and lower payoffs in the future. ∎

The degree to which an individual prefers immediate utility over delayed utility is captured by the *rate* at which a discount function falls.

Definition 2.1 For discount function $D(k)$, the **discount rate** in period $k \geq 1$ is:

$$\rho(k) \equiv -\frac{D(k) - D(k-1)}{D(k)} \tag{2.3}$$

The discount rate is the decline in the discount function relative to its current level. Note that because discount functions are (weakly) decreasing, the negative sign in the above expression implies that the discount rate is expressed as a nonnegative number. In addition, we use rho, ρ, the lowercase Greek letter for r, to indicate that we are measuring a *rate*. We do not use r to denote the discount rate because economists reserve r to indicate the interest rate. And since the discount rate can vary from period to period, it is written as a function of time. Exercise 2.1 asks you to calculate the discount rates for Alex, Betty, and Carlos from Example 2.1.

How do we interpret differences in discount rates across individuals? A high (low) discount rate means that the discount function is declining quickly (slowly). Intuitively, with a higher discount rate, the future is more heavily discounted and the individual places less weight on future utility. Discount rates are often interpreted as measures of *impatience*. Or alternatively, the lower your discount rate, the more patient you are, since the weight on future utility is closer to the weight on present utility.

2.2.2   *Constant Discounting*

The problem of modeling an intertemporal utility function caught the interest of Paul Samuelson when he was a PhD student at Harvard University in the 1930s. Samuelson would become one of the most influential economists of the 20th century (he was the first American to win the Nobel Prize for economics). In his first publication, at the age of only 21, he considered the theoretical implications of assuming that the discount rate does not vary from period to period, but is constant for an individual (Samuelson 1937). In doing so, Samuelson collapsed the many varied psychological reasons for time discounting into a single number, the discount rate.

With a constant discount rate, the discount function takes an exponential form:

$$D(k) = \delta^k \text{ for } \delta \in (0, 1] \tag{2.4}$$

where we use delta, δ, the lowercase Greek letter for d, to indicate discounting. To verify that the exponential discount function gives a constant discount rate, plug (2.4) into (2.3):

$$\rho(k) = -\frac{\delta^k - \delta^{k-1}}{\delta^k} = \frac{1}{\delta} - 1 \tag{2.5}$$

As claimed, the discount rate does not depend on period k with an exponential discount function (all of the k's from the middle term of (2.5) cancel). Note that a constant discount rate does not mean that the *slope* of the discount function is constant. It means that the *percent change* in the discount function is constant, generating an exponential curve. A family of exponential discount functions is plotted in Figure 2.2. For larger discount rates the discount function declines more rapidly.

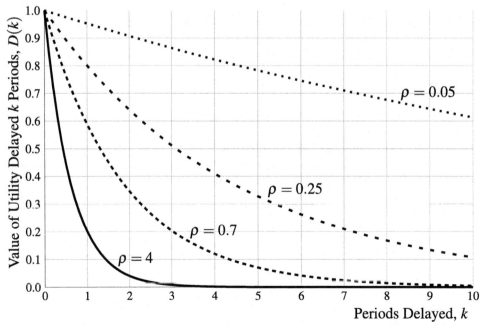

Figure 2.2 Exponential Discount Functions, $D(k) = \delta^k = (1/(1+\rho))^k$

The joint assumptions that preferences over sequences of outcomes are represented by their total discounted utility, with the discount function taking the exponential form, constitute the Discounted Utility (DU) model.

Definition 2.2 The **Discounted Utility (DU) model** evaluates a sequence of outcomes from the perspective of period $t = 0$ as follows:

$$U^0(x_0, x_1, ..., x_T) = u(x_0) + \delta u(x_1) + \delta^2 u(x_2) + \cdots + \delta^T u(x_T)$$

$$= \sum_{k=0}^{T} \delta^k u(x_k)$$

Samuelson was clear when he introduced this model of intertemporal preferences that it is neither a realistic description of how individuals *actually* evaluate outcomes over time, nor a normative ideal of how individuals *should* evaluate outcomes over time. However, most economists focused on the tractability of this elegant model and ignored Samuelson's warnings, adopting the DU model as both a descriptive and normative framework for behavior. The DU model continues to be widely used throughout all of economics and it is therefore our next standard assumption of individual decision making.

Standard Assumption 4 Discounted Utility Model

To make matters confusing, sometimes discounting in the DU model is described in terms of δ instead of the discount rate ρ. Because δ is the *factor* by which utility in the next period is multiplied to obtain the value in the current period, δ is the **discount factor**. By rearranging equation (2.5) to solve for δ, we find that:

$$\delta = \frac{1}{1+\rho}$$

The discount rate and discount factor are inversely related. To heavily discount the future (i.e., care less about the future), is to have a *high* discount rate and a corresponding *low* discount factor. Recall that high discount rates lead to quickly declining discount functions, and since the discount function is $D(k) = \delta^k$, the discount factor δ must be smaller. For instance, in Figure 2.2, the steepest curve has the highest discount rate of $\rho = 4$ (with $\delta = \frac{1}{1+\rho} = \frac{1}{1+4} = 0.2$), and the flattest curve has the lowest discount rate of $\rho = 0.05$ (with $\delta = \frac{1}{1+\rho} = \frac{1}{1+0.05} \approx 0.95$).

2.2.3 Time Consistency

Why is the DU model so widely assumed for economic analysis? It is common, for instance, to assume only a general shape for the instantaneous utility function u without specifying its exact functional form. But it is rare for economists studying intertemporal choice to simply assume that the discount function $D(k)$ is some arbitrary decreasing function with time-varying discount rates. The reason is because constant discounting implies that preferences are internally consistent; they do not shift over time. Otherwise, it is possible that your preferences today about the future might be different than your preferences when you actually arrive in the future. But then which preferences should you use to evaluate outcomes: your preferences today or in the future? Constant discounting eliminates these thorny questions. The following definition and discussion provides precision.

Definition 2.3 Let $U^t(\cdot)$ be the utility function that represents preferences over sequences of outcomes from the perspective of period t. Then the preferences are **time-consistent** if:

$$U^t(x_t, x_{t+1}, ..., x_T) \geq U^t(x_t, \tilde{x}_{t+1}, ..., \tilde{x}_T)$$
$$\text{if and only if}$$
$$U^{t+1}(x_{t+1}, ..., x_T) \geq U^{t+1}(\tilde{x}_{t+1}, ..., \tilde{x}_T)$$

for any two sequences of outcomes $(x_t, x_{t+1}, ..., x_T)$ and $(x_t, \tilde{x}_{t+1}, ..., \tilde{x}_T)$ that share the same outcome in period t.

Intuitively, the definition of time-consistent preferences says the preference for one sequence of outcomes over another does not change based on the time period from which the sequences are evaluated. In other words, preferences *confirm* earlier preferences. If, for example, when 22 years old you make a plan for how much to save at the age of 23, this is the same plan you would make when actually 23. Your 22-year-old plan is therefore confirmed by your 23-year-old plan.

Such time consistency in preferences is tightly linked to constant discounting, an insight first made by Strotz (1955). In particular, suppose preferences are represented by utility function (2.1): $U^t = \sum_{k=0}^{T-t} D(k) u(x_{t+k})$. Then an exponential discount function implies time-consistent preferences and moreover, to guarantee time consistency, the discount function must be exponential. It is in this way that a constant discount rate, an exponential discount function, and time-consistent preferences are all equivalent. Exponential discounting is the standard in economics, not because it would be impossible mathematically to use a different discount function, but because it rules out the possibility that individuals at different points in time disagree with themselves about what they prefer.

Although time consistency is intuitively appealing, if you have ever planned to start a diet or start writing a paper and then failed to follow through, your preferences are not time-consistent, but **time-inconsistent**. If individuals have time-inconsistent preferences, then their preferences cannot be represented by the DU model. In Part II we therefore consider alternatives to the DU model.

Before concluding this section, be careful to note that if the discount function is not exponential, the preceding discussion does not say that preferences will *always* fail to confirm earlier preferences, but only that there *exists* an environment in which preferences will fail to confirm earlier ones. The next example illustrates this possibility.

■ **Example 2.2 — Time Consistency.** Consider the setup of Example 2.1. Let's determine the preferences over the sequences S and V for Alex, Betty, and Carlos from the perspective of Friday ($t = 1$), $U^1(x_1, x_2, x_3) = u(x_1) + D(1)u(x_2) + D(2)u(x_3)$:

$$U^1_{Alex}(S) = 10 + 0.9 \cdot 10 + 0.8 \cdot 10 = 27$$
$$U^1_{Alex}(V) = 14 + 0.9 \cdot 8 + 0.8 \cdot 2 = 22.8$$
$$U^1_{Betty}(S) = 10 + 0.7 \cdot 10 + 0.6 \cdot 10 = 23$$
$$U^1_{Betty}(V) = 14 + 0.7 \cdot 8 + 0.6 \cdot 2 = 20.8$$
$$U^1_{Carlos}(S) = 10 + 0.5 \cdot 10 + 0.25 \cdot 10 = 17.5$$
$$U^1_{Carlos}(V) = 14 + 0.5 \cdot 8 + 0.25 \cdot 2 = 18.5$$

Carlos' preferences have not changed. From the perspective of both period 0 and period 1, he prefers V. We know this must be the case because Carlos has a constant discount rate and therefore has time-consistent preferences.

Betty, on the other hand, is initially indifferent between S and V in period 0, but when period 1 arrives, she strictly prefers S. This shift in preferences demonstrates her time inconsistency, which we expect given that she does not have a constant discount rate.

Finally, Alex too does not have a constant discount rate, but she prefers sequence S in period 0 and in period 1. Although her preferences do not shift in this example, there exists an environment in which Alex's preferences will shift over time. Exercise 2.4 asks you to generate such an example. ∎

2.3 Decision Making with Uncertainty

Imagine that you are a college senior deciding between a risky career at a startup or a more stable career at an established firm. The chances of becoming a millionaire and being laid off are both higher at the startup than at the established firm.

Or perhaps you are facing the decision whether or not to purchase health insurance. You begin by considering the advantages of health insurance; if you get sick or injured, then the cost of seeing a doctor and receiving treatment will be much lower than without insurance. However, you also recognize that health insurance can be expensive and may feel like a waste if you buy the insurance and never use it because you remain healthy.

These are examples of an individual decision problem in a setting with uncertainty. This section introduces the standard approach to studying such problems.

2.3.1 Describing Uncertainty

In the career choice example you are uncertain about what your financial situation will be next year with each job. You could be unemployed, employed, or the recipient of a massive bonus. And in the health insurance context, you have uncertainty about your health status. We describe such uncertainty by assigning a belief to each possible outcome.

Definition 2.4 Given all possible outcomes $(x_1, x_2, \ldots, x_N)$, the **belief** that outcome x_n occurs is denoted by p_n, where:

1 $p_n \geq 0$ for all $n = 1, 2, \ldots, N$; and
2 $p_1 + p_2 + \cdots + p_N = 1$

Remark on Notation: The full set of beliefs is denoted by $p = (p_1, p_2, \ldots, p_N)$. It is also convenient to express beliefs as a function, where $p(x_n)$ is the belief that x_n occurs.

The two conditions in this definition require that beliefs be nonnegative and sum to 1, or 100%. In the health insurance context, beliefs might be $p(\text{Healthy}) = 0.9$ and $p(\text{Sick}) = 0.1$, indicating a 90% belief in being healthy.

But where do beliefs come from? Economists assume that beliefs are **accurate**. That is, they equal the true probability of each possible outcome. This is straightforward when the probability of each outcome is known with certainty. For instance, when flipping a fair coin with a 50% chance of landing on heads, we assume that an individual's belief that the coin lands on heads equals the known probability of 50%. Such *objective* forms of uncertainty are referred to as *risk*.

The uncertainty in most economic decisions, however, does not resemble the flip of a coin, roll of the dice, or spin of a roulette wheel. More often, individuals are faced with uncertain outcomes for which probabilities exist, but are not known with certainty. In the health insurance example the chance of being healthy is not so obvious. But based on your health record, diet, exercise routine, family history, and environment, you should be able to construct a well-informed *subjective* assessment of the chance that you will be healthy in the coming year. It is standard to assume that such subjective beliefs equal the true underlying probabilities.

Economists also assume that beliefs are consistent with the laws of probability. This includes how individuals revise, or update, their beliefs when they learn new information. For instance, how should you update your belief about the chance of being healthy after receiving a negative diagnosis from a possibly faulty test? What if you test positive? There is a statistical rule for updating beliefs conditional on such new information named after Thomas Bayes, an 18th century minister and statistician.

Definition 2.5 Let A denote a set of possible outcomes (or a *state of the world*). Denote the *prior* belief, before observing new information, that A is true by $p(A)$. The prior belief that the state of world is not A is denoted by $p(\neg A)$.

Bayes' rule determines the *posterior* belief, after observing new information or data D, that A is true as follows:

$$p(A \mid D) = \frac{p(D \mid A)p(A)}{p(D \mid A)p(A) + p(D \mid \neg A)p(\neg A)}$$

where $p(D \mid A)$ is the likelihood of observing D given state of the world A, and $p(D \mid \neg A)$ is the likelihood of observing D given that A is not the state of the world.

To see the usefulness of Bayes' rule, consider the following medical diagnosis example that applies Bayes' rule to updating beliefs.

■ **Example 2.3 — Bayes' Rule for Medical Testing.** Sandy is concerned that she may have or soon develop lupus, an autoimmune disease. Before being tested for lupus, she does some research about the prevalence of lupus in the general population and also her particular risk factors. She forms an accurate prior belief of 2% that she has lupus. The antibody test for lupus is informative, but not without error: 98% of people with lupus will test positive, but so will 10% of people without lupus. Suppose that Sandy receives a positive test result. What then is her posterior belief after receiving the positive test result that she has lupus?

Let L indicate the state of the world in which she has lupus, and $T+$ indicate the information of a positive test. The prior beliefs are $p(L) = 0.02$ and $p(\neg L) = 1 - p(L) = 0.98$. The test's accuracy is described by the likelihoods $p(T + \mid L) = 0.98$ and $p(T + \mid \neg L) = 0.1$. Applying Bayes' rule, we compute the posterior belief:

$$p(L \mid T+) = \frac{p(T + \mid L)p(L)}{p(T + \mid L)p(L) + p(T + \mid \neg L)p(\neg L)}$$
$$= \frac{0.98 \cdot 0.02}{0.98 \cdot 0.02 + 0.1 \cdot 0.98} = \frac{1}{6} \approx 16.7\%$$

Sandy's belief that she has lupus has increased from 2% to 16.7%. This may be a smaller increase than you expected. Given a positive result and the fact that 98% of people with lupus test positive for it, you may think that the chance she has lupus is much closer to 100%. If so, you are forgetting that most people do not have lupus and yet many of them, if tested, would test positive. This makes a positive test likely to be a false indicator.

To better understand the intuition for this result, imagine that there is a population of 10,000 people. Sandy initially thinks that 2%, or 200 people, have the disease. If all 200 individuals with lupus took the antibody test, 98% of 200, or 196 people would test positive. If the 9,800 people without lupus also took the antibody test, 10% of 9,800, or 980 people would test positive. In total, 196 + 980 = 1, 176 people test positive. But of these 1,176 people, only 196 actually have the disease. The share of positive tests that are accurate is then 196/1176 = 1/6, as calculated above. ■

Computing beliefs in this way is unintuitive and challenging. Yet the assumption that individuals assess uncertainty with accurate beliefs updated via Bayes' rule permeates economics. This is our next standard assumption of individual decision making.

Standard Assumption 5 Accurate Beliefs updated using Bayes' rule

With an understanding of how uncertainty is characterized with beliefs, we now turn to modeling how individuals evaluate uncertainty.

2.3.2 Evaluating Uncertainty

A set of uncertain outcomes with corresponding probabilistic beliefs is referred to as either a **lottery**, **gamble**, or **prospect**. We will denote a lottery L by merging the possible outcomes $(x_1, x_2, \ldots, x_N)$ with the corresponding beliefs $p = (p_1, p_2, \ldots, p_N)$ as follows:

$$L = (x_1, p_1; x_2, p_2; \ldots; x_N, p_N)$$

We want to characterize how economists model preferences over such lotteries.

Let's start with a simple example in which you currently have $100 in wealth and are offered the choice between two lotteries with prizes determined by the flip of a fair coin. With objective probabilities, accurate beliefs are simply equal to the 50-50 chance of each side of the coin landing up. In the first lottery L_1 you win $80 if the coin lands on heads and nothing if it lands on tails. The second lottery L_2 pays $50 on heads and $25 on tails. With Standard Assumption 2 that individuals evaluate final outcomes, the potential winnings from these lotteries are integrated with the initial $100 of wealth to generate the following lotteries:

$$L_1 = (\$180, 0.5; \$100, 0.5)$$
$$L_2 = (\$150, 0.5; \$125, 0.5)$$

Observe that with lottery L_1 there are two possible utilities that can result: $u(180)$ or $u(100)$, where utility is defined over total wealth. One method for evaluating this lottery is to take a weighted average of these two utilities, using your beliefs as weights, i.e., $0.5u(180) + 0.5u(100)$. This method of evaluating outcomes based on the expected utility is in fact the standard model that economists use for decision making with uncertainty. The general definition is as follows:

Definition 2.6 Given outcomes $(x_1, x_2, \ldots, x_N)$ with beliefs $p = (p_1, p_2, \ldots, p_N)$ and utility function $u(x)$ over outcomes, **expected utility** is:

$$E[u(x) \mid p] = p_1 u(x_1) + p_2 u(x_2) + \cdots + p_N u(x_N)$$
$$= \sum_{n=1}^{N} p_n u(x_n)$$

Remark on Notation: It is convenient to express $E[u(x)|p]$, with a slight abuse of notation, as $E(u(L))$ where $L = (x_1, p_1; x_2, p_2; \ldots; x_N, p_N)$.

Applying this definition to our earlier coin flip example, we have that lottery L_1 is preferred to lottery L_2 if and only if:

$$0.5u(180) + 0.5u(100) \geq 0.5u(150) + 0.5u(125)$$

The expected utility representation of preferences is used throughout economics for studying decision making with uncertainty. It serves as both a descriptive model of behavior and a normative model of how individuals should act.

Standard Assumption 6 Expected Utility

Why is expected utility so dominant? One reason is that as an average, it is an intuitively appealing guide for decision making in the long run. That is, if you experienced the same lottery every day for years, then the average daily utility over this long period would be close to the expected utility. Another reason appeals to theorems that guarantee, along with some technical assumptions, that preferences can be represented by expected utility (Neumann and Morgenstern 1944; Savage 1972).

In fact, you may be wondering how else one could reasonably evaluate uncertainty. Observe that expected utility has two key mathematical properties:

1 Each $u(x_n)$ term is multiplied by the belief p_n (and not by some nonlinear function of p_n like $\ln(p_n)$ or $\sqrt{p_n}$).
2 The expected utility is the sum of the $p_n u(x_n)$ terms.

But it is not obvious that individuals must behave according to these particular mathematical operations. For now, let's practice applying expected utility to a career choice example.

■ **Example 2.4 — Career Choice.** Blake is considering either a safe career at an established firm or a risky career at a tech startup. She has researched the likelihood for each job of becoming laid off and in the case of the startup, being acquired by a larger firm, which could result in a huge bonus. Let's model each of these careers as a lottery with the following possible outcomes and corresponding beliefs:

$$L^{\text{Safe}} = (\text{Unemployed}, 0.05; \ \text{Employed at High Salary}, 0.95)$$
$$L^{\text{Risky}} = (\text{Unemployed}, 0.30; \ \text{Employed at Medium Salary}, 0.68; \ \text{Bonus}, 0.02)$$

Blake has also determined the utility she would obtain from each possible outcome, except for the bonus possibility. The utilities are:

$$u(\text{Employed at High Salary}) = 200$$
$$u(\text{Employed at Medium Salary}) = 175$$
$$u(\text{Unemployed}) = 120$$

Blake's expected utilities from each lottery are therefore:

$$
\begin{aligned}
E(u(L^{\text{Safe}})) &= 0.05 \cdot u(\text{Unemployed}) + 0.95 \cdot u(\text{Employed at High Salary}) \\
&= 0.05 \cdot 120 + 0.95 \cdot 200 \\
&= 196 \\
E(u(L^{\text{Risky}})) &= 0.30 \cdot u(\text{Unemployed}) + 0.68 \cdot u(\text{Employed at Medium Salary}) \\
&\quad + 0.02 \cdot u(\text{Bonus}) \\
&= 0.30 \cdot 120 + 0.68 \cdot 175 + 0.02 \cdot u(\text{Bonus}) \\
&= 155 + 0.02 \cdot u(\text{Bonus})
\end{aligned}
$$

Therefore, Blake prefers the risky career if and only if:

$$
\begin{aligned}
&\Leftrightarrow 155 + 0.02 \cdot u(\text{Bonus}) \geq 196 \\
&\Leftrightarrow u(\text{Bonus}) \geq \frac{196 - 155}{0.02} = 2{,}050
\end{aligned}
$$

Given that the risky startup offers a lower base salary and a higher chance of unemployment than the safe firm, the potential bonus must generate a utility payoff of at least 2,050 to make the risky job preferable. ■

2.3.3   Risk Preferences

An important special case of decision making with uncertainty is when the outcomes refer to different levels of total wealth. For simplicity, economists often assume that the only outcome that individuals care about is their wealth because it is with this wealth that they can purchase goods, services, and experiences that ultimately bring satisfaction. A convenient way to keep track of the utility at each possible level of wealth is to assume a particular functional form for $u(\cdot)$. But what should this utility function look like? While we always assume that utility is increasing, the curvature of the utility function depends on the attitude towards risk, or **risk preference**. Before characterizing risk preferences, we need the following definition:

> **Definition 2.7** Given lottery $L = (x_1, p_1; x_2, p_2; \ldots; x_N, p_N)$ where each x_n indicates a wealth outcome, the **expected wealth** from L is equal to $\sum_{n=1}^{N} p_n x_n$.

Intuitively, the expected wealth of a lottery is the average wealth one would expect to have if the lottery were iterated many times. It is now possible to define the three types of risk preferences.

> **Definition 2.8**
>
> **Risk averse** describes preferences that rank a certain wealth level W higher than a risky lottery with expected wealth W.
>
> **Risk loving/seeking** describes preferences that rank a certain wealth level W lower than a risky lottery with expected wealth W.
>
> **Risk neutral** describes preferences that rank a certain wealth level W equal to a risky lottery with expected wealth W.

To illustrate these definitions, consider the hypothetical decision problem of choosing between two lotteries: L_1 pays \$50 for sure and L_2 pays \$10 or \$90, each with a 50% chance. Because L_1 has no risk, it is an example of a *degenerate* lottery. These two lotteries have the same expected wealth equal to $W + 50$, where W is the chooser's initial wealth. The expected utilities of the lotteries are:

$$E(u(L_1)) = u(W + 50)$$
$$E(u(L_2)) = 0.5 \cdot u(W + 10) + 0.5 \cdot u(W + 90)$$

Figure 2.3a depicts the relationship between utility and wealth. With L_2, the individual is equally likely to be at point A or point B. The midpoint between A and B, labeled as point E, therefore identifies the expected wealth on the horizontal wealth axis and the expected utility on the vertical utility axis. Lottery L_1 gives wealth $W + 50$ and utility $u(W + 50)$ with certainty. Let a point $C = (W + 50, u(W + 50))$ denote this certain outcome in the figure. The utility function $u(x)$ must pass through points A, B, and C as these correspond to the possible lottery outcomes. But where is point C? The answer depends on which lottery the individual prefers.

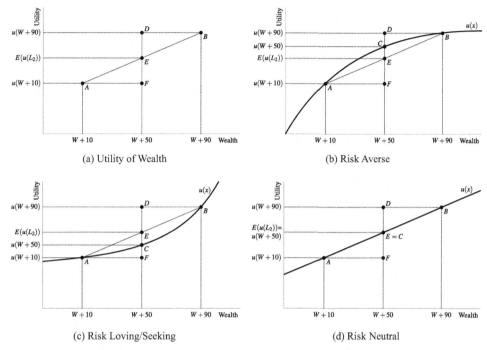

Figure 2.3 Risk Preferences and the Shape of Utility Function $u(x)$

If the individual has risk averse preferences, then by definition she strictly prefers the certain lottery L_1 to the risky lottery L_2:

$$E(u(L_2)) < E(u(L_1)) = u(W + 50) < u(W + 90)$$

where the last inequality follows from assuming that utility is increasing. Therefore, C must fall between D and E. Figure 2.3b shows this case with a utility function that passes through A, B, and C. Notice the concave shape of the utility function.

The preceding example illustrates a general result: with expected utility preferences, risk aversion is equivalent to concave utility over wealth. This result is striking because there exists another distinct motivation for concave utility. In particular, it is reasonable to assume that an additional dollar increases utility by less and less as people become wealthier. Such diminishing marginal utility of wealth means that the slope of the utility function becomes flatter with more wealth, or is concave. So diminishing marginal utility, concave utility, and risk aversion are all equivalent. To develop some intuition for the connection between diminishing marginal utility and risk aversion, consider a lottery in which you can win or lose \$40 with equal probability. If your marginal utility decreases in wealth, the gain of \$40 would increase utility by less than the loss of \$40 would decrease utility. Therefore, the risky lottery would reduce expected utility, inducing you to reject it and stay with your current certain wealth.

There are settings in which risk loving or risk neutral preferences may be more appropriate modeling assumptions. For instance, to understand gambling behavior, we might assume that individuals are risk loving. In the preceding example a risk loving individual prefers risky lottery L_2 to degenerate lottery L_1:

$$E(u(L_2)) > E(u(L_1)) = u(W + 50) > u(W + 10)$$

where once again the last inequality follows from assuming that utility is increasing. Therefore point C must fall between E and F. Tracing a utility function that passes through points A, B, and C generates a convex utility function as in Figure 2.3c. Finally, in the case of risk neutral preferences, the individual is indifferent between the two lotteries:

$$E(u(L_2)) = E(u(L_1)) = u(W + 50)$$

Now point C is equal to point E and the utility function is linear, as in Figure 2.3d.

In sum, with expected utility preferences, we have the following equivalences:

Risk Preference		Utility function		Marginal utility of wealth
Risk Averse	⇔	Concave	⇔	Diminishing
Risk Neutral	⇔	Linear	⇔	Constant
Risk Loving	⇔	Convex	⇔	Increasing

2.3.4 The Expected Utility Model

To conclude this section I want to clarify a subtle distinction. Economists often refer to *the expected utility model* (or theory) when studying decision making with uncertainty. The expected utility model typically assumes:

• Standard Assumption 2: Reference-Independent Preferences;
• Standard Assumption 3: Utility Maximization;
• Standard Assumption 5: Accurate Beliefs updated using Bayes' rule;
• Standard Assumption 6: Expected Utility; and often
• Risk Aversion or Risk Neutrality over wealth.

Importantly, the expected utility model is narrower than Standard Assumption 6 that preferences over uncertain outcomes are represented by expected utility. That is, individuals could evaluate uncertainty with expected utility preferences, but simultaneously evaluate outcomes relative to a reference point (violating Standard Assumption 2) and/or apply inaccurate beliefs (violating Standard Assumption 5). It will prove instructive to consider the role of each standard assumption separately.

2.4 Standard Model of Individual Decision Making

We have now introduced six standard assumptions that economists make when modeling the individual decision problem. These assumptions can be organized into three categories: preferences, beliefs, and the decision process. The following definition restates them.

Definition 2.9 The **standard model of individual decision making** satisfies the following assumptions:

1   **Standard Preferences:**

    a Discounted Utility Model
    b Reference-Independent Preferences
    c Expected Utility
    d Self-Interested Preferences

2   **Standard Beliefs:** Accurate Beliefs updated using Bayes' rule
3   **Standard Decision Process:** Utility Maximization

Taken together, these assumptions admit a stylized representation of the standard model of individual decision making:

$$\max_{(x_0, x_1, \ldots, x_T) \in X} \sum_{k=0}^{T} \delta^k E[u(x_k) \mid p] \qquad \text{(Standard Model)}$$

where $\delta \in (0, 1]$ is the discount factor, $u(\cdot)$ is a function over individual-specific final outcomes, and beliefs p are accurate and updated using Bayes' rule.

This model is the starting point for much of economic theory. The model is tractable and can often be analyzed using standard mathematical tools. It is also general, providing a unified theoretical framework to understand choices related to consumption, savings, labor supply, health, education, and marriage. Not only is the model used as a descriptive (or positive) theory of how individuals actually behave, it also serves as a normative model of how people ought to behave. That is, economists assume that individuals act so as to maximize their exponentially discounted expected utility *and* it is in their best interest to do so.

The primary drawback to the standard model is that it may not be psychologically realistic. If it makes predictions that conflict with observed behavior, then policy recommendations and welfare assessments using this model may not be reliable. We turn to investigating the realism of each standard assumption, one by one, in the six parts of the book that follow.

I conclude this discussion by noting that throughout the book I work under the presumption that preferences are sufficiently well-behaved so as to admit representation by some utility function. The focus is on characterizing the form of the utility function, not its possible nonexistence.

2.5   Rational Behavior

The standard model of individual decision making outlined in this chapter is at times referred to as classical or neoclassical. These labels are not particularly useful for our purposes. The motivation for adopting the "standard model" terminology is to avoid associating the model with a school of thought, and instead with the empirical regularity of how mainstream economists practice economics in their work.

Another label associated with the standard model is rationality. You may have an intuitive understanding of what constitutes rational behavior: perhaps behavior that is sensible, thoughtful, or reasonable. Economists, however, often define rational behavior as that which is consistent with the specific assumptions in the standard model. This is a narrow and technical notion of rationality.

Consider instead the following more general definition of rationality.

> **Definition 2.10** The behavior of an individual is **rational** if it is in the individual's self-determined best interest.

This definition of rational behavior is not vacuous, as it can plausibly rule out behavior that is erratic, impulsive, naive, or overly influenced by persuasion. At the same time, this definition does *not* imply the standard model of decision making (Blume and Easley 2008). It does not imply that individuals are purely self-interested, as one's best interest might include generosity. It also does not imply that individuals evaluate outcomes with exponentially discounted expected utility using accurate beliefs. And it does not necessarily imply that an individual chooses the most preferred alternative if the process of finding this option is not in their best interest (e.g., it would require substantial time and cognitive effort acquiring information or problem solving).

The important takeaway is that as we document **anomalies**, or behavior that is inconsistent with the standard model, it is inappropriate to automatically equate such behavior with irrationality. In fact, I will largely avoid labeling behavior as rational or irrational, as these descriptions implicitly impose a debatable value judgement on how people should go about making decisions. The primary goal is to better understand reality, not rationality.[4]

2.6   Summary

1   The methodological approach of economics is to understand social phenomena in terms of the individual decisions of people in society.
2   An **individual decision problem** consists of a **choice set** and **preferences** over the outcomes that can result from the alternatives in the choice set.
3   It is standard to assume that preferences are self-interested and reference-independent.
4   A **utility function** assigns a numerical score, called **utility**, to each possible outcome. A utility function **represents** preferences if and only if more preferred outcomes are assigned larger utility values.
5   It is standard to assume that individuals make choices that **maximize utility**.
6   It is standard to assume that when faced with an **intertemporal choice** problem, individuals exhibit a preference for the present over the future, or **time discounting**. In addition, sequences of outcomes are evaluated with the **Discounted Utility (DU) model** of preferences, which has the following features:

   a   Total utility is the sum of **instantaneous utilities** in each period discounted by an exponential **discount function**.
   b   The rate at which the discount function declines, the **discount rate**, is constant.
   c   Preferences are **time-consistent**.

7   It is standard to assume that individuals form **accurate beliefs** about the probability of uncertain outcomes and update these beliefs using **Bayes' rule**.

8 It is standard to assume that individuals evaluate a **lottery** with its **expected utility**, which is the belief-weighted average of the utilities from each possible outcome.

9 Attitudes towards risk, or **risk preferences**, are defined by the relative preference between a lottery and a certain outcome equal to the **expected wealth** of the lottery.

10 Risk preference is connected to both the rate at which the marginal utility of wealth changes and the curvature of the utility function over wealth.

11 The **standard model of individual decision making** makes all of the standard assumptions noted in this list.

12 The behavior implied by the standard model is not necessarily equivalent to **rational** behavior.

13 **Anomalies** are real-world behaviors that are inconsistent with the standard model.

2.7   Exercises

Exercise 2.1 — Calculating Discount Rates. Recall the discount functions $D(k)$ for Alex, Betty, and Carlos in Example 2.1. Determine each individual's discount rates $\rho(k)$ for $k = 1$, 2, and 3. Verify that only Carlos exhibits a constant discount rate over time.

Exercise 2.2 — Discounting Profits. Muhammed is considering an investment in his dairy farm which will reduce his profits this year by I, but increase his profits every year thereafter by a constant amount R with certainty. Assume that his preferences are represented by the Discounted Utility model, with annual discount factor $\delta = 0.9$, and instantaneous utility function over profits $u(x) = x$.

a   If Muhammed's time horizon is four years, including the current year (i e , $t = 0$ and $T = 3$), what is the minimum return relative to the investment, R/I, to induce Muhammed to prefer making the investment?

b   Now suppose the return relative to the investment, R/I, equals 15%. What is the minimum time horizon that will induce Muhammed to prefer the investment? *Hint: The sum of a geometric series $\delta + \delta^2 + \ldots + \delta^T$ equals $\delta(1-\delta^T)/(1-\delta)$ if $0 \leq \delta < 1$.*

Exercise 2.3 — Personal Inconsistency. Provide an example from your own personal experience that suggests time inconsistency.

Exercise 2.4 — Finding Time Inconsistency. In Example 2.1 Alex does not discount the future at a constant rate. Therefore, Alex can exhibit time inconsistency: there exist utility sequences $u = (u_0, u_1, u_2, u_3)$ and $\tilde{u} = (u_0, \tilde{u}_1, \tilde{u}_2, \tilde{u}_3)$ such that Alex prefers u in period 0, but prefers $\tilde{u}$ in period 1. Find two sequences u and $\tilde{u}$ such that this is true.

Exercise 2.5 — Proving Time Consistency. Prove that the DU model implies time-consistent preferences. This proof is instructive for confirming your understanding of the notation in this chapter.

Exercise 2.6 — Uncertain Safety. Hugo works a dangerous job in the logging industry. He faces a 2% chance of a non-fatal injury and a 0.1% chance of a fatal injury this year. Hugo holds accurate beliefs about these risks. What does he believe to be the probability that he suffers no injuries this year?

Exercise 2.7 — Bayesian Batteries. Imperium Industries manufactures batteries. About 10% of the batteries produced are bad. The company uses a quality control test that approves every good battery, as well as 5% of the bad batteries. Imperium sells every battery that is approved by this test. With what probability does the company sell a bad battery?

Exercise 2.8 — Viral Statistics. An antibody test for a virus is 99% accurate: 99% of people with the virus will test positive and 99% of people without the virus will test negative. Suppose that v share of the population has the virus, where v is a number between 0 and 1.

a   What is the probability that a randomly selected person who tests positive actually has the virus? Your answer will depend on v.
b   How does your answer in part (a) change with an increase in the virus prevalence v? Interpret.
c   A randomly selected person with a positive test result has at least a 90% chance of having the virus if at least what share of the population has it?

Exercise 2.9 — Utility of Expectations. Recall the two lotteries from Section 2.3.2:

$$L_1 = (\$180, 0.5; \$100, 0.5)$$
$$L_2 = (\$150, 0.5; \$125, 0.5)$$

Maya (M) and Gemma (G) are both expected utility maximizers, but have different utility functions over wealth: $u^M(x) = x$ and $u^G(x) = \ln(x)$. Which of the two lotteries do Maya and Gemma each prefer?

Exercise 2.10 — Healthy Choices. Otto is an expected utility maximizer deciding whether or not to buy health insurance. His utilities with and without insurance depend on whether or not he is healthy, as follows:

	healthy	*sick*
with insurance	$u = 80$	$u = 70$
without insurance	$u = 100$	$u = 10$

Let p denote Otto's belief that he will be sick and $1 - p$ denote his belief that he will be healthy. Assume these beliefs do not depend on his insurance coverage.

a   Determine Otto's expected utility with insurance (in terms of p).
b   Determine Otto's expected utility without insurance (in terms of p).
c   Suppose Otto chooses to purchase insurance. What does this decision imply about the range of possible beliefs Otto must have about his chance of being sick?

Exercise 2.11 — Picturing Risk Preferences. Allison is risk averse and Nate is risk neutral. They have both been offered identical jobs with a base annual salary of $60,000 and a 20% chance of a $20,000 bonus at the end of the year. There is no risk of layoff. For both Allison and Nate sketch a clearly labeled diagram with the following features:

a   utility function over annual income from $60,000 to $80,000;
b   expected income, $E(I)$, from accepting the job;
c   utility of expected income, $u(E(I))$, from accepting the job;

d   expected utility, $E(u(I))$, from accepting the job; and

e   the certain (riskless) annual income, $\hat{I}$, that would make the individual indifferent to accepting the job.

Exercise 2.12 — Degrees of Risk. Caesar is risk averse and faces two lotteries: X and Y. Each lottery offers the chance to win or lose some amount of money. And they both generate the same expected wealth for Caesar. But lottery X offers a bigger win and a bigger loss than lottery Y. Which lottery gives Caesar a larger expected utility?

Exercise 2.13 — Ticket to Riches. There is a $10 lottery ticket that pays $95,000 with probability 0.0001 and nothing otherwise. Would a risk averse expected utility maximizer (with accurate beliefs) ever buy this ticket? Explain.

Notes

1 See Udehn (2001) for a comprehensive review of the methodological individualism that is central to economics.

2 There is evidence that the pattern of firms deviating from simple profit maximization is related to manager ability (Goldfarb and Xiao 2011; Hortaçsu et al. 2019) and has been documented in professional football (Romer 2006; Massey and Thaler 2013) and retail markets (Ellison, Snyder, and Zhang 2018; DellaVigna and Gentzkow 2019).

3 A technical concern is whether there exists a utility function that can represent preferences. While beyond the scope of this book, there are representation theorems that show restrictions on preferences and choice sets that guarantee existence of a utility function. See Kreps (1988) and Kreps (1990, 18–37).

4 For further discussion of rationality in economics, see Blume and Easley (2008), Simon (2008), Sent (2008), Arrow (1990), and Sen (1990).

References

Arrow, Kenneth J. 1990. "Economic Theory and the Hypothesis of Rationality." In *Utility and Probability,* edited by John Eatwell, Murray Milgate, and Peter Newman, 25–37. The New Palgrave. London: Palgrave Macmillan UK. doi:10.1007/978-1-349-20568-4_8.

Blume, Lawrence E., and David Easley. 2008. "Rationality." In *The New Palgrave Dictionary of Economics,* edited by Steven N. Durlauf and Lawrence E. Blume, 5396–5405. London: Palgrave Macmillan UK. doi:10.1007/978-1-349-58802-2_1387.

Collard, David. 1975. "Edgeworth's Propositions on Altruism." *The Economic Journal* 85 (338): 355–360. doi:10.2307/2230997.

DellaVigna, Stefano. 2009. "Psychology and Economics: Evidence from the Field." *Journal of Economic Literature* 47 (2): 315–372. doi:10.1257/jel.47.2.315.

DellaVigna, Stefano, and Matthew Gentzkow. 2019. "Uniform Pricing in U.S. Retail Chains." *The Quarterly Journal of Economics* 134 (4): 2011–2084. doi:10.1093/qje/qjz019.

Edgeworth, Francis Ysidro. 1881. *Mathematical Psychics: An Essay on the Application of Mathematics to the Moral Sciences.* London: C. Kegan Paul & Company.

Ellison, Sara Fisher, Christopher Snyder, and Hongkai Zhang. 2018. "Costs of Managerial Attention and Activity as a Source of Sticky Prices: Structural Estimates from an Online Market." NBER Working Paper 24680. Cambridge, MA: National Bureau of Economic Research. doi:10.3386/w24680.

Goldfarb, Avi, and Mo Xiao. 2011. "Who Thinks about the Competition? Managerial Ability and Strategic Entry in US Local Telephone Markets." *American Economic Review* 101 (7): 3130–3161. doi:10.1257/aer.101.7.3130.

Hortaçsu, Ali, Fernando Luco, Steven L. Puller, and Dongni Zhu. 2019. "Does Strategic Ability Affect Efficiency? Evidence from Electricity Markets." *American Economic Review* 109 (12): 4302–4342. doi:10.1257/aer.20172015.

Kreps, David M. 1988. *Notes on the Theory of Choice.* Boulder, CO: Westview Press Incorporated.

———. 1990. *A Course in Microeconomic Theory.* Princeton: Princeton University Press.

Loewenstein, George. 1992. "The Fall and Rise of Psychological Explanations." In *Choice Over Time,* edited by George Loewenstein and Jon Elster, 3–34. New York: Russell Sage Foundation.

Massey, Cade, and Richard H. Thaler. 2013. "The Loser's Curse: Decision Making and Market Efficiency in the National Football League Draft." *Management Science* 59 (7): 1479–1495. doi:10.1287/mnsc.1120.1657.

Neumann, John von, and Oskar Morgenstern. 1944. *Theory of Games and Economic Behavior.* Princeton: Princeton University Press.

Rabin, Matthew. 2002. "A Perspective on Psychology and Economics." *European Economic Review* 46 (4–5): 657–685. doi:10.1016/s0014-2921(01)00207-0.

Rae, John. 1834. *The Sociological Theory of Capital.* London: Macmillan.

Romer, David. 2006. "Do Firms Maximize? Evidence from Professional Football." *Journal of Political Economy* 114 (2): 340–365. doi:10.1086/501171.

Samuelson, Paul. 1937. "A Note on Measurement of Utility." *The Review of Economic Studies* 4 (2): 155–161. doi:10.2307/2967612.

Savage, Leonard J. 1972. *The Foundations of Statistics.* 2nd edition. New York: Dover Publications, Inc.

Sen, Amartya. 1990. "Rational Behaviour." In *Utility and Probability,* edited by John Eatwell, Murray Milgate, and Peter Newman, 198–216. The New Palgrave. London: Palgrave Macmillan UK. doi:10.1007/978-1-349-20568-4_28.

Sent, Esther-Mirjam. 2008. "Rationality, History of the Concept." In *The New Palgrave Dictionary of Economics,* edited by Steven N. Durlauf and Lawrence E. Blume, 5407–5414. London: Palgrave Macmillan UK. doi:10.1007/978-1-349-58802-2_1389.

Simon, Herbert A. 2008. "Rationality, Bounded." In *The New Palgrave Dictionary of Economics: Volume 1–8,* edited by Steven N. Durlauf and Lawrence E. Blume, 5405–5407. London: Palgrave Macmillan UK. doi:10.1007/978-1-349-58802-2_1388.

Smith, Adam. 1776. *An Inquiry Into the Nature and Causes of the Wealth of Nations.* London: W. Strahan / T. Cadell.

Strotz, R. H. 1955. "Myopia and Inconsistency in Dynamic Utility Maximization." *The Review of Economic Studies* 23 (3): 165–180. doi:10.2307/2295722.

Udehn, Lars. 2001. *Methodological Individualism: Background, History and Meaning.* 1st edition. London: Routledge.

3 Behavioral Welfare Economics

Learning Objectives

★ Understand what economists mean by welfare.

★ Make sense of the difference between experienced utility and decision utility.

★ Evaluate the advantages and disadvantages of nudges.

★ Apply welfare analysis in settings with nonstandard decision makers.

Consider the many ways that your economic life is shaped and directed by government policies. One obvious impact of the government on your life is taxes. Every time you buy something, you likely pay a sales tax. And some goods, like gasoline and cigarettes, are subject to even higher excise taxes. If you are working a job, income and payroll taxes reduce your paycheck to less than what your employer has paid you. Taxes are also levied on profits and property. In fact, governments of rich countries collect 1 out of every 3 dollars of gross domestic product (GDP) in tax revenue on average (OECD 2019).

What does this tax revenue pay for? Much of it is spent funding public education, retirement benefits, health insurance, and income support for the poor. It also purchases public goods like roads, policing, and national defense. In addition to these expenditures, governments manage a complex system of regulations, ranging from the minimum wage and workplace safety rules, to environmental protections and the justice system.

What are the rationales for such government intervention in a market economy? Economists approach this question by imagining a fictional **benevolent social planner** (or benevolent dictator) who aims to improve social welfare and has the full power to unilaterally implement policies of their choosing. This imaginary construct allows us to set aside the complex political economy questions of how governments actually make policy when faced with special interests, lobbying, and strategies for reelection. Two traditional motivations for government intervention are:

1 **redistribution** of income or wealth to reduce inequality; and
2 **correcting a market failure** (e.g., caused by market power, externalities, or asymmetric information) in which, at least theoretically, there is another way to organize resources in society that helps some people and makes no one worse off.

Understanding when and how a benevolent social planner should intervene in the economy is a central concern of welfare economics.

DOI: 10.4324/9780367854072-4

But welfare economics has traditionally ignored the possibility that individuals could benefit from help with their own decision making. Evidence from behavioral economics, introduced throughout this book, reveals that individuals can make mistakes. In such cases the social planner is arguably justified in helping to improve decision making (Thaler and Sunstein 2003). The third rationale for government intervention is therefore:

3 **paternalism**, which aims to promote choices that would make an individual better off.

Paternalism is often viewed with skepticism. Because even if a government is well intentioned, there is no guarantee that it does not substitute its own judgements for what it means to make individuals "better off" (Posner 2011; Sugden 2008). While this is a legitimate concern, I assume for simplicity that the social planner evaluates policies according to citizens' preferences, not its own.

This chapter develops a framework for thinking about welfare, both individual and social. We begin with standard welfare economics in which, without redistributive or market failure concerns, there is no rationale for a social planner to intervene. We then show why paternalistic policies can be justified when there is a gap between what individuals choose and what maximizes their well-being. In such a case, what form should the policies take? Possible policies include changing prices with taxes or subsidies, or more directly mandating or banning certain options. Another strategy is to use what is commonly referred to as a nudge. We explore the consequences of using nudges for policy and conclude the chapter by applying our insights to consumer decisions related to health and energy efficiency. The general framework in this chapter will be referenced and applied throughout the book.

3.1 Welfarism

A central aim of economics is understanding how well individuals are faring in market economies. This is an important question because individual well-being is the foundation for evaluating both the efficiency and equity of market outcomes. But how should we measure individual and social welfare?

One way to measure welfare is to take an opulence approach that uses income or wealth as an indicator of well-being. After all, with more financial resources, an individual can consume more goods and services. At a macro level, the concept of gross domestic product (GDP) — a monetary measure of the value of goods and services produced in a country in a given year — reflects this opulence approach to social welfare. Similarly, the poverty rate measures the share of people below some income threshold and is often used as an indicator of a society's welfare.

A problem with the opulence approach is that it is really a measure of *being well off*, when what economists ultimately care about for evaluating market outcomes is *well-being*. Well-being is concerned with how well (or unwell) an individual feels about their circumstances, and not simply the existence (or absence) of possessions. This focus on the mental state of the individual for evaluating well-being follows from the influential ideas of utilitarian philosophers like Jeremy Bentham and John Stuart Mill.

The standard economics approach is then to measure individual welfare with the happiness, satisfaction, or desire-fulfillment that individuals experience. Although these ideas appear to be quite similar, there can be important differences between them. For instance, it is entirely possible to be unhappy that you are studying for an exam, but simultaneously fulfill your desire for learning. Conversely, receiving a surprise hotel room upgrade could make you happy, even if you do not desire fancy hotel rooms when traveling. In spite of these distinctions, modern economics adopts a simplifying approach of lumping them together into a common concept that we refer to as **experienced utility**. That is, experienced utility refers to actual experienced happiness, satisfaction, or desire-fulfillment achieved from an outcome. Using only experienced utility to measure welfare is known as welfarism (Sen 1979b).

Definition 3.1 Welfarism is a normative approach that measures welfare only in terms of experienced utility. In this approach:

1 **Individual Welfare** is equal to the individual's experienced utility; and
2 **Social Welfare** is a function of the experienced utilities of those in the society. Two canonical social welfare functions include:

- **Utilitarian Social Welfare** is the sum of experienced utilities of everyone in the society; and
- **Rawlsian Social Welfare** is the lowest experienced utility of anyone in the society.[1]

While behavioral economics abandons many of the standard assumptions of the individual decision problem introduced in Chapter 2, it does not abandon welfarism. In this book we will use the welfarism approach to evaluate both individual and social welfare.[2]

It is worth noting that in spite of the widespread use of the welfarism approach throughout economics, it is not without drawbacks. One major limitation is that it neglects the characteristics and conditions of individuals. Consider an impoverished child in the developing world who has come to terms with her unfortunate state, but still experiences high levels of happiness from the simple pleasures of small meals and a community of friends. In the welfarism approach this child could then be viewed as achieving higher individual welfare than a wealthy executive who experiences high levels of stress and unfulfillment from being passed over for a promotion at work. This extreme example illustrates how using experienced utility as a measure of welfare can be misleading if we do not consider additional individual characteristics. Such problems with, and alternatives to, the welfarism approach have been explored comprehensively, but largely remain outside the standard practice of economics (e.g., Sen 1985; Nussbaum 2001).

3.2   Welfare of Standard Decision Making

When you decide how much of your income to spend on clothing or a celebratory dinner, or where to work during the summer, or whether or not to pursue graduate school, the standard assumption is that the choices you make are the ones that, given your set of available alternatives, yield the highest utility (Standard Assumption 3).

Recall that this utility-maximization problem can be expressed mathematically as:

$$\max_{x \in X} \quad U(x)$$

Because the utility function $U(x)$ represents the individual's preferences over possible outcomes *when making a decision*, this utility function is known as **decision utility**. We now have two distinct utility concepts: experienced utility and decision utility (Kahneman, Wakker, and Sarin 1997; Kahneman and Sugden 2005). This distinction is summarized as follows:

Definition 3.2

Decision utility represents preferences when making a decision.

Experienced utility is the experienced happiness, satisfaction, or desire-fulfillment that results from a decision.

Suppose that experienced utility and decision utility are the same. Then when an individual makes a choice by maximizing her decision utility, she is simultaneously choosing the outcome that maximizes the happiness that she will experience from her choice. This is perfectly reasonable in many cases. Why wouldn't you choose to spend your money or time in a way that generates the most satisfying and pleasurable experiences for you? In fact, standard economics adopts this simplifying convention, treating both experienced and decision utility as identical concepts and using the single term "utility" to refer to both interchangeably.

Standard Assumption 7 Experienced utility equals decision utility

This is a nontrivial assumption with important implications for welfare and the role of policy. Because individual welfare is defined as experienced utility, standard economics implicitly assumes that individuals are making choices that maximize their own welfare. If a benevolent social planner were tasked with choosing for the individual an available option that maximizes their individual welfare, she would choose the same outcome that the individual would choose for herself. There is no difference between the social planner's welfare-maximization problem and the individual's utility-maximization problem. As a consequence, there is no role for government intervention by a social planner.

We can visualize the preceding insight with a standard demand curve diagram. An individual demand curve traces out how many units of a good an individual would choose to consume at each possible price of the good, holding all other prices and income constant. How do consumers decide how many units of food, clothing, or entertainment to demand? They do so by maximizing their decision utility. And it turns out that an individual demand curve is determined by the **marginal decision utility** from consuming one additional unit of the good.[3] Consumers will continue to purchase more of the good as long as the additional (or marginal) decision utility from consuming one more unit exceeds the unit price. With marginal decision utility drawn as in Figure 3.1, the consumer will choose Q_1 units at the high price of P_1, but increase their consumption to Q_2 units if the price drops to P_2.

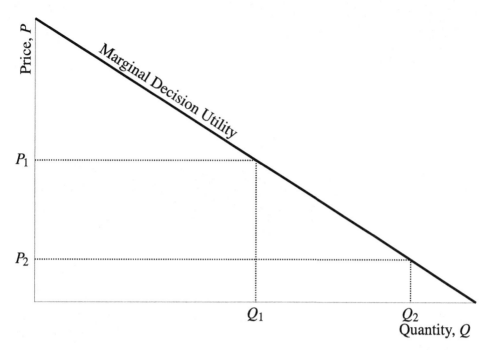

Figure 3.1 Individual Demand Curve as Marginal Decision Utility

While decision utility determines a consumer's choices when faced with different prices, in order to evaluate the consumer's welfare we make use of experienced utility. For each unit consumed, consider the difference between the **marginal experienced utility**, or additional satisfaction from consumption, and the price paid. The sum of these differences across all units consumed equals a welfare measure known as **consumer surplus**. That is, consumer surplus measures the consumer's welfare benefit from consumption minus the cost of consumption.

Graphically, consumer surplus is the area below the marginal experienced utility curve and above the price, up to the quantity consumed. Under the standard assumption that decision and experienced utility are the same, marginal decision and marginal experienced utility are also the same. This case is depicted in Figure 3.2. At a price of P^*, the consumer will choose $Q^* = Q_{Dec}(P^*)$ units because this is where marginal decision utility equals the price. The corresponding consumer surplus is then $A_1 + A_2$, or the area below marginal experienced utility and above the price, up to Q^*.

Could the consumer facing a price of P^* in Figure 3.2 achieve higher consumer surplus by choosing a different quantity other than Q^*? No. To see this, suppose she did not maximize her decision utility and consumed only Q_1 units. Now her consumer surplus is equal to A_1 — she loses out on the potential surplus of A_2 by underconsuming. And if she instead decided to overconsume at Q_2, she would realize negative surplus on the units between Q^* and Q_2 because the price is higher than her marginal experienced utility. Her total consumer surplus would then be $A_1 + A_2 - B$, which is less than if she had simply maximized her decision utility by choosing Q^*.

In summary, when decision and experienced utility coincide, consumers make choices that maximize their own welfare. There are many reasons to be skeptical of this

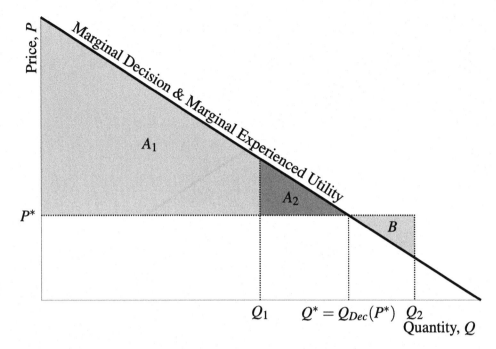

Figure 3.2 Individual Demand Curve as Marginal Decision & Marginal Experienced Utility

assumption. One set of critiques, originating from philosophers, focuses on the observation that by conflating decision with experienced utility, we rule out a rich set of motivations for human decisions that are not consistent with achieving the highest experienced satisfaction. For example, people may make decisions out of a sense of obligation, duty, or sacrifice that do not generate maximal happiness. Economists have traditionally dismissed these critiques by arguing that such motivations are unlikely to be of primary relevance in the more narrow domain of economic decision making.

There is also evidence from psychology and neuroscience that, even in the domain of standard economic decisions, we should not expect decision and experienced utility to be one and the same. In the following section we explore the influence of this evidence on behavioral economics and the implications for welfare.

3.3   Internalities

Suppose that you are making a decision today about whether or not to buy yogurt to eat for breakfast tomorrow morning. To make this decision, you likely need to pause (perhaps only very briefly) to think about how much satisfaction or pleasure you would achieve from eating yogurt tomorrow. How accurately do your expectations at the time of making the decision match your actual experience from eating yogurt?

Under the standard assumption that decision and experienced utility are the same, your forecast of the future experience when making a decision (known sometimes as a *hedonic forecast* or *affective forecast*) is accurate. But an experimental study found that individuals' predictions for how much they expect to like yogurt or music over the course of a week were uncorrelated with their actual experienced satisfaction (Kahneman and

Snell 1992). This may not be surprising since although we usually know what we like and what we do not, when there is a gap between the decision and experience of a good, we may err when trying to forecast future satisfaction. Accurately perceiving the value of packing an umbrella when it is not currently raining or an afternoon snack when breakfast just ended can be challenging.

There is further evidence from neuroscience. Berridge and Robinson (2003) discuss the different brain systems associated with *wanting* and *liking*. Wanting is related to the maximization of decision utility, while liking concerns the evaluation of experienced utility. If the brain processes wanting and liking differently, then the standard economics conflation of decision and experienced utility may not be justified.

Behavioral economists, informed by such evidence, have developed models that allow individuals to make **mistakes**, or choices that do not maximize individual welfare. Such a mistake can occur if the decision utility that an individual maximizes to make a choice doesn't align with the experienced utility they use to evaluate their own welfare from that choice. The gap between between decision making and experienced satisfaction creates an internality.[4]

> **Definition 3.3** An **internality** is the difference between marginal decision utility and marginal experienced utility.

While internalities can be positive or negative and arise for a variety of reasons, they are often due to individuals inaccurately weighting or ignoring the full consequences of their decisions on their own *internal* well-being. For example, diners may decide to eat dessert (partially ignoring the negative health costs) even though their experienced satisfaction (including the negative health costs) would have been higher had they skipped it. Or investors' inaccurate beliefs about stock market movements may induce them to choose investment strategies that do not generate the highest returns, even though that is likely their objective. And online shoppers may ignore shipping costs or taxes when making decisions even though they will experience those added costs in the total amount charged to their credit card.

3.3.1   Welfare Loss of an Internality

How does the existence of an internality change the standard welfare analysis? Consider the positive internality depicted in Figure 3.3 where marginal decision utility is no longer equal to marginal experienced utility, but higher. For concreteness, let's imagine that the good in the figure is an unhealthy snack like potato chips in which the consumer underweights the health consequences. When the price of a potato chip bag is P^*, the consumer maximizes decision utility by choosing the quantity $Q_{Dec}(P^*)$. What is her consumer surplus? Remember that it is the area between marginal experienced utility and the price. So for the first Q^* units she gains consumer surplus equal to area A. But for the remaining units, because her marginal experienced utility is below the price, she loses consumer surplus equal to area B. Her total consumer surplus is therefore $A - B$.

When there is no internality the consumer's decision maximizes her consumer surplus. But we see in Figure 3.3 that this consumer could have achieved a higher consumer surplus by cutting back on her potato chip consumption. In fact, she would have

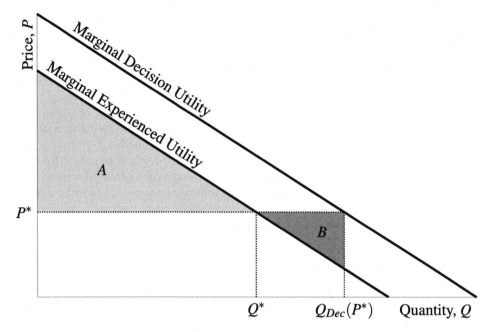

Figure 3.3 Consumer Surplus with an Internality

maximized her consumer surplus had she stopped consuming as soon as her marginal experienced utility dropped below the price. By only consuming Q^* units, she would have achieved her maximum consumer surplus possible, equal to area A.

3.3.2 *Paternalistic Taxation*

With standard decision makers who maximize experienced utility and their own welfare, there is no economic rationale for the government to impose paternalistic policies aimed at protecting people from their own choices. But in a world with internalities, paternalistic policies that improve an individual's welfare — according to the individual's own personal preferences — are now justified. This welfare improvement is possible because if an individual is misperceiving her marginal experienced utility when deciding to consume (perhaps because she is ignoring potato chip calories and fat content), a benevolent social planner could help correct this misperception by incentivizing the individual to align her decisions with her own experienced well-being.

How could such a paternalistic policy be designed? One way to change consumption incentives is to change the price with a per-unit tax. And because the benevolent social planner only wants to help the consumer, let's also assume that all of the tax revenue is rebated back to the consumer in a lump sum — the government is not going to spend the money on some other project or redistribute it to a neighbor. Suppose that the per-unit tax t is set equal to the magnitude of the internality (i.e., the difference between marginal decision and marginal experienced utility) at the welfare-maximizing quantity Q^*. Then, as depicted in Figure 3.4, the price increases from P^* to $P^* + t$.[5] At this higher price the consumer now decides to consume only Q^* units. She obtains consumer surplus equal to area A_1 minus area C, reflecting consumption units with marginal

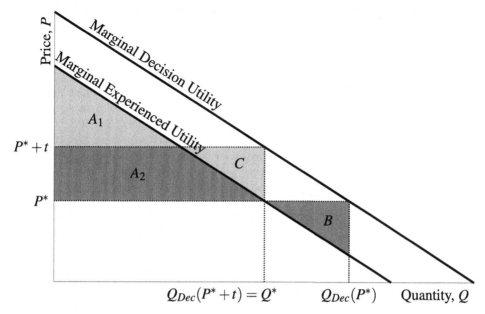

Figure 3.4 Correcting an Internality with a Per-Unit Tax and Rebate

experienced utility initially above, and later below, the tax-inclusive price $P^* + t$. But remember, the government rebates the tax revenue, which equals $t \times Q^* = A_2 + C$. Adding this rebate to consumer surplus we have welfare $(A_1 - C) + (A_2 + C) = A_1 + A_2 = A$. She is now faring better than in the no-tax world when her welfare was only the consumer surplus $A - B$.

This strategy of correcting an internality with a tax is analogous to the standard economic analysis of correcting an externality. In the case of an externality like pollution from some production process, a competitive market will lead to more pollution than is socially optimal because the producer does not take into account the negative impact of the external pollution on others. A per-unit tax (also known as a Pigouvian tax, after its originator Arthur Pigou) on production that equals the difference between the marginal cost to society and the private marginal cost to the producer, evaluated at the socially optimal production level, leads to the social optimum. In effect, the tax on the producer acts to *internalize* the external costs that the producer is imposing on society, incentivizing less production and subsequently less pollution.

The analysis in Figure 3.4 mirrors this logic. By setting the tax equal to the difference between marginal decision utility (i.e., the perceived benefit to the consumer) and the marginal experienced utility (i.e., the actual benefit to the consumer), at the welfare-maximizing quantity, the consumer internalizes the impact of consumption on *their own* experience. As the size of the internality diminishes, the optimal corrective tax shrinks in magnitude, disappearing entirely under the standard assumption of no internalities.

In order to operationalize such a policy, the social planner would need to estimate both marginal decision and marginal experienced utilities. One can make use of data on actual consumer decisions to estimate marginal decision utility. Estimating marginal experienced utility is more challenging as it is not directly revealed by consumer behavior. That is, I can observe how many potato chips people decide to purchase, but not necessarily their experienced satisfaction from potato chip consumption. Behavioral economists, however, have developed various strategies to help identify experienced utility (Chetty 2015).

3.4 Nudges

Consider the wide range of paternalistic public policies that exist to protect consumers from harmful or dangerous choices. Some policies take the form of mandates or bans. Drivers are mandated to wear seat belts in almost every US state. Social Security is a mandated retirement savings program for American workers to protect against poverty in old age. And lead-based house paint has been banned in the US since 1978 due to the neurological problems of lead ingestion, particularly by children. In each of these cases, the policy changes the choice set for consumers by reducing the number of available options.

A policy alternative to mandates and bans is changing relative prices with a subsidy or tax. In order to promote health, a government might subsidize preventative care for citizens. Many states tax cigarettes, alcohol, and cannabis (where it is not banned) to raise prices and discourage consumption of these so-called *sin goods*.

It is standard in economics to restrict public policy interventions to either a mandate, ban, subsidy, or tax. By changing the choice set or relative prices, these policies are predicted to impact consumer behavior. But there are other types of policies aimed at changing behavior that don't change the set of available options or prices. In the 1980s the National Highway Traffic Safety Administration created a series of popular TV commercials with talking crash test dummies to demonstrate the importance of wearing a seat belt while driving. And since the 1990s there have been many public service campaigns warning against the health consequences of tobacco. Such campaigns alone do not prevent anyone from driving without a seatbelt or smoking. They also don't change the economic incentives of these activities. Therefore, the standard model of decision making predicts that consumer behavior will be unaffected.

Suppose that your job is to develop policies to reduce potato chip consumption, as in the previous section. But you know that banning or taxing potato chips is not politically popular. What are some alternative policies? You could create a public awareness campaign with billboards that advertise the negative health effects of junk food. Or you could make the nutritional labels on potato chip bags larger. Or you could require schools to make an apple the default side dish with school lunches and make chips available only upon request. The standard model of decision making predicts that none of these policies will matter for behavior. Consumers presumably already know the nutritional facts from eating chips, so unless you restrict their availability or raise their price, behavior should stay the same. A significant contribution of behavioral economics is the recognition that there are *supposedly irrelevant factors* that do in fact matter (Thaler 2016).

3.4.1 Defining Nudges

A nudge is a policy that steers or guides people in a particular direction, but still allows them to choose their own path. Driving directions from an app like Waze are a nudge because the suggested directions impact the route you take, even though you have the freedom to choose any route you want. Waze is not going to prevent you from going off of its suggested route — in fact, it adapts to you. This concept was popularized in the best-selling book *Nudge* (Thaler and Sunstein 2009).

Definition 3.4 A nudge is an intervention "that alters people's behavior in a pre-dictable way without forbidding any options or significantly changing their eco-nomic incentives."[6]

Let's unpack this definition. Because a nudge cannot forbid any options, mandates and bans are definitely not nudges. And because a nudge cannot significantly change eco-nomic incentives, taxes and subsidies that change relative prices are also not nudges. But nevertheless, a nudge still impacts behavior in a predictable way. Nudges are there-fore referred to as a form of *soft* paternalism, in contrast to the *heavy-handed* paternalism of standard economic policies that limit choices.

Nudges can take many forms. One of the most effective forms is a default. In our potato chips example, changing the default school lunch side from chips to an apple doesn't prevent a student from choosing the chips. Nor does it change the price of chips relative to an apple. All the default does is steer students towards the apple. The factory settings on a new computer or smartphone also act as defaults. And more consequentially, defaults matter for retirement savings and health, as we discuss in Chapter 7.

Nudges can alternatively take the form of a reminder, warning, or information disclo-sure. A text message reminder to schedule a dentist appointment, an alarm clock, a bath-room sign reminding you to wash your hands, and an alert to reply to an important email are all nudges. Clear warnings in large bold fonts on medicine or appliances can similarly impact behavior without changing options or incentives. Simple and uniform informa-tion disclosure about the foods we eat, the credit cards we use, and the student loans we incur also act as nudges.

3.4.2   How Nudges Work

Although nudges don't change the set of options or economic incentives, we can think of nudges as changing the environment in which a choice is made. Driving a car with GPS is a different environment than driving without GPS. Choosing a side to go with lunch when the default is potato chips is a different environment than when the default is an apple. Buying fast food with nutritional labels is a different environment than without. And taking out student loans with clear, easy to understand information about loan repayments is a different environment than when the fees and interest rates are obscured in fine print. Psychologists have long recognized the importance of the environment for decision making and often refer to the environment as the *frame* in which a decision is made. Behavioral economists tend to instead refer to the environ-ment as the *choice architecture*. In any case, the key observation is that the way in which a decision is framed or constructed can impact the choices that people make.

This observation reveals the limitations of the standard framework. In the standard model we assume that people already know how to get where they are going, whether they prefer potato chips or an apple, how much they value different fast food options, and how to read a student loan contract. Changing the environment should then have little to no impact on standard decision makers.

But suppose some individuals mistakenly choose options that do not maximize their own welfare. Perhaps they have an internality, underweighting or ignoring the full consequences of their decisions. Or the decision problem may be so complex that finding the best option is simply too burdensome. If nudges change the environment in such a way that these individuals more clearly perceive or understand their options, then their behavior can change as well.

Over 150 governments around the world have implemented nudges to impact consumer behavior. They are often used to influence health, safety, retirement savings, and energy consumption (Benartzi et al. 2017; Sunstein, Reisch, and Rauber 2018; Loewenstein and Chater 2017). And private companies employ nudges to market and sell products. Given this widespread adoption, we next consider what makes nudges so appealing, as well as some potential drawbacks.

3.4.3   Advantages of Nudging

A key advantage of a nudge relative to traditional policy interventions is that it influences behaviors without changing the choice set. Mandates and bans remove options from the choice set — a mandate to wear a seatbelt eliminates the option to drive without one (or at least increases the chance of paying a fine). And subsidies and taxes distort the choice set — raising the gasoline tax means that individuals can no longer drive as much without cutting back on some other expenditure. Because nudges leave the choice set as is, individuals remain free to choose the same options with or without the nudge. This freedom of choice makes nudges liberty-preserving.

Why is such liberty preservation desirable? There are philosophical reasons to value liberty-preserving policies, grounded in the moral principle of respect for an individual's autonomy to make choices that promote their own flourishing. And there are political reasons for valuing liberty-preserving policies; it may be easier for a democratic government to persuade voters to endorse policies that do not restrict their choices than policies that do.

We can also evaluate nudging from a social welfare perspective. Recall that paternalistic policies are motivated by a concern to improve the welfare of individuals who are making a mistake. For instance, we saw in the previous section how an individual who eats more potato chips than they would like to eat can achieve higher welfare with a tax and rebate policy. And many safety rules (e.g., seatbelt mandates and drug bans) can be viewed as improving the welfare of individuals who underestimate the risks of dangerous activities. But such policies apply to everyone, including those who are not making mistakes. While there are surely some of us who consume more chips than we would like, there are also others for whom there is no difference between what they like and what they choose. If we tax chips, everyone pays the same tax. The overeaters can be made better off with the tax. But the standard decision makers may be worse off with a chip tax that distorts their otherwise welfare-maximizing choice.[6] Similarly, consumers who underestimate the risks of drug use may be better off with a ban or tax on the drug. But standard decision makers who prefer to use a drug after accurately considering all of its costs and benefits are made worse off with a restricted choice set.[7]

A policy maker who only wants to implement policies that increase social welfare must therefore consider a policy's asymmetric effects. Suppose a paternalistic policy increases the individual welfare of consumers whose mistakes are corrected. But it also reduces the individual welfare of standard consumers whose options have been restricted. Whether the net impact on social welfare is positive or negative depends on the magnitudes of the changes on individual welfare, as well as the definition of social welfare (e.g., utilitarian or Rawlsian). And given that a group of policy makers may each define social welfare in a different way, even if they all agree about the effects of the policy on each individual, they may not agree about whether or not it is worth implementing.

Nudges can provide a solution as an *asymmetrically paternalistic* policy, feasibly making no one worse off, while significantly improving the welfare of those making mistakes (Camerer et al. 2003). Suppose that potato chips are replaced with apples as the default side dish in cafeterias, but still remain as an option upon request. This nudge does not change the behavior or individual welfare of standard consumers. But those who would like to eat a healthier diet are made better off by a default that steers them towards choosing a more nutritious option. As long as the implementation costs of the nudge are negligible and producer profits are not reduced, then everyone in society wins from the nudge policy.

More generally, this type of social welfare gain is known as a Pareto improvement.

> **Definition 3.5** A **Pareto improvement** is a change to a new social outcome in which at least one individual is better off and no individual is worse off.

Pareto improvements are arguably unobjectionable because there is at least one winner and no losers. It is therefore easier to generate consensus around a Pareto-improving policy than one that helps some individuals and hurts others, even if the social benefits outweigh the costs. The potential for nudges to create Pareto improvements may explain their popular use by governments around the world.

3.4.4 Disadvantages of Nudging

If nudges only help and never hurt individual welfare, why not replace all paternalistic policies with nudges? Perhaps the most important practical shortcoming of a nudge is that, as its name suggests, it is much weaker than a *shove* (Sunstein 2013). If the objective of a policy is to prevent dangerous drug use, reduce the risk of death in a car accident, or ensure the elderly avoid poverty, then nudges may not be strong enough to achieve the desired outcomes. Standard policy interventions that more directly influence behavior may be required in these cases. But there remain other concerns. I discuss two: the ethics and psychological costs of nudging.[8]

Although nudges preserve choices, if they are influencing behavior without individuals realizing that they are being guided, then perhaps nudges do not truly respect autonomy. If it were revealed to you that a restaurant changed its default side that comes with a sandwich from french fries to a salad in order to encourage you to eat healthier, might you feel manipulated? Or if a social media company set its default privacy settings in a way that maximizes their ability to profit from selling your data (while still leaving you the option to restrict this data access), would you feel violated? And if nudges that take the form of suggestions and reminders are simply propaganda by another name, then we have reason to worry about the ways in which they violate autonomy, whether people know it or not.[9]

To mitigate the concern that nudges violate autonomy, we could require that nudges be transparent. For instance, whether it is a private company or a government that is doing the nudging, the existence and purpose of the nudge could be public information.

But if nudges are effective precisely because people are not fully aware they are being nudged, then transparency, in solving one problem, might create another. If you knew that you were being nudged towards a particular behavior, might you react against the targeted behavior to convince yourself of your free will to reject coercion? This question can be answered empirically by observing responses to nudges with and without transparency. One recent study conducted such a nudging experiment with different levels of transparency (i.e., knowledge of the potential influence of the default, its purpose, or both) and found that the nudge is effective in all cases (Bruns et al. 2018). While more evidence is needed, it appears possible for nudges to be both ethical and effective.

Another critique of nudges is not philosophical, but psychological, in nature. Consider nudges that warn against the dangers of smoking, eating unhealthy foods, or not washing hands after using the bathroom. These nudges, by creating the impression of danger, impose their own psychological cost. For anyone who is contemplating decisions about smoking, eating, and hand washing, the presence of these warnings may reduce experienced utility. Being reminded that a milkshake is bad for you might cause you to order a small instead of a large, but the health reminder still makes for a less pleasurable experience.

The claim that nudges are Pareto improving is no longer true once we introduce psychological costs to nudges.[10] The individuals making mistakes remain better off with the nudge as long as the psychological costs are sufficiently small relative to the welfare gains from the nudged behavior. But if standard decision makers also experience the psychological costs of the nudge, then they are unambiguously worse off since the nudge provides no benefit for their already individually optimal behavior. And if a social planner is going to introduce a policy that imposes a cost on individuals, why not instead use a tax that at least has the benefit of generating government revenue to fund spending on education, the military, or health care? Glaeser (2005) urges skepticism of nudges for this reason, among others.

We turn in the remainder of this chapter to some real-world settings where consumers are prone to make mistakes and nudges can be a useful policy tool.

3.5   Health Mistakes   [Health]

Good health is of fundamental importance for one's well-being. But even though the stakes are high, health choices do not necessarily maximize one's individual welfare. This section explores consumer mistakes in the context of two important health care decisions: choosing health care interventions (e.g., treatments, medicines, diagnostic tests) and choosing health insurance plans.

3.5.1   *Choosing Health Care*

Consider the following true story. A 24-year-old father with a toothache visited the emergency room when his face began to swell. He was prescribed antibiotics and pain medication. Because he could not afford both, he bought only the pain medication. He later died as the tooth infection spread to his brain (Gann 2011). Had he instead chosen the antibiotics, the infection could have been treated, saving his life.

Although this devastating outcome is an extreme example of a mistaken health decision, there are many other settings where consumers are likely not maximizing their own welfare. Consider diabetes. Diabetes medications increase life expectancy and reduce the risk of blindness and limb loss. Despite these significant benefits, fewer than 70% of patients adhere to prescribed treatments (DiMatteo 2004). And while there may be underutilization of diabetes medications, there is simultaneously widespread overutilization of antibiotics. Many patients demand antibiotics for sinus infections that often clear up on their own with saline rinses and decongestants, or even take them for colds and other viral infections, against which antibiotics are useless. The overuse can cause bacteria to adapt and resist the antibiotics. In fact, the Centers for Disease Control and Prevention call antibiotic resistance "one of the world's most pressing public health problems" (CDC 2019a).

Health Care Internalities

To make sense of these decisions, let's apply our decision making framework to the consumer choice of a particular health care intervention (Baicker, Mullainathan, and Schwartzstein 2015). This could be medicine, a treatment, test, or screening. Receiving the intervention delivers a benefit, but the actual benefit may not equal the consumer's perception of the benefit when making a decision. The **experienced benefit**, b^{exp}, is the marginal experienced utility from the intervention. But the **decision benefit**, b^{dec}, is what the consumer believes the benefit to be when making their decision. This corresponds to the marginal decision utility from the intervention.[11]

If the experienced and decision benefits are not equal, then there exists an internality equal to their difference $b^{dec} - b^{exp}$. What can cause such an internality? If consumers are myopically focused on the present, they might underweight the future benefits of their diabetes medication or the future costs of antibiotic resistance. In the case of the man with the tooth infection who chose pain medications over antibiotics, he was likely overweighting the immediate pain symptoms relative to the less salient infection. Similarly, HIV patients adhere more closely to treatment regimens when symptoms are salient relative to the asymptomatic stage (Gao et al. 2000). People also form inaccurate beliefs, including the belief that vaccines cause autism or that certain herbal medicines are effective, despite no credible evidence.

Health care doesn't come for free. Let P be the price of the intervention.[12] The consumer therefore decides to purchase the intervention if and only if the perceived decision benefit exceeds the price:

$$\text{Utilizes} \Leftrightarrow b^{dec} > P$$

But they would maximize their individual welfare by purchasing the intervention if and only if the experienced benefit exceeds the price:

$$\text{Should Utilize} \Leftrightarrow b^{exp} > P$$

The relationship between decisions and individual welfare is illustrated in Figure 3.5. The standard case with no internalities, for which decision and experienced benefits are the same ($b^{dec} = b^{exp}$), corresponds to the dashed 45° line in the figure. Along this line the consumer always chooses what she should. She only purchases the treatment when the actual experienced benefit exceeds the price.

The more interesting cases occur when there is an internality. A positive internality ($b^{dec} > b^{exp}$) corresponds to a point above the 45° line. While a decision can still be

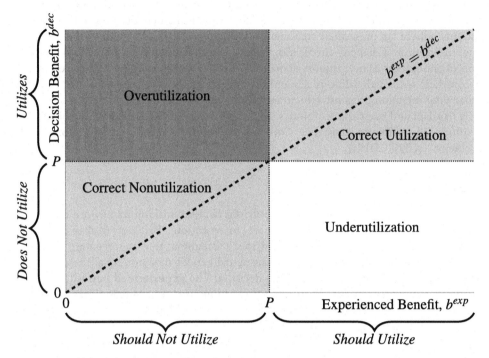

Figure 3.5 Health Care Utilization with Internalities

welfare-maximizing with a positive internality, it is also possible to be in the overutilization region. Examples of overutilization include use of ineffective treatments like antibiotics for sinus or ear infections. There are also expensive treatments that have been shown to deliver minimal, if any, benefits, including arthroscopic surgery for osteoarthritis of the knee and proton-beam therapy for prostate cancer (Chandra and Skinner 2012). Consumers who demand unnecessary tests like MRIs for low back pain would also fall into this region.

A negative internality ($b^{dec} < b^{exp}$) conversely corresponds to a point below the 45° line. In this case, consumers undervalue the benefits of the intervention and can underutilize health care. Diabetes patients who fail to adhere to their treatment regimen are an example. Preventative care, like a vaccine or screening, that delivers a high experienced benefit is also at risk of being underutilized.

Nudging Adherence

When patients make health care choices that do not maximize their own welfare there exists a paternalistic justification for policy intervention. Consider the case of high blood pressure (hypertension). Adherence to medications that reduce blood pressure is important for reducing the risks of heart disease and stroke. Cutler et al. (2007) estimate that anti-hypertensive therapy averts 90,000 premature deaths in a given year. But overall adherence to hypertensive therapies is around 50% to 70%. The observation that many patients underutilize high-value medications suggests a negative internality.

Suppose that a policy objective is to help improve welfare for those who are underutilizing anti-hypertension medication, without changing the incentives or options for those who are adhering. A solution is to nudge individuals towards decisions that better align with their own experienced welfare. Nudges could take the form of patient education, peer support, simplification of dosing schedules, or regular reminders. These interventions do not change the options or economic incentives for patients, but if they help to make the benefits of adherence more salient, they could encourage compliance. There is evidence that in fact, simplified dosing regimens and reminders improve adherence by 10% to 20% (Schroeder, Fahey, and Ebrahim 2004). More generally, nudges hold promise as an effective policy tool for public health.

3.5.2 *Choosing Health Insurance Plans*

Another important health decision (at least in the US) is choosing a health insurance plan. Whether an individual is offered health insurance through their employer, or purchases health insurance in a private marketplace, there is often a menu of plans from which to choose.

Choosing a health insurance plan is a complicated decision. Each plan specifies a different network of doctors and specialists, covered medications, monthly premiums, deductibles, and copays for every possible treatment. This decision is further complicated by the fact that you can only change health insurance plans once per year and must make your choice before you know how healthy or sick you will be in the following year.

Given this complexity, it should not be surprising if many consumers don't choose the plan that would maximize their own welfare, but simply choose to remain in their current plan. The tendency to do nothing is a form of inertia. Handel (2013) studies health plan choice inertia for employees at a large company. He finds that even when employees have the option of switching to another plan that is clearly better for them, the majority remain with their current plan. This inertia causes the average employee to give up over $2,000 a year in savings. Any benefit from not actively shopping across plans, in terms of time and effort saved, comes at a considerable financial cost.

An Unintended Consequence of Nudging Insurance Plans

Policy makers in both public and private settings have worked to implement nudges that make it easier for consumers to evaluate their health insurance options. These nudges include simple standardized benefits descriptions, customized plan recommendations, and default options.

There is, however, a potential drawback to nudging consumers towards choosing the best plan for their own welfare. To see how nudging can backfire, start by imagining a set of health insurance plans that offer different amounts of coverage, where more comprehensive plans are more expensive. In a pre-nudge world with strong inertia, once a consumer selects their first plan, they do not switch plans, even as their health changes over time. The individual who signed up for a comprehensive plan anticipating high medical care needs, but who luckily remained healthy, does not switch to a cheaper plan with less coverage. Similarly, someone who develops conditions or contracts diseases that require expensive treatment does not switch to a plan best suited to their current medical needs.

What happens once we introduce nudges that make it easier to find the best plan each year? The good news is that *if* the insurance plan prices stay fixed, consumers will improve their welfare by making better choices. But prices will not stay fixed. The comprehensive plans will become popular with unhealthy consumers. To cover the higher expenses of insuring a less healthy population, the price of the comprehensive plans will increase. Healthy individuals will then switch towards the cheaper plans with less generous coverage since they do not expect to use health care often. This sorting process is known as *adverse selection* because the comprehensive insurance is selected by the less healthy consumers (who are adverse consumers from the perspective of the insurance company since they cost more to insure). Once we account for the price adjustments as consumers self sort into different plans, social welfare can actually decline substantially. Handel (2013) estimates that social welfare falls by almost 8% when inertia is reduced by nudging. This example illustrates how policy makers must be careful to think through the unintended consequences of nudging for market outcomes.

3.6   Energy-Efficient Light Bulb Underuse   [Energy]

The average American spends almost $1,500 per year on electricity. This is more than spending on groceries for meat, poultry, fish, eggs, and dairy combined (BLS 2020). But by adopting energy-efficient technologies, consumers can realize cost savings. Compact fluorescent light bulbs (CFLs), for instance, last longer and use four times less electricity relative to standard incandescent light bulbs. Switching to a CFL from an incandescent light bulb can save about $5 per year on average. This is not an insignificant saving, especially when adding up the many light bulbs in a home or an office building.

Given the savings from CFLs and only minor drawbacks — they are not dimmable and take a few moments to reach full brightness — we would expect many consumers to adopt this technology. But in 2010, CFLs filled only 28% of available household sockets, costing US households a total of $15 billion by using incandescent bulbs instead of CFLs (Allcott and Taubinsky 2015). More generally, the observation that many consumers do not choose to adopt cost saving energy-efficient products is called the *energy paradox* (Jaffe and Stavins 1994).

The energy paradox looks like the consequence of a consumer mistake. The underutilization of energy-efficient light bulbs is predicted for consumers whose decision benefit is sufficiently below their actual experienced benefit. A consumer may have a low decision benefit because they underweight or misperceive the future energy savings from investing in CFLs. Or they may simply be inattentive to publicly available information about the cost savings. With consumer mistakes, there is a paternalistic motivation for encouraging adoption of energy-efficient light bulbs. This rationale can reinforce other motivations — like correcting market failures induced by externalities or market power — for government intervention in the light bulb market.

Many countries have introduced a mix of bans and subsidies to promote the use of energy-efficient light bulbs. A benefit of such interventions is the improvement in individual welfare for those who are better off buying CFLs, but only do so because of the policy. A drawback is that for standard decision makers who prefer to give up the cost savings of CFLs in exchange for the warm light and bulbous shape of traditional incandescent bulbs, a ban on traditional bulbs makes them worse off.

An alternative policy that does not restrict consumer choice is a nudge. Allcott and Taubinsky (2015) study the impact of a nudge that provides consumers with information about cost savings from CFLs. The standard model predicts that this nudge should have no impact on behavior because the information provided was already publicly available to consumers; why would choices change if you are reminded of something you should already know? But for consumers who are mistaken, inattentive, or uninformed about the cost savings, the nudge provides clarity and can subsequently impact behavior. The authors find that the nudge increases the average willingness to pay for a 60-watt CFL by $2.30. The nudge is therefore effective at boosting demand for energy-efficient light bulbs, without coercion or a restriction of choices. It is also likely that any psychological costs associated with the informational nudge would be small. This is a nudge success story.

3.7   Summary

1   **Welfarism** measures welfare only in terms of **experienced utility**, or the experienced satisfaction from an outcome.
2   Standard economics assumes that individuals make decisions by maximizing **decision utility**, and that it is simultaneously equal to experienced utility. Under these assumptions, there is no paternalistic rationale for government intervention.
3   Behavioral economics allows for settings in which there is a gap between an individual's marginal decision utility and marginal experienced utility. This gap is called an **internality** because individuals are not fully recognizing the consequences of their decisions on their own internal experiences. There is a paternalistic rationale for government intervention when an internality exists.
4   A **nudge** is a form of soft paternalism that changes behavior without forbidding any options or changing economic incentives. Nudges have been used widely by governments, policy makers, and private companies.
5   Nudges have the advantage relative to traditional policy interventions of not restricting choices. Concerns with nudges include their potential to undermine autonomy and impose psychological costs on consumers.
6   Health care is a setting where consumers may make mistakes when choosing care or insurance plans. While nudges can help to improve individual welfare in some contexts, they can also generate unintended negative consequences.
7   Nudging energy-efficient light bulbs, which save consumers money relative to traditional incandescent bulbs, is effective at promoting their use.

3.8   Exercises

Exercise 3.1 — Government Goals. For each of the following government policies, briefly discuss whether the primary motivation for the policy is to redistribute, correct a market failure, or correct an individual mistake (i.e., paternalism).

a   A ban on looking at your phone while crossing the street.
b   Speed limits on highways.
c   National defense.
d   Nutritional support (e.g., food stamps) for low-income families.
e   A ban on plastic straws.
f   Progressive income taxation.
g   Safety regulation of food, drugs, and cosmetics.

Exercise 3.2 — Broad Range of Benevolence. Abbi and Ilana are the only ones in society. There is a fixed set of resources that can be distributed between them. Each

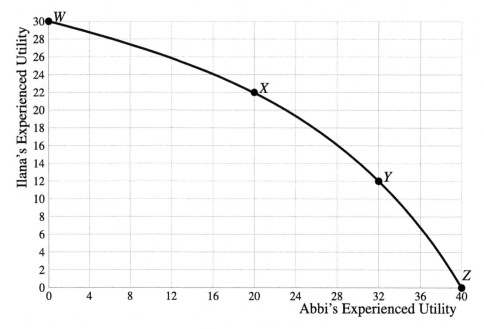

Figure 3.6 Frontier of Possible Experienced Utilities in Exercise 3.2

allocation of resources leads to a different combination of experienced utilities for Abbi and Ilana — the more that one has, the greater is their experienced utility and the lower is the other's experienced utility. This tradeoff between experienced utilities is depicted in Figure 3.6. Rank the four labeled allocations of experienced utilities (*W*, *X*, *Y*, and *Z*) for a benevolent social planner with each of the following social welfare functions:

a   Utilitarian social welfare.
b   Rawlsian social welfare.

Exercise 3.3 — Social Welfare Calculations. Alma and Bruno are the only ones in society. There is a fixed set of resources that can be distributed between them. Each allocation of resources leads to a different combination of experienced utilities for Alma (U_A^{exp}) and Bruno (U_B^{exp}). The set of possible experienced utilities is given by the following constraint:

$$U_A^{exp} + 2U_B^{exp} = 200$$

Observe that the more satisfaction one citizen achieves, less is possible for the other. What allocation of experienced utilities (U_A^{exp}, U_B^{exp}) maximizes social welfare in the following cases?

a   Utilitarian social welfare. *Hint: It is socially optimal to give one person zero experienced utility.*
b   Rawlsian social welfare. *Hint: It is socially optimal to give Alma and Bruno equal experienced utilities.*

c **[Calculus Required]** Bernoulli–Nash social welfare, which is the product of the experienced utilities (don't worry, this was not in the chapter). *Hint: Use calculus to maximize $U_A^{exp} \times U_B^{exp}$ after plugging in the constraint above.*

d Which social welfare criterion strikes you as being the most just or fair? Why?

Exercise 3.4 — Wicked Welfarism (Sen 1979a). There are three social outcomes, X, Y, and Z, with the following experienced utilities for the only two persons in society, Ann and Bob, in each social outcome:

	Social Outcome		
	X	Y	Z
Ann's Experienced Utility	4	7	8
Bob's Experienced Utility	12	9	7

- In social outcome X, Ann is hungry while Bob eats amply.
- In social outcome Y, Bob has been forced to give food to Ann.
- In social outcome Z, Ann is as hungry as in X and Bob is as amply fed, but Ann, who happens to be a sadist, is allowed to torture Bob (who is not a masochist).

a Is any one social outcome a Pareto improvement relative to another? If so, which one? If not, why not?

b In the welfarism approach, how would a utilitarian and a Rawlsian social planner each rank the desirability of the three social outcomes?

c What is a critique of the welfarism approach in the context of this (stylized) example? Briefly discuss how one might modify welfarism to accommodate your critique.

Exercise 3.5 — Internalities in Action. Propose a new context, not discussed in the chapter, where consumers are likely to exhbit a:

a positive internality; and

b negative internality.

Exercise 3.6 — A Case of the School Blues. Edith is deciding how many years of higher education to pursue. Because she underweights the future benefits of higher education, she has a negative internality — her marginal experienced utility is greater than her marginal decision utility. This is depicted in Figure 3.7, where $P^* = \$10,000$ is the market price for an additional year of higher education.

a How many years of higher education does Edith choose? What is her consumer surplus?

b How many years of higher education would maximize Edith's consumer surplus?

c What is Edith's loss in consumer surplus in part (a) relative to her maximum possible consumer surplus in part (b)?

Exercise 3.7 — A Cure for the School Blues. Consider once again Edith's higher education decision in Exercise 3.6. You, as a benevolent social planner, want to help Edith make the choice that maximizes her own consumer surplus. To do so, you

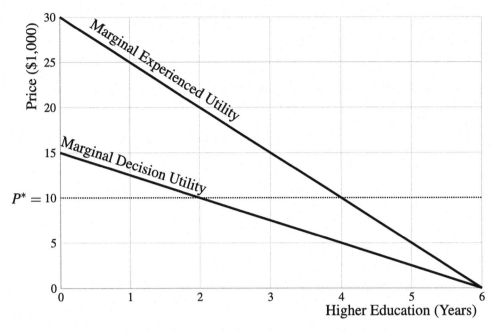

Figure 3.7 Marginal Decision and Experienced Utilities in Exercise 3.6

propose subsidizing higher education by paying Edith $s for each year of education she consumes. Refer to Figure 3.7 to answer the following questions.

a   How large should the per-unit subsidy s be in order to induce Edith to choose the level of education that maximizes her consumer surplus (as found in Exercise 3.6(b))?
b   To finance this subsidy you must also impose a lump-sum tax on Edith equal to the total cost of the subsidy (i.e., the product of s and the quantity of education chosen by Edith in part (a)). What is the size of this lump-sum tax?
c   What is Edith's consumer surplus with the per-unit subsidy in part (a) minus the lump-sum tax in part (b)? How does this compare to her consumer surplus without any government intervention?

Exercise 3.8 — A Tale of Two Nudges. Reflect on the nudges that you encounter in your daily life.

a   What is a nudge you benefit from? In what ways do its advantages outweigh its disadvantages?
b   What is the worst nudge you can think of? Why is it so objectionable?

Exercise 3.9 — Chipping Away at Welfare. Sophal and Madeline consume potato chips. While Sophal is a standard decision maker, Madeline exhibits a positive internality, overconsuming potato chips. You are a benevolent social planner evaluating the impact of a nudge on social welfare. The nudge only impacts Madeline's behavior, reducing her potato chip consumption and increasing her experienced utility from chip consumption. However, the nudge also imposes a psychological cost $C > 0$ on everyone. Let the experienced utilities for each consumer, net of the psychological nudge cost be as follows:

	No Nudge	*With Nudge*
Sophal's Experienced Utility	10	$10 - C$
Madeline's Experienced Utility	8	$14 - C$

a   Does the nudge generate a Pareto improvement? Why or why not?
b   Suppose that you evaluate social welfare as a utilitarian. For what range of C does the nudge improve social welfare?
c   Suppose that you evaluate social welfare as a Rawlsian. For what range of C does the nudge improve social welfare?
d   Suppose that Madeline's experienced utility with the nudge is $20 - C$ instead of $14 - C$. How do your answers in parts (b) and (c) change? Interpret.

Exercise 3.10 — Neighbors as Nudges. [Energy] Schultz et al. (2007) conduct a field experiment to test the impact of nudging consumers in San Marcos, California to conserve electricity. The nudge is a message left at the doors of consumers with information about how their electricity consumption compares to the average household in the neighborhood.

a   The nudge induced households with above average electricity consumption to reduce their consumption by just over 1 kilowatt-hour per day. This is equivalent to turning off ten 100-watt light bulbs for an hour each day. But the nudge also induced households with below average electricity consumption to *increase* their consumption by almost 1 kilowatt-hour per day. Provide a plausible explanation for these two results. Would you recommend this nudge as a policy? Why or why not?
b   The researchers also tested an *enhanced* nudge on a different set of households that included emoticons in the informational message. Households with below average electricity consumption received a happy face on the message, while households with above average consumption received a sad face. This nudge had a stronger impact on above average consumers, who reduced their electricity consumption by 1.7 kilowatt-hours per day. And the nudge had no impact on the electricity consumption of below average consumers. Why do you think the introduction of the emoticons changed the impacts of the nudge? Would you recommend this nudge as a policy? Why or why not?
c   You are a benevolent social planner concerned that individuals are mistakenly overconsuming energy. Would you recommend an informational nudge or a tax on energy to correct this mistake? Justify your answer.

Exercise 3.11 — An Education with No Strings Attached. [Development] In 2008 the government of Morocco was developing a new program aimed at increasing the primary school completion rate for children in rural areas. The program, *Tayssir*, was designed to provide an annual cash transfer paid to fathers equal to about 5% of household expenditures, *conditional* on school enrollment and attendance.

Benhassine et al. (2015) conduct a field experiment in Morocco to evaluate the impact of *Tayssir*. In particular, each of 320 school sectors was randomly assigned to either receive 1) no cash transfer, 2) the conditional cash transfer, or 3) a cash transfer that was *labeled* as an education support program, but not conditional on school enrollment or attendance.

a   Explain why the unconditional labeled cash transfer can be understood as a nudge.
b   Assume that households are standard decision makers. In this case, would you expect the conditional cash transfer or the unconditional labeled cash transfer to be more effective at increasing primary school completion rates?
c   The researchers find large impacts of cash transfers on school participation, with little difference between the conditional and unconditional cash transfers. Explain why this evidence suggests that households may have been making a mistake in this setting. In addition, how might the nudge be working to correct this mistake?

Notes

1   Rawlsian social welfare refers to the work of John Rawls (1971).
2   Excellent references for normative analysis in behavioral economics settings include Bernheim and Rangel (2009) and Mullainathan, Schwartzstein, and Congdon (2012).
3   I make the simplifying assumption of quasilinear decision utility and quasilinear experienced utility functions here, and throughout the book. A quasilinear utility function takes the form $u(Q) + Y$ where Q is the quantity of the good of interest and Y is money spent on other goods.
4   Herrnstein et al. (1993) introduced the internality concept and Mullainathan, Schwartzstein, and Congdon (2012) analyze public policy in the presence of internalities. The internality as defined here is also referred to as the *marginal* internality.
5   In the analysis of a per-unit tax, I am implicitly assuming a horizontal, perfectly elastic, supply curve.
6   It is possible to make everyone better off with a carefully designed tax-rebate policy, as discussed in Section 7.3.
7   There are also potential negative externalities from obesity and drug use that would provide an independent rationale for government intervention.
8   Another objection is an *epistemic* argument that in order to design a nudge, the nudger needs to know the preferences of the nudged better than they themselves do. Sunstein (2015) defends against this criticism and Chetty (2015) discusses policy applications of nudges in the context of uncertainty about individual decision making.
9   See Bovens (2009) for a deeper exploration of the ethical implications of nudging.
10 Jimenez-Gomez (2018) develops a theory of optimal nudging with psychological costs.
11 Both b^{exp} and b^{dec} are measured in monetary terms.
12 For simplicity, I assume that the patient is uninsured and that the price P equals the social marginal cost of providing the treatment. Therefore, what is best for the individual is also best for society. Otherwise, with insurance, the consumer would only pay a fraction of the social cost in the form of a copay. And then it is possible for a treatment to be individually optimal but not socially optimal. This is known as moral hazard.

References

Allcott, Hunt, and Dmitry Taubinsky. 2015. "Evaluating Behaviorally Motivated Policy: Experimental Evidence from the Lightbulb Market." *American Economic Review* 105 (8): 2501–2538. doi:10.1257/aer.20131564.

Baicker, Katherine, Sendhil Mullainathan, and Joshua Schwartzstein. 2015. "Behavioral Hazard in Health Insurance." *The Quarterly Journal of Economics* 130 (4): 1623–1667. doi:10.1093/qje/qjv029.

Benartzi, Shlomo, John Beshears, Katherine L. Milkman, Cass R. Sunstein, Richard H. Thaler, Maya Shankar, Will Tucker-Ray, William J. Congdon, and Steven Galing. 2017. "Should Governments Invest More in Nudging?" *Psychological Science* 28 (8): 1041–1055. doi:10.1177/0956797617702501.

Benhassine, Najy, Florencia Devoto, Esther Duflo, Pascaline Dupas, and Victor Pouliquen. 2015. "Turning a Shove into a Nudge? A 'Labeled Cash Transfer' for Education." *American Economic Journal: Economic Policy* 7 (3): 86–125. doi:10.1257/pol. 20130225.

Bernheim, B. Douglas, and Antonio Rangel. 2009. "Beyond Revealed Preference: Choice-Theoretic Foundations for Behavioral Welfare Economics." *The Quarterly Journal of Economics* 124 (1): 51–104. doi:10.1162/qjec.2009.124.1.51.

Berridge, Kent C., and Terry E. Robinson. 2003. "Parsing Reward." *Trends in Neurosciences* 26 (9): 507–513. doi:10.1016/S0166-2236(03)00233-9.

BLS (Bureau of Labor Statistics). 2020. *Consumer Expenditures Surveys Tables.* Last Modified September 22, 2020, https://www.bls.gov/cex/tables.htm#annual.

Bovens, Luc. 2009. "The Ethics of Nudge." In *Preference Change,* edited by Till Grüne-Yanoff and Sven Ove Hansson, 207–219. Theory and Decision Library 42. Dordrecht: Springer Netherlands. doi:10.1007/978-90-481-2593-7_10.

Bruns, Hendrik, Elena Kantorowicz-Reznichenko, Katharina Klement, Marijane Luistro Jonsson, and Bilel Rahali. 2018. "Can Nudges Be Transparent and yet Effective?" *Journal of Economic Psychology* 65: 41–59. doi:10.1016/j.joep.2018.02. 002.

Camerer, Colin F., Samuel Issacharoff, George Loewenstein, Ted O'Donoghue, and Matthew Rabin. 2003. "Regulation for Conservatives: Behavioral Economics and the Case for 'Asymmetric Paternalism.' " *University of Pennsylvania Law Review* 151 (3): 1211–1254. doi:10.2307/3312889.

CDC (Centers for Disease Control and Prevention). 2019. *Antibiotic Resistance.* Last Reviewed November 21, 2019, https://www.cdc.gov/narms/faq.html.

Chandra, Amitabh, and Jonathan Skinner. 2012. "Technology Growth and Expenditure Growth in Health Care." *Journal of Economic Literature* 50 (3): 645–680. doi:10.1257/jel.50.3.645.

Chetty, Raj. 2015. "Behavioral Economics and Public Policy: A Pragmatic Perspective." *American Economic Review* 105 (5): 1–33. doi:10.1257/aer.p20151108.

Cutler, David M., Genia Long, Ernst R. Berndt, Jimmy Royer, Andrée-Anne Fournier, Alicia Sasser, and Pierre Cremieux. 2007. "The Value Of Antihypertensive Drugs: A Perspective On Medical Innovation." *Health Affairs* 26 (1): 97–110. doi:10.1377/hlthaff.26.1.97.

DiMatteo, M. Robin. 2004. "Variations in Patients' Adherence to Medical Recommendations: A Quantitative Review of 50 Years of Research." *Medical Care* 42 (3): 200–209. doi:10.1097/01. mlr.0000114908.90348.f9.

Gann, Carrie. 2011. "Without Insurance, Man Dies from Toothache." *ABC News,* September 2, 2011. https://abcnews.go.com/Health/insurance-24-year-dies-toothache/story?id=14438171.

Gao, X., D. P. Nau, S. A. Rosenbluth, V. Scott, and C. Woodward. 2000. "The Relationship of Disease Severity, Health Beliefs and Medication Adherence among HIV Patients." *AIDS Care* 12 (4): 387–398. doi:10.1080/09540120050123783.

Glaeser, Edward L. 2005. "Paternalism and Psychology." NBER Working Paper 11789. Cambridge, MA: National Bureau of Economic Research. doi:10.3386/w11789.

Handel, Benjamin R. 2013. "Adverse Selection and Inertia in Health Insurance Markets: When Nudging Hurts." *American Economic Review* 103 (7): 2643–2682. doi:10.1257/aer.103.7.2643.

Herrnstein, Richard J., George Loewenstein, Drazen Prelec, and William Vaughan. 1993. "Utility Maximization and Melioration: Internalities in Individual Choice." *Journal of Behavioral Decision Making* 6 (3): 149–185. doi:10.1002/bdm.3960060302.

Jaffe, Adam B., and Robert N. Stavins. 1994. "The Energy Paradox and the Diffusion of Conservation Technology." *Resource and Energy Economics* 16 (2): 91–122. doi:10.1016/0928-7655(94)90001-9.

Jimenez-Gomez, David. 2018. "Nudging and Phishing: A Theory of Behavioral Welfare Economics." SSRN Scholarly Paper ID 3248503. Rochester, NY: Social Science Research Network. https://papers.ssrn.com/abstract=3248503.

Kahneman, Daniel, and Jackie Snell. 1992. "Predicting a Changing Taste: Do People Know What They Will Like?" *Journal of Behavioral Decision Making* 5 (3): 187–200. doi:10.1002/bdm.3960050304.

Kahneman, Daniel, and Robert Sugden. 2005. "Experienced Utility as a Standard of Policy Evaluation." *Environmental and Resource Economics* 32 (1): 161–181. doi:10.1007/s10640-005-6032-4.

Kahneman, Daniel, Peter P. Wakker, and Rakesh Sarin. 1997. "Back to Bentham? Explorations of Experienced Utility." *The Quarterly Journal of Economics* 112 (2): 375–406. doi:10.1162/003355397555235.

Loewenstein, George, and Nick Chater. 2017. "Putting Nudges in Perspective." *Behavioural Public Policy* 1 (1): 26–53. doi:10.1017/bpp.2016.7.

Mullainathan, Sendhil, Joshua Schwartzstein, and William J. Congdon. 2012. "A Reduced-Form Approach to Behavioral Public Finance." *Annual Review of Economics* 4 (1): 511–540. doi:10.1146/annurev-economics-111809-125033.

Nussbaum, Martha C. 2001. *Women and Human Development: The Capabilities Approach.* Cambridge: Cambridge University Press.

OECD. 2019. "Revenue Statistics 2019." Technical report. Paris: OECD Publishing. doi:10.1787/0bbc27da-en.

Posner, Richard A. 2011. *Economic Analysis of Law.* 8th edition. New York: Aspen Publishers.

Rawls, John. 1971. *A Theory of Justice.* Cambridge, MA: Harvard University Press.

Schroeder, Knut, Tom Fahey, and Shah Ebrahim. 2004. "How Can We Improve Adherence to Blood Pressure-Lowering Medication in Ambulatory Care?: Systematic Review of Randomized Controlled Trials." *Archives of Internal Medicine* 164 (7): 722–732. doi:10.1001/archinte.164.7.722.

Schultz, P. Wesley, Jessica M. Nolan, Robert B. Cialdini, Noah J. Goldstein, and Vladas Griskevicius. 2007. "The Constructive, Destructive, and Reconstructive Power of Social Norms." *Psychological Science* 18 (5): 429–434. doi:10.1111/j.1467-9280.2007.01917.x.

Sen, Amartya. 1979a. "Personal Utilities and Public Judgements: Or What's Wrong With Welfare Economics." *The Economic Journal* 89 (355): 537–558. doi:10.2307/2231867.

———. 1979b. "Utilitarianism and Welfarism." *The Journal of Philosophy* 76 (9): 463–489. doi:10.2307/2025934.

Sen, Amartya. 1985. *Commodities and Capabilities.* North-Holland: Oxford University Press.

Sugden, Robert. 2008. "Why Incoherent Preferences Do Not Justify Paternalism." *Constitutional Political Economy* 19 (3): 226–248. doi:10.1007/s10602-008-9043-7.

Sunstein, Cass R. 2013. "Nudges vs. Shoves." *Harvard Law Review Forum* 127: 210. https://heinonline.org/HOL/Page?handle=hein.journals/forharoc127&id=212&div=&collection=.

———. 2015. *Why Nudge?: The Politics of Libertarian Paternalism.* Reprint edition. New Haven: Yale University Press.

Sunstein, Cass R., Lucia A. Reisch, and Julius Rauber. 2018. "A Worldwide Consensus on Nudging? Not Quite, but Almost." *Regulation & Governance* 12 (1): 3–22. doi:https://doi.org/10.1111/rego.12161.

Thaler, Richard H. 2016. "Behavioral Economics: Past, Present, and Future." *American Economic Review* 106 (7): 1577–1600. doi:10.1257/aer.106.7.1577.

Thaler, Richard H., and Cass R. Sunstein. 2003. "Libertarian Paternalism." *American Economic Review* 93 (2): 175–179. doi:10.1257/000282803321947001.

———. 2009. *Nudge: Improving Decisions About Health, Wealth, and Happiness.* Revised & Expanded. New York: Penguin Books.

Part II

Intertemporal Preferences

A standard assumption in the model of individual decision making (Definition 2.9) is that individuals evaluate sequences of outcomes with the Discounted Utility model of preferences. This means that the instantaneous utilities achieved from the outcomes in each period are discounted by an exponential discount function and then added together. These features of the standard model are highlighted below:

$$\max_{(x_0,x_1,\dots,x_T)\in X} \sum_{k=0}^{T} \delta^k\, E[\, u(x_k)\; |\; p] \qquad \text{(Standard Model)}$$

The objective for this part of the book is to question these highlighted assumptions and consider alternative ways of evaluating a sequence of outcomes. To focus the analysis, I restrict attention to settings without uncertainty. I also maintain the other standard assumptions of self-interested utility maximization with preferences defined over final outcomes.

Part II is organized as follows. Chapter 4 begins by documenting evidence of intertemporal choice that is inconsistent with the behavior predicted by the standard model. In particular, we assess the implications of assuming exponential discounting ($\sum_{k=0}^{T} \delta^k$), along with an instantaneous utility function $u(\cdot)$ that depends only on outcomes in the current period. Chapter 5 considers an alternative nonstandard model by allowing for a non-exponential discount function that captures individuals' bias towards the present. Chapter 6 introduces models of habit formation and anticipation that allow for the instantaneous utility function to depend not only on current outcomes, but on past and future outcomes. And finally in Chapter 7 we consider market and policy responses to individuals who make such nonstandard intertemporal choices.

4 Discounted Utility Model Anomalies

Learning Objectives

★ Evaluate the descriptive accuracy of the Discounted Utility model by comparing its theoretical predictions with evidence from lab experiments.

★ Hypothesize modifications to the Discounted Utility model that could better explain observed behavior.

★ Understand the intuition for, and limitations of, the standard life-cycle consumption and savings problem.

Imagine that you are a pioneering behavioral economist looking to test the standard Discounted Utility (DU) model of preferences (see Section 2.2). This is a challenging task because you cannot directly observe the utility functions of individuals with a pair of binoculars, a microscope, or an MRI machine. And if you ask a friend to tell you their utility function over a sequence of outcomes, they may very well start laughing at such an absurd question.

In this first chapter on intertemporal choice we explore the evidence that early behavioral economists generated from clever lab experiments to convince skeptics that the standard DU model is often *consistently inconsistent* with actual behavior. The discrepancies between the predictions of the DU model and empirical evidence constitute anomalies for the standard model. The following anomalies are identified: time effects, magnitude effects, sign effects, and a preference for improving sequences. The chapter concludes with an analysis of the standard life-cycle model predictions for consumption and savings behaviors over one's life, and the conflicting evidence.

So as to guide our critique of the DU model, it is helpful to recognize that the model is not a single assumption, but in fact summarizes a *set* of assumptions for evaluating a sequence of outcomes. The two key assumptions are:

1   *Constant Discounting*: the discount rate ρ is constant between any two consecutive periods. This is equivalent to assuming an exponential form for the discount function, $D(k) = \delta^k$, where the discount factor δ is equal to $1/(1 + \rho)$. Constant discounting also implies time-consistent preferences.

2   *Consumption Independence*: an outcome's instantaneous utility does not depend on outcomes experienced in past or future periods. For example, today's preference for eating Korean BBQ or Chinese food is independent of having eaten Chinese food yesterday or expecting to eat Chinese food tomorrow.

DOI: 10.4324/9780367854072-6

There are many more implicit assumptions in the DU model that I omit, as we will focus on challenges to the two assumptions above.[1]

4.1   Time Effects

This section considers evidence that individuals discount future outcomes at different rates depending on the length of the delay. In particular, discount rates appear to be smaller for more distant outcomes. This time effect on the discount rate constitutes our first anomaly of the DU model.

4.1.1   *Preference Reversals*

Lab Experiment — Apples Away (Thaler 1981)
Thaler (1981, 202) suggests the following two decision problems, A and B:

A Choose between

   $A.1$ One apple today
   $A.2$ Two apples tomorrow

B Choose between

   $B.1$ One apple in one year
   $B.2$ Two apples in one year plus one day

Decision problem A asks individuals to evaluate the tradeoff between more consumption ($A.2$) and sooner consumption ($A.1$). There is no right or wrong choice here, and it is typical for approximately a third of individuals to select $A.1$. For these individuals, immediate consumption outweighs higher consumption in the future. When faced with decision problem B, however, almost no one chooses $B.1$. It is reasonable that after a year-long delay, most individuals are sufficiently patient to wait one extra day to double the number of apples that they receive.

How does this experimental evidence reveal an anomaly? Although the DU model does not require any particular choices to be made in the above decision problems *in isolation*, it does make a prediction about how an individual's choices *across* these two decision problems are related. In fact, A and B are equivalent decision problems according the DU model. Decision problem B is simply decision problem A shifted forward in time. To see this formally, let's apply the DU model by letting a period be equal to a day, δ be the daily discount factor, and u be the instantaneous utility function defined over the number of apples.[2] Then:

$$B.2 \text{ preferred to } B.1 \quad \Leftrightarrow \quad \delta^{366}u(2) > \delta^{365}u(1)$$
$$\Leftrightarrow \quad \delta u(2) \quad > u(1) \quad \Leftrightarrow \quad A.2 \text{ preferred to } A.1$$

where the second line follows by dividing both sides of the inequality by δ^{365}. This chain of reasoning demonstrates that if an individual prefers *B.2*, then they must also prefer *A.2*. This is true for any $u(\cdot)$ and any δ. And yet, there are individuals (you may be one of them) who will wait an extra day for an additional apple if the apples are received far in the future (prefer *B.2*), and at the same time will not wait for an extra apple today (prefer *A.1*).

This phenomenon is an example of a **preference reversal.** More generally, a preference reversal refers to a situation in which, as two differentially delayed rewards are both brought closer to the present, preferences switch to favor the sooner reward. Such preference reversals have been established in a number of experimental settings. For example, Kirby and Herrnstein (1995) offer 36 individuals the choice between delayed rewards with differing delay lengths. They find that 34 of the subjects (94%) exhibit preference reversals.

Preference reversals have even been documented in non-humans. In one experiment, pigeons were offered a choice between a sooner, but shorter access period to eat grain and a more delayed, but longer access period for feeding. When both opportunities to eat grain were sufficiently delayed, the pigeons chose to wait for the more delayed, but longer eating option. As the two options were shifted closer to the present, all six pigeons in the study reversed preferences in favor of the smaller-sooner reward (Ainslie and Herrnstein 1981).

The DU model rules out the possibility of preference reversals. This is because with time-consistent preferences (as in the DU model), future preferences always confirm earlier preferences — you cannot act differently than you had planned. But with a preference reversal, you make the decision today about apple consumption a year from now and plan to wait an extra day for an extra apple, only to then change your mind a year later and forego the additional apple tomorrow in exchange for immediate consumption. Because the DU model makes a prediction that is inconsistent with empirical evidence from multiple studies, we have reason to reject this model of behavior as universally valid.

How might we then modify the DU model to allow for this observed behavior? Preference reversals can be understood as a **self-control problem** in which individuals (or pigeons) are able to be patient for distant rewards, but become impatient for more immediate rewards and give in to the soonest reward despite it being smaller. Recall that discount rates are often interpreted as a measure of impatience because with a high discount rate, future utility is discounted more and consequently valued less relative to the present. Thus, if individuals are impatient in the short run and more patient in the long run, an alternative model would allow for discount rates to become smaller for more distant outcomes.

Let's confirm that a model with a declining discount rate over the time horizon, or equivalently, an increasing discount factor, can make sense of the observed preference reversal in the Apples Away Lab Experiment. Let δ_S and δ_L be short-run and long-run daily discount factors where $\delta_S < \delta_L$. Suppose that individuals use the short-run discount factor when evaluating decision problem A and the long-run discount factor for decision problem B. In addition, assume there is an individual with a preference reversal who prefers *A.1* over *A.2* and *B.2* over *B.1*. Then:

$$A.1 \text{ preferred to } A.2 \quad \Leftrightarrow \quad u(1) > \delta_S u(2)$$
$$B.2 \text{ preferred to } B.1 \quad \Leftrightarrow \quad \delta_L u(2) > u(1)$$

Both of these inequalities can now be true at the same time if $\delta_L u(2) > u(1) > \delta_S u(2)$. Note that with constant discounting, $\delta_L = \delta_S$ and then these two inequalities cannot both hold simultaneously (because then $\delta u(2) > \delta u(2)$, a mathematical impossibility). By relaxing the assumption that the discount rate, and thereby the discount factor, is the same for all time horizons, we have modified the DU model so that it can be consistent with observed behavior. We now turn to extending this intuition of declining discount rates (or increasing discount factors) to another setting.

4.1.2   Hyperbolic Discounting

Lab Experiment — Winnings Wait (Thaler 1981)

Good News! You have won $15 in a lottery. You can receive the money now or in the future. How much money would you need in 1 year to make you indifferent between waiting and taking the money now?

   Also answer this question if the winnings are $250 or $3,000 instead of $15. How do your answers change if the time horizon is 3 months or 3 years instead of 1 year?

The median responses from University of Oregon students surveyed by Thaler (1981) are as follows:

Table 4.1 Typical Responses to Winnings Wait Lab Experiment

Current Prize Amount	or, equivalently, Receive in		
	3 months	1 year	3 years
$15	$30 (277%)	$60 (139%)	$100 (63%)
$250	$300 (73%)	$350 (34%)	$500 (23%)
$3,000	$3,500 (62%)	$4,000 (29%)	$6,000 (23%)

Note: Each cell contains the median indifference dollar amount, with the implied average annual discount rate in parentheses.

Consider the first scenario in the above lab experiment. A typical respondent is indifferent between receiving $15 today and $60 in one year. The individual therefore needs to be compensated with an additional $45 to wait one year for her winnings. Observe that the more compensation an individual requires for waiting reflects a greater discount rate. For a very patient individual who does not discount the future at all, they are indifferent between $15 today and $15 in the future. But for a very impatient individual who heavily discounts the future, a delay requires a substantial increase in the future payout to remain indifferent. It turns out the implied average annual discount rate is 139% for someone who is indifferent between $15 today and $60 in one year. This and the other corresponding discount rates are reported in parentheses in Table 4.1.[3]

   Regardless of the amount of the winnings today, there is a striking pattern in the results: as the time horizon increases (read the rows in Table 4.1 from left to right), the implied average annual discount rate becomes smaller. If the discount rate were constant at 139%, then receiving $15 today would be equivalent to receiving $21 in 3 months. And yet, the typical respondent reports that they need to be compensated by an additional $30 − $21 = $9 to wait 3 months, reflecting more impatience and a higher discount rate in the near future. Conversely, with a constant discount rate of 139%, receiving $15 today would be equivalent to receiving $971 in 3 years. And yet, the typical respondent reports that they need to be compensated by $971 − $100 = $871 less to wait 3 years, reflecting more patience and a lower discount rate in the more distant future. The same story applies for the $250 and $3,000 prizes. This experiment provides further support for the insight developed in the Apples Away Lab Experiment that discount rates are smaller at longer horizons.

What does the evidence that discount rates diminish at longer horizons imply for the shape of the discount function, $D(k)$? First, let's use the experimental data from Table 4.1 to plot points through which the discount function should pass. For the case of the $15 prize, we know that the discount function for the typical respondent should satisfy $15 = $D(k) \times$ Prize in k months. The discount function is the amount by which the future prize money must be weighted to make it equivalent to the current option of receiving $15. Therefore, plugging in the future equivalent prize amounts, we obtain $D(3 \text{ months}) = $15/$30 = 0.5$, $D(12 \text{ months}) = $15/$60 = 0.25$, and $D(36 \text{ months}) = $15/$100 = 0.15$. These points are plotted in Figure 4.1.

Next, we can try to fit an exponential function through these experimental data points. The figure shows an exponential discount function with a constant annual discount rate of 139% (the solid curve). This function passes exactly through the experimental data at the 1-year horizon, but it is too high at the 3-month horizon and too low at the 3-year horizon. A more empirically accurate discount function would decline faster initially (high discount rate) and then flatten out more at longer horizons (low discount rate). A candidate for such a function is a **hyperbolic function**, which is a

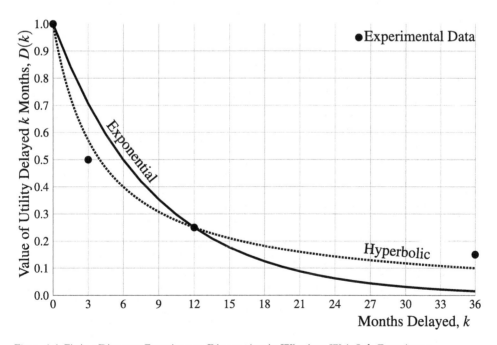

Figure 4.1 Fitting Discount Functions to Discounting in Winnings Wait Lab Experiment

function that describes a hyperbola. An example of a hyperbolic discount function is:[4]

$$D^h(k) = \frac{1}{1 + \alpha k} \text{ for } \alpha > 0$$

The dotted curve in Figure 4.1 plots the hyperbolic discount function $D^h(k)$ with α chosen so that the function passes through the experimental data at the 1-year horizon. While not a perfect fit with the experimental data, the hyperbolic function comes much closer than the exponential function. It declines more quickly at first before becoming flatter. Exercise 4.2 asks you to verify that the discount function with a hyperbolic form indeed generates declining discount rates over the time horizon. In the next chapter we develop an alternative to the DU model that allows for a hyperbolic discount function.

4.1.3 *Poverty and Discounting*   *[Development]*

Debates about the mathematical structure of an individual's discount function may feel esoteric and far removed from the social phenomena of interest to economists. To see the relevance, let's briefly consider how time discounting matters in the context of poverty.

The extreme poverty rate, defined as the share of people living on less than $1.90 per day in 2011 dollars, is near 10% globally (World Bank 2018). This is down from over 40% in the early 1980s. In spite of this substantial improvement, there are still gains to be made. In fact, of the 17 Sustainable Development Goals set forth by the United Nations, the first is to eliminate extreme poverty around the world.

For economists interested in understanding the determinants and persistence of poverty, it is natural to ask how the circumstances of living in poverty impact preferences and choices, which in turn could make poverty harder to escape. A better understanding of these connections can help to improve the design of policies aimed at reducing poverty. But these are challenging questions to answer because economic circumstances are likely both a cause, and a consequence, of decision making.

Given the topic of this chapter, let's narrow our focus to the relationship between poverty and discount rates. Many studies find a negative correlation between discount rates and income both within countries — rich and poor — as well as across countries (e.g., Lawrance 1991; Yesuf and Bluffstone 2008; Pender 1996; Dohmen et al. 2016). This is an interesting observation, but does not itself undermine the standard DU model which allows for discount rates to vary across people. It also doesn't tell us whether high discount rates contribute to the likelihood of being poor or whether living in poverty increases discount rates (or both).

To understand the *causal* impact of poverty on discount rates, economists can turn to lab experiments in which participants are randomly assigned different experimental incomes. This strategy permits an evaluation of the direct impact of income changes on behavior. In one such lab experiment, Haushofer and Fehr (2019) reduce the experimental incomes for some participants and not for others before asking questions similar to those in the Winnings Wait Lab Experiment. The participant responses reveal that the negative income shock increases discount rates over short horizons, but not over long horizons.

This evidence suggests that falling into poverty may increase the likelihood of hyperbolic discounting and self-control problems. For example, you may intend to save some money from a future paycheck (because your long-term discount rate is low), but when the paycheck arrives you might reverse your preferences, spending more and saving less than planned (because your short-term discount rate is high). If poverty makes this gap between planned savings and actual savings larger, then savings for the poor will accumulate only very slowly and an escape from poverty becomes even more challenging. Banerjee and Mullainathan (2010) explore mathematically how such a poverty trap can indeed arise with hyperbolic discounting.

A feedback loop between poverty and discount rates is of course not the only reason why it is difficult for the poor to improve their material conditions. If poverty affects attitudes towards risk taking or impairs cognitive decision making through its impact on stress and mental health, then through these additional channels poverty can reinforce itself (Mullainathan and Shafir 2013; Haushofer and Fehr 2014). And even if the poor have the same preferences as the nonpoor, they face a much smaller set of options (e.g., limited access to low-interest loans, good public schools, health care, and safe neighborhoods). Poverty alleviation may therefore require significant public support.

4.2   Magnitude Effect

Returning to the Winnings Wait Lab Experiment, we can observe an additional anomaly. The experimental evidence in Table 4.1 reveals that as the size of the prize increases (read the columns top to bottom), the discount rate declines. Consider the case of the 3-month waiting period for the delayed prize. The typical individual exhibits a discount rate of 277% for the $15 prize. Suppose that we hold that discount rate fixed as the magnitude of the prize increases. Then the individual would be indifferent between $250 today and $500 in 3 months, but she reports needing only $300 in 3 months for indifference. Similarly, with this discount rate she should be indifferent between $3,000 today and $6,000 in 3 months, but she only needs $3,500 in 3 months for indifference. This **magnitude effect** in which the typical individual exhibits declining discount rates for larger prizes is again inconsistent with the DU model's assumption that discount rates are constant.[5]

The magnitude effect is robust to alternative settings. It is present across small rewards ($2 to $20 in Ainslie and Haendel (1983)) and across large rewards ($10,000 to $1 million in Raineri and Rachlin (1993)). These results are based on lab experiments with student responses to hypothetical situations. A critique of this method is that how participants answer such hypothetical questions may not well represent actual behavior if the monetary stakes were real. To address this concern, Kirby (1997) ran a series of auctions with psychology students at Williams College who bid their own actual money on delayed monetary rewards. For 62 of the 67 participants, their bids reveal lower discount rates for larger rewards. In addition, a hyperbolic discount function fits better than an exponential discount function for 59 of the participants, lending further support for declining discount rates over time. Although the magnitude effect shows up in real behavior, another concern with these experiments is that the participants likely do not have much expertise in economics or finance. But even when experienced economics and finance students are asked to evaluate the value of delayed rewards, the magnitude effect is still present (Benzion, Rapoport, and Yagil 1989).

Why are individuals acting in this way? One possibility is that waiting to receive a prize requires a fixed mental effort. And for larger rewards this fixed cost of waiting is relatively small, inducing more patience (see Exercise 4.3). Let's put this in the language of what you could buy with the different prize winnings. For instance, with $15 you could buy a nice lunch, with $250 you could take a weekend trip to a nearby town, and with $3,000 you could buy a used car. By interpreting the prize amounts in terms of what you can purchase, it makes sense that you might be more patient (with a low discount rate) to receive the big prize that will have a significant impact on your life, while also being quite impatient (with a high discount rate) by demanding a large return in order to wait for a small prize.

4.3   Sign Effect

The following lab experiment is a variation on the Winnings Wait Lab Experiment, where instead of a delayed reward, a penalty is delayed.

Lab Experiment — Losing Later (Thaler 1981)

Bad news! You just got a traffic ticket. You owe a $15 fine which can be paid today or in 1 year. How much would you pay in 1 year to make you indifferent between waiting to pay and paying the current $15 fine now? The ticket will not disappear.

Also answer this question for a fine of $100 or $250. How do your answers change if the time horizon to pay the future fine is 3 months or 3 years instead of 1 year?

The median responses from University of Oregon students surveyed by Thaler (1981) are as follows:

Table 4.2 Typical Responses to Losing Later Lab Experiment

Current Fine Amount	or, equivalently, Pay in		
	3 months	1 year	3 years
$15	$16 (26%)	$20 (29%)	$28 (20%)
$100	$102 (6%)	$118 (16%)	$155 (15%)
$250	$251 (1%)	$270 (8%)	$310 (7%)

Note: Each cell contains the median indifference dollar amount, with the implied average annual discount rate in parentheses.

Ask yourself: how large of a fine due in 1 year would make you indifferent to paying $15 today? You may recognize that there are benefits by waiting to pay the fine. By delaying, you have time to plan for the payment. A delay also means that you don't have to cut back on spending today, but can put off the pain of cutting back on spending to the future. You might also earn more money in the future, making it easier to pay the fine. To maintain indifference between paying $15 today and paying another amount in the future, the future payment then has to be larger than $15 to balance out the benefits of waiting.

The typical respondent reported that paying $20 next year would make them indifferent to paying $15 today. What is surprising is that when framed as a reward in the Winnings Wait Lab Experiment, individuals are indifferent between receiving $15 today and $60 in one year. With a loss, the future is valued at $15/$20= 75% relative to the present, but with a gain the future is valued at $15/$60 = 25% relative to the present. Once again, we find discount rates that are not constant, contrary to the DU model.

The key takeaway from the results in Table 4.2 is the **sign effect**, for which losses are discounted less than gains. The discount rates in Table 4.2 are substantially smaller than the corresponding discount rates in Table 4.1 for a gain. Even though individuals report a need for significant compensation to wait for a gain (generating large discount rates), they are simultaneously unwilling to pay much in order to delay a loss (generating low discount rates). In fact, it is not uncommon for respondents to be indifferent between a $15 loss today and a $15 loss far in the future (in which case the discount rate would be zero).

One possible explanation for this apparent patience for losses is that individuals simply want to get a loss over with. If the specter of a looming future loss generates feelings of dread that counteract the standard benefits of delaying payment, then individuals may become indifferent to paying a fine today and the same fine in the future. And if the feeling of dread is strong enough (e.g., every day you wake up anxious about your future fine that has to be paid), you might even prefer paying $15 today over $15 in the future. Within the standard DU model framework, where dread and anxiety are not accounted for, the discount rate would need to be negative to capture such a preference for paying the fine now (and reducing current consumption) ratherthan in the future. We explore further this idea of valuing future consumption more than present consumption in the next section.

4.4 Preference for Improving Sequences

The previous three anomalies provide evidence inconsistent with a constant discount rate that is independent of the timing, magnitude, or sign of the outcome. In this section, instead of focusing on what impacts the *rate* at which the discount function declines, we consider evidence that the discount function may not be declining at all, but increasing over the time horizon. In such a case the discount rate is negative because it is defined as the *negative* of the rate of change of the discount function.

The DU model assumes positive time preference (in the form of a positive discount rate) to capture the idea that individuals value future utility less than present utility. This preference implies that when faced with a decision of how to order a sequence of outcomes, an individual prefers to start with the best outcome, followed by the second best, and so forth. To do otherwise would be to lower the total discounted utility. The following experiment tests this assumption.

Lab Experiment — Dinner Order (Loewenstein and Prelec 1993)

Loewenstein and Prelec (1993, 93) pose the following questions to 95 Harvard University undergraduates, with the instructions to ignore all preexisting plans.

1   Which would you prefer if both were free?

 A Dinner at a fancy French restaurant
 B Dinner at a local Greek restaurant

For those who prefer French:	**Results:**
2 Which would you prefer?	
C French dinner on Friday in 1 month	[80%]
D French dinner on Friday in 2 months	[20%]
3 Which would you prefer?	
E French dinner on Fri. in 1 mo. & Greek dinner on Fri. in 2 mos.	[**43%**]
F Greek dinner on Fri. in 1 mo. & French dinner on Fri. in 2 mos.	[**57%**]

Let's apply the general discounted utility model of preferences (2.2) to the above experiment. That is, assume individuals discount future utility, but do not assume any particular shape for the discount function $D(k)$. Economic theory makes no predictions about how individuals answer the first question; one can prefer any cuisine they like. For those individuals who prefer French over Greek food, most (80%) also prefer to eat their French dinner sooner rather than later (*C* is preferred to *D*). Therefore, using the discounted utility framework with a period equal to a month, the majority preference implies:[6]

$$D(1)u(French) > D(2)u(French) \Leftrightarrow D(1) > D(2) \tag{4.1}$$

This is as expected since a declining discount function ($D(1) > D(2)$) is the standard assumption and consistent with scheduling good outcomes sooner rather than later.

For the final question in the Dinner Order Lab Experiment, asked only to those who prefer the French dinner, the majority of respondents (57%) prefer to eat the Greek dinner before the French dinner (*F* is preferred to *E*). That is, the majority prefers to delay the most desired outcome, generating an improving sequence and not a worsening sequence. Again using model (2.2), the majority preference implies:

$$\begin{aligned} D(1)u(French) + D(2)u(Greek) &< D(1)u(Greek) + D(2)u(French) \\ \Leftrightarrow \quad D(1)[u(French) - u(Greek)] &< D(2)[u(French) - u(Greek)] \\ \Leftrightarrow \quad D(1) &< D(2) \end{aligned} \tag{4.2}$$

where the last inequality follows from knowing that these individuals already reported preferring French over Greek dinner ($u(French) - u(Greek) > 0$). We have a contradiction. For the same group of individuals, the majority demonstrates a declining discount function in (4.1) and simultaneously demonstrates an increasing discount function in (4.2).

This experiment illustrates our next anomaly, the **preference for improving sequences.** Notice that when the dinner is presented as a single outcome, most individuals want the good outcome close to the present. This choice is consistent with the impatience implied by the assumption of a declining discount function. When framed as a sequence of dinners, impatience should again induce individuals to choose the preferred French dinner first. But the majority instead prefer to delay the French dinner until after the Greek dinner.

The preference for improving sequences has also been studied in contexts that are more realistic than choosing when to schedule a fancy free dinner. Consider, for instance, two identical jobs that will pay you the same total salary over five years. Suppose you can choose between an increasing salary sequence (e.g., $50K, $52K, $54K, $56K, $58K) or a declining salary sequence (e.g., $58K, $56K, $54K, $52K, $50K). Most individuals prefer the increasing sequence (Hsee, Abelson, and Salovey 1991; Loewenstein and Sicherman 1991), even though the standard assumption that individuals prefer the present over the future implies that the declining sequence is better. There is also a financial benefit to the declining salary profile because by saving the initially high earnings, it is possible to support greater consumption. For example, with an annual interest rate on savings of 5%, the declining salary profile can generate an additional $390 per year of consumption relative to the increasing wage profile. The consumption and savings decision problem is explored more fully in the next section.

For unpleasant outcomes, a preference for improving sequences implies that individuals will prefer sequences that start with the worst outcome over those that delay it. This preference has been documented in studies that ask participants to rank sequences of discomfort or pain (Chapman 2000; Varey and Kahneman 1992).

What can explain such preferences? One possibility is that individuals savor or dread future outcomes. If individuals savor future gains, then by saving these gains for the future, they can enjoy the anticipation leading up to the eventual outcome. By experiencing the pleasant outcome immediately, such savoring is cut short. For instance, consider the excitement you might experience by looking forward to an upcoming vacation that would not exist if the vacation were announced as a surprise just hours before leaving. Conversely, if future losses are dreaded, then by moving the loss to the present, the individual prevents the accumulation of anxiety and dread that would accrue over time up until the realization of the future loss. It is not fun awaiting a future dental surgery or future bill payment. Note that present feelings of savoring or dread about future outcomes are ruled out in the standard DU model by the assumption of consumption independence.

Another possible explanation is that individuals adapt to their current outcomes and find it particularly unpleasant to experience a loss in the next period. With the salary sequence example, suppose that you consume all of your income each year. It might then be difficult to take a vacation in year 1 and adapt to regular French dinners, only to find that in subsequent years you no longer have the means to vacation or eat out as frequently. By choosing an improving sequence, no such losses are experienced. This psychological explanation is again ruled out by the standard model.

4.5 Life-Cycle Model

This chapter of anomalies concludes with a widely-used application of the DU model. Economists have long been concerned with understanding the consumption and savings patterns of individuals over time. This topic attracts microeconomists who are interested in the impact of tax policies and welfare programs on individual behavior. Macroeconomists are interested in the relationships between aggregate consumption and savings, and economic growth, business cycles, and monetary policy. In fact, economics as a discipline got its start with Adam Smith's *An Inquiry into the Nature and Causes of the*

Wealth of Nations (1776), which attributes differential living standards across countries to differences in the allocation of resources to consumption versus savings.

The modern economic approach for studying consumption and savings behavior is grounded in the **life-cycle model** of Modigliani and Brumberg (1954). This framework assumes that individuals choose a lifetime consumption sequence that maximizes the DU model of preferences subject to a budget constraint. We first discuss the setup of the problem before comparing its theoretical predictions with empirical evidence.

4.5.1   Preferences

Assume that an individual in period 0 evaluates a sequence of consumption expenditures $(c_0, c_1, \ldots, c_T)$ with the Discounted Utility model:

$$U^0(c_0, c_1, \ldots, c_T) = \sum_{k=0}^{T} \delta^k u(c_k) \tag{4.3}$$

where $0 < \delta \leq 1$. Implicit in this utility function is the assumption that the individual lives for exactly T periods beyond period 0 and knows this. In reality it is uncommon to know exactly how long you will live, but we make this simplifying assumption to abstract away from issues of uncertainty. We also assume that greater consumption increases utility ($u(c)$ is strictly increasing), but that the marginal utility gain is smaller at higher levels of consumption ($u(c)$ is strictly concave).

4.5.2   Budget Constraint

It remains to specify the choice set, which in this case is determined by the **budget constraint** on sequences of consumption expenditures. Without any constraints, the utility-maximizing consumption sequence is to spend infinite amounts of money every period. This is obviously not possible because individuals are constrained by their income y_k in each period k. One possible budget constraint would require that consumption expenditure in period k be at most income in period k (i.e., $c_k \leq y_k$ for every k). This, however, is overly restrictive because it rules out the possibility of borrowing or saving across periods. Instead, we make the following assumptions on the budget constraint:

- *Certain Income*: Individuals know their entire future sequence of income levels with certainty. This is admittedly unrealistic in most cases, but simplifies the analysis and permits us to generate qualitative insights that are robust to introducing uncertainty.
- *No Liquidity Constraints*: Individuals can save or borrow any amount, and earn interest or pay interest, respectively, at a constant known per-period interest rate $r \geq 0$. In reality, individuals often face liquidity constraints in the form of limited access to borrowing (e.g., it might be difficult to convince a bank to give you a loan) or higher interest rates on borrowing than on saving (e.g., even if the bank issues you a loan, the interest you pay to the bank is much more than what the bank pays in interest to savers).
- *Budget Balance*: At the end of life, all debts are repaid and all income and savings are spent. This rules out the ability to die with unpaid debts or leave a bequest to heirs.

Although it is unlikely that individuals finish life with exactly zero assets, this assumption provides a rough approximation.

Given these assumptions, the **intertemporal budget constraint** is:

$$c_0 + \frac{c_1}{R} + \frac{c_2}{R^2} + \cdots + \frac{c_T}{R^T} = y_0 + \frac{y_1}{R} + \frac{y_2}{R^2} + \cdots + \frac{y_T}{R^T}, \text{ or equivalently,}$$

$$\sum_{k=0}^{T} \frac{c_k}{R^k} = \sum_{k=0}^{T} \frac{y_k}{R^k} \tag{4.4}$$

where $R = 1 + r \geq 1$ is the *gross* per-period interest rate.

The intertemporal budget constraint (4.4) has an intuitive interpretation in the language of **present values**. The present value of \$100 received in k periods with a gross interest rate of R is equal to \$100/R^k. This makes sense because saving \$100/R^k today will yield, after k periods of interest, \$100/$R^k \times R^k = \$100$. And the present value of a sequence of money is simply the sum of the present values across each period. Present value is a common concept used in economics, finance, and accounting. The intertemporal budget constraint therefore requires that the present value of lifetime consumption expenditures must equal the present value of lifetime income. In the special case for which the interest rate r is zero, so that $R = 1 + r = 1$, the intertemporal budget constraint becomes even simpler: total lifetime consumption expenditure equals total lifetime income.

4.5.3 The Solution

In the life-cycle model an individual maximizes the discounted utility function (4.3) subject to the intertemporal budget constraint (4.4). Expressed mathematically, we have:

$$\max_{(c_0, c_1, \ldots, c_T)} \sum_{k=0}^{T} \delta^k u(c_k) \text{ such that } \sum_{k=0}^{T} \frac{c_k}{R^k} = \sum_{k=0}^{T} \frac{y_k}{R^k} \tag{4.5}$$

This is a complex optimization problem. To solve it, we have to find an entire sequence of consumption expenditures $(c_0^*, c_1^*, \ldots, c_T^*)$ that both satisfies the intertemporal budget constraint *and* generates at least as much total discounted utility as any other affordable consumption sequence. But there are an infinite number of possible sequences to consider.

The good news is that this problem admits a shockingly simple solution, as long as we make the additional assumption that the discount rate ρ is equal to the interest rate r.[7] Why make this assumption? When $\rho = r$ the individual discounts future utility at the same rate as the interest earned on savings and charged on loans. Intuitively, the individual is exactly as patient as the market for loanable funds. In this special case, it is utility-maximizing for the individual to spend the *same amount* on consumption in every period. This is summarized in the following theorem.

Theorem 4.1 If the discount rate ρ is equal to the interest rate r, then the solution to the life-cycle problem (4.5) satisfies the intertemporal budget constraint with constant consumption expenditure in every period: $c_0^* = c_1^* = \cdots = c_T^*$.

What if the discount rate and interest rate are not equal? Then, the utility-maximizing sequence of consumption expenditures will not be constant, but either increasing over the life cycle or decreasing over the life cycle. To determine how the relationship between ρ and r impacts consumption, it is useful to solve the general problem (4.5) using the tools of calculus. These details are relegated to Appendix 4A. For expositional clarity, the remainder of this chapter retains the simplifying assumption that $\rho = r$.

4.5.4 Implications

The utility-maximizing solution of constant consumption expenditure is at first surprising. Note that it is true regardless of the income pattern over the life cycle. For the tech entrepreneur who becomes rich in her 20s and retires at 35, or the teacher who earns a stable salary until retirement at age 67, or the lifelong student who amasses enormous student debt collecting multiple PhDs before earning an income late in life, this model predicts that each of them will maintain constant consumption over their life. But surely, income must matter.

Differences in lifetime income across individuals matter to the extent that they imply different *levels* of consumption for an entrepreneur versus a teacher. The income differences however do not change the prediction of constant consumption expenditure over time for each individual. To see this mathematically, make the simplifying assumption that the discount rate ρ and interest rate r are not only equal, but also equal to zero (so that $R = 1 + r = 1$). We can then use the intertemporal budget constraint to solve for the level of consumption expenditure in each period, c^* (where I have dropped the time period subscripts since consumption is the same in every period):

$$\sum_{k=0}^{T} y_k = \sum_{k=0}^{T} c^* = (T+1)c^*$$

$$\Rightarrow c^* = \frac{\sum_{k=0}^{T} y_k}{T+1} \tag{4.6}$$

Consumption in each period is just the sum of lifetime income divided by the number of periods.[8] If the rich entrepreneur has a higher total lifetime income than the teacher or lifelong student, she will achieve a higher level of consumption in every period.

How is constant consumption possible when income is variable? Recall that the intertemporal budget constraint assumes no liquidity constraints. Individuals are able to achieve a constant level of consumption in this model by saving when they earn more than c^* and borrowing when they earn less than c^*. Most college students, for example, are earning less than their lifetime average income, so they borrow against their future earnings to finance their education. Then, later in life when they are earning more than their lifetime average income, they can pay back their student loans and accumulate savings for retirement. All the while, consumption remains constant. The following example illustrates a hypothetical income sequence and the corresponding levels of consumption and wealth accumulation that result from maintaining constant consumption. Exercise 4.6 also has you investigate how the pattern of income impacts the sequence of savings.

■ **Example 4.1 — Constant Consumption.** Nia is an 18-year-old college student. She has studied the life-cycle decision problem (4.5) and wants to calculate her utility-maximizing level of consumption. For simplicity, assume that both her discount rate and interest rate are zero. Because $\rho = r$, her consumption sequence is constant. And because the interest rate is zero, consumption in every period is the average of her lifetime income, as in equation (4.6).

Assume the following about Nia's lifetime income. For the next 4 years of college her income is zero, but she borrows $7,500 each year in student loans. In her first job at age 22 she earns an annual salary of $50K. Her salary increases by $2K each year for the next 25 years until the age of 47 at which point her salary is $100K. For the remaining 20 years of her life from age 48 until retirement at age 67, her income remains flat at $100K. She lives for 20 years in retirement with zero income and dies at the end of her 87th year. Let's use this 70-year time horizon to determine her annual consumption level:[9]

$$
\begin{aligned}
c^* &= \frac{4 \times -\$7,500 + \sum_{t=0}^{25}(\$50,000 + \$2,000 \times t) + 20 \times \$100,000 + 20 \times \$0}{70} \\
&= \frac{-\$30,000 + 26 \times \$50,000 + \$2000 \times \sum_{t=0}^{25} t + \$2,000,000}{70} \\
&= \frac{-\$30,000 + \$1,300,000 + \$2000 \times (25 \times 26/2) + \$2,000,000}{70} \\
&= \frac{\$3,920,000}{70} = \$56,000/\text{year}
\end{aligned}
$$

In order to maintain this constant level of consumption throughout her life, Nia will borrow heavily while young, repay her debt when she is older, and accumulate sufficient wealth to finance her retirement. Figure 4.2 plots Nia's lifetime sequences of income, consumption, and wealth.

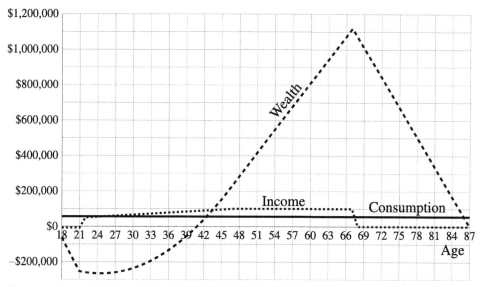

Figure 4.2 Income, Consumption, and Wealth for Example 4.1

Wealth over Nia's lifetime reaches extremes far beyond her annual income. Early in life, as consumption exceeds income, she is accumulating debt that reaches $266,000 at the age of 25. After 25, she begins earning more than she spends, allowing her to pay back her debt and accumulate a total wealth of $1,120,000 by her last year of work. Note that her wealth falls whenever income is below consumption and rises whenever income exceeds consumption.[10] She also ends her life with zero wealth, as required by budget balance.   ∎

This behavior of **consumption smoothing** is one of the key insights of the original life-cycle models of the 1950s. That is, instead of simply spending each year's income in full, the utility-maximizing plan is to *smooth* consumption across periods, reducing adjustments in one's standard of living up and down over time. Note that consumption smoothing does not imply constant consumption. Even when $\rho \neq r$ and the optimal sequence of consumption is always increasing or always decreasing, the consumer is still smoothing consumption across periods (see Appendix 4A for details).

4.5.5   *Life-Cycle Evidence*   *[Household]*

The life-cycle model can be tested against empirical evidence of actual behavior. This section considers five theoretical predictions and the corresponding evidence for American households, adapted from Angeletos et al. (2001).

First, the life-cycle model assumes exponential discounting and therefore time-consistent preferences. Applied to the context of savings decisions, time consistency means that a plan to save in the future is confirmed by actually saving when the future arrives. Individuals should not regularly fail to meet their planned savings objectives. Yet in one survey, 76% of respondents reported that they believe they should be saving more for retirement (Farkas and Johnson 1997). This evidence of an apparent self-control problem suggests that individuals, at least in the context of savings, are not exponential discounters. The DU model therefore cannot accurately describe life-cycle consumption and savings behavior.

Second, consumption smoothing implies that only new information can cause a change in consumption. The intuition is that by taking into account all future certain income (or accurate expectations about future uncertain income), individuals plan to smooth their consumption across periods so that anticipated ups and downs in the income stream have no impact on consumption. Consumption is shifted only when there is new information about future income, like an unexpected promotion or layoff. Because predicted income has already been taken into account when setting consumption, the **marginal propensity to consume** out of changes in *predicted* income, that is how much consumption changes with a change in predicted income, should be zero (Hall 1978). Most estimates of the marginal propensity to consume, however, find that a $1 increase in predicted income leads to a $0.10–$0.30 increase in consumption. Consumption is moving with fluctuations in predicted income, contrary to the prediction of the life-cycle model.

Another implication of consumption smoothing is that individuals anticipate and plan for retirement so as not to experience a decline in living standards upon retirement. This requires building up sufficient wealth before retirement. But the evidence reveals a median 14% decline in consumption for Americans between the years just before and after retirement (Bernheim, Skinner, and Weinberg 2001). There is similar evidence from the United Kingdom (Banks, Blundell, and Tanner 1998) and Italy (Battistin, Blundell, and Lewbel 2009).

The model predicts not only substantial wealth accumulation before retirement, but substantial accumulation of liquid wealth (e.g., cash, checking accounts, and savings accounts). This is in contrast to more illiquid forms of wealth like owning a house. It is this liquid wealth that provides a buffer to protect against low-income years caused by unemployment or illness, as well as a reserve from which to spend out of during retirement. But only 37% of households have liquid wealth in excess of a month's income. This statistic masks substantial differences across people, with only 20% of younger households (ages 20–39) holding at least a month's worth of liquid assets. Many young people are not prepared to continue paying their bills in the event of job loss. What are the implications of the model if we allow for income uncertainty, which we had assumed away for tractability? Individuals are now predicted to reduce consumption relative to the case with income certainty and increase their savings as a precaution against the uncertain future. This only exacerbates the discrepancy between the model's predictions of high savings, and the actual meager savings of many Americans.

Finally, consider the introduction of liquidity constraints to the life-cycle model. If there are limits to borrowing, then to help finance consumption during a future low-income year, the model predicts that individuals will increase their current savings instead of relying on future borrowing. Once again, we have a prediction that is at odds with the low wealth accumulation of many households.[11] An important liquidity constraint in the real world manifests in the form of very high interest rates — often in excess of 20% — on credit card debt. The model predicts that individuals will only resort to borrowing on credit cards in special situations when there are periods of unemployment or illness, and even then will do so in moderation. In reality, 70% of households carry credit card debt, with an average debt of $5,000 (including those with zero debt).

In summary, many of the predictions of the life-cycle model are not supported by evidence. Relaxing the assumptions of income certainty and no liquidity constraints does not help to improve the accuracy of the model. Taken together, we have good reason to reject the life-cycle model as describing the savings and consumption behavior of many Americans. A possible modification to the model would be to do away with the assumption of exponential discounting and time consistency. We take this up in the next chapter.

A more dramatic departure from the life-cycle model would be to assume that regardless of the discount function and constraints on the choice set, the utility-maximization problem might be too difficult to solve. In fact, one analysis suggests that it would take at least a million years of learning by trial and error for an individual to approach the solution in the life-cycle model (Allen and Carroll 2001). If individuals are using simple rules of thumb or other criteria to make consumption and savings decisions, then it is unsurprising that a model predicated on optimization fails to match reality. This concern is explored in Chapter 19.

4.6   Summary

1   There is evidence of behavior in **lab experiments** that is inconsistent with the standard Discounted Utility (DU) model of intertemporal preferences.

2   When two delayed rewards are brought closer to the present, individuals often switch their preference from the more delayed/larger reward to the less delayed/

smaller reward. This type of **preference reversal** suggests a **self-control problem** in which individuals are relatively patient for distant rewards (low discount rate), but become more impatient for immediate rewards (high discount rate). A **hyperbolic discount function** exhibits such a declining discount rate over the time horizon of the delay, as opposed to the constant discount rate assumed in the DU model.

3   Empirically, discount rates decrease in the size of the delayed reward, suggesting more patience for delaying larger rewards. This is the **magnitude effect**.

4   Empirically, delayed losses are discounted less than delayed gains. This **sign effect** is consistent with a preference for getting a loss over sooner than later.

5   When future outcomes are framed as a sequence, individuals often **prefer an improving sequence** instead of shifting the most desired outcomes towards the present, as predicted by the DU model.

6   The **life-cycle model** applies the standard DU model of preferences to an individual's consumption and savings decisions over their lifetime. This model implies **consumption smoothing**, by which individuals borrow and save to smooth out consumption from year-to-year, regardless of the pattern of income. In the case that the discount rate and interest rate are equal, the utility-maximizing consumption expenditure is constant over time.

7   There is empirical evidence of consumption and savings behavior that is inconsistent with the theoretical predictions of the life-cycle model.

4.7   Exercises

Exercise 4.1 — Tax Timing. [Public Finance] Sam expects to receive a sizable income tax refund (more income tax was withheld from his paycheck over the previous year than he actually owed). His tax advisor offers him the option of taking the tax refund as cash in February or depositing the refund in an illiquid savings account where it will earn interest and can be withdrawn in October later in the year.

a   What are the relative pros and cons of taking the tax refund as cash in February?

b   Suppose that Sam has standard preferences represented by the Discounted Utility model. Would Sam's choice be different if he were asked to make this decision in December of the previous year or February of the current year? Explain.

c   Jones and Mahajan (2015) conduct a field experiment with low-income taxpayers to test for time consistency in such a setting. They find evidence of preference reversals. Based on the time effects in this chapter, how would you expect choices to shift between December and February?

Exercise 4.2 — Hyperbolic Discount Rates. Heidi discounts the future with a hyperbolic discount function $D^h(k) = \frac{1}{1+\alpha k}$, where $k \geq 0$ is the number of periods from the present and $\alpha > 0$ is a constant.

a   Compute the discount rate for $D^h(k)$ as a function of k. Recall that the discount rate is defined in Definition 2.1.

b   How does the discount rate that you computed in part (a) change as k increases?

c What does your observation in part (b) suggest about how Heidi's degree of impatience changes from the short run (small k) to the long run (large k)?

Exercise 4.3 — Modeling the Magnitude Effect. To help explain the magnitude effect, let's modify our standard DU model by introducing a *psychic* cost $F \geq 0$ incurred by an individual who has to wait one year to receive a given prize (Thaler 1981). In particular, let the utility function over a prize received today (c_0) and a prize received in one year (c_1) be:

$$U(c_0, c_1) = \begin{cases} c_0 & \text{if } c_1 = 0 \\ c_0 + \delta c_1 - F & \text{if } c_1 > 0 \end{cases} \tag{4.7}$$

where $0 < \delta < 1$ is the discount factor.

a. Discuss how δ and F differ in how they impact the utility of receiving a future prize.Recall from the data in Table 4.1 that the typical respondent is indifferent between: 1) \$15 immediately and \$60 in one year; and 2) \$3,000 immediately and \$4,000 in one year.

b. Suppose that $F = 0$ (i.e., we have the standard DU model of preferences). Show that in this case the model of preferences (4.7) *cannot* reconcile the two preceding indifference conditions. In particular, show that each indifference condition implies a different value for δ.

c. Now let $F > 0$. Show that in this more general case the model of preferences (4.7) *can* reconcile the two indifference conditions. In particular, determine a value for δ and a value for F that are consistent with both indifference conditions.

d. Use the values for δ and F from part (c) to determine how much money received in one year would be equivalent to receiving a prize of \$250 immediately. Compare this with the typical response in Table 4.1. Do you think this model predicts behavior approximately well?

Exercise 4.4 — Sequencing Vacations. Don's preferences over cities, c, to visit are represented by an instantaneous utility function, $u(c)$. He prefers San Francisco (*SF*) to San Diego (*SD*), so $u(SF) > u(SD)$. In addition, his preferences over sequences of cities to visit in the next two months, (c_1, c_2), are represented by a discounted utility function:

$$U(c_1, c_2) = D(1)u(c_1) + D(2)u(c_2)$$

where the discount function $D(k)$ can take any form.

a Don can afford to visit both cities over the next two months. He would rather visit San Diego before San Francisco (i.e., he prefers the sequence (*SD*, *SF*) to (*SF*, *SD*)). Given this preference, determine whether $D(1)$ is larger or smaller than $D(2)$.

b Does Don exhibit an intertemporal choice anomaly? If so, which one? If not, why?

c Do Don's preferences seem reasonable to you? Briefly explain why or why not.

Exercise 4.5 — It's Dinner Times. Consider the following alternative sequences of dinners over the next three weekends (Loewenstein 1987, 678–679):

Alternative	This weekend	Next weekend	Two weekends from now
A	Dinner at a fancy French restaurant	Eat at home	Eat at home
B	Eat at home	Dinner at a fancy French restaurant	Eat at home
X	Dinner at a fancy French restaurant	Eat at home	Fancy lobster dinner
Y	Eat at home	Dinner at a fancy French restaurant	Fancy lobster dinner

a Suppose that individual preferences over a sequence of dinners (c_1, c_2, c_3) are represented by a discounted utility function of the form:

$$U(c_1, c_2, c_3) = D(1)u(c_1) + D(2)u(c_2) + D(3)u(c_3) \tag{4.8}$$

where $D(k)$ is some discount function and $u(c)$ is the instantaneous utility function. If A is preferred to B, does the individual prefer X or Y more?

b Of the 37 Yale University undergraduates asked to choose between A and B — ignoring any possible scheduling conflicts — the majority (84%) preferred sequence B to A. The majority (57%) also preferred sequence X to Y. Explain whether the majority preferences support or contradict the model of preferences (4.8).

c Provide psychologically plausible reasons for the majority preferences in part (b). Can you identify an anomaly of intertemporal choice not discussed in the chapter?

Exercise 4.6 — Mini Life Cycles. Ingrid and Devon are standard maximizers of the Discounted Utility model. Assume that they both have discount rates and interest rates of zero ($\rho = r = 0$). Ingrid knows that for the next 5 years she has an increasing income stream provided in the table below. Devon on the other hand knows that for the next 5 years he has a decreasing income stream also provided in the table. Ingrid and Devon must have zero wealth (no unpaid debts and no unspent savings) at the end of the 5th year. Fill in the rest of the table with their corresponding consumption, savings (which if negative indicates borrowing), and wealth in each period.

	Period t	Income y_t	Consumption c_t	Savings $y_t - c_t$	Wealth $(y_0 - c_0) + \cdots + (y_t - c_t)$
	0	$50,000			
	1	$54,000			
Ingrid	2	$59,000			
	3	$65,000			
	4	$72,000			$0

(Continued)

(Continued)

	Period	Income	Consumption	Savings	Wealth
	t	y_t	c_t	$y_t - c_t$	$(y_0 - c_0) + \cdots + (y_t - c_t)$
Devon	0	$68,000			
	1	$63,000			
	2	$58,000			
	3	$56,000			
	4	$55,000			$0

Comment on the similarities and differences between the consumption and wealth paths for these two consumers over the five years.

Exercise 4.7 — Interest(ed) in the Life Cycle. Example 4.1 assumes that Nia has both a discount rate of zero and faces an interest rate of zero. These assumptions made calculating her constant level of consumption expenditure of $56,000 fairly straightforward. When the discount rate and interest rate are equal, but not necessarily zero, the constant per-period consumption expenditure is c^*, given as follows:

$$c^* = \frac{R-1}{R - 1/R^T} \sum_{k=0}^{T} \frac{y_k}{R^k}$$

Compute (using a computer) Nia's constant annual consumption expenditure in the following cases.

a   Assume that $\rho = r = 0.025$.
b   Assume that $\rho = r = 0.05$.
c   Assume that $\rho = r = 0.1$.
d   Assume that $\rho = r = 0.2$.
e   Explain how increasing the interest and discount rates impacts Nia's annual consumption expenditure. Provide intuition for your findings.

4A   Appendix: The Calculus of the Life-Cycle Model

Intertemporal choice problems, like that of the life-cycle model, are challenging to solve because a utility-maximizing individual must choose an entire sequence of outcomes that generates the highest lifetime utility from among all possible sequences of outcomes in the choice set. This appendix introduces a useful method for solving such multi-dimensional problems. With this method we will prove Theorem 4.1 and show how to solve the life-cycle model when the interest rate and discount rate are not equal.

Economists often model the behavior of consumers and firms as the solutions to **constrained optimization problems**. It is standard to assume that consumers optimize by maximizing a utility function. Without any constraints, many consumers would choose to eat out at fancy restaurants, take exotic vacations, or live in extravagant homes. In reality, most everyone faces constraints, the most important of which is the budget constraint: you can only consume what you can afford (or borrow). Firms, on the other hand, optimize by minimizing costs of production. They are often constrained not by a budget (since they can raise money from investors or banks), but by their technological ability to transform inputs of labor and capital into a good or service to sell.

In its most general form, a constrained optimization problem consists of an *objective function* $f(c_0, c_1, \ldots, c_T)$ that we seek to maximize, subject to the constraint that $g(c_0, c_1, \ldots, c_T) = 0$. We can express this mathematically as:

$$\max_{(c_0, c_1, \ldots, c_T)} f(c_0, c_1, \ldots, c_T) \text{ such that } g(c_0, c_1, \ldots, c_T) = 0 \tag{4A.1}$$

The method of Lagrange converts this difficult constrained optimization problem to an equivalent *un*constrained optimization problem, which is simpler to solve. To do this, we first introduce a new variable λ known as the *Lagrange multiplier*. The **Lagrangian** function $\mathcal{L}$ is then defined as:

$$\mathcal{L}(c_0, c_1, \ldots, c_T, \lambda) = f(c_0, c_1, \ldots, c_T) - \lambda g(c_0, c_1, \ldots, c_T) \tag{4A.2}$$

The Lagrangian is a new function equal to the difference between the objective function $f(\cdot)$ and the constraint function $g(\cdot)$ multiplied by λ.

It turns out that the solution to maximizing the Lagrangian $\mathcal{L}$ is the same as the solution to the original problem (4A.1). And to find the solution that maximizes the Lagrangian, we take its partial derivatives with respect to each of the variables and set them equal to zero (these are the *first order conditions*). The following theorem formalizes this result.

Theorem 4A.1 Let $c^* = (c_0^*, c_1^*, \ldots, c_T^*)$ be a solution to problem (4A.1) and define $\mathcal{L}$ as in (4A.2). Then:

$$\frac{\partial \mathcal{L}}{\partial \lambda} = -g(c_0^*, c_1^*, \ldots, c_T^*) = 0, \text{ and} \tag{4A.3}$$

$$\frac{\partial \mathcal{L}}{\partial c_k} = \frac{\partial f(c_0^*, c_1^*, \ldots, c_T^*)}{\partial c_k} - \lambda \frac{\partial g(c_0^*, c_1^*, \ldots, c_T^*)}{\partial c_k} = 0 \text{ for all } k \in \{0, \ldots, T\} \tag{4A.4}$$

The theorem provides a set of equations that must be satisfied at the solution to the constrained optimization problem (4A.1).[12] The first order condition (4A.3) simply says that the solution must satisfy the constraint, i.e., $g(\cdot) = 0$. The second set of first order conditions (4A.4) consists of $T + 1$ equations. Taken together, you can solve these $T + 2$ equations for the $T + 2$ unknowns: $(c_0^*, c_1^*, \ldots, c_T^*)$ and λ.

Let's apply Theorem 4A.1 to the standard life-cycle problem (4.5):

$$\max_{(c_0, c_1, \ldots, c_T)} \sum_{k=0}^{T} \delta^k u(c_k) \text{ such that } \sum_{k=0}^{T} \frac{c_k}{R^k} - \sum_{k=0}^{T} \frac{y_k}{R^k} = 0$$

Observe that in this constrained optimization problem the objective function is $f(c_0, \ldots, c_T) = \sum_{k=0}^{T} \delta^k u(c_k)$ and the constraint function is $g(c_0, \ldots, c_T) = \sum_{k=0}^{T} c_k/R^k -$

$\sum_{k=0}^{T} y_k / R^k$. The Lagrangian is therefore:

$$\mathcal{L} = \sum_{k=0}^{T} \delta^k u(c_k) - \lambda \left[\sum_{k=0}^{T} \frac{c_k}{R^k} - \sum_{k=0}^{T} \frac{y_k}{R^k} \right]$$

We can now determine the first order conditions of the Lagrangian for each of c_0, c_1, ..., c_T. From calculus we observe that for any arbitrary c_k where $k \in \{0, 1, ..., T\}$,

$$0 = \frac{\partial \mathcal{L}}{\partial c_k} = \delta^k u'(c_k^*) - \lambda \frac{1}{R^k}$$

Rearranging, we obtain:

$$(R\delta)^k u'(c_k^*) = \lambda \text{ for all } k \in \{0, 1, ..., T\} \tag{4A.5}$$

This set of equations provides a theoretical prediction about the behavior of an individual whose consumption decisions are the solutions to the life-cycle problem. Consider the simplifying case from the chapter that the discount rate ρ equals the interest rate r. In this case $R\delta = \frac{1+r}{1+\rho} = 1$, which implies that $(R\delta)^k = 1$ for all k. The conditions in (4A.5) therefore reduce to $u'(c_k^*) = \lambda$ for all k. This says that the slope of the instantaneous utility function evaluated at each of the optimal consumption levels is always equal to the constant λ in every period. What does this look like graphically? Figure 4A.1 plots an instantaneous utility function $u(\cdot)$, which we assumed to be increasing and concave. Because $u'(c_t^*)$ is always the same and there are no two different consumption expenditures that generate the same marginal utility u', the consumption

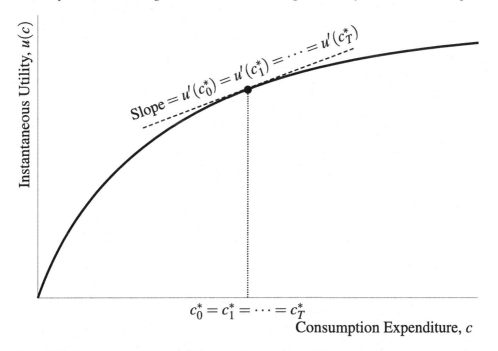

Figure 4A.1 Instantaneous Utility and Constant Consumption with $\rho = r$

expenditures in every period must also be the same. That is, consumption is constant over the entire life cycle: $c_0^* = c_1^* = \ldots = c_T^*$. This is the result from Theorem 4.1.

The result of constant consumption does not depend on the particular functional form of the increasing and concave instantaneous utility function $u(\cdot)$. It does depend crucially on the assumption that the discount and interest rates are equal. Exercise 4A.1 has you characterize the general path of consumption expenditure when $\rho \neq r$ for an arbitrary instantaneous utility function. To determine the actual utility-maximizing sequence of consumption expenditures we need to assume a particular instantaneous utility function and solve the system of equations in (4A.5) together with the intertemporal budget constraint. In Exercise 4A.2 you are asked to do this.

4A.1   Appendix Summary

1   **Constrained optimization problems**, like utility maximization and cost minimization, are common throughout economics. The **method of Lagrange** provides a method for solving such problems.
2   The **life-cycle model** implies that the path of consumption expenditure over time depends entirely on the relative magnitudes of the discount rate and interest rate, and not on the pattern of income.

4A.2   Appendix Exercises

Exercise 4A.1 — Non-Constant Consumption Expenditure. Notice that the right-hand side of the equations in (4A.5) is always the same number λ. This means that $(R\delta)^k u'(c_k^*)$ is the same number for all periods k. Therefore, as k increases, c_k^* must adjust so as to keep $(R\delta)^k u'(c_k^*)$ constant. The path of consumption depends on the magnitude of $R\delta = \frac{1+r}{1+\rho}$.

a   Fill in each of the six blank cells in the following table with the word "increasing" or "decreasing" to make the statements correct.

	Case 1: $r = \rho$	Case 2: $r > \rho$	Case 3: $r < \rho$
$R\delta = \frac{1+r}{1+\rho}$	= 1	>1	<1
	As k increases, then...		
$(R\delta)^k$ is	constant		
	and given that $(R\delta)^k u'(c_k^*)$ must be constant...		
$u'(c_k^*)$ is	constant		
	and given that $u'(c)$ is a decreasing function...		
c_k^* is	constant		

b   The logic in part (a) reveals that consumption expenditures are either constant, increasing, or decreasing and the direction depends entirely on the relationship between the interest rate r and the discount rate ρ. Provide intuition for this result.
c   You have shown that the direction of consumption expenditure over time does not depend on the pattern of income. Discuss the ways in which income impacts consumption expenditure and savings in the life-cycle model.

Exercise 4A.2 — Life-cycle Time Consistency. Consider a three-period ($T = 2$) version of the standard life-cycle model in which Towa inherits $70,000 in period 0 ($y_0 = 70,000$) and must decide how to allocate this money on consumption expenditure over three years. Assume that she earns no other income ($y_1 = y_2 = 0$) and there is no interest on savings or borrowing ($r = 0$, or $R = 1$). Towa's intertemporal budget constraint is therefore: $c_0 + c_1 + c_2 = 70,000$. In addition, assume that her instantaneous utility function $u(c_k) = \ln(c_k)$ and she has a discount factor $\delta = 1/2$ (or $\rho = 1/\delta - 1 = 1$). She therefore evaluates consumption expenditures at time zero as follows:

$$U^0(c_0, c_1, c_2) = \ln(c_0) + \frac{1}{2}\ln(c_1) + \left(\frac{1}{2}\right)^2 \ln(c_2)$$

a Use the method of Lagrange to determine Towa's utility-maximizing consumption expenditure c_0 in period 0, as well as her planned consumption expenditures c_1 and c_2 in the remaining periods.

b Let's check to see if Towa in period 1 actually wants to follow through with her planned consumption expenditure from part (a). You should have found that Towa spends $40,000 in period 0, leaving her with $30,000 for the remaining two periods. Given this observation, Towa's utility-maximization problem from the point of view of period 1 is:

$$\max_{c_1, c_2} \ln(c_1) + \frac{1}{2}\ln(c_2)$$
$$\text{such that} \quad c_1 + c_2 = 30,000$$

Use the method of Lagrange to solve this problem for Towa's actual consumption expenditures in periods 1 and 2.

c Does Towa's actual consumption in periods 1 and 2 (your answers to part (b)) differ from her period-0 plan for future consumption (your answers to part (a))? Briefly discuss and connect to the concept of time consistency.

Notes

1 Frederick, Loewenstein, and O'Donoghue (2002) identify seven additional assumptions of the DU model: (1) *Integration*: new alternatives are integrated with pre-existing plans; (2) *Utility Independence*: only the total utility matters from an outcome sequence and not the pattern of realized utility over time; (3) *Stationary Instantaneous Utility*: the instantaneous utility function does not change over time; (4) *Stationary Discount Function*: the discount function is independent of the time perspective from which a sequence of outcomes is being evaluated; (5) *Independence of Discounting from Consumption*: the discount function is independent of the type of consumption; (6) *Positive Time Preference*: individuals (weakly) prefer utility in the present over delayed utility (i.e., $\rho \geq 0$, or $\delta \leq 1$); and (7) *Diminishing Marginal Utility*.

2 I also assume for simplicity that (1) the outcomes in all other periods are the same across options, (2) apple consumption in the absence of these options is zero, and (3) it is not a leap year.

3 To calculate the implied continuously compounded annual discount rate ρ, we use: Future Prize = Current Prize $\times e^{\rho t}$ where t is years between the current and future payouts. Implicit in this equation is that the instantaneous utility function over the prize money, x, is $u(x) = Ax$ for some $A > 0$ and that existing wealth is ignored or normalized to zero. I maintain this assumption in the remainder of this section.

4 The functional form for $D^h(k)$ was suggested by Herrnstein (1981) and Mazur (1987).

5 Recall from Note 3 that the implied discount rates are calculated assuming that the utility function over money is linear and existing wealth is zero. If the utility function is strongly concave and defined over total wealth, including existing wealth plus prize winnings, then the implied discount rates can be much smaller and similar to each other across the size of the prize, eliminating the magnitude effect as an anomaly.

6 Inequality (4.1) implicitly assumes that $u(French) > 0$ and that in the absence of French dinner the individual always eats a meal with instantaneous utility normalized to zero.

7 Observe that $\rho = r$ is equivalent to $\delta = 1/R$ because in the DU model $\delta = \frac{1}{1+\rho}$.

8 For the more general case in which $\rho = r > 0$, equation (4.6) becomes: $c^* = \frac{R-1}{R-1/R^T} \sum_{k=0}^{T} \frac{y_k}{R^k}$.

9 The third equality follows from the formula for the sum of the first n natural numbers: $n(n + 1)/2$.

10 Wealth is the accumulation of each period's additional savings, which is the gap between income and consumption in each period. Mathematically, wealth in period t is $\sum_{k=0}^{t}(y_k - c_k)$.

11 One important difference between liquidity constraints and income uncertainty is that with limits on borrowing, individuals cannot maintain consumption above income early in life. See Carroll (2001) for further discussion.

12 Theorem 4A.1 provides necessary conditions, i.e., the conditions that necessarily hold at the optimum. In general, these conditions are not sufficient to guarantee that any solution to them must be optimal. However, for all of the applications in this book the conditions (4A.3) and (4A.4) are both necessary and sufficient.

References

Ainslie, George, and Varda Haendel. 1983. "The Motives of the Will." In *Etiologic Aspects of Alcohol and Drug Abuse,* edited by E. Gottheil, K. Durley, T. Skodola, and H. Waxman, 3: 119–140. Springfield, IL: Charles C. Thomas.

Ainslie, George, and Richard J. Herrnstein. 1981. "Preference Reversal and Delayed Reinforcement." *Animal Learning & Behavior* 9 (4): 476–482. doi:10.3758/bf03209777.

Allen, Todd W., and Christopher D. Carroll. 2001. "Individual Learning about Consumption." *Macroeconomic Dynamics* 5 (02): 255–271. doi:10.3386/w8234.

Angeletos, George-Marios, David Laibson, Andrea Repetto, Jeremy Tobacman, and Stephen Weinberg. 2001. "The Hyperbolic Consumption Model: Calibration, Simulation, and Empirical Evaluation." *Journal of Economic Perspectives* 15 (3): 47–68. doi:10.1257/jep.15.3.47.

Banerjee, Abhijit V., and Sendhil Mullainathan. 2010. "The Shape of Temptation: Implications for the Economic Lives of the Poor." NBER Working Paper 15973. Cambridge, MA: National Bureau of Economic Research. doi:10.3386/w15973.

Banks, James, Richard Blundell, and Sarah Tanner. 1998. "Is there a Retirement-Savings Puzzle?" *American Economic Review* 88 (4): 769–788.

Battistin, Erich, Richard Blundell, and Arthur Lewbel. 2009. "Why Is Consumption More Log Normal than Income? Gibrat's Law Revisited." *Journal of Political Economy* 117 (6): 1140–1154. doi:10.1086/648995.

Benzion, Uri, Amnon Rapoport, and Joseph Yagil. 1989. "Discount Rates Inferred from Decisions: An Experimental Study." *Management Science* 35 (3): 270–284.

Bernheim, B. Douglas, Jonathan Skinner, and Steven Weinberg. 2001. "What Accounts for the Variation in Retirement Wealth among U.S. Households?" *American Economic Review* 91 (4): 832–857. doi:10.1257/aer.91.4.832.

Carroll, Christopher D. 2001. "A Theory of the Consumption Function, with and without Liquidity Constraints." *Journal of Economic Perspectives* 15 (3): 23–45. doi:10.1257/jep.15.3.23.

Chapman, Gretchen B. 2000. "Preferences for Improving and Declining Sequences of Health Outcomes." *Journal of Behavioral Decision Making* 13 (2): 203–218. doi:10.1002/(sici)1099-0771 (200004/06)13:2<203::aid-bdm317>3.0.co;2-s.

Dohmen, Thomas, Benjamin Enke, Armin Falk, David Huffman, and Uwe Sunde. 2016. "Patience and the Wealth of Nations." Working Paper 2016-012. Human Capital and Economic Opportunity Working Group. https://econpapers.repec.org/paper/hkawpaper/2016-012.htm.

Farkas, Steve, and Jean Johnson. 1997. *Miles to Go: A Status Report on Americans' Plans for Retirement: A Report from Public Agenda.* Public Agenda.

Frederick, Shane, George Loewenstein, and Ted O'Donoghue. 2002. "Time Discounting and Time Preference: A Critical Review." *Journal of Economic Literature* 40 (2): 351–401. doi:10.1257/jel.40.2.351.

Hall, Robert E. 1978. "Stochastic Implications of the Life Cycle-Permanent Income Hypothesis: Theory and Evidence." *Journal of Political Economy* 86 (6): 971–987. doi:10.1086/260724.

Haushofer, Johannes, and Ernst Fehr. 2014. "On the Psychology of Poverty." *Science* 344 (6186): 862–867. doi:10.1126/science.1232491.

———. 2019. "Negative Income Shocks Increase Discount Rates." Working Paper. Princeton University.

Herrnstein, Richard J. 1981. "Self-control as Response Strength." In *Quantification of Steady-State Operant Behavior,* edited by Christopher M. Bradshaw, Elmer Szabadi, and C. F. Lowe, 3–20. Elsevier.

Hsee, Christopher K., Robert P. Abelson, and Peter Salovey. 1991. "The Relative Weighting of Position and Velocity in Satisfaction." *Psychological Science* 2 (4): 263–267. doi:10.1111/j.1467-9280.1991.tb00146.x.

Jones, Damon, and Aprajit Mahajan. 2015. "Time-Inconsistency and Saving: Experimental Evidence from Low-Income Tax Filers." NBER Working Paper 21272. Cambridge, MA: National Bureau of Economic Research. doi:10.3386/w21272.

Kirby, Kris N. 1997. "Bidding on the Future: Evidence against Normative Discounting of Delayed Rewards." *Journal of Experimental Psychology: General* 126 (1): 54. doi:10.1037/0096-3445.126.1.54.

Kirby, Kris N., and Richard J. Herrnstein. 1995. "Preference Reversals Due to Myopic Discounting of Delayed Reward." *Psychological Science* 6 (2): 83–89. doi:10.1111/j.1467-9280.1995.tb00311.x.

Lawrance, Emily C. 1991. "Poverty and the Rate of Time Preference: Evidence from Panel Data." *Journal of Political Economy* 99 (1): 54–77. doi:10.1086/261740.

Loewenstein, George. 1987. "Anticipation and the Valuation of Delayed Consumption." *The Economic Journal* 97 (387): 666–684. By permission of the Royal Economic Society, doi:10.2307/2232929.

Loewenstein, George, and Drazen Prelec. 1993. "Preferences for Sequences of Outcomes." *Psychological Review* 100 (1): 91–108. Copyright © 1993 by the American Psychological Association, Inc. Adapted with permission, doi:10.1037/0033-295X. 100.1.91.

Loewenstein, George, and Nachum Sicherman. 1991. "Do Workers Prefer Increasing Wage Profiles?" *Journal of Labor Economics* 9 (1): 67–84. doi:10.1086/298259.

Mazur, James E. 1987. "An Adjusting Procedure for Studying Delayed Reinforcement." In *The Effect of Delay and of Intervening Events on Reinforcement Value,* edited by Michael L. Commons, James E. Mazur, John Anthony Nevin, and Howard Rachlin. Hillsdale, NJ: Lawrence Erlbaum Associates, Inc.

Modigliani, Franco, and Richard Brumberg. 1954. "Utility Analysis and the Consumption Function: An Interpretation of Cross-section Data." In *Post-Keynesian Economics,* edited by Kenneth K. Kurihara, 388–436. New Brunswick, N.J.: Rutgers University Press.

Mullainathan, Sendhil, and Eldar Shafir. 2013. *Scarcity: Why Having Too Little Means So Much.* New York: Henry Holt / Company.

Pender, John L. 1996. "Discount Rates and Credit Markets: Theory and Evidence from Rural India." *Journal of Development Economics* 50 (2): 257–296. doi:10.1016/s0304-3878(96)00400-2.

Raineri, Andres, and Howard Rachlin. 1993. "The Effect of Temporal Constraints on the Value of Money and other Commodities." *Journal of Behavioral Decision Making* 6 (2): 77–94. doi:10.1002/bdm.3960060202.

Smith, Adam. 1776. *An Inquiry Into the Nature and Causes of the Wealth of Nations.* London: W. Strahan / T. Cadell.

Thaler, Richard H. 1981. "Some Empirical Evidence on Dynamic Inconsistency." *Economics Letters* 8 (3): 201–207. Reprinting from p 202, Copyright (1981), with permission from Elsevier, doi:10.1016/0165-1765(81)90067-7.

Varey, Carol, and Daniel Kahneman. 1992. "Experiences Extended across Time: Evaluation of Moments and Episodes." *Journal of Behavioral Decision Making* 5 (3): 169–185. doi:10.1002/bdm.3960050303.

World Bank. 2018. "Poverty and Shared Prosperity 2018: Piecing Together the Poverty Puzzle." Technical Report. Washington, DC: World Bank. License: Creative Commons Attribution CC BY 3.0 IGO.

Yesuf, Mahmud, and Randall Bluffstone. 2008. "Wealth and Time Preference in Rural Ethiopia." Discussion Paper Series EfD DP 08-16. Environment for Development.

5 Present Bias

Learning Objectives

★ Understand how the model of present-biased preferences differs from the standard Discounted Utility model.

★ Determine theoretical predictions of present-biased preferences for behavior.

★ Evaluate empirical evidence supportive of present bias.

Self-control problems are commonplace. Despite the best of intentions, many of us struggle to exercise regularly or start working on projects early. It is also challenging to resist the temptation to eat unhealthy snacks or spend beyond our means with a credit card.

In this chapter we allow for such self-control problems by developing an alternative to the standard Discounted Utility (DU) model. This alternative model differs from the standard model by replacing the exponential discount function (and its constant discount rate) with a discount function that discounts the near future at a higher rate than the distant future. In doing so, the model captures a bias towards the present that can help to explain why many individuals fail to follow through with plans to exercise, study, or save.

Although we abandon constant discounting in this chapter, we maintain the other key assumption of the DU model: consumption independence. That is, utility today is independent of consumption in periods other than the present. Consumption dependence is introduced in Chapter 6.

This chapter begins by introducing the new model of present-biased preferences. We then apply this model to two different types of consumer choice problems. The first is a decision *whether or not* to consume a good that generates benefits in one period and costs in another. Going to the gym today, for example, generates a present cost in terms of time, effort, and money, but delivers health benefits in the future. The second application concerns the timing of *when* to complete an activity that must be done before some deadline. Suppose, for instance, that you have a free single-day gym pass that expires at the end of the week and must decide when to use it. In each application we consider how the predictions of present-biased preferences differ from those of the standard DU model. The chapter concludes with a range of empirical evidence — from health, education, and savings contexts — for present bias.

DOI: 10.4324/9780367854072-7

5.1   Present-Biased Preferences

The evidence of preference reversals and self-control problems in the previous chapter suggests that individuals exhibit relative impatience in the short term (high discount rate) and greater patience over the long term (low discount rate). A hyperbolic discount function with declining discount rates over the future time horizon can therefore better match this evidence than the standard exponential discount function with its constant discount rate.

5.1.1   Quasi-Hyperbolic Discounting

Although a hyperbolic discount function improves the descriptive accuracy of the model, it is a significantly more complicated function, making the model less tractable. To balance these competing priorities, consider a hybrid function that maintains the tractability of the exponential discount function, but allows for the declining discount rates characteristic of the hyperbolic discount function. Such a hybrid is the **quasi-hyperbolic discount function**, which takes the following form:

$$D^{qh}(k) = \begin{cases} 1 & \text{if } k = 0 \\ \beta\delta^k & \text{if } k \geq 1, \end{cases} \quad \text{where } 0 < \beta \leq 1$$

This function, popularized by Laibson (1997), is also referred to as the *beta-delta discount function*, in reference to its two parameters β and δ. It is plotted as a dashed curve in Figure 5.1, along with the functions and data from Figure 4.1.[1] The quasi-hyperbolic discount function approximates the hyperbolic shape, dropping faster than the exponential function initially, and then declining slower than the exponential

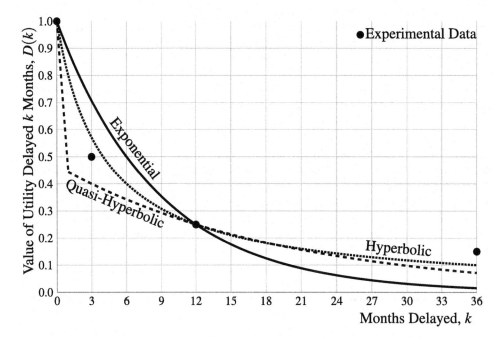

Figure 5.1 Fitting Discount Functions to Discounting in Winnings Wait Lab Experiment

function over longer horizons. It consequently comes closer to the experimental data than the exponential function.

By applying the discount function $D^{qh}(k)$ to the general discounted utility form (see expression (2.1)), we have the following nonstandard model of intertemporal preferences.

Definition 5.1 The **model of present-biased preferences** evaluates a sequence of outcomes as the quasi-hyperbolic discounted sum of instantaneous utilities.[2] In particular, the total discounted utility of the outcome sequence $(x_t, x_{t+1}, \ldots, x_T)$ from the perspective of period t is:

$$U^t(x_t, x_{t+1}, \ldots, x_T; \beta) = D^{qh}(0)u(x_t) + D^{qh}(1)u(x_{t+1}) + D^{qh}(2)u(x_{t+2})$$
$$+ \cdots + D^{qh}(T-t)u(x_T)$$
$$= u(x_t) + \beta\delta u(x_{t+1}) + \beta\delta^2 u(x_{t+2}) + \cdots + \beta\delta^{T-t}u(x_T)$$

where $u(\cdot)$ is the instantaneous utility function and $0 < \beta, \delta \leq 1$.

The quasi-hyperbolic discount function differs only slightly from the standard case. In fact, if $\beta = 1$, then it *is* the standard exponential discount function $D(k) = \delta^k$. This strategy of embedding the standard model as a special case of the nonstandard model is common in behavioral economics (Rabin 2013). By modifying the standard model with a single parameter (in this case, β), empirical estimates of the parameter provide us with a measure of the degree to which preferences differ from those assumed in the standard model (in this case, how far β is from 1).

How exactly does this model of present bias satisfy the goals of tractability and psychological realism? It is tractable because the discount function looks like a standard exponential function for all periods after the current period. In particular, between any two consecutive periods in the future, the discount rate is constant and equal to $1/\delta - 1$:

$$\rho(k) = -\frac{D^{qh}(k) - D^{qh}(k-1)}{D^{qh}(k)} = -\frac{\beta\delta^k - \beta\delta^{k-1}}{\beta\delta^k} = \frac{1}{\delta} - 1 \text{ for all } k \geq 2$$

And yet, it achieves more realism by exhibiting a larger discount rate from the present period to the next period than between all future periods. We can verify this:

$$\rho(1) = -\frac{D^{qh}(1) - D^{qh}(0)}{D^{qh}(1)} = -\frac{\beta\delta - 1}{\beta\delta} = \frac{1}{\beta\delta} - 1 \geq \frac{1}{\delta} - 1$$

This feature aligns with the motivating evidence in the previous chapter. Observe also that the smaller is β, the larger is the immediate discount rate $\rho(1)$, and the greater is the present bias.

5.1.2 Time Inconsistency

Although it may appear to be a minor adjustment to the standard model, introducing the quasi-hyperbolic discount function has significant consequences. Recall from Section 2.2.3 that exponential discounting is equivalent to time-consistent preferences. Therefore, with quasi-hyperbolic discounting, preferences are no longer guaranteed to be time-consistent.

Allowing for time inconsistency generates new problems for the decision maker. If preferences can shift over time, then the individual is in some sense no longer a single decision maker moving through time. Instead, there is a different self making choices in each period, and these multiple selves of the same individual may disagree with each other. For example, my current self might like to go to the gym tomorrow morning before work. But when the alarm clock goes off tomorrow morning, my tomorrow self might prefer to hit the snooze button and go back to sleep. If there are indeed changing versions of the self across time, how aware is any current self of the preferences of future selves? That is, do I know today that I am unlikely to follow through on my plan to go to the gym tomorrow morning?

In order to capture how self-aware individuals are of their future preferences, let $\hat{\beta}$ be the individual's belief of their true β. A sophisticated individual, or **sophisticate**, is fully aware of their future preferences, in which case $\hat{\beta} = \beta$. In the gym example, if I am a sophisticate, I correctly anticipate today that my tomorrow self will not want to go to the gym. Given that I recognize this self-control problem, I might text a friend now to arrange meeting me at the gym in the morning. This is an example of a **commitment strategy** that will make it less likely for my tomorrow self to deviate from my current preferences.

Conversely, a naive individual, or **naif**, believes they have time-consistent preferences, or equivalently an exponential discount function. In this case, $\hat{\beta} = 1$ (because when $\beta = 1$, $D^{qh}(k)$ is exponential). If I am a naif, I do not realize today when planning my trip to the gym in the morning that when tomorrow morning arrives, I am unlikely to actually go to the gym. Therefore, I do not make any plans today to go to the gym with a friend because I do not anticipate failing to follow through. Notice that expectations about future behavior, which depend on $\hat{\beta}$, can impact decisions today.[3]

5.1.3 Welfare with Present Bias

Thinking about welfare for time-inconsistent individuals is complicated because different selves of the same person can disagree with each other over time. Today you may want to go to the gym tomorrow, but tomorrow you may not actually want to exercise. Which version of your self should you satisfy to maximize your welfare?

Let's assume that present-biased individuals evaluate their welfare from a *long-run perspective* before making decisions (O'Donoghue and Rabin 1999). When all outcomes are in the future and there is no decision to make at present, the discount rate between any two consecutive future periods is constant. So although present bias ($\beta < 1$) impacts decisions when they are made, it doesn't matter from the long-run perspective of experienced welfare resulting from those decisions. Just because a present-biased individual discounts the future health benefits of going to the gym at a higher rate when it comes time to decide whether or not to actually go to the gym, the future health benefits of exercise are no less real. The following definition formalizes this welfare approach.

Definition 5.2 The **individual welfare** W from a sequence of outcomes $(x_0, x_1, ..., x_T)$ for an individual with present-biased preferences is

$$W(x_0, x_1, ..., x_T) \equiv u(x_0) + \delta u(x_1) + \delta^2 u(x_2) + \cdots + \delta^T u(x_T)$$

for any β or $\hat{\beta}$.

This definition of individual welfare implies that present-biased decision makers would achieve the highest possible welfare by making choices as if they were time-consistent exponential discounters. But because they are not, choices can fail to maximize welfare. Such welfare losses motivate paternalistic interventions that aim to make those with present bias better off. We explore such policy concerns in Chapter 7. The remainder of this chapter is focused on understanding the consequences of present bias for behavior.

5.2 Consumption of a Good

Let's consider how someone with present-biased preferences would evaluate whether or not to consume a good in the future.[4] This simple decision problem reveals the key features of present-biased decision making.

Assume that there are three periods. Denote the present by period 0, when consumption is planned, but not actually consumed. There is a good x that can be consumed (for free) in period 1, with an immediate payoff of u_1 and a delayed payoff in period 2 of u_2. Assume that not consuming the good generates zero payoff in all periods. If payoffs in both periods are positive ($u_1, u_2 > 0$), the good is always good and the consumer will consume. And if payoffs in both periods are negative ($u_1, u_2 < 0$), the good is always bad and the consumer will not consume.

The more interesting cases are goods that deliver a positive payoff in one period and a negative payoff in the other. An **investment good** (e.g., exercising, job search, dieting, writing a paper) has an immediate cost ($u_1 < 0$) and a delayed reward ($u_2 > 0$). On the other hand, a **leisure good** (e.g., eating dessert, watching TV, smoking) has an immediate reward ($u_1 > 0$) and a delayed cost ($u_2 < 0$). The four types of possible goods are labeled in Figure 5.2, each of which corresponds to one of the four quadrants.

What are the predictions for how a present-biased individual, let's call her Patty, will behave in this example? In period 0 Patty *plans* to consume the good in period 1 if and

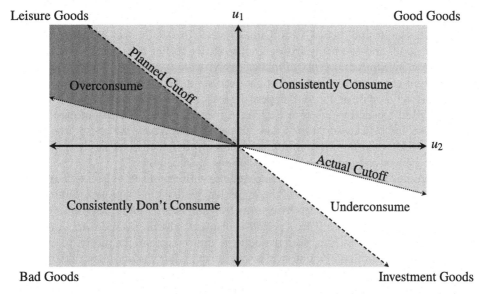

Figure 5.2 Visualizing Consumption with Present Bias

only if the total discounted utility from the good is at least the total discounted utility from not consuming, which we assumed was zero:

$$\text{Plans to Consume} \Leftrightarrow U^0(x;\beta) \geq U^0(0;\beta)$$
$$\Leftrightarrow \beta\delta u_1 + \beta\delta^2 u_2 \geq 0 \Leftrightarrow u_1 + \delta u_2 \geq 0 \tag{5.1}$$

From the perspective of period 0, all payoffs are delayed and hence are all multiplied by β. The β's cancel out and therefore do not impact Patty's period-0 plan. Observe that if Patty had a time-consistent friend Theresa (for whom $\beta = 1$ and δ were the same), Theresa would make the same plan as Patty in period 0. Following through with this period-0 plan would consequently maximize individual welfare.

Patty's decision plan is depicted graphically in Figure 5.2. She plans to consume any good with payoffs that are above the Planned Cutoff dashed line (which has slope $-\delta$). There are both leisure and investment goods that Patty plans to consume, but only if the rewards are sufficiently large relative to the costs.

Next, consider the decision in period 1 to *actually* consume the good, which Patty again does if and only the total discounted utility from the good is at least zero:

$$\text{Actually Consumes} \Leftrightarrow U^1(x;\beta) \geq U^1(0;\beta) \Leftrightarrow u_1 + \beta\delta u_2 \geq 0 \tag{5.2}$$

From the perspective of period 1, there is an undiscounted immediate payoff u_1 and a delayed payoff u_2, the current value of which is discounted by $\beta\delta$.

Compare the inequalities in (5.1) and (5.2). For time-consistent Theresa (with $\beta = 1$), the two inequalities are identical; the plan to consume and actual consumption are aligned. Recall that this is exactly what it means to be time-consistent. For present-biased Patty (with $\beta < 1$), however, her rule in period 0 for planning consumption in period 1 differs from her actual consumption decision rule in period 1. In particular, when period 1 arrives, Patty discounts the delayed payoff u_2 by more than she planned (because $\beta\delta < \delta$).

The higher-than-planned discounting of the future payoff corresponds graphically to a flatter cutoff line in Figure 5.2. Patty actually consumes in period 1 if the payoffs are above the Actual Cutoff dotted line (which has slope $-\beta\delta$). The difference between the Planned Cutoff and Actual Cutoff lines reveals that Patty will consume too few investment goods and too many leisure goods relative to her own plans.

Consider an investment good like exercising, with payoffs $u_1 < 0 < u_2$. For exercise payoffs in the medium gray regions of the lower right quadrant in Figure 5.2, Patty follows through her plan to either exercise or not. But suppose the exercise payoffs are in the unshaded region. In this case Patty's period-0 plan is to exercise in the next period. When making this plan, both the costs and benefits are in the future. In period 1, however, the cost of exercising is immediately felt, while the delayed health benefits are by comparison far away. Her bias towards the present cost induces her to abandon her exercise plan.

Now consider a leisure good like eating dessert, with payoffs $u_1 > 0 > u_2$. For dessert payoffs in the medium gray regions of the upper left quadrant in Figure 5.2, Patty follows through her plan to either eat dessert or not. But suppose the dessert payoffs are in the dark gray region. In this case Patty's period-0 plan is to abstain from dessert in the next period. When making this plan, both the benefits and costs are in the future. In period 1, however, the benefit of enjoying dessert is immediate, while the delayed health costs are by comparison far away. Her bias towards the present cost induces her to abandon her planned abstention. These observations are summarized in the first row of Table 5.1.

Table 5.1 The Effect of Present Bias on Consumption Behavior

	Time-Consistent	Present-Biased	
		Sophisticate	Naif
Plan vs. Actual	accurately plans	underconsumes investment goods & overconsumes leisure goods	
Expectation vs. Actual	accurately anticipates		overestimates investment goods & underestimates leisure goods

Patty's welfare is maximized by acting as if she were time-consistent and following through with her period-0 plan. When she over or underconsumes relative to her plan, she experiences a welfare loss. Note that for smaller values of β, the degree of present bias is stronger and the Actual Cutoff line becomes flatter. The Planned Cutoff line is unaffected. Stronger present bias therefore increases the area of the dark gray and unshaded regions, making over and underconsumption, and the corresponding welfare loss, more likely.

To what extent do present-biased individuals accurately anticipate their future behavior? Recall that $\hat{\beta}$ indicates the individual's belief of their true β. Given this belief, we can think through how an individual in period 0 *expects* to behave in period 1. That is, what does the period-0 self expect her period-1 self to do? She expects to consume if and only if the total discounted utility from the good at time 1, evaluated using her belief of preferences in period 1, is at least zero:

$$\text{Expects to Consume} \Leftrightarrow U^1(x; \hat{\beta}) \geq U^1(0; \hat{\beta}) \Leftrightarrow u_1 + \hat{\beta}\delta u_2 \geq 0 \qquad (5.3)$$

A sophisticate is fully aware of her true preferences ($\hat{\beta} = \beta$) and accurately anticipates actual consumption. This is evident by observing that inequalities (5.2) and (5.3) are identical for the sophisticate. The sophisticate knows she may not go to the gym tomorrow or may eat dessert after dinner, in spite of plans to the contrary. She may therefore pursue commitment strategies that help her to align her plans with her actual behavior (e.g., arranging a schedule to exercise with a gym buddy who can hold her accountable or bringing only enough cash to dinner to pay for an entree and no dessert).

A naif does not realize she has a self-control problem ($\hat{\beta} = 1$) and therefore fails to anticipate actual consumption. In fact, for the naif, inequalities (5.1) and (5.3) are identical; she expects to follow through with her plan. But she may be surprised by her actual period-1 decision. For an investment good she *overestimates* actual consumption because she doesn't anticipate her failure to make the investment. Similarly, for a leisure good she *underestimates* actual consumption because she doesn't anticipate her failure to abstain. These observations are summarized in the second row of Table 5.1.

The model of present-biased preferences generates the type of self-control problems and time inconsistency that we observe in experimental studies, and perhaps in our own behavior. We must be careful when thinking through how individuals with such preferences behave, given that their preferences shift over time and their expectations depend on how self-aware they are. These issues are not present with exponential discounting because in that standard case, plans, expectations, and actual behavior are all one and the same.

5.3   Doing it Once

Instead of evaluating the sequence of payoffs associated with consuming a good, we can also apply the model of present-biased preferences to study the intertemporal choice problem of deciding *when* to do an activity. If you have to write a paper, when do you write it? Do you start writing far in advance or the night before it's due? Or if you have a free movie pass that expires in a month, when do you go to the theater?

In this section we consider settings such as these, where an individual must decide on the timing of an activity. The analysis is adapted from O'Donoghue and Rabin (1999). I first introduce the model and then apply the model to examples that highlight the differential predictions for the behavior of time-consistents, naifs, and sophisticates. These examples illustrate more general insights about behavior that are discussed at the end of this section.

5.3.1   Model Setup

Consider an activity that an individual must complete exactly once within a particular time frame. The activity cannot be avoided and cannot be repeated. Assume that there are T periods within which to complete the activity. In each period 1, 2, ..., T the individual must decide whether or not to complete the activity. Doing the activity in period k generates a reward v_k and a cost c_k. The rewards and costs, however, are not experienced simultaneously. When they are realized depends on the type of activity:

1   Investment activity completed in period k: cost c_k realized immediately in period k and delayed reward v_k realized in period $T + 1$
2   Leisure activity completed in period k: reward v_k realized immediately in period k and delayed cost c_k realized in period $T + 1$

Writing a paper is an investment activity, so the cost of writing is realized when actually writing, but the reward from writing the paper — in terms of the feedback and grade — is realized after the due date. In the movie pass example, seeing a movie is a leisure activity. So the enjoyment of the movie is realized at the theater, but the cost from going to the movies, if any, is realized later.

Preferences

The individual has present-biased preferences. And assume for simplicity that $\delta = 1$. Let $U^t(k)$ denote the total discounted utility from the perspective of period t from completing the activity in period $k \geq t$. Utility depends on the type of activity as follows:

$$\text{Investment Activity}: U^t(k) = \begin{cases} \beta v_k - c_k & \text{if } k = t \\ \beta(v_k - c_k) & \text{if } k > t \end{cases}$$

$$\text{Leisure Activity}: U^t(k) = \begin{cases} v_k - \beta c_k & \text{if } k = t \\ \beta(v_k - c_k) & \text{if } k > t \end{cases}$$

Observe that when the activity is to be completed in a future period $k > t$, both the reward and cost are delayed, so they are both multiplied by β. In this case, the total utility from the perspective of period t is the same for both investment and leisure activities. But when the activity is completed in the current period ($k = t$), utility depends on the type of activity. For the investment activity only the reward is delayed and hence multiplied by β, whereas for the leisure activity only the cost is delayed and multiplied by β.

Strategies

To determine when an individual completes the activity, we must consider whether or not the individual would complete the activity in *every* possible period, assuming that it has not yet been completed. That is, even if the individual completes the activity in period 2, we must determine whether or not they would complete the activity in period 3 if they had not completed it in period 2. Why do we consider such counterfactual situations? Because it is possible for current behavior to depend on expectations about future behavior. Therefore, we specify future behavior that may never occur to help us understand the present. This will become clearer once we work through some examples.

The complete contingent plan for behavior in every period is called a strategy.

Definition 5.3 A **strategy** for a player is $s = (s_1, s_2, \ldots, s_T)$, where for every $t = 1$, $2, \ldots, T$, $s_t \in \{Y, N\}$ denotes that the player does (Y) or does not (N) complete the activity in period t, assuming she has not yet done it.

The individual then actually completes the activity in the first period of the strategy with a Y. Note that regardless of the rewards and costs or type of activity, $s_T = Y$. This is because we have assumed that the activity must be completed by period T, so if it has not yet been completed before this point, the individual must do it in the last period.

We now define how the full strategies are determined for three types of individuals: time-consistents (TCs), naifs, and sophisticates. We begin with TCs who have $\beta = 1$, so $U^t(k) = v_k - c_k$ for all $k \geq t$ and for both types of activities.

Definition 5.4 A **strategy for a time-consistent** is a strategy s^{tc} such that for all $t < T$

$$s_t^{tc} = Y \Leftrightarrow U^t(t) \geq U^t(k) \text{ for all } k > t$$

How should we read this definition? Interpret period t as the current period. Then a TC will do the activity immediately ($s_t^{tc} = Y$) if and only if from the current perspective, doing the activity now is at least as good as doing the activity in *any* future period. This should be fairly intuitive. The individual considers the payoff from doing the activity today and in every future period, and as long as there is no future period in which it would be better to complete the activity, she does it now.

Naifs have present-biased preferences ($0 < \beta < 1$), but they believe they are time-consistent ($\hat{\beta} = 1$), so they make decisions just like the TCs.

> **Definition 5.5 A strategy for a naif** is a strategy s^n such that for all $t < T$
>
> $$s_t^n = Y \Leftrightarrow U^t(t) \geq U^t(k) \text{ for all } k > t$$

Although naifs and TCs share the same reasoning process, they differ in their preferences.

Sophisticates are similarly present-biased ($0 < \beta < 1$), but they conduct a more sophisticated analysis than naifs, since they accurately anticipate their future preferences ($\hat{\beta} = \beta$). In particular, sophisticates first determine when they will complete the activity *if they do not do it now*. They then decide to do the activity now if and only if given their current preferences, doing it now is preferred to waiting for their future self to do it. Suppose for instance that I realize that if I do not write my paper tonight, I will keep procrastinating until the night before it is due. Therefore, I will write it tonight if and only if I prefer writing it tonight to writing it the night before it is due. We can express this logic with math notation as follows:

> **Definition 5.6 A strategy for a sophisticate** is a strategy s^s such that for all $t < T$
>
> $$s_t^s = Y \Leftrightarrow U^t(t) \geq U^t(k') \text{ where } k' \text{ is the smallest integer such that}$$
>
> $$k' > t \text{ and } s_{k'}^s = Y$$

Observe that each period's action depends on the strategic actions in future periods. Because of this, to solve for the sophisticate's full strategy we have to reason backwards. We start by determining s_{T-1}^s, followed by s_{T-2}^s, and so on.

Although naifs and sophisticates share the same preferences, their behavior can differ since a naif does not accurately anticipate how their future selves will behave. In the paper writing example, this can lead a naif to each day convince herself that she will write the paper tomorrow, only to be surprised by continuous procrastination.

5.3.2   Examples

Let's apply this abstract model to some concrete examples, starting with the case of an investment activity.

■ **Example 5.1 — Investment Activity**. You need to write a paper on one of four weekends ($T = 4$), but on each weekend, a different movie is premiering, which you must miss while working on your paper:

- Week 1: A bad movie
- Week 2: A mediocre movie
- Week 3: A good movie
- Week 4: An excellent movie

The cost of writing the paper is the immediate loss of missing a movie premiere. Because the quality of the movie premieres is increasing over time, the cost of writing the paper is also increasing each period. Let $c = (3, 5, 8, 13)$. Assume that the quality of your paper (and its subsequent grade) is independent of when you write the paper. Therefore let the delayed rewards schedule be constant $v = (\bar{v}, \bar{v}, \bar{v}, \bar{v})$. Finally, assume $\beta = 1/2$ for the naïfs and sophisticates.

Time-Consistents

A TC wants to minimize the cost since the reward is constant. Because the costs are increasing over time, in each period the TC prefers to write the paper now rather than wait, assuming it has not yet been written. The TC's strategy is therefore:

$$s^{tc} = (Y, Y, Y, Y)$$

and she writes the paper on the first weekend, missing the bad movie.

Naïfs

A naïf similarly wants to minimize the cost, but because $\beta = 1/2$, she perceives future costs as only half of their realized cost when she arrives in the future. Therefore, in period 1, the cost of writing the paper immediately is 3, while the perceived cost of writing it in the future is 2.5, 4, and 6.5 for the three following weeks, respectively. Because the perceived cost of writing the paper in week 2 is less than writing it in week 1, the naïf delays, believing she will write it in week 2. But when week 2 arrives, the immediate cost is 5, as opposed to a perceived cost of 4 from delaying to week 3, so she again delays. This logic continues until the last week when she must write the paper and miss the excellent movie. Her strategy is therefore:

$$s^n = (N, N, N, Y)$$

The naïf overestimates her future willingness to write the paper. Thus, even though the naïf and TC reason through the decision problem in the same way, the naïf's present-biased preferences lead her to behave very differently.

Sophisticates

A sophisticate reasons backwards as follows:

- In week 4 she must write the paper if she has not yet written it ($s_4^s = Y$).
- In week 3 she can write and lose 8 or wait until week 4 and lose 13 (perceived as a cost of 6.5), so she delays writing the paper ($s_3^s = N$).
- In week 2 she can write and lose 5 or wait, knowing that her period-3 self will delay to the last period, and incur a currently perceived cost of 6.5. She therefore chooses to do it now ($s_2^s = Y$).
- In week 1 she can write the paper at a cost of 3 or wait until week 2, knowing that her period-2 self will write the paper if it has not yet been written, and incur a currently perceived cost of 2.5. She therefore chooses to delay ($s_1^s = N$).

In summary,

$$s^s = (N, Y, N, Y)$$

The sophisticate procrastinates a bit, but accurately anticipates her future procrastination and hence does not wait as long as the naif to write the paper, only missing the mediocre movie in week 2.

Commitment Strategy

Suppose the sophisticate aims to instead behave like the time-consistent, writing the paper in the first week and missing the worst movie. How could she achieve such an outcome? She needs a strategy that helps commit herself to writing the paper the first week. One such possibility is to increase the cost of writing the paper in week 2, from $c_2 = 5$ to $c_2 = 7$, by planning fun social activities with friends or family during that weekend. Let's now re-consider the strategy of the sophisticate in the second and first weeks:

- In week 2 she can write and lose 7 or wait, knowing that her period-3 self will delay to the last period, and incur a currently perceived cost of 6.5. She therefore chooses to wait ($s_2^s = N$).
- In week 1 she can write the paper at a cost of 3 or wait until week 4, knowing that her period-2 and period-3 selves will delay, and incur a currently perceived cost of 6.5. She therefore prefers to write the paper ($s_1^s = Y$).

Now, her full strategy is $s^s = (Y, N, N, Y)$ and she behaves like the TC, as desired.

This example highlights a somewhat counterintuitive logic. By increasing the cost of writing the paper in week 2, the sophisticate has made herself better off (in the sense that she misses out on a worse movie). Higher costs could never make the time-consistent better off. But in a setting with present bias, commitment strategies that increase costs or limit choices can actually help an individual achieve more desirable outcomes. Note that naifs do not seek out such commitment strategies because they (incorrectly) believe that they are time-consistent. ∎

∎ **Example 5.2 — Leisure Activity.** You have been gifted a free movie ticket that you must use on one of four weekends to see a movie premiere, with the movies increasing in quality over time, as in the previous example. Assume that you do not have money to pay for any additional movies. As before, $T = 4$ and $\beta = 1/2$ for the naifs and sophisticates. Seeing a movie is a reward and we assume that the rewards schedule is $v = (3, 5, 8, 13)$. There is no cost to seeing the free movie, so we let $c = (0, 0, 0, 0)$.

Time-Consistents

A TC prefers to wait until the last weekend when the best movie premieres. Therefore:

$$s^{tc} = (N, N, N, Y)$$

Naifs

A naif in the first two weeks prefers to wait to the last week when the perceived value of the best movie is 6.5. But in week 3 the naif gives in and sees the good movie because the immediate reward of 8 is greater than the currently perceived reward of 6.5 from waiting. Therefore:

$$s^n = (N, N, Y, Y)$$

Sophisticates

A sophisticate reasons backwards as follows:

- In week 4 she must use her possibly unused movie pass ($s_4^s = Y$).
- In week 3 she sees the movie immediately ($s_3^s = Y$), just as the naif does in week 3.
- In week 2 she can see the movie immediately and obtain a reward of 5, or delay and know that her period-3 self will go to the theater, yielding a currently perceived reward of 4. She therefore sees the movie immediately ($s_2^s = Y$).
- In week 1 she can similarly obtain a reward of 3 from immediate consumption or delay, knowing that her period-2 self will consume immediately, yielding a currently perceived reward of 2.5. She therefore uses her movie pass immediately ($s_1^s = Y$).

In summary,

$$s^s = (Y, Y, Y, Y)$$

The sophisticate uses her movie pass to see the worst possible movie! Why is the sophisticate seeing a worse movie than the naif? The sophisticate is aware of her future self-control problems and therefore realizes that if she delays, she will use the movie pass in the next period. Given her knowledge that she will not hold out to see the best movie, she reasons that seeing the current movie is always better than waiting one week to see a slightly better movie. The naif, on the other hand, naively believes in the first two weeks that she can hold out to see the best movie and therefore finds it worthwhile to wait. She then surprises herself in week 3 by giving in and seeing the good, but not excellent, movie. ∎

5.3.3 General Results

The previous examples illustrate general features of sophisticate and naif behavior that hold regardless of the particular costs, rewards, number of periods, or magnitude of β. In particular, present bias generates clear predictions for the timing of an activity.

Let's first compare time-consistents and naifs. They differ in their preferences, but not in their beliefs about future behavior (because both believe their future selves to be time-consistent, even though only the TCs are correct). With the investment activity in Example 5.1 the TC writes the paper on the first weekend, while the naif procrastinates until the last weekend. This observation motivates our first general result: naifs always delay making an investment relative to TCs. When it is a leisure activity, however, as in Example 5.2, the TC waits until the last weekend to use the movie pass to see the best movie, while the naif sees a less-than-excellent movie on the third weekend. This observation motivates our second general result: naifs always do leisure activities before TCs. These results confirm the intuition of a self-control problem; when preferences are present-biased, individuals move away from investments and towards leisure activities. The following theorem summarizes.

Theorem 5.1 — Time-Consistents vs. Naifs.

Naifs do an investment activity (weakly) later than time-consistents.
Naifs do a leisure activity (weakly) earlier than time-consistents.

We now turn to comparing sophisticates and naifs, who share the same preferences, but differ in their beliefs about future behavior. In the previous examples the sophisticate does the activity before the naif for both the investment activity and the leisure activity. This turns out to be a general result:

Theorem 5.2 — Sophisticates vs. Naifs.

Sophisticates do activities (weakly) earlier than naifs.

Sophisticates are correct in their pessimism that their future selves will give in to self-control problems, regardless of whether the activity is immediately costly or immediately rewarding. With an investment activity sophisticates anticipate their future preference to delay, and so to mitigate such delays, choose to procrastinate less than naifs. This fits nicely with the intuition that sophistication dampens the severity of the self-control problem. What is more surprising, is that because sophisticates recognize their future impatience with a leisure activity, they have no illusion of patiently waiting to do the leisure activity and reason that if they are going to give in to temptation, they might as well do it sooner than later. This logic induces sophisticates to also do leisure activities before naifs.

The preceding two theorems can be summarized graphically with timelines depicting when each type of individual does the activity, as in Figure 5.3. Observe that for a leisure activity, the timing is unambiguously ordered: first sophisticates, then naifs, and finally

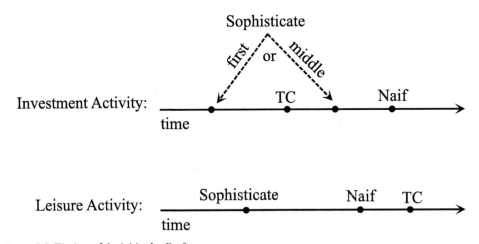

Figure 5.3 Timing of Activities by Preferences

TCs. In the case of an investment activity, we know that naifs do it last, but we do not know whether TCs or sophisticates do the activity first.

It turns out that whether a sophisticate or TC does an investment activity first depends on the specific context. In Example 5.1 the TC writes her paper before the sophisticate. But it is possible to change the rewards and costs associated with writing a paper in such a way that the TC writes the paper *after* the sophisticate. This is possible because there are two competing motivations for a sophisticate to change the activity date relative to a TC. The sophisticate's present bias shifts her behavior towards procrastination. But because a sophisticate correctly anticipates her future preference to delay, she may want to make an investment earlier to avoid such procrastination. Since either effect can dominate, we cannot in general order which type does the activity first.

5.3.4 Welfare

If you could choose, would you prefer to be a naif or a sophisticate? To answer this question, let's consider individual welfare in this setting. Applying the long-run perspective for welfare in Definition 5.2, we have the following definition.

> **Definition 5.7** The **individual welfare** of completing an activity in period k is $W(k) \equiv v_k - c_k$.

In particular, the welfare of doing the activity in a period is simply the reward minus the cost of doing it in that period, no matter the degree of present bias. We can now return to our motivating question: do naifs or sophisticates achieve higher welfare?

With an investment activity, sophisticates achieve higher welfare than naifs. This is because sophistication helps to mitigate the degree of procrastination. Let's confirm that this result is consistent with Example 5.1. The naif writes the paper in the fourth week, achieving welfare $W(4) = \bar{v} - 13$. The sophisticate writes the paper in the second week, achieving welfare $W(2) = \bar{v} - 5$. As expected, it is better to be a sophisticate when facing an activity with immediate costs and delayed rewards.

But sophistication is not always preferable. In Example 5.2 the naif sees a movie in the third week, with welfare $W(3) = 8 - 0 = 8$. The sophisticate realizes that she will give in to seeing a movie in week 3 and also in week 2, so she decides that she might as well see the movie in the first week, obtaining lower welfare of $W(1) = 3 - 0 = 3$. There are also leisure activity scenarios in which the sophisticate's earlier timing relative to the naif is advantageous. You will see such cases in exercises at the end of this chapter.

It is worth underscoring the significance of the observation that the welfare of a naif can be higher than that of a sophisticate. Economists are inclined to view the strategic and forward-looking sophisticate as more rational than the naif. Recall that we previously defined behavior as rational when it is in an individual's own best interest (Definition 2.10). And yet, once we abandon the standard assumption of time consistency, it is possible for naivete to better realize one's own best interest.

The preceding model of an individual choosing when to do an activity effectively illustrates the counterintuitive results that can obtain when the assumptions of standard economics are relaxed. But we are not abandoning standard economics. We are still operating within the standard methodological framework of economics by building models, determining their theoretical predictions, and testing these predictions against empirical evidence. We turn to such evidence in the following section.

5.4 Empirical Evidence of Present Bias

The model of present-biased preferences generates a set of testable predictions for behavior. Although you may intuitively feel that the model is a good or bad descriptive theory for how people behave, we want evidence that goes beyond introspection and intuition. This section provides empirical evidence from a variety of decision-making contexts: health, education, savings, and personal finance. And in each context the data are inconsistent with the predictions of the DU model, but consistent with present bias. The takeaway is not that the DU model is never an accurate model of behavior, but that there exist non-trivial settings in which behavior is better characterized by present bias.

5.4.1 Exercise   [Health]

You may be familiar with the experience of planning to exercise, only to later abandon your plans. But surely there are also times when you have followed through with your exercise plans. We would like to empirically test whether exercise behavior is better explained by time-consistent preferences or present-biased preferences that generate self-control problems.

DellaVigna and Malmendier (2006) examine this question by collecting data from three US gyms. At these gyms customers could choose between different membership contracts. One option was a monthly fee of $80 that allowed unlimited access. Another option was to pay $10 per visit, with no monthly fee. If the standard DU model represents preferences, individuals would choose the monthly contract only if they go to the gym at least eight times per month. Otherwise, it is cheaper to just pay per visit. And yet, members that chose the monthly contract only visited the gym 4.4 times per month on average. In effect, they were paying $80/4.4 \approx $18 per visit — almost double what they could be paying per visit if they cancelled their monthly contract. This evidence is inconsistent the standard DU model.

The evidence of monthly members under-utilizing their gym membership is predicted by the model of present-biased preferences. Because going to the gym is an investment good, we know from the insights summarized in Table 5.1 that present bias leads to underconsumption. The logic is as follows. A present-biased individual who plans to go to the gym at least eight times each month chooses the monthly contract. When making this choice, she is highly discounting both the future disutility of exercising and the future health benefits. Once she has signed the contract and faces the decision to actually go to the gym each day, the immediate disutility of exercising is not discounted, while the future health benefits remain highly discounted. She therefore does not go to the gym as frequently as she had originally planned.

There are two possible explanations for this behavior. If the members were naifs, then they overestimated their future gym attendance, chose the monthly contract, and were surprised that they exercised so little. If they were sophisticates, then they accurately anticipated that their future selves would not want to go to the gym often. In response, they chose the monthly contract to act as a commitment strategy. The monthly contract helps to align actual attendance with planned attendance by lowering the immediate monetary cost of going to the gym from \$10 to \$0 (because the pre-paid \$80 monthly fee is sunk and does not matter when deciding to go to the gym). In essence, a sophisticate realizes that getting to the gym is hard enough without having to hand over \$10 on each visit, so paying a high price in advance to eliminate that per-visit fee is worth it. If the sophisticate had paid per visit, she might have visited even less than 4.4 times per month.

DellaVigna and Malmendier (2006) pursue multiple strategies to disentangle the two explanations of naivete and sophistication. One strategy is to simply survey gym members as to how often they anticipate going to the gym in the next month. The survey evidence reveals that the predicted attendance of 9.5 visits is twice as large as the actual attendance of 4.2 visits. This overestimation is only consistent with naivete. For evidence from an alternative strategy, see Exercise 5.5.

5.4.2   School Work   *[Education]*

Like exercise, education is another investment activity. The costs of attending class, paying attention, completing homework, and studying for exams are immediate. While the benefits of schooling — in terms of higher future earnings, job satisfaction, and health — are delayed.[5] If students are present-biased, then our theory predicts underconsumption. That is, even when students plan to exert significant effort in school, they can fail to follow through when the immediate effort costs loom large relative to the heavily discounted future rewards. But this is only a hypothesis. Let's consider some evidence.

Field Experiment — Cashing in on School (Levitt et al. 2016)

Between 2009 and 2011 students at Chicago-area schools were offered small financial incentives for improvement on a low-stakes test. In a set of randomly selected classrooms (treatment group), students were told that if they improved relative to their previous test score they would receive a cash reward (\$10 or \$20) either immediately after the test, or a month later. Students in other classrooms (control group) were offered no such financial reward. Because of the random assignment, any difference in test score improvements for students in classes with and without financial incentives must be due to the effect of the reward.

Levitt et al. (2016) find that a \$20 reward paid immediately after the test increases test scores relative to the control group. In fact, the improvement induced by this reward is equivalent to five months of learning. But there is no evidence that test scores are increased by a \$10 reward or a delayed reward.

This experimental evidence is surprising for standard economics. If \$20 paid immediately after the test increases effort, then \$20 paid only one month later should have a similar, if slightly dampened, effect. But the short delay appears to eliminate the incentive for greater effort. To make these results consistent with the DU model, students must exhibit an absurdly high discount rate of 800% annually. High discounting of delayed rewards, however, is consistent with present-biased preferences.

If present bias is prevalent among students, then there may be widespread underinvestment in schooling relative to what students would actually like to achieve. Education is just one of many consequential decisions in an individual's lifetime. We next turn to the life-cycle consumption and savings problem introduced at the end of the previous chapter.

5.4.3   Present-Biased Life-Cycle Evidence   *[Household]*

Present-biased preferences may also better explain consumption and savings behaviors over the life cycle than standard time-consistent preferences.

To assess this hypothesis, let's allow for a more realistic budget constraint in the life-cycle model. In particular, assume that income is uncertain and borrowing cannot exceed 30% of the average income for an individual's age group. For instance, if average income is $40,000 for people your age, we assume that no bank will lend you more than $12,000, even though you might prefer to take on greater debt. In addition, assume that individuals can borrow on credit cards at a higher interest rate than what is earned on savings. And finally, individuals can acquire an illiquid asset, like a house, from which it is more difficult to extract cash for spending than from a liquid checking or savings account.

Given the assumptions on the budget constraint, how do the theoretical predictions differ between present-biased and time-consistent preferences? Angeletos et al. (2001) conduct exactly such an analysis, solving for the utility-maximizing consumption sequences via computer simulations in these two cases.[6] I report their theoretical findings and corresponding empirical evidence.

Self-Control Problems

Many households report a desire to save more than they do. Such undersaving relative to one's own intentions is predicted by present-biased preferences. Time-consistents, however, do not experience a self-control problem. Their desired savings and actual savings would be the same.

Wealth Accumulation

Only 37% of households hold liquid wealth — cash, checking, and savings accounts — in excess of one month's income. But the DU model predicts this share to be much higher at 73%. Because of their tendency to give in to instant gratification and spend at higher levels, present-biased households are consequently predicted to accumulate less liquid wealth than time-consistent households. In fact, with present-biased preferences, only 40% of households are predicted to hold at least one month's income in liquid wealth. This is much closer to the observed evidence.

Although present-biased individuals are predicted to hold less liquid wealth, they are predicted to hold *more* illiquid wealth than time-consistents. They are more likely to hold their wealth in an asset like a house than in easily spendable checking and savings accounts. To see why, consider a sophisticate who is aware of her future inclination to spend more than planned. By "locking up" her wealth in a house now, she commits her future self to not overspending. This logic does not apply for a time-consistent. In the absence of a self-control problem, holding wealth in liquid forms is preferable, as it makes it easier to smooth consumption across low-income periods.

Comovement of Predicted Income and Consumption

Typical estimates of the marginal propensity to consume (MPC) out of changes in predicted income range from 0.1 to 0.3. For a $10 increase in predicted income, households increase consumption expenditure by $1 to $3. But, as discussed in the previous chapter, the DU model implies a MPC out of predicted income changes close to zero.

With present-biased preferences, the model generates a MPC out of predicted income changes of 0.17. This falls within the range of empirical estimates. Why is the MPC higher in this case? Because with less liquid wealth, it is more difficult to smooth consumption across periods. Consumption subsequently tracks predictable changes in income, generating the positive MPC. Note that the predicted MPC is significantly below 1; present-biased households are not predicted to live hand to mouth, spending each additional dollar of income entirely on consumption. They are still smoothing consumption across periods, but not to the extreme degree that is predicted for time-consistents.

Retirement

Empirical evidence shows that the average household experiences a 12% decline in consumption around retirement (Bernheim, Skinner, and Weinberg 2001). The DU model predicts only a 3% consumption decline since households are building up sufficient wealth to finance a smooth transition to retirement. With present-biased preferences, the model predicts a much larger consumption drop of 14.5%, which better matches actual behavior. The reason for this difference is the same as that which drives the positive MPC out of changes in predicted income. With lower levels of liquid wealth, the drop in income at retirement, even though it is predictable, leads to a corresponding drop in consumption.

Credit Cards

Finally, we know that many households (70%) carry credit card debt at high levels (average debt of $5,000). The DU model predicts that only 19% of households borrow on their credit cards, with an average credit card debt of $900. These predictions are far below what we observe. In contrast, the model with present-biased preferences predicts that 51% of households borrow on credit cards, with an average debt of $3,400. While still an imperfect prediction, the assumption of present-biased preferences brings the theory closer to the evidence.

Present bias promotes credit card use for two reasons. First, credit cards turn consumption into a leisure good: consumption benefits are enjoyed immediately, while the payment and interest costs are delayed to the future. Present bias therefore leads to overspending on credit cards. Second, given the low liquid wealth of present-biased households, credit cards help to facilitate consumption smoothing during low-income periods. It may appear to be a puzzle that many households borrow heavily with credit cards while simultaneously accumulating significant illiquid wealth in their house. Exercise 5.6 prompts you to think through how present-biased preferences can reconcile these two features of behavior. To conclude, we consider a field experiment with credit card offers.

5.4.4   Credit Card Take-Up [Household]

Field Experiment — Teasing Interest (Ausubel 1999)

A credit company mailed one of three different credit card offers at random to potential customers. Each mailing offered the customer a credit card with an initial low interest rate for the first 6 months (the pre-teaser rate) and a higher interest rate thereafter (the post-teaser rate) as follows:

Offers	Pre-teaser Rate	Post-teaser Rate
Control	6.9%	16%
Pre-Treatment	4.9%	16%
Post-Treatment	6.9%	14%

Relative to the control offer, there were two treatment offers, one that lowered the pre-teaser rate, and the other that lowered the post-teaser rate, each by 2 percentage points. Differences in customer response rates between a treatment group and the control group reflect the impact of reducing the interest rate.

Among those who accepted a credit card offer, the average borrowing balance in the first 6 months was $2000. In the next 15 months, the average borrowing balance was $1000. This implies that over the observed 21-month borrowing history:

- Taking up the pre-treatment offer saves $2\% \times \$2000 \times 6/21 = \$11.43$ relative to the control offer.
- Taking up the post-treatment offer saves $2\% \times \$1000 \times 15/21 = \$14.29$ relative to the control offer.

If everyone were time-consistent, then they would have accurately anticipated their future borrowing and interest payments. Based on the above calculations, customers should have responded more to the post-treatment offer than to the pre-treatment offer, since it provides greater savings. However, Ausubel (1999) finds that the difference in the response rate relative to the control for the pre-treatment offer was 2.5 times larger than for the post-treatment offer.

The evidence from this field experiment — that individuals over-respond to the immediate pre-teaser rate reduction — is inconsistent with time consistency. The evidence instead points to naivete. Naifs underestimate consumption of leisure goods like credit card-financed spending. They believe that their credit card balance will be low after the initial 6-month teaser period because they think they will have paid off their initial purchases and refrained from accumulating additional credit card debt. With such expectations, naifs will respond more to the pre-treatment offer — with its discount on immediate short-term debt — than to a longer-term discount on future debt they do not believe they will have. This prediction is consistent with the evidence. Notice that sophisticates would realize that their future debt would remain high and therefore respond more strongly to the post-treatment offer. In sum, the evidence is suggestive of naive present-biased preferences.

5.5   Summary

1   The **model of present-biased preferences** modifies the standard DU model with a **quasi-hyperbolic discount function** instead of an exponential discount function. This nonstandard discount function features a larger discount rate between the current period and the next period than between any two sequential periods in the future.

2   Present-biased individuals underconsume **investment goods** and overconsume **leisure goods**.

3   Present-biased individuals who are fully aware of their future preferences are called **sophisticates**. Given that they accurately anticipate their future behavior, they may demand **commitment strategies** that limit their choices or increase the costs of particular actions in order to help align their future behavior with their present preferences.

4   Present-biased individuals who incorrectly believe they are time-consistent are called **naifs**. These individuals do not realize that their future selves may behave differently than expected. Naifs overestimate their consumption of investment goods, but underestimate their consumption of leisure goods.

5   Relative to time-consistents, naifs procrastinate doing an investment activity and give in early to a leisure activity. Because sophisticates accurately anticipate their future behavior, they do both investment and leisure activities before naifs.

6   Evidence of gym attendance and credit card take-up supports naive present-biased preferences, as individuals exercise less and spend more than their expectations.

7   A field experiment conducted with school-age children finds that students exhibit very high short-term discount rates that suggest present-biased preferences.

8   A life-cycle model of consumption and savings with present-biased preferences makes more accurate predictions than assuming time-consistent preferences.

5.6   Exercises[7]

Exercise 5.1 — Doing it Once: Sporting Time. O'Donoghue and Rabin (1999, 112) propose the following scenario:

> Suppose you must write a paper this weekend, on Friday night, Saturday or Sunday. You know the paper will be better if written on either Saturday or Sunday (when you have an entire day). However, it is a mid-November weekend with plenty of sports on TV — pro basketball on Friday night, college football on Saturday, and pro football on Sunday. You prefer watching pro football to college football, and prefer college football to pro basketball.

Let's apply the Doing it Once model to this decision problem of when to write the paper. There are three periods ($T = 3$) over which to write the paper, an investment activity. The rewards correspond to the quality of the paper (which is higher if written on a full weekend day instead of Friday night). The costs correspond to the desirability of the sport event that is missed by writing the paper. They are:

$$v = (12, 18, 18)$$

$$c = (3, 8, 13)$$

a   What is the strategy for a time-consistent ($\beta = 1$)? When is the paper written and what is individual welfare?

b   What is the strategy for a naif (with $\beta = 1/2$)? When is the paper written and what is individual welfare?

c   What is the strategy for a sophisticate (with $\beta = 1/2$)? When is the paper written and what is individual welfare? Compare to the time-consistent.

Exercise 5.2 — Doing it Once: Commitment Costs. Recall Example 5.2 in which you are gifted a free movie ticket that must be used on one of four weekends. In that example the sophisticate achieved lower welfare than the naif, going to see the worst movie instead of waiting for a better movie. Suggest a commitment strategy that would help the sophisticate achieve higher welfare.

Exercise 5.3 — Doing it Once: Group Think. It is Wednesday afternoon and a group of students are discussing when to meet to work on a group project that is due on the following Monday. It will only take one meeting to complete the project. The only days that everyone is available to work are Thursday, Friday, and Saturday. The costs are increasing every day since it is worse to give up weekend time than weekday time for a project. In addition, the project will be of lower quality if it is done on Friday, when everyone is exhausted and distracted. We can model this situation as a case of immediate costs in the Doing it Once model with $T = 3$ and the following reward and cost schedules:

$$v = (16, 14, 16)$$

$$c = (6, 8, c_3) \text{ where } 10 < c_3 < 18$$

a   What is the strategy if the students are time-consistent ($\beta = 1$)? When does the group meet?

b   What is the strategy if the students are naifs (with $\beta = 1/2$)? When does the group meet?

c   The strategy for the case in which the students are sophisticates depends on c_3. Assume that $\beta = 1/2$. Find a value of $c_3 \in (10, 18)$ such that the sophisticates meet on the same day as the time-consistents and a value of $c_3 \in (10, 18)$ such that the sophisticates meet on the same day as the naifs.

d   Think about how this problem may have been different for students before the availability of cell phones. Explain how cell phones can be welfare-reducing due to the ease with which they facilitate coordination and planning a time to meet.

Exercise 5.4 — Doing it Once: It Gets Better. Consider the Doing it Once model with an immediate rewards activity that must be done in one of three periods ($T = 3$). The costs of doing it are zero in every period: $c = (0, 0, 0)$. The benefits of doing it are growing exponentially over time at rate $\gamma > 1$ (gamma for "growth"). In particular, the benefit schedule is $v = (V, \gamma V, \gamma^2 V)$ where $V > 0$.

1   Determine the strategy for a time-consistent ($\beta = 1$).
2   Determine the strategy for a naif in terms of β and γ. For a given β, how does a larger γ impact when the naif does the activity? Provide intuition for your answer.
3   Determine the strategy for a sophisticate in terms of β and γ. For a given β, how does a larger γ impact when the sophisticate does the activity? Compare and contrast this to the impact of γ on the naif's timing.
4   Does the naif or sophisticate achieve (weakly) higher welfare in this example?

Exercise 5.5 — Running up Charges. [Health] The DellaVigna and Malmendier (2006) study of exercise behavior using data from gyms finds evidence of present bias. To help determine whether this is due to naive or sophisticated behavior the authors examine the time between a member's last visit and when they cancel their monthly contract (monthly contracts renew automatically until they are cancelled by the member).

Let's use the Doing it Once model to think about a member who has gone to the gym for the last time and must decide when to notify the gym that they want to cancel their membership. In this case T is very large because an individual can delay cancellation for a long time. This investment activity has a small immediate cost — it just takes a few minutes to cancel. The delayed benefits of cancelling are substantial because by cancelling, members save themselves $80 per month for a service they are no longer using. Note then that if members were time-consistent, we would expect them to cancel soon after their last visit, only delaying by a few days.

a   Suppose that members are naifs. Then do you expect them to cancel quickly or delay cancellation for a long time? Explain.
b   Suppose that members are sophisticates. Then do you expect them to cancel quickly or delay cancellation for a long time? Explain.
c   On average, members do not visit the gym at all for 2.3 months before cancelling the contract, which costs over $180. Based on your answers to (a) and (b), does this evidence point to naivete or sophistication of these members?

Exercise 5.6 — Credit Card Conundrum. [Household] Laibson, Repetto, and Tobacman (2007) report the following statistics for the average American household (led by a high school graduate without a college degree):

- high credit card debt (11.7% of annual income); and
- high wealth accumulation, including home equity (260% of annual income among 50–59 year-olds).

a   Explain why the standard DU model cannot explain these two facts simultaneously.
b   Explain how present-biased preferences can reconcile these two facts. Does the evidence point to sophistication or naivete?

Exercise 5.7 — Targeting Work. [Labor] Kaur, Kremer, and Mullainathan (2015) conduct the following 13-month field experiment with data entry workers in India. For the control contract, workers were paid per accurate data entry a standard piece rate. On randomly selected days the workers were offered a treatment contract in which they were asked to choose a target number of entries for the day: if they met the target, they received the standard piece rate, but if they fell short of the target, they received only half the piece rate for their output. In both cases payments were made to workers at the end of each week.

a   Explain the downsides of setting a target greater than zero in the treatment contract.
b   When offered the treatment contract, workers set a positive target for themselves 36% of the time. Explain how this can be explained by workers with present bias.

Exercise 5.8 — Setting Deadlines. [Education] Consider the following field experiment by Ariely and Wertenbroch (2002) using MIT Sloan Business School students as subjects. There are two sections of the same executive-education class that requires three papers and a final project. In one section the students face evenly spaced deadlines for each of the three papers. In the other section students early in the semester can choose a deadline for each paper, but cannot change the deadlines after their selection. In both sections, students suffer a 1% lower grade for each day a paper is late.

a   If the students in the self-imposed deadline section are time-consistent, when should they set their deadlines? Explain.
b   Explain why setting deadlines before the last day of class can be an effective commitment strategy for a present-biased sophisticate.
c   In the self-imposed deadline section, 68% of deadlines were set before the last week of classes. Does this point to time consistency or present-biased sophistication?
d   The average paper grades were higher in the section with evenly spaced deadlines than in the self-imposed deadline section. Interpret this evidence.

Exercise 5.9 — Punctual Proofreading. [Labor] Consider the following field experiment by Ariely and Wertenbroch (2002) with MIT students as subjects. There are three 10-page papers, each purposefully written with 100 spelling and grammatical errors. The school newspaper advertises a student job opportunity to read and detect these errors, with each detected error paying $0.10. The 60 participants were randomly split into three different experimental groups as follows:

1   Evenly spaced deadline (ESD) group: Students had to submit one of the three papers every seven days.
2   End deadline (ED) group: Students had to turn in all of the papers in three weeks.
3   Self-imposed deadline (SID) group: Students could choose their own deadlines for each paper within a three week window.

There was no benefit for turning in papers early, but there was a $1 penalty for each day that a paper was late. Figure 5.4 shows the results of this experiment.

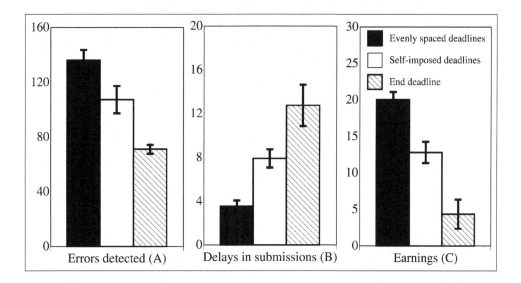

Figure 5.4 Evidence from Proofreading Field Experiment in Exercise 5.9

Source: Reprinted from Dan Ariely and Klaus Wertenbroch. 2002. "Procrastination, Deadlines, and Performance: Self-control by Precommitment." *Psychological Science* 13 (3): 219–224. Copyright ©2002 American Psychological Society, with permission from Sage.

a   Observe that there is lower performance (in terms of errors detected and money earned) for the students in the ED group than in the SID group. Is this evidence of a self-control problem? If so, which form of self-control problem (naivete vs. sophistication) is suggested by this result? Explain. *Hint: It is useful to first consider if TCs would behave differently in the ED and SID groups (and if so, how). Then consider the same question for naifs and sophisticates.*

b   Observe also that more errors were detected by students in the ESD group than in the SID treatment. Discuss what this suggests about the optimality of the students' self-imposed deadlines.

5A   Appendix: The Calculus of the Present-Biased Life-Cycle Model

In this appendix we determine the theoretical predictions of a stylized life-cycle model with present-biased preferences. The analysis makes use of the method of Lagrange, developed in Appendix 4A. Even with this powerful mathematical method, to analytically solve the problem we restrict attention to a simple intertemporal budget constraint with certain income, budget balance, and no liquidity constraints. Allowing for a more realistic budget constraint — as in Section 5.4.3 — dramatically increases the complexity of the problem and requires a computer to solve.

In our stylized model Ares must decide how to allocate his lifetime income on consumption expenditure across three years, where each year is a period $t \in \{0, 1, 2\}$. Ares inherits \$43,500 in year 0 ($y_0 = 43{,}500$) and earns no other income ($y_1 = y_2 = 0$). Assume that there is no interest on savings or borrowing ($r = 0$ and $R = 1 + r = 1$). Ares' intertemporal budget constraint is therefore: $c_0 + c_1 + c_2 = 43{,}500$.

Let Ares' preferences in period t over consumption expenditure sequences be represented by the model of present-biased preferences (Definition 5.1) with instantaneous utility function $u(c_t) = 2\sqrt{c_t}$ and $\delta = 1$:

$$U^t(c_t, c_{t+1}, c_{t+2}; \beta) = 2\sqrt{c_t} + \beta 2\sqrt{c_{t+1}} + \beta 2\sqrt{c_{t+2}}$$

To understand the implications of this nonstandard model we consider three cases:

1   time-consistent ($\beta = 1$);
2   present-biased naif ($\beta = 1/2$, $\hat{\beta} = 1$); and
3   present-biased sophisticate ($\beta = 1/2 = \hat{\beta}$).

In each case we determine the predicted consumption sequence and the corresponding individual welfare W:

$$W(c_0, c_1, c_2) = 2\sqrt{c_0} + 2\sqrt{c_1} + 2\sqrt{c_2}$$

Case 1: Time-consistent ($\beta = 1$)

For the standard case, we know that when the interest rate r and discount rate ρ are equal, as they are in this case ($r = 0$ and $\rho = 1/\delta - 1 = 0$), Ares chooses constant consumption. From the budget constraint we therefore have that the time-consistent Ares chooses:

$$(c_0^{tc}, c_1^{tc}, c_2^{tc}) = (\$14{,}500, \$14{,}500, \$14{,}500)$$

Because he is time-consistent, his future selves will never wish to deviate from this plan. His welfare is:

$$W^{tc} = 2\sqrt{c_0^{tc}} + 2\sqrt{c_1^{tc}} + 2\sqrt{c_2^{tc}} = 6\sqrt{14{,}500} \approx 722.5 \text{ utils, i.e. units of utility}$$

Case 2: Present-biased naif ($\beta = 1/2$, $\hat{\beta} = 1$)

If Ares is present-biased, then because his preferences shift over time we must consider both the consumption sequence that Ares prefers in period 0 and also what he prefers in period 1. And because he is naive, he solves the period-0 problem first, assuming that his period-1 self will be time-consistent.

Case 2a: Period-0 Problem. Ares solves the following problem in period 0:

$$\max_{c_0, c_1, c_2} \quad U^0(c_0, c_1, c_2; \beta = 1/2) = 2\sqrt{c_0} + \sqrt{c_1} + \sqrt{c_2}$$
$$\text{such that} \quad c_0 + c_1 + c_2 = 43{,}500$$

The corresponding Lagrangian is:

$$\mathcal{L} = 2\sqrt{c_0} + \sqrt{c_1} + \sqrt{c_2} - \lambda[c_0 + c_1 + c_2 - 43{,}500]$$

We determine the first order conditions of the Lagrangian (see Theorem 4A.1):

$$\left.\begin{array}{l} 0 = \dfrac{\partial \mathcal{L}}{\partial c_0} = \dfrac{1}{\sqrt{c_0}} - \lambda \\[2mm] 0 = \dfrac{\partial \mathcal{L}}{\partial c_1} = \dfrac{1}{2\sqrt{c_1}} - \lambda \\[2mm] 0 = \dfrac{\partial \mathcal{L}}{\partial c_2} = \dfrac{1}{2\sqrt{c_2}} - \lambda \end{array}\right\} \Rightarrow \sqrt{c_0} = 2\sqrt{c_1} = 2\sqrt{c_2} \Rightarrow c_0 = 4c_1 \text{ and } c_1 = c_2$$

Combining these equations with the budget constraint, we find the consumption plan:

$$\begin{aligned} \$43{,}500 \;&=\; c_0 + c_1 + c_2 = 4c_1 + c_1 + c_1 = 6c_1 \\ &\Rightarrow c_1 = \$43{,}500/6 = \$7{,}250 \\ &\Rightarrow c_2 = c_1 = \$7{,}250 \\ &\Rightarrow c_0 = 4c_1 = 4 \times \$7{,}250 = \$29{,}000 \end{aligned}$$

In sum, the period-0 naif spends \$29,000 in the first year and plans to spend \$7,250 in each of the next two years. This is definitely not the constant consumption preferred by the TC. Because the naif discounts the future more than the TC, he shifts more of his spending to the present. However, once Ares arrives in the next period, he may not follow through with his initial plan. Let's check this possibility.

Case 2b: Period-1 Problem. When Ares arrives in period 1, he has already spent \$29,000 in period 0, and now must decide how to allocate the remaining \$14,500 across the final two periods:

$$\max_{c_1, c_2} \quad U^1(c_1, c_2; \beta = 1/2) = 2\sqrt{c_1} + \sqrt{c_2}$$
$$\text{such that} \quad c_1 + c_2 = 43{,}500 - 29{,}000 = 14{,}500$$

The corresponding Lagrangian is:

$$\mathcal{L} = 2\sqrt{c_1} + \sqrt{c_2} - \lambda[c_1 + c_2 - 14{,}500]$$

We again determine the first order conditions of the Lagrangian:

$$\left.\begin{array}{l} 0 = \dfrac{\partial \mathcal{L}}{\partial c_1} = \dfrac{1}{\sqrt{c_1}} - \lambda \\[2mm] 0 = \dfrac{\partial \mathcal{L}}{\partial c_2} = \dfrac{1}{2\sqrt{c_2}} - \lambda \end{array}\right\} \Rightarrow \sqrt{c_1} = 2\sqrt{c_2} \Rightarrow c_1 = 4c_2$$

Combining this with the budget constraint, we find the consumption plan:

$$\begin{aligned} \$14{,}500 \;&=\; c_1 + c_2 = 4c_2 + c_2 = 5c_2 \\ &\Rightarrow c_2 = \$14{,}500/5 = \$2{,}900 \\ &\Rightarrow c_1 = 4c_2 = 4 \times \$2{,}900 = \$11{,}600 \end{aligned}$$

Ares has become impatient and is not following his initial plan. In year 0 he planned to split his remaining assets equally across the next two years. But when he arrives in year 1, he doesn't spend $7,250 as planned, but instead spends $11,600. This leaves him with only $2,900 in the last year. Observe that he planned to save more of his money in year 1 than he actually saves. Ares suffers from a self-control problem and actually spends the following amounts each year:

$$(c_0^n, c_1^n, c_2^n) = (\$29,000, \ \$11,600, \ \$2,900)$$

which yields welfare:

$$W^n = 2\sqrt{c_0^n} + 2\sqrt{c_1^n} + 2\sqrt{c_2^n} = 2\sqrt{29,000} + 2\sqrt{11,600} + 2\sqrt{2,900} \approx 663.7 \text{ utils}$$

This is almost a 10% loss in welfare relative to what is possible by consuming like the TC.

Case 3: Present-biased sophisticate ($\beta = 1/2 = \hat{\beta}$)

If Ares is a sophisticate, then he is fully aware of his future preferences. That is, when deciding how much to consume in period 0, he thinks through how his current consumption will affect his future behavior. Although he will not be surprised by his self-control problem like the naif, he still experiences a self-control problem of giving in to too much spending relative to the TC.

To solve this decision problem we must solve it backwards; the only way the period-0 self can decide how much to consume is to have first thought through the behavior of his future period-1 self. Notice that this is analogous to the backward solving method for the sophisticate in the Doing it Once model of Section 5.3.

Case 3a: Period-1 Problem. When Ares arrives in period 1 he will have assets equal to the $43,500 less whatever he spent in period 0. Since we are solving the period-1 problem first, we don't yet know how much he spends in period 0. Therefore, let $a_1 = \$43,500 - c_0$ indicate Ares' assets at the start of period 1. He then solves the following problem:

$$\max_{c_1, c_2} \quad U^1(c_1, c_2; \beta = 1/2) = 2\sqrt{c_1} + \sqrt{c_2}$$
$$\text{such that} \quad c_1 + c_2 = a_1$$

The corresponding Lagrangian is:

$$\mathcal{L} = 2\sqrt{c_1} + \sqrt{c_2} - \lambda[c_1 + c_2 - a_1]$$

We again determine the first order conditions of the Lagrangian:

$$\left.\begin{aligned} 0 = \frac{\partial \mathcal{L}}{\partial c_1} = \frac{1}{\sqrt{c_1}} - \lambda \\ 0 = \frac{\partial \mathcal{L}}{\partial c_2} = \frac{1}{2\sqrt{c_2}} - \lambda \end{aligned}\right\} \Rightarrow \sqrt{c_1} = 2\sqrt{c_2} \Rightarrow c_1 = 4c_2$$

Combining this with the budget constraint, we find the consumption plan:

$$a_1 = c_1 + c_2 = 4c_2 + c_2 = 5c_2$$
$$\Rightarrow c_2 = 0.2a_1$$
$$\Rightarrow c_1 = 4c_2 = 0.8a_1$$

Notice that the consumption plan depends on the assets available in period 1. Regardless of how much money Ares has to spend in period 1, he will spend 80% of his assets immediately in period 1, leaving 20% of his assets for consumption expenditure in period 2. This is exactly what the naif does when he arrives in period 1 with $14,500 ($c_1^n = 0.8 \times \$14,500 = \$11,600$). The sophisticate, unlike the naif, anticipates that he will behave in this way when period 1 arrives. Let's see how this impacts the sophisticate's period-0 problem.

Case 3b: Period-0 Problem. Ares takes as given his future behavior (i.e., $c_1 = 0.8a_1$ and $c_2 = 0.2a_2$) and therefore solves the following period-0 problem:

$$\max_{c_0, a_1} U^0(c_0, 0.8a_1, 0.2a_1; \beta = 1/2) = 2\sqrt{c_0} + \sqrt{0.8a_1} + \sqrt{0.2a_1}$$
$$\text{such that} \quad c_0 + a_1 = 43{,}500$$

It is important to observe that we have plugged Ares' future behavior directly into his utility function *before* we compute any derivatives.[8] Although this problem looks slightly different than the problems we have been studying because the choice variables are a consumption expenditure and an asset level, we can still apply the method of Lagrange to find the solution. The corresponding Lagrangian is:

$$\mathcal{L} = 2\sqrt{c_0} + \sqrt{0.8a_1} + \sqrt{0.2a_1} - \lambda[c_0 + a_1 - 43{,}500]$$

The first order conditions of the Lagrangian are (making use of chain rule):

$$\left. \begin{array}{l} 0 = \dfrac{\partial \mathcal{L}}{\partial c_0} = \dfrac{1}{\sqrt{c_0}} - \lambda \\[2ex] 0 = \dfrac{\partial \mathcal{L}}{\partial a_1} = \dfrac{.8}{2\sqrt{0.8a_1}} + \dfrac{.2}{2\sqrt{0.2a_1}} - \lambda \end{array} \right\} \Rightarrow \sqrt{a_1} = \sqrt{c_0}\left(\dfrac{0.4}{\sqrt{0.8}} + \dfrac{0.1}{\sqrt{0.2}}\right)$$

This in turn implies that $a_1 = c_0\left(\frac{0.4}{\sqrt{0.8}} + \frac{0.1}{\sqrt{0.2}}\right)^2 = 0.45c_0$. Combining this with the budget constraint, we find the consumption plan:

$$\$43{,}500 = c_0 + a_1 = c_0 + 0.45c_0 = 1.45c_0$$
$$\Rightarrow c_0 = \$43{,}500/1.45 = \$30{,}000$$
$$\Rightarrow a_1 = 0.45c_0 = 0.45 \times \$30{,}000 = \$13{,}500$$

By spending $30,000 in year 0, Ares has $13,500 to spend in the remaining two years. From our previous work we know that in year 1 he spends 80% of his year-1 assets, or $0.8 \times \$13{,}500 = \$10{,}800$. In summary, the sophisticate's consumption sequence is:

$$(c_0^s, c_1^s, c_2^s) = (\$30{,}000, \ \$10{,}800, \ \$2{,}700)$$

Notice that relative to the naif, the sophisticate actually consumes more in the first period, generating lower consumption in the last two periods. Because consumption is even further away from the constant consumption benchmark of the TC, the sophisticate achieves even lower welfare than the naif:

$$W^s = 2\sqrt{c_0^s} + 2\sqrt{c_1^s} + 2\sqrt{c_2^s} = 2\sqrt{30{,}000} + 2\sqrt{10{,}800} + 2\sqrt{2{,}700} \approx 658.2 \text{ utils}$$

Why is the sophisticate worse off than the naif? Because the sophisticate anticipates his future self-control problem, he reasons that if he is going to give in to temptation and consume 80% of his assets in period 1 (and not 50% like the naif incorrectly believes), he might as well give in to temptation from the beginning, consuming more in the first period than the naif.

Discussion

This stylized example illustrates the importance of the discount function. With standard exponential discounting Ares is time-consistent and finds it best to spend an equal amount each year. With present-biased preferences Ares consumes approximately two-thirds of his lifetime income in the first period (instead of only one third in each period) and has very little to spend in the final period. The consequently smaller savings and the considerable drop in consumption in the last period are consistent with empirical evidence that many households have little liquid wealth and experience consumption declines at retirement.

We conclude by noting that the general results from the Doing it Once model in Section 5.3.3 are consistent with Ares' decision of how to spend his income over time. Because consumption is not an activity that is done once, the models do not align perfectly. In spite of this, we can interpret consumption as a leisure activity since consuming generates an immediate reward and a delayed cost (in the form of reducing future consumption possibilities). From Theorems 5.1 and 5.2 we know that sophisticates do leisure activities before naifs, who do them before TCs. Applying this logic to Ares' consumption problem, we would expect that sophisticates would consume the most in the first period, followed by naifs, and then TCs. This is exactly what we found: $c_0^s = \$30{,}000$, $c_0^n = \$29{,}000$, and $c_0^{tc} = \$14{,}500$.

In the end-of-appendix exercises you will have an opportunity to apply the methods of solving the TC, naif, and sophisticate problems to more general settings that include allocating effort across periods and choosing when to retire.

5A.1 *Appendix Summary*

1   Relative to a time-consistent exponential discounter, an individual with present-biased preferences chooses to shift consumption to the present and consequently save less for the future.
2   A naif achieves higher welfare than a sophisticate in the stylized life-cycle model. This is because unlike the naif, who does not anticipate their future impatience, the sophisticate accurately anticipates their future impatience and decides that they should therefore give in even more to the immediate satisfaction of consumption.

5A.2 *Appendix Exercises*[9]

Exercise 5A.1 — Presently Biased Consumption. Enyo, like Ares in the text, must decide how to allocate her lifetime income on consumption expenditure across three years, where each year is a period $t \in \{0, 1, 2\}$. Enyo inherits \$300,000 in year 0 ($y_0 = 300{,}000$) and earns no other income ($y_1 = y_2 = 0$). Assume that there is no interest on savings or borrowing ($r = 0$). Enyo's intertemporal budget constraint is therefore: $c_0 + c_1 + c_2 = 300{,}000$.

Enyo's preferences in period t over consumption expenditure sequences are represented by the model of present-biased preferences with instantaneous utility function $u(c_t) = \ln(c_t)$ and $\delta = 1$:

$$U^t(c_t, c_{t+1}, c_{t+2}; \beta) = \ln(c_t) + \beta \ln(c_{t+1}) + \beta \ln(c_{t+2})$$

a If Enyo is time-consistent with $\beta = 1$, determine her choice of consumption in each period.

b If Enyo is a naif with $0 < \beta < 1$, determine her choice of consumption in each period. Note that your answers will depend on β. How does her consumption in each period change as β decreases from 1? Interpret.

c If Enyo is a sophisticate with $0 < \beta < 1$, show that she chooses the same consumption sequence as if she were a naif. *Note: This is a special result due to the properties of the natural logarithm instantaneous utility function.*

Exercise 5A.2 — Paper Procrastination. It is Monday morning and time-consistent Tracy, naive Nancy, and sophisticated Sophie are in a class with a term paper due on Thursday morning. The students therefore have three days to write the paper. Suppose that each student knows it will take 13 hours to do the necessary research and write the paper.

Let's model this decision problem like the life-cycle model except instead of allocating income across years, the students are allocating homework time across days. For any day $t \in \{\text{Monday } (M), \text{Tuesday } (T), \text{Wednesday } (W)\}$, let x_t be the number of hours that a student works on the paper that day. The students' preferences on day t over sequences of writing hours are represented by the model of present-biased preferences with instantaneous utility function $u(x_t) = -x_t^2$ and $\delta = 1/2$:

$$U^t(x_t, x_{t+1}, x_{t+2}; \beta) = -x_t^2 - \beta \frac{1}{2} x_{t+1}^2 - \beta \frac{1}{4} x_{t+2}^2$$

a We first consider this problem for time-consistent Tracy, for whom $\beta = 1$.

   i On Monday morning Tracy makes a plan for finishing the term paper that maximizes her Monday utility function:

$$U^M(x_M, x_T, x_W; 1) = -x_M^2 - \frac{1}{2} x_T^2 - \frac{1}{4} x_W^2$$

   subject to $x_M + x_T + x_W = 13$. Use the method of Lagrange to determine how many hours Tracy plans to work on Monday, Tuesday, and Wednesday.

   ii You should have found that Tracy spent $13/7 \approx 1.86$ hours working on the project on Monday. On Tuesday morning, her utility function is now

$$U^T(x_T, x_W; 1) = -x_T^2 - \frac{1}{2}x_W^2$$

If she maximizes her Tuesday utility function subject to the constraint that $x_T + x_W = 13 - 13/7$, how much will she work on Tuesday and Wednesday? Do the hours chosen for Tuesday and Wednesday agree with the plans she set on Monday? Why or why not?

   iii Compute Tracy's individual welfare, W.

b   We now consider the same problem for naive Nancy, for whom $\beta = 1/2$.

   i On Monday morning Nancy makes a plan for finishing the term paper that maximizes her Monday utility function:

$$U^M(x_M, x_T, x_W; 1/2) = -x_M^2 - \frac{1}{4}x_T^2 - \frac{1}{8}x_W^2$$

subject to $x_M + x_T + x_W = 13$. Use the method of Lagrange to determine how many hours Nancy plans to work on Monday, Tuesday, and Wednesday.

   ii On Tuesday morning Nancy must decide how much to actually work on Tuesday and Wednesday, given that she already worked her Monday hours. She does so by maximizing her Tuesday utility function:

$$U^T(x_T, x_W; 1/2) = -x_T^2 - \frac{1}{4}x_W^2$$

subject to the constraint that $x_T + x_W = 13 - x_M^n$ where x_M^n is the number of hours that she worked on Monday (as you found in part (b.i)). How much does she work on Tuesday and Wednesday? Does Nancy have time-consistent preferences? Explain.

   iii Compute Nancy's individual welfare, W.

c   Finally, consider the same decision problem for sophisticated Sophie, for whom $\beta = 1/2$ (just like naive Nancy). Because Sophie is sophisticated, though, she realizes that she has a self-control problem.

   i On Monday morning Sophie realizes that when she wakes up on Tuesday she will not follow the plan that maximizes her Monday preferences, but instead will observe that she already worked x_M hours and choose to allocate the remainder of the task so as to maximize:

$$U^T(x_T, x_W; 1/2) = -x_T^2 - \frac{1}{4}x_W^2$$

subject to the constraint that $x_T + x_W = 13 - x_M$. Use the method of Lagrange to determine, as a function of x_M, how much Sophie will work on Tuesday, $x_T(x_M)$ and Wednesday, $x_W(x_M)$.

ii On Monday she takes into account how her choice of work on Monday impacts how much she will actually work when Tuesday arrives. Using the functions you found in part (c.i), she chooses x_M to maximize:

$$U^M\left(x_M, x_T(x_M), x_W(x_M); 1/2\right) = -x_M^2 - \frac{1}{4}x_T(x_M)^2 - \frac{1}{8}x_W(x_M)^2$$

This is an *un*constrained optimization problem. To solve it, determine the first order condition with respect to x_M. How much does Sophie work on Monday, Tuesday, and Wednesday?

iii Compute Sophie's individual welfare, W.

d Compare the sequence of hours worked over the week for Tracy, Nancy, and Sophie. Does Nancy or Sophie achieve higher welfare? Provide intuition.

Exercise 5A.3 — Resolving to Retire (Diamond and Köszegi 2003). It is Regina's 25th birthday and she knows that she will live for 60 more years. Partition these remaining years into three 20-year periods: early (age 25–44), middle (age 45–64), and late (age 65–84). Let $t = 0, 1, 2$ indicate the early, middle, and late periods, respectively. Assume that the interest rate r is zero.

In her early period she works and earns $2,100,000 in total (i.e., $105,000 per year on average). And in her late period she is retired and earns no income. But in her middle period she must decide whether or not to work part time. If she works part time in her middle period she earns an additional $900,000 in total, but also incurs a utility cost of 1.4 utils in this period. This utility cost captures the idea that time spent working in this period is less time that she can devote to being with family and traveling.

Assume that Regina's preferences are represented by the model of present-biased preferences (Definition 5.1).

In the early period she plans her consumption expenditure over time and her labor supply decision for her middle years. Let w be an indicator variable that equals 1 if Regina decides to work at $t = 1$ and equals 0 if she starts retirement at $t = 1$. Her period-0 problem is then:

$$\max_{c_0, c_1, c_2, w} \ln(c_0) + \beta \ln(c_1) + \beta \ln(c_2) - \beta \times 1.4w$$

such that $c_0 + c_1 + c_2 = 2,100,000 + 900,000w$

where $0 < \beta \le 1$, $\delta = 1$, and her instantaneous utility function is $u(c) = \ln(c)$. Note that the $-\beta \times 1.4w$ term reflects the (discounted) utility cost of working at $t = 1$.

Her problem at period $t = 1$ (given c_0) is then:

$$\max_{c_1, c_2, w} \ln(c_1) + \beta \ln(c_2) - 1.4w$$

such that $c_1 + c_2 = 2,100,000 + 900,000w - c_0$

Notice that total wealth in this period-1 problem is reduced by the consumption expenditure in period 0. Also, the utility cost of working in period 1, $-1.4w$, is not discounted as in the period-0 problem because here the work is in the present and not the future.

a   Start by assuming that Regina is time-consistent ($\beta = 1$). We want to solve for her consumption (c_0, c_1, c_2) and period-1 work choice (w). Because w is not a continuous variable, we must solve the period-0 consumption expenditure problem twice: first assuming that $w = 0$ and then assuming that $w = 1$. Whichever case generates the largest utility will be Regina's utility-maximizing choice. We proceed in steps:

   i   Suppose that Regina does not work in period 1 ($w = 0$). Use the method of Lagrange to solve for (c_0, c_1, c_2) in her period-0 utility-maximization problem.
   ii Now suppose that Regina does work in period 1 ($w = 1$). Use the method of Lagrange to solve for (c_0, c_1, c_2) in her period-0 utility-maximization problem.
   iii Use Regina's period-0 lifetime utility function to evaluate the two previous cases and determine her preferred labor supply and consumption decisions.

b   Now assume that $\beta = 1/2$ and Regina is a naif. That is, in period 0 she makes a plan for the future and decides how much to consume in period 0 based on this plan. She doesn't take into account that her period-1 self may not want to follow the plan of her period-0 self. We proceed in steps:

   i   Solve her period-0 utility-maximization problem. Again, it is necessary to consider the two cases of working and not working in period 1. Does she plan to work in period 1? And how much does she spend on consumption in period 0?
   ii Given her consumption decision in period 0, solve her period-1 utility-maximization problem. Note that she is not bound by her labor supply plan from period 0. Therefore, it is again necessary to consider the two cases of working and not working in period 1. Does she work in period 1? And how much does she spend on consumption in periods 1 and 2?
   iii Comment on how the naif's behavior compares with that of the time-consistent.

c   Maintain the assumption that $\beta = 1/2$, but now assume that Regina is a sophisticate. That is, she takes into account the behavior of her self at $t = 1$ when making her plans at $t = 0$. *Warning: This is a challenging problem.*

   i   Start with her period-1 utility-maximization problem, taking the unknown c_0 as given. Again, it is necessary to consider the two cases of working and not working in period 1. You should determine a plan that is contingent on c_0. That is, both the level of consumption (c_1, c_2) and the decision to work w depend on c_0.
   ii Her period-0 self anticipates her period-1 self following through on her period-1 plan. Therefore, solve her period-0 problem, taking into account her period-1 plan. Does she work in period 1? And how much does she spend on consumption in each period?
   iii Comment on how the sophisticate's behavior compares with that of the naif.

Notes

1 Different values of δ are used to plot the exponential and quasi-hyperbolic discount functions so that both functions pass through the same point at the 12 month horizon.
2 The term "present-biased" was coined by O'Donoghue and Rabin (1999). Bernheim and Taubinsky (2018) suggest calling such preferences "present-focused."

3 It is possible to define partial naivete as $1 > \hat{\beta} > \beta$, but for simplicity, I ignore this intermediate case.
4 Section 5.2 is adapted from the simple model in DellaVigna (2009), which was originally developed by DellaVigna and Malmendier (2004).
5 See Psacharopoulos and Patrinos (2018) and Oreopoulos and Salvanes (2011) for reviews of the financial and nonfinancial benefits of schooling, respectively.
6 The reported life-cycle model predictions with present-biased preferences assume sophistication. The predictions are similar if one assumes naivete.
7 Exercises 5.3, 5.4, and 5.9 are adapted from exercises by Lorenz Goette.
8 Formally, the sophisticate's decision problem is a noncooperative game between the period-0 and period-1 selves. The solution we determine is the outcome of the subgame perfect equilibrium of this game.
9 Exercise 5A.2 is adapted from Bergstrom and Varian (2010, 371-374) and Exercise 5A.3 is adapted from an exercise by Glenn Ellison.

References

Angeletos, George-Marios, David Laibson, Andrea Repetto, Jeremy Tobacman, and Stephen Weinberg. 2001. "The Hyperbolic Consumption Model: Calibration, Simulation, and Empirical Evaluation." *Journal of Economic Perspectives* 15 (3): 47–68. doi:10.1257/jep.15.3.47.

Ariely, Dan, and Klaus Wertenbroch. 2002. "Procrastination, Deadlines, and Performance: Self-control by Precommitment." *Psychological Science* 13 (3): 219–224. doi:10.1111/1467-9280.00441.

Ausubel, Lawrence M. 1999. "Adverse Selection in the Credit Card Market." Unpublished.

Bergstrom, Theodore C., and Hal R. Varian. 2010. *Workouts in Intermediate Microeconomics.* 8th edition. New York: W.W. Norton & Company.

Bernheim, B. Douglas, Jonathan Skinner, and Steven Weinberg. 2001. "What Accounts for the Variation in Retirement Wealth among U.S. Households?" *American Economic Review* 91 (4): 832–857. doi:10.1257/aer.91.4.832.

Bernheim, B. Douglas, and Dmitry Taubinsky. 2018. "Behavioral Public Economics." In *Handbook of Behavioral Economics: Foundations and Applications,* edited by B. Douglas Bernheim, Stefano DellaVigna, and David Laibson, vol. 1. North-Holland.

DellaVigna, Stefano. 2009. "Psychology and Economics: Evidence from the Field." *Journal of Economic Literature* 47 (2): 315–372. doi:10.1257/jel.47.2.315.

DellaVigna, Stefano, and Ulrike Malmendier. 2004. "Contract Design and Self-Control: Theory and Evidence." *The Quarterly Journal of Economics* 119 (2): 353–402. doi:10.1162/0033553041382111.

———. 2006. "Paying Not to Go to the Gym." *American Economic Review* 96 (3): 694–719. doi:10.1257/aer.96.3.694.

Diamond, Peter, and Botond Köszegi. 2003. "Quasi-hyperbolic Discounting and Retirement." *Journal of Public Economics* 87 (9): 1839–1872. doi:10.1016/S0047-2727(02)00041-5.

Kaur, Supreet, Michael Kremer, and Sendhil Mullainathan. 2015. "Self-Control at Work." *Journal of Political Economy* 123 (6): 1227–1277. doi:10.1086/683822.

Laibson, David. 1997. "Golden Eggs and Hyperbolic Discounting." *The Quarterly Journal of Economics* 112 (2): 443–477. doi:10.1162/003355397555253.

Laibson, David, Andrea Repetto, and Jeremy Tobacman. 2007. "Estimating Discount Functions with Consumption Choices over the Lifecycle." NBER Working Paper 13314. Cambridge, MA: National Bureau of Economic Research. doi:10.3386/w13314.

Levitt, Steven D., John A. List, Susanne Neckermann, and Sally Sadoff. 2016. "The Behavioralist Goes to School: Leveraging Behavioral Economics to Improve Educational Performance." *American Economic Journal: Economic Policy* 8 (4): 183–219. doi:10.1257/pol.20130358.

O'Donoghue, Ted, and Matthew Rabin. 1999. "Doing It Now or Later." *American Economic Review* 89 (1): 103–124. doi:10.1257/aer.89.1.103.

Oreopoulos, Philip, and Kjell G. Salvanes. 2011. "Priceless: The Nonpecuniary Benefits of Schooling." *Journal of Economic Perspectives* 25 (1): 159–184. doi:10.1257/jep.25.1.159.

Psacharopoulos, George, and Harry Anthony Patrinos. 2018. "Returns to Investment in Education: A Decennial Review of the Global Literature." *Education Economics* 26 (5): 445–458. doi:10.1080/09645292.2018.1484426.

Rabin, Matthew. 2013. "An Approach to Incorporating Psychology into Economics." *American Economic Review* 103 (3): 617–622. doi:10.1257/aer.103.3.617.

6 Consumption Dependence

Learning Objectives

★ Consider two nonstandard models with consumption dependence: habit formation and anticipation.

★ Apply the model of habit formation to understand addictive behaviors.

★ Apply the model of anticipation to explain two of the Discounted Utility model's anomalies: the sign effect and the preference for improvement.

★ Interpret evidence that supports the models of habit formation and anticipation.

Recall that the standard Discounted Utility (DU) model of intertemporal preferences makes two key assumptions: constant discounting and consumption independence. The previous chapter explored the implications of abandoning the assumption of a constant discount rate. But it maintained the assumption of consumption independence, that utility obtained in a particular period depends only on consumption in that period.

In this chapter we relax the assumption of consumption independence in two key ways. We begin by letting *past* consumption impact present utility. This allows us to develop a model of habit formation, where habitual behaviors emerge because doing an activity yesterday makes doing it today more desirable. We apply this model to understand addictive activities like drug use and consider the different theoretical predictions when habit formation preferences are either time-consistent or present-biased. And we conclude this first half of the chapter with empirical evidence of habit formation in the contexts of voting and tobacco use.

Alternatively, anticipation of *future* consumption can also impact present utility. This possibility is explored in the second half of the chapter with a model of anticipatory utility. The model is applied to make sense of DU anomalies in Chapter 4 that we have yet to explain, namely the sign effect and preference for improvement. The chapter concludes with evidence that anticipation of bad future outcomes, or anxiety, can impact decisions related to personal health and long-term investing.

6.1 Habit Formation

People develop habits of regular behaviors or routines. Some habits, like regular exercise, a morning coffee, washing hands, or spiritual practices can be beneficial. Others, like smoking, snacking, playing video games, gambling, lying, or stealing may be harmful.

DOI: 10.4324/9780367854072-8

Such habits, if not moderated, can limit a person's capacity to flourish, or lead to illness or even legal prosecution. The key feature of habit formation is that past consumption, whether it is of exercise, coffee, or tobacco, reinforces the taste for current consumption. In order to capture this effect, we must allow current preferences to depend on what was consumed in the past.

Recall that the Discounted Utility model of preferences over a sequence of outcomes (from the perspective of period 0) takes the following form:

$$U^0 = u_0 + \delta u_1 + \delta^2 u_2 + \cdots + \delta^T u_T \tag{6.1}$$

where u_t is the instantaneous utility realized in period t and δ is the discount factor. The DU model goes further and also assumes consumption independence, i.e., utility in each period depends only on consumption in that period. Mathematically, this requires that $u_t = u(x_t)$, where $u(\cdot)$ is the instantaneous utility function and x_t is consumption in period t. This assumption rules out habit formation because, for instance, how much tobacco I consumed yesterday has no impact on my valuation of smoking tobacco today.

We introduce habit formation by letting instantaneous utility depend not only on current consumption, but also on consumption in the previous period. In math notation, this means that $u_t = u(x_t, x_{t-1})$, with the utility function $u(\cdot)$ taking two inputs instead of only one.[1]

This is not enough — we also want to ensure that past consumption x_{t-1} increases demand for current consumption x_t. A key principle of economic theory is that demand for a good increases if the marginal utility of consumption increases, holding all else constant. Therefore, *past* consumption must increase the marginal utility of *current* consumption. This relationship is illustrated in Figure 6.1, where the solid curve shows instantaneous utility as a function of current consumption, holding past consumption fixed at some high level. The dashed curve shows the same relationship between instantaneous utility and current consumption, but for a lower fixed level of

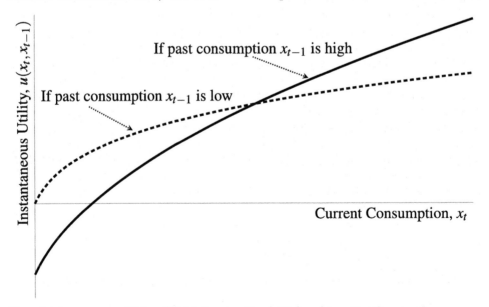

Figure 6.1 Instantaneous Utility of Habit-Forming Good: High and Low Past Consumption

past consumption. Because the slope of the utility function measures the marginal utility of current consumption, higher past consumption rotates the utility curve to make it steeper. Intuitively, for greater past consumption, the additional satisfaction from increasing current consumption is higher. Or equivalently, the reduction in satisfaction from decreasing current consumption is higher, making it harder to stop consuming. The following definition summarizes.

Definition 6.1 A habit formation model assumes that instantaneous utility at time t is $u_t = u(x_t, x_{t-1})$, where past consumption x_{t-1} increases the marginal utility of current consumption x_t.

Math Note: Expressed with calculus notation, we have: $\frac{\partial}{\partial x_{t-1}}\left[\frac{\partial u_t}{\partial x_t}\right] > 0$.

There are multiple habit formation models. This is true for two key reasons. The first is that it is possible to allow for more complicated channels through which past consumption impacts current utility. In the above definition, only consumption in the previous period matters for the present. In reality, past consumption over many periods can generate a cumulative effect on the present. There is likely a difference between current tastes for tobacco by someone who started smoking yesterday and someone who started smoking 10 years prior. Although the specification of our model is too simple to make such distinctions, it is still capable of generating the central insights from a more complex analysis.

The second reason is that the instantaneous utility function from a habit formation model can be paired with either standard exponential discounting or present biased quasi-hyperbolic discounting. The discount function is particularly relevant when modeling addictive activities as habit formation.

With exponential discounting, a habit formation model of preferences over an addictive good is referred to as one of **rational addiction**. The mathematical representation of such preferences follows from plugging $u_t = u(x_t, x_{t-1})$ into equation (6.1):

$$U^0 = u(x_0) + \delta u(x_1, x_0) + \delta^2 u(x_2, x_1) + \cdots + \delta^T u(x_T, x_{T-1}) \tag{6.2}$$

Rational addiction may sound like an oxymoron, especially if one associates addiction with irrationality. But the "rational" modifier is applied in this case because even though habit formation is a nonstandard form of preferences, individuals are arguably acting in their own self-determined best interest. They remain time-consistent, following through with their plans to consume (or not) a habit-forming good. Becker and Murphy (1988) introduce such a rational addiction model in which forward-looking individuals weigh the long-run costs of addiction against the benefits of consumption to make their choices. According to this framework, individuals consume addictive goods while fully recognizing the costs of their consumption in terms of future addiction.

Alternatively, individuals may exhibit habit-forming preferences while simultaneously being present-biased. In contrast to rational addiction, individuals would now underweight future costs relative to the present benefits and therefore not fully recognize the addictive nature of their choices (Gruber and Köszegi 2001). Mathematically, preferences over a sequence of outcomes would be represented by:

$$U^0 = u(x_0) + \beta\delta u(x_1, x_0) + \beta\delta^2 u(x_2, x_1) + \cdots + \beta\delta^T u(x_T, x_{T-1}) \tag{6.3}$$

for some $\beta < 1$. And as we explored in the previous chapter on present bias, the extent to which an individual is sophisticated or naive to their own present bias will impact their behavior. These implications are best demonstrated with an example, which we turn to in the next section.

6.2　Drug Use

To illustrate how the two ways of discounting — exponentially or quasi-hyperbolically — matter for consumption of an addictive good, in this section we work through a stylized example of drug use (adapted from O'Donoghue and Rabin 1999). Although the example is somewhat artificial, it reveals the key implications of a habit formation model.

Consider an individual who lives for three periods: $t = 1, 2, 3$. In each period, she can decide whether to consume a habit-forming drug ("hit") or not consume ("refrain"). Consumption is free, but it leads to being "hooked" in the next period. Refraining leads to being "unhooked" in the next period. She starts period 1 unhooked. Our objective is to determine the predicted behavior of this individual in each period, depending on whether they are time-consistent or present-biased.

Her instantaneous utility depends on both whether she hits or refrains in the current period, and whether she is hooked or unhooked. These payoffs are represented graphically in Figure 6.2. Notice that regardless of past behavior, hitting is enjoyable — it generates higher current utility than refraining. But utility when hooked is less than utility when unhooked, no matter current behavior. This negative effect of past drug use on current utility captures the potentially harmful consequences for one's health or career prospects, as well as the diminished satisfaction from developing a tolerance to the drug. The key feature generating habit formation, however, is that the marginal utility of current

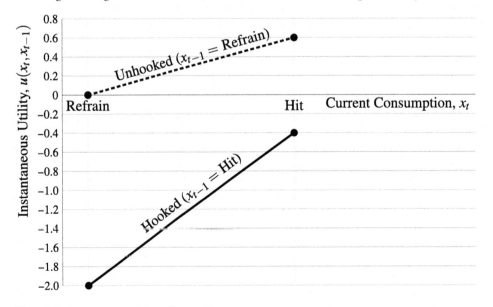

Figure 6.2 Instantaneous Utility of Drug Use

consumption, or the slope of the utility function, is greater when hooked $(-0.4 - (-2) = 1.6)$ than when unhooked $(0.6 - 0 = 0.6)$. In other words, hitting the drug (and becoming hooked) increases the marginal benefit from hitting again in the next period.

Before we determine how this individual is predicted to behave, it is helpful to recognize that since her payoffs are affected by her current addiction status, which is in turn determined by past decisions, we can reason through the decision process by starting in period 3 and working backwards. In particular, for each period we will determine whether or not she finds it optimal to hit, both if she is hooked and if she is unhooked.

Case 1: Time-Consistent Rational Addiction

Consider first the case of rational addiction in which she exponentially discounts her future instantaneous utility, as in equation (6.2), with discount factor $\delta = 1$. Let's start in the last period $t = 3$. If she arrives in this period unhooked she can hit and earn a payoff of 0.6 or refrain for a payoff of 0. She therefore hits. If she were hooked in this period, she could hit for a payoff of -0.4 or refrain for a payoff of -2. Again, she decides to hit. Since there is no future period and drug use is enjoyable, she always decides to hit in period 3.

Let's roll back to period 2, using the knowledge that she will always hit in period 3. If she is unhooked in period 2 she can hit for an immediate payoff of 0.6, but then she will be hooked in period 3 and hit again for a payoff of -0.4, or 0.2 in total. If instead she refrains, her immediate payoff is 0, followed by a payoff of 0.6 from hitting while unhooked in period 3. She therefore prefers to refrain in period 2 if unhooked. But what if she is hooked in period 2? Then hitting generates an immediate payoff of -0.4 followed by another hit while hooked in period 3, for a total payoff of -0.8. By refraining, her immediate payoff drops to -2, followed by another hit while unhooked in period 3, for a total payoff of -1.4. To summarize, in period 2 she refrains if unhooked, but hits if already hooked.

All that remains is to consider her decision in the first period when we know she is unhooked (by assumption). By hitting in the first period, she will be hooked in the second period and therefore hit again, before finally hitting once more in the last period. Alternatively, she could refrain in period 1, and by remaining unhooked in period 2, will refrain then, before hitting for the first time in period 3. Adding up the corresponding payoffs from these two options we find that she prefers to refrain in period 1. This analysis is summarized in Table 6.1.

Table 6.1 Payoffs and Actions: Time-Consistent Drug Use

		If Unhooked in Period t		If Hooked in Period t	
$t = 3$	Hit	$U^3 = 0.6$		$U^3 = -0.4$	✓
	Refrain	$U^3 = 0$	⊘	$U^3 = -2$	
$t = 2$	Hit	$U^2 = 0.6-0.4 = 0.2$		$U^2 = -0.4-0.4 = -0.8$	✓
	Refrain	$U^2 = 0+0.6 = 0.6$	⊘	$U^2 = -2+0.6 = -1.4$	
$t = 1$	Hit	$U^1 = 0.6-0.4-0.4 = -0.2$			
	Refrain	$U^1 = 0+0+0.6 = 0.6$	⊘		

Notes: Checks indicate preferred action in each period contingent on addiction status. Circled checks indicate actual behavior in each period.

Table 6.2 Payoffs and Actions: Naive Drug Use

		If Unhooked in Period t		**If Hooked in Period t**	
$t = 3$	Hit	$U^3 = 0.6$	✓	$U^3 = -0.4$	⊘
	Refrain	$U^3 = 0$		$U^3 = -2$	
$t = 2$	Hit	$U^2 = 0.6 - \frac{1}{2}0.4 = 0.4$	⊘	$U^2 = -0.4 - \frac{1}{2}0.4 = -0.6$	✓
	Refrain	$U^2 = 0 + \frac{1}{2}0.6 = 0.3$		$U^2 = -2 + \frac{1}{2}0.6 = -1.7$	
$t = 1$	Hit	$U^1 = 0.6 - \frac{1}{2}0.4 - \frac{1}{2}0.4 = 0.2$			
	Refrain	$U^1 = 0 + \frac{1}{2}0 + \frac{1}{2}0.6 = 0.3$	⊘		

Notes: Checks indicate preferred action in each period contingent on addiction status. Circled checks indicate actual behavior in each period.

As a time-consistent she therefore refrains for the first two periods, deciding to hit only in the last period when there are no future costs from hitting.

Case 2: Naive Present-Biased Addiction

Let's now allow the individual to be naively present-biased with preferences as in equation (6.3), with $\delta = 1$ and $\beta = 1/2$. Her naivete implies that she believes herself to be time-consistent — she thinks that her future self will act like the time-consistent in Case 1.

In period 3 the naif conducts the same reasoning as the time-consistent and decides to always hit. The naif's reasoning in period 2 is almost identical to that of the time-consistent, except she discounts her future payoffs by $\beta = 1/2$. Inspect Table 6.2 to see the corresponding algebra. This extra discounting has the effect of inducing her to hit while unhooked in period 2, unlike the time-consistent who preferred to refrain. She therefore always hits in period 2, as well as in period 3.

In the first period the unhooked naif makes her decision under the false belief that she will only hit if she is hooked in period 2 (like the time-consistent), when in fact she will actually always hit in period 2. If she hits in period 1, she correctly expects to hit while hooked in the next two periods. But if she refrains in period 1, she incorrectly expects her unhooked period-2 self to refrain, when in fact she will hit. She then also expects her period-3 self to be unhooked when she hits. Adding up her expected payoffs in each period and discounting the future payoffs by β, we find that she prefers to refrain in the first period.

In summary, the naif refrains in period 1 because she thinks that she will refrain in period 2 before giving in to the drug in the last period. In actuality, her abstention in the first period is followed by drug use in the next two periods. Compared to the time-consistent, the naif indulges more in the addictive activity. This is a general consequence of naivete that is not specific to the current example. It is also similar to the result in the previous chapter that when a leisure activity — like drug use — is to be done once, naifs indulge earlier than time-consistents (Theorem 5.1).

Case 3: Sophisticated Present-Biased Addiction

In our final case we maintain the same preferences as the naif ($\delta = 1$ and $\beta = 1/2$), but assume that the individual is a sophisticate who is fully aware of her present bias. She accurately anticipates her future behavior when making decisions in the present.

Table 6.3 Payoffs and Actions: Sophisticated Drug Use

		If Unhooked in Period t		If Hooked in Period t	
$t = 3$	Hit	$U^3 = 0.6$	✓	$U^3 = -0.4$	⊘
	Refrain	$U^3 = 0$		$U^3 = -2$	
$t = 2$	Hit	$U^2 = 0.6 - \frac{1}{2}0.4 = 0.4$	✓	$U^2 = -0.4 - \frac{1}{2}0.4 = -0.6$ ⊘	
	Refrain	$U^2 = 0 + \frac{1}{2}0.6 = 0.3$		$U^2 = -2 + \frac{1}{2}0.6 = -1.7$	
$t = 1$	Hit	$U^1 = 0.6 - \frac{1}{2}0.4 - \frac{1}{2}0.4 = 0.2$	⊘		
	Refrain	$U^1 = 0 + \frac{1}{2}0.6 - \frac{1}{2}0.4 = 0.1$			

Notes: Checks indicate preferred action in each period contingent on addiction status. Circled checks indicate actual behavior in each period.

The decision process for the sophisticate is identical to that of the naif in period 3 because there is no future period. And because the naif and sophisticate share the same preferences and the same beliefs about behavior in period 3 — that they will always hit — they also share the same decision in period 2 to always hit.

In the first period the sophisticate is not guaranteed to behave identically to the naif because in this period her expectations of period-2 behavior differ. The sophisticate correctly expects to always hit in period 2, whereas the naif naively believes that she will refrain if unhooked in period 2. By the algebra in the last rows of Table 6.3 we observe that the sophisticate prefers to hit in period 1. Because she expects to hit in the next two periods, the future benefit from refraining is smaller, which induces her to indulge in the drug immediately and hit in every period. Exercise 6.4 asks you to consider the implications of present bias for welfare in this example.

6.3 Empirical Evidence of Habit Formation

Let's now turn from theory to empirical evidence of habit formation in relation to voting and tobacco use.

6.3.1 *Voting Habits*   [Politics & Law]

Democratic governments provide most adult citizens with the opportunity to participate in the political processes that govern their lives through voting. The right to vote has been hard fought throughout history. And yet, many eligible voters do not exercise this right. In the United States, typically 40% of eligible voters do not vote in presidential elections (McDonald 2019).

Can the standard model explain this low voter turnout? A standard decision maker will vote only if the costs of voting (in terms of the time and effort to show up at a polling location or submit an absentee ballot) are less than the expected benefits. But in an election with millions of voters where the candidate with a plurality of votes wins, it is very unlikely for any single person's vote to be the pivotal vote that determines the winner. In other words, given all of the other votes, any single vote will almost surely not affect the outcome. With a small benefit from voting, the standard model in fact predicts low voter turnout.

The puzzle is therefore not why turnout is so low, but why turnout is as high as it is. This puzzle is known as the paradox of voting (Downs 1957). To explain this paradox researchers have considered nonstandard motivations for voting. For instance, voters might obtain a benefit from the act of voting and not simply from the small chance of impacting the election outcome. Voters may also feel social pressure to participate in elections or an obligation to fulfill their civic duty (see Section 15.4.1).

Another explanation for observed turnout is that voters are doing so out of habit. In particular, if voting once significantly increases the marginal utility of voting in the next election, then we would expect individuals to maintain their voting participation over time. Let's consider the following test of this hypothesis.

Quasi-Experiment — Voting Habits (Fujiwara, Meng, and Vogl 2016)

Rainfall on election days is a natural phenomenon outside the control of economists. It also acts to create quasi-experimental variation — some areas of the country experience rain on an election day, while others do not. Rainfall is relevant for voting because it increases the cost of voting (commuting to a polling place in the rain is more burdensome) and therefore reduces turnout.

If voting is habit forming, then voters who experienced rainfall in the *previous* election were less likely to vote in that election, which reduces their likelihood of voting in the *current* election. Conversely, if voting is not habit forming, then the weather from 4 years prior should have no impact on the likelihood of voting in the current election. By estimating the effect of past rainfall on current turnout rates, it is possible to disentangle these two hypotheses.

Fujiwara, Meng, and Vogl (2016) consider voter turnout and local rainfall on US presidential election days from 1952 to 2012. They find that rainfall 4 years prior has a negative impact on current voter turnout. And moreover, the likelihood of voting in the current election is impacted more by rainfall 4 years ago than rainfall in the 2 weeks before the current election. This evidence strongly suggests that voting is in fact habit forming.

The evidence that voting is habit forming has significant implications for policies aiming to increase voter turnout. For instance, it might not be necessary to make voting compulsory for all citizens (as is the case in 21 countries ranging from Argentina to Uruguay (CIA 2019)), but only for first-time voters. This has been proposed as a way to start the voting habit, or equivalently to prevent the habit of not voting (Lodge and Birch 2012). Alternatively, get-out-the-vote campaigns aimed at young people may generate long-term civic engagement and increase turnout over time.

6.3.2   Tobacco   [Health]

Tobacco use is widespread. The increased risk of various cancers, heart disease, and diabetes from smoking make it the leading preventable cause of death in the United States. An average of 1,300 people die each day in the United States from cigarette use, including diseases caused by secondhand smoke. And smokers can expect to live 10 fewer years than nonsmokers. This is a global health issue, with smoking responsible for 7 million deaths per year worldwide (CDC 2019).

A model of habit formation can help to make sense of the decision to smoke. Even if the satisfaction obtained from smoking is initially modest relative to the high health costs, once an individual starts smoking, a habit formation model predicts that the marginal utility from future smoking increases, leading to greater future demand.

This is in contrast to the standard DU model with consumption independence, where the marginal utility stays constant over time regardless of past smoking behavior. In this case, we would expect regular smoking only for those who obtain the greatest pleasure from smoking, with consumption benefits that outweigh the massive health costs.

Although it is probably not surprising that tobacco addiction can be explained by a model of habit formation, we have not discussed whether tobacco use is better explained by rational addiction or present-biased addiction. The answer to this question matters for the design of public policy. We discuss each theoretical possibility in turn.

Rational Tobacco Addiction

Suppose that observed tobacco use is explained by the rational addiction model in which individuals are time-consistent. Then the decision to smoke is determined by weighing the immediate enjoyment of smoking against both the health costs from current consumption and the costs of future addiction. Because individuals are forward looking, if they expect higher tobacco prices next year (due perhaps to an impending tax increase), they would anticipate a reduction in their future tobacco consumption and therefore reduce tobacco consumption today (Becker and Murphy 1988). Otherwise, the disutility from reducing future consumption would be greater. There are many studies that confirm this key empirical prediction of the rational addiction model (e.g., Becker, Grossman, and Murphy 1994).

If rational addiction describes well the behavior of smokers, then individuals are making choices that maximize their own welfare. From a policy perspective the only rationale for government intervention is to correct externalities from smoking. That is, the government need only be concerned about the external effects of smoking on nonsmokers. And by setting a tax on cigarettes equal to the magnitude of these external costs, smokers internalize the impact of their behavior on others and reduce consumption to the socially optimal level.

The external costs of smoking include higher health insurance costs, secondhand smoke, low birth weights, and reduced worker productivity. There is also a perverse external benefit of smoking: by shortening life expectancies, tobacco use reduces the cost to the government of providing benefits in old age like health care (Medicare) and income support (Social Security). Empirical studies estimate total external costs that range from 33 cents to $1.75 per pack of cigarettes (Gruber 2001). These estimated externality costs are well below the combined US federal and median state excise tax of $2.71 per pack (Boonn 2020), suggesting that US cigarette taxes are excessively high.

Present-Biased Tobacco Addiction

Suppose instead that observed smoking behavior is due to habit formation with present bias. As with rational addiction, individuals are forward looking, even if they are somewhat myopic. The empirical evidence that a future tobacco price increase reduces current consumption is consistent with forward looking behavior. So while the evidence is supportive of rational addiction, it does not rule out present bias. How then can we disentangle the two theories?

The primary difference is that with present-biased preferences, the plans that smokers make for their own future behavior can differ from actual behavior. A time-consistent smoker who plans to quit would actually do so. But it is possible for a present-biased smoker to make a plan to quit, only to repeatedly fail to follow through. In fact, many smokers fail to follow through with their stated intention to quit (Gruber 2001) and overestimate the likelihood of their future abstinence from smoking by over 100% (Chaloupka, Levy, and White 2019). The fact that actual behavior deviates from desired behavior is strong evidence against the rational addiction model, and for present bias. The following quasi-experiment provides further evidence.

Quasi-Experiment — Cigarette Taxes (Gruber and Mullainathan 2005)

Consider the theoretical predictions for the effect of a cigarette tax on the individual welfare of smokers. In the rational addiction model the tax increases cigarette prices and reduces consumption of a pleasurable good, making smokers worse off.

Suppose instead that smokers are present-biased and overconsume cigarettes relative to their own plans. Then although the tax again reduces consumption, smokers can be made better off by smoking less and better aligning their actions with what they desire.

Gruber and Mullainathan (2005) collect data from the United States and Canada to estimate the effect of cigarette taxes on self-reported happiness, a measure of individual welfare. To identify this effect, they leverage the quasi-experimental variation induced by different states and provinces independently changing cigarette taxes over time. The difference in the self-reported happiness of smokers (relative to nonsmokers) between high and low tax settings measures the effect of tax changes.

The researchers find that smokers report greater happiness when cigarette taxes are higher — both in the Canadian and American data. This result is further evidence in favor of present-biased preferences over time consistency.

If present-biased habit formation is the better descriptive model, as the evidence suggests, then smokers are not consistently making choices that align with their desired plans. As a consequence, individual welfare losses from smoking can be significant. Chaloupka, Levy, and White (2019) estimate that according to smokers' own preferences, they suffer a welfare loss of $400 *each week*.

There is now a paternalistic motivation for taxing cigarettes, in addition to correcting externalities. Cigarette taxes help present-biased smokers internalize the delayed but serious health costs of smoking on their future self. And by smoking less, they are made better off. Gruber and Kőszegi (2001) estimate that with present bias, the socially optimal tax rate on a pack of cigarettes is at least $1 higher than what it would be if the social planner were only concerned with correcting externalities. Adding this additional $1 to the upper end of the externality cost estimate of $1.75 per pack, the total optimal tax of $2.75 is quite close to the actual median tax of $2.71. We explore optimal policy for present-biased consumers further in the next chapter.

6.4   Anticipation

Imagine that you have just booked a vacation. Surely you will experience the enjoyment of reading on the beach or exploring historical sites while actually on vacation. But your enjoyment need not be limited to the specific dates of your holiday. In fact, you may be savoring the anticipated pleasure right now, well before your departure.

The observation that anticipated pleasure matters is not new. William Stanley Jevons, a late 19th century economist, argued exactly this point. Writing about a planned vacation, he observed:

> The intensity of anticipation will be greater ... the more intensely one expects to enjoy it when the time comes. In other words, the amount of pleasure expected is one factor determining the intensity of anticipal pleasure. Again, the nearer the date fixed for leaving home approaches, the greater does the intensity of anticipal pleasure become: at first when the holiday is still many weeks ahead, the intensity increases slowly; then, as the time grows closer, it increases faster and faster, until it culminates on the eve of departure. (Jevons 1871/1905, 64)

Such *currently* felt pleasure from the anticipation of *future* consumption was ruled out with the development of the DU model in the early 20th century. The DU model's assumption of consumption independence restricts the instantaneous utility obtained in a particular period to consumption in that period. To allow for anticipated pleasures (or pains), we modify the DU model so that future consumption can impact current utility, as in Loewenstein (1987).

Let's begin by imagining a decision maker Annie who is evaluating some future outcome, like a fancy dinner, bonus salary, jury duty, or final exam. Annie knows that this outcome will occur in period $T > 0$ and deliver instantaneous utility v in that period. For simplicity, let her instantaneous utility from all other consumption in each period be equal to zero, so $v > 0$ indicates a future pleasure and $v < 0$ indicates a future pain.

In the standard DU model, instantaneous utility u_t in each period t before the outcome occurs does not depend on the future outcome. Therefore, $u_t = 0$ for every period $t < T$. The only nonzero instantaneous utility occurs in period T when $u_T = v$. This standard instantaneous utility function is represented by the dotted graph in Figure 6.3, where v is assumed to be positive. Observe that instantaneous utility jumps from zero to v in period T.[2]

But Annie anticipates the future outcome in each period leading up to period T. Let her anticipal pleasure (with $v > 0$) be consistent with Jevons' description above. That is, her instantaneous utility u_t in periods $t < T$ is both increasing as she gets closer to the future outcome in period T, and increasing at an increasing rate. As time passes and she approaches her fancy dinner, for example, she experiences increasingly more pleasure until the day of the dinner when she realizes the actual benefit v. Some possible instantaneous utility functions are graphed in Figure 6.3, corresponding to different degrees of anticipation. Notice that although Annie obtains zero utility *from consumption* in each period before T, she experiences positive utility *from anticipation* in each of these periods.

We can express Annie's instantaneous utility function mathematically as follows:

$$u_t(T, v) = A^{T-t}v \qquad \text{for } 0 \leq t < T \tag{6.4}$$

where $0 \leq A < 1$ is a measure of the intensity of her anticipation. This is the function that is graphed in Figure 6.3, with higher values of A corresponding to greater instantaneous utility from anticipation. In the extreme case that A approaches 1, Annie would

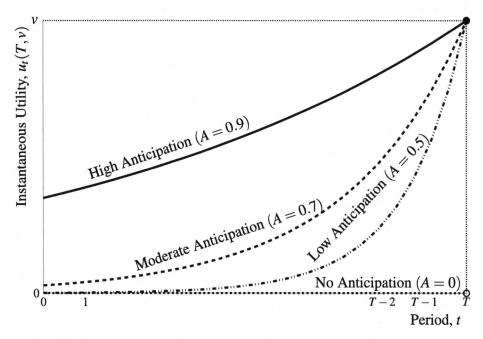

Figure 6.3 Instantaneous Utility from Anticipation of Outcome in Period *T*

experience anticipated pleasure almost equal to the actual pleasure *v* in every period leading up to the outcome.

Observe that with this functional form, Annie's anticipal pleasure exactly matches Jevons' claims that:

1   it is greater "the more intensely one expects to enjoy it when the time comes" — $u_t(T, v)$ increases in *v*, the enjoyment from the outcome when it occurs;
2   it is greater "the nearer the date fixed for [the future outcome] approaches" — $u_t(T, v)$ increases in *t*, the time leading up to the outcome; and
3   "as the time grows closer, it increases faster and faster" — $u_t(T, v)$ increases at an increasing rate in *t*.

Although we have been focused on a future pleasure, the instantaneous utility function in (6.4) can be equally applied to the case of a future pain with $v < 0$. A plot of $u_t(T, v)$ when $v < 0$ would look like the graphs in Figure 6.3 reflected across the horizontal axis. In this case, instead of ignoring the future pain, Annie would experience anticipal *dis*pleasure in the periods leading up to the outcome. We can think of such feelings as dread or anxiety that grow more extreme the closer Annie approaches period *T*.

We can now plug the instantaneous utility function $u_t(T, v)$, into the DU framework with discount factor δ to complete our model of anticipatory preferences.

Definition 6.2 In the **anticipatory model**, the total discounted utility from the perspective of period 0 of experiencing a future payoff *v* in period $T > 0$, is:

$$U(T,v) = u_0(T,v) + \delta u_1(T,v) + \cdots + \delta^{T-1} u_{T-1}(T,v) + \delta^T v \qquad (6.5)$$

where $0 < \delta < 1$. Instantaneous utility $u_t(T, v) = A^{T-t} v$ for $t < T$ and $0 \le A < 1$.

The instantaneous utility in each period t is discounted by δ^t, as is standard in the DU model. This is analogous to the model of rational addiction introduced earlier in this chapter, where instantaneous utility is discounted exponentially, but with utility in each period depending on *past* consumption. Note also that in the last period T instantaneous utility is simply v because there is no more anticipation and only the experience of the outcome.

The preferences represented by the anticipatory model are not necessarily time-consistent, even though the discount function is exponential. The way in which time inconsistency manifests in this model, however, is different from the time inconsistency induced by quasi-hyperbolic discounting. In the model of present-biased preferences, individuals choose more leisure (e.g., watch TV) and less investment (e.g., write a paper) than they had planned. With anticipation, Annie's time inconsistency works in the reverse direction. Because a future leisure activity is pleasurable, Annie might plan to watch two episodes of TV tonight, but then only watch one episode so that she can savor the anticipation of watching the second episode in the future. Similarly, Annie's plan to write a paper next week might cause her sufficient anxiety that she just decides to write the paper immediately to avoid the dread.

6.5 Anticipation Explanations of Anomalies

The anticipatory model of preferences can shed light on the remaining unexplained anomalies of the DU model from Chapter 4. In particular, it can make sense of the sign effect, in which individuals do not discount all outcomes at the same rate, but appear to discount future bad outcomes at much lower discount rates than future good outcomes.[3] It can also predict the common preference for delaying good outcomes and getting bad outcomes over with.

6.5.1 Sign Effect

We begin by reviewing the evidence from the Winnings Wait and Losing Later Lab Experiments in Chapter 4. When faced with delaying a prize by 1 year, the typical respondent reported indifference between receiving $15 immediately and $60 in 1 year. Conversely, when faced with delaying the payment on a traffic ticket, the typical respondent was indifferent between paying the $15 fine immediately and paying a $20 fine in 1 year.

These two indifference preferences cannot be reconciled in the DU framework with a constant discount rate. To delay a prize, individuals appear to be very impatient, needing substantial compensation of an additional $45 to wait for their winnings. The implied annual discount rate is 126%. But this level of impatience diminishes dramatically in the context of paying a fine — a phenomenon known as the sign effect. Individuals are only willing to pay an extra $5 to delay the fine, implying a discount rate of only

29%. The fact that a single discount rate cannot explain these two observations simultaneously poses a threat to the descriptive validity of the DU model.

Let's instead apply the anticipatory model of preferences in Definition 6.2 to the experimental evidence above — with one modification. Assume that a period is equal to a year, so that individuals in period 0 are considering an outcome in period 0 or period 1. And let the instantaneous utility of the actual outcome, v, be the amount of money received or paid. The modification we make is to allow for anticipation of bad future outcomes (i.e., dreading) to be more intense than anticipation of good future outcomes (i.e., savoring). This assumption is motivated by the observation that future bad outcomes are always unpleasant — there is nothing pleasant about an upcoming root canal — while waiting for a future good outcome like receiving a year-end bonus can be both exciting and frustrating. In the language of our model, we are assuming that A is equal to A_G for good outcomes and equal to A_B for bad outcomes, with $A_G < A_B$.

Using equation (6.5), with the modification that dreading is stronger than savoring, the total discounted utilities of $\$v$ now ($T = 0$) and $\$v$ next year ($T = 1$) are therefore:

$$U(0,v) = v \tag{6.6}$$

$$U(1,v) = u_0(1,v) + \delta v = \begin{cases} A_G v + \delta v & \text{if } v > 0 \\ A_B v + \delta v & \text{if } v < 0 \end{cases} \tag{6.7}$$

The immediate outcome generates the full payoff v. But when delayed, the individual experiences anticipatory utility in period 0, in addition to the discounted payoff in period 1.

We can now combine the experimental evidence with the anticipatory preferences represented by the utility functions in equations (6.6) and (6.7). Indifference between receiving $\$15$ now and $\$60$ in 1 year means that:

$$U(0,15) = U(1,60) \Rightarrow 15 = A_G 60 + \delta 60$$

And the indifference between paying $\$15$ now and $\$20$ in 1 year means that:

$$U(0,-15) = U(1,-20) \Rightarrow -15 = -A_B 20 - \delta 20$$

With a little algebra it is possible to show that these two indifference equations can hold simultaneously, as long as $A_B = 0.5 + A_G$. That is, by introducing differential anticipation for good and bad outcomes, with a single fixed value of δ the model can reconcile the observed evidence on preferences for delaying winnings and losses.[4] The anomalous behavior of the sign effect is no longer surprising once we enrich the DU model with anticipation.

Beyond the math, what is the intuition for why the anticipatory model is able to explain the sign effect? Observe that the introduction of anticipatory utility increases the presently perceived weight placed on a future outcome because it delivers utility not only in the period when it occurs, but in every prior period as well. In our example, the delayed payoff is not simply weighted by δ, but by $A + \delta$. For an economist empirically estimating discount rates, anticipatory utility has the effect of inflating the estimated discount factor (from δ to $A + \delta$), or equivalently, deflating the estimated discount rate. This is the key observation: anticipation dampens the estimated discount rate. So for outcomes where we expect anticipation to be stronger, such as unpleasant ones, the estimated discount rates should appear smaller, as the sign effect confirms. Exercise 6.7 has you apply this same intuition to explain the magnitude effect.

6.5.2 Timing of Outcomes

Recall the experimental evidence in Section 4.4 that many people express a preference to delay good outcomes and accelerate bad outcomes (e.g., eating the most desired meal last, earning the highest salary last, and experiencing discomfort or pain quickly). This evidence is inconsistent with the predictions of the DU model that individuals would want to experience good outcomes as soon as possible and delay bad outcomes as far into the future as possible. We concluded our previous discussion by noting that anticipation may be able to explain this anomaly. Let's confirm this hypothesis.[5]

Our objective is to apply the anticipatory model of preferences in Definition 6.2 to determine how long a decision maker would like to delay a good or bad outcome, if at all.[6] That is, we want to determine the outcome period T that maximizes $U(T, v)$. We should expect that our answer may very well depend on whether or not the outcome is a pleasure ($v > 0$) or pain ($v < 0$). It may also depend on the intensity of anticipation A and the discount factor δ.

The first step in our analysis is to simplify the complicated expression for $U(T, v)$ in equation (6.5). It turns out that this expression can be simplified to the following:

$$U(T,v) = \left[A\left(\frac{\delta^T - A^T}{\delta - A}\right) + \delta^T \right] v \tag{6.8}$$

Although this function may not appear to be much of a simplification, it permits us to make three helpful observations about the effects of changing T on utility:

1   $U(0, v) = v$, i.e., when there is no delay ($T = 0$), total discounted utility is equal to the instantaneous utility of the outcome v;
2   $U(T, v)$ has the same sign as v for all T because the term in square brackets is always positive; and
3   if the outcome is infinitely delayed ($T \to \infty$), then $U(T, v)$ converges to zero because δ^T and A^T both approach zero as T increases.

Good Outcome

Consider the case of a future pleasurable outcome, so that $v > 0$. Given the above observations, we have a good idea about what the graph of $U(T, v)$ as a function of T must look like.[7] We know it starts at v, remains positive for all T, and eventually approaches zero. But we don't know whether it increases above v before decreasing towards zero, or whether it is always decreasing from v towards zero. Figure 6.4 depicts these two possibilities as curvy C and decreasing D, respectively.

If an individual — let's call her Annie — has a total discounted utility function that looks like curve C, then she maximizes utility by delaying the good outcome by 3 periods, at which point the curve peaks. If, however, curve D represents Annie's preferences, her utility is maximized by consuming the good outcome immediately with no delay.

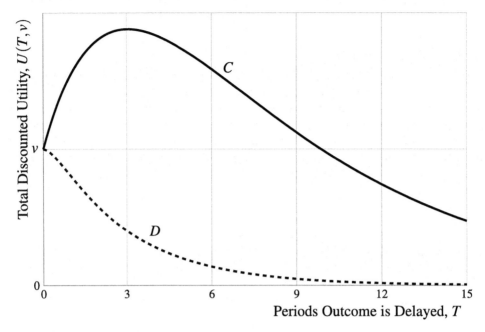

Figure 6.4 Total Discounted Utility from Delaying a Good Outcome *T* Periods

But what determines whether $U(T, v)$ looks like curve C or D? Observe that $U(T, v)$ will look like curve C if an initial delay by one period increases total discounted utility, i.e., $U(1, v) > U(0, v)$. Otherwise, it will look like curve D because once the curve starts to decrease, it never increases again. Combining this observation with Annie's utility-maximizing behavior noted above, and expression (6.8), we have the following set of logical equivalences:

$$\text{Delay Good Outcome} \quad \Leftrightarrow U(T, v) \text{ looks like curve C}$$
$$\Leftrightarrow U(1, v) > U(0, v)$$
$$\Leftrightarrow \left[A\left(\frac{\delta - A}{\delta - A}\right) + \delta \right] v > v$$
$$\Leftrightarrow A > 1 - \delta$$

To summarize, the anticipatory model of preferences predicts that Annie will prefer to delay a good outcome if and only if $A > 1 - \delta$. Intuitively, Annie is balancing two opposing motivations when evaluating how far to delay the outcome. With strong anticipatory utility, corresponding to a large A, Annie wants to enjoy the anticipation by delaying the outcome. Consuming too quickly deprives her of the opportunity to savor the upcoming pleasure. But with a high discount rate, corresponding to a small δ (or large $1 - \delta$), Annie is impatient and does not place much weight on her future utility from either anticipation or consumption. She therefore wants to enjoy the good outcome soon. It should therefore not be surprising that in order for Annie to prefer a delay, the anticipation motive must be sufficiently strong to dominate the impatience motive, or mathematically A must be larger than $1 - \delta$.

Finally, even when Annie prefers to delay a good outcome, she does not want to do so indefinitely. We know this mathematically because curve *C* must peak at some point before declining towards zero. To understand the intuition, suppose Annie has strong anticipation utility and considers delaying a good outcome to infinity so that there are an infinite number of periods during which to experience the pleasure of anticipation. But the presence of even minimal discounting implies that much of the future anticipatory utility will be sufficiently discounted to make it negligible from the perspective of period 0. Therefore, she will still choose to experience the outcome in finite time.

By integrating anticipation into the DU framework, we now have a theoretical prediction consistent with the observed evidence that for some people, delaying a good outcome is preferred. And this anticipatory model still permits individuals to exhibit the standard preference not to delay — corresponding to a sufficiently small value of *A*. In fact, when $A = 0$ and there is no anticipation, the model reduces back to the standard DU model.

Bad Outcome

It remains as an exercise for you in Exercise 6.10 to consider the implications of the model for the case of a bad outcome with $v < 0$. You should similarly conclude that the relative magnitudes of A and $1-\delta$ impact the predicted timing of the future unpleasantness.

6.6 Empirical Evidence of Anxiety

In this final section we consider evidence that anticipation of future bad outcomes, or anxiety, can have a significant impact on one's decision making and health.

6.6.1 *Avoiding Health Information*   *[Health]*

It is increasingly possible to obtain detailed health information about one's genetic predisposition to various diseases. Private companies, like 23andMe, offer services to test your DNA for the chance of developing health conditions like type-2 diabetes and Alzheimer's disease. And of course there are traditional diagnostic tests that screen for the existence of various cancers, including breast, ovarian, and colon cancer.

What is the standard DU model's prediction of individual demand for such medical testing? Given the relatively low price of these tests (at least for those with comprehensive health insurance) and the large benefits from early detection and treatment, we would expect that standard decision makers would want to gather as much medical information as possible. Only very high discounting of one's future health could make sense of avoiding such useful and potentially life-extending information.

And yet, many people avoid obtaining important health information. Consider tests for the susceptibility to cancer. Among patients with the highest risk of breast and ovarian cancer who were offered such a test, 40% declined (Lerman et al. 1996). Perhaps even more surprising, among high-risk individuals who had been tested for colon cancer, 57% did not want to know the results (Lerman et al. 1999). There is also survey evidence that after observing breast cancer symptoms, individuals often delay visiting a doctor for an official diagnosis by months (Facione 1993). And delays are longer for women with family members previously diagnosed with breast cancer than those without (Meechan, Collins, and Petrie 2002). Although individuals may hope the symptoms will improve on their own, delaying only makes treatment more challenging.

Anticipation can provide a plausible explanation for the above evidence. With anticipatory utility, learning bad news about one's future health outcomes generates presently felt feelings of anxiety or dread. And if such feelings are sufficiently strong relative to the standard benefits of early detection, it is less puzzling as to why many individuals choose to avoid or delay potentially bad health news.

Köszegi (2003) verifies this intuition with a model of utility that depends on anxiety about future health outcomes. The model predicts that when there is a small chance of learning bad news, people will go to the doctor. But they are more likely to avoid the doctor if they believe very bad news is possible. This aligns well with the empirical evidence of health testing and diagnosis decisions. "For example, a woman might be too afraid to go to the doctor when she notices a lump in her breast, but at the same time have no qualms about going with an equally annoying inflammation, in which case cancer is very unlikely" (1079). But keep in mind that this is exactly the opposite prediction of standard decision making. Without anxiety, individuals should be more likely to go to the doctor when the benefit of the doctor's visit is greater, i.e., when the chance of learning bad news is higher and early treatment is more valuable.

The next topic considers the impact of anxiety not on decisions of health, but finance.

6.6.2   *Stock Market Fluctuations*   *[Finance]*

Investing money in the stock market is one method for earning a return on savings. Although the stock market is a risky place to invest, with significant price fluctuations, it has historically outperformed most other investments that are available to the average individual. In spite of the advantages of long-term investing in the stock market, only half of American households own stock shares. And the richest 10% of households own 84% of the total value of stock shares (Wolff 2017).

While there are many possible reasons as to why participation in the stock market is not more widespread, let's focus on the role of anxiety. For an investor with anticipal utility, their current instantaneous utility depends not only on current consumption, but also on their anticipated future consumption. And because current savings are future consumption, a stock market decline that reduces savings (and future consumption) should then have an immediate negative effect on well-being. On the day of a significant stock market decline an anxious investor might start worrying about their ability to afford their child's college education or an early retirement. The impact of such anxiety on current utility would have the effect of reducing the investor's willingness to participate in the stock market (Caplin and Leahy 2001).

In the standard DU model without anticipal utility, the prospect of diminished future consumption following a stock market decline would not impact current instantaneous utility. It would only matter for the instantaneous utility realized far in the future, and since that future utility is exponentially discounted, it would have only a modest impact on current well-being. The following quasi-experiment provides evidence to suggest that anxiety is in fact relevant for investors.

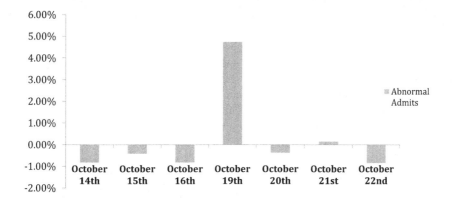

Figure 6.5 Abnormal Hospital Admissions and Black Monday Crash of October 19, 1987

Source: Reprinted from Joseph Engelberg and Christopher A. Parsons. 2016. "Worrying about the Stock Market: Evidence from Hospital Admissions." *The Journal of Finance* 71 (3): 1227-1250. Copyright ©2016 The American Finance Association, with permission from John Wiley and Sons.

Quasi-Experiment — Worrying about the Stock Market (Engelberg and Parsons 2016)

Consider the possible impact of stock market fluctuations on hospital admissions for psychological distress (e.g., anxiety, panic disorder, and depression). If stock market declines increase hospital admissions, then we can conclude that anticipation of future consumption impacts current well-being, and that investor preferences include anticipal utility.

Because day-to-day fluctuations in the stock market should be unrelated to other factors that could lead to changes in hospital admissions rates (e.g., flu season or long-run health trends), we can think of daily stock market returns as creating a quasi-experiment. That is, by comparing hospital admissions rates on the days in which the stock market declines significantly to the admissions rates on other days, we can be confident that any difference is due to the stock market decline.

Figure 6.5 depicts hospital admissions in the days surrounding one particular event, the October 19, 1987 "Black Monday" crash of the stock market by 25%. On the day of the crash hospital admissions jumped by 5% relative to what would have been normally expected. Notice also that the increase in admissions is isolated to the day of the crash, underscoring the immediacy of the effect.

More generally, using California data from 1983 to 2011, Engelberg and Parsons (2016) find that a decline in stock prices by one standard deviation (approximately -1.5%) increases hospital admissions by approximately 0.2% over the next two days. The effect is primarily concentrated in psychological disorders on the first day. This evidence provides strong evidence for anticipal utility. The authors also estimate that the distress induced by stock market declines increases California hospital costs by at least $100 million each year.

But what about stock market increases? For investors with anticipal utility, as supported by the above quasi-experimental evidence, a positive return on savings should generate immediate pleasure from savoring the expansion in future consumption possibilities. And given that the stock market goes up more often than it goes down over sufficiently long horizons, this logic would suggest that with more frequent feelings of pleasure than dread, individuals should not be so reluctant to invest in the stock market.

Engelberg and Parsons (2016) also estimate the impact of large stock market increases on hospital admissions, but find no effect. One explanation for this null effect is that hospital admissions likely only decline due to a reduction in the prevalence of acute pain, and not necessarily due to an improvement in well-being. Investors may therefore be experiencing immediate anticipal pleasure from a stock market increase — we just cannot observe it in the hospital data.

Alternatively, stock market increases may generate much weaker anticipal pleasure than stock market decreases generate anxiety. Recall that we made exactly this assumption when explaining the sign effect in the previous section. The low stock market participation rate is then not so surprising. We explore the idea that losses generate a more intense response than equivalent gains in Part III.

6.7 Summary

1 Habit formation can be modeled by permitting past consumption to impact current instantaneous utility.

2 One particular **habit formation model** assumes that consumption in the previous period increases the marginal utility of current consumption.

3 In a **rational addiction** model, habit-forming preferences are discounted exponentially. In this case, individuals are time-consistent and make welfare-maximizing choices.

4 Preferences over addictive goods can alternatively be modeled as habit formation with a quasi-hyperbolic discount function. In this case, the preferences are present-biased and consumption of an addictive leisure good can be greater than planned.

5 Empirical evidence suggests that voting can be habit-forming and that the behavior of cigarette consumers aligns better with present bias than time-consistent rational addiction.

6 Anticipation can be modeled by permitting future consumption to impact current instantaneous utility.

7 One particular **anticipatory model** assumes that:

   a instantaneous utility from a future outcome increases (in magnitude) at an increasing rate as one approaches the future outcome; and

   b the sequence of instantaneous utilities is discounted exponentially.

8 If anticipation is more intensely felt for future bad outcomes than future good outcomes, the anticipatory model predicts the sign effect.

9 The anticipatory model can explain the DU anomaly of a preference for improvement. In particular, for sufficiently intense anticipation, it predicts a preference to delay a good outcome and accelerate a bad outcome to the present.

10 Anxiety can explain the evidence that many individuals decline or delay health status information. Anxiety can also be induced by stock market declines, leading to low stock market participation.

6.8   Exercises

Exercise 6.1 — Soap Solution. [Development] Washing hands is important for reducing the spread of germs that lead to disease, particularly in children. Hussam et al. (2017) conduct a field experiment in India that distributes soap dispensers to households. The soap dispensers include a time-stamped sensor to allow the researchers to monitor soap use for handwashing. Only some households are specifically informed that the researchers are monitoring their daily handwashing for the next four months. This monitoring message increases handwashing rates by 23% in the short term.

a   Suppose that the Indian households in the study do not have habit-forming preferences. What do you expect to happen to handwashing rates after the four months of monitoring in the households that knew they were being monitored? Would it stay the same or decrease? Explain.

b   Answer part (a) again, but under the assumption that the households have habit-forming preferences.

c   The researchers find that the higher handwashing rates continue after the first four months. Does this point to habit formation?

d   The researchers find that children in households receiving a soap dispenser are less likely to experience diarrhea and acute respiratory infections relative to those in households not receiving a dispenser. Use this information to make a policy recommendation.

Exercise 6.2 — Cash for Cardio. [Health] You want to test whether or not exercise is habit-forming. To do so, you offer financial incentives for a limited period of time that pay people to visit the gym. You observe the impact on gym attendance from introducing the financial incentives and from withdrawing the incentives.

a   Compare and contrast the predictions of the standard and habit formation models of preferences for your experiment.

b   Charness and Gneezy (2009) conduct such a study and find that the limited financial incentives lead to a large increase in gym attendance that persists (over 7 weeks) after the financial incentives are stopped. Does this evidence suggest standard or habit-forming preferences?

c   Carrera et al. (2018) also conduct such a study and find that the financial incentives lead to a small increase in gym attendance that does not persist after the financial incentives are stopped. Does this evidence suggest standard or habit-forming preferences?

Exercise 6.3 — Taxing Oneself. Julie has been a smoker for the past few years. She decides that she wants to quit smoking. To do so, she self-imposes a daily cigarette limit that gradually declines to zero over time. And she also commits to donating a dollar to charity for every cigarette that she smokes above her self-imposed daily limit. Does Julie's strategy for quitting provide evidence for or against the rational addiction model? Explain.

Exercise 6.4 — Drug Welfare. Consider the numerical example of drug use in Section 6.2. Individual welfare W from the sequence of choices over the three periods is the sum of instantaneous utilities in each period, without discounting by β (as in Definition 5.2). And because the discount factor $\delta = 1$, we have $W = u_1 + u_2 + u_3$, where u_t is the instantaneous utility in period t.

a   Compute individual welfare for the time-consistent.
b   Compute individual welfare for the naif.
c   Compute individual welfare for the sophisticate.
d   Is the naif or sophisticate worse off? Explain.

Exercise 6.5 — Addiction Intensity. Jane faces the decision problem of whether to hit or refrain from a habit-forming drug over three periods, exactly as described in Section 6.2. The only difference from the in-chapter example is that Jane's instantaneous utility from refraining while hooked is only -1.1 (instead of -2).

a   What is Jane's marginal utility of hitting when unhooked? What is her marginal utility of hitting when hooked? Are these marginal utilities consistent with the habit formation model assumption that past consumption increases the marginal utility of current consumption?
b   Is the drug more or less addictive for Jane than for the individual with preferences as in Section 6.2? Explain your reasoning.
c   If Jane is time-consistent, what is her drug use in each period? Compare to the time-consistent in Section 6.2.
d   If Jane is a naif, what is her drug use in each period? Compare to the naif in Section 6.2. In particular, explain how the intensity of addiction (see your answer to part (b)) impacts the frequency of drug use for the naif.

Exercise 6.6 — Sav(or)ing. Igor is young and struggles to motivate himself to save for retirement, which feels distant and abstract. He is much more motivated to save for a specific purchase, like a new phone, car, or vacation. Discuss how anticipatory utility can make sense of Igor's behavior.

Exercise 6.7 — Magnitudes of Anticipation. Recall from Section 4.2 that the magnitude effect refers to the phenomenon in which individuals appear to discount more valued outcomes at a lower rate. In particular, the Winnings Wait Lab Experiment shows that the median individual is simultaneously indifferent between $15 today and $60 next year (139% discount rate) and indifferent between $3,000 today and $4,000 next year (29% discount rate). Let's apply the anticipatory model of preferences to make sense of this magnitude effect.

a   Denote the intensity of anticipation A for a small prize by A_S. Apply equation (6.5) to the small prize indifference condition $U(0, 15) = U(1, 60)$. Solve for A_S in terms of δ.
b   Denote the intensity of anticipation A for a large prize by A_L. Apply equation (6.5) to the large prize indifference condition $U(0, 3000) = U(1, 4000)$. Solve for A_L in terms of δ.
c   Is A_S smaller or larger than A_L? Provide intuition for this ranking.

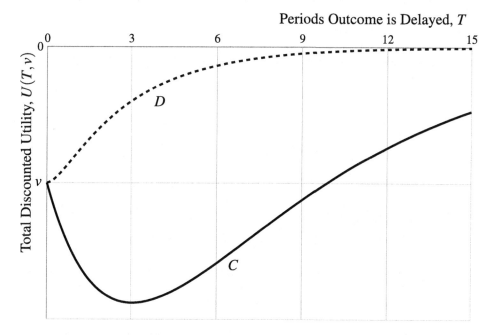

Figure 6.6 Anticipatory Utility of a Bad in Exercise 6.10

Exercise 6.8 — Delay Tactics. Provide a real-world example in which people repeatedly delay consumption of a good so as to prolong the savoring of future consumption.

Exercise 6.9 — TV Guides. All 10 episodes of a new season of your favorite streaming TV show will be released tomorrow. Discuss both your plans for TV watching and your actual TV watching tomorrow under each of the following preferences.

a   Habit-forming preferences with

   1   time consistency;
   2   present-biased naivete; and
   3   present-biased sophistication.

b   Anticipatory model of preferences.

Exercise 6.10 — Shockingly Bad Timing (Loewenstein 1987). Consider the timing of a future bad outcome ($v < 0$), like receiving a non-lethal, but strong electric shock. Figure 6.6 shows two possible plots of $U(T, v)$, as given by equation (6.8).

a   If $U(T, v)$ looks like curve C, when is the optimal time T to receive the shock? If $U(T, v)$ looks like curve D, when is the optimal time T to receive the shock?

b   Now suppose you must receive the shock by period 9 at the latest. Re-answer the two questions from part (a) given this constraint.

c   Observe that $U(T, v)$ looks like curve C if and only if $U(1, v) < U(0, v)$. Apply equation (6.8) to this inequality to derive a bound on A for which $U(T, v)$ looks like curve *C*. Provide intuition for the connection between this condition and your results in parts (a) and (b).

Exercise 6.11 — That's Two Bad. Explain how the anticipatory model can simultaneously predict that individuals 1) want to get a bad outcome over with quickly (like paying a parking ticket) and also 2) want to delay a bad outcome (like visiting the doctor after observing possible skin cancer symptoms). *Hint: Apply your insights from Exercise 6.10.*

Exercise 6.12 — Timing is Everything. [Calculus Required] Consider a good future outcome with payoff $v > 0$ in T periods and per-period discount factor $\delta = 0.9$. Suppose that you can choose how long to delay the good outcome.

a Use calculus to determine the length of delay T that maximizes the anticipatory utility function in equation (6.8). Your answer will depend on *A*. *Hint: If $f(T) = b^T$, then $f'(T) = \ln(b) \cdot b^T$. Also note that we are implicitly assuming in this calculation that* T *is a real number, even though the chapter assumes that* T *is an integer.*

b How does the optimal delay T that you found in part (a) depend on the intensity of anticipation *A*? Does greater anticipation induce the individual to speed up or delay the outcome? Provide intuition.

Notes

1 See Duesenberry (1952) for the first economic consideration of habit formation and Pollak (1970) and Ryder and Heal (1973) for early formal treatments.
2 Formally, u_t is only defined over discrete periods, but Figure 6.3 graphs u_t as if time were continuous for easier visualization.
3 The sign effect and magnitude effect are alternatively explained by assuming a reference-dependent utility function (Loewenstein and Prelec 1992; al-Nowaihi and Dhami 2009).
4 It also follows from algebra that $\delta = 0.25 - A_G$. We therefore need $A_G < 0.25$, so that $0 < \delta < 0.25$.
5 Although the empirical evidence in Section 4.4 emphasized preferences over sequences of outcomes, in the present section we consider a simpler context in which preferences are defined over the timing of a single good or bad outcome relative to the status quo.
6 We restrict attention to the preferred delay period only from the perspective of period 0. That is, we ignore the possible time inconsistency by which an individual might prefer to change the timing of the outcome as it approaches. This is consistent with the types of decisions faced by participants in the experiments documenting a preference for improvement.
7 Formally, $U(T, v)$ is only defined at integer values of T, but for ease of visualization, we treat the graph of $U(T, v)$ as the smooth interpolation through the function's discrete values.

References

Becker, Gary S., Michael Grossman, and Kevin M. Murphy. 1994. "An Empirical Analysis of Cigarette Addiction." *American Economic Review* 84 (3): 396–418.

Becker, Gary S., and Kevin M. Murphy. 1988. "A Theory of Rational Addiction." *Journal of Political Economy* 96 (4): 675–700.

Boonn, Ann. 2020. *State Excise Tax Rates & Rankings*. Updated June 29, 2020, https://www.tobaccofreekids.org/assets/factsheets/0097.pdf.

Caplin, Andrew, and John Leahy. 2001. "Psychological Expected Utility Theory and Anticipatory Feelings." *The Quarterly Journal of Economics* 116 (1): 55–79. doi:10.1162/003355301556347.

Carrera, Mariana, Heather Royer, Mark Stehr, and Justin Sydnor. 2018. "Can Financial Incentives Help People Trying to Establish New Habits? Experimental Evidence with New Gym Members." *Journal of Health Economics* 58: 202–214. doi:10.1016/j. jhealeco.2018.02.010.

CDC (Centers for Disease Control and Prevention). 2019. *Smoking & Tobacco Use Fact Facts.* Last Reviewed May 21, 2020, https://www.cdc.gov/tobacco/data_statistics/fact_sheets/fast_facts/index.htm.

Chaloupka, Frank J., Matthew R. Levy, and Justin S. White. 2019. "Estimating Biases in Smoking Cessation: Evidence from a Field Experiment." NBER Working Paper 26522. Cambridge, MA: National Bureau of Economic Research. doi:10.3386/w26522.

Charness, Gary, and Uri Gneezy. 2009. "Incentives to Exercise." *Econometrica* 77 (3): 909–931. doi:10.3982/ECTA7416.

CIA (Central Intelligence Agency). 2019. *The World Factbook: Suffrage Status by Country.* Accessed September 12, 2019, https://www.cia.gov/library/publications/the-world-factbook/fields/311.html.

Downs, Anthony. 1957. *An Economic Theory of Democracy.* New York: Harper Collins.

Duesenberry, James. 1952. *Income, Saving, and the Theory of Consumer Behavior.* Cambridge, MA: Harvard University Press.

Engelberg, Joseph, and Christopher A. Parsons. 2016. "Worrying about the Stock Market: Evidence from Hospital Admissions." *The Journal of Finance* 71 (3): 1227–1250. doi:10.1111/jofi.12386.

Facione, Noreen C. 1993. "Delay versus Help Seeking for Breast Cancer Symptoms: A Critical Review of the Literature on Patient and Provider Delay." *Social Science & Medicine* 36 (12): 1521–1534. doi:10.1016/0277-9536(93)90340-A.

Fujiwara, Thomas, Kyle Meng, and Tom Vogl. 2016. "Habit Formation in Voting: Evidence from Rainy Elections." *American Economic Journal: Applied Economics* 8 (4): 160–188. doi:10.1257/app.20140533.

Gruber, Jonathan. 2001. "Tobacco at the Crossroads: The Past and Future of Smoking Regulation in the United States." *Journal of Economic Perspectives* 15 (2): 193–212. doi:10.1257/jep.15.2.193.

Gruber, Jonathan H., and Sendhil Mullainathan. 2005. "Do Cigarette Taxes Make Smokers Happier." *The B.E. Journal of Economic Analysis & Policy* 5 (1). doi:10.2202/1538-0637.1412.

Gruber, Jonathan, and Botond Köszegi. 2001. "Is Addiction Rational? Theory and Evidence." *The Quarterly Journal of Economics* 116 (4): 1261–1303. doi:10.1162/003355301753265570.

Hussam, Reshmaan, Atonu Rabbani, Giovanni Reggiani, and Natalia Rigol. 2017. "Habit Formation and Rational Addiction: A Field Experiment in Handwashing." SSRN Scholarly Paper ID 3040729. Rochester, NY: Social Science Research Network. https://papers.ssrn.com/abstract=3040729.

Jevons, William Stanley. 1905. *Theory of Political Economy.* London: Macmillan. Original publication date: 1871.

Köszegi, Botond. 2003. "Health Anxiety and Patient Behavior." *Journal of Health Economics* 22 (6): 1073–1084. Reprinting from p 1079, Copyright (2003), with permission from Elsevier, doi:10.1016/j.jhealeco.2003.06.002.

Lerman, Caryn, Chanita Hughes, Bruce J. Trock, Ronald E. Myers, David Main, Aba Bonney, Mohammad R. Abbazadegan, et al. 1999. "Genetic Testing in Families with Hereditary Nonpolyposis Colon Cancer." *JAMA* 281 (17): 1618–1622. doi:10.1001/jama.281.17.1618.

Lerman, Caryn, Steven Narod, Kevin Schulman, Chanita Hughes, Andres Gomez-Caminero, George Bonney, Karen Gold, et al. 1996. "BRCA1 Testing in Families With Hereditary Breast-Ovarian Cancer: A Prospective Study of Patient Decision Making and Outcomes." *JAMA* 275 (24): 1885–1892. doi:10.1001/jama.1996.03530480027036.

Lodge, Guy, and Sarah Birch. 2012. "The Case for Compulsory Voting." *New Statesman,* April 28, 2012. https://www.newstatesman.com/blogs/politics/2012/04/case-compulsory-voting.

Loewenstein, George. 1987. "Anticipation and the Valuation of Delayed Consumption." *The Economic Journal* 97 (387): 666–684. By permission of the Royal Economic Society, doi:10.2307/2232929.

Loewenstein, George, and Drazen Prelec. 1992. "Anomalies in Intertemporal Choice: Evidence and an Interpretation." *The Quarterly Journal of Economics* 107 (2): 573–597. doi:10.2307/2118482.

McDonald, Michael P. 2019. *United States Elections Project.* Accessed August 12, 2019, http://www.electproject.org/.

Meechan, Geraldine, John Collins, and Keith Petrie. 2002. "Delay in Seeking Medical Care for Self-detected Breast Symptoms in New Zealand Women." *The New Zealand Medical Journal* 115 (1166).

al-Nowaihi, Ali, and Sanjit Dhami. 2009. "A Value Function that Explains the Magnitude and Sign Effects." *Economics Letters* 105 (3): 224–229. doi:10.1016/j.econlet. 2009.08.004.

O'Donoghue, Ted, and Matthew Rabin. 1999. "Addiction and Self-Control." In *Addiction: Entries and Exits,* edited by Jon Elster, 331. New York: Russell Sage Foundation.

Pollak, Robert A. 1970. "Habit Formation and Dynamic Demand Functions." *Journal of Political Economy* 78 (4, Part 1): 745–763. doi:10.1086/259667.

Ryder, Harl E., and Geoffrey M. Heal. 1973. "Optimal Growth with Intertemporally Dependent Preferences." *The Review of Economic Studies* 40 (1): 1–31. doi:10.2307/2296736.

Wolff, Edward N. 2017. "Household Wealth Trends in the United States, 1962 to 2016: Has Middle Class Wealth Recovered?" NBER Working Paper 24085. Cambridge, MA: National Bureau of Economic Research. doi:10.3386/w24085.

7 Market & Policy Responses to Present Bias

Learning Objectives

★ Understand how selling to present-biased consumers impacts profit-maximizing pricing strategies.

★ Consider the evidence of default effects and the implications for both firm behavior and public policy.

★ Evaluate the tradeoffs of both nudges and taxes as policies aimed at promoting welfare for populations with standard and present-biased consumers.

Imagine that a health club has hired you as a consultant. The club is looking to you for pricing guidance. They don't know if they should set a single price per visit for everyone, or offer customers the opportunity to sign up as members and pay a monthly fee to gain unlimited access. They also want advice on how high to set prices. In order to answer these questions you must first learn about the preferences of the health club's customers. How is your pricing recommendation different for time-consistent customers versus naive or sophisticated customers with present bias?

Or perhaps you have just opened a new coffee shop. When setting up your register you have the option of selecting default tip suggestions. Does suggesting a 15%, 20%, or 25% tip matter for how much your customers will actually tip on their latte and cookie order? And if it does matter, what would you do?

You may alternatively find yourself working as a policy maker in the government or at a think tank concerned with the rising obesity rate. For which types of policies might you advocate to encourage individuals to exercise more and eat fewer calories? And how do your recommendations depend on whether or not individuals are time-consistent?

This chapter explores the answers to these motivating questions. We begin with an examination of profit-maximizing pricing behavior when consumers are present-biased. We then consider the evidence that default options have a significant impact on behavior. This evidence can be explained by present-biased preferences and has implications for both profit-maximizing firms and policy. We conclude with an analysis of policy that can take the form of a nudge or tax, as applied to discouraging consumption of "sin" goods like unhealthy food.

DOI: 10.4324/9780367854072-9

7.1   Two-Part Tariffs

For many goods and services, you pay a price per unit. Each apple and gallon of gas is the same price no matter how many units you buy. There are also subscription services for television, music, and phones in which you do not pay per show, song, or chat, but instead pay a fixed monthly fee that gives you unlimited access. And if you have ever been to a county fair, you have seen a hybrid of these two pricing schemes — you pay an entrance fee to get into the fair, but then also pay an additional price for each amusement ride. This last case is an example of what is called a **two-part tariff** because the fair is charging a price with two parts (we can think of tariff as a synonym for price here). The first part is the entrance or access fee and the second part is the price per unit of consumption. In fact, we can even think of the pricing of apples as a simple two-part tariff where the access fee is zero. And the subscription service is a two-part tariff where the per-unit price is zero.

Two-part tariffs are widespread, at least when companies have market power. We see this type of pricing at gyms and country clubs where members pay a monthly or annual fee to access the facility, but then also pay per visit or round of golf. Bars that charge a cover fee and then also charge per drink are using a two-part tariff. Credit cards often charge an annual fee and then additional interest rates (the per-unit price) on balances that are not paid in full at the end of the billing cycle.

Notice that in each of these cases, consumers are making decisions over time. First they decide whether or not to go to the county fair or join the golf club or sign up for the credit card, and then they decide how intensively to use the product (e.g., how many rides to ride, how many days to golf, or how much to spend). In this section we apply our previous insights about intertemporal choice to understand how firms choose the profit-maximizing two-part tariff when they face standard exponential discounters, as well as possibly naive or sophisticated present-biased consumers. We also consider the welfare consequences of such pricing strategies that aim to exploit the present bias of consumers. This analysis is adapted from DellaVigna and Malmendier (2004).

7.1.1   Pricing for Time-Consistent Consumers

Let's begin by considering two-part tariff pricing for standard consumers. An amusement park faces a population of identical time-consistent customers who have the same preferences for rides. When consumers are time-consistent there is no difference between the number of rides that a customer plans to ride, expects their future self to ride, and actually rides. We can therefore represent these consistent preferences for rides with a single downward sloping demand curve — a higher per-unit price for a ride means that the customer will go on fewer rides. Such a demand curve, D, is drawn in Figure 7.1. Also assume for simplicity that the amusement park has no fixed costs and a constant marginal cost of supplying each additional ride. Finally, we assume that the park knows the demand curve for the individual, perhaps through market research.

Suppose the amusement park sets a per-ride price P above marginal cost as in Figure 7.1. Then it is earning profits on each of the Q rides demanded by the consumer, equal to the difference between the price and the marginal cost. But if the park chooses to offer a two-part tariff, an access fee will increase its profits further. How large can it set such an access fee? The firm wants to set it as high as possible without the consumer turning away from the park. Because the consumer achieves a surplus equal to the difference

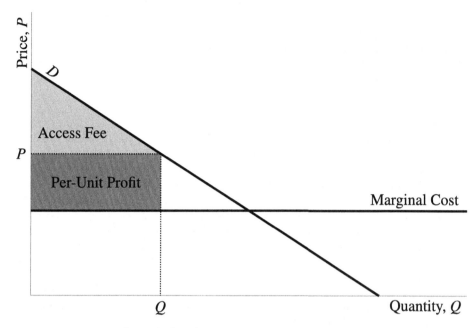

Figure 7.1 Two-Part Tariff: Standard Preferences

between what they are willing to pay (as measured by the demand curve) and the price they actually pay per ride, the park can set the access fee equal to this consumer surplus, transferring this surplus from the consumer to the park. Consumers will be left with zero consumer surplus and the park will have achieved profits from this consumer equal to the trapezoidal area between the demand curve and marginal cost curve, up to Q.

What per-unit price and access fee would lead then to the largest profits for the park? Following the logic above, since a two-part tariff allows the park to earn as profits the area between the demand curve and marginal cost curve, it wants to choose a per-unit price that maximizes this area. It should not be difficult to convince yourself that the firm maximizes profit by setting its per-unit price P^* equal to marginal cost and then charging an access fee equal to consumer surplus. This is illustrated in Figure 7.2. Although the firm is not earning any per-unit profits on each ride, it is earning large profits on the access fee.

For an amusement park like Disneyland where the marginal cost of providing an additional ride is essentially zero, this analysis suggests that they should set their price per ride at zero and instead earn their revenue from charging a high entrance fee equal to consumer surplus. This is in fact what they, and many other amusement parks, do. For bars and country clubs with market power where the marginal cost of a drink or round of golf is positive, they will maximize profit by charging both a price per unit *and* a cover or membership fee, as is common.

7.1.2   *Pricing Investment Goods for Present-Biased Consumers*

How does our analysis of profit-maximizing two-part tariffs change if consumers are present-biased? Let's consider investment goods for which there is an immediate cost and a delayed reward. Going to the gym is a classic example of such an investment

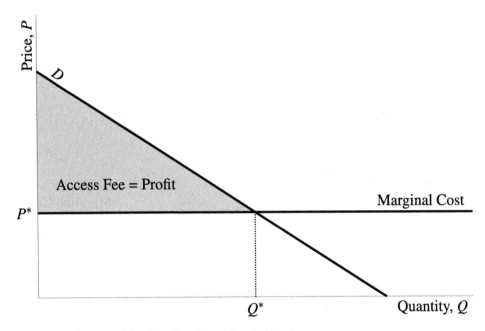

Figure 7.2 Profit-Maximizing Two-Part Tariff: Standard Preferences

good, and also a setting where we often see two-part tariffs. Should a gym still set its per-visit price equal to marginal cost if its customers are present-biased (as suggested by evidence in Section 5.4.1)? And does it matter whether customers are naive or sophisticated about their present bias?

We know from Chapter 5 that present-biased consumers underconsume investment goods relative to their plans. That is, an individual might plan to go to the gym three times per week when all of the costs and rewards of exercise are in the future, but then only go once each week when the cost of going to the gym is in the present and the health benefits remain far away.

To illustrate this wedge between what an individual plans to do and what they actually do, let's modify our two-part tariff analysis by allowing for two different demand curves. Let D_{Plan} be the individual's demand curve indicating how often they plan to go to the gym, before they have actually signed up as a member. This curve corresponds to their marginal *experienced* utility of going to the gym and is therefore relevant when determining consumer surplus. In addition, let D_{Actual} be the individual's demand curve indicating how often they actually visit the gym, which corresponds to the marginal *decision* utility of a gym visit. This demand curve is drawn to the left of D_{Plan} in Figure 7.3 because at every price, actual visits are less than planned.

Potential customers must make a decision whether or not to sign up for the gym and pay the membership fee before they decide how often to actually visit the gym. We therefore also need to consider the individual's expected demand for their future self if they join the gym. Naïfs are not aware of their present bias and therefore expect their plans for the future to be accurate. They are surprised when they use the gym so infrequently. Their expectation of future demand is D_{Plan}. Sophisticates, however, are fully aware of their present bias and expect their future demand to be D_{Actual}.

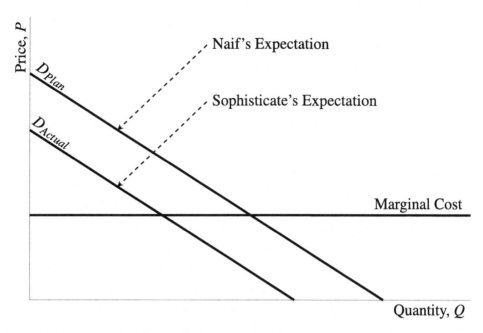

Figure 7.3 Present-Biased Preferences for Investment Good

This difference in expectations matters because when setting a two-part tariff, the gym cannot set a membership fee that exceeds an individual's consumer surplus based on their *expectation* of future use. Otherwise, the individual will reject the gym's pricing contract and not become a member. We now turn to the case for naifs, followed by sophisticates.

Naifs

Suppose the gym knows its customer is a naif and follows the profit-maximizing rule for time-consistent consumers by setting a per-visit price equal to marginal cost P^*, as in Figure 7.4. A naif expects to consume Q^*_{Plan} visits upon joining the gym and therefore expects their consumer surplus to be area $A = A_1 + A_2 + A_3$. If the gym charges this area as its fee, the naif will join and the gym's profit on this customer will be A.

Can the gym make even more money from this customer? Suppose they lower the per-visit price below marginal cost to P^L. In this case the naif expects to consume Q^L_{Plan} visits, yielding an expected consumer surplus of $A + B + C$. The gym can charge a membership fee equal to this expected consumer surplus. But because they are pricing below marginal cost they lose money on each actual visit of the naif to the gym. The naif actually visits only Q^L_{Actual} times, generating a loss to the gym equal to area B. Subtracting this loss from the membership fee, the gym's total profit from the customer is $A+C$. By lowering its per-visit price the gym has increased its profits by C.

This surprising result is due to the naif's overestimation of their future behavior. Because they believe they will go to the gym more often than they actually do, they expect their consumer surplus to also be larger than it actually will be. The gym can exploit this misperception and lower the per-visit price, inflating the naif's expected consumer surplus, and increasing their willingness to pay for an upfront membership fee.

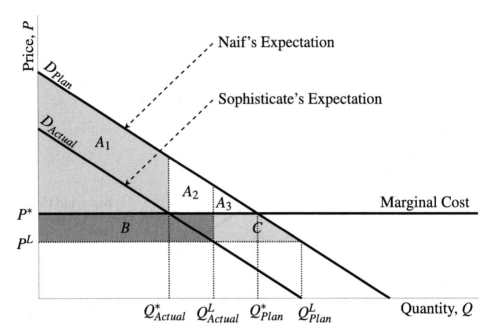

Figure 7.4 Two-Part Tariff on Investment Good: Present-Biased Preferences

The gain from this higher membership fee offsets the loss from lowering the per-visit fee because the naif does not actually visit very often.

What is the naif's actual consumer surplus under this two-part tariff? Because they visit only Q^L_{Actual} times, their consumer surplus is $A_1 + A_2 + B$ minus the membership fee of $A + B + C$. Consumer surplus is therefore negative, and equal to $-(A_3 + C)$. They would be better off rejecting the contract, but they do not realize this when joining.

Sophisticates

Now suppose the gym faces a sophisticate. If it sets a per-visit price equal to P^*, the sophisticate correctly expects their future consumption to be Q^*_{Actual} and consumer surplus to be A_1. The gym therefore charges A_1 as the membership fee and makes A_1 in total profit.

Once again, let's see what happens if the gym were to lower its per-visit price to P^L. The sophisticate expects their future consumption to be Q^L_{Actual}, with a corresponding expected consumer surplus of $A_1 + A_2 + B$. The gym's profit on this customer is then equal to the fee (which equals the expected consumer surplus of $A_1 + A_2 + B$) minus the loss on each of the sophisticate's visits (B). The net profits are therefore $A_1 + A_2$. The gym has increased its profits by A_2.

This result is perhaps even more surprising than for the naif. Sophisticates do not over-estimate their future behavior and yet the gym is still able to increase its profits by charging a per-visit price below marginal cost. The key insight to make sense of this result is that sophisticates demand commitment strategies to help them better align their actual consumption with planned consumption. In this case they are willing to pay a higher membership fee up front in return for a lower per-visit price, which will help them

Table 7.1 Summary Analysis of Two-Part Tariffs for Investment Goods

	Naif		Sophisticate	
Per-Unit Price	P^*	P^L	P^*	P^L
Expected Q	Q^*_{Plan}	Q^L_{Plan}	Q^*_{Actual}	Q^L_{Actual}
Expected Consumer Surplus = Access Fee	A	$A + B + C$	A_1	$A_1 + A_2 + B$
Actual Q	Q^*_{Actual}	Q^L_{Actual}	Q^*_{Actual}	Q^L_{Actual}
Profit	$A \quad < $	$A + C$	$A_1 \quad <$	$A_1 + A_2$
Actual Consumer Surplus (Net of Access Fee)	$-(A_2 + A_3)$	$-(A_3 + C)$	0	0

Notes: Entries refer to the prices, quantities, and areas labeled in Figure 7.4. $A = A_1 + A_2 + A_3$.

commit to more frequent gym attendance. Otherwise, without the lower price, they rightly know that their future selves will not go as often as they had planned. The value to the consumer of increasing their gym use is transferred to the gym via a higher membership fee, the magnitude of which outweighs the gym's loss on lowering its price.

Does the sophisticate, like the naif, regret choosing this two-part tariff? No. The sophisticate is indifferent between choosing and rejecting the two-part tariff because the membership fee exactly equals their actual consumer surplus, yielding a net zero consumer surplus after the fee is paid. Sophistication therefore prevents the negative consumer surplus that the naif experiences.

The foregoing analysis of profit maximizing two part tariffs for investment goods is summarized in Table 7.1. Exercise 7.1 asks you to repeat the analysis of two-part tariffs for the case of leisure goods like credit cards, where the benefit of consumption is immediate and the high interest payments are delayed.

Evidence

The above analysis provides a theoretical rationale for profit-maximizing firms to set per-unit prices below their marginal cost. That is, if they have reason to believe that their customers are either naifs or sophisticates, they can exploit the present bias for profit. There is evidence that some firms may be doing just this. Let's consider evidence from gyms and vacation timeshares.

In their study on gym memberships, DellaVigna and Malmendier (2004) estimate the marginal cost of a gym visit to be \$3–\$6, capturing the costs of providing towels, maintaining gym equipment, and paying employees. Given that many gyms offer two-part tariffs with a positive monthly access fee and zero per-visit price, these gyms are pricing visits \$3–\$6 below marginal cost. This evidence suggests that gyms are aware of their customers' self-control problems and have designed contracts to maximize their profits.

Planning a vacation is another example of an investment activity with immediate costs (e.g., logistics and payments), followed by the delayed reward of the actual vacation. One popular way for individuals to take vacations is by purchasing a timeshare, which allows a one-week stay at a resort condominium each year. This is a multi-billion dollar industry in the United States. Timeshares are priced as a two-part tariff — there is an initial fee followed by an annual price for property maintenance. When selling to naifs who over-estimate how often they will use the timeshare, or sophisticates who know they will not take vacations as often as they would like unless the per-vacation price is low, timeshare companies have an incentive to set an annual price below marginal cost and a high initial fee. According to the American Resort Development Association, in 2018 the average annual price was under $1,000 (likely below marginal cost) and the average initial fee was a staggering $22,180. This pricing appears consistent with the predictions of our model.

7.2   Defaults

Suppose you are signing up for a new social media service. All of your posts will be shared with everyone else using the platform, as well as advertisers. But because the social media company values your privacy, they make it easy for you to limit others' access to your content (e.g., with only your friends, with your friends and friends of your friends, etc.). Think about how you might control your privacy in this setting.

Now imagine that when signing up for the social media service all of your posts are automatically private and only visible to you. The point of course is to be somewhat social, so the company makes it easy for you to select who is permitted to access your content. Would the access you provide to others be the same as in the first scenario above?

Because you have the same options in both scenarios, standard economic theory predicts that individuals would share the same amount of information, regardless of whether they opted out of sharing everything or opted in to sharing something. But in a lab experiment that surveyed college students to answer exactly these questions, students on average shared a third more information in the first case when the option was to limit access than in the second case when the option was to grant access (Steffel, Williams, and Pogacar 2016).

When Walt Disney World changed its default sides and beverages for kids' meals to healthier options — without preventing anyone from choosing the less healthy french fries and soda — consumption of calories, fat, and sodium all decreased (Peters et al. 2016).

In both of these examples, the **default** option acts like a magnet — choices appear to be attracted to the default. If the default is to share data widely, people share more data than if the default were to keep data private. Individuals are more likely to choose the default sides and beverages, whatever they happen to be.

The power of defaults to change behavior is an important insight. It is so significant because defaults are seemingly irrelevant in the individual decision problem. And yet, we find examples everywhere in which behavior is predictably shifted by defaults. They are the most well-known form of a nudge (Section 3.4).

How can we make sense of default effects? Based on where we are in this book, it should not come as a surprise that they are predicted by naive present-biased preferences.[1] To see why, think of the decision to choose a non-default option as an investment activity. The benefits of choosing the most preferred privacy settings, for instance, are not realized until the future, while the small cost of filling out a privacy checklist is immediate. From the Doing it Once model (Section 5.3) we know that naifs procrastinate doing investment activities. A naif might each day plan to update their privacy settings tomorrow, only to put it off day after day. In fact, O'Donoghue and Rabin (2001) show that even a small degree of self-control problems with naivete can induce *infinite* procrastination.

A present-biased sophisticate is not predicted to be as influenced by defaults. Although sophisticates can also procrastinate, their procrastination is less severe because they realize that if they want a non-default option and do not make that choice quickly, they will keep putting it off. We therefore expect them to act more like time-consistents and choose their most preferred option with minimal delay, independent of the default. The empirical evidence of strong default effects is therefore more consistent with naivete.

7.2.1 Suggested Tips   *[Industrial Organization]*

In the previous section we saw how firms can adjust prices to achieve higher profits when faced with present-biased consumers. But are there other ways a firm could profit from their customers' present bias without changing prices?

One strategy would be to leverage default effects. It is common in many retail environments, like cafes, for customers to be prompted upon paying with a credit card to select a tip amount from a touch screen. After ordering a latte, for example, you might be prompted to tip 15%, 20%, or 25%, or to enter a custom tip amount. We can think of the suggested tip percentages as a menu of defaults. For customers who want to tip at one of these amounts, it is quite easy to tap the desired amount. But if you want to tip 10% or 18% you have to take a few seconds to enter a custom tip.

Because you always have the option of choosing your own desired tip, standard economics predicts that changing the default tip options should have no effect on actual tipping behavior. But in a world where at least some customers only select from the default options, a business might find it profitable to increase their default tips. Let's consider some evidence from the field.

Field Experiment — Tipping Taxis (Haggag and Paci 2014)

In 2004 New York City mandated that taxi cabs allow riders to pay with a credit card. By 2008 all taxi cabs had installed credit card machines that displayed the base fare on a payment screen at the end of a ride. Before paying, riders were prompted to enter a tip or select one of three suggested default tips.

A large share of taxi cabs were outfitted with credit card machines that suggested different tips based on the fare. For fares under $15, the tip suggestions were $2, $3, or $4. But for fares over $15, the suggestions were 20%, 25%, or 30%. This creates a jump in the suggested tips for fares just below and above $15. The table below shows how the suggested tips change for similar fares near the $15 cutoff.

Base Fare	Low Tip	Medium Tip	High Tip
$14.90	**$2.00** (13%)	**$3.00** (20%)	**$4.00** (27%)
$15.10	$3.02 (**20%**)	$3.78 (**25%**)	$4.53 (**30%**)

Haggag and Paci (2014) analyze data on all licensed taxi rides in 2009 paid via credit card with the above tip suggestions — a total of over 7 million rides.

Figure 7.5 shows the average tip percentage for base fares between $5 and $25. The key takeaway from the figure is the discontinuous increase in the tip percentage from fares just below to just above $15. If riders had ignored the default tip suggestions, and simply entered custom tips at the level they thought was appropriate, then the average tip percentage should have changed smoothly. We observe such smooth changes in the tip percentage everywhere except at $15. The only thing that changes for riders at a fare of $15 is the default tip suggestions. We can therefore be confident that the increased tipping is caused by the higher default tips. In fact, the researchers estimate that the higher suggested tips increased tips by 10%.

Does the evidence that higher default tips increase tipping imply that businesses should start raising their default tip amounts ever higher and higher? If default effects exist, then this appears to be the profit-maximizing response. One important consideration, however, is that customers may react negatively to very high tip suggestions that are outside social norms of acceptable tipping behavior and respond by tipping nothing. Indeed, Haggag and Paci (2014) find that the increase in tip suggestions for taxi cab fares above $15 increased the probability that riders tipped nothing. A local business might therefore want to tread lightly when deciding how high to raise suggested tips, so as not to insult its customers. We return to such issues of reciprocity in Part V.

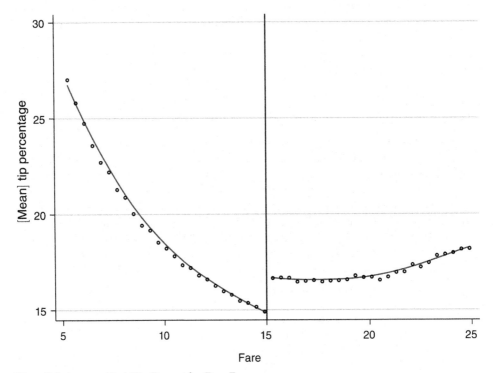

Figure 7.5 Average Taxi Tip Percent by Base Fare

Source: Haggag and Paci (2014). Copyright American Economic Association; reproduced with permission of the *American Economic Journal: Applied Economics*.

7.2.2 Organ Donations [Health]

Beyond increasing business profits, defaults can also be leveraged as a policy tool to promote social welfare. Let's see how default effects can help save lives.

The Organ Shortage

Over 100,000 people in the United States are on the waiting list for a lifesaving organ transplant, particularly a kidney (UNOS 2020). Economists, health professionals, and philosophers have all suggested ways to increase the supply of organs for donation. Economists see the introduction of financial incentives for living donors (most people have two kidneys and need only one) as a possible solution to reduce the waiting list (Becker and Elias 2007). Iran allows financial incentives and there have been experiments in the Philippines and China, but in most of the world financial incentives are banned. The prohibition on market exchange of organs is motivated by ethical concerns about treating the human body as a commodity and the potential exploitation of the poor to provide organs for the rich. In response, some economists have considered non-financial incentives to encourage organ donation, such as giving priority on waiting lists to those who have previously registered as donors (Kessler and Roth 2012).

Defaulting Donations

Instead of relying on incentives (financial or otherwise) to encourage donations, let's consider the impact of default policies for organ donations. Some countries like the United States require *explicit* consent to be an organ donor — the default is that no citizen is an organ donor until they register to be one. Most US states make it easy to register as an organ donor by filling out a short form online or in person. Other countries operate under a *presumed* consent system in which everyone is a donor unless they register not to be one. In both systems individuals have the same choice set and the cost of changing one's donor status is small. Standard economic theory therefore predicts that the default should have very little impact (if at all) on the decision to register as a donor.

In a survey of European countries, Johnson and Goldstein (2003) find that while the average consent rate is 15% in explicit consent countries, it is 98% in presumed consent countries. The country-specific consent rates are depicted in Figure 7.6. Defaults clearly matter in this context. Note that because consent is necessary, but not sufficient for donations to actually occur (e.g., family objections and organ incompatibility can prevent consenting donors from donating), the gap in consent rates overstates the impact of defaults on donations. Yet, Johnson and Goldstein (2003) still find that presumed consent increases the donation rate by 16%. This evidence suggests that switching from explicit to presumed consent could be a life-saving policy change.

7.2.3 Retirement Savings [Public Finance]

Workers typically aim to retire in their sixties, leaving time to enjoy a work-free life in older age. Achieving this goal requires individuals to save for retirement throughout their working life. Many rich countries also provide income support for the elderly, as Social Security does in the United States. But are there other policies, like defaults and nudges, that could help individuals save? Before answering this question, let's first review some features of retirement savings.

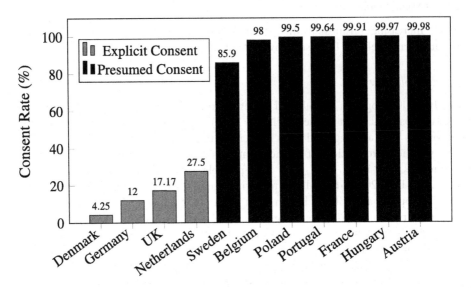

Figure 7.6 Organ Donation Consent Rates by Country
Data Source: Johnson and Goldstein (2003).

United States Retirement Savings

Americans can save for retirement by making use of individual retirement accounts that provide tax advantages. One type of account is an employer-sponsored 401(k) plan, named after the corresponding section of the US tax code. A 401(k) plan works as follows: employees allocate a portion of their pre-tax earnings to an account that offers a menu of stocks and bonds in which to invest. Employers can encourage such savings by matching employee contributions up to some limit. As an example, an employer might offer a 50% match on the first $5,000 of employee contributions each year. For an employee saving at least $5,000 in their 401(k) in a given year, the employer contributes an extra $2,500 to their account. The invested money then accumulates over time to be withdrawn and spent later in life. There is also a 10% penalty if 401(k) balances are withdrawn before age $59\frac{1}{2}$, so as to discourage workers from consuming their savings before retirement.

Financial planners often provide rules of thumb to help people decide how much they should be contributing to their 401(k) or other retirement accounts so as to smooth their consumption spending into retirement. Some planners recommend saving 15% of your salary each year. Others make benchmark recommendations, like achieving total savings equal to your salary by age 30, six times your salary by age 50, and ten times your salary by retirement. This may sound high, but revisit Example 4.1, where the life-cycle model predicts that in the last year of employment, the standard decision maker accumulates savings equal to 11.2 times annual salary. In contrast, 41% of Americans aged 55–64 have zero savings in retirement accounts. And among the remaining 59% with some retirement savings, a quarter of them have saved less than $26,000 (GAO 2015). This is definitely nowhere near ten times a typical worker's salary.

Retirement income is supplemented by Social Security benefits. Social Security is a pay-as-you-go program in which current workers and employers contribute a share of wages to a government fund that pays benefits to current retirees. Although Social Security benefits are modest, replacing less than 40% of pre-retirement earnings for the average worker, they are responsible for lifting millions of the elderly out of poverty (CBPP 2020). And because many Americans do not save much, if at all, for retirement, these benefits account for a large share of total income for individuals over 65. For half of the elderly population, Social Security benefits account for at least 50% of total family income and for half of this population, the benefits exceed 90% of total family income (Dushi, Iams, and Trenkamp 2017).

Defaulting Savings

What is to be done from a policy perspective about the meager retirement savings of the average American, which limits their ability to smooth consumption into retirement? One reaction is to do nothing, trusting that individuals are consistently saving exactly what they intend and cannot be made better off. The observed low savings rates could reflect high discount rates in the standard Discounted Utility model — people simply prefer to save little for retirement so as to enjoy present consumption.

But the evidence suggests that typical savings behavior may be better explained by present-biased preferences (Section 5.4.3). In this case, individuals suffer from self-control problems and save less than they intend, leading to individual welfare losses. A paternalistic government intervention that aims to make people better off is now justified. The forced savings required of Social Security can be understood as exactly such an intervention.

In reality, there are likely some of us who are time-consistent savers and others who experience self-control problems of varying degrees. Defaults (and nudges more generally) make for an appealing policy tool in this case because they have the potential to help those with self-control problems align their actual savings with their planned savings, while simultaneously maintaining a full unaltered set of options for those who are already saving as they desire. Social Security, conversely, does not permit individuals to save less for retirement than required by law. Let's see if, and how, defaults impact savings behavior.

Quasi-Experiment — 401(k) Default (Madrian and Shea 2001)

A publicly traded Fortune 500 company offered its employees a 401(k) plan with a match that worked as follows: for every dollar that a worker put into their 401(k) account, the company pitched in an additional $0.50, but stopped matching once the employee had contributed 6% of their salary.

The company changed its default 401(k) participation for new employees on April 1, 1998, without changing any of the contribution rules or the types of employees hired:

- Before April 1: Default for new hires was nonparticipation in the 401(k).
- After April 1: New hires were automatically defaulted into contributing 3% of their salary to the 401(k).

All employees, regardless of their hiring date, had the option to override the default with a phone call or by filling out a form.

The change in participation default creates a quasi-experiment. In particular, any difference in the 401(k) participation rates for employees hired just before and just after April 1, 1998 must be due to the change in default.

Madrian and Shea (2001) find that the 401(k) plan participation rate was 37% among employees with the nonparticipation default, but 86% for employees with the participation default. The default clearly matters.

What can we infer from the above evidence about the share of employees who are naifs versus time-consistents (for simplicity, ignore sophisticates who are predicted to behave similarly to time-consistents)? Naifs are predicted to follow the default, whatever it is, because they always procrastinate initiating a change (Exercise 7.5 asks you to verify this claim). Time-consistents would instead ignore the default and participate in the 401(k) if and only if the benefits outweigh the costs. Because the behavior of the time-consistents is the same regardless of the default, the difference in participation rates with different defaults is entirely due to the naifs. In particular, the share of employees who are naifs must equal 49% — the difference between 86% participation with the participation default and 37% participation with the nonparticipation default. The other 51% of employees are therefore time-consistent. And finally, because the time-consistents are the only participants with the nonparticipation default, 73% (= 37%/ 51%) of them chose to participate.

Madrian and Shea (2001) is a highly influential study that prompted a series of follow-up analyses investigating the power of defaults to impact savings behavior. Across different industries and countries, there is consistent evidence that 40%–50% of individuals follow the savings default (e.g., Choi et al. 2004; Cronqvist and Thaler 2004). Setting a default is therefore a policy choice of great consequence for welfare. And the optimal 401(k) default depends on both the nature and distribution of worker preferences (Carroll et al. 2009; Bernheim, Fradkin, and Popov 2015).

Nudging Beyond Defaults

As an alternative to defaults, let's consider two other nudges that can empower naifs to overcome their self-control problems: financial education and precommitment strategies.

A reasonable hypothesis for why savings rates are low is that deciding how to save for retirement is simply too complex of a problem. Under this hypothesis, if individuals had better access to financial education and personalized recommendations from qualified experts, then they would more clearly understand the significant benefits of contributing to an individual retirement account throughout their life, and act accordingly.

The evidence suggests that the effect of such financial education is quite modest. Duflo and Saez (2003) conduct a field experiment at a large university and find that only 12% of non-contributing individuals who attended an informational benefits fair start contributing to their retirement account in the months after the fair. This is significantly lower than the additional 40%–50% of employees who start contributing when the default changes to automatic enrollment.

What might explain this limited effectiveness of financial education? Contributing to an individual retirement account imposes an immediate cost and a delayed benefit.

Suppose financial education increases the perceived magnitude of the delayed benefit. Then workers not contributing to their 401(k) plan should become more inclined to contribute. In fact, Choi et al. (2002) report that 100% of non-401(k) participants who attended a financial seminar reported that they planned to enroll in the 401(k). But only 14% actually enrolled. While this gap between plans and actions is not predicted by time-consistent preferences, it is exactly what we expect with present-biased preferences. Increasing the perceived magnitude of a delayed benefit shifts one's current plans for the future, but has only a muted effect on actions when the benefit is heavily discounted relative to the more immediate cost of reducing consumption today.

To help individuals align their plans with their actual behavior, Thaler and Benartzi (2004) propose a precommitment savings program that goes beyond education. It is cleverly named the Save More Tomorrow™ (SMarT) Program and works as follows. Employees who sign up for the program agree to have a small portion of their salary invested in their 401(k) beginning with their first paycheck following a raise. If, for instance, the employee receives a raise of 3% at the end of the year, this triggers an automatic 1% contribution to her 401(k). Her paycheck then increases by only 2%, with the other 1% going to savings. In some sense, her retirement savings are hidden from her. And as she receives additional raises in the future, her 401(k) contribution rate is also increased up to a preset maximum. The program still permits employees to exit at any time.

As opposed to simply enrolling in a 401(k) plan today, committing to the SMarT program does not trigger an immediate cost. The cost of taking money out of your paycheck to fund a retirement account is delayed to a future date. And when both costs and benefits are delayed, our theory predicts present-biased individuals to act consistently with their plans to save.

For employees at a midsize manufacturing company who enrolled in the SMarT program, 80% remained enrolled after four pay raises. And by the fourth raise, savings rates for these employees had increased from 3.5% to 13.6% (Thaler and Benartzi 2004). This dramatic increase in savings rates illustrates the power of leveraging behavioral economics insights to design policies that can help individuals realize welfare gains.

7.3   Nudging and Taxing Sin Goods

Saving for retirement is not the only setting where we might be concerned that individuals are making mistakes. Consider the consumption of non-essential foods and beverages that are high in calories, sugar, salt, or fat. Increased calorie consumption has been a primary driver of the growing obesity rate in America (Cutler, Glaeser, and Shapiro 2003). And with obesity comes a greater risk of diabetes, heart disease, and certain cancers. The annual cost of treating obesity in the United States accounts for over 16% of the total spending on all medical care (Cawley and Meyerhoefer 2012).

If individuals have self-control problems and overconsume calories, then there is a justification for paternalistic policies that help align actual behavior with desired behavior. In fact, the World Health Organization has urged countries to introduce policies aimed at reducing obesity rates. Hungary and Mexico have introduced taxes on unhealthy foods and beverages. And the United States has banned artificial trans fats in processed foods.

In this section we consider the design of policy directed at reducing consumption of unhealthy "sin" goods when at least some, but not all, of the population is present-biased. We assume away any possible externalities from consumption of sin goods, so as to focus exclusively on the paternalistic motivation for policy. For concreteness, the two specific policies we consider are a dessert nudge and a cookie tax. But the insights apply more generally to other sin goods.

7.3.1　Welfare with Sin Goods

Sin goods are leisure goods. They generate immediate gratification from consumption followed by a delayed cost in the form of health effects. Time-consistents weigh these benefits and costs against each other and make individual welfare-maximizing choices.

With present-biased preferences, individuals make decisions as if the future health costs they will experience are smaller than they actually are. In particular, they choose consumption by maximizing decision utility, which includes their present bias. But their individual welfare is given by experienced utility, for which present bias is absent. This gap between decision and experienced utilities generates an internality (Definition 3.3). By partially ignoring the internal effects of present consumption on the health of their future self, they overconsume sin goods and realize a welfare loss.

A policy intervention aimed at reducing sin good consumption will have different welfare effects on time-consistents and present-biased consumers. To evaluate the net impact of a policy on social welfare, we adopt a utilitarian social welfare function. That is, a policy improves social welfare if it increases the sum of individual welfare across the population. And we refer to a policy as *optimal* if it generates the highest social welfare from among a set of possible policy alternatives.

7.3.2　Nudging Dessert

To illustrate the welfare effects of nudging both time-consistent and present-biased consumers, let's consider a common decision: whether or not to order dessert at a restaurant. The nudge is designed to help present-biased diners better perceive the future health costs of eating a sugary dessert (corresponding to a larger β in the model of present-biased preferences). Perhaps the nudge appears on the menu as a nutritional label or a warning about the long-run health effects of sugar consumption. Or the desserts are listed on the alcohol beverage menu, framing them as an unhealthy choice.

Although the nudge does not change the available choices or economic incentives of ordering dessert, we assume that it imposes a small psychological cost on those who choose to consume dessert; being reminded of sugar's negative health effects reduces the enjoyment of dessert consumption. Let's work through a specific nudging example (adapted from Jimenez-Gomez 2018).

■ **Example 7.1 — Dessert Nudges for All**. There are both present-biased and time-consistent consumers who are considering whether or not to purchase a $6 dessert. Our job is to evaluate the welfare impact of introducing an anti-dessert nudge.

The experienced benefit of eating dessert is equal to the immediate satisfaction minus $8 in future health costs and a $1 psychological cost of the nudge (when the nudge is in effect). Assume that time-consistents obtain $18 worth of immediate satisfaction from dessert, compared to $11 in satisfaction for present-biased consumers.

Consumers will purchase dessert as long as the decision benefit from the dessert is at least the $6 price.[2] For time-consistents, the decision benefit is equal to the experienced benefit. But for present-biased consumers, the future health costs are discounted by $\beta = 1/2$. Assume that the nudge increases β to 3/4.

In summary, the experienced and decision benefits from consumption for time-consistent and present-biased consumers (with and without the nudge) are as follows:

Benefits (in $):	No Nudge		Nudge	
	Experienced	Decision	Experienced	Decision
Time-Consistent	$18 - 8 = 10$	$18 - 8 = 10$	$18 - 8 - 1 = 9$	$18 - 8 - 1 = 9$
Present-Biased	$11 - 8 = 3$	$11 - \frac{1}{2}8 = 7$	$11 - 8 - 1 = 2$	$11 - \frac{3}{4}8 - 1 = 4$

Without the nudge, everyone consumes dessert because the decision benefits exceed the $6 price. Dessert makes the time-consistent better off because the experienced benefit of $10 exceeds the $6 price, generating a $4 welfare gain. The present-biased consumer, however, would be better off not consuming because her experienced benefit of $3 is less than the price. Her satisfaction from the dessert is not enough to make it worth eating, but she eats it anyways because she doesn't fully internalize the future health costs.

Introducing the nudge does not stop the time-consistent from eating dessert — her decision benefit of $9 still exceeds the price. But the nudge stops the present-biased consumer from choosing dessert since it lowers her decision benefit below the price to $4.

To determine whether or not it is worthwhile to implement this nudge, we must evaluate the effect of the nudge on social welfare. The social benefit of the nudge is that it stops the overconsumption of dessert by the present-biased consumers. By refraining, each of these consumers foregoes the $3 experienced benefit of consumption, but saves the $6 price. The net effect is a welfare gain of $3. The social cost of the nudge is borne by the time-consistents who endure the $1 psychological cost when eating dessert. The nudge will therefore increase utilitarian social welfare if there are enough present-biased consumers obtaining the $3 welfare benefit from the nudge to outweigh the $1 welfare cost of the nudge to each time-consistent. In particular, as long as more than 25% of the consumers are present-biased, the nudge increases social welfare.

The main takeaway from this example is that nudges can generate both welfare gains for those whose mistakes are corrected, and welfare losses for standard consumers. The net effect on social welfare depends on the magnitudes of these gains and losses, as well as the prevalence of mistakes in the population.[3] Exercise 7.9 asks you to repeat the welfare analysis in Example 7.1, but with alternative psychological nudge costs. ∎

7.3.3 Sin Taxes

Suppose that instead of nudging, the government taxes sin goods — let's call them cookies — to help present-biased consumers reduce their overconsumption. Taxes not only influence behavior, but also generate government revenue. Because nudges can impose a psychological cost on consumers without collecting any revenue in the process, taxes have this advantage over nudges (Glaeser 2005). We will verify that when there are at least some present-biased consumers, it is theoretically possible to tax cookies and return the revenue back to consumers in such a way that not only increases social welfare, but makes *each* individual better off. In contrast, recall from Example 7.1 that even if the nudge increased social welfare, it still made time-consistents worse off.

Our policy of interest is a per-unit tax t that increases the price of a cookie from $1 to $1 + t$. In addition, the government rebates back to each consumer an equal share of the

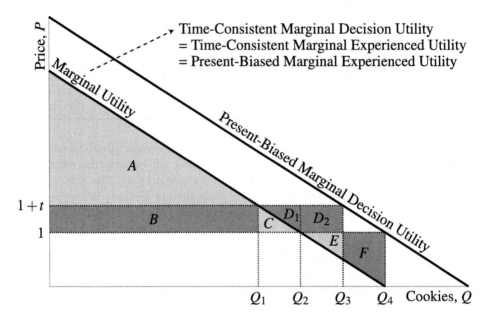

Figure 7.7 Welfare Analysis of Cookie Tax *t*

total cookie tax revenue. Notice that this rebate is the same for everyone — high cookie consumers receive the same rebate as low cookie consumers. By rebating all revenue back to consumers, the government is not making or losing money. See O'Donoghue and Rabin (2006) for a full analysis of this tax policy, from which this section is adapted.

Assume that cookie consumers all share the same marginal experienced utility from an additional cookie. For time-consistent consumers, this marginal experienced utility is also their marginal decision utility. Present-biased consumers discount future health costs by $\beta < 1$. Because these consumers do not fully internalize the future health costs they will experience from cookie consumption when making a decision, their marginal decision utility exceeds marginal experienced utility. The marginal utilities are depicted in Figure 7.7.[4]

With this figure we can evaluate the effects of the cookie tax policy on individual and social welfare. We measure individual welfare by consumer surplus — the difference between marginal experienced utility and the price for each cookie consumed — plus the tax rebate. And social welfare is utilitarian. We first consider the optimal tax that maximizes social welfare and then show how the tax policy can make everyone better off.

Optimal Tax Rate

The optimal cookie tax is straightforward to determine when all consumers share the same preferences. If everyone is time-consistent, the optimal tax is zero. Without any internalities, each time-consistent eats the number of cookies that maximizes their individual welfare. Any distortion of their behavior makes them worse off. Conversely, if everyone is equally present-biased, the optimal tax is positive and equal to the magnitude of the internality (see Exercise 7.10 to work through the details).

Given that a cookie tax makes time-consistents worse off, but can make present-biased consumers better off, what do we do when there are both types of consumers who all pay the same tax rate? It turns out that the optimal tax rate is still positive. The reason for a positive cookie tax is that the welfare gain to present-biased consumers from reducing their overconsumption of cookies is larger than the welfare loss to time-consistents whose choices are distorted by the tax.

To visualize this reasoning, let's examine the effect of a tax on individual welfare for each type of consumer separately. In particular, imagine that the government has the ability to pay an individualized rebate to each person equal to the amount they paid in cookie taxes (i.e., the rebate equals the tax rate t multiplied by the individual's cookie consumption). Although this is an unrealistic assumption, *how* government revenue is rebated paid back to consumers does not matter for social welfare here.

Consider first the time-consistent in Figure 7.7. Without the tax she consumes Q_2 cookies and achieves consumer surplus equal to the area $A+B+C$. The tax t reduces her consumption to Q_1. Her consumer surplus shrinks to A, but with an individualized rebate equal to B ($= t \times Q_1$), her welfare is $A+B$. The tax policy therefore reduces her welfare by C.

Repeating the same logic for the present-biased consumer, we observe that without the tax she consumes Q_4 cookies. On the first Q_2 cookies she achieves consumer surplus equal to $A+B+C$, but because she continues consuming cookies that provide marginal experienced utility below the price, her consumer surplus is reduced to $A+B+C-E-F$. The tax t reduces her consumption to Q_3, yielding consumer surplus $A - D_1 - D_2 - E$. But once we add the individualized rebate $B+C+D_1+D_2$ ($= t \times Q_3$), her welfare is $A+B+C - E$. The tax policy therefore increases her welfare by F. Table 7.2 summarizes.

This analysis confirms that the welfare loss for the time-consistent (equal to triangle C) is smaller than the welfare gain for the present-biased consumer (equal to trapezoid F). And it turns out that no matter how few present-biased consumers exist in the population, as long as they exist, the optimal tax rate is still positive.

The optimality of a positive tax rate does not tell us, however, how high it should be. The magnitude of the optimal tax rate can vary substantially, depending on a variety of

Table 7.2 Summary Welfare Analysis of Cookie Tax t in Figure 7.7

	Time-Consistent		*Present-Biased*	
Cookie Price	1	$1 + t$	1	$1 + t$
Quantity (Q)	Q_2	Q_1	Q_4	Q_3
Consumer Surplus	ABC	A	$ABC-E-F$	$A-D-E$
Rebate				
Individual ($t \times Q$)	0	B	0	$B + C + D$
Uniform		$B + C + D_1$		$B + C + D_1$
Welfare: Consumer Surplus +				
Individ. Rebate	ABC	$A + B$	$ABC-E-F$	$ABC-E$
Uniform Rebate		$ABC + D_1$		$ABC-E-D_2$

Notes: Entries refer to the prices, quantities, and areas labeled in Figure 7.7, with $ABC = A + B + C$ and $D = D_1 + D_2$ used for brevity of notation. Uniform rebate assumes equal numbers of time-consistent and present-biased consumers.

factors that include the prevalence of present-biased consumers, how severe the present bias is, the magnitude of future health costs, and the responsiveness of consumption to price changes. For instance, the optimal tax rate is only 5% when half the population is present-biased with $\beta = 0.99$ and the other half is time-consistent. But it jumps to over 60% when $\beta = 0.9$ for the present-biased half of the population. Intuitively, when present bias is more severe (i.e., when β is further from 1), cookie overconsumption is more severe, and corrective taxes that reduce consumption are of greater social value.

Pareto-Improving Taxes

Part of the challenge with actually implementing tax policy in the real world is that even if the policy improves social welfare, there can still be winners and losers — and the losers will protest the tax or hire lobbyists to protest on their behalf. A goal in welfare economics is therefore to find policies that, at least in theory, make everyone a winner. Recall that a Pareto improvement refers to a change in which everyone is made better off (Definition 3.5). Incredibly, there exists such a Pareto-improving cookie tax policy, as long as the present-biased consumers are sufficiently responsive to the tax.

What is the intuition for Pareto-improving taxes? First observe that time-consistents consume fewer cookies than those with present bias at every price. Therefore, when the cookie tax revenue is collected and rebated back to everyone uniformly, income is redistributed from those with self-control problems who pay more in taxes to time-consistents who pay less in taxes.

In Figure 7.7 each time-consistent pays B in taxes, while each present-biased consumer pays $B+C+D_1 + D_2$. With equal numbers of each type of consumer, the uniform rebate is the average of these two tax payments: $\frac{1}{2}(B + B + C + D_1 + D_2) = B + C + D_1$, where I have made use of the fact that $C = D_1 = \frac{1}{2}D_2$. This uniform rebate exceeds the time-consistent's consumer surplus loss of $B + C$ from the tax, making them better off.

Present-biased consumers, who are paying more in taxes than they receive back from the government as a rebate, are only better off if the welfare gain from reducing their cookie consumption is sufficiently large. From the *Consumer Surplus* row of Table 7.2, we see that the tax changes the present-biased consumer surplus by $F - B - C - D_1 - D_2$. Adding in the uniform rebate, the change in welfare for a present-biased consumer is $F - D_2$. Area F measures the benefit of the tax from discouraging cookie consumption from Q_4 to Q_3. And area D_2 is the gap between total taxes paid and the smaller rebate received. Therefore, the present-biased consumers are better off when the benefit F exceeds the loss D_2. In our figure, $F > D_2$, so they are better off, yielding a Pareto improvement in society. Although this is true here and in many cases, it is possible to construct examples where present-biased consumers are worse off. For instance, if the tax does not induce present-biased consumers to reduce their cookie consumption by very much, then the benefit F could be too small to compensate for the tax transfer of D_2 to the time-consistents.

The magnitude of the maximum Pareto-improving tax rate is similar to the optimal tax rate. This similarity reveals that the optimal tax rate not only maximizes social welfare, but also provides an upper bound on a policy that can make everyone better off relative to a world with no taxes on cookies.

7.4   Summary

1   The profit-maximizing **two-part tariff** with standard consumers sets the per-unit price equal to marginal cost and the access fee equal to consumer surplus.

2   When selling an investment good to present-biased consumers, the profit-maximizing two-part tariff sets the per-unit price *below* marginal cost and the access fee equal to *expected* consumer surplus. This increases profits relative to using the two-part tariff designed for standard consumers. The intuition for the result depends on the beliefs that the present-biased consumer has about their future consumption:

    a   Naifs overestimate their future use and are therefore willing to pay an access fee that exceeds their actual consumer surplus.

    b   Sophisticates are willing to pay a larger access fee in exchange for a lower per-unit price in order to help commit their future selves to better follow through with their planned consumption.

3   There is empirical evidence in the contexts of food consumption, tipping, organ donations, and retirement savings that many consumers choose **default** options.

4   The power of defaults to impact behavior can be explained by naive present bias.

5   Financial education has little impact on retirement savings decisions. Precommitment strategies are effective at increasing retirement savings.

6   With present-biased preferences there exists an internality. And when an internality exists, policies that help to align actual behavior with desired behavior can improve individual welfare.

7   In a population with both present-biased and time-consistent consumers:

    a   a nudge improves social welfare if the benefits from nudging actual behavior closer to desired behavior exceed the psychological costs of the nudge;

    b   it is always possible (given our model) to introduce a positive tax on a sin good that improves social welfare; and

    c   it is sometimes possible to introduce a positive tax on a sin good that makes everyone better off.

7.5   Exercises[5]

Exercise 7.1 — Leisurely Two-Part Tariff (DellaVigna and Malmendier 2004).
We know from the chapter that firms with market power who want to maximize their profits with a two-part tariff will set their per-unit price below marginal cost — *if* they are selling an investment good. But what would a firm selling a leisure good do?

To answer this question, we again represent the decision process for a present-biased consumer graphically, as in Figure 7.8. Because a leisure good delivers immediate benefits with delayed costs, we know that present-biased consumers overconsume leisure goods relative to their plans. In this case, the demand curve D_{Plan} that indicates the consumer's planned consumption, is drawn to the left of D_{Actual}, the demand curve indicating actual consumption at every possible per-unit price. As with investment goods, we use the D_{Plan} curve to measure the individual's true experienced welfare from the leisure good.

a   Complete Table 7.3, referencing the labels in Figure 7.8.
b   By how much do profits change by increasing the per-unit price from P^* to P^H when the customer is naive? And if they are instead sophisticated?
c   Provide intuition for your results in part (b). *Hint: The intuition for naifs and sophisticates consuming a leisure good is similar to the investment good case.*

Exercise 7.2 — Making Sense of Credit Cards and Gambling. Completing Exercise 7.1 should convince you that with present-biased consumers, firms have a profit motive to increase the per-unit price and to decrease the access fee relative to the case with standard consumers.

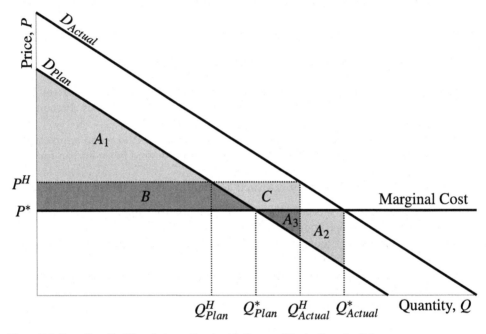

Figure 7.8 Two-Part Tariff on Leisure Good with Present Bias in Exercise 7.1

Table 7.3 Analysis of Two-Part Tariffs for Leisure Good in Exercise 7.1

	Naif		Sophisticate	
Per-Unit Price	P^*	P^H	P^*	P^H
Expected Q				
Expected Consumer Surplus = Access Fee				
Actual Q				
Profit				
Actual Consumer Surplus (Net of Access Fee)				

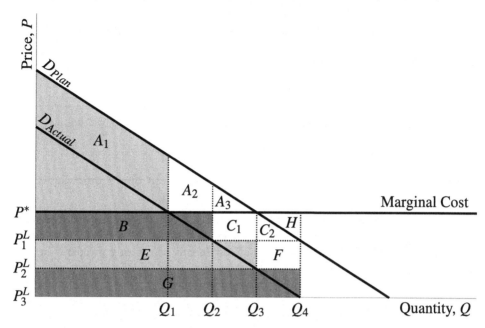

Figure 7.9 Picturing the Two-Part Tariff for Sophisticated Gym-Goers in Exercise 7.4

For each of the following leisure goods, discuss how selling to present-biased consumers is predicted to impact the profit-maximizing two-part tariff. Do these predictions seem consistent with what you see in the real world?

a   **Credit cards:** Credit card-financed consumption is a leisure good because individuals can enjoy immediate consumption while delaying payment to the future. Credit card companies can offer two-part tariffs with the interest rate on unpaid balances as the per-unit price, and an annual membership fee as the access fee.

b   **Las Vegas hotels:** Gamblers experience an immediate benefit from the thrill of gambling, but in most cases lose money and therefore face the delayed cost of lower consumption in the future. Las Vegas hotels integrate the gambling experience with accommodations. We can think of these hotels as offering a two-part tariff in which the expected loss per gambling game is the per-unit price of gambling, and the cost of a hotel room is the access fee.

Exercise 7.3 — Crafty Creditors (Heidhues and Kőszegi 2010). Recall the evidence in Section 5.4.4 that consumers respond much more to credit card offers that reduce the interest rate in the first few months than to ones that offer a delayed, but longer-term reduction in the interest rate. This is in spite of the fact that most people would be better off with a lower interest rate in the long term. Such a mistake is consistent with naively present-biased consumers.

What does this evidence imply for the types of perks that a profit-maximizing credit card company will offer? Can you think of some real-world examples consistent with the predicted firm behavior?

Table 7.4 Analyzing the Two-Part Tariff for a Gym in Exercise 7.4

	Sophisticate			
Per-Unit Price	P^*	P_1^L	P_2^L	$P_3^L = 0$
Expected Q	Q_1	Q_2		
Expected Consumer Surplus = Access Fee	A_1	$A_1 + A_2 + B$		
Actual Q	Q_1	Q_2		
Profit	A_1	$A_1 + A_2$		
Actual Consumer Surplus (Net of Access Fee)	0	0		

Exercise 7.4 — Gym Pricing: How Low to Go? (DellaVigna and Malmendier 2004). We know that a gym with present-biased customers can increase its profits by decreasing its per-visit price below marginal cost (relative to setting the per-visit price equal to marginal cost). But our analysis, summarized in Table 7.1, does not tell us *how low* the per-visit price should be to maximize profits.

a　**Sophisticates:** Suppose the gym is facing a population of sophisticated customers with planned (D_{Plan}) and actual (D_{Actual}) demand curves given as in Figure 7.9. Recall that sophisticates correctly expect demand to be actual demand, but achieve consumer surplus equal to the area below the D_{Plan} curve and above the per-visit price. We already know the firm's profits when the per-visit price is P^* and P_1^L.

　　i　Complete Table 7.4, referencing the labels in Figure 7.9, with the profit and consumer surplus when the per-visit price is P_2^L. Repeat your analysis for the case with a zero per-visit price, $P_3^L = 0$. Assume no fixed costs.
　　ii　Are profits largest when the per-visit price is P_1^L, P_2^L, or P_3^L? What is consumer surplus and quantity of gym visits at this profit-maximizing per-visit price?
　　iii　Compare your answers in the previous part to the consumer surplus and quantity consumed of standard consumers (for whom actual demand is D_{Plan}) that are charged a two-part tariff with a per-visit price equal to marginal cost. Is there any reason for regulating gyms to help sophisticates? Justify your answer.

b　**Naifs: [Calculus Required]** Now suppose instead that the gym is facing a population of naive customers, each with individual demand curves as follows:

$$D_{Plan} : P = 12 - Q \qquad \text{and} \qquad D_{Actual} : P = 12\beta - Q$$

where $0.5 < \beta < 1$. Recall that naifs incorrectly expect demand to be their planned demand and that consumer surplus is equal to the area below the D_{Plan} curve and above the per visit price. In addition, assume that the gym has no fixed costs and a constant marginal cost of \$6 per visit.

　　i　Write down an expression for the firm's profit from a single naif that is charged a two-part tariff with a per-visit price $P < 6$ (we already know the profit-maximizing per-visit price is below marginal cost) and an access fee equal to the naif's expected consumer surplus. Profit should depend on P and β.

ii Determine the P that maximizes your profit expression. It should depend on β.

iii How does the profit-maximizing P change as β shrinks away from 1? Provide intuition.

iv Does the naif realize a positive or negative consumer surplus (net of the access fee)? Is there any reason for regulating gyms to help naifs? Justify your answer.

Exercise 7.5 — Default Decisions. Time-consistent Terri and naive Nash have preferences over an infinite sequence of daily payoffs (u_0, u_1, u_2, ...) given by

$$U^0(u_0, u_1, u_2...; \beta) = u_0 + \beta \sum_{k=1}^{\infty} \delta^k \cdot u_k$$

where $\delta = 0.9999$ is the daily discount factor, $\beta = 1$ for Terri, and $\beta < 1$ for Nash. You will want to make use of the fact that $\sum_{k=1}^{\infty} \delta^k = \delta/(1 - \delta)$.

Terri and Nash have been hired at a company that pays them each a \$60,000 annual salary. The company offers a 401(k) with a 50% employer match, but the default is non-participation. In order to begin allocating money from their paycheck to the 401(k), they must fill out a form and select the funds in which they want to invest their money. This process takes at most 3 hours and therefore imposes an immediate time and effort cost of $c - \$90$ (corresponding to the three hours spent enrolling instead of making \$30/hour).

By enrolling in the 401(k) they gain the benefit of delayed consumption, which is enhanced by the employer match and the tax advantages of the plan. Based on current tax rates and a 6% savings rate, this is approximately a \$5 daily benefit.

Each day that they have not enrolled in the 401(k) they have a choice to make — either enroll or do not enroll today. Let's now see what Terri and Nash decide to do.

a   **Time-Consistent Terri ($\beta = 1$):** Terri either enrolls immediately, earning utility $U^0(-c, 5, 5, 5, ...;1)$, or never enrolls, earning utility $U^0(0, 0, 0, 0, ...;1)$. How large does the cost of signing up, c, have to be to make her not enroll? Does she enroll when $c = 90$?

b   **Naive Nash ($\beta < 1$):** Nash believes that his future selves are time-consistent and therefore that tomorrow he will behave like Terri. From part (a) we know that Terri enrolls when $c = 90$, so Nash believes that if he doesn't enroll today, he will do so tomorrow. Therefore, Nash enrolls today if and only if his utility from enrolling today, $U^0(-90, 5, 5, 5, ...;\beta)$, is at least his utility today from enrolling tomorrow, $U^0(0, -90, 5, 5, ...;\beta)$.

i   Calculate $U^0(-90, 5, 5, 5, ...;\beta)$ and $U^0(0, -90, 5, 5, ...;\beta)$.

ii Determine the range of β for which Nash does not enroll today.

iii Briefly discuss your answer and explain what it means for Nash's decision process if $\beta = 0.8$.

Exercise 7.6 — Nudging Farmers to Fertilize. [Development] Duflo, Kremer, and Robinson (2011) study the use of fertilizer by Kenyan farmers. Fertilizer is a key input to productive farming. The researchers find that while 98% of the farmers in their study report that they plan to use fertilizer in the following season, only 36% follow through with their plan. In fact, the researchers estimate that 69% of the farmers are present-biased.

a   Is fertilizer an investment or leisure good? Explain how present-biased preferences can predict the observed difference between planned and actual behavior.
b   Offering free home delivery of fertilizer early in the season increases fertilizer use by 70%. Explain why this policy is likely so effective and why such a large impact would not be predicted if farmers were time-consistent.
c   Discuss the advantages of the free home delivery policy relative to a more standard fertilizer subsidy policy that has the same effect on fertilizer use.

Exercise 7.7 — Dropping the College Dropout Rate. [Education] Despite the significant benefits of a college degree, over half of students who enroll in a US four-year college drop out within six years (College Atlas 2018).

a   Explain how present-biased preferences may better explain the low college completion rate than the standard model of decision making with time-consistent preferences.
b   Suggest at least one nudge that could help students who have already successfully attained the impressive achievement of being accepted into college, remain enrolled and on track to graduate.

Exercise 7.8 — Convenient Calories. [Health] Cutler, Glaeser, and Shapiro (2003) survey the evidence on why Americans have become more obese since the mid 1960s. They argue that the increase in obesity rates is driven at least in part by the rise of mass food preparation. Thanks to technological advances in food processing and packaging, consumers can rely much more on prepared foods that decades ago were prepared at home from scratch. In fact, the average family spent 130 minutes per day on food preparation and cleanup in 1965, but that time fell by half over the following decades.

These technological advances have the effect of reducing the time between an individual's initial desire to consume food and the actual consumption of the food. And when the immediate benefit of consuming increases (because the time cost of preparation has declined), food consumption is predicted to increase for all consumers.

a   For standard time-consistent consumers, does the reduction in the time cost of food preparation increase or decrease individual welfare? Explain.
b   Explain how it is possible for the reduction in the time cost of food preparation to reduce individual welfare for a present-biased consumer with self-control problems.
c   Recommend a policy in the context of food consumption that could improve social welfare. Justify your recommendation.

Exercise 7.9 — To Nudge or Not. Let's modify Example 7.1, considering how the magnitude of the nudge's psychological cost impacts the welfare analysis. Answer the following questions when the psychological cost of the nudge is i) $0, ii) $2, and iii) $5.

a   Is the nudge effective at preventing mistakes?

b   Present-biased consumers must be at least what share of the population for the nudge to increase utilitarian social welfare?

Exercise 7.10 — Uniform Sin, Optimally Taxed (O'Donoghue and Rabin 2006). We know from Chapter 3 that when there is a gap between marginal decision utility and marginal experienced utility, then the optimal corrective per-unit tax is equal to this difference, evaluated at the welfare-maximizing quantity. Let's apply this insight to the case of a sin tax on cookies that are consumed by a population of equally present-biased individuals.

Let marginal experienced utility of consuming the xth cookie be:

$$MU^{exp}(x) = MV(x) - MC(x)$$

where $MV(x) > 0$ is the marginal value of enjoying the cookie in the present and $MC(x) > 0$ is the delayed marginal health cost of eating the cookie.

Because of present bias, the marginal decision utility of consuming the xth cookie is:

$$MU^{dec}(x) = MV(x) - \beta MC(x)$$

where $0 < \beta < 1$.

a   Determine the optimal per-unit cookie tax, $t^* = MU^{dec}(x^*) - MU^{exp}(x^*)$, where x^* is the welfare-maximizing level of cookie consumption. Your answer should depend on β and $MC(x^*)$.

b   How does the optimal cookie tax change with an increase in β? Or with an increase in $MC(x^*)$? Provide intuition for your answers.

Exercise 7.11 — Nicotine Nudge. Consider the following two-period model of cigarette consumption, where c_1 and c_2 are the number of cigarette packs consumed in years 1 and 2. For simplicity assume that cigarettes are free, $c_2 \geq c_1$, and that only smoking in period 2 has negative health effects (given by $-c_2/2$). Experienced utility in each year is:

Year 1 : $$U_1^{exp}(c_1|n) = \frac{2}{n}\sqrt{c_1}$$

Year 2 : $$U_2^{exp}(c_2|c_1, n) = \frac{2}{n}\sqrt{c_2 - c_1} - \frac{c_2}{2}$$

where $n \in (0, 1]$ measures the intensity of a nudge that discourages tobacco use.

a   How do the utility functions above capture the idea that cigarettes are habit forming (Definition 6.1)? In particular, comment on how consuming more cigarettes in the first period impacts both the utility and marginal utility of consumption in the second period.

Total lifetime experienced utility (assuming $\delta = 1$), and therefore individual welfare, is then given by:

$$W = U^{exp} = U_1^{exp}(c_1|n) + U_2^{exp}(c_2|c_1, n) = \frac{2}{n}\sqrt{c_1} + \frac{2}{n}\sqrt{c_2 - c_1} - \frac{c_2}{2}$$

Assume that individuals are present-biased and do not fully perceive the future health costs of smoking. Total lifetime decision utility is given by:

$$U^{dec} = \frac{2}{n}\sqrt{c_1} + \frac{2}{n}\sqrt{c_2 - c_1} - n \cdot \frac{c_2}{2}$$

b   Holding fixed cigarette consumption, how does an increase in the nudge (n) impact lifetime experienced utility? How does it impact lifetime decision utility? Provide intuition.

c   Consider three different levels of the anti-smoking nudge: $n = 1/2$, $3/4$, and 1. Below is a table showing how many packs of cigarettes a consumer who is maximizing decision utility, U^{dec}, will choose to consume for each value of n:

	$n = 1/2$	$n = 3/4$	$n = 1$
c_1	64	12.64	4
c_2	128	25.28	8

How does the nudge impact cigarette consumption? Compute individual welfare with each level of the nudge using the information in the table. How does the nudge impact welfare? Which of these three nudges achieves the highest welfare?

d   Suppose the government is deciding between helping smokers to reduce cigarette consumption by either nudging or taxing cigarettes directly. Discuss one reason why nudging (e.g., via public health campaign) might be preferable and one reason why taxation might be preferable.

e   **[Calculus Required]** None of the nudge levels in part (c) achieves the highest possible individual welfare. Determine the nudge n that maximizes individual welfare, taking into account the impact of the nudge on decisions. What is cigarette consumption and welfare at this maximum?

Notes

1 There are alternative explanations for default effects. For example, a default may be interpreted as a recommendation or social norm that acts to persuade. Or individuals may simply forget to change away from defaults, or find a decision problem overly complex and thus stick with the default to avoid expending additional cognitive effort.

2 Recall from Section 3.5 that the experienced benefit is the marginal experienced utility from consumption, while the decision benefit is the marginal decision utility from consumption, each measured in dollars.

3 I assume when evaluating the social welfare effects of a nudge that the nudge is costless to implement and profits are unaffected.

4 Formally, I assume quasilinear utility functions over Q cookies and Y spending on other goods, i.e., $U^{exp} = v(Q) - c(Q) + Y$ and $U^{dec} = v(Q) - \beta c(Q) + Y$ where $v(Q)$ measures immediate gratification and $c(Q)$ measures the delayed health costs.

5 Exercise 7.5 is adapted from an exercise by Stefano DellaVigna.

References

Becker, Gary S., and Julio Jorge Elias. 2007. "Introducing Incentives in the Market for Live and Cadaveric Organ Donations." *Journal of Economic Perspectives* 21 (3): 3–24. doi:10.1257/089533007781798311.

Bernheim, B. Douglas, Andrey Fradkin, and Igor Popov. 2015. "The Welfare Economics of Default Options in 401(k) Plans." *American Economic Review* 105 (9): 2798–2837. doi:10.1257/aer.20130907.

Carroll, Gabriel D., James J. Choi, David Laibson, Brigitte C. Madrian, and Andrew Metrick. 2009. "Optimal Defaults and Active Decisions." *The Quarterly Journal of Economics* 124 (4): 1639–1674. doi:10.1162/qjec.2009.124.4.1639.

Cawley, John, and Chad Meyerhoefer. 2012. "The Medical Care Costs of Obesity: An Instrumental Variables Approach." *Journal of Health Economics* 31 (1): 219–230. doi:10.1016/j.jhealeco.2011.10.003.

CBPP (Center on Budget and Policy Priorities). 2020. *Policy Basics: Top Ten Facts about Social Security.* Updated August 13, 2020, https://www.cbpp.org/research/social-security/policy-basics-top-ten-facts-about-social-security.

Choi, James J., David Laibson, Brigitte C. Madrian, and Andrew Metrick. 2002. "Defined Contribution Pensions: Plan Rules, Participant Choices, and the Path of Least Resistance." *Tax Policy and the Economy* 16: 67–113. doi:10.1086/654750.

———. 2004. "For Better or for Worse: Default Effects and 401(k) Savings Behavior." In *Perspectives on the Economics of Aging,* edited by David A. Wise, 81–126. Chicago, IL: University of Chicago Press.

College Atlas. 2018. *U.S. College Dropout Rate and Dropout Statistics.* Updated June 29, 2018, https://www.collegeatlas.org/college-dropout.html.

Cronqvist, Henrik, and Richard H. Thaler. 2004. "Design Choices in Privatized Social-Security Systems: Learning from the Swedish Experience." *American Economic Review* 94 (2): 424–428. doi:10.1257/0002828041301632.

Cutler, David M., Edward L. Glaeser, and Jesse M. Shapiro. 2003. "Why Have Americans Become More Obese?" *Journal of Economic Perspectives* 17 (3): 93–118. doi:10.1257/089533003769204371.

DellaVigna, Stefano, and Ulrike Malmendier. 2004. "Contract Design and Self-Control: Theory and Evidence." *The Quarterly Journal of Economics* 119 (2): 353–402. doi:10.1162/0033553041382111.

Duflo, Esther, Michael Kremer, and Jonathan Robinson. 2011. "Nudging Farmers to Use Fertilizer: Theory and Experimental Evidence from Kenya." *American Economic Review* 101 (6): 2350–2390. doi:10.1257/aer.101.6.2350.

Duflo, Esther, and Emmanuel Saez. 2003. "The Role of Information and Social Interactions in Retirement Plan Decisions: Evidence from a Randomized Experiment." *The Quarterly Journal of Economics* 118 (3): 815–842. doi:10.1162/00335530360698432.

Dushi, Irena, Howard M. Iams, and Brad Trenkamp. 2017. "The Importance of Social Security Benefits to the Income of the Aged Population." *Social Security Bulletin* 77 (2): 1–12. https://www.ssa.gov/policy/docs/ssb/v77n2/v77n2p1.html.

GAO (U.S. Government Accountability Office). 2015. "Retirement Security: Most Households Approaching Retirement Have Low Savings." Report GAO-15-419. GAO. https://www.gao.gov/products/GAO-15-419.

Glaeser, Edward L. 2005. "Paternalism and Psychology." NBER Working Paper 11789. Cambridge, MA: National Bureau of Economic Research. doi:10.3386/w11789.

Haggag, Kareem, and Giovanni Paci. 2014. "Default Tips." *American Economic Journal: Applied Economics* 6 (3): 1–19. doi:10.1257/app.6.3.1.

Heidhues, Paul, and Botond Koszegi. 2010. "Exploiting Naïvete about Self-Control in the Credit Market." *American Economic Review* 100 (5): 2279–2303. https://www.aeaweb.org/articles?id=10.1257/aer.100.5.2279.

Jimenez-Gomez, David. 2018. "Nudging and Phishing: A Theory of Behavioral Welfare Economics." SSRN Scholarly Paper ID 3248503. Rochester, NY: Social Science Research Network. https://papers.ssrn.com/abstract=3248503.

Johnson, Eric J., and Daniel Goldstein. 2003. "Do Defaults Save Lives?" *Science* 302 (5649): 1338–1339. doi:10.1126/science.1091721.

Kessler, Judd B., and Alvin E. Roth. 2012. "Organ Allocation Policy and the Decision to Donate." *American Economic Review* 102 (5): 2018–2047. doi:10.1257/aer. 102.5.2018.

Madrian, Brigitte C., and Dennis F. Shea. 2001. "The Power of Suggestion: Inertia in 401(k) Participation and Savings Behavior." *The Quarterly Journal of Economics* 116 (4): 1149–1187. doi:10.1162/003355301753265543.

O'Donoghue, Ted, and Matthew Rabin. 2001. "Choice and Procrastination." *The Quarterly Journal of Economics* 116 (1): 121–160. doi:10.1162/003355301556365.

———. 2006. "Optimal Sin Taxes." *Journal of Public Economics* 90 (10–11): 1825–1849. doi:10.1016/j.jpubeco.2006.03.001.

Peters, John, Jimikaye Beck, Jan Lande, Zhaoxing Pan, Michelle Cardel, Keith Ayoob, and James O. Hill. 2016. "Using Healthy Defaults in Walt Disney World Restaurants to Improve Nutritional Choices." *Journal of the Association for Consumer Research* 1 (1): 92–103. doi:10.1086/684364.

Steffel, Mary, Elanor F. Williams, and Ruth Pogacar. 2016. "Ethically Deployed Defaults: Transparency and Consumer Protection through Disclosure and Preference Articulation." *Journal of Marketing Research* 53 (5): 865–880. doi:10.1509/jmr.14. 0421.

Thaler, Richard H., and Shlomo Benartzi. 2004. "Save More Tomorrow[TM]: Using Behavioral Economics to Increase Employee Saving." *Journal of Political Economy* 112 (S1): 164–187. doi:10.1086/380085.

UNOS (United Network Organ Sharing). 2020. *Organ Transplant Trends*. Accessed November 15, 2020, https://unos.org/data/transplant-trends/.

Part III

Reference-Dependent Preferences

A standard assumption in the model of individual decision making (Definition 2.9) is that preferences are reference-independent. That is, individuals evaluate outcomes on their own independent terms, and not as gains or losses relative to some point of reference. This assumption is featured in the standard model by the *absence* of any reference point in the utility function $u(\cdot)$ highlighted below:

$$\max_{(x_0, x_1, \ldots, x_T) \in X} \sum_{k=0}^{T} \delta^k E[\, u(x_k) \mid p] \qquad \text{(Standard Model)}$$

The objective of Part III is to question this assumption and instead consider reference-*dependent* preferences that depend not only on the final outcome, but on the outcome's comparison to the status quo, an expectation, an aspiration, or another possible point of reference. To focus the analysis, we maintain the other standard assumptions of decision making. Individuals are still assumed to be self-interested expected utility maximizers with accurate beliefs. And for simplicity, we assume away the intertemporal decisions that were the focus of the previous part.

Part III is organized as follows. Chapter 8 begins by documenting evidence that is inconsistent with the behavior predicted by reference-independent preferences. These anomalies suggest that individuals evaluate outcomes as gains and losses, and that losses are experienced more intensely than equivalent gains. Given this evidence, Chapter 9 introduces a nonstandard utility function that captures such an aversion to losses. Chapter 10 explores the policy implications and market responses to consumers with reference-dependent preferences, with applications to the environment, education, compensation, and auctions.

Before we begin, note that I apply the term "reference-dependent" specifically to settings where individuals evaluate outcomes as gains or losses relative to a reference point. There are other types of nonstandard preferences that depend on reference points, but not as gains or losses. For example, the habit formation model in Section 6.1 assumes that current preferences depend on the reference point of past consumption. And in Section 14.3 we consider social preferences that depend on the reference point of what other people have. These topics are outside our present scope.

8 Reference-Independence Anomalies

Learning Objectives

★ Understand the endowment effect and the characteristics of those who exhibit it.

★ Develop intuition for how the model of reference-independent expected utility can generate seemingly inconsistent and absurd predictions.

★ Understand the equity premium puzzle and what it implies about investor attitudes towards the stock market.

★ Hypothesize modifications to the standard reference-independent model of preferences to better explain observed behavior.

When a coach tells her team, "win some, lose some," she is no doubt reacting to a recent loss. More generally, this idiom underscores the mix of outcomes, both good and bad, that characterize life. But what makes an outcome good or bad? Is finishing a night of gambling with $200 in your pocket a good outcome or a bad outcome? It surely depends on whether you started the night with $1000 or $10 in your pocket. Or is renting your own one bedroom apartment a good or bad outcome? It is likely good if you had previously been living in a dorm room with two roommates. But the same outcome may be perceived as a loss by someone who moved only because they lost their two bedroom home in a foreclosure.

In order to determine whether an outcome is a win or loss, we must know how it compares to some reference point. The reference point could be a previous recent outcome, like wealth before gambling or housing before moving. When a baseball team expects to make it to the World Series, but is eliminated in the quarterfinals, their perceived loss is relative to the reference point of their expectations.

In any case, the standard model of decision making assumes that preferences do not depend on — they are independent of — reference points. So although individuals can prefer more money to less, and more bedrooms to fewer, the actual quantity of money or bedrooms is all that matters. The path by which an individual arrives at a final outcome is assumed to be irrelevant for their evaluation of that outcome. This is a convenient assumption because we only need to know an individual's observable outcome, and not also how it compares to a potentially unobservable reference point. Although this assumption helps to make the standard model simpler and more tractable, it potentially does so at the expense of accurately describing behavior in the real world.

DOI: 10.4324/9780367854072-11

This chapter documents anomalous behaviors that are inconsistent with reference-independent preferences. We begin with evidence that, contrary to the standard prediction, individuals value an object in their possession more than if the same object were not in their possession. The next section considers choices between risky wins and losses. And we conclude with a famous anomaly from finance: the equity premium puzzle. This puzzle identifies the failure of the standard model to explain the relative magnitude of stock market returns. The evidence throughout the chapter comes from a wide range of methods, including lab experiments, field experiments, thought experiments, and observational data.

Each anomaly points to preferences that not only depend on reference points, but that weight losses more than gains. This insight motivates the nonstandard model of preferences introduced in Chapter 9.

8.1   Endowment Effect

The **endowment effect** describes the phenomenon by which an individual values a good in their possession, or endowment, more highly than when it is not in their possession, all else equal (Thaler 1980). According to standard economics, we would not expect your valuation of a coffee mug, for instance, before you buy it to differ from your valuation once you own it, assuming it works as expected. Whether or not it is in your possession does not change the functionality or aesthetic pleasure of the mug. And yet, experimental evidence from both the lab and the field demonstrates that possession matters, constituting a puzzle for standard economics.

8.1.1   Early Evidence from the Lab

Consider the following early lab experiment documenting the endowment effect.

Lab Experiment — Mug Exchange (Knetsch 1989)

Three groups of students at the University of Victoria were offered a choice between two free objects: a coffee mug or a Swiss chocolate bar. These were not exotic items — the mugs were sold in the university bookstore for $4.95 and the chocolate bar could be purchased at local stores for $6.

The only difference between the three otherwise similar groups of students was whether or not they were given (or endowed with) the mug or chocolate before making the decision between the goods. For example, students in one group were each given a mug before being asked if they would like to exchange the mug for the chocolate.

The initial endowments for the three groups were:

1   No endowment before choosing mug or chocolate.
2   Endowed with mug before choosing to keep mug or exchange for chocolate.
3   Endowed with chocolate before choosing to keep chocolate or exchange for mug.

The following table shows the percent of students in each group who chose the mug versus the chocolate.

Endowment	Choose Mug	Choose Chocolate	# of Students
None	56%	44%	55
Mug	89%	11%	76
Chocolate	10%	90%	87

The evidence from this experiment is striking. To see why, first consider the predicted behavior under the standard assumption that preferences are defined over final outcomes. In this case, students either prefer the final outcome of receiving a mug or a chocolate bar. Changing the endowment before the decision should have no effect on preferences for these familiar goods. And given that the endowments were randomly assigned to three similar groups of students, we would expect to observe a similar preference for mugs relative to chocolate in each of the groups.

What do we actually observe? When there is no endowment and students simply indicate their preferred gift, preferences are split almost evenly, with 56% choosing the mug. To repeat, standard economics then predicts that approximately half of the students in the other groups should also choose the mug. But for the group of students who were first endowed with the mug, 89% choose to keep the mug instead of exchanging for the chocolate. Mugs are suddenly highly desired. This strong preference for mugs then collapses when students are endowed with the chocolate bar — only 10% choose the mug in this case.

In summary, individuals appear to value a good — no matter whether it is a mug or chocolate — much more when it is in their possession, even if only for a few minutes, than when it is not. This evidence confirms the hypothesis of the endowment effect.

The Mug Exchange Lab Experiment shows that endowments impact preferences. But how intense is this impact? To answer this question we can compare an individual's maximum willingness to pay (WTP) for a good to the minimum price they are willing to accept (WTA) to sell the same good. The standard model predicts WTP to equal WTA.[1] If you value a coffee mug at $5, then you should be willing to pay at most $5 to buy it. And if you already own it, you should be willing to sell it for any price over $5. But the endowment effect changes this logic. If a seller, by virtue of already possessing the mug, values it more highly than a buyer (who does not yet possess it), then the seller's WTA will be greater than the buyer's WTP. The gap between WTA and WTP therefore measures the magnitude of the endowment effect. The following experiment elicits such values in a lab setting.

Lab Experiment — Monetizing Mugs (Kahneman, Knetsch, and Thaler 1990)

Seventy-seven students at Simon Fraser University were randomly assigned to one of three groups as follows:

- Sellers were given a coffee mug and asked their minimum willingness to accept (WTA) to sell the mug.
- Buyers were asked their maximum willingness to pay (WTP) for a mug that they did not yet possess.

- Choosers, who were not given a mug, were asked how much money would make them exactly indifferent between choosing the money and choosing the mug.

The median responses were as follows:

- Seller WTA: $7.12
- Buyer WTP: $2.87
- Chooser Indifference Price: $3.12

There are two important takeaways from this evidence. First, observe that the median WTA of $7.12 is much larger than the median WTP of $2.87. The mug's value is almost 2.5 times greater to those who possess it than to those who do not. Horowitz and McConnell (2002) survey 50 different studies and find that the average WTA is typically 2.6 times greater than the average WTP. This robust result is consistent with a strong endowment effect. Kahneman, Knetsch, and Thaler (1990) also conduct a follow-up experiment identical in structure to the one above, except for one difference: price tags are left on the mugs. Incredibly, the results are even more extreme in this case, with a median WTA that is 3.5 times greater than the median WTP. The endowment effect is therefore not arising simply because individuals do not understand a mug's market value.

We would also like to know the extent to which the difference between WTA and WTP is due to the sellers' reluctance to give up the mug (which increases their WTA) versus the buyers' reluctance to give up money (which decreases their WTP). The choosers can help us answer this question because unlike the other two groups, choosers do not have to give up anything in their decision — they either gain a mug or gain money. Their median indifference price of $3.12 for the mug is therefore a "true" valuation, exempt from any possible influence of losing an endowment. This valuation is much closer to the buyer WTP than the seller WTA. Therefore, our second takeaway is that the difference between WTA and WTP is the consequence of a strong reluctance to sell ($7.12 is much larger than $3.12) and only a small reluctance to buy ($2.87 is slightly less than $3.12).

What alternative model of preferences could explain the endowment effect? One option is to allow preferences to depend not only on the final outcome, but also on how the final outcome compares to the reference point of an individual's initial endowment. And if losing part of an endowment is weighted more than adding to one's endowment, then we would expect individuals to value retaining an endowed good more than acquiring it — exactly as we observe in the lab experiments. We develop such a model in the next chapter. For now, let's continue exploring further evidence of the endowment effect.

8.1.2 Further Evidence from the Field

Although we have strong evidence of the endowment effect from controlled lab experiments, this does not guarantee that the endowment effect exists in settings outside of a university classroom. Perhaps the decisions facing students in the lab experiments to trade and value coffee mugs fail to represent the types of actual economic decisions that individuals face in their daily lives.

How exactly do real-world interactions differ from the previous lab environments? When individuals exchange goods in real markets, they are often experienced with the act of trading. Buyers and sellers of stocks, bonds, advertising, electricity, business supplies, and real estate are presumably familiar with the markets in which they trade. But for the lab participants, the experiment was likely the first time they had ever been prompted to exchange or explicitly value a coffee mug. In addition, the lab participants were not a representative sample from the global population. Instead, they were most likely a homogenous group of young adults who grew up in industrialized societies.

Does the endowment effect still hold when participants are experienced traders? Or does it still hold for those from non-industrialized societies? We answer these questions in turn, with evidence from two experiments outside the lab.

Sportscard Trading Experience   *[Sports]*

To examine the role of trading experience on the endowment effect, List (2003) replicates versions of the Mug Exchange and Monetizing Mugs Lab Experiments in real-world marketplaces, as described below.

Field Experiment — Sportscard Show (List 2003)

John List attended a sportscard show in Orlando, Florida. He approached individuals at the show and asked if they would be willing to fill out a short 5 minute survey. For each of the 148 individuals who agreed, he randomly offered them one of two sports memorabilia gifts in return for completing the survey.[2] With the gift in hand, participants completed the survey. Upon completion, participants were then offered the opportunity to exchange their initial gift for the other sports memorabilia gift. Participants were permitted to inspect both goods before making their decision. Because the two sports memorabilia gifts were of comparable value and randomly assigned, standard economics predicts that half of the participants initially received their less preferred gift option and would therefore switch.

In a follow-up field experiment at a Tucson, AZ sportscard show he elicited from 60 participants their maximum WTP for a sheet of basketball trading cards. Another 60 participants were physically gifted the sheet of basketball trading cards before reporting their minimum WTA in order to sell. Standard economics predicts that the two similar groups should value the cards equally and therefore report similar WTPs and WTAs.

List (2003) reports the results of these experiments separately for participants who were professional dealers and ordinary consumers with less trading experience. These two groups share similar demographic characteristics (e.g., age, gender, education, and income). They differ only in the frequency with which they trade (16 times per month vs. 6 times per month) and years of market experience (10 years vs. 7 years). Therefore, any differences in behavior between these two groups can reasonably be attributed to the difference in market experience.

	Orlando, FL Percent Trade	Tucson, AZ WTA	WTP	WTA/WTP
Nondealers (all)	23.0%	$18.53	$3.32	5.6
with below average experience	6.8%			
with above average experience	46.7%			
Dealers	44.6%	$8.15	$6.27	1.3

The foregoing evidence provides a more nuanced understanding of the endowment effect. First, we observe that the endowment effect survives outside the lab in real-world markets. But it is not a universal phenomenon exhibited by everyone equally. The endowment effect is strongest for inexperienced nondealers, 93.2% of whom retain the first good they are endowed. The more experienced nondealers, as well as the professional dealers, trade their initial gift almost 50% of the time, exactly as predicted by standard economics. Greater trading experience appears to eliminate the endowment effect.[3] We observe a similar pattern by comparing WTA with WTP. Nondealers report a minimum selling price that is 5.6 times larger than their maximum buying price, while dealers report a WTA that is approximately equal to WTP. The field evidence therefore lends support to the standard model of preferences, as long as we restrict attention to experienced market participants. If our interest, however, is to understand market settings where individuals are less experienced (e.g., taking out student loans for college or buying a first house), the standard model is likely to make poor predictions.

Exposure to Modern Society   [Development]

Let's now consider to what extent the endowment effect is a phenomenon of the industrialized societies in which it is often examined. One possibility is to conduct an endowment exchange experiment with people from different global regions and compare the results across cultures (see e.g., Henrich et al. 2001, 2006). A drawback to such an approach is that because cultures differ along so many dimensions, it is difficult to identify which specific cultural features amplify or diminish the magnitude of the endowment effect. The following study solves this problem by comparing the behavior of individuals from the same population, but with different levels of exposure to modern society.

Quasi-Experiment — Hunter-Gatherer Exchange (Apicella et al. 2014)

The Hadza Bushmen are one of the last remaining hunter-gatherer populations in the world. As such, they provide an insight into the behavior of our pre-agricultural ancestors. The Hadza reside in Northern Tanzania in a remote region long isolated from modern culture. They are an egalitarian society in which decisions are made collectively, and food and resources are shared close to equally.

In recent years the Hadza living near the village of Mangola have been increasingly visited by ethno-tourists exploring nearby safari or hunting parks. In response, Hadza have begun selling bows and arrows to tourists and purchasing food and alcohol in the village. A lake and mountains separate Mangola from the Hadza living elsewhere in the region, making exposure to tourists uncommon for Hadza far from Mangola.

This setting creates a quasi-experiment in which the Hadza who happen to live near Mangola are exposed to modern culture, while those who happen to live further away are not. And given that there is very little evidence of migration across the region, any differences in Hadza behavior based on distance to Mangola can plausibly be attributed to modern culture.

In 2010, 91 Hadza adults — 46 living near Mangola and 45 living further away — participated in a version of the Mug Exchange Lab Experiment. Instead of mugs and chocolate, the goods were two familiar and comparable packages of biscuits.

Apicella et al. (2014) find that among the Hadza living close to Mangola, only 25% switched their initial endowment, providing evidence of an endowment effect. But for those living further away, there was no endowment effect, with 53% choosing to switch their initial endowment.

Figure 8.1 illustrates the evidence by plotting the fraction of participants who switched their endowed gift in each camp against the camp's distance from Mangola. The size of each camp's marker is proportional to the number of participants. We see that for camps with high exposure to tourists and close to Mangola, switching is much less common than retaining the endowed gift. But the participants in camps more than 30km from Mangola are about equally likely to switch or keep their endowment.

This evidence significantly enriches our understanding of the endowment effect. If we assume that the behavior of the isolated Hadza approximates that of our pre-agricultural ancestors, then early humans did not exhibit an endowment effect. And the fact that the endowment effect only exists for the Hadza who are exposed to the market-oriented behavior of tourists suggests that the evolution of culture over time led to its emergence in industrialized societies.

But how do we reconcile this inference with the previous evidence that market experience diminishes, not introduces, the endowment effect? One speculative hypothesis is

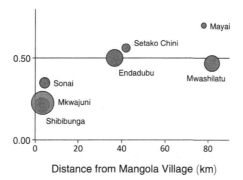

Figure 8.1 Fraction of Hadza Subjects Switching Endowed Item, by Camp

Source: Apicella, Azevedo, Christakis, and Fowler (2014). Copyright American Economic Association; reproduced with permission of the *American Economic Review*.

that in a hunter-gatherer world without concepts of private ownership, there is no endowment effect because individuals do not value an object based on who possesses it — everyone in the community owns it equally. But with the emergence of markets and private property, the endowment effect may develop as individuals experience strong attachments to their possessions. And it is only through high levels of market interaction in which individuals come to expect constant exchange that this attachment to possessions diminishes. In the next chapter we consider the impact of such expectations on the endowment effect.

8.2   Coding Lotteries

The assumption that preferences are reference-independent also generates anomalies when individuals choose between risky options. Trading a coffee mug, sports memorabilia, or biscuits for another comparable item is essentially risk free. But there are many decisions — about health, investments, career, and education — where uncertainty is pervasive.

In this section we consider simple decisions between lotteries. The standard model assumes that individuals prefer the lottery with the largest expected utility, where utility is defined over final outcomes. We illustrate how this assumption generates predictions at odds with actual behavior. Instead, individuals appear to evaluate outcomes as gains or losses relative to their current wealth.

8.2.1   Recoding a Lottery

Lab Experiment — Gain-Loss Equivalence (Kahneman and Tversky 1979)

A participant pool of 138 Israeli students was split, at random, into two groups. Each group was presented with one of the following two hypothetical problems. For context, at the time of the study the median net monthly income for a family was approximately I£3,000, where I£ refers to the Israeli pound.

1   In addition to whatever you own, you have been given I£1,000. You are now asked to choose between:

                                                              Results:

   A   Win I£1,000 with a 50% chance   **[16%]**
   B   Win I£500 for sure   **[84%]**

2   In addition to whatever you own, you have been given I£2,000. You are now asked to choose between:

   C   Pay I£1,000 with a 50% chance   **[69%]**
   D   Pay I£500 for sure   **[31%]**

Notice that each group of participants above is faced with two consecutive outcomes. First, they are told that they have been gifted some certain amount of money: I£1,000 or I£2,000. And then, they are prompted to choose between another certain outcome or a lottery. Under the standard assumption that preferences are defined over final outcomes, individuals integrate the initial gift into their evaluation of the two options. In so doing, the options for individuals in Group 1 are to choose either a lottery with equal chances of winning I£2,000 in total or I£1,000 in total (option *A*), or the certain outcome of winning I£1,500 in total (option *B*). But you should verify that these are exactly the same two options facing Group 2, once the initial I£2,000 gift is integrated into options *C* and *D*. In summary, the final outcomes are:

$A = C$: equal chance of winning I£2,000 or I£1,000
$B = D$: win I£1,500 for sure

Given that Groups 1 and 2 face the same decision over final outcomes, if preferences are defined only over final outcomes then we should expect the individuals in both groups to make similar choices. But instead, 84% of Group 1 prefers I£1,500 for sure, while less than a third of Group 2 prefers this outcome.

The only difference between the two problems is how the final outcomes are presented to the subjects. For Group 1, the final outcomes are *coded* as gains. But for Group 2, the same final outcomes are coded as losses. This **coding**, or redefining of final outcomes as gains or losses before individuals evaluate their options, must therefore be the cause of the difference in majority choices. It appears that individuals neglect the initial gift when evaluating their options. They care about changes in outcomes relative to prior wealth, and not simply the final outcome.[4]

8.2.2   *Aversion to Small-Stakes Lotteries*

Let's now consider a more extreme example illustrating how the standard assumption that preferences are defined over final outcomes leads to absurd predictions for choosing lotteries (Rabin 2000). Note that this is a theoretical thought experiment, as opposed to the previous anomalies in this chapter that have been identified by empirical evidence.

▪ *Example 8.1   Absurd Lottery Preferences*

Suppose that Kate is a standard decision maker who prefers lotteries that generate the largest expected utility. In addition, assume that Kate, no matter her wealth, would always reject a lottery in which she is equally likely to win $10 or lose $9. Perhaps Kate views the chance of losing $9 as too high, or the chance of winning $10 too low, for her to accept such a bet. This may not match your own preferences, but Kate's preferences are nonetheless arguably reasonable.

Given these preferences, do you think Kate would accept a lottery in which she has equal chances of losing $180 or winning $1,000? The standard model predicts that she would reject this lottery as well. What if instead of winning $1,000, the prize were $10,000? She again would reject the lottery. In fact, the standard model predicts that even if Kate were offered an even bet between losing $180 or winning $20 trillion (the annual GDP of the United States), she would still say no. This is clearly absurd. ▪

Why is the standard model generating such unreasonable predictions? Let's start by thinking carefully about what Kate's seemingly reasonable preference over the small-stakes lottery actually means. We assumed that Kate would always reject a lottery with equal chances of winning $10 or losing $9. Therefore, her utility from keeping a certain amount of wealth W must be greater than her expected utility from the even bet between wealth outcomes of $W+10$ or $W-9$. Expressed mathematically, we have:

$$u(W) > 0.5u(W+10) + 0.5u(W-9) \text{ for any } W$$

where $u(\cdot)$ is her utility function over final wealth outcomes (see Definition 2.6). By multiplying this inequality by 2 and rearranging, it can be equivalently expressed as:

$$\overbrace{u(W) - u(W-9)}^{\text{Potential Utility Loss}} \quad > \quad \overbrace{u(W+10) - u(W)}^{\text{Potential Utility Gain}} \text{ for any } W$$

In words, Kate rejects this lottery because the decrease in utility from potentially losing $9 is larger than the increase in utility from potentially winning $10. Graphically, her utility function $u(\cdot)$ must therefore be sufficiently concave, as depicted by the curve in Figure 8.2(a). Otherwise, with a linear (or close to linear) utility function, as drawn in Figure 8.2(b), the gain in utility from a win would be greater than the drop in utility from a loss and she would accept the lottery. Kate's concave utility function also implies that she is risk averse.

The next step is to recognize that because Kate would reject this small-stakes lottery at *every* wealth level, her utility function must be sufficiently concave at *every* wealth level. But this concavity at every wealth level implies that the entire utility function, when viewed over a large range of possible wealth levels, must be extremely concave. Such extreme concavity corresponds to extreme risk aversion because large increases in

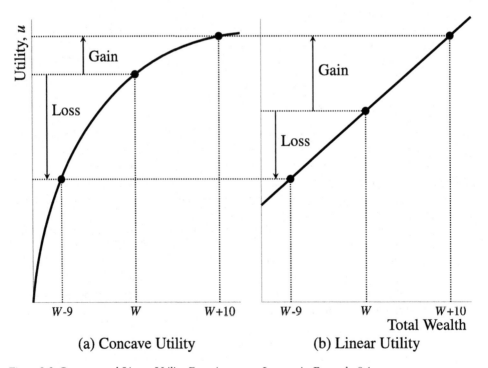

Figure 8.2 Concave and Linear Utility Functions over Lottery in Example 8.1

wealth have little positive impact on utility, while modest decreases in wealth have a more substantial negative impact on utility. And in Kate's case, her preferences over the small-stakes lottery imply that her utility function must be so concave that winning trillions of dollars increases her utility by less than the drop in utility from losing $180. For the mathematically curious, Appendix 8A formalizes this intuition.

It is also instructive to think through this logic in reverse. Under the standard expected utility model, for Kate to accept the lottery with a 50% chance of winning trillions of dollars, she *cannot* reject the small-stakes lottery at every wealth. That is, *reasonable risk aversion over large stakes implies low levels of risk aversion over small stakes.* Geometrically, a concave utility function over large changes in wealth is approximately linear over small changes in wealth. And because the utility function has very little curvature when wealth changes are small, the expected utility model predicts that individuals should behave as if they were approximately risk neutral over small stakes. Yet, there is evidence that many individuals are like Kate and averse to small-stakes lotteries (Thaler et al. 1997).

How can we avoid the absurd conclusions of this thought experiment? As the evidence in the Gain-Loss Equivalence Lab Experiment suggests, we could allow individuals to code lottery outcomes as wins or losses relative to their wealth. And if losses are weighted more than wins, as suggested by the endowment effect, then the logic above breaks down. In this case, we would expect individuals to reject even bets with potential wins and losses of similar magnitudes, while simultaneously accepting even bets where the potential wins are much larger than the potential losses.

8.3   Equity Premium Puzzle   [Finance]

One of the most famous anomalies in economics, the equity premium puzzle, concerns the relative returns on safe and risky investments. Before describing the anomaly, let's review some important concepts from finance.

8.3.1   Returns and Investments

We begin with a foundational concept. The **return on investment** is the change in the value of an investment relative to its initial cost:

$$\text{Return} = \frac{\text{Current Value} - \text{Initial Cost}}{\text{Initial Cost}}$$

Because the return is the ratio of one dollar amount to another, it is expressed as a percent. For example, if an initial investment of $500 is worth $600 the following year, then the annual return on this investment was $\frac{\$600 - \$500}{\$500} = 0.20$, or 20%.

Financial markets treat short-term debt issued by the United States federal government as among the safest of investments. In particular, the US government sells **Treasury Bills (T-Bills)** to investors in order to finance government operations and expenditures. These T-Bills act as IOUs, in which the government promises to pay the T-Bill holder a fixed amount of money on a specific date (usually three months after they are issued). Investors earn a positive return by buying T-Bills for less than what the government will pay in the future. For example, a T-Bill that pays $100 in 3 months and sells for $99 today, earns a 3-month return of $\frac{\$100 - \$99}{\$99} = 0.0101 = 1.01\%$, or an annualized return of $4 \times 1.01\% = 4.04\%$. Because the chance that the US defaults on this short-

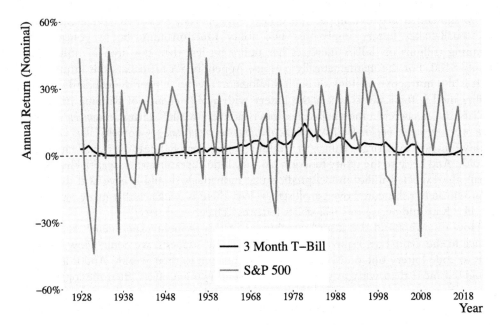

Figure 8.3 Annual Nominal Returns on S&P 500 and 3-Month Treasury Bill, 1928-2018

Data Source: Damodaran (2019).

term promise is very low, T-Bills are considered a relatively riskless or **risk-free asset**. The black line in Figure 8.3 shows the nominal annual return for 3 month T-Bills from 1928 to 2018. Observe that the returns on T-Bills have been quite stable, earning a low, but positive return that has rarely exceeded 7%.

Investors can also purchase shares of a publicly traded company, referred to as **stocks** or **equities**. Companies sell shares for the same reason that the government sells T-Bills — to raise money. Stock holders earn a positive return by selling stocks for more than they paid or receiving payouts of company earnings as dividends. Stocks are much riskier investments because while companies can experience huge profits, they can also make substantial losses and even shut down.

To help mitigate the risk of buying stocks in individual companies, investors can invest their money in a fund that holds stocks in many companies. The return on a fund is then equal to the average return of the stocks in the fund. For example, an S&P 500 index fund delivers a return equal to the (share-weighted) average return of the 500 large companies in the S&P 500. The performance of the S&P 500 is often taken as an indicator of the aggregate US stock market. The gray line in Figure 8.3 shows the nominal annual return for the S&P 500 (inclusive of dividends) over time. Relative to T-Bills, the S&P 500 is much more volatile, with alternating years of large positive and large negative returns. But the positive returns are far more frequent than the negative returns.

8.3.2   The Equity Premium

To appreciate the difference between investing in T-Bills and an S&P 500 index fund, consider the following hypothetical. Suppose that you (or your great grandparents) were deciding where to invest $100 on January 1, 1928. What do you think the nominal value (not adjusting for inflation) of that initial $100 investment would be at the end of 2018 if the money and its returns were continuously re-invested in T-Bills? And what if it were continuously re-invested in the S&P 500? Make a guess before reading on.

If invested in the risk-free T-Bills, the initial $100 would have grown to $2,063. This corresponds to an average annual return of 3.38%. This is clearly better than leaving the $100 bill under a mattress or in a piggy bank. But if it had been invested in the S&P 500, it would have grown to the enormous sum of $382,850. The average annual stock market return is significantly larger, at 9.49% (Damodaran 2019). Observe that this average return includes the Great Depression, World War II, the 1973 oil crisis, the dot-com crash of the early 2000s, and the more recent Great Recession. And yet it is still this large.

The additional return on stocks (or equities) relative to the return on risk-free assets is called the **equity premium**. Taking the average over the past 90 years in the US,

$$\text{Equity Premium} = \text{StockReturn} - \text{Risk-Free Return}$$
$$= 9.49\% - 3.38\% = 6.11\%$$

This difference reveals a 6.11% premium from investing in stocks relative to risk-free assets. And as we saw above, this equity premium compounded over many years leads to massive differences in the total return on investment. A similar equity premium exists in many other industrialized countries as well.

The existence of a positive equity premium is not a puzzle. In fact, it is exactly what standard economics predicts. To understand why, suppose to the contrary that there were no equity premium so that stocks and T-Bills generated the same average return, but that stock returns were still more variable. For instance, if stock returns were equally likely to be either +12% or −8% each year, while T-Bills generated a certain 2% return each year, there would be no equity premium over time. A risk averse investor would then not invest any money in the stock market because she could earn the same average return without the risk (to which she is averse) by simply investing all of her money in safe T-Bills. Companies would be unable to attract investments and raise money.

The average return on stocks must therefore be higher than on a risk-free asset in order to induce investors to accept the risk of investing in the stock market. We can consequently interpret the equity premium as the additional return that investors demand in order to invest in the stock market.

8.3.3   The Puzzle

If the standard model predicts an equity premium and that is what we observe, where is the promised puzzle? The issue is not with the existence of an equity premium, but with its size. The **equity premium puzzle** is that the historical equity premium is too large to be explained by the standard model of decision making (Mehra and Prescott 1985).

To understand what is meant by "too large," let's consider the implications of the standard model. Suppose that investors are standard decision makers with instantaneous utility of consumption given by

$$u(c) = \frac{c^{1-A}}{1-A}$$

where $A > 0$. This specific utility function is commonly used because it admits the useful interpretation that for a 1% increase in consumption, marginal utility decreases by A%.[5] Typical estimates of A range between 1 and 4, with an average value of 2. That is, for a 1% increase in consumption, it is typical for individuals to act as if their marginal utility decreases by 2%.

But in order for the standard model to predict the observed equity premium of 6.11%, A must be equal to 46 (see Exercise 8.9 for details). This is an extreme result that requires the utility function to be very concave — a 1% increase in consumption must reduce the slope of the utility function by 46%. Such extreme concavity of the utility function implies an extreme degree of risk aversion. To appreciate just how extreme, with $A = 46$ an investor would prefer to have a certain wealth of $50,800 rather than accept a lottery with equal chances of holding wealth of either $50,000 or $100,000. But surely, almost everyone would take an even bet where the loss is only $800, while the potential winnings are over $49,000. In summary, only absurd aversion to risk explains why investors demand a 6.11% equity premium for investing in risky stocks.

If investors exhibit a standard degree of risk aversion, with $A = 2$, then the predicted equity premium is only 0.26%. The actual equity premium is almost 6 percentage points higher than this prediction. So although the stock market is risky and risk averse investors demand compensation in the form of an equity premium to invest in stocks, the actual volatility of the stock market justifies only a modest equity premium. The very high returns of the stock market appear to overcompensate investors for accepting the risk. And yet many Americans avoid stocks completely, as if they are terrified of any risk.

It is important to remember that the equity premium puzzle is only a puzzle relative to the standard model. There are many dimensions along which the standard model may fail to capture actual decision making. And in fact, numerous alternative models of decision making have been proposed to generate predictions of a larger equity premium.[6]

Based on the previous anomalies in this chapter, it should not be surprising that this anomaly may be a consequence of assuming reference-independent preferences. In particular, the strong aversion to investing in stocks suggested by the equity premium puzzle may be driven by investors who focus on the ups and downs of the stock market, with the downs perceived as more extreme than equivalent ups. This would surely make the stock market appear less appealing as an investment option. We are now ready to introduce a model of exactly these preferences and consider its implications in the following chapter.

8.4 Summary

1 The **endowment effect** is the phenomenon by which an individual values a good in their possession, or endowment, more highly than when it is not in their possession.

2 The endowment effect is evidenced by lab and field experiments in two ways:

a   a reluctance to trade any good that has been recently gifted; and
b   a significantly larger minimum willingness to accept than maximum willingness to pay for the same good.

3 There is evidence that the endowment effect varies across individuals with different market experience and exposure.
4 The way in which final outcomes are **coded**, or redefined as gains or losses, impacts choices.
5 With standard preferences, risk aversion over small-stakes lotteries implies an absurd level of risk aversion over lotteries with large stakes. Equivalently, reasonable risk aversion over large-stakes lotteries implies essentially risk neutrality over small-stakes lotteries.
6 The **return on investment** is the change in the value of an investment relative to its initial value.
7 **Treasury Bills** are a (relatively) **risk-free asset** with low variability and a low average return on investment.
8 **Stocks**, or **equities**, are a risky asset with high variability and a high average return on investment.
9 The **equity premium** is the difference between the average annual return on the stock market and risk-free assets. The historical equity premium in the United States is approximately 6%.
10 The **equity premium puzzle** is the phenomenon that the empirical equity premium is too large to be explained by the standard model of decision making.
11 Each anomaly in the chapter suggests that individuals care about outcomes relative to a reference point and weight losses more than gains.

8.5   Exercises

Exercise 8.1 — Endowment Effect Examples. Explain how each of the following examples from Thaler (1980, 43-44) can be explained by the endowment effect. In particular, what is the endowment in each example? And what do standard reference-independent preferences predict?

a   Mr. R bought a case of good wine in the late 50s for about $5 a bottle. A few years later his wine merchant offered to buy the wine back for $100 a bottle. He refused, although he has never paid more than $35 for a bottle of wine.
b   Mr. H mows his own lawn. His neighbor's son would mow it for $8. He wouldn't mow his neighbor's same-sized lawn for less than $20.
c   Two survey questions:

   i   Assume you have been exposed to a disease which if contracted leads to a quick and painless death within a week. The probability you have the disease is 0.001. What is the maximum you would be willing to pay for a cure?
   ii Suppose volunteers were needed for research on the above disease. All that would be required is that you expose yourself to a 0.001 chance of contracting the disease. What is the minimum payment you would require to volunteer for this program? (You would not be allowed to purchase the cure.)

   Typical answers are (i) $650 and (ii) $33,000.

Exercise 8.2 — Value Variation. A common problem in environmental economics is determining the value of goods that are not traded and therefore do not have a market price. For example, what is the value of saving a species that is close to extinction or protecting natural environments from development and industry? One method for estimating such values, known as contingent valuation, is to survey individuals.

Suppose that a group of individuals are surveyed about their valuation of the Amazon rainforest. Half of the individuals are asked how much they would be willing to pay to preserve 100 acres of currently unprotected rainforest. The other half are asked how much they would need to receive in order to be in favor of selling 100 acres of currently protected rainforest to a logging company that will deforest the land.

a   Based on the evidence in this chapter, which group do you expect to report a higher valuation for the 100 acres of rainforest?

b   Which question does an environmentalist want to ask in order to make their case? What about an industrialist?

c   Explain why contingent valuation may not be the best way to value non-market goods.

Exercise 8.3 — Endowed Status. *Status quo bias* refers to the phenomenon by which individuals exhibit an affinity for status quo options, like voting for an incumbent candidate, investing more in the same investments, or buying products from the same brands. Samuelson and Zeckhauser (1988) document the status quo bias with experimental evidence from the lab. Explain how the endowment effect could give rise to a status quo bias. Can you think of an alternative explanation for the status quo bias?

Exercise 8.4 — Endowing IPOs in India. [Finance] Anagol, Balasubramaniam, and Ramadorai (2018) study a quasi-experimental setting in India where initial public offering (IPO) shares in a newly public company are randomly assigned to applicants. Among those who apply, some are randomly granted the opportunity to purchase the shares at an initial IPO issue price (the winners), while others (the losers) must wait until the stock begins to trade freely to purchase shares at the market price.

Because of the random assignment, winners and losers should share identical preferences on average. Standard economics therefore predicts that soon after everyone is able to trade shares, there should be no difference between the two groups in their likelihood to hold company stock. The researchers find, however, that the winners are much more likely to hold the stock (and buy more of it) than the losers, even two years after the stock was made public.

a   Provide an explanation for this result using the insights from this chapter.

b   Suppose that the researchers restricted their comparison between winners and losers to only those applicants with the most trading experience. Based on the evidence from the Sportscard Show Field Experiments, how would you expect the stock holdings of these two subgroups to compare to each other over time?

Exercise 8.5 — Endowments for Primates. There is evidence that chimpanzees and capuchin monkeys exhibit an endowment effect (Brosnan et al. 2007; Lakshminaryanan, Chen, and Santos 2008), as do great apes, but only for food items (Kanngiesser et al. 2011).

a   Interpret this evidence. In particular, what does it suggest about the origins of the endowment effect?

b   Can you reconcile this evidence with the findings of the Hunter–Gatherer Exchange Field Experiment in the chapter?.

Exercise 8.6 — Effects of Endowments and Income. The chapter claims that the standard model predicts the maximum willingness to pay (*WTP*) to buy a good equals the minimum willingness to accept (*WTA*) to sell the good. Let's explore this claim in the context of buying and selling coffee mugs.

Assume that an individual, Willie, is a participant in the Monetizing Mugs Lab Experiment. He has preferences over mugs (*M*) and wealth (*W*) represented by a utility function $u(M, W)$. Willie initially has no mugs ($M = 0$) and \$8 of wealth ($W = 8$). His *WTP* is the amount of money he can give up in exchange for gaining a mug that makes him indifferent to just keeping his initial endowments. Mathematically, his *WTP* is then defined by the following indifference condition:

$$u(0, 8) = u(\text{Don't Buy}) = u(\text{Buy for } \$WTP) = u(1, 8 - WTP) \tag{8.1}$$

If Willie is gifted a mug, then his *WTA* is the amount of money he can accept in exchange for losing the mug that makes him indifferent to just keeping the mug. Mathematically, his *WTA* is defined by:

$$u(1, 8) = u(\text{Don't Sell}) = u(\text{Sell for } \$WTA) = u(0, 8 + WTA) \tag{8.2}$$

a   Suppose that $u(M, W) = 12\sqrt{M + 1} + W$. Use equations (8.1) and (8.2) to predict Willie's *WTP* and *WTA*.

b   Now suppose that $u(M, W) = (M + 1) \times W$. Use equations (8.1) and (8.2) to predict Willie's *WTP* and *WTA*.

You should have found that *WTA* = *WTP* in one of these cases and that *WTA* > *WTP* in the other. This illustrates that *WTA* need not always equal *WTP*. But what accounts for the difference in results? With the utility function in part (a), Willie's valuation of a mug does not change if his income goes up or down (i.e., no income effect). Whereas with the utility function in part (b), Willie's valuation of a mug increases with his income (i.e., a positive income effect).

c   Provide intuition for the connection between (i) income effects and (ii) the relationship of *WTA* to *WTP*. *Hint: By virtue of being gifted a mug, sellers have higher "incomes" than buyers.*

d   Which utility function do you think is more likely in the mug exchange context? Why?

Exercise 8.7 — Framing Cancer Treatment. [Health] McNeil et al. (1982) asked patients, physicians, and graduate students to choose between two alternative treatments for lung cancer: surgery or radiation. The main tradeoff between these two treatments is that although surgery has a higher long-term survival rate than radiation therapy, it also has a higher short-term risk of death. Before choosing which treatment they would prefer, half of the respondents were provided information about the survival probabilities (i.e., the risk of surviving treatment and being alive in 1 or 5 years) for each treatment. The other half of respondents were provided the same exact information, but in terms of mortality probabilities (i.e., the risk of dying during treatment and dying within 1 or 5 years).

a   Suppose that respondents have standard preferences. Would you expect the two groups (survival vs. mortality data information) to have similar or different preferences over the treatment options? Why?

b   The researchers find that radiation is preferred to surgery 25% of the time for those given the survival data and 42% of the time for those given the mortality data. Explain what this evidence suggests about the respondents' preferences. How is the evidence related to evidence from this chapter?

Exercise 8.8 — Equity Premium Investment Strategy. Suppose that we interpret the standard model of decision making as a normative criterion for how individuals ought to behave. In this case, what does the equity premium puzzle imply about how individuals should be investing their savings over long horizons? That is, should they be investing more or less in the stock market? Explain.

Exercise 8.9 — Predicting the Equity Premium (Mehra 2003). The standard model of decision making with utility $u(c) = c^{1-A}/(1 - A)$ implies the following relationship between the average annual return on stocks (R_S), the average annual return on a risk-free asset (R_F), and A:

$$\frac{\ln (1 + R_S) - \ln (1 + R_F)}{0.00125} = A \tag{8.3}$$

You can verify that if $R_S = 0.0949$ and $R_F = 0.0338$, then $A = 46$ as noted in the chapter.

a   Suppose that $A = 4$ (which is at the upper end of typical estimates for A). In addition, assume that the risk-free return is $R_F = 0.0338$, as observed. Use equation (8.3) to compute the equity premium $R_S - R_F$ in this case. How does this compare to the observed equity premium of 6.11%?

b   Suppose that $A = 0$.

   i   What is the shape of the utility function u in this case? Is it concave, linear, or convex?

   ii   What does the shape of u imply about whether individuals are risk averse, risk neutral, or risk loving? See Section 2.3.3 to review these concepts.

   iii   Use equation (8.3) to determine the equity premium, $R_S - R_F$.

   iv   Provide intuition for why the risk preferences in part (b.ii) imply the equity premium in part (b.iii).

8A   Appendix: The Math of Absurd Lottery Preferences

Theorem 8A.1 — Calibration Theorem (Rabin 2000). Let an individual be an expected utility maximizer where utility u is defined over total wealth. In addition, assume that $.5u(W + 10) + .5u(W - 9) \leq u(W)$ for all W. Then, $.5u(\infty) + .5u$ $(W - 180) \leq u(W)$ for all W. That is, the individual prefers to reject a lottery with

equal chances of winning any positive amount of money or losing $180.
Remark on Notation: $u(\infty) \equiv \lim_{x \to \infty} u(x)$

Proof. We proceed in four steps.

1 **Derive an upper bound on the curvature of the utility function, *u*.**
   Given that $.5u(W + 10) + .5u(W - 9) \le u(W)$ for all W, multiplying by 2, we have:

   $$u(W + 10) + u(W - 9) \le 2u(W) = u(W) + u(W) \text{ for all } W$$

   or equivalently,

   $$u(W + 10) - u(W) \le u(W) - u(W - 9) \text{ for all } W \qquad (8A.1)$$

Because u is concave, we also know that line segment A is steeper than line segment B in Figure 8A.1. This implies the following inequality:

$$\underbrace{u(W + 10) - u(W + 9)}_{\text{slope of } B} \le \underbrace{\frac{u(W + 10) - u(W)}{10}}_{\text{slope of } A} \text{ for all } W \qquad (8A.2)$$

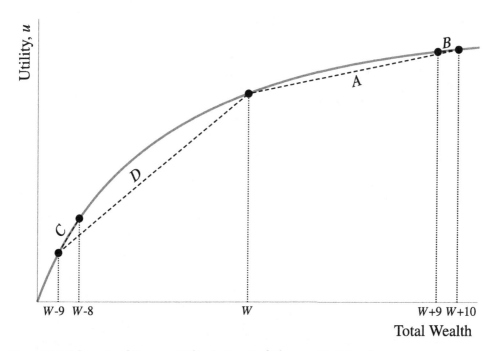

Figure 8A.1 Schematic of Concave Utility in Step 1 of Theorem 8A.1 Proof

Similarly, line segment C is steeper than line segment D, implying:

$$\overbrace{\frac{u(W) - u(W - 9)}{9}}^{\text{slope of } D} \leq \overbrace{u(W - 8) - u(W - 9)}^{\text{slope of } C} \text{ for all } W \tag{8A.3}$$

Define $MU(x) = u(x) - u(x - 1)$ as the marginal utility of the xth dollar. Then, combining the above inequalities, we obtain

$$
\begin{aligned}
MU(W + 10) \quad &= u(W + 10) - u(W + 9) \\
&\leq \frac{u(W + 10) - u(W)}{10} \text{ by inequality (8A.2)} \\
&\leq \frac{u(W) - u(W - 9)}{10} \text{ by inequality (8A.1)} \\
&\leq \frac{9(u(W - 8) - u(W - 9))}{10} \text{ by inequality (8A.3)} \\
&= \frac{9}{10} MU(W - 8)
\end{aligned}
$$

And since this holds for all W,

$$MU(W + 18) \leq 0.9 MU(W) \text{ for all } W \tag{8A.4}$$

Inequality (8A.4) says that the marginal utility, or slope of the utility function, at a wealth level with an additional \$18 must be at most 90% of the current marginal utility.

2   **Use Step 1 to derive an upper bound on $u(\infty)$.**
Consider the line tangent to the utility function at wealth W. The slope of this line is $MU(W)$, and is labeled as such in Figure 8A.2. Because u is concave, the utility function at $W + 18$ must be below this tangent line at $W + 18$. The value of this tangent line at $W + 18$ is equal to $u(W) + 18MU(W)$. Therefore,

$$u(W + 18) \leq u(W) + 18MU(W) \tag{8A.5}$$

By the same logic also illustrated in Figure 8A.2,

$$u(W + 36) \leq u(W + 18) + 18MU(W + 18) \tag{8A.6}$$

Combining the previous three inequalities we obtain the following upper bound on $u(W + 36)$:

$$
\begin{aligned}
u(W + 36) \quad &\leq u(W + 18) + 18MU(W + 18) \text{ by inequality (8A.6)} \\
&\leq u(W) + 18MU(W) + 18MU(W + 18) \text{ by inequality (8A.5)} \\
&\leq u(W) + 18MU(W) + 18 \cdot 0.9MU(W) \text{ by inequality (8A.4)} \\
&= u(W) + 18MU(W)[1 + 0.9] \tag{8A.7}
\end{aligned}
$$

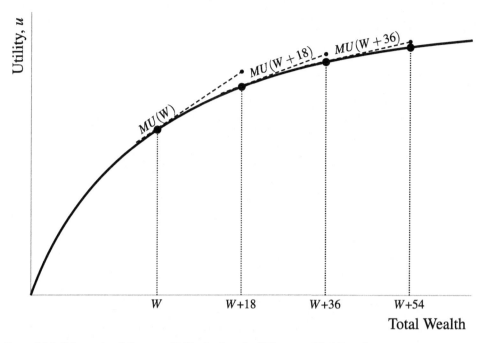

Figure 8A.2 Schematic of Concave Utility in Step 2 of Theorem 8A.1 Proof

With analogous steps, we can also obtain an upper bound on $u(W + 54)$:

$$
\begin{aligned}
u(W + 54) \ &\le u(W + 36) + 18MU(W + 36) \text{ by concavity of } u \\
&\le u(W) + 18MU(W)[1 + 0.9] + 18MU(W + 36) \text{ by (8A.7)} \\
&\le u(W) + 18MU(W)[1 + 0.9] + 18 \cdot 0.9MU(W + 18) \text{ by (8A.4)} \\
&\le u(W) + 18MU(W)[1 + 0.9] + 18 \cdot 0.9 \cdot 0.9MU(W) \text{ by (8A.4)} \\
&= u(W) + 18MU(W)[1 + 0.9 + 0.9^2] \quad\quad\quad\quad\quad (8A.8)
\end{aligned}
$$

You should recognize a pattern with the upper bounds in (8A.5), (8A.7), and (8A.8). It turns out that for any integer $n \ge 1$,

$$
u(W + 18n) \le u(W) + 18MU(W)[1 + 0.9 + 0.9^2 + \cdots + 0.9^{n-1}] \quad (8A.9)
$$

We can take the limit as n approaches infinity on both sides of (8A.9) to obtain (with use of the geometric series formula):

$$
u(\infty) \le u(W) + 18MU(W)\left[\frac{1}{1 - 0.9}\right] = u(W) + 180MU(W) \quad (8A.10)
$$

3 **Derive an upper bound on $u(W - 180)$.**

Consider the line tangent to the utility function at wealth W, with slope $MU(W)$. Because u is concave, the utility function at $W - 180$ must be below the tangent line at $W - 180$. The value of this tangent line at $W - 180$ is equal to $u(W) - 180MU(W)$.

Therefore,

$$u(W - 180) \leq u(W) - 180MU(W) \qquad (8A.11)$$

4 Combine Steps 2 and 3 to derive the desired result.

Divide inequalities (8A.10) and (8A.11) by 2 to obtain:

$$0.5u(\infty) \leq 0.5u(W) + 90MU(W)$$
$$0.5u(W - 180) \leq 0.5u(W) - 90MU(W)$$

Then add these two inequalities to obtain our desired inequality:

$$0.5u(\infty) + 0.5u(W - 180) \leq u(W)$$

Notes

1 The standard model allows for WTA to be greater than WTP if there are transaction costs or income effects. These are unlikely explanations for the evidence in this section where transaction costs are eliminated and any possible income effects are negligible.
2 The two gifts were a Kansas City Royals ticket stub for the game in which Cal Ripken Jr. broke the world record for consecutive games played and a dated certificate commemorating the game in which Nolan Ryan won his 300th game. John List had access to numerous units of each gift from his previous attendance at each of these events.
3 An alternative interpretation of these data is that individuals without the endowment effect choose to participate in markets more often. List (2003) provides evidence against this hypothesis by comparing the traders with themselves over time to control for unobservable individual-specific characteristics.
4 The evidence from the Gain-Loss Equivalence Lab Experiment also illustrates a more general phenomenon that Kahneman and Tversky (1979) refer to as the *isolation effect*, by which choices depend on how outcomes are isolated from each other within a multistage decision problem.
5 To see this result, first note that marginal utility is $MU(c) = c^{-A}$. The percent change in MU following a 1% change in c is then $\frac{dMU(c)}{dc} \frac{c}{MU(c)} = -Ac^{-A-1} \frac{c}{c^{-A}} = -A$.
6 Siegel and Thaler (1997) provide an accessible overview of different approaches to explaining the equity premium puzzle.

References

Anagol, Santosh, Vimal Balasubramaniam, and Tarun Ramadorai. 2018. "Endowment Effects in the Field: Evidence from India's IPO Lotteries." *The Review of Economic Studies* 85 (4): 1971–2004. doi:10.1093/restud/rdy014.

Apicella, Coren L., Eduardo M. Azevedo, Nicholas A. Christakis, and James H. Fowler. 2014. "Evolutionary Origins of the Endowment Effect: Evidence from Hunter-Gatherers." *American Economic Review* 104 (6): 1793–1805. doi:10.1257/aer.104.6. 1793.

Brosnan, Sarah F., Owen D. Jones, Susan P. Lambeth, Mary Catherine Mareno, Amanda S. Richardson, and Steven J. Schapiro. 2007. "Endowment Effects in Chimpanzees." *Current Biology* 17 (19): 1704–1707. doi:10.1016/j.cub.2007.08.059.

Damodaran, Asmath. 2019. *Annual Returns on Stock, T.Bonds and T.Bills: 1928—Current*. Accessed August 22, 2019, http://pages.stern.nyu.edu/~adamodar/New_Home_Page/datafile/histretSP.html.

Henrich, Joseph, Robert Boyd, Samuel Bowles, Colin F. Camerer, Ernst Fehr, Herbert Gintis, and Richard McElreath. 2001. "In Search of Homo Economicus: Behavioral Experiments in 15 Small-Scale Societies." *American Economic Review* 91 (2): 73–78. doi:10.1257/aer.91.2.73.

Henrich, Joseph, Richard McElreath, Abigail Barr, Jean Ensminger, Clark Barrett, Alexander Bolyanatz, Juan Camilo Cardenas, Michael Gurven, and Edwins Gwako. 2006. "Costly Punishment across Human Societies." *Science* 312 (5781): 1767–1770. doi:10.1126/science.1127333.

Horowitz, John K., and Kenneth E. McConnell. 2002. "A Review of WTA/WTP Studies." *Journal of Environmental Economics and Management* 44 (3): 426–447. doi:10.1006/jeem.2001.1215.

Kahneman, Daniel, Jack L. Knetsch, and Richard H. Thaler. 1990. "Experimental Tests of the Endowment Effect and the Coase Theorem." *Journal of Political Economy* 98 (6): 1325–1348. doi:10.1086/261737.

Kahneman, Daniel, and Amos Tversky. 1979. "Prospect Theory: An Analysis of Decision under Risk." *Econometrica* 47 (2): 263–291. doi:10.2307/1914185.

Kanngiesser, Patricia, Laurie R. Santos, Bruce M. Hood, and Josep Call. 2011. "The Limits of Endowment Effects in Great Apes (Pan paniscus, Pan troglodytes, Gorilla gorilla, Pongo pygmaeus)." *Journal of Comparative Psychology* 125 (4): 436–445. doi:10.1037/a0024516.

Knetsch, Jack L. 1989. "The Endowment Effect and Evidence of Nonreversible Indifference Curves." *American Economic Review* 79 (5): 1277–1284.

Lakshminaryanan, Venkat, M. Keith Chen, and Laurie R. Santos. 2008. "Endowment Effect in Capuchin Monkeys." *Philosophical Transactions of the Royal Society B: Biological Sciences* 363 (1511): 3837–3844. doi:10.1098/rstb.2008.0149.

List, John A. 2003. "Does Market Experience Eliminate Market Anomalies?" *The Quarterly Journal of Economics* 118 (1): 41–71. doi:10.1162/00335530360535144.

McNeil, Barbara J., Stephen G. Pauker, Harold C. Sox Jr, and Amos Tversky. 1982. "On the Elicitation of Preferences for Alternative Therapies." *The New England Journal of Medicine* 306 (21): 1259–1262. doi:10.1056/NEJM198205273062103.

Mehra, Rajnish. 2003. "The Equity Premium: Why Is It a Puzzle?" *Financial Analysts Journal* 59 (1): 54–69. http://www.jstor.org/stable/4480451.

Mehra, Rajnish, and Edward C. Prescott. 1985. "The Equity Premium: A Puzzle." *Journal of Monetary Economics* 15 (2): 145–161.

Rabin, Matthew. 2000. "Risk Aversion and Expected-Utility Theory: A Calibration Theorem." *Econometrica* 68 (5): 1281–1292. doi:10.1111/1468-0262.00158.

Samuelson, William, and Richard Zeckhauser. 1988. "Status Quo Bias in Decision Making." *Journal of Risk and Uncertainty* 1 (1): 7–59. doi:10.1007/BF00055564.

Siegel, Jeremy J., and Richard H. Thaler. 1997. "Anomalies: The Equity Premium Puzzle." *Journal of Economic Perspectives* 11 (1): 191–200. doi:10.1257/jep.11.1. 191.

Thaler, Richard H. 1980. "Toward a Positive Theory of Consumer Choice." *Journal of Economic Behavior & Organization* 1 (1): 39–60. Reprinting from pp 43–44, Copyright (1980), with permission from Elsevier, doi:10.1016/0167-2681(80)90051-7.

Thaler, Richard H., Amos Tversky, Daniel Kahneman, and Alan Schwartz. 1997. "The Effect of Myopia and Loss Aversion on Risk Taking: An Experimental Test." *The Quarterly Journal of Economics* 112 (2): 647–661. doi:10.1162/003355397555226.

9   Reference Dependence

Learning Objectives

★   Understand how the model of reference-dependent preferences with loss aversion differs from the standard model.

★   Apply the model of reference-dependent preferences to explain anomalies in settings with both certainty and risk.

★   Evaluate empirical evidence of reference-dependent preferences.

★   Appreciate the sensitivity of predicted behavior to the reference point and the bracketing of a decision problem.

The anomalies in the previous chapter illustrate the shortcomings of assuming that individuals have standard reference-independent preferences. This assumption generates predictions that are inconsistent with behaviors in lab settings, real-world marketplaces, and the stock market. In each case, the evidence points to the plausible alternative that individuals code outcomes as gains or losses. And losses are experienced more intensely than gains of the same magnitude.

This chapter begins by integrating these insights into a nonstandard model of preferences that are reference-*dependent*. To do so, we expand the utility function to depend not only on the final outcome, but on a point of reference. This reference point might be a function of past outcomes or future expectations. Sensations of losses are also assumed to be greater than equivalent gains. The model is sufficiently general to be applied across a wide range of settings, with and without certainty.

The remainder of the chapter puts the model to work. The first applications make sense of the anomalies in Chapter 8: the endowment effect, seemingly absurd risk preferences, and the equity premium puzzle. We conclude with evidence from labor markets, job search, and life-cycle consumption that can be explained by our new model (and not the standard one). The end-of-chapter exercises further illustrate the applicability of the model to understanding behaviors ranging from golf putts to tax evasion.

9.1   Reference-Dependent Preferences

In this section we build a model of reference-dependent utility. Let's begin with a simple model before embedding it into a more general framework.

DOI: 10.4324/9780367854072-12

9.1.1 Gain-Loss Utility

Suppose that you just found a $20 bill on an empty sidewalk. You are now $20 richer. With standard reference-independent preferences, you would evaluate your newly found wealth with a utility function $u(x)$ where x is your *total wealth*. That is, if your wealth before the fortuitous find was W, your utility has increased from $u(W)$ to $u(W + 20)$. But what if you don't actually care about your total wealth, and only the fact that your wealth has increased by $20? In other words, your utility depends on the *difference* between the final outcome of $W + 20$ and your initial wealth W.

Now suppose that instead of finding a $20 bill, you find a $20 parking ticket on your car. Because your total wealth is now $W - 20$, the standard model requires your utility to be $u(W - 20)$. But if all you care about is the fact that you lost money, then your utility should depend on the *difference* between the final outcome of $W-20$ and your initial wealth W. And if losing $20 feels much worse than finding $20, the drop in utility from the loss should be larger in magnitude than the increase in utility from the gain.

We can mathematically represent such concerns with gains and losses as follows:

Definition 9.1 The **(linear) gain-loss value function** over a final outcome x and reference point r is:

$$v(x \mid r) = \begin{cases} x - r & \text{if } x \geq r \\ \lambda(x - r) & \text{if } x < r \end{cases}$$

where $\lambda \geq 1$ is the **coefficient of loss aversion**.

To develop intuition for the above definition, let's apply this gain-loss value function as a measure of utility to the examples above. Note that in both scenarios we assumed that outcomes are evaluated relative to the reference point of initial wealth (i.e., $r = W$).

$$\text{Winning } \$20: \quad v(W + 20 \mid W) = W + 20 - W = 20$$
$$\text{Losing } \$20: \quad v(W - 20 \mid W) = \lambda(W - 20 - W) = -20\lambda$$

Observe that the utility from winning $20 does not depend on the wealth level — it is just 20. Similarly, the utility from losing $20 is independent of the wealth level. But there is a difference between the gain and the loss. With a loss utility is multiplied by lambda, λ, the lowercase Greek letter for l, chosen because it is applied to *losses*. And since $\lambda \geq 1$, the negative utility is at least as large in magnitude as the positive utility. The parking ticket lowers utility more than the equally sized $20-find increases it. This is consistent with the proposed valuations above.

The gain-loss value function, depicted graphically in Figure 9.1, provides a nonstandard utility representation of preferences. In particular, it exhibits the following two key features that are not present in the standard model.

1   **Reference Dependence:** The utility assigned to a final outcome x is a function of the difference between that outcome and a reference point r. When the outcome is exactly equal to the reference point, utility is zero. Outcomes above the reference

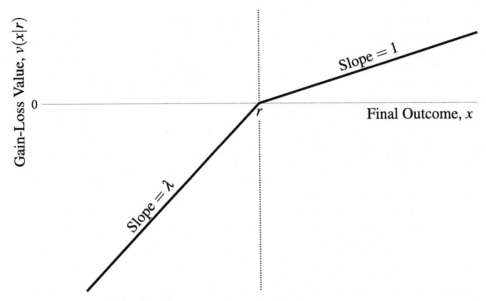

Figure 9.1 Gain-Loss Value Function

point generate positive utility, while outcomes below the reference point generate negative utility. Because a change in the reference point impacts utility, holding the final outcome fixed, the utility in this case is **reference-dependent**. For example, finding $20 on the sidewalk can generate negative utility instead of positive utility if the point of reference is the hopeful expectation of finding $50 on the sidewalk.

2   **Loss Aversion:** The magnitude of λ measures the degree to which individuals overweight losses relative to equally sized gains, i.e., are **loss averse**. Graphically, λ is the slope of the value function over losses, while the slope of the value function over gains is 1. Larger values of λ create a more severely kinked value function at the reference point r. If $\lambda = 1$, then the value function is an unkinked straight line with slope 1 and there is no loss aversion.

The gain-loss value function can be applied to understand a wide range of decision problems, including choices over certain and risky outcomes.[1] The broad applicability of this model of preferences is due in part to the fact that the reference point is not specified. But such flexibility of the reference point warrants caution. If the model's predictions depend on the reference point and we are uncertain about what the relevant reference point is for decision makers, then our predictions may be unreliable. We must therefore be careful in applications to think carefully about what makes for a reasonable reference point given the particulars of the decision context.

Gain-loss utility illuminates another feature of decision making: bracketing. In any economic model of decision making, standard or not, we must specify the bounds of the available choice set (denoted by X in our standard model). When choosing between 12 different types of toothpaste at the drugstore, are you also integrating this toothpaste choice with all of your other decisions in life (e.g., how often to go to the dentist, whether or not to buy dental floss, how much money to spend on cosmetics, etc.)? It is typical to assume that individuals are not doing such a grand integration of choices and are instead evaluating each choice separately. This assumption of narrow mental brackets around each choice is called **narrow bracketing** (or narrow framing). But the standard reference-independence assumption that individuals evaluate final wealth outcomes, integrating monetary gains and losses with total wealth, is a form of **broad bracketing**. Thinking about total current wealth, or even lifetime wealth, requires a broad perspective.

The bounds of the mental brackets can matter more with gain-loss utility than standard utility.[2] This is because preferences, and therefore behavior, shift so abruptly at the reference point. And with narrower brackets, outcomes are often closer to this reference point. In one study, 89% of people bracket narrowly, suggesting that broad bracketing can be a poor model of behavior (Rabin and Weizsäcker 2009). When applying gain-loss utility we must therefore be careful to also consider the mental bracket for the decision of interest.

9.1.2 A Model of Reference-Dependent Preferences

The gain-loss value function is a compelling alternative model of utility, particularly for evaluating changes in wealth, like finding or losing $20. But it has two important limitations: the standard **intrinsic utility** from the final outcome is neglected and only one good — like wealth — can be considered at a time. Let's build an enriched reference-dependent model of preferences that address these two limitations in turn.[3]

The Role of Intrinsic Utility

Imagine two scenarios. In one, your wealth is $200 and in the other, your wealth is $10,000. Now suppose that in each scenario you discover a $20 parking ticket on your car. If we use the gain-loss value function to represent preferences, then no matter your wealth, you always feel the same about the parking ticket, with a utility of -20λ. But your absolute level of wealth may also impact your utility.

One solution is not to discard standard intrinsic utility completely, but to "merge" it with gain-loss utility. In particular, let preferences over an outcome x, given a reference point r, be represented by utility function $U(x|r)$ as follows:

$$U(x \mid r) = u(x) + \eta \cdot v(u(x) \mid u(r))$$
$$= u(x) + \begin{cases} \eta(u(x) - u(r)) & \text{if } u(x) \geq u(r) \\ \eta\lambda(u(x) - u(r)) & \text{if } u(x) < u(r) \end{cases} \quad (9.1)$$

where $u(x)$ is the standard intrinsic utility from consuming x, and $v(\cdot)$ is the gain-loss value function. The parameter eta, η, measures the weight placed on gain-loss utility.

With this model, the intrinsic utility of the final outcome now has a role. In fact, it has two roles. Its first role can be clearly seen by considering the special case with $\eta = 0$. Then no weight is attached to the gain-loss utility and $U(x|r) = u(x)$; we are back to the standard reference-independent case where intrinsic utility is all that matters. But for $\eta > 0$, total reference-dependent utility U is the weighted sum of intrinsic utility and gain-loss utility. And observe that intrinsic utility now shows up again, inside the gain-loss utility function $v(\cdot)$. This means that when individuals evaluate gains and losses, they are specifically evaluating the *gains and losses of intrinsic utility*, and not the gains and losses of the outcomes directly. Although equation (9.1) is quite complicated, its advantage is that it evaluates outcomes entirely in terms of intrinsic utility and only two parameters: λ and η.

To see equation (9.1) in action, let's apply it to the two scenarios above with a $20 parking ticket at different wealth levels. Let the reference point be wealth before the ticket ($r = W$) and the final outcome be wealth after the ticket ($x = W - 20$). In addition, assume that intrinsic utility of wealth is $u(x) = 5x$. The reference-dependent utility of receiving the ticket is therefore:

$$
\begin{aligned}
U(W - 20 \mid W) &= u(W - 20) + \eta\lambda[u(W - 20) - u(W)] \\
&= 5(W - 20) + \eta\lambda[5(W - 20) - 5W] \\
&= 5W - (1 + \eta\lambda)100
\end{aligned}
$$

Observe the following characteristics of this expression:

1   Utility U is increasing in the absolute level of wealth W. Being rich with a parking ticket generates more utility than being poor with a parking ticket.
2   Utility U is decreasing in the coefficient of loss aversion λ. Being more averse to losses lowers the utility from a parking ticket.
3   Utility U is decreasing in the weight attached to gain-loss utility η. Caring more about gains and losses relative to intrinsic utility lowers the utility from a loss.

These are intuitively appealing properties of a utility function.

Allowing Multiple Goods

The utility function $U(x|r)$ is limited by its application to only one good, which in all of our examples thus far has been wealth. But for many economic decisions, particularly those without risk, the choice is not one of trading off different amounts of money, but trading off money against a good or service. Every time you buy something, you are exchanging money for a good. The reverse exchange characterizes selling. And in a barter setting, you might ask your roommate for a haircut in return for cleaning the bathroom — with no money exchanged at all.

Our next step is then to allow reference-dependent utility U to apply to two goods (one of which can still be wealth). Note that with two final outcomes, denoted by x_1 and x_2, there must be two corresponding reference points, r_1 and r_2. A straightforward method for accommodating two goods is to compute reference-dependent utility for each using equation (9.1) and then add them up.[4] Doing so completes our model.

> **Definition 9.2**   The **model of reference-dependent preferences** evaluates final outcomes (x_1, x_2), given corresponding reference points (r_1, r_2), as follows:
>
> $$
> \begin{aligned}
> U((x_1, x_2) \mid (r_1, r_2)) &= u_1(x_1) + \eta \cdot v(u_1(x_1) \mid u_1(r_1)) \\
> &\quad + u_2(x_2) + \eta \cdot v(u_2(x_2) \mid u_2(r_2))
> \end{aligned}
> $$

where $\eta \geq 0$, $u_1(\cdot)$ and $u_2(\cdot)$ are the intrinsic utility functions over goods 1 and 2, and $v(\cdot)$ is the gain-loss value function in Definition 9.1.

Pay careful attention to what has a subscript and what does not in the above utility expression. The subscripts indicate differentiation between the two goods. With subscripts on the intrinsic utility functions, $u_1(\cdot)$ and $u_2(\cdot)$, the model allows for different intrinsic preferences for each good. Otherwise, if the two goods were wealth and coffee mugs, \$10 would have to generate the same intrinsic utility as 10 coffee mugs. Conversely, $v(\cdot)$ and η do not have subscripts. This means that an individual applies the same coefficient of loss aversion λ to utility losses of each good and equally weights the gain-loss utility of each good.[5] In sum, *all* utility gains are multiplied by η and *all* utility losses are multiplied by $\eta\lambda$.

This model is best understood through its application — not by staring at subscripts and Greek letters. So let's start applying.

9.2   Application: Endowment Effect

Recall the evidence of the endowment effect in both lab and field settings from the previous chapter. One implication of the endowment effect is that an individual's maximum willingness to pay (WTP) for a good is much lower than their minimum willingness to accept (WTA) to sell the same good. Our objective is to explain this phenomenon by applying the model of reference-dependent preferences to the decision problems facing buyers and sellers of mugs. We end this section by exploring the importance of determining what counts as a reference point.

9.2.1   Endowment-Based Reference Points

Let Eddie be a decision maker with the reference-dependent utility function $U(\cdot)$ as in Definition 9.2. He is narrowly concerned with the number of mugs (m) that he has and his total wealth today (w). Assume that his intrinsic utility functions over these two goods are:

$$\text{Intrinsic Mug Utility}: u_m(m) = B \cdot m \text{ where } B > 0 \text{ is a mug's marginal benefit}$$
$$\text{Intrinsic Wealth Utility}: u_w(w) = w$$

In addition, Eddie's reference points for mugs and wealth are his endowments of each. And for simplicity, let's assume that he is initially endowed with zero mugs and zero wealth. Our last assumption is that $\eta = 1$, so intrinsic utility is weighted equally to gain-loss utility.

Buying

Consider the buying decision. If Eddie buys a mug at a price P, then he has a mug ($m = 1$), but his wealth has dropped by the price paid ($w = -P$). Alternatively, he could do nothing and enjoy his mug-less life (with $m = w = 0$). Let's compute his utility U for each of these cases. Remember that his reference points are zero mugs and zero wealth ($r_m = r_w = 0$).

$$\text{Buy}: U((1, -P) \mid (0, 0)) = B \cdot 1 - P + v(B \cdot 1 \mid B \cdot 0) + v(-P \mid 0)$$
$$= B - P + B - \lambda P$$
$$= 2B - (1 + \lambda)P$$
$$\text{Don't Buy}: U((0, 0) \mid (0, 0)) = B \cdot 0 + 0 + v(B \cdot 0 \mid B \cdot 0) + v(0 \mid 0) = 0$$

Observe that when buying a mug Eddie obtains standard intrinsic utility $B-P$. But he also experiences the gain utility of B from acquiring the mug and the loss utility of $-\lambda P$ from paying for the mug. For greater loss aversion, λ is larger and the utility loss from spending money is magnified. If Eddie maintains the status quo and does nothing, his intrinsic utility is zero. And since there have been no gains or losses, his gain-loss utility is also zero.

What, then, is Eddie's WTP? His WTP is the tipping point at which any higher price would induce him to switch from buying to not buying. In other words, it is the price that makes him exactly indifferent between buying and not. We can therefore equate the above two utilities and solve for the indifference price, denoting it by *WTP*:

$$\overbrace{0 = U((0, 0) \mid (0, 0))}^{\text{Don't Buy Utility}} = \overbrace{U((1, -WTP) \mid (0, 0)) = 2B - (1 + \lambda)WTP}^{\text{Buy Utility}}$$

$$\Rightarrow WTP = \left(\frac{2}{1 + \lambda}\right)B$$

The WTP depends on two parameters: B and λ. It is increasing in the marginal benefit of the mug B. Intuitively, Eddie is willing to pay more for mugs if he likes them more. And if he is not loss averse, then $\lambda = 1$ and his WTP is simply B. Why would he pay more for the mug than the marginal benefit that it brings him? But if he is loss averse, then $\lambda > 1$ and his WTP is less than B. That is, loss aversion amplifies the loss of money relative to the gain of the mug, making him less willing to purchase. The negative relationship between loss aversion and WTP is plotted with the dashed curve in Figure 9.2.

Selling

Let's repeat the above analysis, but in the case that Eddie has been endowed with a mug ($r_m = 1$) and must decide whether or not to sell it. If he sells the mug at a price P, then he no longer has any mugs ($m = 0$), but his wealth has increased by the sales price ($w = P$). His other option is to maintain the status quo and retain the mug ($m = 1$ and $w = 0$). His reference-dependent utilities from these two options are then:

$$\text{Sell}: U((0, P) \mid (1, 0)) = B \cdot 0 + P + v(B \cdot 0 \mid B \cdot 1) + v(P \mid 0)$$
$$= P - \lambda B + P$$
$$= 2P - \lambda B$$
$$\text{Don't Sell}: U((1, 0) \mid (1, 0)) = B \cdot 1 + 0 + v(B \cdot 1 \mid B \cdot 1) + v(0 \mid 0) = B$$

In this case selling generates standard intrinsic utility of P, as well as loss utility from giving up the mug and gain utility from receiving payment. And by maintaining the status quo, Eddie simply obtains the intrinsic utility of keeping the mug.

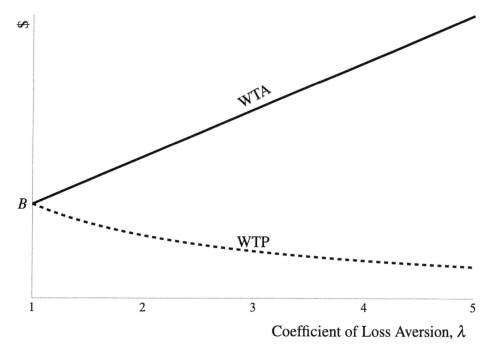

Figure 9.2 WTP and WTA with Loss Aversion

Eddie's WTA is the tipping point at which any lower price would induce him to switch from selling the mug to retaining it. It is therefore the price, *WTA*, that makes him indifferent between selling and not, determined as follows:

$$\overbrace{2WTA - \lambda B}^{\text{Sell Utility}} = U((0, WTA) \mid (1,0)) = \overbrace{U((1,0) \mid (1,0)) = B}^{\text{Don't Sell Utility}}$$

$$\Rightarrow WTA = \left(\frac{1+\lambda}{2}\right)B$$

Without loss aversion ($\lambda = 1$), he is willing to sell the endowed mug for exactly its marginal benefit B. He would not sell at a lower price. But with loss aversion, the loss of the mug is amplified relative to the gain of the payment. He therefore requires a higher price as compensation for giving up the mug. This increases his WTA above B. And for greater loss aversion, Eddie's WTA is larger, as plotted by the solid curve in Figure 9.2.

Estimating Loss Aversion

Putting the preceding buying and selling decisions together, we see that WTA is now predicted to be larger than WTP. This is exactly what we observe empirically with the endowment effect. It is only in the case of no loss aversion that the model of reference-dependent preferences makes the standard prediction that WTA and WTP are equal.

The model also makes a more specific prediction about the relationship between WTA and WTP. It is not simply that loss aversion creates a gap between the two, but for larger coefficients of loss aversion λ the gap grows, as illustrated in Figure 9.2. Mathematically, the relative size of WTA to WTP is predicted to be:

$$\frac{WTA}{WTP} = \frac{\left(\frac{1+\lambda}{2}\right)B}{\left(\frac{2}{1+\lambda}\right)B} = \left(\frac{1+\lambda}{2}\right)^2 \tag{9.2}$$

This is a very useful equation. Because although we do not observe λ, we do know how much larger WTA is relative to WTP. We can therefore pin down the unique value of λ that generates the observed WTA/WTP gap. In the Monetizing Mugs Lab Experiment (Section 8.1.1) the median WTA was \$7.12, while the median WTP was only \$2.87. Plugging these values into equation (9.2), and solving for λ, we obtain:

$$\frac{\$7.12}{\$2.87} = \left(\frac{1+\lambda}{2}\right)^2 \quad \Rightarrow \quad \lambda = 2\sqrt{7.12/2.87} - 1 \approx 2.2$$

The evidence is consistent with a loss aversion coefficient λ that is approximately 2. That is, individuals must be weighting losses twice as much as equivalent gains in order to explain observed behavior. Of course, this conclusion depends on us believing that our modeling assumptions for Eddie match the preferences of subjects in the experiment.

9.2.2   Expectations-Based Reference Points

The model of reference-dependent preferences is a success in that it predicts the well-documented endowment effect. But recall that not everyone exhibits the endowment effect to the same degree. In the Sportscard Show Field Experiment (Section 8.1.2), participants with the most trading experience exhibited the weakest endowment effect.

One explanation for this observation is that trading experience diminishes loss aversion. By trading regularly, individuals may come to not care about losses with greater intensity than equivalent gains. If experienced traders have a smaller value of λ, then we would expect a smaller difference between WTA and WTP. Note that this hypothesis requires the magnitude of λ to vary across individuals.

There is another explanation for the impact of experience on the endowment effect that maintains uniform loss aversion. That is, experienced traders share the same degree of loss aversion as inexperienced traders. The difference in behavior is then explained not by differences in loss aversion, but by differences in the point of reference. In particular, suppose that gains and losses are coded relative to *expectations* instead of endowments. And assume the following expectations for each type of trader after being gifted an object in the field experiment:

- *Inexperienced traders* expect to walk out of the experiment with the endowed object. In this case, their expectation remains equal to their endowment. So with an expectations-based reference point they should behave exactly as Eddie does with his endowment-based reference point, i.e., exhibiting the endowment effect.
- *Experienced traders* expect to be equally likely to keep the endowed object or sell it. With such random expectations as the point of reference, giving up the object then only feels like a loss the 50% of the time that the expectation is to keep it. The other

50% of the time selling is expected, so giving up the object is not coded as a loss. The net result is a diminished likelihood of experiencing a loss. And it turns out that once we introduce such random reference points, the model no longer predicts an endowment effect — even with loss aversion. *WTA* is predicted to equal *WTP*. For the mathematical details, see Appendix 9A.

In summary, suppose that all traders share the same reference-dependent preferences and the same degree of loss aversion. And in addition, their reference points are based on their expectations. Then plausible differences in these expectations based on their trading experience fully explain the evidence that experience diminishes the endowment effect. This is good news for the robustness of the model of reference-dependent preferences.

9.3 Application: Aversion to Small-Stakes Lotteries

Reference-dependent preferences can also apply to choices over risky options, like lotteries. A common lottery is one in which an individual can either win or lose money. And the decision between such lotteries is often bracketed to include an evaluation of total wealth, but exclude any other concerns. In this section we see how reference dependence can explain the aversion to small-stakes lotteries that is inconsistent with the standard model.

9.3.1 Expected Gain-Loss Utility

Consider the following lottery: with probability p you gain g and otherwise, with probability $1 - p$, you lose l. In addition, you have prior wealth W. The two possible final outcomes from accepting this lottery are then a total wealth of either $W + g$ or $W - l$. This lottery can be compactly expressed as $L = (W + g, p; W - l, 1 - p)$.

The standard expected utility model (Section 2.3.4) assumes that this lottery is evaluated as follows:

$$E(u(L)) = pu(W + g) + (1 - p)u(W - l) \tag{9.3}$$

where $u(\cdot)$ is the utility function over total wealth.

Let's introduce reference-dependent utility to this expected utility form of preferences. To do so, replace the utility function $u(\cdot)$ with the gain-loss value function $v(\cdot)$.[6] A natural choice for the reference point in this setting is to assume that individuals code lottery outcomes as gains or losses relative to their prior wealth W.

Definition 9.3 Expected gain-loss utility from a monetary lottery $L = (W + g, p; W - l, 1 - p)$ with reference point W is:

$$\begin{aligned} E(v(L \mid W)) &= pv(W + g \mid W) + (1 - p)v(W - l \mid W) \\ &= pg - (1 - p)\lambda l \end{aligned} \tag{9.4}$$

where $v(\cdot)$ is the gain-loss value function in Definition 9.1.

Remark: Excuse the abuse of notation in writing $E(v(L|W))$ as the expectation of $v(x|W)$ for outcomes x induced by lottery L. This mirrors the convention of writing $E(u(L))$ for the expected utility of lottery L.

Observe that the gain and loss are each weighted by their corresponding probabilities, but the loss is amplified by the coefficient of loss aversion λ. Notice also that prior wealth W is cancelled out by the gain-loss value function and does not appear in equation (9.4).[7]

9.3.2   Revisiting Absurd Lottery Preferences

Example 8.1 from the previous chapter illustrates that with preferences represented by standard expected utility (as in equation (9.3)), plausible risk aversion over small-stakes lotteries generates absurd conclusions. Let's apply expected gain-loss utility to this example instead. Recall the premise that Kate always rejects a lottery in which she has equal chances of gaining $10 or losing $9, no matter her wealth. With gain-loss utility relative to her wealth W, she evaluates this small-stakes lottery $L^S = (W+ 10, 0.5; W- 9, 0.5)$ as:

$$E(v(L^S \mid W)) = 0.5 \cdot 10 - 0.5 \cdot \lambda \cdot 9 = 5 - 4.5\lambda$$

If she instead rejects the lottery, then her final outcome is simply her wealth, implying that $v(W|W) = 0$. Kate therefore rejects the lottery if $5 - 4.5\lambda < 0$, or equivalently, if $\lambda > 5/4.5 = 1.1$. And based on the endowment effect evidence in the previous section, λ is at least 2. Expected gain-loss utility therefore predicts Kate to indeed reject these small-stakes gambles at every wealth because the loss of $9 feels significantly worse relative to the gain of $10.

The standard expected utility model also allows Kate to reject these small-stakes gambles. But in doing so, then requires her to reject an even bet between losing $180 and winning *any* amount of money g. With expected gain-loss utility, such a big-stakes lottery $L^B = (W + g, 0.5; W- 180, 0.5)$ is rejected if and only if:

$$0 = v(W \mid W) > E(v(L^B \mid W)) = 0.5 \cdot g - 0.5 \cdot \lambda \cdot 180 = 0.5g - 90\lambda$$
$$\Leftrightarrow g < 180\lambda$$

Kate is no longer predicted to reject this big-stakes lottery for any g. In fact, with a typical loss aversion coefficient of $\lambda = 2$, she only rejects the lottery for gains less than $360. But for a potential gain of $361, let alone trillions of dollars, she would accept. This prediction is more realistic.

Expected gain-loss utility avoids the absurd conclusions of standard expected utility.[8] It allows individuals to simultaneously be averse to small-stakes lotteries and willing to accept big-stakes lotteries with high expected winnings.

9.3.3   Loss Aversion vs. Risk Aversion

A common source of confusion is distinguishing loss aversion from risk aversion. Risk aversion in the standard expected utility model implies that the utility function over

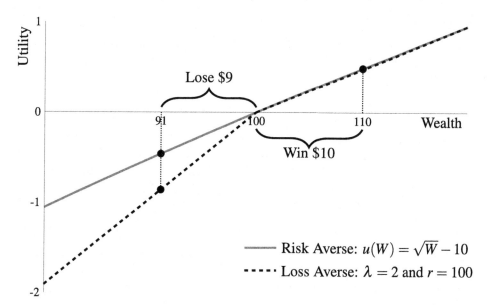

Figure 9.3 Picturing Loss Aversion vs. Risk Aversion with a Small-Stakes Lottery

wealth is concave. And given a concave utility function, a decrease in wealth lowers utility more than an equally sized increase in wealth raises utility. But this sounds a lot like loss aversion, where relative to a reference point, losses are weighted more than equivalent gains.

A key difference is demonstrated by considering the predictions for loss aversion and risk aversion when evaluating a small-stakes lottery like $L^S = (W+ 10, 0.5; W- 9, 0.5)$. Observe that this lottery has a positive expected payout — if you played it over and over many times, you would expect to gain \$0.50 per round on average.

A loss averse individual who weights losses twice as much as gains will nevertheless reject this lottery. This is illustrated in Figure 9.3 with a loss averse utility function (the dashed lines) and reference point of \$100 in wealth.[9] The utility lost from losing \$9 clearly exceeds the utility gained from winning \$10. The average of these equally likely utility changes is therefore negative.

A standard risk averse individual has a concave utility function over total wealth, suggesting that she might also reject this risky lottery. But when we "zoom in" to look at a concave utility function over small gains and losses, it is almost a straight line. Figure 9.3 plots a standard concave utility function that indeed looks almost linear over a \$40 wealth range. And with an almost linear utility function over small-stakes lotteries, the individual is essentially risk neutral, weighting gains and losses almost equally. The utility gained from winning \$10 is slightly larger than the utility lost from losing \$9. She should therefore accept the lottery with its positive expected winnings.

In summary, the standard expected utility model with risk aversion predicts that individuals are approximately risk neutral over gain-loss lotteries with small stakes. Loss aversion, however, implies strong aversion to such lotteries. Exercise 9.7 further demonstrates this distinction with a numerical example.

9.4   Application: Equity Premium Puzzle   [Finance]

It remains to provide an explanation for the equity premium puzzle, the last anomaly in Chapter 8. Recall the puzzle: the standard model predicts a much smaller premium on equity returns relative to safe asset returns than what we observe. In particular, the large equity premium suggests that individuals are absurdly risk averse, requiring a massive premium as compensation for accepting the risk of investing in the stock market.

To motivate our proposed resolution to this puzzle, consider the following abstract model of the stock market. Imagine that investing in the stock market is a lottery with known risks where each day the investment is equally likely to experience a gain of $250 or a loss of $150. If you faced this lottery only once, would you accept or reject it? What if the lottery were played twice? What if you faced a long sequence of this lottery, played once every day? It is not uncommon for an individual to reject the one-time lottery, but accept two or more repetitions (Gneezy and Potters 1997). Such seemingly reasonable preferences are impossible with the standard expected utility model of preferences (Samuelson 1963).

Suppose instead that individuals evaluate lotteries with expected gain-loss utility and loss aversion coefficient $\lambda = 2$. The one-time bet is the lottery $L^1 = (W+ 250, 0.5; W - 150, 0.5)$ where W is prior wealth. With two iterations, there is a 25% chance of winning both times and a 25% chance of losing both times. The only other possibility is to win once and lose once, which has a 50% chance. Putting this together, the repeated lottery is $L^2 = (W+ 500, 0.25; W+ 100, 0.5; W - 300, 0.25)$. And the corresponding expected gain-loss utilities with $\lambda = 2$ are then:

$$E(v(L^1 \mid W)) = 0.5 \cdot 250 - 0.5 \cdot \lambda \cdot 150 = 125 - 75\lambda = -25 < 0$$
$$E(v(L^2 \mid W)) = 0.25 \cdot 500 + 0.5 \cdot 100 - 0.25 \cdot \lambda \cdot 300 = 175 - 75\lambda = 25 > 0$$

Loss aversion therefore predicts what was not possible with standard expected utility: reject the one-time lottery, but accept the repeated lottery.

What is the intuition for this result? With a one-time lottery, experiencing a loss is just as likely as a gain. Even though the gain is larger in magnitude, loss aversion makes this lottery unattractive. But when the lottery is repeated, a gain is now three times as likely as a loss. The aversion to losses is counterbalanced by the lower probability of a loss and this repeated lottery is now perceived as better than the status quo.

Observe the importance of bracketing. Suppose that each day a decision maker has the option to accept or reject a single iteration of this lottery. With narrow bracketing, each lottery is evaluated in isolation. And because the single lottery is always rejected, the decision maker never accepts any risk. But with broader bracketing that integrates the accumulation of outcomes over a longer horizon (2 days is sufficient in our example), a decision maker accepts a sequence of lotteries, that if evaluated in isolation would be rejected. In fact, with a broad bracket that considers a long sequence of lotteries, the expected daily outcome is a $50 win and the possibility of netting a total loss is very low. For instance, over 87 iterations, the chance of a negative total monetary payoff is less than 1%.

Benartzi and Thaler (1995) apply the insights of this toy model to explain the equity premium puzzle. Like the one-time version of the lottery, over the short horizon of a day, or even a year, the stock market has a high chance of underperfoming safe bonds. If investors have short-sighted, or myopic, investment horizons due to narrow

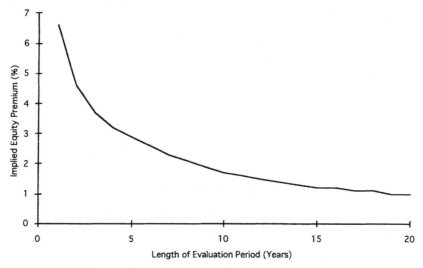

Figure 9.4 Implied Equity Premium vs. Evaluation Period

Source: Shlomo Benartzi and Richard H. Thaler, "Myopic Loss Aversion and the Equity Premium Puzzle," *The Quarterly Journal of Economics*, 1995, 110, 1, 73–92, by permission of Oxford University Press.

bracketing, then the stock market appears quite risky. And with loss aversion, each downturn in the stock market is weighted more than equivalent upturns. **Myopic loss averse** investors therefore exhibit strong aversion to the stock market. They consequently require substantial compensation in the form of high returns in order to make equity investments attractive.

But with a longer investment horizon over many years, it becomes increasingly unlikely that the stock market underperforms safe bonds. Recall that historically, the ups of the stock market are more frequent and larger in magnitude than the downs, delivering high positive returns over time. With such a broader bracket for investment decisions, the stock market appears much less risky. And investors would therefore require only a modest equity premium for accepting the additional risk of the stock market.

This logic implies that in a world with loss averse investors, the equity premium should decline as investors evaluate their investment returns over longer horizons. As illustrated by Figure 9.4, Benartzi and Thaler (1995) show that the observed large equity premium is in fact predicted by loss averse investors who evaluate their investments with only a 1-year horizon. They also estimate that if instead, investors used a 20-year horizon, a reasonable length for retirement planning, the equity premium would fall from over 6% to 1.4%. That is, investors would accept the risk of the stock market with a premium of only 1.4%. From this perspective, the actual equity premium of 6.1% makes the stock market a great investment.

9.5 Empirical Evidence of Reference Dependence

In this final section we consider evidence of labor and consumption behaviors that are explained well by reference-dependent preferences with loss aversion. The key implication of such preferences is that individuals have a greater incentive to avoid a loss than to achieve a gain. But what counts as a loss or gain will depend on the specifics of each decision-making context. The end-of-chapter exercises introduce evidence from additional settings, including tax evasion, housing, golf, and entrepreneurship. This wide range of evidence strongly supports reference dependence as an important feature of decision making.

9.5.1   Targeting Income   [Labor]

Suppose that your hourly wage just increased. Assuming you can choose your work hours, would you work more or less? The standard theory of labor supply predicts that you would choose to work more hours.[10] The reason is that with a higher wage the marginal benefit of working — or equivalently, the marginal cost of *not* working — is greater.

The predicted positive relationship between wages and labor supply is a foundation of economic theory. But it presumes standard preferences. What if workers instead care not only about their total income, but how their income compares to an **income target**? That is, I might set a mental income target of making $100 today as a rideshare driver. Earning more than $100 is coded as a gain and falling short is coded as a loss. Let's first consider the predictions of such income targeting, followed by supporting empirical evidence.

Generating Predictions

Let's represent reference-dependent preferences with loss aversion relative to an income target r as follows:

$$U(h \mid r) = \begin{cases} wh - r - 2h^2 & \text{if } wh \geq r \\ \lambda(wh - r) - 2h^2 & \text{if } wh < r \end{cases} \tag{9.5}$$

where w is the hourly wage, h is hours supplied, and their product wh is income.[11] Utility depends on two components. The first is how income compares with the income target. Losses relative to this reference point are weighted more than gains, with a coefficient of loss aversion $\lambda \geq 1$. Notice that the point of reference is not an endowment or prior wealth, as we have typically seen throughout this chapter, but a forward-looking expectation of income. The second component of utility is the $-2h^2$ term. This captures the cost of supplying labor effort — holding income fixed, working more hours decreases utility.

Suppose that a worker chooses labor hours to maximize utility function (9.5). The utility-maximizing choice of hours h for each possible wage w is plotted in Figure 9.5. Consider first the standard case with no loss aversion ($\lambda = 1$). Then the predicted labor supply is always increasing in the wage, depicted by the dashed line in the figure.

When loss aversion is present ($\lambda > 1$), the labor supply function takes on the oddly shaped solid line in the figure. What accounts for this shape? When the worker's wage is low and she is below her income target, higher wages incentivize her to work more hours. This is for the same reason as the standard case. But once her wage is high enough that she meets her income target (at $w = w^t$), further wage increases induce her to work less and simply maintain her income target. When wages are sufficiently high ($w \geq w^T$), she once again chooses to work more. Note also that her labor

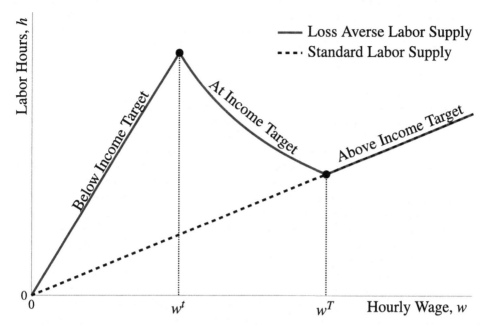

Figure 9.5 Labor Supply Functions with Standard and Loss Averse Preferences

supply function is steeper for low wages than high wages because at low wages she has the additional incentive to avoid a loss by reaching her income target.

The two labor supply functions in Figure 9.5 illustrate a clear testable prediction of reference-dependent preferences. Namely, evidence that labor supply is decreasing in the wage allows us to reject the standard model. Be careful to observe that evidence of labor supply increasing in the wage is consistent with both models.

Testing Predictions

Although the standard and reference-dependent models of preferences generate different predictions, testing these predictions with observational data is quite challenging. The first issue is that a worker's wage doesn't vary that much over time. And even when it does, most workers have very little control over the precise number of hours they work.

We therefore want to examine jobs where wages fluctuate frequently and workers have a great degree of control over their hours. It is perhaps not surprising that much of the economics research on this question has focused on occupations like taxi drivers and bike messengers. These are exactly the types of jobs where workers choose their hours. And moreover, hourly wages fluctuate from day to day. These fluctuations are not because cab fares and delivery rates jump around randomly. Instead, random factors like bad weather increase demand for taxi rides and delivery services, which in turn make each hour of work more profitable on these days.

In an early study estimating the slope of the labor supply function, Camerer et al. (1997) examine the hours worked and daily earnings of New York City cab drivers.

Their statistical analysis of these observational data suggests that there is indeed a negative relationship between wages and hours, a finding that rejects the standard model. This result is supported by evidence from a variety of settings (Goette, Huffman, and Fehr 2004). The following field experiment details one such setting.

Field Experiment — Loss Averse Bike Messengers (Fehr and Goette 2007)

Forty-two bike messengers in Zurich, Switzerland were randomly assigned to one of two groups. Each group received a 25% increase in their delivery commission rate in one of two different months.

Because the wage was randomly increased for some messengers and not others at a given moment in time, any difference in labor supply behavior between the two groups must be due to the wage difference.

Fehr and Goette (2007) estimate two key effects of the higher wage on labor supply:

1   Messengers work approximately *30% more* shifts.
2   Within each shift, messengers make *6% fewer* deliveries.

The first result implies an upward-sloping labor supply function that is consistent with both the standard and the reference-dependent models.

The second result is consistent with income targeting. Messengers with higher wages can reach their target income with fewer deliveries. But it could also be consistent with standard preferences if the higher wage induces messengers to work more shifts (see the first result) and as a result get tired sooner and put in less effort on each shift.

To disentangle the income targeting and fatigue explanations for the second result, the researchers used a lottery choice experiment to evaluate whether each messenger exhibited loss aversion or not.[12] Incredibly, when treated with the higher wage the loss averse messengers reduced their deliveries, while the others did not. This is only consistent with an income targeting explanation for the second result, and not fatigue. In sum, only income targeting can explain both of the observed results.

9.5.2   Job Search Effort   *[Labor]*

A persistent feature of the labor market is unemployment. Many rich countries pay unemployment benefits for a limited duration to those who have lost their job and are looking for work. These benefits replace a share of past wages and help people to smooth consumption between jobs, particularly if they have limited savings.

An important decision for those receiving unemployment benefits is how much effort to exert searching for a new job. This search decision requires individuals to trade off the benefit of securing a new job quickly (and before unemployment benefits expire) against the costs of job hunting and giving up available unemployment benefits. Although economists cannot directly observe job search effort, we can observe unemployment durations. From these data it is possible to calculate, week by week, the rate at which the unemployed exit unemployment. And given that greater search effort increases the exit rate from unemployment, we can test competing models of preferences by comparing their predictions for the exit rate with the evidence.

With standard preferences, the newly unemployed are predicted to initially exert low search effort. But as time passes without finding a job, they increase search effort so as to avoid the possible loss of unemployment benefits while still jobless. And once benefits have expired, they maintain a constant level of search effort. This predicted behavior implies an increasing unemployment exit rate over time that plateaus once benefits expire.[13]

The evidence of unemployment exit rates contradicts this standard prediction. Instead, the exit rate 1) begins high, 2) declines as unemployment persists, 3) spikes just as benefits expire, and 4) declines gradually once benefits are no more. This pattern holds in many countries, including the United States, Hungary, Austria, Germany, and France.

DellaVigna et al. (2017) demonstrate that a model of reference-dependent preferences predicts this four-stage pattern of unemployment exit rates. The key to understanding this result is recognizing that larger losses incentivize greater search effort — because search effort increases the chance of finding a job and avoiding the loss. But a loss relative to what? The authors show that the model is most accurate when the reference point is a continuously moving average of the past 6 months of earnings, including the unemployment benefit. Intuitively, workers adapt as their earnings change, evaluating current outcomes in relation to their recent past. Let's apply such preferences to a worker's (unsuccessful) search efforts over the full cycle of unemployment benefits.

1   Initially, search effort is high because unemployment benefits constitute a significant loss relative to past earnings from employment and she wants to curtail this loss. With intense search effort she may be able to quickly find a new job and restore her full earnings.

2   As the unemployment spell continues, the reference point of average past earnings declines. With a lower reference point, unemployment benefits represent a smaller loss and she searches less.

3   As the unemployment benefit expiration date approaches, she considers the large potential loss from losing benefits and therefore increases search efforts once again.

4   Once benefits have expired and she still remains jobless, her average recent earnings and reference point continue to decline, reducing the perceived loss of unemployment and subsequently her search effort.

Reference-dependent preferences are a success. They predict job search behavior that exactly matches the pattern of observed unemployment exit rates. But this finding rests on two assumptions that are worth emphasizing. The first is the reference point. In this chapter we have considered reference points equal to both endowments and forward-looking income targets. The backward-looking reference point in this setting is new. Alternative reference points — e.g., fixed at earnings in the previous job or expected future earnings — do not match the job search evidence as well. The principal takeaway is that our theoretical analysis is sensitive to assumptions about the particular reference point.

The second assumption concerns present bias (see Chapter 5). The reference-dependent model best fits the data if we also assume present-biased preferences. Present bias implies that workers consume most of their earnings in each period. So as earnings fall with a job loss and the later expiration of unemployment benefits, consumption falls as well. It is these consumption losses that drive the observed pattern of search effort. Conversely, standard exponential discounting predicts employed workers to save as a precaution in case of unemployment. In doing so, their consumption remains stable when they lose their job or unemployment benefits, mitigating the losses they experience. More generally, this underscores the importance of considering multiple behavioral models simultaneously when explaining real-world phenomena.

9.5.3   Life-Cycle Consumption Expectations   *[Household]*

Understanding consumption and savings patterns over an individual's life is a classic concern of economics. The primary prediction of the standard life-cycle model is for individuals to save and borrow so as to smooth their consumption spending over time, maintaining constant consumption in certain cases (Theorem 4.1). But key empirical facts contradict the implications of this standard model. For example, consumption 1) is hump-shaped, increasing early in life and decreasing at its end, 2) drops at retirement, and 3) initially underresponds to permanent changes in income (see e.g., Attanasio and Weber 2010).

Pagel (2017) shows that a model with reference-dependent preferences predicts all three of these empirical facts. The model assumes that in each period individuals obtain standard intrinsic utility from consumption and gain-loss utility from comparing actual consumption to expected consumption. But this life-cycle model goes further by including an additional anticipatory component to gain-loss utility. That is, when a consumer receives good or bad news today about her future income, perhaps from a promotion or layoff, she experiences gain-loss utility *today* from comparing her new expectations of future consumption to her prior expectations of future consumption. Notice that in this comparison the reference point is her expectation of future consumption before receiving the news. This form of gain-loss utility is consequently known as **news utility** (Köszegi and Rabin 2009).

The foregoing analysis highlights the role of expectations in shaping reference points, which in turn influence behavior. This insight is developed further in the end-of-chapter appendix.

9.6   Summary

1 The **(linear) gain-loss value function** evaluates final outcomes as gains and losses relative to a reference point. As a model of preferences, it features **reference dependence**.

2 The **coefficient of loss aversion** λ is the weight on losses relative to gains in the gain-loss value function. For $\lambda > 1$, the function features **loss aversion**.

3 The **model of reference-dependent preferences** evaluates final outcomes as the (weighted) sum of standard **intrinsic utility** from the final outcome and the gain-loss utility relative to a reference point.

4 **Bracketing** refers to how narrowly or broadly a single decision is integrated into the full set of choices that an individual makes. Models of decisions with reference-dependent preferences often assume narrow bracketing around the reference point.

5 The endowment effect is consistent with reference-dependent preferences where losses are weighted twice as much as gains.

6 To evaluate lotteries, **expected gain-loss utility** is the expectation of the gain-loss value function applied to the lottery outcomes, weighted by the lottery probabilities.

7 Expected gain-loss utility predicts strong risk aversion over small-stakes lotteries with a win and loss. Standard expected utility with risk aversion instead predicts essentially risk neutral preferences over small-stakes lotteries.

8 **Myopic loss aversion** can explain the large equity premium.

9 Loss aversion introduces a greater incentive to avoid a loss than to achieve a gain.

10 Empirical evidence of effort exerted by workers is consistent with reference-dependent preferences where the reference point for the employed is an **income target** and for the unemployed is an average of recent earnings.

11 Life-cycle consumption anomalies are explained by reference-dependent preferences with gain-loss utility relative to expectations of future consumption, or **news utility**.

9.7 Exercises[14]

Exercise 9.1 — Tempering Expectations. Alexander Pope, an 18th century English poet, wrote in a letter: "Blessed is the man who expects nothing, for he shall never be disappointed" (Pope 1725/1886, 104). Connect this 300-year-old sentiment to the concepts of reference dependence and loss aversion.

Exercise 9.2 — Insurance Losses. When an individual purchases an insurance policy (for their home, car, health, etc.) there are two distinct prices. The premium is the price paid, often monthly, for being insured. The premium is paid whether or not the individual experiences an accident (from a home theft, car accident, illness, etc.). In the event of an insured accident, the individual must then also make a second type of payment to cover part of the total cost of the accident. This is known as co-insurance and can include deductibles or copays. According to Novemsky and Kahneman (2005), individuals may be loss averse over co-insurance payments, but not premium payments. What does this suggest about the formation of reference points?

Exercise 9.3 — March Madness, Indeed. [Sports] The Duke University men's basketball team is competing in the NCAA Final Four tournament tomorrow. A Duke student, Josh, is a basketball fan and wants to go to the game. He has reference-dependent preferences over basketball tickets (t) and wealth (w), with reference points (r_t and r_w) equal to his endowments of each. His utility function is:

$$U((t,w) \mid (r_t, r_w)) = Bt + w + v(Bt \mid Br_t) + v(w \mid r_w)$$

where $v(x \mid r) = \begin{cases} x - r & \text{if } x \geq r \\ \lambda(x - r) & \text{if } x < r \end{cases}$

and $B > 0$ is the intrinsic marginal benefit of a ticket. Because Josh's preferences are identical in form to those of Eddie in Section 9.2.1, Josh's willingness to pay (WTP) and willingness to accept (WTA) for a ticket are, like Eddie's for a mug, given by:

$$WTP = \left(\frac{2}{1+\lambda}\right)B \qquad WTA = \left(\frac{1+\lambda}{2}\right)B$$

Carmon and Ariely (2000) survey 93 Duke student basketball fans about their WTP for a ticket if they did not have one and their WTA if they did. The median responses were WTP = \$150 and WTA = \$1,500.

a   Assuming that the surveyed students have preferences like Josh, compute their coefficient of loss aversion, λ, and marginal benefit of a ticket, B.

b   How does this estimate of λ compare to the evidence with mugs where $\lambda \approx 2.2$? Provide a psychological rationale for any difference between these two estimates.

Exercise 9.4 — Choice Mugs. In Section 9.2.1 we computed Eddie's willingness to pay (WTP) for a mug as a buyer and his willingness to accept (WTA) as a seller. Consider now the possibility that Eddie is a "chooser." That is, he has the option to choose a mug or an amount of money P. Assume that Eddie has the same utility function $U(\cdot)$, endowments, and reference points ($r_m = r_w = 0$) as in the chapter. *Note that your answers to parts (a)–(c) below may depend on the parameters B and/or λ.*

a   Determine Eddie's utility from choosing the mug.

b   Determine Eddie's utility from choosing an amount of money P.

c   Determine the amount of money, P_C, that makes Eddie indifferent between accepting the mug or the money.

d   How does P_C depend on B and/or λ, if at all? Provide intuition for your answers.

e   How does P_C compare in magnitude to the expressions for WTP and WTA in the chapter (the ranking does not depend on B or λ)? Does the ranking of these three values match the evidence in the Monetizing Mugs Lab Experiment in Section 8.1.1?

Exercise 9.5 — Limited Loss Aversion. Let Edna be the fraternal twin of Eddie from Section 9.2.1. Edna shares the same utility function $U(\cdot)$, endowments, and reference points as Eddie — *except* she is loss averse over mugs, but not wealth. She still experiences gain-loss utility from wealth, but she weights gains and losses equally. In other words, her coefficient of loss aversion for mugs is $\lambda > 1$, and for wealth is 1.

a   Determine Edna's willingness to pay (WTP) for a mug in terms of B and λ. How does this compare to Eddie's WTP? Explain.

b   Determine Edna's willingness to accept (WTA) for a mug in terms of B and λ. How does this compare to Eddie's WTA? Explain.

c   Use the empirical evidence from Kahneman, Knetsch, and Thaler (1990) that WTA = \$7.12 and WTP = \$2.87 to estimate Edna's coefficient of loss aversion for mugs λ. How does this compare to the estimate of Eddie's uniform coefficient of loss aversion? Provide intuition for your answer.

Exercise 9.6 — Weight Gains and Losses. Jenny has reference-dependent preferences over mugs (m) and wealth (w), with reference points equal to her current endowments of each: three mugs and \$100 of wealth. Her utility function is:

$$U((m, w) \mid (3, 100)) = 5m + w + \eta v(5m \mid 15) + \eta v(w \mid 100)$$

where $\eta > 0$ and $v(x \mid r) = \begin{cases} x - r & \text{if } x \geq r \\ 2(x - r) & \text{if } x < r \end{cases}$

Note that this utility function implicitly assumes $u_m(m) = 5m$, $u_w(w) = w$, and $\lambda = 2$.

a What is Jenny's willingness to pay (WTP) for one more mug? How does a larger η impact WTP? Explain.

b What is Jenny's willingness to accept (WTA) to sell one of her three mugs? How does a larger η impact WTA? Explain.

c What amount of money P_C would make Jenny indifferent between accepting the money and accepting one more mug? How does a larger η impact P_C? Explain.

d Rank WTP, WTA, and P_C (the ranking does not depend on η).

Exercise 9.7 — Aversion to Losses and Risks. Leon and Renata have the same current wealth, W. They both face the decision to accept or reject the following two lotteries:

$$\begin{aligned} \text{Big-stakes Lottery} : L^B &= (W + 0.75W, 0.5; W - 0.5W, 0.5) \\ \text{Small-stakes Lottery} : L^S &= (W + 0.03W, 0.5; W - 0.02W, 0.5) \end{aligned}$$

The big-stakes lottery is an even bet between increasing wealth by 75%, or losing 50% of wealth. The small-stakes lottery is also an even bet of winning 50% more than the potential loss, but with much smaller gains and losses.

Leon is loss averse relative to his current wealth W, with coefficient of loss aversion $\lambda = 2$. He evaluates lotteries with their expected gain-loss utility (as in equation (9.4)). Renata has standard risk averse preferences, with utility of final wealth outcome x given by $u(x) = \ln(x)$. She evaluates lotteries with their expected utility (as in equation (9.3)).

a Does Leon he accept the big-stakes lottery? What about the small-stakes lottery?

b Repeat part (a) for Renata. You can do this without knowing her wealth W. *Hint: use log rules.*

c Compare and contrast the choices that Leon and Renata make for each lottery. What does this reveal about the difference between loss aversion and risk aversion?

Exercise 9.8 — Lost Profits and Loss Aversion. [Development]. Esau possesses wealth of 900 Kenyan shillings (Ksh). He is offered a gift of 100Ksh. He can either accept the certain money or instead choose a lottery that has equal chances of paying out 250Ksh or paying out nothing.

a   Suppose that Esau has standard risk averse preferences, with utility of final wealth outcome x given by $u(x) = \sqrt{x}$. He evaluates lotteries with their expected utility (as in equation (9.3)). Does he take the certain money or the lottery?

b   Now suppose that Esau is loss averse relative to his newly current wealth of 1,000Ksh, with coefficient of loss aversion $\lambda = 2$. He evaluates lotteries with their expected gain-loss utility (as in equation (9.4)). Does he accept the lottery or reject it?

c   Kremer et al. (2013) offer a similar choice to small-scale retail shop owners in Western Kenya. In fact, shop owners can choose how much of the 100Ksh they want to keep and how much they want to allocate to the lottery. Shop owners who allocate more to the lottery in this experiment are more likely to maintain higher inventories and subsequently earn higher profits. Does this evidence suggest that loss aversion promotes or diminishes profits?

Exercise 9.9 — The Look of Losses. Explain why it might be an advantageous investment strategy *not* to closely follow financial news everyday.

Exercise 9.10 — Driving the (Reference) Point Home (DellaVigna 2009). [Calculus Required] Layla is a cab driver who works h hours per day, earns an hourly wage of w, and targets a daily income of $r = \$100$. She has reference-dependent preferences represented by:

$$U(h \mid 100) = \begin{cases} wh - 100 - 2h^2 & \text{if } wh \geq 100 \\ \lambda(wh - 100) - 2h^2 & \text{if } wh < 100 \quad \text{where } \lambda \geq 1 \end{cases}$$

a   Determine Layla's labor supply function, $h(w)$, when she is not loss averse ($\lambda = 1$). *Hint: Labor supply is determined by maximizing utility.*

b   Now assume that Layla is loss averse with $\lambda > 1$. To determine her loss averse labor supply function, $h^L(w; \lambda)$, you will consider three cases depending on whether, at her utility-maximizing outcome, she surpasses, misses, or exactly meets her daily income target of $100.

  i   Assume that income exceeds $100. Determine $h^L(w; \lambda)$. Then, given this supply function, find the minimum wage w^T for which income $wh^L(w; \lambda)$ actually exceeds $100 as assumed.

  ii   Assume that income is less than $100. Determine $h^L(w; \lambda)$. Then, given this supply function, find the maximum wage w^t for which income $wh^L(w; \lambda)$ actually falls short of $100 as assumed.

  iii   Assume that income exactly equals $100. Determine $h^L(w; \lambda)$. *Hint: This should be immediate. No calculus required.* Note that this supply function is valid for wages between w^t and w^T.

c   Sketch the complete reference-dependent labor supply function, $h^L(w; \lambda)$, from part (b) — it should look like the loss averse labor supply in Figure 9.5. Label w^t and w^T in your plot. How does the shape of this function change as λ approaches 1? Interpret.

Exercise 9.11 — Expectations to Boot (Köszegi and Rabin 2006). Coco has reference-dependent preferences over pairs of shoes (s) and wealth (w), with reference points r_s and r_w, represented by:

$$U((s, w) \mid (r_s, r_w)) = 60s + w + v(60s \mid 60r_s) + v(w \mid r_w)$$

where $v(x \mid r) = \begin{cases} x - r & \text{if } x \geq r \\ 2(x - r) & \text{if } x < r \end{cases}$

Note that this utility function implicitly assumes $u_s(s) = 60s$, $u_w(w) = w$, $\lambda = 2$, and $\eta = 1$. For mathematical simplicity, assume that Coco is endowed with zero shoes and zero wealth. She is considering whether or not to buy a pair of shoes. Her reference points are equal to her *expected* outcomes (not her endowments).

a   Suppose that Coco expects to buy the pair of shoes at price P, so her reference point is $(r_s, r_w) = (1, -P)$. Find the range of prices such that she in fact buys the shoes.

b   Now suppose that Coco expects *not* to buy the pair of shoes, so her reference point is $(r_s, r_w) = (0, 0)$. Find the range of prices such that she in fact *doesn't* buy the shoes.

c   Using your answers to the previous two parts, can you determine if Coco will buy shoes at a price of $65? Provide an intuitive explanation, making sure to discuss the role of reference-dependent preferences on her decision-making.

Exercise 9.12 — Keeping up with Yourself. [Calculus Required] Joan lives for two periods ($t = 1, 2$): youth and middle age. Denote her consumption expenditure in each period by c_1 and c_2 (measured in millions of dollars). She must divide her lifetime income of $2 million between these two periods. Her budget constraint is:

$$c_1 + c_2 = 2$$

She has reference-dependent preferences over lifetime consumption represented by:

$$U((c_1, c_2) \mid (0.6, r_2)) = \ln(c_1) + \ln(c_2) + v(\ln(c_1) \mid \ln(0.6)) + v(\ln(c_2) \mid \ln(r_2))$$

where $v(x \mid r) = \begin{cases} x - r & \text{if } x \geq r \\ 2(x - r) & \text{if } x < r \end{cases}$

This utility function implicitly assumes $u_1(c_1) = \ln(c_1)$, $u_2(c_2) = \ln(c_2)$, $\lambda = 2$, and $\eta = 1$.

Observe that Joan's reference point for consumption in period 1 is $600,000 (i.e., $r_1 = 0.6$). Her reference point for period-2 consumption is a weighted (geometric) average of her period-1 reference point and her period-1 consumption. In particular,

$$r_2 = c_1^\theta \times 0.6^{(1-\theta)} \text{ for } 0 \leq \theta \leq 1$$

a   What is r_2 when $\theta = 0$? What is r_2 when $\theta = 1$? How does an increase in θ impact Joan's period-2 reference point?

b   Guess that Joan's utility-maximizing lifetime consumption is never a loss: $c_1 \geq 0.6$ and $c_2 \geq r_2$. Solve for Joan's utility-maximizing consumption, c_1 and c_2 (which will depend on θ). You can verify that her preferred consumption in each period exceeds the reference points, as guessed. *Hint: Solve either by replacing c_2 with $2 - c_1$ in the utility function, or by using the method of Lagrange (see Appendix 4A).*

c   Are c_1 and c_2 from part (b) increasing or decreasing in θ? Provide intuition.

d   Connect your results in part (c) to the life-cycle consumption evidence that individual consumption is not flat over time, but increasing early in life.

Exercise 9.13 — No Place Like Home. [Household] Genesove and Mayer (2001) verify with evidence from the Boston condominium market in the 1990s that seller preferences are reference-dependent, with a reference point equal to the initial condo purchase price. Suppose that Dorothy is such a seller. She has reference-dependent preferences over the sale price P, given that she originally paid P_0 for the condo, represented by:

$$U(P \mid P_0) = \begin{cases} P - P_0 & \text{if } P \geq P_0 \\ \lambda(P - P_0) & \text{if } P < P_0 \end{cases}$$

where $\lambda > 1$.

a   Unfortunately for Dorothy, the housing market has dipped since she bought the condo and she must sell at a loss. Do you expect her to choose a higher or lower sale price than someone with standard preferences ($\lambda = 1$) when selling at a loss? Explain.

b   Based on the Sportscard Show Field Experiment evidence in Section 8.1.2, do you expect your prediction in part (a) to be more dramatic if the condo is Dorothy's residence or if it is one of many investment properties she owns and rents for income?

Exercise 9.14 — Bye Bye Birdie. [Sports] The objective of a golf tournament is to finish with the lowest number of strokes over 72 holes. Each hole is assigned a recommended number of strokes, known as *par*. When a hole is completed one stroke under par, it is known as a *birdie*.

a   Suppose that golfers have standard reference-independent preferences and care only about their total strokes in a tournament. In this case, should their putting effort depend on whether they are putting for a score of par or putting for a birdie? Explain.

b   Now suppose that golfers have loss averse reference-dependent preferences that are narrowly bracketed over the number of strokes on each hole, with par as the reference point. In this case, should their putting effort depend on whether they are putting for a score of par or putting for a birdie? Explain.

c   Pope and Schweitzer (2011) study the putting success of professional golfers across tournaments from 2004 to 2008. This data set includes over 2.5 million putts. Their data are summarized in Figure 9.6. How does putting success depend on whether making the putt earns the golfer par or birdie?

d   Apply your predictions in parts (a) and (b) to the evidence in part (c). Is putting behavior suggestive of standard or reference-dependent preferences?

Exercise 9.15 — Tax Tricks. [Public Finance] Throughout the year American workers are required to pay income taxes on their earnings to the federal government.

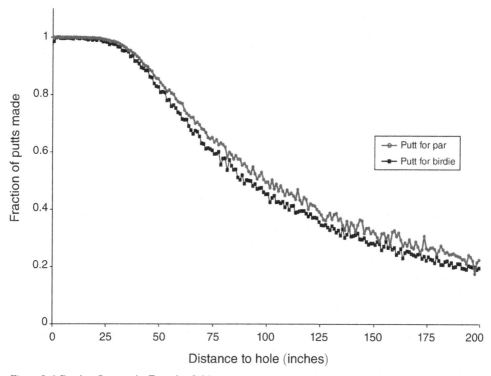

Figure 9.6 Putting Success in Exercise 9.14

Source: Pope and Schweitzer (2011). Copyright American Economic Association; reproduced with permission of the *American Economic Review*.

These tax payments are an estimate of the total tax bill that the individual will owe for the year. On tax day, April 15th each year, individuals must report to the Internal Revenue Service (IRS) the difference between what they have already paid in taxes and their total tax liability. If they have overpaid, they receive a refund. And if they have underpaid, they make an additional payment.

The complexity of the US tax code also allows for some margin of manipulation or evasion of taxes (e.g., overstating deductions or underreporting income sources that the government is unlikely to observe). Rees-Jones (2018) estimates that taxpayers pursue an additional $34 of tax reductions when faced with owing money to the IRS, relative to receiving a refund, on tax day. Explain how this evidence is predicted by the model of reference-dependent preferences, but not by standard preferences over total wealth. In particular, what is the reference point that taxpayers are likely using?

9A   Appendix: The Math of Random Reference Points

A benefit of the model of reference-dependent preferences in Definition 9.2 is its flexibility — the reference point can take on many forms. It can be prior wealth, an expected income target, or an average of recent earnings. In each of these cases the reference point is certain. But what if the point of reference is not a single certain outcome, but a *set* of uncertain outcomes with corresponding probabilities? In this appendix we adapt the model to the case with a referent that is such a lottery. We then apply this framework to understand the impact of trading experience on the endowment effect.

To allow for random reference points, we follow the framework of Köszegi and Rabin (2006). The basic idea is to compute the reference-dependent utility separately for *each possible reference point* and then take the weighted average of these reference-dependent utilities, using the probabilities of each possible reference point as the weights.[15] This approach is formalized in the following definition.

Definition 9A.1 The **model of reference-dependent preferences with random reference points** evaluates final outcomes (x_1, x_2), given a corresponding referent lottery $R = ((r_1^A, r_2^A), p; (r_1^B, r_2^B), 1 - p)$, as follows:

$$
\begin{aligned}
U((x_1, x_2) \mid R) &= pU((x_1, x_2) \mid (r_1^A, r_2^A)) + (1 - p)U((x_1, x_2) \mid (r_1^B, r_2^B)) \\
&= u_1(x_1) + u_2(x_2) + p\eta \cdot \left[v(u_1(x_1) \mid u_1(r_1^A)) + v(u_2(x_2) \mid u_2(r_2^A)) \right] \\
&\quad + (1 - p)\eta \cdot \left[v(u_1(x_1) \mid u_1(r_1^B)) + v(u_2(x_2) \mid u_2(r_2^B)) \right]
\end{aligned}
$$

where $\eta \geq 0$, $u_1(\cdot)$ and $u_2(\cdot)$ are the intrinsic utility functions over goods 1 and 2, and $v(\cdot)$ is the gain-loss value function in Definition 9.1.

▪ **Example 9A.1 — Experienced Expectations.** Let's apply this model of preferences to Eddie's buying and selling decisions of a mug in Section 9.2.1. Recall the assumptions that $\eta = 1$ and the intrinsic utility functions over mugs and wealth are $u_m(m) = Bm$ and $u_w(w) = w$.

Assume that Eddie is an experienced trader of mugs. Because of his experience, he expects with a 50% chance to keep his endowment and with a 50% chance to change his endowment. Let his referent be this random expectation.

Buying: As a potential buyer of a mug, Eddie has an endowment of zero mugs and zero wealth ($r_m = r_w = 0$). He expects with a 50% chance to keep this endowment and with a 50% chance to buy a mug at a price P ($r_m = 1$ and $r_w = -P$). His referent is then the lottery $R = ((0, 0), 0.5; (1, -P), 0.5)$. Applying Definition 9A.1, we can compute Eddie's utility U from buying and not buying a mug as follows:

$$
\begin{aligned}
\text{Buy}: U((1, -P) \mid R) &= 0.5U((1, -P) \mid (0, 0)) + 0.5U((1, -P) \mid (1, -P)) \\
&= B - P + 0.5[v(B \mid 0) + v(-P \mid 0)] \\
&= B - P + 0.5(B - \lambda P) \\
&= 1.5B - (1 + 0.5\lambda)P \\
\text{Don't Buy}: U((0, 0) \mid R) &= 0.5U((0, 0) \mid (0, 0)) + 0.5U((0, 0) \mid (1, -P)) \\
&= 0.5[v(0 \mid B) + v(0 \mid -P)] \\
&= 0.5(-\lambda B + P)
\end{aligned}
$$

Eddie's WTP is the price that makes him indifferent between buying and not buying:

$$\overbrace{0.5(-\lambda B + WTP)}^{\text{Don't Buy Utility}} = U((0,0) \mid R) = \overbrace{U((1, -WTP) \mid R) = 1.5B - (1 + 0.5\lambda)WTP}^{\text{Buy Utility}}$$

$$\Rightarrow WTP = B$$

This is a striking result. With the random reference point Eddie's WTP for a mug is exactly equal to his marginal benefit of the mug, B. His WTP does *not* depend on λ. For any degree of loss aversion he is always willing to pay at most B. Why does this happen? With a certain endowment-based reference point, as in the chapter, Eddie only experiences a loss when he buys the mug — he loses money. But in this setting that loss is dampened because half the time he expects to lose the money from buying a mug. And maintaining the status quo also generates a loss because half the time he expects to buy and in not buying, he loses out on not having a mug. These losses, from both buying and not buying "wash out" so that loss aversion does not impact his WTP.

Selling: Now consider the case where Eddie is endowed with a mug and zero wealth ($r_m = 1$ and $r_w = 0$). He expects with a 50% chance to keep this endowment and with a 50% chance to sell the mug at a price P ($r_m = 0$ and $r_w = P$). His referent is then the lottery $R = ((1, 0), 0.5;(0, P),0.5)$. Applying Definition 9A.1, we can compute Eddie's utility U from selling and not selling the mug as follows:

$$
\begin{aligned}
\text{Sell}: U((0, P) \mid R) &= 0.5U((0, P) \mid (1,0)) + 0.5U((0, P) \mid (0, P)) \\
&= P + 0.5[v(0 \mid B) + v(P \mid 0)] \\
&= P + 0.5(-\lambda B + P) \\
&= 1.5P - 0.5\lambda B
\end{aligned}
$$

$$
\begin{aligned}
\text{Don't Sell}: U((1,0) \mid R) &= 0.5U((1,0) \mid (1,0)) + 0.5U((1,0) \mid (0, P)) \\
&= B + 0.5[v(B \mid 0) + v(0 \mid P)] \\
&= B + 0.5(B - \lambda P) \\
&= 1.5B - 0.5\lambda P
\end{aligned}
$$

Eddie's WTA is the price that makes him indifferent between selling and not selling. It should be obvious from the above expressions that they are equal at a price of B. That is, $WTA = B$ and as with his WTP, it is independent of the degree of his loss aversion. The intuition is similar. Whether Eddie sells or not, he expects a loss 50% of the time. These losses cancel out so that loss aversion does not impact his WTA.

No Endowment Effect: In summary, not only are Eddie's WTP and WTA independent of the coefficient of loss aversion λ, they are equal to each other. He exhibits no endowment effect; he values the mug at B, is willing to pay at most B for it, and will sell it for no less than B. This confirms the claim in the chapter that expectations-based random reference points can explain why greater trading experience is associated with a weaker (or non-existent) endowment effect   ∎

This example reveals an important insight: reference-dependent preferences with loss aversion do not necessarily imply an endowment effect. What they do is make the endowment effect possible. But whether or not the preferences lead to an endowment effect depends on the nature of the reference point. Once again, the model's predictions are only as good as the reference point is accurate. The following exercises prompt you to apply this model to additional settings of shopping and saving.

9A.1   Appendix Exercises[16]

Exercise 9A.1 – Moderately Experienced Expectations. Suppose that in Example 9A.1 Eddie has an intermediate level of trading experience and therefore expects with a 75% chance to keep his endowment and with a 25% chance to change his endowment.

a Determine his WTP (which may depend on B and λ).
b Determine his WTA (which may depend on B and λ).
c Does he exhibit an endowment effect (i.e., WTA/WTP > 1)? How does the ratio of WTA to WTP compare to the cases when he expects to keep his endowment with certainty and with only a 50% chance? Discuss this comparison.

Exercise 9A.2 — Sandwich Surprises (Karle, Kirchsteiger, and Peitz 2015). Jayden likes turkey sandwiches (t) more than meatball sandwiches (m). In particular, his intrinsic utility functions over these sandwiches and wealth (w) are $u_t(t) = 13t$, $u_m(m) = 10m$, and $u_w(w) = w$. He currently has no sandwiches and no wealth. He knows that when he gets to the store one of the sandwiches will be priced at \$8 and one will be priced at \$7. But before arriving at the store, he doesn't know whether the price of the turkey sandwich (P_t) will be higher or lower than the price of the meatball sandwich (P_m). He expects that it is equally likely that he will buy the cheaper or the more expensive sandwich. Jayden's reference-dependent preferences with this random reference point for buying each type of sandwich are therefore represented by the following utilities:

$$\text{Buy Turkey Sandwich: } U_t = 13 - P_t + 0.5v(-P_t \mid -7) + 0.5v(-P_t \mid -8)$$
$$\text{Buy Meatball Sandwich: } U_m = 10 - P_m + 0.5v(-P_m \mid -7) + 0.5v(-P_m \mid -8)$$

where $v(x \mid r) = \begin{cases} x - r & \text{if } x \geq r \\ \lambda(x - r) & \text{if } x < r \end{cases}$

Note that these utility functions implicitly assume $\lambda \geq 1$, $\eta = 1$ and the referent lottery $R = ((1, -7), 0.5; (1, -8), 0.5)$ where the first good is sandwiches and the second is wealth.

a Show that if the turkey sandwich is the cheaper sandwich ($P_t = 7$), he will always buy it, i.e, $U_t > U_m$.
b Now suppose that the turkey sandwich is the more expensive sandwich ($P_t = 8$). For what range of λ will he still buy the turkey sandwich?
c Provide intuition for the result in part (b). That is, why is it that for sufficiently strong loss aversion Jayden will act differently than standard theory predicts?

Exercise 9A.3 — Precautionary Savings (Köszegi and Rabin 2009). [Calculus Required] In our analysis of the standard life-cycle model in Section 4.5 we assumed that income was predictable and known. In fact, future income may be random. Let's now think about the role of uncertain future income on savings decisions with both standard preferences and reference-dependent preferences. Precautionary savings refers to the extra savings caused by future income being uncertain rather than certain.

Consider the following setting: there are two periods ($t = 1, 2$) in which an individual has to divide her assets of 1 over consumption in each period, with zero interest rate and zero discount rate. In addition, there is a random, mean–zero shock in period 2, either increasing or decreasing her assets by z, each with probability 0.5. In particular, if she consumes c_1 in period 1, then consumption in period 2 will be either $1 - c_1 + z$ or $1 - c_1 - z$, each equally likely.

Let her standard intrinsic utility of consumption in each period be given by the per-period utility function, $u(c)$, where we assume that $u' > 0$, $u'' < 0$. In summary, her lifetime expected utility is given by:

$$u(c_1) + 0.5u(1 - c_1 + z) + 0.5u(1 - c_1 - z) \tag{9A.1}$$

a   Assume that there is no risk (i.e., $z = 0$). Simplify expression (9A.1) and determine her utility-maximizing consumption in period 1. *Hint: Don't forget chain rule.*

b   Now assume that there is risk (i.e., $z > 0$) and determine the first order condition for maximizing (9A.1). Write your expression with only $u'(c_1)$ on the left side of the equation. *Note: It can be shown using Jensen's inequality that if marginal utility is convex ($u''' > 0$), then her first period savings are higher with risk than in part (a). These are precautionary savings.*

Now assume that she also experiences gain-loss utility *only over second period consumption*. Her reference point for second period consumption is random: given the choice of c_1, the reference point in period 2 is equally likely to be $1 - c_1 + z$ or $1 - c_1 - z$. Note that for a given level of c_1, for *each* possible consumption level in period 2 she compares this period-2 consumption to $1 - c_1 + z$ and $1 - c_1 - z$. In particular, her lifetime expected utility is:

$$u(c_1) \quad +0.5[u(1 - c_1 + z) + 0.5 \cdot 0 + 0.5v(u(1 - c_1 + z) \mid u(1 - c_1 - z))]$$
$$+0.5[u(1 - c_1 - z) + 0.5v(u(1 - c_1 - z) \mid u(1 - c_1 + z)) + 0.5 \cdot 0] \tag{9A.2}$$

where zeros indicate no gain or loss and $v(x \mid r) = \begin{cases} x - r & \text{if } x \geq r \\ \lambda(x - r) & \text{if } x < r \end{cases}$

c   Apply the gain-loss value function $v(\cdot)$ to lifetime expected utility (9A.2) and arrange terms so that lifetime expected utility takes the following form:

$$u(c_1) \quad +0.5u(1 - c_1 + z) + 0.5u(1 - c_1 - z)$$
$$+G(\lambda) \cdot (u(1 - c_1 + z) - u(1 - c_1 - z)) \tag{9A.3}$$

where $G(\lambda)$ is some function of λ. Find $G(\lambda)$ and provide intuition for how λ impacts the expression in (9A.3) relative to the standard case in (9A.1).

d   Determine the first order condition for maximizing your expression for lifetime expected utility in part (c). Arrange this first order condition with only $u'(c_1)$ on the left side of the equation. Will the utility-maximizing c_1 be higher or lower than in part (b)? Provide intuition for how loss aversion impacts savings.

Notes

1 A more general nonlinear version of this gain-loss value function was originally proposed by Kahneman and Tversky (1979) as one feature of their theory of decision making with risk. This theory, known as prospect theory, is presented in Chapter 12.
2 Barberis, Huang, and Thaler (2006) argue for the importance of narrow bracketing.
3 The model is adapted from Köszegi and Rabin (2006), which itself is related to the earlier model of reference-dependent preferences over certain outcomes proposed by Tversky and Kahneman (1991).
4 It is also possible to allow more than two goods, adding up the reference-dependent utility for each.
5 In theory, we could allow a different λ and a different η for each good. But doing so in general increases the complexity of the model without generating significantly distinct insights for our purposes.
6 An alternative is to replace $u(\cdot)$ with $U(\cdot)$ in Definition 9.2. But since the lottery consists of changes in one good (i.e., wealth), we can generate the same insights by using the simpler gain-loss value function $v(\cdot)$.
7 The expected gain-loss utility model is a *partial* version of prospect theory (Kahneman and Tversky 1979) that is developed more fully in Chapter 12.
8 Wakker (2005) provides a different resolution to the absurd conclusions of the expected utility model with probability weighting, a concept introduced in Chapter 12
9 The slopes of the loss averse utility function in Figure 9.3 are adjusted to align with the risk averse utility function. But the slope below \$100 remains twice as steep as the slope above \$100.
10 The positive impact of wages on labor supply assumes a substitution effect (to work more) that dominates the income effect (to work less). The income effect describes the increased purchasing power from a wage increase that induces workers to demand more leisure time, or equivalently, to supply less labor. Our focus is on settings where income effects are negligible.
11 The labor supply utility function in equation (9.5) is adapted from DellaVigna (2009).
12 The test for loss aversion was the option to accept an even bet of winning 8 Swiss francs or losing 5 Swiss francs. Rejecting this lottery is consistent with expected gain-loss utility and $\lambda = 2$. Accepting it suggests standard, approximately risk neutral, preferences over small-stakes lotteries.
13 See Mortensen (1986) for a review of standard job search models.
14 Exercises 9.6 and 9.12 are adapted from exercises by Botond Köszegi.
15 See O'Donoghue and Sprenger (2018, Sec. 6) for an excellent comprehensive review of theoretical and empirical work on expectations-based reference points.
16 Exercise 9A.3 is adapted from an exercise by Lorenz Goette.

References

Attanasio, Orazio P., and Guglielmo Weber. 2010. "Consumption and Saving: Models of Intertemporal Allocation and Their Implications for Public Policy." *Journal of Economic Literature* 48 (3): 693–751. doi:10.1257/jel.48.3.693.

Barberis, Nicholas, Ming Huang, and Richard H. Thaler. 2006. "Individual Preferences, Monetary Gambles, and Stock Market Participation: A Case for Narrow Framing." *American Economic Review* 96 (4): 1069–1090. doi:10.1257/aer.96.4.1069.

Benartzi, Shlomo, and Richard H. Thaler. 1995. "Myopic Loss Aversion and the Equity Premium Puzzle." *The Quarterly Journal of Economics* 110 (1): 73–92. doi:10.2307/2118511.

Camerer, Colin F., Linda Babcock, George Loewenstein, and Richard H. Thaler. 1997. "Labor Supply of New York City Cabdrivers: One Day at a Time." *The Quarterly Journal of Economics* 112 (2): 407–441. doi:10.1162/003355397555244.

Carmon, Ziv, and San Ariely. 2000. "Focusing on the Forgone: How Value Can Appear so Different to Buyers and Sellers." *Journal of Consumer Research* 27 (3): 360–370. doi:10.1086/317590.

DellaVigna, Stefano. 2009. "Psychology and Economics: Evidence from the Field." *Journal of Economic Literature* 47 (2): 315–372. doi:10.1257/jel.47.2.315.

DellaVigna, Stefano, Attila Lindner, Balázs Reizer, and Johannes F. Schmieder. 2017. "Reference-Dependent Job Search: Evidence from Hungary." *The Quarterly Journal of Economics* 132 (4): 1969–2018. doi:10.1093/qje/qjx015.

Fehr, Ernst, and Lorenz Goette. 2007. "Do Workers Work More if Wages are High? Evidence from a Randomized Field Experiment." *American Economic Review* 97 (1): 298–317. doi:10.1257/aer.97.1.298.

Genesove, David, and Christopher Mayer. 2001. "Loss Aversion and Seller Behavior: Evidence from the Housing Market." *The Quarterly Journal of Economics* 116 (4): 1233–1260. doi:10.1162/003355301753265561.

Gneezy, Uri, and Jan Potters. 1997. "An Experiment on Risk Taking and Evaluation Periods." *The Quarterly Journal of Economics* 112 (2): 631–645. doi:10.1162/003355397555217.

Goette, Lorenz, David Huffman, and Ernst Fehr. 2004. "Loss Aversion and Labor Supply." *Journal of the European Economic Association* 2 (2–3): 216–228. doi:10.1162/154247604323067934.

Kahneman, Daniel, Jack L. Knetsch, and Richard H. Thaler. 1990. "Experimental Tests of the Endowment Effect and the Coase Theorem." *Journal of Political Economy* 98 (6): 1325–1348. doi:10.1086/261737.

Kahneman, Daniel, and Amos Tversky. 1979. "Prospect Theory: An Analysis of Decision under Risk." *Econometrica* 47 (2): 263–291. doi:10.2307/1914185.

Karle, Heiko, Georg Kirchsteiger, and Martin Peitz. 2015. "Loss Aversion and Consumption Choice: Theory and Experimental Evidence." *American Economic Journal: Microeconomics* 7 (2): 101–120. doi:10.1257/mic.20130104.

Köszegi, Botond, and Matthew Rabin. 2006. "A Model of Reference-Dependent Preferences." *The Quarterly Journal of Economics* 121 (4): 1133–1165. doi:10.1162/qjec.121.4.1133.

———. 2009. "Reference-Dependent Consumption Plans." *American Economic Review* 99 (3): 909–936. doi:10.1257/aer.99.3.909.

Kremer, Michael, Jean Lee, Jonathan Robinson, and Olga Rostapshova. 2013. "Behavioral Biases and Firm Behavior: Evidence from Kenyan Retail Shops." *American Economic Review* 103 (3): 362–368. doi:10.1257/aer.103.3.362.

Mortensen, Dale T. 1986. "Job Search and Labor Market Analysis." In *Handbook of Labor Economics,* 2: 849–919. Elsevier. doi:10.1016/S1573-4463(86)02005-9.

Novemsky, Nathan, and Daniel Kahneman. 2005. "The Boundaries of Loss Aversion." *Journal of Marketing Research* 42 (2): 119–128. doi:10.1509/jmkr.42.2.119. 62292.

O'Donoghue, Ted, and Charles Sprenger. 2018. "Reference-Dependent Preferences." In *Handbook of Behavioral Economics: Foundations and Applications,* edited by B. Douglas Bernheim, Stefano Della-Vigna, and David Laibson, 1: 1–77. North-Holland.

Pagel, Michaela. 2017. "Expectations-Based Reference-Dependent Life-Cycle Consumption." *The Review of Economic Studies* 84 (2): 885–934. doi:10.1093/restud/rdx003.

Pope, Alexander. 1886. "Gay and Pope to Fortescue, September 23, 1725." In *The Works of Alexander Pope,* vol. IX. London: John Murray.

Pope, Devin G., and Maurice E. Schweitzer. 2011. "Is Tiger Woods Loss Averse? Persistent Bias in the Face of Experience, Competition, and High Stakes." *American Economic Review* 101 (1): 129–157. doi:10.1257/aer.101.1.129.

Rabin, Matthew, and Georg Weizsäcker. 2009. "Narrow Bracketing and Dominated Choices." *American Economic Review* 99 (4): 1508–1543. doi:10.1257/aer. 99.4.1508.

Rees-Jones, Alex. 2018. "Quantifying Loss-Averse Tax Manipulation." *The Review of Economic Studies* 85 (2): 1251–1278. doi:10.1093/restud/rdx038.

Samuelson, Paul. 1963. "Risk and Uncertainty: A Fallacy of Large Numbers." *Scientia* 57 (98): 108.

Tversky, Amos, and Daniel Kahneman. 1991. "Loss Aversion in Riskless Choice: A Reference-Dependent Model." *The Quarterly Journal of Economics* 106 (4): 1039–1061. doi:10.2307/2937956.

Wakker, Peter P. 2005. "Formalizing Reference Dependence and Initial Wealth in Rabin's Calibration Theorem." Mimeo. Econometric Institute, Erasmus University Rotterdam.

10 Market & Policy Responses to Loss Aversion

Learning Objectives

★ Consider welfare interpretations of loss aversion.

★ Understand why incentives can have a stronger effect on behavior when framed as losses instead of gains.

★ Evaluate the implications of loss aversion for policies, contracts, and market rules that aim to incentivize particular behaviors.

Environmental policy advocates seek to incentivize reductions in the consumption and disposal of single-use plastics. School principals seek to improve student learning and test scores by incentivizing high quality instruction. Similarly, business managers seek to compensate workers in a way that incentivizes high effort and productivity, without constant oversight. And when an art collector auctions off a painting, she hopes that the auction rules incentivize aggressive bidding that leads to a high selling price.

No matter the specific context, each of these scenarios illustrates a common economic problem: which policies, contracts, or rules most effectively incentivize behaviors in a particular direction? Incentives can take the form of rewards for desired behaviors (as subsidies or bonuses), or punishments for undesired behaviors (as taxes or fines). From the perspective of a standard decision maker, a reward for doing an activity has the same incentive effect as an equivalent punishment for *not* doing the activity.

When individuals are loss averse, as evidenced in the previous two chapters, equivalent rewards and punishments no longer share the same incentive effects. A loss averse individual is predicted to exert greater effort to avoid a punishment than to achieve a reward. This observation generates novel insights for the design of public policy and private contracts.

This chapter explores each of the four scenarios above. We begin with a brief discussion of individual welfare interpretations for loss averse individuals. The following two sections on incentivizing the use of reusable shopping bags and incentivizing instructional quality highlight the policy implications of loss aversion. And the consequences of loss aversion for profit maximization are explored in the final two sections, with applications to worker contracts and auction design.

DOI: 10.4324/9780367854072-13

10.1 Welfare Interpretations of Loss Aversion

When an individual evaluates a loss more intensely than an equivalent gain, is she making a mistake? Recall that a mistake refers to a decision that does not maximize an individual's own self-determined welfare, where welfare is given by *experienced* utility (Section 3.2).

In the previous chapter we constructed a nonstandard model of *decision* utility with reference dependence and loss aversion. We then demonstrated that if consumers make decisions by maximizing this nonstandard decision utility function, the predicted behavior aligns well with observed behavior across a variety of settings.

Such behavior constitutes a mistake only if the model of decision utility fails to represent experienced utility. Suppose that decision utility measures actual feelings of pleasure and pain associated with perceived gains and losses. Then it also measures experienced utility. Under this interpretation, there is no mistake and no welfare loss.

But even though gain-loss utility impacts decision making, perhaps what matters most for welfare is the experienced satisfaction from the final outcome, after making the decision. Then experienced utility may deviate from decision utility. In this case, decisions can constitute mistakes, justifying paternalistic policy interventions.

Both interpretations — loss aversion as part of experienced utility or not — have merit. As a consequence, this chapter does not aim to evaluate the welfare losses from loss aversion (if any exist), but instead considers the ways in which loss averse behaviors impact how we think about policy and profit-maximization strategies.

10.2 Reusable Bag Use [Environment]

10.2.1 Background and Evidence

Plastic bags are a lightweight, durable, compact, and subsequently convenient means of transporting groceries and other goods. They were first introduced to American consumers at grocery stores in the late 1970s, usually free of charge, and have since become ubiquitous. This use adds up to approximately 100 billion plastic bags consumed each year in the United States and over a trillion plastic bags worldwide (Clapp and Swanston 2009). Although plastic bags are usually recyclable, the Environmental Protection Agency estimates that only 12.8% of plastic bags, sacks, and wraps in the United States were recycled in 2015 (EPA 2018). Instead, plastic bags often end up in landfills, where they degrade at slow rates. And those not in landfills make their way to rivers and oceans, introducing a hazard to aquatic and marine life.

Concern with the environmental damage caused by plastic bags has motivated governments around the world to discourage their use with a variety of policies. This includes South Africa (Hasson, Leiman, and Visser 2007), Ireland (Convery, McDonnell, and Ferreira 2007), and China (He 2010). In the early 2000s, California cities and counties began banning retailers from providing plastic bags to consumers (Taylor and Villas-Boas 2016). And on January 1, 2010, Washington DC was the first US city to require food retailers to charge a $0.05 tax at checkout for each single-use plastic or paper bag. A portion of this tax revenue was kept by the retailer, while the remainder was used to support cleanup of the heavily polluted Anacostia River. Prior to the implementation of the tax, some grocery stores in the Washington DC area incentivized shoppers to bring their own bags by paying them a subsidy of $0.05 for each reusable bag the customer used (Homonoff 2018). Whether a ban, tax, or subsidy, each of these policies is aimed at reducing the consumption of single-use plastics that generate negative externalities. The following quasi-experiment estimates the differential impacts on behavior of a tax and subsidy.

Quasi-Experiment — Incentivizing Disposable Bag Use (Homonoff 2018)

Consider two similar policies aimed at reducing disposable (plastic and paper) bag use at grocery stores in the Washington DC area: a $0.05 tax on each disposable bag used and a $0.05 subsidy for each reusable bag used instead of a disposable bag. Homonoff (2018) examines the effects of these policies with data on bag use behavior from more than 16,000 customers over six months from late 2011 to early 2012.

To study the effect of the tax, she leverages the quasi-experiment induced by the introduction of the tax in Montgomery County, Maryland on January 1, 2012. Customers in this county were treated with the introduction of the tax. Customers in nearby counties (Washington, DC and Arlington County, Virginia) where there was no change in the disposable bag use policy during this period serve as a control group. By comparing the change in bag use in the treated county to the change in bag use in the control counties, we can be confident that any differential change in bag use behavior is due to the introduction of the tax.

To study the effect of the subsidy, she compares the customer bag use at stores offering the bonus to otherwise similar stores not offering the bonus.

The results of the tax policy analysis are illustrated in Figure 10.1. Observe that the share of customers using disposable bags remained essentially flat in the controls of Washington, DC (where a tax was in effect for the entire observation period) and Arlington County (where no tax was in effect for the entire observation period). In the absence of the tax, we would then expect shoppers in Montgomery County to similarly continue using disposable bags at the same rate as they were before the tax. But the implementation of the tax in Montgomery County led to a 42 percentage point decline in disposable bag use. This is a very strong response, particularly given the relatively small magnitude of the $0.05 per-bag tax.

In contrast to the tax, the subsidy had virtually no impact on decreasing disposable bag use.

10.2.2 Modeling Loss Averse Shoppers

The drastically different impacts of the tax and subsidy in the above quasi-experiment are not predicted by standard economics. If customers were standard decision makers, then both the tax and the subsidy should have the same impact on disposable bag use. This is because both policies provide customers with a $0.05 incentive to use a reusable bag instead of a disposable bag.

Instead, customers only responded to the tax. But if customers are loss averse, then by coding the tax as a loss and the subsidy as a gain, the incentive effect of the tax would be larger than the incentive effect of an equivalent bonus to use a reusable bag.

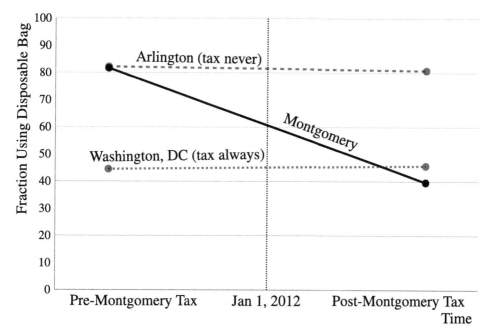

Figure 10.1 Disposable Bag Taxes and Use

Data Source: Homonoff (2018).

Let's verify this intuition. Suppose that a shopper has reference-dependent preferences and is loss averse relative to her wealth in the absence of any bag-use incentive policy. Denote this wealth reference point by W. In addition, let b equal 1 or 0 to indicate that the shopper brings or does not bring her own reusable bag. Denote the per-bag tax by $t \geq 0$ and the per-bag subsidy by $s \geq 0$. The introduction of these incentives generates total wealth of $W + sb - t(1 - b)$, since wealth increases by s if a reusable bag is used and decreases by t if it is not used. Preferences can then be represented by the following utility function:

$$U(b \mid W) = \begin{cases} W + sb - t(1 - b) - W - bc & \text{if } W + sb - t(1 - b) \geq W \\ \lambda[W + sb - t(1 - b) - W] - bc & \text{if } W + sb - t(1 - b) < W \end{cases}$$

$$= \begin{cases} sb - t(1 - b) - bc & \text{if } sb \geq t(1 - b) \\ \lambda[sb - t(1 - b)] - bc & \text{if } sb < t(1 - b) \end{cases} \quad (10.1)$$

where $\lambda \geq 1$ is the coefficient of loss aversion and c is the utility cost of bringing your own reusable bag. This cost will be higher for individuals who find it challenging to remember to bring a bag. The cost could even be negative for those who obtain satisfaction from bringing their own bag.

We can simplify this utility function considerably by considering the tax and subsidy policies separately. Suppose that there is a tax $t > 0$ and no subsidy $s = 0$. Then by bringing a bag ($b = 1$), the shopper avoids the tax, has no gain or loss in wealth, and only pays

Table 10.1 Bag Use Reference-Dependent Utilities $U(b|W)$, from Equation (10.1)

Policy	Reusable Bag $b = 1$	Disposable Bag $b = 0$	Choose Reusable Bag $U(1 \mid W) \geq U(0 \mid W)$
Tax: $t > 0$, $s = 0$	$U(1 \mid W) = -c$	$U(0 \mid W) = -\lambda t$	$c \leq \lambda t$
Subsidy: $s > 0$, $t = 0$	$U(1 \mid W) = s - c$	$U(0 \mid W) = 0$	$c \leq s$

the utility cost c of bringing the reusable bag. If she does not bring her own bag ($b = 0$), then the utility loss of paying the tax is $-t\lambda$.

With the subsidy policy $s > 0$ and no tax $t = 0$, a shopper who brings a bag ($b = 1$) receives the subsidy gain s and pays the utility cost c. By using a disposable bag ($b = 0$), she experiences no wealth gains or losses, yielding utility of zero. These values are summarized in Table 10.1.

The final column of Table 10.1 indicates the upper bound on the cost c for which a shopper will bring her own reusable bag. In the absence of loss aversion ($\lambda = 1$) we have the prediction that shoppers will bring their own bags as long as c is less than the magnitude of the incentive. So for a tax and subsidy of equal magnitude, a shopper's bag choice should be the same under either policy. This confirms the standard prediction that the $0.05 tax and the $0.05 subsidy should have the same impact on behavior.

What are the predictions for the effects of a $0.05 subsidy and a $0.05 tax on loss averse shoppers ($\lambda > 1$)? With the subsidy, any shopper with $c \leq 0.05$ will choose to bring their own reusable bag. With the tax, all of the shoppers incentivized by the subsidy, plus shoppers with utility cost c up to $\lambda 0.05 > 0.05$, will be induced to bring their own bags. That is, more shoppers are impacted by the tax than the subsidy. This is because the tax is perceived as a wealth loss, and to avoid this loss, more shoppers are willing to incur the hassle of bringing their own reusable bags to the grocery store.

In sum, loss aversion predicts the tax to incentivize more people to use disposable bags than the equivalent subsidy. This qualitative prediction is consistent with the evidence from the quasi-experiment. But in order for loss aversion alone to explain the massive reduction in disposable bag use from a small tax, Homonoff (2018) estimates that the coefficient of loss aversion must be very large, with $\lambda = 5.3$. Recall that typical estimates find λ in the range of 2 to 2.5.

10.2.3   *Explanations Beyond Loss Aversion*

The large estimate of λ suggests that loss aversion may not be the only factor driving customer responsiveness to the tax. One way in which the tax differs from the subsidy is that the tax changes disposable bags from being free to costing something. With the subsidy, disposable bags remain free (ignoring the opportunity cost of saving $0.05 with a reusable bag). And if customers obtain additional utility from free goods (as in Shampanier, Mazar, and Ariely 2007), then by eliminating the free price, the tax is predicted to have a larger impact on behavior than the subsidy.

The tax and subsidy also differ in that the tax was the consequence of a law, whereas the bonus was a voluntary store policy. If laws communicate social norms about what types of behaviors are socially desirable, then the change in behavior from the tax may be driven in part by changing perceptions about the benefits of reusable bags.

For this hypothesis to explain the data in Figure 10.1, it must be that social norms only shift for shoppers at the moment when the county in which they shop imposes the bag tax. But the proximity of the counties to each other means that most shoppers were likely aware of the bag tax law in the area, even if it did not apply to them. It is more likely that social norms were therefore shifting throughout the region over time, and not simply for Montgomery County shoppers after January 1, 2012.

The key insight illustrated by this example is that behavior responds more to a policy that consumers code as a loss than an equivalent policy coded as a gain. This has important implications for policy makers interested in effectively incentivizing behavior to improve social welfare. The insight can also be leveraged by firms looking to incentivize particular behaviors from workers. The next sections consider such settings.

10.3   Teacher Compensation   [Education]

The United States government spends over $700 billion annually on public elementary and secondary education. This amounts to almost $14,000 per student. And approximately 80% of the expenditures go to teacher compensation (NCES 2019). Given the significant resources allocated to public education, economists are interested in studying policies that promote the best outcomes for students.

A pathway for improving student outcomes is to ensure high quality teachers. One method for quantifying teacher quality is a value-added approach that measures how much a teacher increases their students' test scores on average. Chetty, Friedman, and Rockoff (2014) find that students of teachers with high value-added scores not only score higher on tests in the short run, but also benefit in the long run. They are more likely to attend college, earn higher salaries, and less likely to have children as teenagers. The authors further estimate that replacing a very low value-added teacher with an average teacher increases the collective future earnings of students in the classroom by $250,000 (in present value).

Given the significant public resources allocated to paying teachers and the importance of teacher quality on student outcomes, policy makers have considered financial incentives for teachers based on student outcomes. The impact of such incentives is theoretically ambiguous. If teachers are already doing their best to improve student achievement, incentives may have no effect. Alternatively, if the incentives motivate additional teacher effort towards curriculum development or family engagement, then we may see student improvements. But if the student improvements, as measured by test scores, are the consequence of teaching-to-the-test at the expense of developing important foundational skills, then such test score improvements may not lead to better long-term student outcomes. In fact, the empirical evidence of teacher financial incentives is mixed, with small and sometimes negative effects (Springer et al. 2010; Fryer 2013).[1]

How might a policy maker leverage the evidence of loss aversion to more effectively incentivize teacher performance? Recall that in the context of exerting effort, a loss averse individual will exert greater effort to avoid a loss than to achieve a gain (as evidenced by labor supply and job search effort in Section 9.5). Therefore, with loss averse preferences, teachers would be predicted to put forth greater instructional effort to avoid a decrease in their compensation than to increase their compensation. The following field experiment tests this hypothesis.

Field Experiment – Incentivizing Teachers (Fryer et al. 2012)

Consider the following field experiment across nine schools in Chicago Heights, Illinois during the 2010–2011 academic year. At the start of the school year teachers were randomly assigned to one of three groups:

1   Control group: no financial incentive for student achievement.
2   Gain group: traditional financial incentive in the form of a year-end bonus for gains in student achievement.
3   Loss group: nontraditional financial incentive in the form of a lump sum payment at the start of the year that would have to be paid back (in part or in full) for lack of student achievement.

In both the Gain and Loss treatment groups student achievement was measured by test score improvements relative to other similar students (based on their previous test scores and demographic characteristics). Because of the random assignment, any differences in student outcomes across these groups can credibly be attributed to the difference in financial incentives.

The financial incentives were constructed so that teachers with the same student achievement received the same additional compensation at the year's end, regardless of whether they were in the Gain or Loss group. Therefore, with standard preferences, the Gain and Loss groups face the same financial incentives for student achievement.

Suppose instead that teachers are loss averse relative to the reference point of their start-of-year bonus. Then teachers in the Gain group, who get no start-of-year bonus, code the financial incentive as a gain. But teachers in the Loss group, who receive a start-of-year bonus, but might be required to pay part of it back, code the financial incentive as a loss. The Loss group teachers face a greater incentive to improve student achievement.

Fryer et al. (2012) find that students with teachers in the Loss group achieved large improvements in math test scores relative to students with teachers in the Control group. In contrast, the researchers find no significant difference in math test scores between students with teachers in the Gain and Control groups. This evidence is consistent with the prediction for loss averse teachers, and inconsistent with standard preferences.

The above results provide important insights for education policy. The fact that financial incentives can impact student test scores demonstrates that at least some teachers have the capacity to further improve student outcomes. But the structure of incentives matters for their effectiveness. In particular, the ineffectiveness of traditional bonus incentives is consistent with the prior studies showing small to zero effects of such incentives. By framing incentives as avoiding a loss, policy makers can leverage loss averse preferences to achieve student gains without spending additional resources.

Although framing incentives as loss avoidance increases student test scores in the short run, we do not know the long-run effectiveness of these incentives. If teachers are motivated to develop strategies that increase student test scores at the expense of developing foundational skills and knowledge, then the incentives may not improve the long-run student outcomes that are most relevant for welfare. In addition, the effectiveness of the incentives to increase test scores may erode, if over time, teachers adjust their reference point. For example, teachers who do not improve their students' test scores may come to anticipate returning most of the start-of-year bonus at year-end. In this case, they may not perceive the repayment of the provisional bonus as a loss, eliminating any additional incentive effect driven by loss aversion.

In sum, while the evidence lends support to broader implementation of teacher incentive programs informed by behavioral economics insights, further evaluation of nonstandard incentive schemes is warranted. The next section considers a similar loss-avoidance incentive program in a manufacturing setting where the quality of work and the long-run effectiveness can be measured.

10.4   Worker Bonuses   [Business]

The previous two sections identify instances where policy makers can leverage loss aversion to improve a social outcome: either to reduce the external damage from disposable plastic bag use or to enhance the efficiency of public education. We turn our attention in this section to a market setting where a firm is seeking to maximize profit.

A central question for a business manager is how to compensate employees. The simplest methods are to pay each worker a fixed salary for the year (e.g., teachers) or an hourly wage (e.g., construction workers). But if the worker's compensation is not contingent on their effort, a self-interested worker has an incentive to shirk their responsibilities. To incentivize high effort, some employers pay a bonus for work that achieves an individual or company-wide goal (e.g., investment bankers). Workers may instead earn a commission (e.g., salespersons) or tips (e.g., taxi drivers) in addition to their base salary. Organizations can also adopt tournament-style systems where compensation is tied to one's rank within the company — and promotions are prizes for outperforming others. These alternative incentive schemes are studied in the field of personnel economics (Lazear and Shaw 2007).

With potentially loss averse workers, managers must consider not only the magnitude and structure of their compensation contracts, but how the incentives are coded as either gains or avoided losses. The evidence from the Incentivizing Teachers Field Experiment documents the strong incentive effects of loss avoidance in the not-for-profit setting of public schools. The following field experiment similarly tests the impact of framing incentives, but in a factory setting. In addition to observing the effects on worker productivity, the study also examines the effects on production quality and productivity over time.

Field Experiment – Incentivizing Factory Workers (Hossain and List 2012)

Consider the following field experiment conducted with the cooperation of Wanlida Group Company, a major Chinese producer and distributor of consumer electronics. From July 2008 to January 2009, 165 workers at the company's Nanjing factory experienced randomly assigned changes in the structure of their compensation for meeting weekly production targets. Because of random assignment, any differences in productivity or quality of work for an employee across the compensation contracts can be credibly attributed to differences in the financial incentives.

Each worker experienced each of the following compensation schemes (paid in renminbi (RMB)) at some point during the experiment:

1   Control: no financial incentive for productivity.
2   Gain incentive: bonus of RMB 80 ($\approx$ \$12) for each week that productivity exceeds the production target (to be paid at the end of 4 weeks).
3   Loss incentive: provisional bonus of RMB 320 that is reduced by RMB 80 for each week that productivity does not meet the production target (to be paid at the end of 4 weeks).

Observe that for a given level of productivity, the Gain and Loss financial incentives pay the same total bonus at the same time. The production targets were set so that they could be met 60%–80% of the time. And the weekly bonus was substantial, equal to 25% of the base weekly salary for a typical worker.

With standard preferences, the workers are expected to exert the same effort with both the Gain and Loss financial incentives. But loss aversion relative to the provisional bonus (RMB 0 for the Gain incentive and RMB 320 for the Loss incentive) predicts greater effort to avoid losing RMB 80 each week than to gain RMB 80 each week.

Hossain and List (2012) document the following results (for employees who work in a team):

1   *Financial Incentives vs. Control:* Both the Gain and Loss financial incentives increased productivity, by 8.5% and 9.5% respectively.
2   *Gains vs. Loss Incentives:* The Loss incentive increased productivity by more than the Gain incentive.
3   *Production Quality:* Higher productivity from financial incentives had no observable impact on production quality or defects.
4   *Profitability:* With higher productivity (and no reduction in quality), the incentive schemes reduced the marginal cost of production by at least 7%.
5   *Long-Run Effects:* The higher productivity from both financial incentives persists over time (i.e., it does not initially spike and then decline).

This evidence supports the standard economics prediction that financial incentives have the effect of increasing productivity. And if the long-run gains in productivity exceed the higher labor costs, profits increase.

The evidence is also consistent with loss aversion, which predicts greater productivity by framing the incentive as one of avoiding a loss instead of achieving a gain. But in contrast to the Incentivizing Teachers Field Experiment, the difference is relatively small in this factory context. To see why, consider how the losses are structured in each experiment. In the teacher context, teachers were actually given a bonus payment at the start of the school year. The failure to improve student outcomes was then associated with a real financial loss in the form of an end-of-year payment — a requirement with which 98% of teachers complied. The factory workers, however, did not receive their provisional bonus at the start of the experiment. Instead, they were simply notified in a letter of their eligibility to receive a large bonus in 4 weeks, but that it would be reduced based on productivity. Because they were never required to make a payment, any perceived loss was psychologically weaker. This comparison underscores the connection between the incentive effects from avoiding a loss and the perceived intensity of that loss.

10.5   Auctions

Salvator Mundi, a painting by Leonardo da Vinci, sold for $450.3 million in 2017 at Christie's auction house. This record-setting auction price made headlines around the world. But auctions are not limited to the sale of famous art or unique artifacts. The reality TV show *Storage Wars* follows individuals who bid on unpaid storage lockers in auctions, hoping to find valuable treasures inside. The US government often uses auctions to buy goods and services. And the targeted advertisements you see while browsing the internet are the outcomes of fast real-time auctions with advertisers bidding to display their product.

10.5.1   Auction Types

Auctions are a widely used allocation mechanism because they have a number of desirable features. Their clear rules make them transparent, they are often difficult to manipulate, and in most cases they achieve the socially efficient outcome of giving the good to the bidder who values it most. There are also many different ways to structure an auction. A common type of auction depicted in the movies is one with an auctioneer announcing ever-increasing prices to a room full of bidders indicating that they would purchase the good at the currently announced price. Once the price is high enough that there are no more bidders, the last bidder who was willing to buy the item wins (and pays the highest bid). This is known as an English auction.

Alternatively, auctions can be organized with sealed bids. In this case each bidder writes down a bid and submits it to the auctioneer, without knowing the bids of anyone else. The highest bidder then wins the auction. What the bidders pay, however, can depend on the auction rules. There are three canonical sealed-bid auctions that differ in what the participants pay. They are:

- **First-price auction**: The winner pays their bid and the losers pay nothing.
- **Second-price auction**: The winner pays the second-highest bid, or equivalently, the highest losing bid. The losers again pay nothing.
- **All-pay auction**: Everyone pays their bid, whether they win or lose. This auction rule is used as a way to think about political lobbying or campaign contributions where everyone pays up front, but only some get their desired outcome.

A key decision for a seller is choosing the auction rules that generate the most revenue. And for a seller who has studied behavioral economics, she also wants to know whether it matters if bidders are loss averse.

Before answering these questions, a clarifying note is in order. Bidding behavior and the subsequent auction revenue depends on how individuals value the good being auctioned. When Treasury bills, portions of the electromagnetic spectrum, and oil fields are auctioned off, their value is the same to all bidders (even if each bidder has different information about what this value actually is). These are known as **common value auctions** because the value of the oil field is the same, or common, to any oil company that owns the land. This is distinct from a **private value auction** in which, as the name suggests, each bidder has a private value for the object. Goods auctioned off for consumption, like a bottle of wine, are likely to be valued differently by each bidder based on their private preferences.

We restrict our analysis to private value auctions where each bidder's private valuation is independent of everyone else. Of course, many goods, like fine art and houses, are a mix of private and common values. While each person may privately value a sculpture differently, if bidders are interested in possibly reselling the sculpture in the future, their current valuation depends not only on their private preference, but on the common assessment of the sculpture's value by other art collectors. To learn more about auction design, see Krishna (2010) and Milgrom (2004).

10.5.2   *Auction Revenue with Standard Bidders*

Suppose there is a group of individuals bidding on a single good G. Each bidder has their own independent private value θ for this good. Let each bidder's preferences over the good and their wealth W be represented by the following utility function:

$$U(G, W) = \theta G + W \tag{10.2}$$

where $G = 1$ if they win the good in the auction and $G = 0$ otherwise.

With these standard reference-independent preferences, each of the three types of sealed-bid auctions induces a different optimal bidding strategy, as follows.[2]

- Second-price auction: A higher bid increases the chance of winning the good, but does not impact the price paid since the winner pays someone else's bid (i.e., the second-highest bid). It is therefore optimal for each bidder to increase their bid up to their true value θ. This is the same optimal strategy as in English auctions — stay in the auction until the price exceeds your private valuation.
- First-price auction: A higher bid again increases the chance of winning the good, but it also increases the amount the bidder must pay if she wins. Because of this cost from increasing the bid (that does not exist with the second-price auction), it is optimal for each bidder to bid less than their true value θ. By reducing bids below θ, the winner ensures that she receives a gain upon winning. Otherwise, by bidding exactly θ, the winner gets an object worth θ, but pays θ for it.
- All-pay auction: A higher bid once again increases the chance of winning the good, but also increases the amount the bidder must pay — whether she wins or loses. Because everyone pays their bid, no matter the outcome, the cost of a high bid is even greater than in the first-price auction. It is therefore optimal for each bidder to bid even less in an all-pay auction than in the first-price auction.

Let's now think about these three auctions from the seller's perspective. In moving from a second-price auction to a first-price auction, the seller receives lower bids, but gets paid the highest bid instead of the second-highest bid. It is not obvious which will generate more revenue. And in moving to the all-pay auction, bids are even lower, but the seller receives payment from everyone, not just the winner. Again, it is not obvious if this leads to an overall increase or decrease in revenue.

It turns out that all three auctions generate the same exact (expected) revenue. This deep result, known as the **revenue equivalence theorem**, is one of the most important in all of auction theory. It also extends beyond the special cases of the three auctions considered here. In fact, revenues are the same across a broad range of auctions. For the original development of this finding, see Vickrey (1961).

The main takeaway is that it does not matter which payment scheme a seller chooses for an independent private-value sealed-bid auction — the expected revenue is always the same. This result hinges crucially, however, on bidders with utility functions as in (10.2).

10.5.3   *Auction Revenue with Loss Averse Bidders*

Does the revenue equivalence result still hold for bidders with loss averse preferences? And if not, which type of auction would a seller choose to extract the most revenue?

To answer these questions, suppose that each bidder evaluates the final outcome (G, W) with the model of reference-dependent utility (Definition 9.2) as follows:

$$ U((G, W) \mid (r_G, r_W)) = \theta G + W + v(\theta G \mid \theta r_G) + v(W \mid r_W) \qquad (10.3) $$

where r_G and r_W are the reference points for the good and wealth, and $v(\cdot)$ is the gain-loss value function with coefficient of loss aversion $\lambda = 2$. Because bidding in an auction is risky — both winning and payment are uncertain — assume that bidders have reference points given by their expectation that winning and losing are both possible. See Appendix 9A for the math behind such random reference points.

Given this setup, whether a bidder wins or loses an auction, she always expects the possibility that the outcome could have been otherwise. Consider an auction loser. She experiences loss utility from not winning the good that she had expected some chance of winning. A winner of a first-price or second-price auction also experiences loss utility. Because she had expected some chance of losing — and not making a payment — by winning and making a payment she experiences loss utility in wealth.

This loss utility is weighted twice as much as the gain utility from unexpected wins and unexpected non-payments. Bidders are therefore more averse to auctions that expose them to greater risk of a loss. And in response, they lower their bids and subsequently the seller's revenue. In other words, a less risky auction payment rule will lead to higher bids and greater seller revenue.

Let's apply this intuition to a comparison of first-price and second-price auctions. A first-price auction is less risky because it eliminates the uncertainty of payment for a winner. By paying their own bid upon winning, a bidder avoids the loss utility of paying more than expected (a possibility with a second-price auction) and is therefore willing to bid more. As a result, sellers earn more revenue from a first-price than a second-price auction (Lange and Ratan 2010).

By the same logic, an all-pay auction is even less risky than the first-price auction because bidders know they will pay their bid, win or lose. The all-pay auction eliminates entirely loss utility in wealth, which induces bidders to bid more aggressively, generating higher revenue than the first-price auction (Eisenhuth and Grunewald 2020). And in fact, there is no other auction format that generates higher revenue for the seller than an all-pay auction with loss averse bidders (Eisenhuth 2019).

There is one important caveat to the revenue ranking of all-pay over first-price auctions. This result follows from assuming that bidders evaluate gains and losses in the intrinsic utility of the good θG and the intrinsic utility of wealth W separately, as in equation (10.3). Such narrow bracketing makes sense when a non-monetary good is being auctioned, like a painting or a bottle of wine.

But suppose that bidders adopt a broader bracket and evaluate gains and losses in *total* intrinsic utility $\theta G + W$ relative to expectations. That is,

$$U((G, W) \mid (r_G, r_W)) = \theta G + W + v(\theta G + W \mid \theta r_G + r_W)$$

From this integrated perspective, the all-pay auction is now riskier, as it requires a bidder to make a certain payment and face the risk of losing the auction. The first-price auction is relatively less risky because even though there remains the same risk of losing the auction, payment is only required upon winning. The less risky first-price auction therefore implies higher revenue than the all-pay auction (Eisenhuth and Grunewald 2020). And the first-price auction maximizes the revenue a seller could receive from any possible auction format (Eisenhuth 2019).

In lab experiments of auctions, seller revenue is significantly higher in first-price auctions than all-pay auctions (Eisenhuth and Grunewald 2020). This is true whether the auctioned item is a real object or money. The empirical dominance of first-price auctions contradicts the revenue equivalence predictions of standard (risk-neutral) preferences. It also contradicts loss averse narrow bracketing. Instead, this lab evidence is consistent with loss averse bidders who broadly bracket total utility gains and losses from auction participation.

While standard theory predicts sellers to be indifferent across a variety of auction mechanisms, the choice of a first-price auction is rationalized by recognizing that bidders evaluate gains and loss as they do, and not as standard theory imagines them to. In sum, our analysis highlights the ways in which profit-maximizing sellers can respond to loss averse consumers.

10.6   Summary

1   The decisions of loss averse consumers may or may not constitute mistakes.
2   In a quasi-experiment, a tax on using disposable shopping bags had a much stronger effect on their use than an equivalent bonus for using reusable shopping bags. This evidence is consistent with loss averse shoppers.
3   In a field experiment, student test scores improved when teachers were faced with returning a start-of-year bonus for lack of student achievement. Paying teachers a year-end bonus for improved test scores had no impact. This evidence is consistent with loss averse teachers.
4   In a field experiment, a bonus for meeting production targets increased worker productivity by less than a provisional bonus that would be reduced for not meeting production targets. This evidence is consistent with loss averse factory workers.
5   The three canonical sealed-bid auction formats — **first-price**, **second-price**, and **all-pay** — differ in the rules for what auction participants pay.

6   When standard (risk–neutral) bidders have independent **private values** of an item for auction, the three canonical auction formats generate the same (expected) revenue for the seller. This result is a consequence of the **revenue equivalence theorem**.

7   When bidders are loss averse with random reference points equal to their expectations of possible outcomes, they bid more aggressively in auctions that mitigate a perceived loss. The (expected) seller revenue is therefore greater for less risky auction payment rules.

   a   With narrow bracketing, revenue is decreasing from all-pay to first-price to second-price auctions.

   b   With broad bracketing, revenue is decreasing from first-price to all-pay to second-price auctions.

10.7   Exercises

Exercise 10.1 — Too Much Loss Aversion. Recall that Homonoff (2018) estimates shopper responses to the disposable bag tax and reusable bag subsidy as consistent with a large coefficient of loss aversion, $\lambda = 5.3$. This evidence suggests that loss aversion may not be the only factor leading to the substantial reduction in disposable bag use following the tax. Hypothesize an additional factor, beyond those discussed in the chapter, that may be generating this result.

Exercise 10.2 — Long-Run Shopping. Homonoff (2018) estimates the impact of a disposable bag tax in the first three months following its implementation. Consider the possible longer-run impacts of the tax over the course of the following year.

   a   If shoppers are loss averse, how might their reference points change over time? How would these longer-run changes in the reference point impact their likelihood of using a disposable bag?

   b   Now suppose that shoppers are both loss averse and have habit-forming preferences. In this case, explain whether habit formation would lead to larger or smaller decreases in disposable bag use in the long run (relative to your answer in part (a)).

Exercise 10.3 — Teacher Policy. Recall the loss incentive for teachers in the Fryer et al. (2012) study. Would you support such an incentive being implemented for all teachers? Explain why or why not.

Exercise 10.4 — Group Work Works. [Labor] The chapter reports the results from the Hossain and List (2012) study of incentivizing factory workers for employees who work in a team. The study also examines the impact of the gain and loss incentives on individuals who work independently. For individuals, there is no (statistically significant) difference in the impact of the gain and loss incentives on productivity.

   a   Does this evidence suggest that loss aversion is stronger for individuals working alone or in groups?

   b   Provide a possible explanation for your answer in part (a).

Exercise 10.5 — Auction Bracketing. Recall that in lab experiments with auctions, Eisenhuth and Grunewald (2020) find evidence that is consistent with loss averse bidders who broadly bracket total utility gains and losses. Discuss the difference between narrow and broad bracketing of auction outcomes. What does broad bracketing suggest about how bidders perceive an auctioned good?

Exercise 10.6 — Saving Smarts. Section 7.2.3 discusses the Save More Tomorrow™, or SMarT, Program proposed by Thaler and Benartzi (2004). This program is designed to help employees increase their savings for retirement. For employees who join the program, upon receiving future pay raises, their savings rate is automatically increased. The increases in the savings rate are always less than the increases in pay. Discuss why loss averse workers will find this program appealing.

Exercise 10.7 — Making Profits with Losses. Apple Music offers new users a free 3-month trial. If a customer wants to continue using Apple Music after the free trial, the price is \$9.99/month. Suppose that consumers have reference-dependent preferences over a month of Apple Music (A) and wealth (W) given by:

$$U((A, W) \mid (r_A, r_W)) = M \cdot A + W + v(M \cdot A \mid M \cdot r_A) + v(W \mid r_W)$$

where $A \in \{0, 1\}$ indicates whether or not the customer has access to Apple Music, M is the intrinsic benefit of Apple Music, and

$$v(x \mid r) = \begin{cases} x - r & \text{if } x \geq r \\ \lambda(x - r) & \text{if } x < r \end{cases}$$

with $\lambda > 1$. The reference point for Apple Music, r_A, is equal to Apple Music access in the previous month. Normalize the reference point for wealth, r_W, to zero.

a   Suppose that there is *no* free trial for customers considering an Apple Music sub-scription, so that the reference point is $(r_A, r_W) = (0, 0)$. Find the maximum will-ingness to pay per month for Apple Music. *Note: Your answer may depend on λ and* M.

b   Now suppose that there *is* a free trial for customers considering an Apple Music subscription. An individual finishing the last month of the free trial has the reference point $(r_A, r_W) = (1, 0)$. Find such an individual's maximum willingness to pay to use Apple Music in the month after the free trial. *Note: Your answer may depend on λ and* M.

c   Compare your answers to parts (a) and (b). Use this comparison to provide intuition for why, with loss averse consumers, Apple Music might find it profitable to offer a free trial for its service.

Exercise 10.8 — Trade-In Incentive (Novemsky and Kahneman 2005). Car deal-erships offer consumers the opportunity to trade in their old car for a new one, reducing the price of the new car by the value of the old one. Use the concept of loss aversion to hypothesize why car dealerships find it worthwhile to offer this marketing strategy.

Exercise 10.9 — Uniform Prices. [Industrial Organization] An important puzzle in economics is the uniformity of prices. For example, even though each movie has a different cost of production and different consumer demand, a movie theater charges the same ticket price for every movie every day of the year (Orbach and Einav 2007). And ticket prices across different movie theaters are often similar, even with different customer bases and different operating costs. This uniform pricing has also been docu-mented for groceries (DellaVigna and Gentzkow 2019), rental cars (Cho and Rust 2010), and online music (Shiller and Waldfogel 2011). It is a puzzle because standard theories of profit maximization predict that prices should adjust much more to differences in costs and demand than they do.

Suppose that profit-maximizing firms are selling to loss averse consumers who code prices above their expected purchase price as a loss. Provide intuition for why the introduction of loss averse consumers may be able to explain this empirical puzzle.[3]

Notes

1 There is evidence that the effects of teacher incentives on student test scores are positive, large, and significant in the developing world context (Duflo, Hanna, and Ryan 2012; Glewwe, Ilias, and Kremer 2010; Muralidharan and Sundararaman 2011).
2 Formally, the bidding strategies are symmetric Bayesian Nash equilibria of each auction game. Determining these strategies is beyond the scope of this book.
3 See Heidhues and Kőszegi (2008) for a formal treatment of this problem.

References

Chetty, Raj, John N. Friedman, and Jonah E. Rockoff. 2014. "Measuring the Impacts of Teachers II: Teacher Value-Added and Student Outcomes in Adulthood." *American Economic Review* 104 (9): 2633–2679. doi:10.1257/aer.104.9.2633.

Cho, Sungjin, and John Rust. 2010. "The Flat Rental Puzzle." *The Review of Economic Studies* 77 (2): 560–594. doi:10.1111/j.1467-937x.2009.00556.x.

Clapp, Jennifer, and Linda Swanston. 2009. "Doing Away with Plastic Shopping Bags: International Patterns of Norm Emergence and Policy Implementation." *Environmental Politics* 18 (3): 315–332. doi:10.1080/09644010902823717.

Convery, Frank, Simon McDonnell, and Susana Ferreira. 2007. "The Most Popular Tax in Europe? Lessons from the Irish Plastic Bags Levy." *Environmental and Resource Economics* 38 (1): 1–11. doi:10.1007/s10640-006-9059-2.

DellaVigna, Stefano, and Matthew Gentzkow. 2019. "Uniform Pricing in U.S. Retail Chains." *The Quarterly Journal of Economics* 134 (4): 2011–2084. doi:10.1093/qje/qjz019.

Duflo, Esther, Rema Hanna, and Stephen P. Ryan. 2012. "Incentives Work: Getting Teachers to Come to School." *American Economic Review* 102 (4): 1241–1278. doi:10.1257/aer.102.4.1241.

Eisenhuth, Roland. 2019. "Reference-Dependent Mechanism Design." *Economic Theory Bulletin* 7 (1): 77–103. doi:10.1007/s40505-018-0144-9.

Eisenhuth, Roland, and Mara Grunewald. 2020. "Auctions with Loss-Averse Bidders." *International Journal of Economic Theory* 16 (2): 129–152. doi:https://doi.org/10.1111/ijet.12189.

EPA (Environmental Protection Agency). 2018. "Advancing Sustainable Materials Management: 2015 Tables and Figures." Report. Washington, DC: EPA.

Fryer, Roland G. 2013. "Teacher Incentives and Student Achievement: Evidence from New York City Public Schools." *Journal of Labor Economics* 31 (2): 373–407. doi:10.1086/667757.

Fryer, Jr, Roland G., Steven D. Levitt, John A. List, and Sally Sadoff. 2012. "Enhancing the Efficacy of Teacher Incentives through Loss Aversion: A Field Experiment." NBER Working Paper 18237. Cambridge, MA: National Bureau of Economic Research. doi:10.3386/w18237.

Glewwe, Paul, Nauman Ilias, and Michael Kremer. 2010. "Teacher Incentives." *American Economic Journal: Applied Economics* 2 (3): 205–227. doi:10.1257/app.2.3. 205.

Hasson, Reviva, Anthony Leiman, and Martine Visser. 2007. "The Economics of Plastic Bag Legislation in South Africa." *South African Journal of Economics* 75 (1): 66–83. doi:10.1111/j.1813-6982.2007.00101.x.

He, Haoran. 2010. "The Effects of an Environmental Policy on Consumers: Lessons from the Chinese Plastic Bag Regulation." Working Papers in Economics 453. University of Gothenburg.

Heidhues, Paul, and Botond Köszegi. 2008. "Competition and Price Variation when Consumers Are Loss Averse." *American Economic Review* 98 (4): 1245–1268. doi:10.1257/aer.98.4.1245.

Homonoff, Tatiana A. 2018. "Can Small Incentives Have Large Effects? The Impact of Taxes versus Bonuses on Disposable Bag Use." *American Economic Journal: Economic Policy* 10 (4): 177–210. doi:10.1257/pol.20150261.

Hossain, Tanjim, and John A. List. 2012. "The Behavioralist Visits the Factory: Increasing Productivity Using Simple Framing Manipulations." *Management Science* 58 (12): 2151–2167. doi:10.1287/mnsc.1120.1544.

Krishna, Vijay. 2010. *Auction Theory.* 2nd edition. San Diego: Academic Press.

Lange, Andreas, and Anmol Ratan. 2010. "Multi-dimensional Reference-Dependent Preferences in Sealed-Bid Auctions – How (Most) Laboratory Experiments Differ from the Field." *Games and Economic Behavior* 68 (2): 634–645. doi:10.1016/j.geb. 2009.08.008.

Lazear, Edward P., and Kathryn L. Shaw. 2007. "Personnel Economics: The Economist's View of Human Resources." *Journal of Economic Perspectives* 21 (4): 91–114. doi:10.1257/jep.21.4.91.

Milgrom, Paul R. 2004. *Putting Auction Theory to Work.* Cambridge: Cambridge University Press.

Muralidharan, Karthik, and Venkatesh Sundararaman. 2011. "Teacher Performance Pay: Experimental Evidence from India." *Journal of Political Economy* 119 (1): 39–77. doi:10.1086/659655.

NCES (National Center for Education Statistics). 2019. "The Condition of Education 2019." Technical report 2019-144. NCES. https://nces.ed.gov/programs/coe/indicator_cmb.asp.

Novemsky, Nathan, and Daniel Kahneman. 2005. "The Boundaries of Loss Aversion." *Journal of Marketing Research* 42 (2): 119–128. doi:10.1509/jmkr.42.2.119. 62292.

Orbach, Barak Y., and Liran Einav. 2007. "Uniform Prices for Differentiated Goods: The Case of the Movie-Theater Industry." *International Review of Law and Economics* 27 (2): 129–153. doi:10.1016/j.irle.2007.06.002.

Shampanier, Kristina, Nina Mazar, and Dan Ariely. 2007. "Zero as a Special Price: The True Value of Free Products." *Marketing Science* 26 (6): 742–757. doi:10.1287/mksc.1060.0254.

Shiller, Ben, and Joel Waldfogel. 2011. "Music for a Song: An Empirical Look at Uniform Pricing and Its Alternatives." *The Journal of Industrial Economics* 59 (4): 630–660. doi:10.1111/j.1467-6451.2011.00470.x.

Springer, Matthew G., Dale Ballou, Laura S. Hamilton, Vi-Nhuan Le, J. R. Lockwood, Daniel F. McCaffrey, Matthew Pepper, and Brian M. Stecher. 2010. "Teacher Pay for Performance: Experimental Evidence from the Project on Incentives in Teaching." Report. National Center on Performance Incentives.

Taylor, Rebecca L., and Sofia B. Villas-Boas. 2016. "Bans vs. Fees: Disposable Carryout Bag Policies and Bag Usage." *Applied Economic Perspectives and Policy* 38 (2): 351–372. doi:10.1093/aepp/ppv025.

Thaler, Richard H., and Shlomo Benartzi. 2004. "Save More Tomorrow™: Using Behavioral Economics to Increase Employee Saving." *Journal of Political Economy* 112 (S1): 164–187. doi:10.1086/380085.

Vickrey, William. 1961. "Counterspeculation, Auctions, and Competitive Sealed Tenders." *The Journal of Finance* 16 (1): 8–37. doi:10.1111/j.1540-6261.1961.tb02789.x.

Part IV

Preferences over Uncertainty

A standard assumption in the model of individual decision making (Definition 2.9) is that preferences over risk and uncertainty are represented by expected utility. That is, individuals evaluate a lottery by taking the expectation, or weighted average, of the possible utilities that could occur, using the belief of each utility outcome as its weight. The expected utility assumption is featured in the standard model by the expectation operator E, highlighted below:

$$\max_{(x_0, x_1, \ldots, x_T) \in X} \sum_{k=0}^{T} \delta^k \, \boxed{E} \, [u(x_k) \mid p] \qquad \text{(Standard Model)}$$

The objective of Part IV is to evaluate this assumption and consider alternative models of evaluating risk and uncertainty. To focus the analysis, we maintain the other standard assumptions of decision making. Individuals are still assumed to be self-interested utility maximizers with accurate beliefs. And we assume away intertemporal choice problems. The only exception is that we allow for reference-dependent preferences, the subject of Part III. It is therefore recommended, but not necessary, to read this part after Part III.

Part IV is organized as follows. Chapter 11 introduces a number of famous anomalies and paradoxes illustrating how individuals make decisions that are inconsistent with expected utility preferences. Given this evidence, Chapter 12 presents two alternative models of preferences that can reconcile the observed anomalies. We also explore how the nonstandard models can help to explain a variety of puzzling behaviors in personal finance. Finally, note that unlike the rest of the book, there is no separate chapter on market and policy responses. Although Chapter 12 includes some brief discussion of relevant policy insights.

11 Expected Utility Anomalies

Learning Objectives

★ Apply expected utility to make predictions for decision making with risk and uncertainty.

★ Identify expected utility anomalies.

★ Understand the different predictions for risk averse and risk loving preferences.

★ Hypothesize modifications to the expected utility model that could better explain the empirical evidence in this chapter.

Many are drawn to lotteries, games of chance, and speculative investments. At the same time, people pursue strategies to protect against the uncertain risks of natural disaster, theft, and other catastrophes.

To understand decision making with uncertainty, economists assume that individuals choose the available lottery with the largest expected utility. Recall from Chapter 2 that the expected utility of a lottery is the weighted average of utilities from each possible outcome, with weights equal to the probabilistic belief that each outcome occurs. This expected utility form of preferences is intuitively appealing and provides powerful insights for a wide range of economic decisions. But there are also puzzling behaviors that are difficult to reconcile with this model.

In this relatively short chapter, we highlight some of the most well-known anomalies of the expected utility model. These anomalies show that no matter the utility level that individuals assign to each possible outcome in a lottery, choices are often inconsistent with the expected utility form of preferences. That is, individuals do not appear to make decisions as if they are choosing the lottery with the highest expected utility. We also challenge the common ancillary assumption that individuals are always risk averse. The next chapter applies these insights to consider alternative ways in which people may actually be translating their beliefs and utilities over uncertain outcomes into decisions.

The anomalies in this chapter are organized in two sections. In the first, we consider decision problems with known objective probabilities for each possible outcome. The second section turns to settings with uncertainty where there is ambiguity about the probabilities. In both cases the standard expected utility form of preferences fails to explain typical preferences.

DOI: 10.4324/9780367854072-15

11.1   Anomalies with Objective Probabilities

Let's begin our exploration of expected utility anomalies by evaluating monetary lotteries with objective probabilities. The possible outcomes of flipping a coin, rolling a die, or spinning a roulette wheel are all determined by such objective probabilities. There is a 1 in 2 chance that a coin lands on heads, a 1 in 6 chance that a die lands on 3, and a 2 in 38 chance that an American roulette wheel lands on a green space. More generally, we assume that decision makers hold beliefs equal to the true probabilities of each possible outcome in a lottery.

Consider a lottery L in which you can win either $\$x_1$, $\$x_2$, or 0. The "winnings" are permitted to be negative, in which case we interpret the outcomes as monetary losses that you must pay. Winning $\$x_n$ occurs with objective probability $p_n \geq 0$, where $p_1 + p_2 \leq 1$. And for simplicity, assume that current wealth is zero, so that the final wealth outcome of winning $\$x_n$ is also $\$x_n$.[1]

It is convenient to compactly denote this lottery as $L = (x_1, p_1; x_2, p_2)$. Observe that if $p_1 + p_2 < 1$, the lottery includes a third possible outcome of winning nothing with probability $1 - p_1 - p_2 > 0$. In the special case that x_1 is certain (i.e., $p_1 = 1$), we write the lottery simply as (x_1). And in the special case that x_1 is not certain, but is the only nonzero outcome (i.e., $x_2 = 0$), we write the lottery as (x_1, p_1).

The standard model of individual decision making assumes that lottery L is evaluated by its expected utility:

$$E(u(L)) = p_1 u(x_1) + p_2 u(x_2) + (1 - p_1 - p_2)u(0)$$

where $u(\cdot)$ is a strictly increasing and strictly concave utility function of wealth. Recall that the concavity of the utility function implies risk aversion. And to simplify the

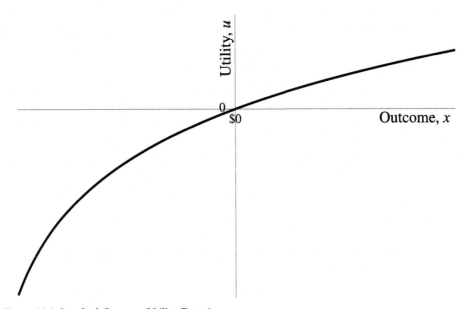

Figure 11.1 Standard Concave Utility Function

analysis, I normalize the utility function so that $u(0) = 0$. Figure 11.1 illustrates such a utility function. With this normalization, the expected utility expression simplifies to:

$$E(u(L)) = p_1 u(x_1) + p_2 u(x_2) \tag{11.1}$$

The expected utility model of preferences makes predictions about how individuals decide between alternative lotteries. In the remainder of this section we highlight a set of anomalies — evidence that contradicts these predictions. The evidence comes from simple lab experiments in which college students and faculty were asked to answer hypothetical questions (Kahneman and Tversky 1979). As you read, you should also consider how you would answer each of these hypothetical questions. Your choices may be more or less anomalous than the typical respondent.

11.1.1 Allais Paradox

The first example is adapted from Allais (1953). Known as the **Allais paradox**, it is the best known counterexample to expected utility.

Lab Experiment — Allais Paradox (Kahneman and Tversky 1979)	
Choose between:	**Results:**
A (2500, 0.33;2400, 0.66)	[18%]
B (2400)	[82%]
Choose between:	
C (2500, 0.33)	[83%]
D (2400, 0.34)	[17%]

Why do the majority choices, *B* and *C*, violate the predictions of expected utility? Let's begin with the first choice. Relative to the certainty of winning \$2,400 with lottery *B*, lottery *A* offers a 33% chance of winning an additional \$100 and a 1% chance of winning nothing. Most respondents prefer the certainty of lottery *B*. If individuals evaluate these lotteries with expected utility as in equation (11.1), the following must be true for the majority:

$$u(2400) = E(u(B)) > E(u(A)) = 0.33u(2500) + 0.66u(2400)$$

The inequality would be reversed for the 18% who prefer *A*. It is important to recognize that there is *no* anomaly in this first decision problem. Expected utility allows for some individuals to prefer *B* and others to prefer *A* — any difference in preferences would be due to differences in the utilities of \$2,500 and \$2,400.

Let's now rearrange the above inequality by subtracting $0.66u(2400)$ from both sides:

$$(1 - 0.66)u(2400) > 0.33u(2500)$$

This inequality reveals a preference ordering over lotteries C and D:

$$E(u(D)) = 0.34u(2400) = (1 - 0.66)u(2400) > 0.33u(2500) = E(u(C))$$

In sum, preferring B to A implies a preference for D over C. And yet, the majority simultaneously prefers B to A and C to D. This is impossible with expected utility, no matter the utility function.

The Allais paradox is an elegant example of how expected utility makes predictions at odds with typical preferences. To understand what is driving this anomaly, think first about why C is more appealing than D. Individuals are likely perceiving the probabilities of winning (33% and 34%) as essentially identical. And they therefore choose the lottery with the higher potential winnings: lottery C. As the algebra of expected utility demonstrates, preferring C implies a preference for A in the first choice. What then is drawing people towards B? The clear benefit of B relative to A is the certainty of winning.

The tendency of individuals to overweight certain outcomes relative to those that are only probable is known as the **certainty effect**. By modifying expected utility to allow for the certainty effect, it may be possible to develop a model of decision making that predicts preferences for both B and C, as observed.

Consider the following simpler illustration of the certainty effect.

Lab Experiment — Simple Allais Paradox (Kahneman and Tversky 1979)

Choose between: **Results:**

  A (4000, 0.80)   [20%]
  B (3000)   [80%]

Choose between:

  C (4000, 0.20)   [65%]
  D (3000, 0.25)   [35%]

Once again, the majority choices of B and C in the two decision problems above are inconsistent with expected utility preferences. The step-by-step logic is as follows:

C is preferred to D $\Leftrightarrow E(u(C)) > E(u(D))$
$\Leftrightarrow 0.2u(4000) > 0.25u(3000)$
$\Leftrightarrow 0.8u(4000) > u(3000)$ by multiplying both sides by 4
$\Leftrightarrow E(u(A)) > E(u(B))$
$\Leftrightarrow A$ is preferred to B

Although the majority preference for C is predicted to generate a majority preference for A, the actual majority preference for the certain lottery B again illustrates the certainty effect.

The Simple Allais Paradox example above suggests another reason why expected utility fails to make accurate predictions. Observe that both the first and second choices offer the chance to win $4,000 or $3,000, and that the probability of the larger win is always 80% of the probability of the smaller win. Because the chance of winning $4,000 relative to the chance of winning $3,000 is the same across the two decision problems, expected utility predicts that preferring *A* (*B*) is equivalent to preferring *C* (*D*). But preferences appear to depend not only on the *relative* probabilities of each win, but also the *magnitudes* of the probabilities. That is, when winning is likely or probable (as with *A* and *B*), individuals prefer the lottery with the higher chance of winning (*B*). But when the probabilities are scaled down to make winning less likely, but still possible (as with *C* and *D*), individuals prefer the lottery with the higher potential winnings (*C*). This observation is confirmed in the following experiment where no lottery is certain.

Lab Experiment — Probable vs. Possible (Kahneman and Tversky 1979)

Choose between:	**Results:**
A (6000, 0.45)	[14%]
B (3000, 0.90)	[86%]

Choose between:	
C (6000, 0.001)	[73%]
D (3000, 0.002)	[27%]

For both choices, the probability of winning $3,000 is twice the probability of winning $6,000. Expected utility once again predicts that preferring *A* (*B*) is equivalent to preferring *C* (*D*). And once again, the majority preferences are for *B* and *C*. When winning is probable, individuals choose the lottery with the higher probability (*B* over *A*). And when winning is only possible (but not probable), individuals choose the lottery with the higher possible payoff (*C* over *D*). In the next chapter we enrich the expected utility model to account for this feature of decision making, as well as the certainty effect.

11.1.2   Reflection Effect

The previous lotteries all involved winning money. How do people make choices over lotteries with monetary losses? For an answer, the following experiment flips all of the winnings in the Simple Allais Paradox to losses, maintaining the same probabilities.

Lab Experiment — Simple Allais Paradox Losses (Kahneman and Tversky 1979)

Choose between:	**Results:**
A (−4000, 0.80)	[92%]
B (−3000)	[8%]

Choose between:

C (−4000, 0.20)   [42%]
D (−3000, 0.25)   [58%]

This example illustrates three key observations about behavior with risky losses. The first is that the majority choices of *A* and *D* are inconsistent with expected utility. As with risky gains, because the relative probabilities of the two possible outcomes are the same in the first and second choices (i.e., the chance of losing $4,000 is always 80% of the chance of losing $3,000), the preference ordering should also be the same.

Second, the majority preferences in each choice are now switched from when the outcomes were gains. With losses, individuals switch from lottery *B* to *A* and from *C* to *D*. By *reflecting* the potential wins across zero to make them losses, the preference order reverses. This phenomenon is the **reflection effect**.

Before turning to the final observation, observe that none of the anomalies documented in this chapter thus far have depended on the shape of the utility function $u(\cdot)$. The two majority preferences in each experiment are inconsistent with expected utility, for *any* increasing utility function. This insight highlights the predictive deficiency of expected utility, independent of $u(\cdot)$.

Let's now think through what risk averse expected utility preferences imply for the choice between lotteries *A* and *B* above. The expected outcome of lottery *A* is to lose $3,200 (= −$4,000 × 0.8). Intuitively, if this lottery were repeated day after day, over a long horizon 80% of the time you would lose $4,000 and 20% of the time you would lose nothing. The average daily losses would be $3,200. The definition of risk aversion is that losing $3,200 with certainty must be preferred to the risky lottery *A* with an expected loss of $3,200. This is depicted graphically in Figure 11.2 where the utility of losing $3,200 for sure is greater than the expected utility of lottery *A*. But losing $3,000 for sure (as with lottery *B*) is obviously better than losing $3,200 for sure. In sum, lottery *B* should be preferred to lottery *A*. And yet, 92% of respondents prefer *A* over *B*. No other decision problem in this chapter elicits such a one-sided preference.

The almost unanimous preference for *A* over *B* reveals our third observation: in the context of lottery losses, individuals appear to be risk loving, not risk averse. That is, relative to a certain loss, an individual may instead prefer a lottery that is both risky and has a larger expected loss. No risk averse individual would make such a choice. Intuitively, with risk loving preferences the benefit of potentially losing nothing in the risky lottery outweighs the cost of expecting to lose more on average.

It is instructive to note that risk loving preferences over losses are consistent with the certainty effect identified earlier. Recall that the certainty effect refers to the overweighting of certain outcomes. When the outcomes are gains, overweighting certainty amplifies the aversion to risk. But when the outcomes are losses, overweighting certain losses (as in lottery *B* above) induces a preference for risky lotteries that provide some chance of avoiding or reducing a loss (as in lottery *A*).

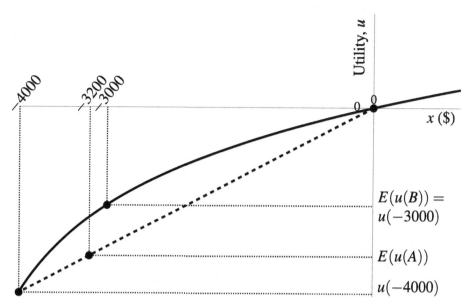

Figure 11.2 Simple Allais Paradox Losses Lab Experiment with Concave Utility Function

11.1.3 Overweighting Unlikely Outcomes

Lab Experiment — An Unlikely Win (Kahneman and Tversky 1979)

Choose between: **Results:**

  A (5000, 0.001)   [72%]
  B (5)   [28%]

The above experiment presents a different challenge to the expected utility model. Lottery *A* offers the chance to win $5,000 with a 0.1% probability. The expected outcome from this lottery is to win $5. A risk averse expected utility decision maker should therefore prefer lottery *B*. It guarantees a certain $5 win, as opposed to winning $5 in expectation, but with much more risk. Contrary to this prediction, over 70% of respondents prefer lottery *A*.

There are two possible ways we can explain this majority preference. One is that individuals are actually risk loving — not risk averse. That is, they choose lottery *A* because the utility of winning $5,000 is more than 1,000 times greater than the utility of winning $5. But there is strong evidence throughout economics that individuals are risk averse over gains. In fact, the majority choices for lottery *B* over lottery *A* in the first three experiments of this section imply risk aversion over gains.

An alternative explanation is that when deciding between the two lotteries, individuals weight the unlikely $5,000 win by more than the 0.001 weight used with expected utility. If such unlikely outcomes are sufficiently overweighted by decision makers, then an individual could have concave utility over gains *and* still prefer risky lottery

A. This will be an important feature of the alternative theory of decision making in the next chapter.

11.2   Ellsberg Paradox

For each of the lotteries in the previous section the probabilities were objectively known. But what if there is not a given objective probability for each possible outcome? In such settings the standard assumption that individuals evaluate uncertainty with expected utility remains. The only difference is that individuals must now form subjective beliefs for each potential outcome. These beliefs, like standard objective probabilities, should be nonnegative and add up to 100% across all possible outcomes.

The following famous experiment illustrates what can go wrong with using expected utility as a model of preferences over uncertain outcomes.

Lab Experiment — Three-Color Urn (Ellsberg 1961)

There is an opaque urn containing 90 balls. You know that 30 of the balls are red. And each of the remaining 60 balls are either black or yellow — but you do not know how many are black and how many are yellow. You draw a single ball at random from the urn. Consider the following two decision problems based on the color of the ball that you draw from the urn.

Choose between the following two bets:

A   Win $100 if the ball is red
B   Win $100 if the ball is black

Choose between the following two bets:

C   Win $100 if the ball is either red *or* yellow
D   Win $100 if the ball is either black *or* yellow

Ellsberg (1961) hypothesized that most individuals when faced with such bets would prefer *A* over *B* and prefer *D* over *C*. The rationale for this hypothesis is that individuals are averse to ambiguity, or exhibit **ambiguity aversion**.

Lottery *A* provides a 1/3 chance of winning, whereas the chance of winning with lottery *B* is ambiguous — it could be anywhere from 0 to 2/3. If individuals like lotteries with known as opposed to ambiguous probabilities, then they will prefer lottery *A*.

Similarly, lottery *D* provides a known 2/3 chance of winning since 60 of the 90 balls are either black or yellow. The chance of winning in lottery *C* could be anywhere from 1/3 (since there are 30 red balls) to 100% (since there could be no black balls). A preference for unambiguous probabilities will induce individuals to choose *D* over *C*.

Ellsberg's conjecture has been confirmed in numerous lab experiments (Chipman 1960; Fellner 1961; Becker and Brownson 1964; Maccrimmon 1968; Slovic and Tversky 1974; Curley and Yates 1989).

The ambiguity aversion demonstrated by the typical choices above cannot be explained by standard expected utility. To see this formally, let the utility of winning nothing be zero and the utility of winning \$100 be $u(100) > 0$. In addition, let (p_R, p_B, p_Y) be an individual's subjective beliefs over the three possible outcomes of drawing a red, black, or yellow ball from the urn, respectively. Note that different people may have different subjective beliefs about the likelihood of drawing a ball of each color.

With expected utility preferences, the typical preference for lottery A over lottery B implies the following:

$$
\begin{aligned}
A \text{ preferred to } B \quad &\Leftrightarrow E(u(A)) > E(u(B)) \\
&\Leftrightarrow p_R \cdot u(100) > p_B \cdot u(100) \\
&\Leftrightarrow p_R > p_B
\end{aligned}
$$

That is, expected utility maximizers who prefer A over B must do so because they believe that drawing a red ball is more likely than drawing a black ball from the urn.

By applying expected utility preferences to the typical preference for lottery D over lottery C, we have:

$$
\begin{aligned}
D \text{ preferred to } C \quad &\Leftrightarrow E(u(D)) > E(u(C)) \\
&\Leftrightarrow (p_B + p_Y)u(100) > (p_R + p_Y)u(100) \\
&\Leftrightarrow p_B + p_Y > p_R + p_Y \\
&\Leftrightarrow p_B > p_R
\end{aligned}
$$

Preferring D over C now requires that individuals believe the draw of a black ball to be more likely than the draw of a red ball. But with such a belief, they should have preferred lottery B over lottery A.

In sum, expected utility suggests that individuals simultaneously believe the urn to contain more red balls than black balls *and* more black balls than red balls. This contradiction, known as the **Ellsberg paradox**, is therefore an anomaly for expected utility. These paradoxical preferences have been documented across a variety of subjects, including managers, executives, trade union leaders, and actuaries.[2] Given this widespread evidence, in the next chapter we consider an alternative to the expected utility representation of preferences that captures such ambiguity aversion.

11.3   Summary

1   The **Allais paradox** is a famous anomaly that reveals how typical lottery preferences are inconsistent with expected utility. It highlights two features of decision making with risk that are not captured by expected utility:

   a   Individuals tend to overweight certain outcomes relative to those that are only probable. This is known as the **certainty effect**.

   b   When winning is probable in each of two lotteries, individuals prefer the lottery with the higher chance of winning. But when winning is only possible (but unlikely) in the two lotteries, individuals prefer the lottery with the better possible outcome.

2   When two lotteries offering potential winnings are changed to offering potential losses (of the same magnitude and with the same probabilities), individuals typically

switch their preference ranking of the lotteries. This is known as the **reflection effect**.

3 Individuals act as if they are risk averse over gains and risk loving over losses.
4 Individuals appear to overweight unlikely outcomes.
5 The **Ellsberg paradox** is a famous anomaly in a setting with uncertainty. It demonstrates that individuals exhibit **ambiguity aversion**.

11.4   Exercises

Exercise 11.1 — Expecting Allais (Allais 1953). Normalize Robin's initial wealth to zero. She has utility function over wealth, $u(\cdot)$. She faces two decision problems. In the first, she can choose between the following two lotteries:

A ($1 million)
B ($1 million, 0.89; $5 million, 0.10)

In the second, she can choose between the following two lotteries:

C ($1 million, 0.11)
D ($5 million, 0.10)

a Most people choose A and D when faced with the two hypothetical problems above. Explain intuitively why people would make such choices.
b Suppose that Robin is a standard expected utility maximizer. Write down the inequality that must hold for Robin to choose lottery A over B.
c Write down the inequality that must hold for Robin to choose lottery D over C (again assuming that she is a standard expected utility maximizer).
d Compare your answers to parts (b) and (c). Interpret.

Exercise 11.2 —European Vacation. Consider another set of choices asked of participants by Kahneman and Tversky (1979).

Choose between:

A 50% chance of winning a three-week tour of England, France, and Italy.
B 100% chance of winning a one-week tour of England.

Choose between:

C 5% chance of winning a three-week tour of England, France, and Italy.
D 10% chance of winning a one-week tour of England.

The majority of participants preferred B over A and C over D.

a Why do you think that B and C are popular choices?
b Are the choices of B and C consistent or inconsistent with the expected utility model? Explain.

Exercise 11.3 — No Love, No Neutrality. For each of the first three lab experiments in the chapter:

a   Compare the expected winnings between lottery *A* and lottery *B*.
b   Determine the choice of *A* vs. *B* for risk neutral expected utility maximizers.
c   Determine the choice of *A* vs. *B* for risk loving expected utility maximizers.

Observe that in each of these first three lab experiments in the chapter at least 80% of subjects prefer lottery *B* to lottery *A*.

d   Use your answers to parts (b) and (c) to conclude what this evidence implies about typical risk preferences.

Exercise 11.4 — Trading Trials. Martha is accused of insider trading. She is offered a plea bargain in which she can pay $1 million or she can go to trial where there is a 10% chance she will be convicted and have to pay $15 million. If found innocent, she pays nothing. She decides to go to trial. If she is an expected utility maximizer, does her decision show that she is risk averse of risk loving? Explain.

Exercise 11.5 — An Unlikely Loss. Consider another choice asked of participants by Kahneman and Tversky (1979). Choose between:

A   (−5000, 0.001)
B   (−5)

Of the participants, 83% preferred lottery *B* to lottery *A*.

a   When the above choice is for wins instead of losses, recall that 72% of participants preferred the 0.1% chance to win $5,000 over winning $5 for sure. Together, these two decision problems illustrate which phenomenon discussed in the chapter?
b   Is the majority preference for *B* over *A* consistent with risk averse expected utility preferences? Explain.
c   The chapter provides suggestive evidence that individuals are risk loving over losses. If an individual has such preferences, provide a possible explanation for the preference of *B* over *A*.

Exercise 11.6 — A Fiery State (Kahneman and Tversky 1979). Sonny owns a home in fire-prone California, where there is a 50% chance of wildfires igniting and damaging his home and property this year. He has a utility function over wealth, $u(w) = \sqrt{w}$, and an initial wealth of $160,000. Suppose that in the event of fire, the damage done will cost Sonny $120,000 to repair.

a   What is Sonny's expected wealth?
b   What is Sonny's expected utility?
c   Sonny has the option to buy a full insurance policy for the year that, in the case of fire, will reimburse him for all of the fire damage repair costs. What is the maximum amount that he would pay for a such an insurance policy? *Hint: Compare his expected utility without insurance from part (b) to the utility of buying the full insurance policy.*
d   Now suppose a sprinkler salesperson offers to sell Sonny industrial strength sprinklers to install around his property to help mitigate the damage of a possible wildfire. The sprinkler system costs $7,000. Unfortunately, the sprinklers cannot stop the fire, but

only limit the damage. In particular if there is a fire, then there will be a 10% chance that the damage will now only cost $63,000 to repair, but a 90% chance that the damage will cost $113,000 to repair. Note that these repair costs do not include the price of the sprinkler system. Does Sonny prefer the sprinkler insurance policy or the full insurance policy at the maximum price in part (c)? Explain whether or not Sonny's decision is surprising to you.

Exercise 11.7 — Two-Urn Ellsberg Paradox. The following decision problem is from Ellsberg (1961). You face two opaque urns, each of which contains 100 balls, either red or black. The distribution of red and black balls in Urn I is unknown to you. But you know that Urn II contains exactly 50 red balls and 50 black balls.

Choose between the following two bets:

A Draw a ball from Urn I and win $100 if the ball is red
B Draw a ball from Urn II and win $100 if the ball is red

Choose between the following two bets:

C Draw a ball from Urn I and win $100 if the ball is black
D Draw a ball from Urn II and win $100 if the ball is black

a   Explain why most people faced with the setting above choose *B* over *A*. If individuals have expected utility preferences, what does this choice imply for the subjective belief about the number of red balls in Urn I?

b   Explain why most people faced with the setting above choose *D* over *C*. If individuals have expected utility preferences, what does this choice imply for the subjective belief about the number of black balls in Urn I?

c   Use your answers to parts (a) and (b) to explain why the majority choices (*B* and *D*) are inconsistent with expected utility preferences.

Exercise 11.8 — Four-Color Ellsberg Paradox. The following decision problem is also from Ellsberg (1961). You face a single opaque urn that contains 200 balls. There are 50 green balls and 50 yellow balls. The remaining 100 balls are either red or black. You will draw a ball at random from this urn.

Choose between the following two bets:

A Win $100 if the ball is red or black
B Win $100 if the ball is green or black

Choose between the following two bets:

C Win $100 if the ball is red or yellow
D Win $100 if the ball is green or yellow

a   What do you expect to be the typical choice between *A* and *B*? If individuals have expected utility preferences, what does this choice imply for the subjective belief about the number of red balls in the urn?

b   What do you expect to be the typical choice between *C* and *D*? If individuals have expected utility preferences, what does this choice imply for the subjective belief about the number of red balls in the urn?

c   Use your answers to parts (a) and (b) to explain why the likely typical choices are inconsistent with expected utility preferences.

Notes

1   With the simplifying assumption that current wealth is zero, there is no difference between utility defined over final outcomes and utility defined over gains and losses. If instead, current wealth is $W > 0$, then winning x generates final outcome $W + x$.

2   Machina and Siniscalchi (2014) provide an excellent overview of both the empirical evidence and theoretical models of ambiguity aversion.

References

Allais, Maurice. 1953. "Le Comportement de l'Homme Rationnel devant le Risque: Critique des Postulats et Axiomes de l'Ecole Americaine." *Econometrica* 21 (4): 503–546. doi:10.2307/1907921.

Becker, Selwyn W., and Fred O. Brownson. 1964. "What Price Ambiguity? or the Role of Ambiguity in Decision-Making." *Journal of Political Economy* 72 (1): 62–73. doi:10.1086/258854.

Chipman, John S. 1960. "Stochastic Choice and Subjective Probability." In *Decisions, Values, and Groups,* edited by Dorothy Willner. London: Pergamon Press.

Curley, Shawn P., and J. Frank Yates. 1989. "An Empirical Evaluation of Descriptive Models of Ambiguity Reactions in Choice Situations." *Journal of Mathematical Psychology* 33 (4): 397–427. doi:10.1016/0022 2496(89)90019-9

Ellsberg, Daniel. 1961. "Risk, Ambiguity, and the Savage Axioms." *The Quarterly Journal of Economics* 75 (4): 643–669. doi:10.2307/1884324.

Fellner, William. 1961. "Distortion of Subjective Probabilities as a Reaction to Uncertainty." *The Quarterly Journal of Economics* 75 (4): 670–689. doi:10.2307/1884325.

Kahneman, Daniel, and Amos Tversky. 1979. "Prospect Theory: An Analysis of Decision under Risk." *Econometrica* 47 (2): 263–291. doi:10.2307/1914185.

Maccrimmon, Kenneth R. 1968. "Descriptive and Normative Implications of the Decision-Theory Postulates." In *Risk and Uncertainty: Proceedings of a Conference held by the International Economic Association,* edited by Karl Borch and Jan Mossin, 3–32. International Economic Association Conference Volumes, Numbers 1–50. London: Palgrave Macmillan UK. doi:10.1007/978-1-349-15248-3_1.

Machina, Mark J., and Marciano Siniscalchi. 2014. "Ambiguity and Ambiguity Aversion." In *Handbook of the Economics of Risk and Uncertainty,* vol. 1. North-Holland.

Slovic, Paul, and Amos Tversky. 1974. "Who Accepts Savage's Axiom?" *Behavioral Science* 19 (6): 368–373. doi:10.1002/bs.3830190603.

12 Non-Expected Utility

Learning Objectives

★ Understand how prospect theory and maxmin expected utility differ from standard expected utility preferences.

★ Apply these nonstandard models to explain anomalies of the standard model.

★ Evaluate the models against empirical evidence from personal finance decisions.

In the face of risk and uncertainty, many individuals make decisions that are not consistent with the standard assumption that preferences are represented by an expected utility form. The previous chapter illustrates such inconsistencies across a variety of lab experiments, including the famous Allais and Ellsberg paradoxes. These anomalies suggest that decision making under uncertainty may better be described by alternative models — ones that do not simply use beliefs as weights on the possible utility outcomes.

This chapter introduces two popular alternative models. The first is prospect theory. For a given lottery, prospect theory assumes that individuals weight the possible outcomes, not with the actual probabilities, but with a *transformation* of the probabilities. In doing so, we can elegantly make sense of the multiple anomalies identified in the first half of the previous chapter. The second alternative model is maxmin expected utility. This model provides an explanation for the observed ambiguity aversion that individuals exhibit in the Ellsberg paradox. It does so by assuming that when faced with ambiguity about probabilities, individuals believe they are facing the worst-case scenario. Hence, they maximize not expected utility, but the *minimum* expected utility.

After introducing each nonstandard model, we apply it to make sense of our motivating anomalies. We then consider how the nonstandard models help to explain the empirical evidence for seemingly contradictory attitudes towards risk. For instance, individuals tend to over-insure themselves against modest risks, while simultaneously seeking out lotteries that increase their exposure to risk. Many people also avoid the risk of investing their savings in the stock market, but those that do increase their risk by insufficiently diversifying their investments. By taking a step away from expected utility, we enrich our understanding of such behaviors and can begin to think in novel ways about the scope for policy to improve individual welfare.

DOI: 10.4324/9780367854072-16

12.1   Prospect Theory

Motivated by the anomalies of decision making with risk documented in the previous chapter, Kahneman and Tversky (1979) propose prospect theory, an alternative theory of preferences over lotteries, or prospects. Prospect theory makes four modifications to the standard expected utility model of preferences over lotteries.

Consider a lottery $L = (x_1, p_1; x_2, p_2; \ldots ; x_N, p_N)$ where each possible monetary outcome x_n occurs with probability $p_n \geq 0$ and $p_1 + p_2 + \cdots + p_N = 1$. The standard expected utility model assumes that preferences over lottery L are represented as follows:

$$E(u(L)) = p_1 u(x_1) + p_2 u(x_2) + \cdots + p_N u(x_N) \tag{12.1}$$

where $u(\cdot)$ is a strictly increasing and weakly concave function. The assumption of weak concavity allows for risk averse or risk neutral preferences, but rules out risk loving preferences.

The first two modifications to the expected utility model proposed by prospect theory are (1) *reference dependence* and (2) *loss aversion*. These assumptions account for the evidence that individuals appear to evaluate final monetary outcomes relative to a reference point — often their initial wealth — and weight losses more than equivalent gains. These two features of prospect theory are the subject of Part III. The expected gain-loss utility given in Definition 9.3 provides a *partial* formulation of prospect theory that includes these two features. In particular, an individual with reference-dependent preferences who is loss averse relative to her initial wealth W evaluates lottery L as follows:

$$E(v(L \mid W)) = p_1 v(x_1 \mid W) + p_2 v(x_2 \mid W) + \cdots + p_N v(x_N \mid W) \tag{12.2}$$

Recall that in this context $v(\cdot)$ is the linear gain-loss value function:

$$v(x \mid W) = \begin{cases} x - W & \text{if } x \geq W \\ \lambda(x - W) & \text{if } x < W \end{cases} \tag{12.3}$$

where $\lambda \geq 1$ is the coefficient of loss aversion. Chapter 9 applies this model to explain the strong aversion to small-stakes lotteries, as well as the equity premium puzzle.

Although the expected gain-loss utility representation of preferences in equation (12.2) modifies the standard expected utility model in equation (12.1), it maintains the standard assumption that preferences take the expected utility form. That is, it still computes the weighted average of payoffs using the probabilities as weights.

The *full* version of prospect theory additionally assumes a non-expected utility form of preferences over risk. It is defined as follows:

Definition 12.1 The **prospect theory** model of preferences evaluates lottery $L = (x_1, p_1; x_2, p_2; \ldots ; x_N, p_N)$, given initial wealth W, as:

$$V(L \mid W) = \omega_1 v(x_1 \mid W) + \omega_2 v(x_2 \mid W) + \cdots + \omega_N v(x_N \mid W)$$

where $v(\cdot)$ is a gain-loss value function exhibiting diminishing sensitivity, and ω_n is the **decision weight** on the payoff from outcome x_n.

This definition integrates the final two features of prospect theory that we have yet to consider: (3) *diminishing sensitivity* and (4) *probability weighting*. Diminishing sensitivity refers to the shape of the gain-loss value function $v(\cdot)$. While the value function still exhibits loss aversion relative to a reference point, it is no longer restricted to be linear as in equation (12.3). And probability weighting allows individuals to weight the payoff from each possible outcome x_n with a decision weight ω_n that can differ from the probability p_n. This last assumption breaks from the standard assumption that preferences take the expected utility form.[1]

We now turn to exploring these two features of prospect theory further. As in the previous chapter, we simplify the exposition by normalizing initial wealth to zero ($W = 0$). We can therefore interpret lotteries with gains and losses as the final outcomes and suppress the reference point in the gain-loss value function by writing $v(x)$ instead of $v(x \mid 0)$.

12.1.1   Diminishing Sensitivity

Consider the utility difference from winning $150 instead of winning only $100. Now imagine the utility difference from winning $1,050 instead of winning only $1,000. For most people the first difference is larger than the second. The additional $50 typically provides a greater increase in satisfaction when it is closer to initial wealth than when it is further away. This may be due to the calculation that $150 is 50% larger than $100, while $1,050 is only 5% larger than $1,000. Similarly, losing $150 instead of $100 is likely to generate a larger utility drop than the utility drop from losing $1,050 instead of $1,000. Kahneman and Tversky (1979) identify this tendency of individuals to be less sensitive to changes in outcomes that are further from initial wealth as **diminishing sensitivity**.

The linear gain-loss value function (12.3) fails to capture such diminishing sensitivity. In the linear case, an additional $50 of winnings always increases utility by 50, no matter how far the gain is from initial wealth. And losing an additional $50 always decreases utility by 50λ, no matter how far the loss is from initial wealth.

Instead of a linear form, diminishing sensitivity implies that the gain-loss value function $v(\cdot)$ is concave over gains and convex over losses. Such a function is illustrated in Figure 12.1. Observe that the value function in the figure exhibits loss aversion: the function is steeper over losses than equivalent gains. Loss aversion, however, will not play a significant role in this chapter's analysis.

12.1.2   Probability Weighting

The final new feature of prospect theory is **probability weighting**, where the possible payoffs from a lottery are not weighted by their probabilities p_n, but instead by decision weights ω_n. The expected utility form of preferences implicitly assumes that the decision weights are simply the probabilities. But prospect theory allows for the decision weights to diverge from these probabilities.

It is important to emphasize that the decision weights should not be interpreted as measuring an individual's beliefs about the likelihood of each outcome. For example, if $\omega_n > p_n$, it does not mean that the individual overestimates the likelihood of outcome x_n. She knows that the probability of outcome x_n is p_n, but evaluates the desirability of the lottery by applying the decision weight ω_n to the payoff from x_n. We explore the role of nonstandard beliefs in Part VI.

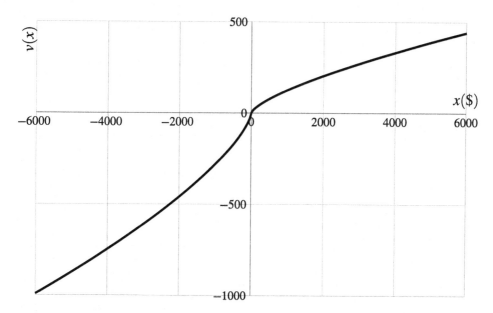

Figure 12.1 Prospect Theory Gain-Loss Value Function

Note: This value function takes the functional form suggested by Tversky and Kahneman (1992): $v(x) = x^\alpha$ for $x \geq 0$ and $v(x) = -\lambda(-x)^\alpha$ with $\alpha = 0.7$ and $\lambda = 2.25$.

But how are decision weights computed? In prospect theory they are determined by means of a **probability weighting function** $\pi(\cdot)$ that transforms probabilities. One such function is illustrated in Figure 12.2. Kahneman and Tversky (1979) assume that the decision weight ω_n equals the probability weighting function applied to probability p_n:

$$\omega_n = \pi(p_n)$$

We maintain this assumption for our analysis. But note that since the original development of prospect theory in 1979, alternative formulations of decision weights have been proposed and adopted for economic analysis.[2]

Let's take a closer look at the decision weights determined by the probability weighting function in Figure 12.2. Observe that the function is increasing: higher probabilities are transformed into larger decision weights. In addition, probabilities equal decision weights at the probability extremes of 0% and 100%: $\pi(0) = 0$ and $\pi(1) = 1$. But the function is not a straight 45-degree line with a slope of one. In fact, if it were the 45-degree line, then $\pi(p) = p$ and decision weights would equal probabilities, as in the standard expected utility case. The inverse-S shape is motivated by the anomalies in the previous chapter. In particular, the function exhibits the following three key features.

Overweighting Unlikely Outcomes

Starting from a zero probability outcome, the probability weighting function initially increases above the 45-degree line. This captures the tendency of individuals to overweight low-probability outcomes. Mathematically, $\pi(p) > p$ for small $p > 0$.

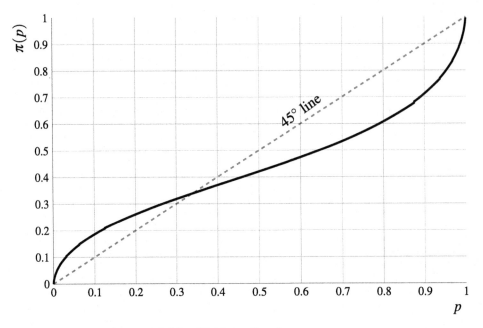

Figure 12.2 Prospect Theory Probability Weighting Function

Note: This probability weighting function takes the functional form suggested by Tversky and Kahneman (1992): $\pi(p) = p^{\gamma}/(p^{\gamma} + (1-p)^{\gamma})^{1/\gamma}$ with $\gamma = 0.61$.

Subcertainty

Consider a lottery with two possible outcomes, one of which occurs with probability 20% and the other with probability 80%. What is the sum of the decision weights on these two complementary outcomes? The decision weight on the first outcome, from visual inspection of Figure 12.2, is about 0.26. But the decision weight on the outcome with an 80% chance is about 0.61. The sum of these decision weights is then 0.26 + 0.61 = 0.87, which is clearly less than 100%.

This example illustrates a general feature of the probability weighting function, known as **subcertainty**. In particular, for any two complementary outcomes, neither of which is certain, the sum of their decision weights is less than the decision weight of a certain outcome. Or expressed mathematically:

$$\pi(p) + \pi(1-p) < \pi(1) = 1 \text{ for all } 0 < p < 1$$

Observe that subcertainty and the overweighting of unlikely outcomes together imply the underweighting of likely (but not certain) outcomes. Graphically such underweighting is evidenced by the fact that the probability weighting function is below the 45-degree line for a wide range of likely outcomes. We can also show this algebraically by considering an outcome that occurs with probability $1 - p < 1$ where p is small:

$$\pi(1-p) \quad < 1 - \pi(p) \text{ by subcertainty}$$
$$< 1 - p \text{ by overweighting unlikely outcomes}$$

In words, for a likely outcome with probability $1 - p$ the decision weight is less than $1 - p$.

The overweighting of unlikely outcomes and underweighting of likely outcomes imply that away from the endpoints the probability weighting function is flatter than the 45-degree line. That is, individuals are less sensitive to changes in probabilities than is predicted by expected utility. For example, increasing the probability of an outcome from 50% to 51% is associated with an increase in the decision weight by less than one percentage point.

Subproportionality

The last feature of the probability weighting function concerns the ratio of probabilities. Consider, for example, the ratio of 20% to 80% and the ratio of 5% to 20%. In both cases the ratio is 1 to 4: 20% is a quarter of 80% and 5% is a quarter of 20%. But the ratio of the decision weights in these two cases is not constant. From Figure 12.2 we observe the following:

$$\frac{\pi(0.2)}{\pi(0.8)} \approx \frac{0.26}{0.61} \approx 0.43 \quad \text{and} \quad \frac{\pi(0.05)}{\pi(0.2)} \approx \frac{0.13}{0.26} = 0.5$$

This numerical example illustrates the property of **subproportionality**. Namely, for a fixed ratio of probabilities, the corresponding ratio of decision weights is larger when the magnitudes of the probabilities are smaller. Mathematically, this requires that

$$\frac{\pi(pq)}{\pi(p)} < \frac{\pi(pqr)}{\pi(pr)} \quad \text{for any } 0 < p, q, r < 1$$

Applying this notation to our example above, $p = 0.8$ and $q = r = 0.25$. Subproportionality places even further restrictions on the shape of the probability weighting function.

12.2 Application: Anomalies with Objective Probabilities

In this section we apply the prospect theory model of preferences to make sense of the anomalous choices illustrated by the lab experiments in Section 11.1. As in that setting, normalize initial wealth to zero ($W = 0$) so that we can interpret final outcomes as gains or losses. And recall that each lottery L can be denoted by $L = (x_1, p_1; x_2, p_2)$, with $p_1 + p_2 \leq 1$. In the case that $p_1 + p_2 < 1$, we interpret lottery L as including the possible third outcome of winning nothing with probability $1 - p_1 - p_2 > 0$. Prospect theory preferences over lottery L, with decision weights $\omega_n = \pi(p_n)$ are therefore represented by:

$$V(L) = \pi(p_1)v(x_1) + \pi(p_2)v(x_2) \tag{12.4}$$

where $v(\cdot)$ is an increasing function, with $v(0) = 0$, that is concave over gains and convex over losses. The probability weighting function $\pi(\cdot)$ overweights unlikely outcomes and exhibits both subcertainty and subproportionality.

12.2.1 Allais Paradox

Let's begin with the famous Allais paradox. Recall that the majority of subjects prefer lottery $C = (2500, 0.33)$ over lottery $D = (2400, 0.34)$. According to prospect theory, this preference implies:

$$\pi(0.33)v(2500) = V(C) > V(D) = \pi(0.34)v(2400)$$

In addition, the majority prefer lottery $B = (2400)$ to lottery $A = (2500, 0.33; 2400, 0.66)$. Putting these two preferences together, we have:

$$V(B) > V(A) \;\Rightarrow\; v(2400) > \pi(0.33)v(2500) + \pi(0.66)v(2400)$$
$$\Rightarrow (1 - \pi(0.66))v(2400) > \pi(0.33)v(2500) \text{ by algebra}$$
$$\Rightarrow (1 - \pi(0.66))v(2400) > \pi(0.34)v(2400) \text{ because } V(C) > V(D)$$
$$\Rightarrow 1 - \pi(0.66) > \pi(0.34) \text{ by algebra}$$
$$\Rightarrow \pi(0.66) + \pi(0.34) < 1 \text{ by algebra}$$

This logic reveals that preferring C and B implies subcertainty: the decision weights on two complementary outcomes (with probabilities 66% and 34%) sum to less than 1. Probability weighting with subcertainty is therefore essential for resolving the Allais paradox. Intuitively, subcertainty predicts the observed certainty effect because the decision weight on the certain outcome is greater than the sum of decision weights on complementary uncertain outcomes. Observe also that without probability weighting, $\pi(p) = p$ and the majority preferences would then imply that $0.66 + 0.34 < 1$, which is clearly impossible.

Consider next the anomaly illustrated by a choice between probable versus merely possible outcomes. In it, the majority prefer lottery $B = (3000, 0.9)$ over $A = (6000, 0.45)$ and lottery $C = (6000, 0.001)$ over $D = (3000, 0.002)$. With the prospect theory model of preferences we therefore have:

$$V(B) > V(A) \;\Rightarrow\; \pi(0.9)v(3000) > \pi(0.45)v(6000) \Rightarrow \frac{v(3000)}{v(6000)} > \frac{\pi(0.45)}{\pi(0.9)}$$

$$V(C) > V(D) \;\Rightarrow\; \pi(0.001)v(6000) > \pi(0.002)v(3000) \Rightarrow \frac{v(3000)}{v(6000)} < \frac{\pi(0.001)}{\pi(0.002)}$$

These majority preferences therefore imply subproportionality with $\frac{\pi(0.45)}{\pi(0.9)} < \frac{\pi(0.001)}{\pi(0.002)}$. Even though the probability of winning \$3000 is half the probability of winning \$6,000 in both decisions, the ratio of decision weights is larger for the smaller probabilities. Intuitively, if individuals choose the higher probability lottery when winning is likely, subproportionality accommodates the tendency to switch to the lottery with the larger potential payoff (and lower probability) when winning is unlikely. Observe also that without probability weighting, $\pi(p) = p$ and the majority preferences would then imply that $\frac{0.45}{0.9} < \frac{0.001}{0.002}$, which is clearly impossible.

12.2.2   Reflection Effect

Prospect theory assumes that the value function is concave over gains and convex over losses. Recall that we motivated this S-shape by appealing to the logic of diminishing sensitivity over increasingly large certain gains and certain losses relative to a reference point. What are the consequences of such a value function in a setting with risk?

Without probability weighting, the S-shaped value function implies risk aversion over risky gains and risk seeking preferences over risky losses. Indeed, the lab evidence that most individuals would prefer \$3,000 for sure rather than a lottery with an 80% chance of winning \$4,000 implies risk aversion. And the reflection effect by which individuals would instead prefer to take a lottery with an 80% chance of losing $4,000 over accepting a certain loss of $3,000 implies risk seeking.

But prospect theory integrates both probability weighting and an S-shaped value function to model preferences over risk. To confirm the descriptive accuracy of this model, consider the following lab experiment.

Lab Experiment — Reflecting the Value Function (Kahneman and Tversky 1979)

Choose between: **Results:**

  A (6000, 0.25)   [18%]
  B (4000, 0.25; 2000, 0.25)   [82%]

Choose between:

  C (−6000, 0.25)   [70%]
  D (−4000, 0.25; −2000, 0.25)   [30%]

Observe that this experiment once again illustrates the robustness of the reflection effect — preferences switch when gains are reflected to be losses. Applying the prospect theory model, the majority preferences in each choice imply:

$$V(B) > V(A) \quad \Rightarrow \pi(0.25)[v(4000) + v(2000)] > \pi(0.25)v(6000)$$
$$\Rightarrow v(4000) + v(2000) > v(6000)$$
$$\Rightarrow v(\cdot) \text{ is concave in this positive range}$$
$$V(C) > V(D) \quad \Rightarrow \pi(0.25)v(-6000) > \pi(0.25)[v(-4000) + v(-2000)]$$
$$\Rightarrow v(-4000) + v(-2000) < v(-6000)$$
$$\Rightarrow v(\cdot) \text{ is convex in this negative range}$$

Therefore, even with probability weighting, the S-shaped value function remains consistent with the majority preferences.

12.2.3   *Overweighting Unlikely Outcomes*

The final anomaly to rationalize is the typical preference for a risky lottery with an unlikely win. Recall that the majority of subjects prefer a lottery with a 0.1% chance of winning $5,000 over winning $5 with certainty. Applying the prospect theory model of preferences to this example, we have:

$$\pi(0.001)v(5000) \quad > v(5)$$
$$\Rightarrow \pi(0.001) \quad > \frac{v(5)}{v(5000)} > \frac{5}{5000} = 0.001$$

where the second inequality is a consequence of $v(\cdot)$ being concave over gains.[3] By allowing the decision weight on the 0.1% outcome to be greater than the objective probability of 0.1%, prospect theory accommodates the common preference for the unlikely win. This is in spite of the risk aversion over gains promoted by diminishing sensitivity.

In summary, diminishing sensitivity in the value function promotes (1) risk aversion over gains and (2) risk seeking over losses. But the overweighting of unlikely outcomes promotes (3) risk seeking over small-probability gains. Intuitively, the additional weight on the unlikely win makes the risk more appealing. Symmetrically, the overweighting of unlikely outcomes promotes (4) risk aversion over small-probability losses (see Exercise 12.5 for an example). These four features of risk preferences implied by prospect theory, and summarized in Table 12.1, are considerably more complex than the standard expected utility model assumption of universal risk aversion over total wealth. With this complexity, however, we gain a more accurate descriptive model of behavior.

12.3 Empirical Evidence of Probability Weighting

Probability weighting generates a non-expected utility form of preferences that explains hypothetical choices across a variety of lab experiments. It also provides a unifying explanation for otherwise puzzling real-world behaviors. In particular, individuals simultaneously seek out insurance to reduce their exposure to modest risks and pay for lottery tickets that increase their exposure to risk. The preference for insurance suggests risk aversion over unlikely losses. And the preference for lotteries suggests risk seeking over unlikely gains. These are precisely the risk preferences promoted by the overweighting of unlikely outcomes, as summarized in Table 12.1. Note that without probability weighting, the diminishing sensitivity of the prospect theory value function would predict the opposite behaviors, i.e., little demand for insurance over modest losses and aversion to lotteries.

In this section we explore insurance and lottery-like market settings to illustrate how probability weighting, especially overweighting unlikely outcomes, can make sense of the empirical evidence. We conclude by briefly considering creative ways in which policy makers might leverage individuals' overweighting of unlikely outcomes to encourage desirable behaviors.

12.3.1 Insurance

The risk of adverse events is a feature of life. A primary function of most rich industrialized countries is in fact to protect citizens against major risks by providing various forms of (often mandatory) insurance. Unemployment insurance, health insurance, natural disaster insurance, and retirement benefit systems provide financial support in the

Table 12.1 Prospect Theory's Four-Fold Pattern of Risk Preferences

	Over Gains	Over Losses
Diminishing Sensitivity Promotes	Risk Aversion	Risk Seeking
Overweighting Unlikely Outcomes Promotes	Risk Seeking	Risk Aversion

event of job loss, illness, home damage from environmental catastrophe, and income loss in old age. But not all risks generate losses of such large magnitude.

Over-Insuring Modest Losses

Individuals must decide for themselves whether or not to insure against the risk of modest losses for which the government is not involved. For example, car rental companies and cell phone manufacturers typically offer insurance to protect against the risk of damage. And many electronics, ranging from DVD players to vacuums, offer extended warranties as a form of insurance against product failure.

The expected utility model is the standard economic approach to modeling the consumer decision to purchase insurance. A key implication of this standard model is that although individuals are assumed to be risk averse over total lifetime wealth, they are approximately risk neutral over gambles with *modest* stakes that are less than a couple thousand dollars (Rabin 2000). This observation is discussed in the context of small-stakes gambles in Section 9.3. And with approximately risk neutral preferences over modest losses, insurance provides little value to consumers. This prediction contradicts the widespread consumption of insurance for the modest potential losses associated with car rentals, cell phones, and electronics.

But the demand for insurance against modest losses is not so puzzling if consumers overweight unlikely losses. Intuitively, the additional weight on the modest loss decreases the value of not insuring. As a result, insurance becomes relatively more desirable. To appreciate the magnitude by which individuals over-insure relative to the predictions of the standard model, consider the following evidence from the home insurance market.

Home Insurance   *[Household]*

Although almost all American homeowners purchase home insurance to protect against losses due to theft, accidents, and fire, they can choose different levels of home insurance coverage. In particular, suppose that customers are offered the option of a policy with either a $1,000 deductible or a $500 deductible. The deductible is the maximum amount that the homeowner pays in the event of a loss. The insurance company fully covers all losses over the deductible. For example, with a $4,000 loss from theft, the insurance company would cover $3,000 with the $1,000 deductible, but $3,500 with the $500 deductible. Lower deductible policies provide more complete insurance coverage for the homeowner, but are also more costly for the insurance company and as a result are priced higher.

Sydnor (2010) examines 50,000 home insurance policies for which individuals had the option to choose among a menu of insurance options. In particular, customers could choose a $1,000 deductible, or pay an additional $100 annually to reduce their deductible to $500. Approximately three times as many customers chose the more expensive $500-deductible policy over the cheaper $1,000-deductible policy. In addition, 4.3% of customers who chose the more generous coverage filed a claim for a loss.

These data are puzzling. To see why, assume that individuals are risk neutral over the modest loss, as is standard, from paying a deductible of either $500 or $1,000. With a 4.3% chance of experiencing this financial loss, the expected savings from choosing the lower deductible policy is $0.043 \times (\$1,000 - \$500) = \$21.50$. That is, individuals should expect to save $21.50 annually by paying out $500 with a 4.3% probability rather than paying $1,000 with a 4.3% probability.[4] But those who chose the $500-deductible policy paid an additional $100 annually for this extra insurance coverage. They are paying almost five times more for the low deductible than it is worth.

Can the overweighting of unlikely outcomes explain this behavior?[5] In this case, the expected savings from choosing the lower deductible policy is now $\pi(0.043) \times \$500$ where $\pi(p)$ is the probability weighting function. Using the probability weighting function from Figure 12.2, $\pi(0.043) = 0.12$, implying that the customer expects to save $0.12 \times \$500 = \$60$ with the lower deductible policy. This is still less than the $100 extra that customers actually paid. But if customers also code the deductible payment as a loss relative to the reference point of not paying any deductible, then with a coefficient of loss aversion $\lambda = 2.25$, their willingness to pay for the lower deductible increases to $2.25 \times \$60 = \$135$. This is greater than the actual $100 difference in the policies. It is no longer surprising why the more generous low-deductible policy is so popular.

In sum, probability weighting predicts individuals to pay much more for insurance over modest losses than expected utility predicts. And when combined with loss aversion, we have a theory of decision making over risk that can explain observed insurance choices.

12.3.2 Lotteries

The average American household spends almost $600 each year on lottery tickets (US Census Bureau 2019). For comparison, Americans spend more on lottery tickets than sports tickets, books, video games, and movie tickets *combined* (Isidore 2015). A typical state-run lottery distributes a share of the revenue to the winner, keeping the remainder to fund public goods or offset taxes. For instance, if 1,000,000 people each buy a lottery ticket for $1, the state might keep 40% of the revenue, or $400,000. The lottery winner then receives $600,000. Note that the expected winnings are $600,000 \times 1/1,000,000 = \$0.60$, which is less than the price of the ticket.

By purchasing a lottery ticket an individual is taking on risk with a negative expected payoff. And if individuals are risk averse over gains, as is the standard assumption in the expected utility model and promoted by the prospect theory value function, then lottery tickets are a lose-lose purchase. But they do not need to be lose-lose if individuals overweight the unlikely outcome of winning. With a decision weight on the win in excess of the true probability, the lottery becomes more attractive. Individuals may subsequently find it worthwhile to play the lottery.[6]

To verify this intuition mathematically, we can apply the prospect theory model of preferences in expression (12.4) to the lottery ticket example above. Let's use the value function $v(\cdot)$ and probability weighting function $\pi(\cdot)$ depicted in Figures 12.1 and 12.2. Assuming exactly one winner, the lottery L offers a one-in-a-million chance of gaining $599,999 (the winnings minus the $1 cost of the ticket), with the complementary outcome of simply losing the $1 ticket price. That is, $L = (\$599999, 0.000001; -\$1, 0.999999)$.

$$
\begin{aligned}
V(L) &= \pi(0.000001) \cdot v(599,999) + \pi(0.999999) \cdot v(-1) \\
&\approx 0.0002187 \cdot 599,999^{0.7} + 0.999642 \cdot -2.25 \\
&\approx 0.17 > 0
\end{aligned}
$$

The payoff from the lottery ticket is now positive and therefore better than maintaining the status quo with a payoff of zero. This prediction relies crucially on the probability weighting, where the decision weight on winning is over 200 times greater than the actual probability. Without probability weighting, the lottery payoff would be:

$$E(v(L)) = 0.000001 \cdot v(599,999) + 0.999999 \cdot v(-1)$$
$$= 0.000001 \cdot 599,999^{0.7} + 0.999999 \cdot -2.25$$
$$\approx -2.24 < 0$$

That is, the cost of losing the $1 ticket dominates the very unlikely benefit of winning and the model predicts no lottery participation.

Stocks as Lotteries   *[Finance]*

Stocks traded in financial markets can also look like lottery tickets. Suppose you buy a share in a publicly traded company at its current stock price. Over the next month that stock price could go up or down, earning you a positive or negative return. If the stock returns are distributed normally, as depicted by the "No Skew" bell curve in Figure 12.3, then stock returns are equally likely to be positive or negative. This surely doesn't look like a lottery ticket. But if instead the returns are positively skewed, with a right tail that is longer than its left tail, there is a large chance of a modest loss and a small chance of a large gain. This much more closely approximates the structure of a lottery ticket.

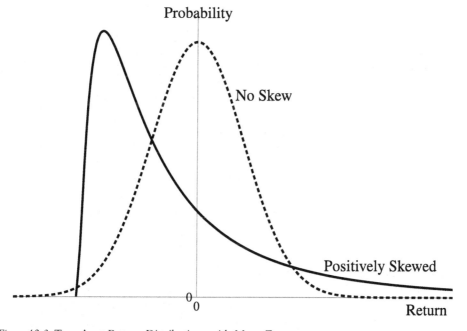

Figure 12.3 Two Asset Return Distributions with Mean Zero

Given that probability weighting promotes a preference for lottery tickets, it also promotes a preference for lottery-like assets with highly skewed return distributions. Barberis and Huang (2008) formalize this intuition. In particular, they show that investors who overweight unlikely outcomes with prospect theory preferences are more likely to buy stocks with skewed returns, causing these stocks to become overpriced relative to the prediction with expected utility preferences.[7] And when skewed stocks become more expensive to purchase, the returns on these stocks consequently fall. Although we might expect this overpricing to be mitigated by standard investors who can profit off of the mispricing — e.g., by short-selling overpriced stocks — the risks and costs of doing so can limit the use of such strategies. Overpriced stocks with skewed returns can therefore persist in the market.

This is not merely a theoretical prediction. There is empirical evidence that assets with skewed distributions are in fact overpriced and earn low average returns. Consider the case of initial public offerings (IPOs), when a private company first issues shares to the public. IPOs have historically earned low returns (Ritter 1991). IPO returns are also highly skewed, since as relatively young companies with uncertain future profitability, modest positive or negative returns are likely outcomes and a very large return is a low-probability event. Investors who purchased IPO shares in Google, Apple, Amazon, or Microsoft, for instance, made massive profits. But these companies represent a tiny fraction of all companies that go public. If investors overweight the chance of highly unlikely superstar performers, they will purchase IPOs in spite of the low expected returns. Green and Hwang (2012) verify that even among IPOs, those with greater expected skewness experience greater first-day returns, but lower returns in the following one to five years. This result is exactly what is predicted by probability weighting: high skewness generates high demand initially, leading to overpricing, and subsequently lower returns over time.[8]

Lotteries as Policy   *[Public Finance]*

How can the preference for lotteries promoted by probability weighting be leveraged to achieve policy aims?[9] One strategy is to use lotteries as an incentive for particular desirable behaviors. Although a lottery is not predicted to incentivize standard risk averse decision makers, there is evidence that it can be an effective policy tool.

Consider the policy goal of increasing household savings. As discussed in Section 4.5, many Americans do not save enough to cover moderate financial emergencies or to smooth their consumption into retirement. The benefit of earning interest by putting money in a traditional savings account does not appear to be a sufficiently appealing incentive to save for the typical household. An alternative is a Prize Linked Savings (PLS) account. Instead of paying interest, PLS accounts enter depositors into a lottery that periodically pays out a large reward (as cash or non-cash), with higher deposits increasing the chance of winning. Although they are not available in the United States for legal reasons, they have existed since at least 1694 in the United Kingdom and are common in Latin America, Europe, and South Asia. Kearney et al. (2011) review the history and effectiveness of PLS accounts, noting their appeal, particularly for low-income households. While evidence in the United States is limited, policy makers may want to revisit the legality of such accounts if they help individuals to align their actual savings levels with what they desire.

Another potential policy goal is the mitigation of obesity. The following experiment tests the impact of lotteries as an incentive for weight loss.

Field Experiment — Weight Loss Lottery (Volpp, John, et al. 2008)

A group of obese individuals (with body mass index between 30 and 40) aged 30–70 years was recruited in 2007 to participate in an evaluation of weight loss strategies. All participants met individually with a dietician at the start of the experiment to review diet and exercise strategies for weight loss. The goal for all participants was weight loss of 16 pounds over 16 weeks. Each participant was weighed every 4 weeks to track progress towards the goal.

Participants were randomized into a control group and a lottery treatment group.[10] The control group participants did not receive any financial incentives for weight loss. But the lottery treatment group was incentivized to meet the weight loss goal as follows:

- Weigh themself each morning and self-report this weight by noon each day.
- Only if the reported weight was at or below their weight loss goal were they eligible for a daily lottery prize.
- Daily lotteries offered a 1 in 5 chance of winning $10 and a 1 in 100 chance of winning $100.
- Accumulated daily lottery winnings were paid out once per month, conditional on verification that actual weight loss met the monthly weight loss goal.

Because the control and treatment groups were randomly assigned, any differences in weight loss over the 16 weeks must be due to the lottery incentive structure.

Volpp, John, et al. (2008) report the following results:

Measure	Control Group	Lottery Group
Average Weight Loss	3.9 lbs.	13.1 lbs.
Met 16 lb. Weight Loss Goal	10.5%	52.6%

The above experiment shows that the opportunity to enter a lottery in return for meeting a weight loss goal increases both the total weight lost and the likelihood of meeting the goal. This finding provides further evidence for the effectiveness of lotteries as a policy intervention. More generally, the evidence casts doubt on the standard model of individuals as risk averse expected utility maximizers and is instead consistent with the probability weighting of prospect theory.

12.4   Maxmin Expected Utility

Recall the Ellsberg paradox from Section 11.2. This famous anomaly reveals an aversion to gambles with ambiguous probabilities. Such ambiguity aversion cannot be reconciled with consistent beliefs applied within the expected utility framework.

The empirical evidence for ambiguity aversion has motivated the development of a multitude of alternative models to expected utility (Machina and Siniscalchi 2014). A popular alternative is to assume that individuals evaluate ambiguity by assuming the worst-case scenario. To make this more precise, suppose that you are faced with an ambiguous gamble for which you only know the *set* of possible probability distributions over the uncertain outcomes — not the actual probability distribution. You then compute the expected utility of this gamble for each of the possible probability distributions. And because the ambiguity makes you pessimistic, you presume that the actual probability distribution for the gamble is the one that generates the lowest expected utility. You therefore make your decision about accepting or rejecting the gamble based on this worst-case scenario.

Such a model for evaluating ambiguity is known as the **maxmin expected utility** model (Gilboa and Schmeidler 1989). Its name follows from the observation that individuals make choices that maximize the lowest, or minimum, expected utility. Like probability weighting in prospect theory, maxmin expected utility deviates from the standard expected utility form of preferences over uncertainty.[11] In the next section we apply the maxmin expected utility model to make sense of the Ellsberg paradox.

12.5   Application: Ellsberg Paradox

In the Three-Color Urn Lab Experiment (Section 11.2) there is an urn with 90 balls, 30 of which are known to be red. The remaining 60 balls are either black or yellow. The probability distribution over drawing a red, black, or yellow ball from the urn is therefore $(p_R, p_B, p_Y) = (1/3, p_B, p_Y)$. The ambiguity over the contents of the urn means that the black and yellow balls can constitute anywhere from zero to two-thirds of the total balls, i.e., $0 \leq p_B, p_Y \leq 2/3$. Recall that each winning bet pays \$100, and \$0 otherwise.

Consider first the choice between bet A that pays off from drawing a red ball and bet B that pays off from drawing a black ball. Bet A has no ambiguity, so maxmin expected utility is just standard expected utility. But bet B is ambiguous: the probability of drawing a black ball could be as high as 2/3, or as low as zero. With maxmin expected utility, individuals assume the worst, that there are no black balls in the urn ($p_B = 0$). Assuming that $u(\$0) = 0$, the maxmin expected utilities of these two bets are therefore:

$$\min_{p_R=1/3} E(u(A)) = \min_{p_R=1/3} p_R \cdot u(100) = 1/3 \cdot u(100) > 0$$

$$\min_{p_B \in [0,2/3]} E(u(B)) = \min_{p_B \in [0,2/3]} p_B \cdot u(100) = 0 \cdot u(100) = 0$$

Bet A is therefore preferred over B.

The next choice is between bet C that pays off from drawing a red or yellow ball and bet D that pays off from drawing a black or yellow ball. Bet C is ambiguous, while bet D has a known probability distribution. The probability of winning with bet C is at least 1/3 because of the 30 red balls, but could also be a sure bet if the remaining balls all are yellow. The former is the worst-case scenario. The maxmin expected utilities are consequently:

$$\min_{p_R+p_Y\in[1/3,1]} E(u(C)) = \min_{p_R+p_Y\in[1/3,1]} (p_R + p_Y) \cdot u(100) = 1/3 \cdot u(100)$$
$$\min_{p_B+p_Y=2/3} E(u(D)) = \min_{p_B+p_Y=2/3} (p_B + p_Y) \cdot u(100) = 2/3 \cdot u(100)$$

Bet *D* is therefore preferred over *C*.

The joint preferences for bets *A* and *D* are exactly what Ellsberg (1961) hypothesized, and what we showed to be impossible with expected utility preferences in Section 11.2. Intuitively, the maxmin expected utility model allows an individual to change their subjective beliefs about the composition of the urn depending on the bet they face. With bet *B* the individual pessimistically believes the urn contains no black balls (and implicitly 60 yellow balls). Yet with bet *C* she pessimistically believes the urn contains no yellow balls.

12.6   Personal Finance with Ambiguity Aversion   [Finance]

The Ellsberg urn experiments clearly identify the tendency for people to be ambiguity averse. But how does such ambiguity aversion matter in more consequential real-world decisions? Consider the problem of deciding how to invest in risky financial assets. First you must decide whether or not to invest your savings in the stock market. And if you do, you must then choose from a large set of options. It turns out that typical households do not make these decisions in the ways predicted by the standard model.

Given that financial markets are rife with both risk, and ambiguity about the nature of that risk, perhaps the gap between standard theory and empirical evidence can be bridged by allowing for ambiguity averse preferences. To evaluate this hypothesis we first consider the logic for how ambiguity aversion could make sense of puzzling household financial investment decisions. We then review some supporting evidence.

12.6.1   The Logic of Ambiguity Aversion

Non-Participation Puzzle

Standard economic theory with expected utility predicts that everyone should participate in the stock market (Merton 1969; Heaton and Lucas 1997). Intuitively, in spite of its risk, the stock market yields sufficiently high returns over time that it is in everyone's interest to invest heavily in stocks. And yet, less than half of US households hold stocks and less than a third hold at least $10,000 in stocks (Wolff 2017). This phenomenon is known as the **non-participation puzzle**.

The non-participation puzzle is not so puzzling, however, if potential investors are ambiguity averse. To see why, begin with the premise that the underlying risk of stock market returns is ambiguous. Depending on which information investors are looking at, or which historical time horizon, they might consider a range of possible scenarios for the riskiness of the stock market. While a standard expected utility investor would base their investment decision on a typical or average scenario, an ambiguity averse investor is inclined to consider a worst-case scenario (as with maxmin expected utility). In doing so, the ambiguity averse investor is much more pessimistic and subsequently reluctant to participate in the stock market.[12]

Observe that the preceding logic also provides a possible explanation for the equity premium puzzle introduced in Section 8.3. The equity premium puzzle refers to the fact that risky stocks (i.e., equities) earn a much higher return relative to safe riskless assets (like Treasury bills) than is predicted by standard preferences. We can interpret this large premium earned by equities as the additional compensation that investors demand in order to entice them to invest in risky assets. Why then are investors so averse to investing in equities? In Section 9.4 we showed that loss aversion could explain the strong aversion to equities, and subsequently the equity premium. But ambiguity aversion also makes investors reluctant to invest in equities. It has been verified that the observed equity premium can be explained, at least partially, in models with ambiguity averse investors (e.g., Maenhout 2004; Ju and Miao 2012; Collard et al. 2018).

Preference for the Familiar

Conditional on deciding to participate in the stock market, investors must also make decisions about which stocks to choose. People can invest directly in company stocks (including the company at which they work) or buy shares in a mutual fund. And there are different stock markets around the world, from the New York Stock Exchange to the Japan Exchange Group and the London Stock Exchange. Standard economic theory predicts that individuals will seek to minimize their risk by diversifying their investments across a broad range of assets around the globe. In doing so, they help to protect against being invested heavily in a particular stock that happens to yield very low returns. Contrary to this standard prediction, many investors instead appear to exhibit a **preference for the familiar**, sacrificing diversification (and less risk) for stocks with which they are familiar.

A striking example of this preference for the familiar is illustrated by the allocation of investments across countries. French and Poterba (1991) estimated that Americans held 94% of their equity investments in the United States. And Americans were not alone in investing so little abroad. The Japanese allocated 98% of their equity investments to Japan and the British allocated 82% to the United Kingdom. In doing so, investors unnecessarily expose themselves to the risk that their home stock markets crash, while the average foreign stock market does not. This **home-bias puzzle** extends to investments within the United States. Investors have been found to invest more in local companies than those that are further away (Huberman 2001; Seasholes and Zhu 2010).

An even more extreme manifestation of this phenomenon is the **own-company stock puzzle**, whereby individuals invest their savings heavily in the company where they work. Benartzi (2001) estimates that employees at publicly traded companies invest about a quarter of their savings in their own company's stock. This is a particularly risky strategy because an employer's stock value is highly correlated with an employee's job security and income. If a company fails — as has happened famously to Enron, Kodak, Woolworth's, and Lehman Brothers — then exactly at the moment when an employee is likely to be laid off and must rely on savings, the value of their savings invested in their employer has likely collapsed. It is more prudent to therefore invest savings at other companies.

Ambiguity aversion can help to explain this preference for stocks that are familiar. Although all stocks generate uncertain returns, individuals may perceive less ambiguity about potential returns for a familiar stock than one with which they are unfamiliar. As a consequence, the worst-case scenario for an unfamiliar stock may seem substantially worse than for a familiar stock, leading to a preference for the familiar. Boyle et al. (2012) and Cao et al. (2011) explore the role of familiarity more formally.

12.6.2   *Empirical Evidence of Ambiguity Aversion*

To empirically evaluate the theoretical predictions of ambiguity aversion on investment behavior, researchers have conducted surveys, in both the lab and the field, that measure attitudes towards ambiguity and actual investment behaviors. For instance, in a representative survey of US households, Dimmock et al. (2016) measure ambiguity aversion using Ellsberg urn-style questions. They find that just over half of those surveyed are ambiguity averse, while another 38% are in fact ambiguity-seeking. The remaining 10% are ambiguity-neutral, as implicitly assumed by the standard expected utility model. Moreover, they find that ambiguity aversion is negatively associated with stock market participation and foreign stock ownership, but positively associated with own-company stock ownership. In summary, the puzzles of non-participation, home bias, and own-company investing can be attributed — at least in part — to ambiguity aversion.

The evidence that ambiguity aversion exists and matters for decision making raises new and interesting policy questions. One possible policy instrument is to encourage financial literacy that mitigates individuals' perceptions of ambiguity. By reducing perceived ambiguity, the ambiguity-averse may be more inclined to participate in the stock market and diversify their investment portfolios (see e.g., Dimmock et al. 2016; Anantanasuwong et al. 2019). More widespread stock market participation could reduce inequality and greater diversification would help to smooth consumption improving individual welfare. Reducing perceived ambiguity may also provide important benefits in the developing world context for farmers considering the adoption of new and uncertain technologies (Bryan 2019). Further policy insights await the continued investigation of ambiguity and its perception.

12.7   Summary

1   The **prospect theory** model of preferences is characterized by the following features:

    a   reference dependence and loss aversion (the topic of Part III);

    b   **diminishing sensitivity**, i.e., changes in outcomes that are further from a reference point generate smaller changes in the value function; and

    c   **probability weighting**, i.e., uncertain payoffs are weighted by decision weights.

2   Decision weights in prospect theory are determined by a **probability weighting function** that features **subcertainty**, **subproportionality**, and the **overweighting of unlikely outcomes**. These assumptions restrict the shape of the probability weighting function to a particular inverse-S shape.

3   Subcertainty and subpropotionality reconcile the Allais paradox anomalies.

4   Diminishing sensitivity promotes risk aversion over gains and risk seeking over losses, explaining the reflection effect anomaly.

5   The overweighting of unlikely outcomes promotes risk aversion over unlikely losses and risk seeking over unlikely gains. This is consistent with the empirical evidence that individuals over-insure against the unlikely risk of a modest loss, and also buy lottery tickets that introduce the risk of an unlikely gain.

6   The **maxmin expected utility** model of preferences assumes that individuals make choices that maximize the minimum expected utility.

7   The ambiguity aversion exhibited in the Ellsberg paradox is consistent with the maxmin expected utility model.

8   Personal finance behaviors that are not predicted by the standard model (e.g., the **non-participation puzzle** and a **preference for the familiar**) are consistent with an aversion to ambiguity. Survey evidence supports the role of such ambiguity aversion in these behaviors.

12.8   Exercises

Exercise 12.1 — The Heat is On. Kahneman and Tversky (1979) note that most people would find it easier to differentiate between a 3° change and a 6° change in room temperature than to differentiate between a change of 13° and a change of 16°. What does this example illustrate about how people sense and perceive changes in their environment? Which feature(s) of prospect theory capture this phenomenon?

Exercise 12.2 — Recoding Revisited. Let's revisit the Gain-Loss Equivalence Lab Experiment from Section 8.2. In the experiment students were first granted some certain amount of money (in Israeli pounds). They were then faced with a choice between two lotteries. The choices suggested that many students evaluated the two lotteries as changes relative to their current wealth (inclusive of the initial monetary grant). This provided evidence for a reference-dependent value function defined over gains and losses. Let's now evaluate what the students' choices also suggest about the shape of this reference-dependent value function. Assume no probability weighting.

a   Some students were initially granted 1,000. They preferred an additional 500 with certainty over a 50% chance of winning another 1,000. What do these preferences imply about the students' risk preferences (i.e., risk averse, risk neutral, or risk seeking) and the shape of the value function (i.e., concave, linear, or convex) over gains?

b   Other students were initially granted 2,000. They preferred paying 1,000 with a 50% chance over paying 500 for sure. What do these preferences imply about the students' risk preferences and the shape of the value function over losses?

c   Do your answers in parts (a) and (b) match with prospect theory's assumption of diminishing sensitivity?

Exercise 12.3 — Explaining the Simple Allais Paradox. Normalize Alice's wealth to zero and assume that she has prospect theory preferences over lotteries L represented by $V(L)$ as in expression (12.4).

a   Write down the inequality that must hold for Alice to choose 3,000 for sure over 4,000 with an 80% chance.

b   Write down the inequality that must hold for Alice to choose 4,000 with a 20% chance over 3,000 with a 25% chance.

c Alice's choices assumed in parts (a) and (b) match the majority choices in the Simple Allais Paradox Lab Experiment from Section 11.1.1. Which assumption on the probability weighting function allows for these choices?

Exercise 12.4 — Explaining a Modified Allais Paradox. Normalize Robin's wealth to zero and assume that she has prospect theory preferences over lotteries L represented by $V(L)$ as in expression (12.4).

a Write down the inequality that must hold for Robin to choose $1 million for sure over the lottery ($1 million, 0.89; $5 million, 0.10).

b Write down the inequality that must hold for Robin to choose a lottery with a 10% chance of winning $5 million over a lottery with an 11% chance of winning $1 million.

c Robin's choices assumed in parts (a) and (b) match the typical choices described in Exercise 11.1. Which assumption on the probability weighting function allows for these choices?

Exercise 12.5 — Explaining an Unlikely Loss. Normalize Lucy's wealth to zero and assume that she has prospect theory preferences over lotteries L represented by $V(L)$ as in expression (12.4).

a Write down the inequality that must hold for Lucy to choose losing $5 for sure over a lottery with a 0.1% chance of losing $5,000.

b Lucy's choice assumed in part (a) matches the typical choice described in Exercise 11.5. What assumption on the probability weighting function allows for this choice?

Exercise 12.6 — What's Your Damage Worth? Mac pays $10 each month for smart phone insurance that fully covers the repair costs of a cracked screen or other damage. The chance of damage each month is 1%, and the average repair cost without insurance is $300.

a Is Mac a standard risk neutral expected utility maximizer? How do you know?

b Can Mac's insurance choice be explained by the value function in prospect theory? Explain.

c Can Mac's insurance choice be explained by the probability weighting function in prospect theory? Explain.

Exercise 12.7 — Home Security. [Household] Sydnor (2010) examines home insurance policy choices. This chapter reviews the evidence from this study on customer choices between the $1000-deductible and $500-deductible policies. Customers could also choose an even more generous policy with only a $250 deductible. Over a third of the customers in the sample made this choice. And among those who chose the $250 deductible policy, 4.9% filed a claim for a loss.

a What are the expected annual savings for a customer who chooses the $250-deductible instead of the $500-deductible policy?

b The $250-deductible policy was $74/year more expensive than the $500-deductible policy. In light of your answer to part (a), explain which of the two policies a standard risk neutral individual would choose.

c   Explain how prospect theory preferences could explain the preference for the $250-deductible policy.

Exercise 12.8 — Lottery Lower Limits. Evy and Patty are each contemplating whether or not to buy a lottery ticket for $1 that generates a gain of $G with a one-in-a-million chance. Normalize their initial wealth to zero. Buying a lottery ticket is therefore equivalent to choosing the lottery $L = (\$G-1, 0.000001; -\$1, 0.999999)$. Both Evy and Patty use the same value function $v(\cdot)$, pictured in Figure 12.1, to evaluate potential gains and losses:

$$v(x) = \begin{cases} x^{0.7} & \text{if } x \geq 0 \text{ (i.e., } x \text{ is a gain)} \\ -2.25 \times (-x)^{0.7} & \text{if } x < 0 \text{ (i.e., } x \text{ is a loss)} \end{cases}$$

a   Evy evaluates lotteries by taking the expected value of her value function $v(x)$, as follows:

$$E(v(L)) = 0.000001 \times v(G-1) + 0.999999 \times v(-1)$$

What is the minimum lottery gain G such that Evy will choose to buy a ticket?

b   Patty evaluates lotteries with *full* prospect theory preferences that include probability weighting, as follows:

$$V(L) = \pi(0.000001) \times v(G-1) + \pi(0.999999) \times v(-1)$$
$$= 0.0002187 \times v(G-1) + 0.999642 \times v(-1)$$

where $\pi(\cdot)$ is the probability weighting function in Figure 12.2. What is the minimum lottery gain G such that Patty will choose to buy a ticket?

c   Is Evy or Patty more likely to buy a lottery ticket? Explain the role of probability weighting in your answer.

Exercise 12.9 — Buying Stocks to the Max. [Finance] Bali, Cakici, and Whitelaw (2011) study stock market returns from 1962 to 2005. They find that stocks which experienced the highest maximum daily returns over the previous month significantly underperform the returns on other stocks. Explain how this evidence is consistent with individuals overweighting unlikely outcomes.

Exercise 12.10 — Horsing around with Probability. [Sports] A famous anomaly in economics is the favorite-longshot bias (Griffith 1949). It refers to the pattern of horse race-track betting in which bettors value longshots too much (given how rarely they win), and value favorites too little (given how often they win). Because of this pattern, bettors could increase their expected winnings by always betting on the favorites (which are underpriced given that so few people bet on them).

Snowberg and Wolfers (2010) study the data on all 6.4 million horse race starts in the United States from 1992 to 2001. With this evidence they find that probability weighting can accurately predict the favorite-longshot bias. Provide an intuitive explanation for how such nonstandard preferences could explain this anomaly.

Exercise 12.11 — Prizing Patients. [Health] Suppose that you want to test the effectiveness of using lotteries to incentivize patients to adhere to their prescribed medication regimen (e.g., Volpp, Loewenstein, et al. (2008) examine patient adherence to blood clot medication). Explain how you would ideally design an experiment to evaluate such an intervention.

Exercise 12.12 — Maxmin-ing the Two-Urn Ellsberg Paradox. Maxine has preferences represented by the maxmin expected utility model. She is faced with the Two-Urn Ellsberg paradox described in Exercise 11.7.

a   Most people prefer bet *B* over *A*. What does Maxine choose?
b   Most people prefer bet *D* over *C*. What does Maxine choose?

Exercise 12.13 — Maxmin-ing the Four-Color Ellsberg Paradox. Maxine has preferences represented by the maxmin expected utility model. She is faced with the Four-Color Ellsberg paradox described in Exercise 11.8.

a   Does Maxine choose bet *A* or *B*?
b   Does Maxine choose bet *C* or *D*?

Exercise 12.14 — When Trade Breaks Down (Dow and Werlang 1992). Suppose there is a risky financial asset that pays a return of either \$100 or \$0. The asset's current price is *P*. Traders evaluate whether to buy the asset, short-sell it, or neither, based on their subjective probability, p, with which they believe the asset will yield a positive return. By buying the asset, a trader pays *P* and expects to receive a payoff of \$100 with probability p. By short-selling the asset, a trader receives *P*, but expects to pay \$100 with probability p. Assume that all traders have initial wealth of zero and evaluate their wealth with utility function $u(x) = x$.

a   Sarah has standard expected utility preferences. She believes the asset will yield a positive return with probability p^*.

   i   Determine the range of prices *P* for which Sarah will prefer to buy than do nothing. Your answer should depend on p^*.
   ii   Now determine the range of prices *P* for which Sarah will prefer to short-sell than do nothing. Again, your answer should depend on p^*.
   iii   Is there any price *P* for which Sarah wants to neither buy nor short-sell the asset? Explain.

b   Max has maxmin expected utility preferences. He believes there is a range of possible probabilities with which the asset will yield a positive return, from a low probability p_L to a high probability p_H.

   i   Determine the range of prices *P* for which Max will prefer to buy than do nothing. Your answer should depend on p_L or p_H.
   ii   Now determine the range of prices *P* for which Max will prefer to short-sell than do nothing. Again, your answer should depend on p_L or p_H.

iii Is there any price P for which Max wants to neither buy nor short-sell asset? Explain.

Notes

1 The idea of using decision weights in place of objective probabilities predates prospect theory, as evidenced by work in psychology, e.g., Edwards (1962).

2 A prominent approach introduced by Quiggin (1982) and further developed by Tversky and Kahneman (1992) assumes that decision weights depend on the probability weighting function $\pi(\cdot)$ applied to *cumulative* probabilities. See O'Donoghue and Sprenger (2018, Sec. 8) for an excellent discussion of these differing models of decision weights.

3 To understand the role of concavity in the example, observe that with $v(\cdot)$ concave, the ray from the origin to the point $(5, v(5))$ must be steeper than the ray from the origin to the point $(5000, v(5000))$. And the slopes of each ray are $v(5)/5$ and $v(5000)/5000$. Therefore, $v(5)/5 > v(5000)/5000$ and rearranging generates the desired inequality.

4 The home insurance calculations assume that losses always exceed \$1,000. If some losses are less than \$1,000, then the \$500 deductible is worth even less and individuals save less than \$21.50.

5 Sydnor (2010) considers and rejects a range of alternative explanations for the high willingness to pay for low deductible policies. They include liquidity constraints, overestimation, menu effects, and the role of sales agents.

6 An alternative explanation for lottery participation by standard risk averse consumers is that individuals receive sufficient enjoyment or entertainment from the act of playing the lottery to compensate them for the expected negative financial return.

7 There exist alternative models that similarly predict the overpricing of highly skewed return distributions (see e.g., Brunnermeier and Parker 2005; Brunnermeier, Gollier, and Parker 2007; Mitton and Vorkink 2007).

8 Barberis and Huang (2008) discuss how probability weighting can help to reconcile a range of additional puzzles in asset pricing, beyond IPO returns.

9 Prospect theory preferences can also be exploited by profit-maximizing firms (e.g., Azevedo and Gottlieb 2012).

10 Volpp, John, et al. (2008) include an additional treatment group to leverage possible loss aversion.

11 There are also models of ambiguity aversion that deviate more dramatically from the expected utility form and make use of insights from prospect theory (see e.g., Tversky and Fox 1995; Tversky and Koehler 1994; Chew and Sagi 2008; Abdellaoui et al. 2011).

12 Studies that explore the role of ambiguity aversion in explaining the non-participation puzzle include Bossaerts et al. (2010), Cao, Wang, and Zhang (2005), Dow and Werlang (1992), Easley and O'Hara (2009), and Epstein and Schneider (2010).

References

Abdellaoui, Mohammed, Aurélien Baillon, Laetitia Placido, and Peter P. Wakker. 2011. "The Rich Domain of Uncertainty: Source Functions and Their Experimental Implementation." *American Economic Review* 101 (2): 695–723. doi:10.1257/aer. 101.2.695.

Anantanasuwong, Kanin, Roy Kouwenberg, Olivia S. Mitchell, and Kim Peijnenberg. 2019. "Ambiguity Attitudes about Investments: Evidence from the Field." NBER Working Paper 25561. Cambridge, MA: National Bureau of Economic Research. doi:10.3386/w25561.

Azevedo, Eduardo M., and Daniel Gottlieb. 2012. "Risk-Neutral Firms Can Extract Unbounded Profits from Consumers with Prospect Theory Preferences." *Journal of Economic Theory* 147 (3): 1291–1299. doi:10.1016/j.jet.2012.01.002.

Bali, Turan G., Nusret Cakici, and Robert F. Whitelaw. 2011. "Maxing Out: Stocks as Lotteries and the Cross-Section of Expected Returns." *Journal of Financial Economics* 99 (2): 427–446. doi:10.1016/j.jfineco.2010.08.014.

Barberis, Nicholas, and Ming Huang. 2008. "Stocks as Lotteries: The Implications of Probability Weighting for Security Prices." *American Economic Review* 98 (5): 2066–2100. doi:10.1257/aer.98.5.2066.

Benartzi, Shlomo. 2001. "Excessive Extrapolation and the Allocation of 401 (k) Accounts to Company Stock." *The Journal of Finance* 56 (5): 1747–1764. doi:10.1111/0022-1082.00388.

Bossaerts, Peter, Paolo Ghirardato, Serena Guarnaschelli, and William R. Zame. 2010. "Ambiguity in Asset Markets: Theory and Experiment." *The Review of Financial Studies* 23 (4): 1325–1359. doi:10.1093/rfs/hhp106.

Boyle, Phelim, Lorenzo Garlappi, Raman Uppal, and Tan Wang. 2012. "Keynes Meets Markowitz: The Trade-Off Between Familiarity and Diversification." *Management Science* 58 (2): 253–272. doi:10.1287/mnsc.1110.1349.

Brunnermeier, Markus K., Christian Gollier, and Jonathan A. Parker. 2007. "Optimal Beliefs, Asset Prices, and the Preference for Skewed Returns." *American Economic Review* 97 (2): 159–165. doi:10.1257/aer.97.2.159.

Brunnermeier, Markus K., and Jonathan A. Parker. 2005. "Optimal Expectations." *American Economic Review* 95 (4): 1092–1118. doi:10.1257/0002828054825493.

Bryan, Gharad. 2019. "Ambiguity Aversion Decreases the Impact of Partial Insurance: Evidence from African Farmers." *Journal of the European Economic Association* 17 (5): 1428–1469. doi:10.1093/jeea/jvy056.

Cao, H. Henry, Bing Han, David Hirshleifer, and Harold H. Zhang. 2011. "Fear of the Unknown: Familiarity and Economic Decisions." *Review of Finance* 15 (1): 173–206. doi:10.1093/rof/rfp023.

Cao, H. Henry, Tan Wang, and Harold H. Zhang. 2005. "Model Uncertainty, Limited Market Participation, and Asset Prices." *The Review of Financial Studies* 18 (4): 1219–1251. doi:10.1093/rfs/hhi034.

Chew, Soo Hong, and Jacob S. Sagi. 2008. "Small Worlds: Modeling Attitudes toward Sources of Uncertainty." *Journal of Economic Theory* 139 (1): 1–24. doi:10.1016/j.jet.2007.07.004.

Collard, Fabrice, Sujoy Mukerji, Kevin Sheppard, and Jean-Marc Tallon. 2018. "Ambiguity and the Historical Equity Premium." *Quantitative Economics* 9 (2): 945–993. doi:10.3982/QE708.

Dimmock, Stephen G., Roy Kouwenberg, Olivia S. Mitchell, and Kim Peijnenburg. 2016. "Ambiguity Aversion and Household Portfolio Choice Puzzles: Empirical Evidence." *Journal of Financial Economics* 119 (3). 559 577. doi:10.1016/j.jfineco. 2016.01.003.

Dow, James, and Sérgio Ribeiro da Costa Werlang. 1992. "Uncertainty Aversion, Risk Aversion, and the Optimal Choice of Portfolio." *Econometrica* 60 (1): 197–204. doi:10.2307/2951685.

Easley, David, and Maureen O'Hara. 2009. "Ambiguity and Nonparticipation: The Role of Regulation." *The Review of Financial Studies* 22 (5): 1817–1843. doi:10.1093/rfs/hhn100.

Edwards, Ward. 1962. "Subjective Probabilities Inferred from Decisions." *Psychological Review* 69 (2): 109–135. doi:10.1037/h0038674.

Ellsberg, Daniel. 1961. "Risk, Ambiguity, and the Savage Axioms." *The Quarterly Journal of Economics* 75 (4): 643–669. doi:10.2307/1884324.

Epstein, Larry G., and Martin Schneider. 2010. "Ambiguity and Asset Markets." *Annual Review of Financial Economics* 2 (1): 315–346. doi:10.1146/annurev-financial-120209-133940.

French, Kenneth R., and James M. Poterba. 1991. "Investor Diversification and International Equity Markets." *American Economic Review* 81 (2): 222–226. https://www.jstor.org/stable/2006858.

Gilboa, Itzhak, and David Schmeidler. 1989. "Maxmin Expected Utility with Non-unique Prior." *Journal of Mathematical Economics* 18 (2): 141–153. doi:10.1016/0304-4068(89)90018-9.

Green, T. Clifton, and Byoung-Hyoun Hwang. 2012. "Initial Public Offerings as Lotteries: Skewness Preference and First-Day Returns." *Management Science* 58 (2): 432–444. doi:10.1287/mnsc.1110.1431.

Griffith, R. M. 1949. "Odds Adjustments by American Horse-Race Bettors." *American Journal of Psychology* 62 (2): 290–294. doi:10.2307/1418469.

Heaton, John, and Deborah Lucas. 1997. "Market Frictions, Savings Behavior, and Portfolio Choice." *Macroeconomic Dynamics* 1 (1): 76–101. doi:10.1017/S1365100597002034.

Huberman, Gur. 2001. "Familiarity Breeds Investment." *The Review of Financial Studies* 14 (3): 659–680. doi:10.1093/rfs/14.3.659.

Isidore, Chris. 2015. "Americans Spend more on the Lottery than on …" *CNNMoney*, February 11, 2015. https://money.cnn.com/2015/02/11/news/companies/lottery-spending/index.html.

Ju, Nengjiu, and Jianjun Miao. 2012. "Ambiguity, Learning, and Asset Returns." *Econometrica* 80 (2): 559–591. doi:10.3982/ECTA7618.

Kahneman, Daniel, and Amos Tversky. 1979. "Prospect Theory: An Analysis of Decision under Risk." *Econometrica* 47 (2): 263–291. doi:10.2307/1914185.

Kearney, Melissa S., Peter Tufano, Erik Hurst, and Jonathan Guryan. 2011. "Making Savings Fun: An Overview of Prize-Linked Savings." In *Financial Literacy: Implications for Retirement Security and the Financial Marketplace,* edited by Olivia Mitchell and Ammamaria Lusardi. Oxford: Oxford University Press.

Machina, Mark J., and Marciano Siniscalchi. 2014. "Ambiguity and Ambiguity Aversion." In *Handbook of the Economics of Risk and Uncertainty,* vol. 1. North-Holland.

Maenhout, Pascal J. 2004. "Robust Portfolio Rules and Asset Pricing." *The Review of Financial Studies* 17 (4): 951–983. doi:10.1093/rfs/hhh003.

Merton, Robert C. 1969. "Lifetime Portfolio Selection under Uncertainty: The Continuous-Time Case." *The Review of Economics and Statistics* 51 (3): 247–257. doi:10.2307/1926560.

Mitton, Todd, and Keith Vorkink. 2007. "Equilibrium Underdiversification and the Preference for Skewness." *The Review of Financial Studies* 20 (4): 1255–1288. doi:10.1093/revfin/hhm011.

O'Donoghue, Ted, and Charles Sprenger. 2018. "Reference-Dependent Preferences." In *Handbook of Behavioral Economics: Foundations and Applications,* edited by B. Douglas Bernheim, Stefano Della-Vigna, and David Laibson, 1:1–77. North-Holland.

Quiggin, John. 1982. "A Theory of Anticipated Utility." *Journal of Economic Behavior & Organization* 3 (4): 323–343. doi:10.1016/0167-2681(82)90008-7.

Rabin, Matthew. 2000. "Risk Aversion and Expected-Utility Theory: A Calibration Theorem." *Econometrica* 68 (5): 1281–1292. doi:10.1111/1468-0262.00158.

Ritter, Jay R. 1991. "The Long-Run Performance of Initial Public Offerings." *The Journal of Finance* 46 (1): 3–27. doi:10.1111/j.1540-6261.1991.tb03743.x.

Seasholes, Mark S., and Ning Zhu. 2010. "Individual Investors and Local Bias." *The Journal of Finance* 65 (5): 1987–2010. doi:10.1111/j.1540-6261.2010. 01600.x.

Snowberg, Erik, and Justin Wolfers. 2010. "Explaining the Favorite–Long Shot Bias: Is It Risk-Love or Misperceptions?" *Journal of Political Economy* 118 (4): 723–746. doi:10.1086/655844.

Sydnor, Justin. 2010. "(Over)insuring Modest Risks." *American Economic Journal: Applied Economics* 2 (4): 177–199. doi:10.1257/app.2.4.177.

Tversky, Amos, and Craig R. Fox. 1995. "Weighing Risk and Uncertainty." *Psychological Review* 102 (2): 269–283. doi:10.1037/0033-295X.102.2.269.

Tversky, Amos, and Daniel Kahneman. 1992. "Advances in Prospect Theory: Cumulative Representation of Uncertainty." *Journal of Risk and Uncertainty* 5 (4): 297–323. doi:10.1007/BF00122574.

Tversky, Amos, and Derek J. Koehler. 1994. "Support Theory: A Nonextensional Representation of Subjective Probability." *Psychological Review* 101 (4): 547–567. doi:10.1037/0033-295X.101.4.547.

US Census Bureau. 2019. *2017 Annual Survey of State Government Finances Tables.* Accessed November 26, 2019, https://www.census.gov/data/tables/2017/econ/state/historical-tables.html.

Volpp, Kevin G., Leslie K. John, Andrea B. Troxel, Laurie Norton, Jennifer Fassbender, and George Loewenstein. 2008. "Financial Incentive-Based Approaches for Weight Loss: A Randomized Trial." *JAMA* 300 (22): 2631–2637. doi:10.1001/jama. 2008.804.

Volpp, Kevin G., George Loewenstein, Andrea B. Troxel, Jalpa Doshi, Maureen Price, Mitchell Laskin, and Stephen E. Kimmel. 2008. "A Test of Financial Incentives to Improve Warfarin Adherence." *BMC Health Services Research* 8 (1): 272. doi:10.1186/1472-6963-8-272.

Wolff, Edward N. 2017. "Household Wealth Trends in the United States, 1962 to 2016: Has Middle Class Wealth Recovered?" NBER Working Paper 24085. Cambridge, MA: National Bureau of Economic Research. doi:10.3386/w24085.

Part V

Social Preferences

A standard assumption in the model of individual decision making (Definition 2.9) is that preferences are purely self-interested. That is, individual behaviors are motivated only by how they impact one's own private payoffs. The outcomes for others are not relevant. Such self-interested preferences are featured in the standard model by the *absence* of anyone else's outcomes in the utility function $u(\cdot)$, highlighted below:

$$\max_{(x_0, x_1, \ldots, x_T) \in X} \sum_{k=0}^{T} \delta^k E[\, \boxed{u(x_k)} \mid p] \qquad \text{(Standard Model)}$$

The objective of Part V is to question the assumption that self-interest alone is sufficient for understanding economic behaviors and social outcomes, and to instead consider alternative models of social preferences. Social preferences are those that deviate from pure self-interest by taking into account the payoffs, actions, or beliefs of others in society besides the self. To focus the analysis, we maintain the other standard assumptions that individuals are discounted expected utility maximizers with accurate beliefs.

Part V is organized as follows. Chapter 13 illustrates the seemingly non-self-interested behaviors of individuals in the field and in lab games. Given this evidence, Chapter 14 introduces nonstandard models of social preferences that can help explain otherwise anomalous behaviors. And Chapter 15 explores the market and policy responses to individuals with social preferences. Applications include labor markets, voting, and public finance.

13 Self-Interested Preference Anomalies

Learning Objectives

★ Appreciate how self-interest can explain seemingly non-self-interested behaviors.

★ Consider the limitations of self-interest as the only motivation for philanthropy and tipping.

★ Compare the predictions of self-interested preferences in dictator, ultimatum, and public good games with empirical evidence.

★ Hypothesize alternative motivations for altruism, generosity, and cooperation beyond self-interest.

We humans, as social creatures, are generous in a multitude of ways. We donate our time, money, and bodies (e.g., blood, kidneys, eggs, sperm) to benefit our families, communities, and those we may never meet. Even the effort of kindness in daily interactions with others reflects a spirit of generosity. Given the standard assumption that individuals have self-interested preferences and therefore make decisions with regard to only their own interest, how can we make sense of such seemingly altruistic behaviors?

One possible answer is that what looks like altruism, generosity, and self-sacrifice is in fact just self-interest in disguise. Although there are multiple theories for this hypothesis, the unifying idea is that altruism is in one's self-interest when the immediate cost of being generous is outweighed by a future benefit. From an evolutionary perspective, humans (and organisms more generally) may find it beneficial to help relatives if doing so promotes the success of the family (Hamilton 1964). Or in the context of a repeated interaction, an individual may exhibit generosity towards another with the expectation that it will be returned in kind (Trivers 1971). And more broadly, groups may be able to induce generous behaviors by adopting punishments or sanctions for members who fail to conform to the group norms (Boyd and Richerson 1992). Together, these theories suggest that self-interested people, embedded in long-run strategic interactions, can exhibit apparently non-self-interested behaviors (see e.g., Bowles and Gintis 2008).

But generosity exists even when there is no reasonable expectation of a future reward or punishment. The last time you visited a coffee shop, rode in a cab, or ate at a restaurant, you probably left a tip for someone you will never meet again. And you have likely

DOI: 10.4324/9780367854072-18

given money to a charitable cause, even if only a modest amount, that benefits people you will never meet at all.

In this chapter we review evidence of generous behaviors that are not so neatly explained away by purely self-interested motivations. We begin with observational evidence from the field, focusing on two major forms of generosity: philanthropy and tipping. In the second half of the chapter we turn to evidence from experimental settings in the lab. The advantage of lab games is that it is possible to plausibly eliminate the self-interested incentives for generosity. And the fact that individuals still demonstrate generosity towards others in these settings suggests that the assumption of self-interest is inadequate. Motivated by this evidence, alternative theories are taken up and assessed in Chapter 14.

13.1   Giving in the Field

Let's begin with evidence of some familiar behaviors that are difficult to reconcile with self-interest alone.

13.1.1   *Philanthropy*   *[Public Finance]*

Americans donate over $400 billion to charities each year (Giving USA 2019), with similar giving patterns throughout the income distribution. Both the rich and poor donate almost 2% of their income, and give most generously to houses of worship and charities that provide basic needs (Meer and Priday 2020). And although the nonprofit sector in the US is more reliant on philanthropy than in other countries, there are high rates of giving in countries around the world (Andreoni 2006).

Is it possible for such generous philanthropic giving to be a consequence of self-interested preferences? Imagine that you are motivated only by self-interest. It does not follow that you must never give to charity. For instance, you might donate money to support a local public radio station that plays music and news you enjoy. Or, knowing that you are at high risk for breast cancer, you might donate to a breast cancer research center, with the intention that you may someday benefit from new treatments or therapies funded in part by your gift. You might also volunteer your time to plant trees in your neighborhood, which has the effect of increasing the price of your house. And you might only sign up to be an organ donor if doing so gives you priority in the event that you need an organ transplant in the future (Stoler et al. 2017). In each of these cases, your giving yields a private benefit, and is therefore consistent with self-interest.

But these examples clearly do not exhaust the full scope of charitable giving. Some give to help alleviate poverty for those in distant countries they will never visit. Others donate to environmental causes to protect lands, oceans, and animals they will never encounter. And for those who leave bequests to future generations, their gifts are received by individuals who have yet to be born. Giving of this form is more challenging to reconcile with self-interest.

How might we modify the standard model to better explain the motivations for philanthropy without private benefit? Individuals may give because they are altruistic, exhibiting a selfless concern for the well-being of others. Or they may derive fulfillment from the act of helping others. Alternatively, individuals may give only because of social pressure to do so. We explore the evidence for such possibilities in the next chapter.

13.1.2   Tipping   *[Industrial Organization]*

Almost $40 billion in tips is given annually in the US (Shierholz et al. 2017). And while this is an order of magnitude smaller than charitable giving, it is likely a more regular part of your daily life. Tips are paid to workers across a wide range of professions: 33 service professions, in fact, according to one account (Lynn, Zinkhan, and Harris 1993). Although there is uncertainty about the precise origins of tipping, from the Roman Empire to the Middle Ages and Tudor England, tipping is clearly an enduring and widespread social phenomenon (Azar 2004). It is also culturally specific; travel guides typically provide information to would-be tourists about appropriate tipping conventions for restaurants, bars, taxis, hotel housekeepers, and the like.

Let's once again ask, as we did with philanthropy, whether it is possible that tipping is predicted by standard self-interested preferences. Imagine that you have such preferences and are dining in a restaurant at which you are a regular customer. Not leaving a tip has the clear benefit of reducing the cost of your dining experience. But there is another factor that you may care about in addition to the money in your pocket: the quality of the service. Ideally, the restaurant manager would provide the appropriate incentives for your server to work hard (e.g., promotions for excellence and demotions or dismissal for low performance). But because you, as the customer, more directly observe the service quality, your tip can act as a bonus to incentivize good service. This logic presumes that you and the server meet repeatedly, allowing the server to learn how the magnitude of the tip they receive from you depends on their efforts. In sum, tipping is not necessarily inconsistent with self-interest if its effect is to buy high-quality service.[1]

A key prediction of the tipping model with standard consumers is that better service leads to higher tips. While there is a wide body of empirical evidence to support this prediction, the magnitude of the effect is modest (Azar 2007). Because tips do not vary much with service quality, there is little incentive for servers to provide excellent service. This in turn means that there is little incentive for customers to tip at all. And yet tipping persists.

Recall that the logic in the preceding scenario depends on repeated interactions between a customer and a waiter. For a self-interested customer eating at a restaurant to which they never intend to return, there is no longer any rationale for leaving a tip. Tipping is financially costly and there is no opportunity to develop a relational contract with the server where bad service is punished with a lower tip. We would therefore expect repeat customers to tip more than one-time customers. Contrary to this prediction, there is evidence that tips vary little between repeat and one-time customers (Bodvarsson and Gibson 1997; Kahneman, Knetsch, and Thaler 1986).[2] Once again, we have good reason to doubt that self-interest alone can explain tipping behaviors.

Reflect on your own motivations, beyond self-interest, for tipping. Perhaps you tip out of a sense of fairness, helping to compensate workers who rely on tips as a primary source of income. Or tipping may be a way to avoid deviating from accepted social norms of what is expected. We consider these nonstandard motivations in the next chapter.

13.2   Giving in the Lab

The fact that many people give to charities and tip their baristas is suggestive of motivations beyond self-interest. But a skeptical economist might not yet be convinced that this observational evidence constitutes an anomaly for the standard model.

How might you convince such a skeptic? One strategy is to consider controlled settings where individuals have every incentive to act in their own self-interest. In particular, we would like to know how people give when their (possibly) selfish behavior cannot be sanctioned by others. Such an environment can be artificially constructed with an anonymized lab experiment.

In this section we consider three classic games played by participants in lab experiments: the dictator game, ultimatum game, and public good game. In each game we find evidence that a non-trivial share of the players exhibit generosity, even when there is no private benefit in doing so. Such lab experiments, of course, are not without their own methodological drawbacks (see Section 1.4.3). But taken together with the observational evidence from the field, it becomes more difficult to maintain the position that self-interest alone drives our economic lives.

13.2.1   Dictator Game

The **dictator game** is so simple it is barely a game. The following lab experiment describes a standard version of this game (see Kahneman, Knetsch, and Thaler (1986) for the first iteration).

Lab Experiment — Dictator Game (Forsythe et al. 1994)

Among a group of participants, half are randomly assigned to the role of proposer (i.e., the dictator). Each proposer is matched to a receiver, but neither the proposer nor the receiver knows with whom they are matched. Proposers are each given $10 and must decide how much of the $10 to gift to their matched receiver. Proposers keep any money that they do not gift. The game then ends.

Forsythe et al. (1994) find that 64% of proposers gift a positive (non-zero) amount.

Why is the outcome of the dictator game so surprising? With standard self-interested preferences, proposers have no incentive to give away any money. The anonymity of the dictator game eliminates any motivation to enjoy social acclaim for generosity or avoid criticism for selfishness. And yet, the majority of subjects gift a share of their money. Therefore, participants likely consider some notions of fairness or equity when making their decisions.

The simplicity of the dictator game has inspired a multitude of variations. Researchers have compared one-shot versus repeated versions of the game, student participants versus non-student participants, earned versus unearned money to split, and small versus large monetary stakes. By 2011, there were 129 published studies on the dictator game, including over 600 different variations (Engel 2011). Consistent with the evidence from the early lab experiment above, Engel (2011) finds that across this large literature 64% of proposers give something and 30% give at least half to the receiver. Incredibly, over 5% of proposers give practically everything away. This distribution of generosity is illustrated in Figure 13.1. For an alternative summary measure of generosity, note that on average, proposers keep 72% of the initial stake for themself.

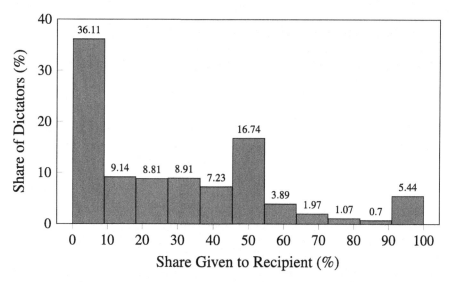

Figure 13.1 Distribution of Giving Generosity in Dictator Games

Data Source: Engel (2011).

Researchers have also explored the extent to which the variation in giving behavior is correlated with demographic characteristics of the participants. For instance, non-students give more than students, women give more than men, the old give more than the young, and people from indigenous societies are more likely to split the money evenly than those from developed Western societies. There are no measured differences by race (Engel 2011). This evidence suggests that preferences towards giving are not universal, but instead can possibly be shaped by education, social roles, and cultural differences.

13.2.2 Ultimatum Game

Let's now consider the **ultimatum game**, which is similar in structure to the dictator game, but with an important twist: namely, the introduction of an ultimatum.[3]

Lab Experiment — Ultimatum Game (Fehr and Schmidt 1999)

Among a group of participants, half are randomly assigned to the role of proposer. Each proposer is matched to a responder, but neither the proposer nor the responder knows with whom they are matched. Proposers are each given an amount of money (known to all) and must decide what share of the money to offer to their matched responder. Responders, upon receiving an offer, have one of two options:

1   Accept the offer; or
2   Reject the offer, in which case both the proposer and responder receive nothing.
Payments, if applicable, are then made and the game ends.

In a survey of the experimental evidence Fehr and Schmidt (1999) find the following four regularities:

1	Proposers almost never offer more than 50%
2	Proposers typically offer between 40% and 50%
3	Proposers almost never offer less than 20%
4	Responders frequently reject offers below 30%

Observe that the proposer in this game can no longer dictate the final outcome. Instead of facing a passive receiver, the proposer makes an ultimatum, which a responder has the option to reject. But unlike a more real-world bargaining situation where a rejection is followed by a counteroffer, here rejection ends the game and destroys the payoffs to both parties.

Before we discuss the evidence, let's first think through the logic of this game under the assumption that participants care only about the money they earn in the game and nothing else. We reason backwards, beginning with the decision faced by a responder. Because any positive amount of money is better than no money, the responder should accept all positive offers. The proposer anticipates this response and should therefore offer very little, perhaps $1, so as to keep the most for herself.[4]

But the actual evidence from the ultimatum game contradicts this theoretical prediction. Instead of offering close to nothing, proposers typically offer just under 50%. Perhaps proposers are so generous because they care about the material well-being of their partner, as suggested by the dictator game. Alternatively, proposer generosity may simply be a self-interested response to an accurate expectation that responders will reject low offers. That is, to avoid getting nothing, proposers choose to offer enough to guarantee that the responders accept. The real puzzle, then, is why responders so frequently reject low, but positive offers. They are never made worse off by accepting an offer, and still they reject.

The ultimatum game evidence is robust across studies from multiple countries and with monetary stakes both large and small. It presents a challenge to the assumption of self-interest, at least for the responders. Consider why you might reject an offer of $10 when you know the proposer keeps $90. What motivations would lead you to turn down $10 for $0? We explore some possible explanations in the following chapter.

13.2.3 *Public Good Game*

We conclude this chapter with one final classic game in economics: the public good game. A **public good** is a special type of good that is available for everyone (i.e., the public) to consume.[5] Canonical examples include national defense, lighthouses, national parks, fireworks displays, and mosquito abatement. In each case, everyone can equally enjoy the benefits of the good.

Individuals in a private market are generally predicted to provide too few public goods relative to what is socially optimal (Samuelson 1954). This underprovision arises because of the **free rider problem**: people would prefer to let others pay for the public good and still enjoy the benefits for free. But the prediction of free riding is conditional on the standard assumption that individuals are purely self-interested. The free rider problem would be mitigated if individuals were motivated to contribute for other reasons. We would therefore like to know empirically the degree to which people actually free ride. To answer this question in a controlled environment, economists have turned to lab settings where participants decide how much to personally contribute to a good that benefits everyone. A standard **public good game** is our next lab experiment.

Lab Experiment — Public Good Game

Five participants, anonymous to each other, are each given 10 tokens. Each token they keep for themself is worth $1. And for every token they contribute towards a common fund, the participants each earn $0.50. The common fund mimics a public good since a private contribution is costly, but everyone equally benefits.

Participants make their decisions simultaneously. The monetary payoff depends on both an individual's own contribution to the common fund and that of the other participants. This game can be played once or repeated multiple times.

Researchers have documented similar behaviors in the public good game across a variety of settings. The game can be modified by changing the number of players in a group, the value of the tokens, and the ability of players to communicate with each other before the game starts. Across these variations, the following regularities emerge:

1   Participants contribute 40%–60% of their resources to the public good in a one-shot game (Marwell and Ames 1981) and in the early rounds of a repeated game (Fehr and Schmidt 1999).
2   Participants contribute less to the public good as the game is repeated (Isaac, McCue, and Plott 1985; Ledyard 1995).
3   In the final period of a repeated game, 73% of participants contribute nothing to the public good (Fehr and Schmidt 1999).

To understand the implications of the above evidence, consider first the problem facing a participant in the final round of a (one-shot or repeated) public good game. Each token that she keeps for herself generates $1. While each token that she gives to the common fund/public good generates only $0.50 for herself. If she is concerned only with her monetary payoff, then she would therefore not contribute anything to the public good. Applying this logic to every player, the common fund would collect nothing — i.e., maximal free riding — and each individual would earn $10.

But participants do not always free ride in the public good game. Participants typically contribute about half of their tokens in the one-shot game. What is each player's payoff if everyone contributes half of their 10 tokens to the public good? The common fund then has 25 tokens (5 players × 5 tokens/player), each of which pays out $0.50 to *every* participant. That is, each participant makes $12.50 from the public good, plus the $5 in tokens they keep, for a total of $17.50. Although this is better than earning only $10, each player still has an incentive to contribute nothing. By letting the four other players contribute 5 tokens each, a player who keeps all 10 tokens for herself could make $10 + \$0.50 \times 20$ common fund tokens $= \$20$. The puzzle therefore remains; no matter how generous or not the other players are, a player always maximizes her own monetary payoff by giving nothing to the public good.

This evidence, which has also been corroborated outside lab settings (List 2004), calls into question the underlying assumption of pure self-interest. People must have some other motivations for public good contributions, even if doing so lowers their own payoff.

What are we to make of the evidence that public good contributions tend to fall as the game is repeated? One conjecture is that the most generous contributors to the public good at the start of the game do so out of a concern for fairness or kindness to others. But as they observe the less generous contributions of the other participants, they become discouraged or angry. And in response, they seek to "punish" the free riders by decreasing their own public good contributions in subsequent rounds. This logic is also consistent with the low level of public good contributions in the last round of a repeated game.

Fehr and Gächter (2000) find supporting evidence for this hypothesis in a modified public good game that introduces a punishment phase after each round. That is, after observing the contributions of the other players, each player has the option to reduce the earnings of any other player. But doing so is costly for the punisher. With purely self-interested preferences, the opportunity to punish should not change the game. It is in the best interest of participants to still contribute nothing to the public good and never spend money on punishment. Contrary to this prediction, the authors find that participants punish those players who deviate the most from the average contributions of the group. And moreover, this punishment is effective at sustaining public good contribution rates in excess of 80% (out of 20 tokens per participant per round). As illustrated in Figure 13.2, when the punishment phase is removed after ten rounds of the game, free riding once again increases.

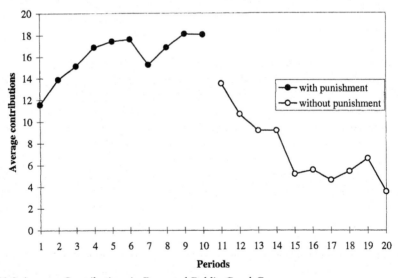

Figure 13.2 Average Contributions in Repeated Public Good Game

Source: Fehr and Gächter (2000). Copyright American Economic Association; reproduced with permission of the *American Economic Review*.

The fact that individuals are willing to give up money by contributing to a public good or by punishing another player, when self-interest predicts otherwise, further motivates the work of the next chapter. In it, we consider a variety of alternatives to the standard model of self-interested preferences.

13.3   Summary

1   Some forms of philanthropy can be consistent with self-interest.
2   Evidence on tipping behavior suggests that self-interest alone is an inadequate explanation.
3   The majority of participants in the **dictator game** give money to strangers.
4   In the **ultimatum game** proposers typically split the total money almost evenly and responders often reject low positive offers.
5   The assumption of self-interest predicts that **public goods** will be underprovided relative to the social optimum because of the **free rider problem**.
6   **Public good games** reveal that participants free ride less than is predicted by standard preferences. And cooperation can be sustained with the ability to punish those who free ride the most.

13.4   Exercises

Exercise 13.1 — Present Time. People spend hundreds of dollars on holiday gifts each year.[6]

a   In what contexts might gift-giving be predicted by self-interest?
b   For what reasons, other than self-interest, might individuals choose to give holiday gifts?

Exercise 13.2 — Tip Drivers. [Industrial Organization] Chandar et al. (2019) study private tipping behavior in ride-shares across a sample of over 40 million Uber trips in the United States during a single month in 2017. They find that 16% of rides are tipped, 60% of riders never tip, and 1% of riders tip on every trip. Do these facts provide support for or against the standard assumption that individuals have self-interested preferences? Explain.

Exercise 13.3 — Cultural Offerings. [Household] Henrich et al. (2001) study how participants play the ultimatum game in 15 small-scale societies across 12 countries on five continents. Consider the following summary evidence from two of the societies:

Society (Country)	Offer (as a Proportion)		Rejection Rate
	Average	Most Common	
Lamalera (Indonesia)	0.58	63% offer 0.5	20%
Gnau (Papua New Guinea)	0.38	32% offer 0.4	40%

a   Are the behaviors of the Lamalera and Gnau predicted by the standard model of self-interested preferences? Explain.
b   Consider the following brief background information:

- For the whale hunting Lamalera "a large catch, always the product of cooperation among many individual whalers, is meticulously divided into predesignated parts and carefully distributed among the members of the community" (Gintis et al. 2003, 159).
- For the Gnau, accepting a gift generates an obligation to reciprocate.

Discuss how the behaviors in the ultimatum game reflect the cultural and/or economic features of each society.

Exercise 13.4 — Fair Competitions. The standard ultimatum game is a game between two players. In this exercise we consider the following two variations to this standard set-up with three players:

- *Responder Competition:* There are two responders to the offer made by the single proposer. Each responder independently decides whether to accept or reject the proposer's offer. If both responders reject the offer, then everyone earns zero. If exactly one responder accepts the offer, only that responder receives the offer. And if both responders accept, a coin flip determines which responder receives the offer.
- *Proposer Competition:* There are two proposers who independently make offers to a single responder. The responder can accept one or neither of the offers, in which case everyone earns zero. The responder cannot accept both offers.

a   Assume that all players have standard self-interested preferences. In this case, for both the responder and proposer competition, provide a prediction for whether offers will be high or low. *Hint: Remember to reason backwards, starting first with the decision for the responder(s).*

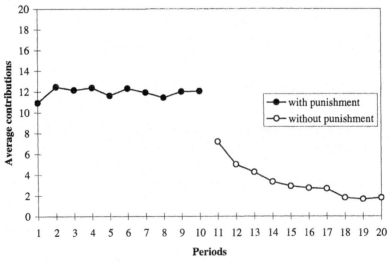

Figure 13.3 Average Contributions in Repeated Public Good Game with Changing Group Composition in Exercise 13.5

Source: Fehr and Gächter (2000). Copyright American Economic Association; reproduced with permission of the *American Economic Review*.

b   Fischbacher, Fong, and Fehr (2009) study these ultimatum games in a set of lab experiments. They find that the average accepted offer in the standard two-person ultimatum game is 43% of the total pie available to split. But with responder competition the average accepted offer is 26% of the pie and with proposer competition the average accepted offer is 68%. Does the competition induced by adding an additional player to the game lead to behaviors that are closer to, or further from, the self-interested predictions in part (a)? Interpret.

Exercise 13.5 — Time and Punishment. Figure 13.2 illustrates the average contributions to the common fund in a public good game repeated 20 times. Recall that after each of the first 10 rounds, players have the ability impose a costly punishment on other players. The ability to punish is removed for the last 10 rounds. In addition, the participants, whose identities are unknown to each other, play with the same group of players in every round.

Fehr and Gächter (2000) also study a variation of this game that is identical in every respect except that now the participants are randomly matched with a different group of players in each of the 20 rounds. The average contributions to the common fund in this variation of the public good game are illustrated in Figure 13.3.

a   Compare Figures 13.2 and 13.3. How does changing the group's composition across rounds impact the average generosity to funding the public good?
b   Provide an interpretation for your observations in part (a).

Notes

1 For theoretical models of tipping as an implicit service contract with standard consumers see Ben-Zion and Karni (1977), Jacob and Page (1980), and Sisk and Gallick (1985).
2 Lynn and McCall (2000) and Conlin, Lynn, and O'Donoghue (2003) find that tips increase with patronage frequency.
3 Gäth, Schmittberger, and Schwarze (1982) provide the first experimental evidence of the ultimatum game.
4 The ultimatum game with self-interested players has a unique (subgame perfect) equilibrium in which the proposer offers nothing and the responder accepts it.
5 A pure public good is defined by two properties: 1) people cannot be excluded from consuming it (nonexcludable) and 2) one individual's consumption of the good cannot diminish another consumer's enjoyment of the same good (non-rival).
6 See Waldfogel (1993) for an analysis of the inefficiency of holiday gift-giving.

References

Andreoni, James. 2006. "Philanthropy." In *Handbook of the Economics of Giving, Altruism and Reciprocity,* edited by Serge-Christophe Kolm and Jean Mercier Ythier, 2:1201–1269. Elsevier. doi:10.1016/S1574-0714(06)02018-5.

Azar, Ofer H. 2004. "The History of Tipping — from Sixteenth-Century England to United States in the 1910s." *The Journal of Socio-Economics* 33 (6): 745–764. doi:10.1016/j.socec.2004.09.043.

———. 2007. "The Social Norm of Tipping: A Review." *Journal of Applied Social Psychology* 37 (2): 380–402. doi:10.1111/j.0021-9029.2007.00165.x.

Ben-Zion, Uri, and Edi Karni. 1977. "Tip Payments and the Quality of Service." In *Essays in Labor Market Analysis,* edited by Orley Ashenfelter and Wallace E. Oates, 37–44. New York: John Wiley & Sons.

Bodvarsson, öRn B., and William A. Gibson. 1997. "Economics and Restaurant Gratuities: Determining Tip Rates." *American Journal of Economics and Sociology* 56 (2): 187–203. doi:10.1111/j.1536-7150.1997.tb03460.x.

Bowles, Samuel, and Herbert Gintis. 2008. "Cooperation." In *The New Palgrave Dictionary of Economics*, 2nd edition, edited by Steven N. Durlauf and Lawrence E. Blume, 1124–1130. London: Palgrave Macmillan UK. doi:10.1007/978-1-349-58802-2_316.

Boyd, Robert, and Peter J. Richerson. 1992. "Punishment Allows the Evolution of Cooperation (or Anything Else) in Sizable Groups." *Ethology and Sociobiology* 13 (3): 171–195. doi:10.1016/0162-3095(92)90032-Y.

Chandar, Bharat, Uri Gneezy, John A. List, and Ian Muir. 2019. "The Drivers of Social Preferences: Evidence from a Nationwide Tipping Field Experiment." NBER Working Paper 26380. Cambridge, MA: National Bureau of Economic Research. doi:10.3386/w26380.

Conlin, Michael, Michael Lynn, and Ted O'Donoghue. 2003. "The Norm of Restaurant Tipping." *Journal of Economic Behavior & Organization* 52 (3): 297–321. doi:10.1016/S0167-2681(03)00030-1.

Engel, Christoph. 2011. "Dictator Games: A Meta Study." *Experimental Economics* 14 (4): 583–610. doi:10.1007/s10683-011-9283-7.

Fehr, Ernst, and Simon Gächter. 2000. "Cooperation and Punishment in Public Goods Experiments." *American Economic Review* 90 (4): 980–994. doi:10.1257/aer. 90.4.980.

Fehr, Ernst, and Klaus M. Schmidt. 1999. "A Theory of Fairness, Competition, and Cooperation." *The Quarterly Journal of Economics* 114 (3): 817–868. doi:10.1162/003355399556151.

Fischbacher, Urs, Christina M. Fong, and Ernst Fehr. 2009. "Fairness, Errors and the Power of Competition." *Journal of Economic Behavior & Organization* 72 (1): 527–545. doi:10.1016/j.jebo.2009.05.021.

Forsythe, Robert, Joel L. Horowitz, N. E. Savin, and Martin Sefton. 1994. "Fairness in Simple Bargaining Experiments." *Games and Economic Behavior* 6 (3): 347–369. doi:10.1006/game.1994.1021.

Gintis, Herbert, Samuel Bowles, Robert Boyd, and Ernst Fehr. 2003. "Explaining Altruistic Behavior in Humans." *Evolution and Human Behavior* 24 (3): 153–172. Reprinting from p 159, Copyright (2003), with permission from Elsevier, doi:10.1016/S1090-5138(02)00157-5.

Giving USA. 2019. "Giving USA: The Annual Report on Philanthropy for the Year 2018." Report. Indiana University Lilly Family School of Philanthropy.

Güth, Werner, Rolf Schmittberger, and Bernd Schwarze. 1982. "An Experimental Analysis of Ultimatum Bargaining." *Journal of Economic Behavior & Organization* 3 (4): 367–388. doi:10.1016/0167-2681 (82)90011-7.

Hamilton, W. D. 1964. "The Genetical Evolution of Social Behaviour. II." *Journal of Theoretical Biology* 7 (1): 17–52. doi:10.1016/0022-5193(64)90039-6.

Henrich, Joseph, Robert Boyd, Samuel Bowles, Colin F. Camerer, Ernst Fehr, Herbert Gintis, and Richard McElreath. 2001. "In Search of Homo Economicus: Behavioral Experiments in 15 Small-Scale Societies." *American Economic Review* 91 (2): 73–78. doi:10.1257/aer.91.2.73.

Isaac, R. Mark, Kenneth F. McCue, and Charles R. Plott. 1985. "Public Goods Provision in an Experimental Environment." *Journal of Public Economics* 26 (1): 51–74. doi:10.1016/0047-2727(85)90038-6.

Jacob, Nancy L., and Alfred N. Page. 1980. "Production, Information Costs, and Economic Organization: The Buyer Monitoring Case." *American Economic Review* 70 (3): 476–478. https://www.jstor.org/stable/1805238.

Kahneman, Daniel, Jack L. Knetsch, and Richard Thaler. 1986. "Fairness as a Constraint on Profit Seeking: Entitlements in the Market." *American Economic Review* 76 (4): 728–741. https://www.jstor.org/stable/1806070.

Ledyard, John O. 1995. "Public Goods: A Survey of Experimental Research." In *The Handbook of Experimental Economics*, edited by John H. Kagel and Alvin E. Roth, 111–194. Princeton, NJ: Princeton University Press.

List, John A. 2004. "Young, Selfish and Male: Field Evidence of Social Preferences." *The Economic Journal* 114 (492): 121–149. doi:10.1046/j.0013-0133.2003. 00180.x.

Lynn, Michael, and Michael McCall. 2000. "Gratitude and Gratuity: A Meta-analysis of Research on the Service-Tipping Relationship." *The Journal of Socio-Economics* 29 (2): 203–214. doi:10.1016/S1053-5357(00)00062-7.

Lynn, Michael, George M. Zinkhan, and Judy Harris. 1993. "Consumer Tipping: A Cross-Country Study." *Journal of Consumer Research* 20 (3): 478–488. doi:10.1086/209363.

Marwell, Gerald, and Ruth E. Ames. 1981. "Economists Free Ride, Does Anyone Else?: Experiments on the Provision of Public Goods, IV." *Journal of Public Economics* 15 (3): 295–310. doi:10.1016/0047-2727(81)90013-X.

Meer, Jonathan, and Benjamin A. Priday. 2020. "Generosity across the Income and Wealth Distributions." NBER Working Paper 27076. Cambridge, MA: National Bureau of Economic Research. doi:10.3386/w27076.

Samuelson, Paul. 1954. "The Pure Theory of Public Expenditure." *The Review of Economics and Statistics* 36 (4): 387–389. doi:10.2307/1925895.

Shierholz, Heidi, David Cooper, Julia Wolfe, and Ben Zipperer. 2017. "Employers would Pocket $5.8 Billion of Workers' Tips under Trump Administration's Proposed 'Tip Stealing' Rule." Technical report. Washington, DC: Economic Policy Institute. https://www.epi.org/publication/employers-would-pocket-workers-tips-under-trump-administrations-proposed-tip-stealing-rule/.

Sisk, David E., and Edward C. Gallick. 1985. "Tips and Commissions: A Study in Economic Contracting." Working Paper 125. Bureau of Economics, Federal Trade Commission.

Stoler, Avraham, Judd B. Kessler, Tamar Ashkenazi, Alvin E. Roth, and Jacob Lavee. 2017. "Incentivizing Organ Donor Registrations with Organ Allocation Priority." *Health Economics* 26 (4): 500–510. doi:10.1002/hec.3328.

Trivers, Robert L. 1971. "The Evolution of Reciprocal Altruism." *The Quarterly Review of Biology* 46 (1): 35–57. doi:10.1086/406755.

Waldfogel, Joel. 1993. "The Deadweight Loss of Christmas." *American Economic Review* 83 (5): 1328–1336. https://www.jstor.org/stable/2117564.

14 Social Preferences

While self-interest is a strong motivator, it alone cannot explain the generosity we observe in a variety of field and lab settings. In this chapter we therefore explore non-standard preferences that, in contrast to purely self-interested preferences, take into account the payoffs, actions, or beliefs of others in society besides the self. Such **social preferences** can explain a multitude of otherwise anomalous behaviors.

In leaving behind the confines of self-interest, we consider multiple hypotheses for social preferences. We disentangle these competing hypotheses by evaluating their theoretical predictions against a range of empirical evidence. While some models perform better than others, there is no single "correct" model. Social preferences vary across people. And even within a single decision, individuals may be motivated by multiple social concerns.

The topics in this chapter are ordered to approximately align with the chronology of economic thinking on social preferences since the 1970s.[1] This history is as follows. The earliest models introduced altruism, in which individuals value the payoffs obtained by others. In the 1980s economists considered the possibility that individuals also value the *act* of giving itself. The next two decades saw models in which individuals care about the distribution of payoffs, as well as how the actions of others generate those payoffs. More recently, economists have investigated the relevance of social pressure and social norms. It is worth noting that in taking more seriously the role of society in shaping individual decisions, economists are reducing the methodological gap with other social scientists.[2]

14.1 Altruism

A natural extension to the standard assumption that individuals are egoists, focused only on themselves, is that they may also be (at least in part) **altruists**, exhibiting a selfless concern for the well-being of others. These others could include people who live in different places around the world, or even people in future generations who have yet to be

DOI: 10.4324/9780367854072-19

born. In this section we consider the key features of altruistic preference models and the extent to which they can explain real-world giving behaviors.

We begin with some helpful notation. Because this chapter is concerned with how an individual evaluates outcomes for both their own self and those of others, we use s to indicate the self and o to indicate others. And to differentiate the altruism model from the subsequent models in this chapter, AL abbreviates altruism. Equipped with this notational shorthand, we define altruistic preferences as follows.

Definition 14.1 In the **altruism model of preferences** the self evaluates both their personal outcome x_s, and the outcome x_o for another individual, by:

$$U_s^{AL} = u(x_s) + a \cdot u(x_o)$$

where $u(\cdot)$ is a utility function and $a \geq 0$ is the **altruism parameter**.

The altruism model is intuitively appealing. In it, the self cares both about their own personal utility, $u(x_s)$, and also the utility realized by the other, $u(x_o)$. Because the self may not weight these two utilities equally, the parameter a allows for varying degrees of altruism. For instance, $a = 1$ corresponds to a high level of altruism, implying that the self is indifferent between an increase in their own utility and an equal increase in the other's utility. Perhaps more likely is a moderate level of altruism, with $0 < a < 1$. This implies that while the self still feels altruistically towards the other, she would prefer a utility gain for herself over an equal utility gain for the other. And in the event that $a = 0$, we return to the standard case without altruism.

To better understand the implications of altruistic preferences, we apply this model to the decision problem of philanthropic giving.

14.1.1   Modeling Altruistic Philanthropy

The previous chapter began by noting how gift-giving could be consistent with pure self-interest, as long as the giver reasonably expects a personal benefit in return for their generosity. With altruistic preferences this is no longer necessary. An altruist can give to another, not for hope of reward or fear of punishment, but simply because the utility gain for the recipient is intrinsically valuable to the giver.

Altruistic feelings can extend beyond a single individual to groups of people. This is particularly relevant in the context of philanthropy where individuals donate money to schools, religious organizations, hospitals, and art museums that benefit entire populations (e.g., students, the poor, the sick, or art goers, respectively).

Let's model the problem for an altruist deciding how generously to donate to a charitable organization. To do so, let $C(G)$ describe the charity's production function: the amount of charitable services it can produce when it receives total giving G. It is these charitable services that provide satisfaction for altruistic donors.[3] We can then express utility as follows.

Definition 14.2 In the (pure) **altruism model of giving**, the self with personal wealth W_s evaluates their giving g_s to a charity, that receives total donations G_o

from others, by:

$$U_s^{AL} = u(W_s - g_s) + a \cdot C(g_s + G_o)$$

where $u(\cdot)$ is a utility function, $C(\cdot)$ is the (increasing and concave) charity production function, and $a \geq 0$ is the altruism parameter.

How does this expression for altruistic utility U_s^{AL} differ from the more general case in Definition 14.1? First, in the giving context the relevant personal outcome for the self x_s, is their wealth after making a gift, $W_s - g_s$. Second, the object of altruistic feelings is not another person's utility $u(x_o)$, but the total supply of charitable services $C(G)$, which depends on total giving $G = g_s + G_o$.

The altruism model of giving highlights an important tradeoff. Giving g_s reduces wealth and therefore personal utility. But it also increases charitable services from which the giver derives satisfaction. A utility-maximizer will therefore continue giving until the marginal utility cost to the self exceeds the marginal altruism benefit derived from helping others.

14.1.2   *Evaluating Altruistic Philanthropy*   [Public Finance]

Altruism provides a theoretical motivation for philanthropic giving. But is the selfless concern for the well-being of others indeed the primary motivation for why people donate to charitable causes? In this section we consider two tests of the altruism model for explaining philanthropy.

Our first test is concerned with how charitable donations respond to donations by others. Suppose, for instance, that the government provides a grant to the charity. From the perspective of an individual altruistic donor, the grant increases G_o, which in turn increases utility U_s^{AL}, assuming that the donor does not change her giving g_s. But the grant might induce the donor to reduce her own giving.

A reduction in giving caused by an increase in giving by others is known as **crowding out**. And the altruism model of giving predicts strong crowding out.[4] That is, for each additional dollar given by others, the altruistic donor reduces her own giving by nearly a dollar. This result follows from recognizing that the altruist cares only about the total supply of giving to the charity. Giving by others acts as a substitute for one's own giving and therefore induces the donor to reduce her own giving and increase private consumption, without sacrificing any decrease in total charitable services provided.

The prediction of strong crowding out can be tested with data. In an early investigation of the crowding out hypothesis Roberts (1984) argues that the increase in US government support for the poor during the Great Depression reduced private charitable giving aimed at poverty relief, evidence that would be consistent with the altruism model. But in subsequent research, economists have found limited evidence for high levels of crowding out (e.g., Payne 1998; Hungerman 2005; Gruber and Hungerman 2007). This evidence suggests that altruism cannot be the main motivation for giving.[5]

For our second test, consider what the altruism model predicts for how donors allocate giving across multiple charities. While we defined altruistic utility in terms of only one charity, we could extend our definition, adding in additional charity production functions. With multiple charities from which to choose, utility-maximizing altruists would choose to spend each donation dollar on the charity that is best able to transform their donations into charitable services. For instance, while you may care about supporting the homeless, arts education, and the environment, as an altruist you would give all of your charitable donations to the single organization where your donations generate the biggest impact. But this prediction is at odds with the evidence. People typically spread their donations across multiple charities. In fact, almost half of all Americans give money to three to five charitable organizations and 15% give to at least six (Yu and Adkins 2016).

In sum, the altruism model of giving fails to match actual giving behaviors. What is wrong with this model? And what is an alternative? We take up answering these questions in the next section.

14.2   Warm-Glow Giving

An important limitation of the altruism model for giving is that it neglects the possibility that individuals care about the *process* by which charities receive donations. Only two things matter for an altruist: their own final wealth and the total donations received by a charity. For example, consider an altruist who last year gave nothing to a charity that received a total of $100,000 in donations from other sources. This year the altruist is $1,000 wealthier and donates $1,000 to the charity, which still receives a total of $100,000 from all sources. In both years the altruist has the same wealth (after making donations) and the charity receives the same total donations. The altruist is therefore indifferent between these two scenarios.

But would you actually be indifferent? Even though the charity is no better or worse off in either case, you may enjoy the feeling of your own generosity in the second scenario. Or you may experience negative feelings of guilt from not giving in the first scenario. Regardless of the particular reason, it is intuitively plausible that individuals care directly about how much they personally contribute to a charity, and not only about the total supply of gifts. This benefit that accrues from the *act* of giving is known as **warm-glow** (Andreoni 1989, 1990). The following definition formalizes this concept.

Definition 14.3 In the (pure) **warm-glow model of giving**, the self with personal wealth W_s evaluates their giving g_s to a charity by:

$$U_s^{WG} = u(W_s - g_s) + \omega(g_s)$$

where $u(\cdot)$ is a utility function and $\omega(\cdot)$ is the (increasing and concave) warm-glow giving function.

As with altruism, the warm-glow giving model assumes that individuals care about their own wealth after making a gift. But the models differ in how gifts increase satisfaction. With altruism, larger gifts increase satisfaction only to the extent that they increase the total supply of charity. With warm-glow, larger gifts increase satisfaction simply by giving, no matter the donations to the charity by anyone else.

The seemingly subtle distinction between the altruism and warm-glow models of giving generates very different theoretical predictions. Consider first the prediction for crowding out. As opposed to the strong crowding out predicted by pure altruism, pure warm-glow predicts no crowding out. Because giving by others G_o does not show up in the expression for U_s^{WG}, it has no impact on personal giving. So if a charity receives a large grant, warm-glow givers will continue to give; the grant cannot substitute for the enjoyment obtained from the act of one's own giving.

We can further consider a more general model in which individuals are simultaneously altruistic and experience warm-glow from giving:

$$U_s = u(W_s - g_s) + a \cdot C(g_s + G_o) + \omega(g_s)$$

Such *impure altruism*, or simply *warm-glow giving*, is a hybrid of the pure altruism and pure warm-glow in Definitions 14.2 and 14.3. In this case, giving by others is an imperfect substitute for one's own giving. Whereas one's own giving might fall by almost $100 in response to a $100 gift by others with pure altruism, it would fall by much less than $100 with impure altruism. Warm-glow in some sense makes giving "sticky," or less responsive to giving by others. This prediction aligns with the empirical evidence of low and incomplete crowding out.

Warm-glow givers also prefer to diversify their charitable donations across multiple charities, a common feature of philanthropic giving. That way they can experience the joy of giving to each charity. This contrasts with the pure altruist who would find it best to allocate all of their giving to the charity for which their donation would generate the largest increase in charitable services. Warm-glow giving therefore does a better job at explaining charitable giving patterns than does the pure altruism model.

A more surprising prediction is that with a large number of donors, all of whom exhibit impure altruism for a charity, the amount that each donor gives depends *only* on the degree to which they experience warm-glow. The magnitude of altruistic feelings is not relevant (Ribar and Wilhelm 2002). In other words, warm-glow "dominates" altruism when there are many donors (see Exercise 14.2). This result makes sense when you consider a typical donor who makes a modest $50 donation to the American Red Cross, which collects over $1.5 million in donations each year. The $50 donation has no real impact on the total supply of charitable services. But it does give the donor warm-glow from giving. In summary, we should expect warm-glow to play a significant role in explaining philanthropic giving.

14.3   Distributional Preferences

We now turn to the giving anomalies in classic lab games. Recall from the previous chapter, for instance, that in the ultimatum game responders frequently reject positive monetary offers in favor of nothing. Altruism, pure or impure, cannot explain such decisions. In fact, quite the opposite of altruism appears to be at play. Responders seem displeased when the proposer keeps most of the money available to distribute. They would rather everyone receive nothing than allow the proposer to walk away with almost all of the stake. That is, the distribution of payoffs matters.

14.3.1   *Modeling Distributional Preferences*

To account for distributional concerns we develop a new model of preferences over monetary outcomes. But instead of discarding altruism altogether, let's enrich the altruism model. Begin with a simple version of the pure altruism model in Definition 14.1:

$$U_s^{AL} = (1 - \rho)x_s + \rho x_o$$

where $1 > \rho \geq 0$.[6] If $\rho = 0$, the self cares only about herself, as is standard. But if $\rho > 0$, the self is altruistic towards the other. And the larger is ρ, the more the self cares about the other's outcome and the less about her own. That is, the self's utility is a weighted average of the outcome for herself and for the other, with $1 - \rho$ as the weight on herself and ρ as the weight on the other. If $\rho = 0.5$ the monetary outcomes are equally weighted and the self is indifferent between an extra dollar going to herself or the other.

A limitation of this baseline altruism model is that it implicitly assumes the self is equally altruistic no matter whether she has more or less than the other. But an individual may feel less altruistic or envious towards another who has more. To accommodate this possibility, we enrich the above model as follows.[7]

Definition 14.4 In the **distributional model of preferences** the self evaluates their personal outcome x_s, and the outcome x_o for another individual, by:

$$U_s(x_s, x_o) = \begin{cases} (1 - \rho)x_s + \rho x_o & \text{if } x_s \geq x_0 \\ (1 - \sigma)x_s + \sigma x_o & \text{if } x_s < x_0 \end{cases}$$

where $1 > \rho \geq \sigma$.

Baseline altruism is nested within this distributional model when $\rho = \sigma$. But if $\rho > \sigma$ the self weights the other's outcome more when her own outcome is greater. To develop intuition, we consider two cases that differ based on the sign of σ.

The distributional model above represents **differential altruism** in the case that $\rho > \sigma > 0$. Because ρ and σ are both positive, the self exhibits altruism towards the other, no matter the outcomes for either individual. This representation implies a preference for efficiency because individuals like outcome improvements for *anyone* in society. But the assumption that $\rho > \sigma$ implies the self benefits more so from the gains of another when she is ahead than when she is behind. Or stated differently, altruism is stronger towards those with less than those with more; it is more natural to feel generous towards the poor than the rich.

An alternative interpretation of the distributional model emerges if we instead assume that $\rho > 0 > \sigma$. Because $\rho > 0$, the self remains altruistic when she is better off; she enjoys higher outcomes for the other. But when worse off, the self applies the negative weight $\sigma < 0$ to the other's outcome; she prefers the other to experience a lower outcome. Together, these two motivations imply that the self prefers to reduce differences between herself and the other. This is therefore a model of **difference** or **inequality aversion**.[8]

But does the distributional model of preferences make reasonable predictions? And if so, do most people exhibit differential altruism of inequality aversion? We take up these questions in the context of lab games next.

14.3.2 *Distributional Preferences in Lab Games*

Imagine that players in the dictator, ultimatum, and public good games make decisions according to the distributional model of preferences. Let's think through how they would play these games.

Dictator Game

Suppose the dictator/proposer is staked with $10 to keep, or share with a recipient. The majority of proposers give something. And among this majority, the most common gift is an even split of $5 for each (see Figure 13.1). This can indeed be the prediction for dictators with distributional preferences. To see how, let g be the gift from the dictator to the recipient. Then the utility for the dictator who keeps $10 - g$ for herself and gives $\$g$ away is:

$$U_s(10 - g, g) = \begin{cases} (1 - \rho)(10 - g) + \rho g & \text{if } 10 - g \geq g \\ (1 - \sigma)(10 - g) + \sigma g & \text{if } 10 - g < g \end{cases}$$

$$= \begin{cases} 10(1 - \rho) + g(2\rho - 1) & \text{if } g \leq 5 \\ 10(1 - \sigma) + g(2\sigma - 1) & \text{if } g > 5 \end{cases}$$

where the second equality follows from some algebraic rearranging.

The cumbersome utility expression above is better understood visually. Figure 14.1 plots the dictator's utility as a function of their gift, with a $5 gift as the utility-maximizing choice. Observe that the utility function only has this shape if it is increasing for gifts

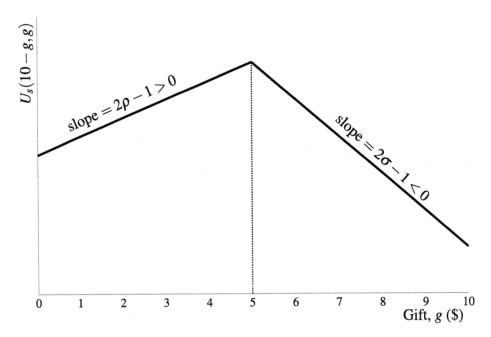

Figure 14.1 Dictator's Distributional Preferences for Giving

less than $5 and decreasing for gifts greater than $5. Mathematically, this requires that:

U_s increasing for $g \leq 5 \iff U_s$ slope $= 2\rho - 1 > 0 \iff \rho > 0.5$
U_s decreasing for $g < 5 \iff U_s$ slope $= 2\sigma - 1 < 0 \iff \sigma < 0.5$

That is, for $\rho > 0.5 > \sigma$, the distributional preferences model predicts equal sharing by the dictator. Intuitively, the dictator must have sufficiently high altruism when she is ahead (i.e., $\rho > 0.5$) to want to gift anything, but sufficiently low altruism when she is behind (i.e., $\sigma < 0.5$) so as not to transfer all $10 to the recipient.

This analysis shows how the distributional model can predict generous sharing in the dictator game, a prediction completely at odds with standard self-interested preferences. But the analysis above does not allow us to disentangle differential altruism ($\sigma > 0$) from inequality aversion ($\sigma < 0$). For further evidence, consider the ultimatum game.

Ultimatum Game

In the ultimatum game responders frequently reject low offers. Consider, for example, the choice for a responder between accepting an offer of $2 from a proposer who keeps $8 (assuming a $10 stake) and rejecting the offer, in which case both players get nothing. The responder's utility from each choice is:

Accept : $U_s(2, 8) = (1 - \sigma)2 + \sigma 8 = 2 + 6\sigma$
Reject : $U_s(0, 0) = (1 - \rho)0 + \rho 0 = 0$

Rejection is preferred as long as $2 + 6\sigma < 0$, or equivalently, $\sigma < -1/3$.

We can therefore explain actual responder behaviors with our distributional preferences model. And moreover, because rejection of low offers requires σ to be negative, responders reveal themselves to be inequality averse. They are willing to forego a few dollars in exchange for nothing because this monetary loss is smaller than the utility gain they experience from eliminating inequality between themself and the proposer.

Public Good Game

The behaviors in the public good game can similarly be explained by inequality aversion. Recall that with standard self-interested preferences, players should not contribute to the public good (100% free riding). And yet, in repeated public good games players typically begin with generous contributions to the public good, but reduce their contributions over subsequent rounds. This pattern makes sense if individuals are inequality averse. In particular, the highest contributors observe the lower contributions of others after each round and can reduce the payoff difference between players by adjusting their contributions downward in the next round. As this process iterates, contributions are predicted to fall with each repetition, as observed in the lab.

We also saw that contributions remain high when players have the ability to impose a costly punishment on others after each round of a public good game (see Figure 13.2). This too can be explained by inequality aversion. Contributors who dislike inequality would be willing to impose punishments that reduce their own payoffs if doing so incentivizes generous contributions from everyone, thereby promoting a more equitable distribution of final payoffs.

Summary

In sum, the anomalous behaviors in our three lab games can all be explained by inequality-averse preferences.[9] This is not to say that everyone is inequality averse. Many players in lab games still act in accordance with the predictions of standard self-interested preferences (e.g., the third of dictators who gift nothing). And even if only some players are inequality averse, the common knowledge of this fact can induce self-interested players to change their behavior (e.g., self-interested proposers who share generously in the ultimatum game to prevent a rejection).

An important takeaway is that there is heterogeneity in preferences. One notable form of heterogeneous preferences is between economists and non-economists, as illustrated by the following lab experiment.

Lab Experiment – Economist and Non-Economist Dictators (Fehr, Naef, and Schmidt 2006)

A dictator decides unilaterally the monetary payoffs for herself and two other players. She must choose an allocation of the form (S, O_1, O_2), where S is the payoff to herself, and O_1 and O_2 are the payoffs for the other two players. The allocations are:

A (4, 5, 14)
B (4, 6, 11)
C (4, 7, 8)

Note that the choice has no impact on the dictator's own payoff, which is always 4. Allocation A (C) generates the largest (smallest) total payoff equal to 23 (19). In addition, allocation A (C) is the least (most) equal distribution.

Choosing A therefore reflects a concern for efficiency (i.e., make the economic pie as large as possible) over equality (i.e., how evenly the economic pie is distributed). This is the predicted choice for an altruistic dictator.

Choosing C instead reflects a concern of equality over efficiency, and is the predicted choice for an inequality-averse dictator.

Fehr, Naef, and Schmidt (2006) report the following results:

	Choose A	*Choose B*	*Choose C*
Economics Student ($n = 197$)	57%	14%	29%
Not Economics Student ($n = 281$)	29%	18%	53%
Preference for Efficiency Prediction	✓		
Inequality Aversion Prediction			✓

While the majority of economics students are concerned with efficiency (as evidenced by their choice of A), the majority of non-economics students are concerned with equality (as evidenced by their choice of C). This result could occur because those who care most about efficiency choose to study economics, or similarly those who care most about equality choose not to study economics. Or it could reflect the effect of mainstream economics education on student preferences (Etzioni 2015). Similar to economics students, medical students, law students, and Republican voters are also more concerned with efficiency than the average American (Fisman et al. 2015; Fisman, Jakiela, and Kariv 2017; Li, Dow, and Kariv 2017). The heterogeneity in preferences across individuals provides a warning to economics experimenters: relying exclusively on economics students as study participants invites the risk of results that do not reflect typical preferences for the general population.

14.4   Reciprocity

The distributional model of preferences, as the name suggests, assumes that the distribution of payoffs matters, and is all that matters. By doing so, it can make sense of otherwise anomalous behaviors. But it neglects the possibility that preferences are responsive to the perceived intentions of others. For instance, individuals may exhibit reciprocity, responding to perceived kind intentions with kindness, or **positive reciprocity**, and perceived unkind intentions with unkindness, or **negative reciprocity**.[10] This section presents evidence from lab and field experiments documenting the role of reciprocity in shaping decisions.

Before turning to the evidence, note that we can accommodate the role of intentions within our distributional model of preferences. Instead of assuming the parameters ρ and σ in Definition 14.4 are fixed for each individual, we can think of them as functions that depend on an individual's perceived intentions of others. Perceived kindness would increase the parameters, shifting the utility weight towards the outcomes of others and away from the self. Perceived unkindness would symmetrically decrease the parameters.[11]

14.4.1   Ultimatum Game

The ultimatum game behaviors that we attributed to inequality aversion in the previous section may in fact be motivated by reciprocity. To see how, consider an individual facing the decision between (Self, Other) payoffs of ($2, $8) or ($0, $0). This is exactly the decision faced by a responder in the ultimatum game who has been offered $2 of a $10 pie. We know that most responders in this situation reject the offer, in effect choosing the ($0, $0) payoffs. And yet, when individuals are simply asked to choose between these two payoff distributions, outside the context of the ultimatum game, no one chooses the ($0, $0) payoffs (Charness and Rabin 2002). What is going on here?

In both settings an individual faces the exact same decision between two payoff distributions. And yet, individuals make very different choices. A distributional model of preferences like inequality aversion, that depends only the distribution of payoffs, cannot possibly explain the difference in choices.

But these choices begin to make sense if we allow for reciprocity. The only difference in the above two decision problems is what precedes the decision. In the ultimatum game the responder knows that the proposer could have offered any split of the $10 pie, but chose to offer only $2. The responder's decision to reduce the proposer's payoff to zero can be understood as a punishment for the perceived unkind offer.

This contrasts with the second decision problem in which an individual is simply faced with the choice between ($2, $8) and ($0, $0), with no other player's actions responsible for this particular pair of options. Because the individual has no reason to suspect mal-intent, they are now willing to accept an unequal outcome.

We can also identify the relevance of positive and negative reciprocity in a variation on the ultimatum game, as outlined in the following lab experiment.

Lab Experiment — Mini Ultimatum Game (Falk, Fehr, and Fischbacher 2003)

Consider a *mini* ultimatum game in which the proposer has $10 to share, but cannot choose any split of the $10 between herself and the responder. Instead, she faces a limited set of offers. The responder is fully aware of the available offers from which the proposer can choose. As is standard, upon receiving an offer the responder accepts or rejects, in which case both players get nothing.

There are three versions of this mini ultimatum game, each with a different set of available offers:

A   Offer $2 to the responder
B   Offer $2 or $0 to the responder
C   Offer $2 or $5 to the responder

Falk, Fehr, and Fischbacher (2003) find that responders who are offered $2 reject the offer as follows:

Mini Ultimatum Game	*Rejection Rate of $2 Offer*
A Proposer has no other option	18%
B Proposer could have offered $0	9%
C Proposer could have offered $5	44%

The mini ultimatum games reveal the importance of reciprocity, both positive and negative. First observe that inequality aversion alone cannot explain the above results. If responders cared only about the distribution of payoffs, then the decision to reject a $2 offer should be the same in every game — once a proposer offers $2, the alternative not offered has no impact on the payoffs. But rejection rates differ substantially across the games.

Next observe that because the proposer has no alternative but to offer $2 in game *A*, responders have no reason to perceive the $2 offer as reflecting either good or bad intentions by the proposer. The 18% rejection rate therefore captures the extent of inequality aversion among the responders without reciprocal motivations. When proposers have the option to offer nothing in game *B*, receiving an offer of $2 is perceived as a kind gesture, leading to a 50% reduction in the rejection rate (from 18% to 9%). But when proposers have the option to offer an even split in game *C*, the $2 offer is perceived as selfish and unkind, leading to an almost 150% increase in the rejection rate (from 18% to 44%). So while reciprocity exists in both positive and negative forms, negative reciprocity is substantially stronger. This insight holds in other settings, to which we turn next.

14.4.2   Gift Exchange   *[Labor]*

Reciprocity is also at play in the context of gift giving. Upon receiving a gift, one typically feels an obligation to reciprocate, even without the threat of formal sanctions. Consider for instance how compelled you feel to respond to the gift of a friendly "Hello" with your own greeting, or your feelings of inadequacy upon receiving a lavish or thoughtful holiday gift from a friend for whom you do not have a gift in return. In fact, the obligatory cost of reciprocating a gift is reflected in the etymological root of *gift*, which is also the root of *poison* in both ancient German and Greek. While anthropologists and sociologists have long recognized the central role of reciprocity in gift exchange (see e.g., Mauss 1954; Belshaw 1965), it was not until the 1980s that economists began to consider the implications of reciprocity for understanding markets.

Consider the labor market relationship between workers and employers. At first glance this does not appear to be a market characterized by gift exchange. In the simplest setting, workers must supply a minimum level of effort to avoid being fired. And employers must pay sufficiently high wages to prevent their workers from quitting. But we can think of efforts and wages above these minima as mutually reciprocal gifts (Akerlof 1982). When workers are treated well by their employer they may exert additional effort as a reciprocal "gift" to their co-workers and the company more generally. Symmetrically, employers who benefit from the "gift" of high effort from their employees may reciprocate by paying a fair wage above what is minimally required. In sum, reciprocal gift exchange in the labor market predicts a positive relationship between wages and effort. The following lab experiment tests this hypothesis.

Lab Experiment — Fair Wage–Effort Game (Fehr, Kirchsteiger, and Riedl 1993)

Student participants are each assigned to play the role of either a worker or a firm that is seeking to hire exactly one worker. Workers and firms are placed in separate rooms so that labor contracts are anonymous.

Firms offer wages to workers, who upon accepting an offer choose their effort. Effort is costly to the worker, but benefits firm profits. This game is repeated 12 times.

With standard self-interested preferences, workers in the game should exert minimal effort since higher effort is costly and does not lead to any future reward (anonymity assures that firms never learn the identity of their employee). Anticipating minimal worker effort no matter the wage, firms should then offer the lowest wage necessary to induce workers to accept the job.

Fehr, Kirchsteiger, and Riedl (1993) find that 1) firms offer wages above the minimum required to attract a worker, 2) workers exert costly effort, and 3) workers receiving higher wages exert greater effort.

The results of the fair wage–effort game support the gift-exchange theory of labor markets. Workers reciprocate high wages (perceived as a kind intention) with higher effort. And anticipating this reaction, firms have an incentive to offer fair wages substantially above the minimum to induce profit-enhancing worker effort. This evidence has been corroborated in subsequent lab experiments with non-student populations (Fehr et al. 1998) and with multiple workers at each firm (Maximiano, Sloof, and Sonnemans 2007). Therefore, even in competitive settings where players have every incentive to be self-interested, we observe behaviors that are inconsistent with the standard model, but consistent with reciprocity.

We may be concerned that the experimental evidence from the lab is contingent on the artificial setting and may not reflect real-world interactions. To address this concern, consider the field experiment below.

Field Experiment — Library Gift Exchange (Kube, Maréchal, and Puppe 2006)

A job advertisement in Germany offered students the opportunity to enter book data into a library database over a single six-hour shift, paying €15 per hour. When students showed up, they were randomly assigned to one of three groups:

1   Control: Wage equal to €15 per hour, as advertised.
2   Kind Treatment: Wage equal €20 per hour, a surprise wage increase.
3   Unkind Treatment: Wage equal €10 per hour, a surprise wage decrease.

Because wages are not tied to performance and the employment relationship is one-shot with no reputational concerns, standard self-interested student workers should always exert the same minimal effort regardless of their wage. This would yield the same average worker productivity across the randomly assigned groups.

Figure 14.2 illustrates student worker productivity, as measured by the average number of books logged every 90 minutes. In all groups average productivity increased over time, reflecting learning on the job. Relative to the control, students in the kind treatment logged more books, whereas students in the unkind treatment logged fewer books. The productivity gap between the control and unkind group is larger than between the control and kind group.

The evidence above rejects standard preferences and instead illustrates how unkindness induces a larger behavioral response than kindness. That is, negative reciprocity is stronger than positive reciprocity. The Mini Ultimatum Game Lab Experiment demonstrated the same qualitative result. And even when positive reciprocity has been documented in other field experiments, it diminishes after a few hours (Gneezy and List 2006).

What can account for the strength of negative, relative to positive, reciprocity? One explanation appeals to the concepts of reference dependence and loss aversion (explored in Part III). Suppose that individuals expect moderate kindness from others. Then perceived unkind intentions are coded as a loss, inducing a strong negative experience that triggers unkindness in the form of negative reciprocity. In contrast, the gain of being treated with more kindness than expected fails to generate a positive experience of the same magnitude and therefore weaker positive reciprocity.

Although we have focused on the role of gift exchange in labor markets, we can apply the same intuition to other behaviors, like charitable giving and tipping. For instance, donors are

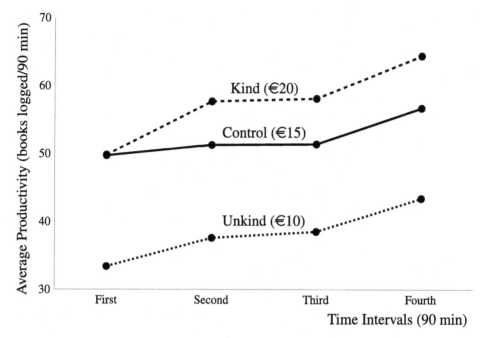

Figure 14.2 Average Worker Productivity
Data Source: Kube, Maréchal, and Puppe (2006).

more generous when charities include small gifts with their solicitations (Falk (2007), as described in Exercise 14.9). And restaurant diners leave larger tips to servers who gift pieces of chocolate upon delivering the bill (Strohmetz et al. 2002). We further examine charitable giving and tipping behaviors in the context of social pressure next.

14.5   Social Pressure

Beyond altruism, warm-glow, inequality aversion, and reciprocity, social pressure is another way by which individuals' social, as opposed to purely private, concerns can impact their behavior. Our decisions about how much to donate or tip, how hard to study in school, which job to take, and even how many children to have may be significantly influenced by social pressures to act in particular ways. This section begins with a simple framework for thinking about social pressure in decision making. We then review field experiments identifying the relevance of social pressure for a variety of economic decisions. And finally we consider the role of social norms as a source of social pressure.

14.5.1   *Modeling Social Pressure*

Let's begin with the self-evident observation that most people care about their **social image**, i.e., how they are perceived by others in society. Some may care about being perceived as smart, successful, happy, or care-free. Others may care about being viewed as kind, generous, or charitable. Social media serves as a platform for people to construct and project such social images. We can accommodate these social image concerns within an economic decision making framework as follows.[12]

> **Definition 14.5** An individual with **social image concerns** evaluates a socially observable action x by:
>
> $$U(x) = B(x) - C(x) + \gamma \cdot S(x)$$
>
> where $B(x)$ and $C(x)$ are the benefit and cost of action x, independent of all social image concerns. $S(x)$ is the positive social image of action x and γ measures the degree to which the individual is concerned with a positive social image.

There are three components to this abstract model of social image concerns. The first is the standard net benefit $B(x) - C(x)$ associated with an action x. The second is the positive social image $S(x)$. It captures how well others view the decision maker, as a function of their observable actions. Note that $S(x)$ is contingent on what the relevant social group regards as socially desirable. For instance, one social group may view environmentally conscious actions that reduce one's carbon footprint as socially desirable, while another social group would perceive such actions with indifference or even hostility. Finally, the parameter γ measures the degree to which the decision maker cares about promoting a positive social image. If $\gamma = 0$, the individual is unconcerned with how they are perceived by others. But if $\gamma \neq 0$, the individual cares in some way about their social image.

The existence of social image concerns introduces **social pressure** to act in ways other than what would be predicted by simply trading off standard costs and benefits. For $\gamma > 0$, individuals will feel social pressure to enhance their social image by choosing actions that *conform* to what others view as socially desirable. If instead $\gamma < 0$, individuals will experience a different form of social pressure to act *contrary* to society's view of what is regarded as desirable.

Let's illustrate this general framework with the specific example of a student's decision about how much effort to invest in their education. Without social image concerns ($\gamma = 0$) the student would make the educational investment decision by optimally trading off the benefits of school work (e.g., intrinsic joy of learning, higher lifetime earnings) against the costs (e.g., effort, foregone leisure). A student who cares positively about their social image ($\gamma > 0$) in a society where academic success is regarded as socially desirable would then experience social pressure to exert additional effort. They might spend more time in the library studying or more actively participate in class discussions. These additional efforts are worthwhile because they enhance their social image as a particularly serious student. If, however, the student is primarily concerned about their social image among a peer group that values indifference towards school as socially desirable, then social pressure would induce the student to invest less in their education, at least publicly. And a contrarian student ($\gamma < 0$) would experience social pressure to study less when studiousness improves their social image, and study more otherwise.

The education investment example highlights two important observations about social image concerns. The first is that individuals may face competing social pressures from multiple groups that disagree about what is socially desirable. Parents, teachers, and employers may value high effort in school, while peer groups may not.[13] Second, individuals can choose actions with varying degrees of social observability. For instance, to simultaneously promote one's social image among parents and teachers who value education and friends who do not, a student can study at home, not in the school library. They can similarly ask their teachers questions via email or after school, not by participating during class.

Finally, note that the model of social image concerns admits an alternative interpretation where $S(x)$ instead refers to an individual's own **self-image** or **identity** (Akerlof and Kranton 2000; Bénabou and Tirole 2006). That is, we may at times be concerned with taking actions that improve how we perceive ourselves or remind us what type of person we are. Consider an individual who signs up to speak at an intimidating professional event, in part to demonstrate self-confidence to themself, or the individual who volunteers for a political cause to remind themself of their commitment to social justice. Self-image concerns can also inhibit actions. For instance, people may not take up support in the form of welfare assistance or mental health care if doing so would require them to admit to themselves that they are in need of help. Note that in contrast to social image concerns, where the visibility of actions is important for changing how others perceive you, actions motivated by self-image concerns can be entirely private.

14.5.2 Social Pressure in the Field

You may be sufficiently convinced that social pressure matters simply from introspection of your own actions in life. But just because social pressure is consistent with certain behaviors, does not mean that it is actually responsible for them.

How can we isolate the impact of social pressure? We want to look for settings where there is a change in the social image associated with an action, $S(x)$, but where the underlying benefits and costs of the action, $B(x)$ and $C(x)$, remain the same. Suppose for instance that an action that was previously private can now be observed by others, but all other consequences of the action for the individual, both good and bad, remain the same. Without social image concerns ($\gamma = 0$), the degree to which the action is observable by others would have no effect on the individual's utility and therefore no effect on behavior; only standard benefits and costs matter. If, however, the individual responds to this change in observability, then they care about their social image ($\gamma \neq 0$) and are subject to social pressure.

In this section we review experimental evidence from the field that applies the above reasoning to identify the relevance of social pressure for a variety of behaviors.[14]

Peer Pressure   *[Education]*

School is commonly perceived to be a setting where students are particularly concerned with their social image. Choices of how to dress, speak, or act may all be influenced by a desire to be perceived positively by one's peers. It is also possible that student decisions about how seriously to invest in education are motivated by social image concerns. The following field experiment tests this hypothesis.

Field Experiment — SAT Peer Pressure (Bursztyn and Jensen 2015)

In early 2014, eleventh-grade students at public high schools in Los Angeles were offered complimentary access to an online prep course for the SAT, a standardized test for college admissions in the US. The students were randomly assigned to receive one of two sign-up forms that differed only in their privacy guarantees, as follows:

1   Private Form: Student decision to sign up would be kept private from everyone, *including* the other students in the classroom.
2   Public Form: Student decision to sign up would be kept private from everyone, *except* the other students in the classroom.

Because of random assignment, any difference in sign-ups across the two groups implies that students are concerned with the impact of their sign-up decision on how others in the classroom perceive them.

Bursztyn and Jensen (2015) find that in non-honors classes the sign-up rate is 11 percentage points lower for students who received the public form relative to the private form. There is no sign-up difference in honors classes.

The above field experiment reveals two important insights. The first is that social image concerns impact educational investments. When the decision to enroll in a SAT prep course is made observable to one's peers, without changing any benefits or costs of taking the course, students in non-honors classes are less likely to sign-up. If SAT prep courses reveal a concern for academics, then it appears that some students prefer to project a social image of not taking academics too seriously.

The experiment also reveals the context-dependence of social image concerns. Students in honors classes do not change their behavior based on the observability of their sign-up choice. Perhaps by virtue of taking an honors class, these students have already generated for themselves a social image of someone who cares a great deal about scholastics. Signing up (or not) for a SAT prep course does little to change this social image in the minds of their class peers. Therefore, even if they care about their social image, students in honors classes make the same sign-up decision with and without observability of their choice. Social image concerns extend beyond school and into adulthood, as explored next.

Conspicuous Consumption   *[Household]*

Although individuals surely evaluate their well-being based on their own consumption, they may also care how their consumption compares to that of others. This hypothesis that people are concerned with their *relative* economic status among their peers is an old idea in economics dating back to at least Veblen (1899). And more recent empirical evidence gives support for the impact of relative income on happiness (Clark, Frijters, and Shields 2008).

One mechanism by which an individual can improve others' perception of their own economic status is through **conspicuous consumption**. This is the behavior of consuming *visible* goods and services motivated by the effect of consumption on one's perceived status (Frank 1985). For example, a family — call them the Joneses — may purchase a car that is bigger and more luxurious than the cars of their neighbors. And assuming that the Joneses do not hide the car away in storage, they can enjoy an enhanced social image from the neighbors' admiration and envy. Notice that the neighbors, if similarly concerned with status, experience social pressure to upgrade their own car or buy another *status good* to avoid falling behind in the social ranking (see Exercise 14.13). In fact, this social pressure is sufficiently commonplace that there is an English-language idiom for it: *keeping up with the Joneses*. While perhaps intuitive, the following quasi-experiment provides us with credible evidence for such social status concerns.

Quasi-Experiment — Lucky Neighbors (Kuhn et al. 2011)

The *Nationale Postcode Loterij* is the second largest national lottery in the Netherlands. Each week a postal code is selected and everyone living in that postal code who bought a lottery ticket is awarded €12,500. This is a substantial reward, equal to eight months of average income. Over 2,000 households, including both winners and non-winners, were surveyed about their demographic characteristics, lottery participation, and consumption behaviors.

Consider the surveyed households that did not participate in the lottery. Because of the randomized structure of lotteries, we can think of nonparticipant households who happen to live close to a lottery winner as "treated" by their neighbors' higher economic status, as follows:

1   Control: Live in a nonwinning postal code.
2   Neighbor Treatment: Live in a winning postal code within two doors of a winner.
3   Next-Door Treatment: Live in a winning postal code next door to a winner.

Any difference in average consumption behaviors between the control and treatment groups can be attributed to the economic success of a neighbor.

Kuhn et al. (2011) find that the share of households who had recently bought a car differed across the groups as follows:

1   Control: 17.3%
2   Neighbor Treatment: 23.4%
3   Next-Door Treatment: 26.5%

That is, having a close neighbor win the lottery significantly increases the probability that a household will buy a car in the next few months. In fact, this neighbor effect is larger than the increase in car consumption for lottery winners themselves.

The evidence from this quasi-experiment is consistent with keeping-up-with-the-Joneses behaviors. Similarly, Agarwal, Mikhed, and Scholnick (2016) find that Canadian households who live next to lottery winners are more likely to file for bankruptcy, suggesting high spending in an attempt to keep up with the neighbors. These behaviors, in aggregate, can shape macroeconomic trends. For instance, the decline in US personal savings rates may be driven by middle-class households spending a greater share of their income, particularly on visible goods and services, in response to the growing income and consumption of neighboring top earners (Bertrand and Morse 2016).

In this, and the education setting before, we have focused on the perceptions of peers and neighbors. For our next setting we consider how even the perceptions that strangers have of us can impact our decisions.

Giving Pressure   *[Public Finance]*

Recall that this chapter began by evaluating competing theories for philanthropic giving. In particular, we argued that warm-glow giving could better explain typical giving behaviors than pure altruism. We now introduce social pressure as a third possible explanation.

Suppose individuals are motivated by neither altruism nor warm-glow concerns, but care that others do not perceive them as ungenerous. When directly asked to donate, they would be motivated to say yes if doing so protects their social image as a charitable person who cares about the disadvantaged. Or alternatively, the utility cost to their social image by saying no could be greater than the cost of simply making a small donation. For example, social pressure could induce someone to give when a neighbor is at the door asking for donations to help the local children's hospital, or a student at one's alma mater is on the phone seeking donations to support scholarships.

Observe a key distinction between warm-glow giving and giving motivated by such social image concerns. With warm-glow, individuals seek out opportunities to give so as to experience the joy of giving. But with social image concerns, individuals avoid situations where they might be asked to give. The following field experiment leverages this insight to disentangle these two possible explanations.

Field Experiment — Door-to-Door Fundraising (DellaVigna, List, and Malmendier 2012)

From April to October of 2008, over 7,500 households in the Chicago area were approached via a door-to-door fundraising drive for charity. Households were randomly assigned to one of three groups:

1   Control: Solicitor knocks on door asking for charitable contribution.
2   Simple Flyer Treatment: A flyer is left on the doorknob notifying the household of the time during the next day when the solicitor would arrive.
3   Opt-Out Flyer Treatment: Same as above, expect the flyer also includes an option for the household to indicate that they do not want to be disturbed (by checking a box and leaving the flyer on the doorknob for the solicitor to see the next day).

Because of random assignment, any difference in average giving behaviors across the households in these groups must be due to the flyers. If households are primarily motivated to give because of altruism and/or warm-glow, the flyers would encourage individuals to be home when the solicitor arrives the next day so that they can give and enhance their utility. But if households are instead primarily motivated to give because of social pressure, the flyers would discourage individuals to be home or answer the door when the solicitor arrives the next day so as to avoid the damage to their social image by telling the solicitor face-to-face that they do not want to donate.

DellaVigna, List, and Malmendier (2012) document the following results:

1   Both flyers reduce the probability that a household opens the door.
2   Overall giving is unaffected by the simple flyer.
3   Overall giving is reduced by 28% with the opt-out flyer. This decrease is due entirely to fewer small donations (under $10), with no change in larger donations.

This field experiment identifies the important, but not exclusive, role of social pressure in charitable giving.[15] Consistent with social pressure, when households are informed about an upcoming opportunity to give, they seek to avoid the interaction by not answering the door. But if only social pressure mattered, the simple flyer should have also reduced overall giving. The fact that it is unaffected implies that the reduction in giving from those avoiding the door is counterbalanced by an increase in giving from altruistic/warm-glow givers who use the flyer information to make themselves available for giving. Finally, the reduction in small, but not larger, donations caused by the opt-out flyer once again points to social pressure. Those who give only to avoid saying no are most likely to give small amounts, and the opt-out box allows these households to easily ignore the solicitation request and avoid making the small gift.

Our discussion has focused on why individuals would make small donations to avoid an undesirable social image. But it is also entirely possible that wealthy individuals, similarly motivated by social image concerns, make large visible donations primarily to enhance their social prestige. Thus, conspicuousness can matter in giving, just as it does in consuming.

14.5.3   Social Norms   *[Industrial Organization, Development]*

The desires to cultivate a social image as the type of person who is popular, economically successful, and/or generous are reasonable motivations for behavior beyond standard costs and benefits. We may also aim to be perceived by others (and ourselves) as someone who upholds **social norms**, or shared expectations for appropriate behavior. For instance, we may seek to avoid the social disapproval, disrespect, or exclusion that follows a deviation from the norm. Even in the absence of external social pressures, self-image concerns may motivate adherence to the norm so as to avoid embarrassment, shame, or guilt.[16]

Social norms are culturally specific, varying in significant ways across social groups both large and small. Altruism and reciprocity, for example, can be understood as social norms. While some cultures may have a strong norm for positive reciprocity, with an obligation to return acts of kindness with kindness, others may not share this social expectation. In fact, survey evidence from 80,000 people across 76 countries reveals substantial regional differences in altruistic and reciprocal social preferences

(Falk et al. 2018). At a smaller scale, the evidence from the SAT Peer Pressure Field Experiment suggests that the social norm for school effort differs across honors and non-honors classes within the same school. In the remainder of this section we review economic evidence of social norms for tipping, fertility, and gender roles.

Recall the restaurant tipping puzzle (Section 13.1.2): actual tipping behaviors are inconsistent with the assumption that diners have standard self-interested preferences. Suppose instead that tipping is motivated by adherence to a social norm of fairly rewarding a server for their effort. Then by tipping less than what is considered socially fair, a customer violates the social norm and consequently experiences external disapproval (e.g., from dining partners, the waiter, restaurant manager) and/or internal feelings of guilt. This potential disutility incentivizes more tipping than we would expect without such social or self-image concerns. Conlin, Lynn, and O'Donoghue (2003) find, using US data, that the responsiveness of tipping to a multitude of factors, including age, gender, group size, and dining frequency, is indeed consistent with tipping as a social norm. The dramatically different tipping behaviors across countries therefore suggests differences in social norms for what it means to fairly reward a server.

Given that social norms can influence behavior, where do they come from? While there is evidence that social norms of the present are strongly influenced by the institutions and practices of the distant past (Alesina, Giuliano, and Nunn 2011; Lowes et al. 2017), they are also malleable over short horizons. Television programming in particular can be a powerful influence for shaping social norms. In Brazil, the families portrayed on soap operas are much smaller than is typical for the country. And Brazilian women with access to these soap operas in turn have fewer children than those without access, suggesting adherence to a media-produced norm (La Ferrara, Chong, and Duryea 2012). Similar evidence from India finds that the introduction of cable TV is associated with lower fertility and a significant decrease in the reported acceptability of domestic violence towards women (Jensen and Oster 2009). The social norms established by TV can therefore impact important family decisions and attitudes within a short period.

Finally, it is possible that people misperceive social norms. Bursztyn, González, and Yanagizawa-Drott (2020) find that most young married men in Saudi Arabia privately support women working outside the home, although for only 4% are their wives doing so. Notably, the same men underestimate the level of this support among other men, including their neighbors. When men are informed about the actual higher support among others, thereby correcting their perception of what is acceptable in the eyes of the community, they become much more likely to help their wives search for a job. In effect, the information diminishes the expectation of social sanction for their wives pursuing outside employment. This evidence illustrates how behavior is responsive not simply to underlying social norms, but to how they are understood and perceived. In the next chapter we explore the ways in which social norms can be leveraged to pursue policy goals.

14.6 Summary

1 **Altruists** care directly about the utility achieved by others.
2 In the **altruism model of giving** the self values the supply of charitable services supported by giving.

3 In the **warm-glow model of giving** the self values the act of giving.

4 The empirical evidence of philanthropic giving (i.e., incomplete **crowding-out** and giving to multiple charities) is better explained by warm-glow (or impure altruism) than pure altruism.

5 In the **distributional model of preferences** the self cares about the distribution of outcomes across individuals. Two special cases are:

    a **differential altruism**, for which distributions with better outcomes for anyone are preferred; and

    b **difference/inequality aversion**, for which more equal distributions are preferred.

6 Empirical evidence from lab games is consistent with difference/inequality-averse preferences.

7 **Positive (negative) reciprocity** occurs when individuals respond to perceived kind (unkind) intentions with kindness (unkindness).

8 Reciprocity can explain behaviors in the lab (ultimatum game) and the field (gift exchange, labor effort).

9 **Social image concerns** introduce **social pressure** as an influence on observable actions. Individuals may be further motivated to maintain a particular **self-image** or **identity**.

10 Evidence from field and quasi-experiments demonstrates that social pressure matters for student effort, **conspicuous consumption**, and philanthropic giving.

11 **Social norms** are shared expectations for appropriate behavior. There is evidence that social image concerns with upholding such norms can influence a range of behaviors, from tipping to fertility and women's labor supply.

14.7 Exercises[17]

Exercise 14.1 — Putting in Your Two Cents. [Calculus Required] Aatiya is deciding how much of her \$1,200 wealth to give to two possible charities (call them charities 1 and 2). Both charities have the same charity production function $C(G) = \ln(G)$ where G is total donations received. Aatiya is a pure altruist, with preferences represented by:

$$U_{Aatiya}^{AL} = \ln\left(1200 - g_1 - g_2\right) + a_1 \cdot \ln\left(g_1 + G_o\right) + a_2 \cdot \ln\left(g_2 + 600\right)$$

where a_1 and a_2 are her altruism parameters for the two charities, and g_1 and g_2 are her monetary gifts to the two charities, respectively. Observe that charity 1 receives G_o from others and charity 2 receives \$600 from others.

    a Suppose that Aatiya feels altruistically only towards charity 1, so that $a_1 > 0$ and $a_2 = 0$. She therefore gives nothing to charity 2 ($g_2 = 0$). Determine how much she gives to charity 1, in terms of a_1 and G_o. How does her giving change when a_1 increases? When G_o increases? Interpret your answers.

    b Now suppose that Aatiya feels equally altruistic towards the charities, with $a_1 = a_2 = 1$. In addition, assume that charity 1 gets no other donations ($G_o = 0$). Determine how much she gives to each charity.

Aatiya's friend Basit also has \$1,200 of wealth to give to the two charities, but he is motivated only by warm-glow, with preferences represented by:

$$U_{Basit}^{WG} = \ln(1200 - g_1 - g_2) + \ln(g_1) + \ln(g_2)$$

Observe that Basit is unconcerned with giving by others and applies the same warm-glow giving function $\omega(g) = \ln(g)$ when giving to either charity.

c   Determine how much Basit gives to each charity.
d   Compare Basit's giving to the two charities (in part c) to Aatiya's giving to the two charities (in part b). Which model of giving better aligns with the evidence that people typically give to multiple charities?

Exercise 14.2 — Warmth in Numbers (Ribar and Wilhelm 2002). [Calculus Required] Soleil has \$1,000 of wealth to allocate between spending on herself or giving to a charity. She has preferences represented by the following utility function:

$$U_s = \ln(1000 - g_s) + a \cdot \ln(g_s + G_o) + w \cdot \ln(g_s)$$

where g_s is her own charitable gift and G_o is total giving to the charity by others. The parameter $a \geq 0$ is the altruism parameter and $w \geq 0$ captures the intensity of warm-glow.

a   Interpret each of the three components of this utility function. What is the name for such preferences?
b   Determine Soleil's first order condition that characterizes her utility-maximizing gift g_s (assuming that she observes, but has no control over G_o).
c   Soleil lives in a community of N people (including herself), each with identical wealth and preferences for giving. Because everyone is identical, each of the other $N - 1$ individuals will make the same size donation as Soleil. We can write this mathematically as $G_o = (N - 1)g_s$. Plug this into your first order condition in part (b) to eliminate G_o and solve for g_s in terms of N, a, and w. This is the equilibrium level of individual giving in the community. How do increases in a and w impact your answer? Interpret.
d   To what level does individual giving g_s in part (c) converge if the population size N approaches infinity? How do increases in a and w impact this limit? What do your answers reveal about the motivations for giving when there is a very large number of donors?

Exercise 14.3 — Playing with Distributions. Alice (A) and Ben (B) are anonymously paired with each other to play a lab game. They have distributional preferences represented by the following utility functions:

$$U_A(x_A, x_B) = \begin{cases} (1 - \rho)x_A + \rho x_B & \text{if } x_A \geq x_B \\ 2x_A - x_B & \text{if } x_A < x_B \end{cases}$$

$$U_B(x_A, x_B) = \begin{cases} x_B & \text{if } x_B \geq x_A \\ 2x_B - x_A & \text{if } x_B < x_A \end{cases}$$

where $0 < \rho < 1$, and x_A and x_B are the monetary outcomes for Alice and Ben, respectively.

a   Does Alice exhibit a preference for differential altruism or inequality aversion? What about Ben?

b   Suppose they play the dictator game in which Alice is given $120 and may transfer any amount to Ben. If $\rho = 0.4$, how much money will Alice give to Ben? What if $\rho = 0.6$?

c   Suppose that instead of playing the dictator game, the two players play the ultimatum game with Alice again as the proposer with $120 to split. How much of the $120 will Alice transfer to Ben if $\rho = 0.4$? What if $\rho = 0.6$? *Hint: Think first about Ben's reject/accept decision and assume that when indifferent, he will accept. Then consider Alice's best decision given Ben's response.*

Exercise 14.4 — Distributing Charity. Provide at least two reasons for why the distributional model of preferences in Definition 14.4 is unlikely to explain actual charitable giving behaviors in the real world.

Exercise 14.5 — Moonlighting. Falk, Fehr, and Fischbacher (2008) run lab experiments of the moonlighting game. In this game two players, call them A and B, are each given $12. The game proceeds in two stages:

1   A can gift at most $6 to B, and for every $1 gifted, B receives $3. A can alternatively choose to take up to $6 *away* from B for herself.

2   B observes A's choice in stage 1 and then makes a choice. B can gift money to A. Or, B can "pay" the experimenter up to $6 to take money away from A, with every dollar paid by B reducing A's payoff by $3.

Let's focus on the preferences of player B.

a   Suppose that B is self-interested. What is the prediction for B's choice in stage 2?

b   No B players behave according to the prediction of self-interested preferences. Suppose instead that B has distributional preferences that depend only on how the money is distributed. To test this hypothesis, the experimenters introduce a randomized version of the above moonlighting game in which the choice by A in stage 1 is determined at random by rolling a pair of dice. With distributional preferences, would you expect B players to behave similarly or differently across the original and randomized versions of the game? Explain.

c   The experimenters find that in the original game 76% of B players rewarded a gift (with a gift) or punished a take (with a sanction) by player A. But only 39% of B players rewarded or punished in the randomized version of the game. Is this evidence consistent with your prediction in part (b)? If not, what does the evidence suggest about B's preferences?

Exercise 14.6 — The Road Not Taken. Two players A and B have distributional preferences as follows:

$$
U_A(x_A, x_B) = \begin{cases} \dfrac{1}{2}x_A + \dfrac{1}{2}x_B & \text{if } x_A \geq x_B \\ (1 - \sigma)x_A + \sigma x_B & \text{if } x_A < x_B \end{cases}
$$

$$
U_B(x_A, x_B) = \begin{cases} \dfrac{1}{2}x_B + \dfrac{1}{2}x_A & \text{if } x_B \geq x_A \\ (1 - \sigma)x_B + \sigma x_A & \text{if } x_B < x_A \end{cases}
$$

where $\sigma < \frac{1}{2}$. They play the following game: A makes a choice between monetary outcome $(x_A, x_B) = (-8, -10)$ or letting B choose between two outcomes: $(x_A, x_B) = (0, 0)$ or $(x_A, x_B) = (6, 0)$.

a   Which option would B choose if given the choice? Anticipating this, which option does A choose? Your answers may depend on σ. Interpret. *Note: Do not worry about values of σ that cause indifference for either player.*

b   Suppose that A instead has an option between $(x_A, x_B) = (4, 12)$ or giving player B the same choice as in part (a). Repeat part (a) for this variation.

c   Suggest intuitively plausible real-world behaviors in these two games that are inconsistent with any single value of σ. What does this suggest about a shortcoming for this model of social preferences?

Exercise 14.7 — Model Student. [Calculus Required] Recall the Library Gift Exchange Field Experiment. Let's model the student worker behavior in this setting. Let w denote the total worker earnings over the 6-hour shift. Assume that the disutility of labor effort $e \geq 0$ is $ce^2/2$, with $c > 0$. For each unit of worker effort, the library gains a benefit $v > 0$. Suppose that the worker's utility function is:

$$U(e) = w - c\frac{e^2}{2} + a(ve - w)$$

where a is a constant.

a   Provide an interpretation of this utility function. In particular, what do the first two terms capture? What does the $ve-w$ term capture? And what is the intuition for a positive, zero, or negative?

b   Determine the worker's utility-maximizing effort level, $e^* \geq 0$. *Note: Be sure that your answer for* e^* *is non-negative for all possible values of* a. Discuss your answer, providing intuition for how e^* depends on a, v, and c.

c   Introduce reciprocity to the model by assuming that surprise wage changes impact the value of a. Given your work in part (b), discuss how this model of reciprocity could explain the empirical evidence in the Library Gift Exchange Field Experiment.

Exercise 14.8 — The Thought Counts. [Labor] Kube, Maréchal, and Puppe (2012) study worker effort in the following field experiment. Workers were recruited to enter book information into an electronic database for 3 hours at an announced wage of €12 per hour. A control group was paid the promised €36 for their work. A "Money" treatment group was surprised with an additional cash gift of €7. A different "Bottle" treatment group was surprised with a thermos bottle gift (worth €7). The average productivities, as measured by characters entered per 30 minute interval, are pictured in Figure 14.3. How do each of the treatments compare with the control group? Discuss what these results suggest about the workers' preferences and motivations.

Exercise 14.9 — Drawing Out Donations. [Public Finance] Falk (2007) conducts a field experiment in which almost 10,000 mailings were sent to residents in Zurich, Switzerland soliciting donations for schools in Dhaka, Bangladesh. Some solicitations included postcards with colored paintings by school children from Dhaka, while others did not.

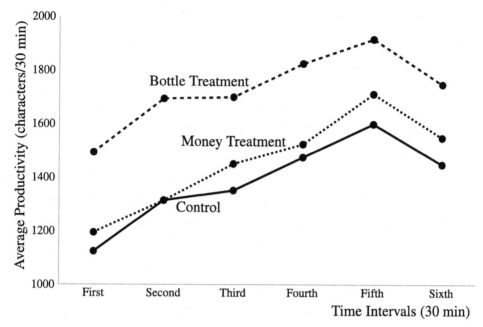

Figure 14.3 Average Worker Productivity in Exercise 14.8

Data Source: Kube, Maréchal, and Puppe (2012).

Randomized Groups	Postcards in Solicitation	Donation Rate
Control	Zero	12.2%
Small Treatment	One	14.4%
Large Treatment	Four	20.6%

What does the evidence from this field experiment reveal about the motivations for giving?

Exercise 14.10 — Marriage Matters. [Labor] Bursztyn, Fujiwara, and Pallais (2017) conduct a field experiment with MBA students on their first day of the MBA program. The students met with a career counselor to complete a standard questionnaire about their job preferences. There were two versions of the questionnaire that differed only in the observability of the students' answers. The public version indicated that "your" answers would be discussed in the career class, while the private version indicated that "anonymized" answers would be discussed. These two versions were randomly assigned to students.

a   With standard preferences, do you expect answers to differ on average across the two questionnaire versions? What if students have social image concerns? Explain.

b   Responses by men and non-single women did not differ across the two questionnaires. But single women reported lower ambition and desired future salaries, less willingness to travel for work or to work long hours, and weaker leadership skills when their responses would be public. What does this evidence suggest about the different motivations for decision making by gender and relationship status?

Exercise 14.11 — Bending a Soccer Ball Game. [Sports] Garicano, Palacios-Huerta, and Prendergast (2005) measure the length of extra time that referees assign at the end of soccer game due to lost time for unusual stoppages. In this extra time both teams have the opportunity to score. Despite official rules for determining the length of extra time, referees typically assign twice as much extra time (4 minutes instead of 2) when the home team is one goal behind than when it is one goal ahead. This difference is even larger towards the end of the season and when stadium attendance is bigger. Interpret this evidence and discuss what it suggests about the nonstandard motivations for referee behavior.

Exercise 14.12 — Credit Where Credit's Due (Ariely, Bracha, and Meier 2009). Priya lives in environmentally-conscious Berkeley, California and is shopping for a new car. She is deciding between a standard sedan and a comparable, but more expensive, environmentally-friendly hybrid sedan.

a　Explain how Priya's concern with her positive social image would influence her car-buying decision (relative to someone without such concerns)?

b　Suppose California implements a large tax credit for those who buy a hybrid car. Discuss how the tax credit influences Priya's decision. In particular, how does it change the standard benefits and costs of a hybrid car? And how might it change the impact of buying a hybrid on Priya's social image (assuming that everyone in the state is fully aware of this tax benefit)?

c　Based on your answer in part (b), are tax credits for adopting environmentally-friendly technologies likely to have a bigger impact on consumer behavior if the technologies are publicly observable (e.g., a hybrid car) or not publicly observable (e.g., an energy-efficient home appliance)? Explain.

Exercise 14.13 — Strategic Consumption. [Calculus Required] Two neighbors, Alan (A) and Bridget (B), each choose how much of their $100 budget to spend on conspicuous consumption c. Money not spent on conspicuous consumption can be spent on other non-observable goods like groceries. They have utility functions as follows:

$$U_A(c_A, c_B) = 25c_A - 75c_B - c_A^2/2 + \gamma c_A c_B$$
$$U_B(c_B, c_A) = 25c_B - 75c_A - c_B^2/2 + \gamma c_B c_A$$

where c_A and c_B are the levels of spending on conspicuous consumption by Alan and Bridget, respectively. Assume that $0 \leq \gamma \leq 3/4$ captures how much individuals care about their perceived social status.

a　Does an increase in conspicuous consumption by one's neighbor increase or decrease one's own utility? How does the magnitude of this effect depend on one's own level of conspicuous consumption? Do your answers seem plausible for individuals who are concerned with their perceived social status?

b If Alan observes Bridget's consumption fixed at c_B, what is his utility-maximizing choice of conspicuous consumption (which depends on c_B and γ)?

c If Bridget observes Alan's consumption fixed at c_A, what is her utility-maximizing choice of conspicuous consumption (which depends on c_A and γ)?

d Using your answers in parts (b) and (c), how does more conspicuous consumption by a neighbor change an individual's own level of conspicuous consumption? What is the phenomenon called?

e Use the two equations in parts (b) and (c) to solve for c_A and c_B (in terms of γ). This is the equilibrium outcome for this neighborhood game. How does the equilibrium level of conspicuous consumption change with an increase in γ? Interpret your answer.

Exercise 14.14 — Warm-Glow Images. The model of warm-glow giving assumes that individuals value the act of giving, but is agnostic as to why this is so. Explain how both social image and self-image concerns could generate warm-glow.

Exercise 14.15 — Normal Spending. Recall the standard life-cycle model of consumption and savings decisions over one's lifetime (Section 4.5). This model predicts that individuals anticipate their future income and then smooth their consumption over time by spending their long-run average income each year. So as income fluctuates in predictable ways (e.g., up with a first job, up with promotions, down with retirement), spending on consumption remains constant. Instead, the empirical evidence reveals that consumption much more closely tracks fluctuations in income. One way to explain this sensitivity of consumption to income is with present-biased preferences (Section 5.4.3). Akerlof (2007) proposes an alternative explanation: social norms influence how much income we feel entitled or obligated to spend. Propose a scenario in which there is a social norm to spend more or less than one's long-run average income.

Notes

1 Arrow (1972) provides an early and prescient analysis of social preferences.

2 Weber (1949) articulates the traditional distinction between economists, who derive social relationships from the behaviors of individuals, and sociologists, who begin with the meaning of actions by social groups.

3 More formally, altruistic feelings transform the object of those feelings into a public good. This insight originates with Hochman and Rodgers (1969) and Kolm (1969), followed by a formal development by Becker (1974).

4 Crowding out is complete for government grants funded by lump sum taxes that do not exceed donors' private donation in the absence of the grant (Bergstrom, Blume, and Varian 1986).

5 See Andreoni (2006, Section 3.3) for a further discussion of the "absurd" predictions implied by the altruism model of giving.

6 To transform the altruism model in Definition 14.1 to the linear model $U_s^{AL} = (1 - \rho)x_s + \rho x_o$, let the utility function be $u(x) = (1 - \rho)x$ and the altruism parameter be $a = \rho/(1 - \rho)$.

7 The distributional model of preferences is a simple version of the model in Charness and Rabin (2002), which itself is influenced by the model in Fehr and Schmidt (1999).

8 See Bolton (1991) and Bolton and Ockenfels (2000) for alternative models of inequality aversion.

9 Charness and Rabin (2002) find that a social-welfare model of preferences like differential altruism, not inequality aversion, best fits behavior across a wide range of lab games.

10 Note that by reciprocity we assume away reputational concerns. In repeated interactions individuals may find it in their own self-interest to reciprocate kindness at some personal cost in order to obtain a future private benefit. This type of reputational reciprocity is consistent with standard preferences.

11 Models that integrate reciprocity with distributional concerns are developed by Charness and Rabin (2002), Falk and Fischbacher (2006), and Cox, Friedman, and Gjerstad (2007).

12 See Bénabou and Tirole (2006) and Bursztyn and Jensen (2017) for more formal developments of social image models, from which the definition of social image concerns here is adapted.

13 See Austen-Smith and Fryer (2005) for a signaling model in an education setting with multiple audiences.

14 Bursztyn and Jensen (2017) provide an excellent review of social pressure evidence from the field.

15 Andreoni, Rao, and Trachtman (2017) conduct a related field experiment with Salvation Army solicitors in front of one or both entrances of a grocery store. While their findings of donor avoidance are consistent with social pressure, they conclude that a better explanation for the observed behavior is an intentional moderation of empathic stimuli to regulate emotions.

16 To learn more about social norms in economics, see Elster (1989), Posner and Rasmusen (1999), Basu (2001), and Bénabou and Tirole (2011).

17 Exercises 14.3, 14.6, and 14.7 are adapted from exercises by Lorenz Goette, Botond Kőszegi, and Stefano DellaVigna, respectively.

References

Agarwal, Sumit, Vyacheslav Mikhed, and Barry Scholnick. 2016. "Does Inequality Cause Financial Distress? Evidence from Lottery Winners and Neighboring Bankruptcies." SSRN Scholarly Paper ID 2731562. Rochester, NY: Social Science Research Network. https://papers.ssrn.com/abstract=2731562.

Akerlof, George A. 1982. "Labor Contracts as Partial Gift Exchange." *The Quarterly Journal of Economics* 97 (4): 543–569. doi:10.2307/1885099.

———. 2007. "The Missing Motivation in Macroeconomics." *American Economic Review* 97 (1): 5–36. doi:10.1257/aer.97.1.5.

Akerlof, George A., and Rachel E. Kranton. 2000. "Economics and Identity." *The Quarterly Journal of Economics* 115 (3): 715–753. doi:10.1162/003355300554881.

Alesina, Alberto, Paola Giuliano, and Nathan Nunn. 2011. "Fertility and the Plough." *American Economic Review* 101 (3): 499–503. doi:10.1257/aer.101.3.499.

Andreoni, James. 1989. "Giving with Impure Altruism: Applications to Charity and Ricardian Equivalence." *Journal of Political Economy* 97 (6): 1447–1458. doi:10.1086/261662.

———. 1990. "Impure Altruism and Donations to Public Goods: A Theory of Warm-Glow Giving." *The Economic Journal* 100 (401): 464–477. doi:10.2307/2234133.

———. 2006. "Philanthropy." In *Handbook of the Economics of Giving, Altruism and Reciprocity*, edited by Serge-Christophe Kolm and Jean Mercier Ythier, 2:1201–1269. Elsevier. doi:10.1016/S1574-0714 (06)02018-5.

Andreoni, James, Justin M. Rao, and Hannah Trachtman. 2017. "Avoiding the Ask: A Field Experiment on Altruism, Empathy, and Charitable Giving." *Journal of Political Economy* 125 (3): 625–653. doi:10.1086/691703.

Ariely, Dan, Anat Bracha, and Stephan Meier. 2009. "Doing Good or Doing Well? Image Motivation and Monetary Incentives in Behaving Prosocially." *American Economic Review* 99 (1): 544–555. doi:10.1257/aer.99.1.544.

Arrow, Kenneth J. 1972. "Gifts and Exchanges." *Philosophy & Public Affairs* 1 (4): 343–362. https://www.jstor.org/stable/2265097.

Austen-Smith, David, and Roland G. Fryer. 2005. "An Economic Analysis of 'Acting White'." *The Quarterly Journal of Economics* 120 (2): 551–583. doi:10.1093/qje/120.2.551.

Basu, Kaushik. 2001. "The Role of Social Norms and Law in Economics: An Essay on Political Economy." In *Schools of Thought: Twenty-Five Years of Interpretive Social Science*, edited by Joan Wallach Scott and Debra Keates, 154–178. Princeton, NJ: Princeton University Press.

Becker, Gary S. 1974. "A Theory of Social Interactions." *Journal of Political Economy* 82 (6): 1063–1093. https://www.jstor.org/stable/1830662.

Belshaw, Cyril S. 1965. *Traditional Exchange and Modern Markets*. 1st ed. Englewood Cliffs, NJ: Prentice Hill.

Bénabou, Roland, and Jean Tirole. 2006. "Incentives and Prosocial Behavior." *American Economic Review* 96 (5): 1652–1678. doi:10.1257/aer.96.5.1652.

Bénabou, Roland, and Jean Tirole. 2011. "Laws and Norms." NBER Working Paper 17579. Cambridge, MA: National Bureau of Economic Research. doi:10.3386/w17579.

Bergstrom, Theodore, Lawrence Blume, and Hal R. Varian. 1986. "On the Private Provision of Public Goods." *Journal of Public Economics* 29 (1): 25–49.

Bertrand, Marianne, and Adair Morse. 2016. "Trickle-Down Consumption." *The Review of Economics and Statistics* 98 (5): 863–879. doi:10.1162/REST_a_00613.

Bolton, Gary E. 1991. "A Comparative Model of Bargaining: Theory and Evidence." *American Economic Review* 81 (5): 1096–1136. https://www.jstor.org/stable/2006908.

Bolton, Gary E., and Axel Ockenfels. 2000. "ERC: A Theory of Equity, Reciprocity, and Competition." *American Economic Review* 90 (1): 166–193. doi:10.1257/aer. 90.1.166.

Bursztyn, Leonardo, Thomas Fujiwara, and Amanda Pallais. 2017. "'Acting Wife': Marriage Market Incentives and Labor Market Investments." *American Economic Review* 107 (11): 3288–3319. doi:10.1257/aer.20170029.

Bursztyn, Leonardo, Alessandra L. González, and David Yanagizawa-Drott. 2020. "Misperceived Social Norms: Women Working Outside the Home in Saudi Arabia." *American Economic Review* 110 (10): 2997–3029. doi:10.1257/aer.20180975.

Bursztyn, Leonardo, and Robert Jensen. 2015. "How Does Peer Pressure Affect Educational Investments?" *The Quarterly Journal of Economics* 130 (3): 1329–1367. doi:10.1093/qje/qjv021.

———. 2017. "Social Image and Economic Behavior in the Field: Identifying, Understanding, and Shaping Social Pressure." *Annual Review of Economics* 9 (1): 131–153. doi:10.1146/annurev-economics-063016-103625.

Charness, Gary, and Matthew Rabin. 2002. "Understanding Social Preferences with Simple Tests." *The Quarterly Journal of Economics* 117 (3): 817–869. doi:10.1162/003355302760193904.

Clark, Andrew E., Paul Frijters, and Michael A. Shields. 2008. "Relative Income, Happiness, and Utility: An Explanation for the Easterlin Paradox and Other Puzzles." *Journal of Economic Literature* 46 (1): 95–144. doi:10.1257/jel.46.1.95.

Conlin, Michael, Michael Lynn, and Ted O'Donoghue. 2003. "The Norm of Restaurant Tipping." *Journal of Economic Behavior & Organization* 52 (3): 297–321. doi:10.1016/S0167-2681(03)00030-1.

Cox, James C., Daniel Friedman, and Steven Gjerstad. 2007. "A Tractable Model of Reciprocity and Fairness." *Games and Economic Behavior* 59 (1): 17–45. doi:10.1016/j.geb.2006.05.001.

DellaVigna, Stefano, John A. List, and Ulrike Malmendier. 2012. "Testing for Altruism and Social Pressure in Charitable Giving." *The Quarterly Journal of Economics* 127 (1): 1–56. doi:10.1093/qje/qjr050.

Elster, Jon. 1989. "Social Norms and Economic Theory." *Journal of Economic Perspectives* 3 (4): 99–117. doi:10.1257/jep.3.4.99.

Etzioni, Amitai. 2015. "The Moral Effects of Economic Teaching." *Sociological Forum* 30 (1): 228–233. doi:10.1111/socf.12153.

Falk, Armin. 2007. "Gift Exchange in the Field." *Econometrica* 75 (5): 1501–1511. doi:10.1111/j.1468-0262.2007.00800.x.

Falk, Armin, Anke Becker, Thomas Dohmen, Benjamin Enke, David Huffman, and Uwe Sunde. 2018. "Global Evidence on Economic Preferences." *The Quarterly Journal of Economics* 133 (4): 1645–1692. doi:10.1093/qje/qjy013.

Falk, Armin, Ernst Fehr, and Urs Fischbacher. 2003. "On the Nature of Fair Behavior." *Economic Inquiry* 41 (1): 20–26. doi:10.1093/ei/41.1.20.

———. 2008. "Testing Theories of Fairness — Intentions Matter." *Games and Economic Behavior* 62 (1): 287–303. doi:10.1016/j.geb. 2007.06.001.

Falk, Armin, and Urs Fischbacher. 2006. "A Theory of Reciprocity." *Games and Economic Behavior* 54 (2): 293–315. doi:10.1016/j.geb.2005.03.001.

Fehr, Ernst, Erich Kirchler, Andreas Weichbold, and Simon Gächter. 1998. "When Social Norms Overpower Competition: Gift Exchange in Experimental Labor Markets." *Journal of Labor Economics* 16 (2): 324–351. doi:10.1086/209891.

Fehr, Ernst, Georg Kirchsteiger, and Arno Riedl. 1993. "Does Fairness Prevent Market Clearing? An Experimental Investigation." *The Quarterly Journal of Economics* 108 (2): 437–459. doi:10.2307/2118338.

Fehr, Ernst, Michael Naef, and Klaus M. Schmidt. 2006. "Inequality Aversion, Efficiency, and Maximin Preferences in Simple Distribution Experiments: Comment." *American Economic Review* 96 (5): 1912–1917. doi:10.1257/aer.96.5.1912.

Fehr, Ernst, and Klaus M. Schmidt. 1999. "A Theory of Fairness, Competition, and Cooperation." *The Quarterly Journal of Economics* 114 (3): 817–868. doi:10.1162/003355399556151.

Fisman, Raymond, Pamela Jakiela, and Shachar Kariv. 2017. "Distributional Preferences and Political Behavior." *Journal of Public Economics* 155: 1–10. doi:10.1016/j. jpubeco.2017.08.010.

Fisman, Raymond, Pamela Jakiela, Shachar Kariv, and Daniel Markovits. 2015. "The Distributional Preferences of an Elite." *Science* 349 (6254). doi:10.1126/science. aab0096.

Frank, Robert H. 1985. "The Demand for Unobservable and Other Nonpositional Goods." *American Economic Review* 75 (1): 101–116. https://www.jstor.org/stable/1812706.

Garicano, Luis, Ignacio Palacios-Huerta, and Canice Prendergast. 2005. "Favoritism under Social Pressure." *The Review of Economics and Statistics* 87 (2): 208–216. doi:10.1162/0034653053970267.

Gneezy, Uri, and John A. List. 2006. "Putting Behavioral Economics to Work: Testing for Gift Exchange in Labor Markets Using Field Experiments." *Econometrica* 74 (5): 1365–1384. doi:10.1111/j.1468-0262.2006.00707.x.

Gruber, Jonathan, and Daniel M. Hungerman. 2007. "Faith-Based Charity and Crowd-out During the Great Depression." *Journal of Public Economics* 91 (5): 1043–1069. doi:10.1016/j.jpubeco.2006.11.004.

Hochman, Harold M., and James D. Rodgers. 1969. "Pareto Optimal Redistribution." *American Economic Review* 59 (4): 542–557. https://www.jstor.org/stable/1813216.

Hungerman, Daniel M. 2005. "Are Church and State Substitutes? Evidence from the 1996 Welfare Reform." *Journal of Public Economics* 89 (11): 2245–2267. doi:10.1016/j.jpubeco.2004.12.009.

Jensen, Robert, and Emily Oster. 2009. "The Power of TV: Cable Television and Women's Status in India." *The Quarterly Journal of Economics* 124 (3): 1057–1094. doi:10.1162/qjec.2009.124.3.1057.

Kolm, S. Ch. 1969. "The Optimal Production of Social Justice." In *Public Economics: An Analysis of Public Production and Consumption and their Relations to the Private Sectors*, edited by J. Margolis and H. Guitton, 145–200. London: Macmillan Press.

Kube, Sebastian, Michel André Maréchal, and Clemens Puppe. 2006. "Putting Reciprocity to Work — Positive Versus Negative Responses in the Field." SSRN Scholarly Paper ID 944393. Rochester, NY: Social Science Research Network. doi:10.2139/ssrn. 944393.

———. 2012. "The Currency of Reciprocity: Gift Exchange in the Workplace." *American Economic Review* 102 (4): 1644–1662. doi:10.1257/aer.102.4.1644.

Kuhn, Peter, Peter Kooreman, Adriaan Soetevent, and Arie Kapteyn. 2011. "The Effects of Lottery Prizes on Winners and Their Neighbors: Evidence from the Dutch Postcode Lottery." *American Economic Review* 101 (5): 2226–2247. doi:10.1257/aer.101.5.2226.

La Ferrara, Eliana, Alberto Chong, and Suzanne Duryea. 2012. "Soap Operas and Fertility: Evidence from Brazil." *American Economic Journal: Applied Economics* 4 (4): 1–31. doi:10.1257/app.4.4.1.

Li, Jing, William H. Dow, and Shachar Kariv. 2017. "Social Preferences of Future Physicians." *Proceedings of the National Academy of Sciences* 114 (48): E10291–E10300. doi:10.1073/pnas.1705451114.

Lowes, Sara, Nathan Nunn, James A. Robinson, and Jonathan L. Weigel. 2017. "The Evolution of Culture and Institutions: Evidence from the Kuba Kingdom." *Econometrica* 85 (4): 1065–1091. doi:10.3982/ECTA14139.

Mauss, Marcel. 1954. *The Gift: Forms and Functions of Exchange in Archaic Societies*. Translated by Ian Cunnison. London: Cohen / West.

Maximiano, Sandra, Randolph Sloof, and Joep Sonnemans. 2007. "Gift Exchange in a Multi-Worker Firm." *The Economic Journal* 117 (522): 1025–1050. doi:10.1111/j.1468-0297.2007.02065.x.

Payne, A. Abigail. 1998. "Does the Government Crowd-out Private Donations? New Evidence from a Sample of Non-profit Firms." *Journal of Public Economics* 69 (3): 323–345. doi:10.1016/S0047-2727(98)00005-X.

Posner, Richard A., and Eric B. Rasmusen. 1999. "Creating and Enforcing Norms." *International Review of Law and Economics* 19 (3): 369–382. doi:10.1016/S0144-8188(99)00013-7.

Ribar, David C., and Mark O. Wilhelm. 2002. "Altruistic and Joy-of-Giving Motivations in Charitable Behavior." *Journal of Political Economy* 110 (2): 425–457. doi:10.1086/338750.

Roberts, Russell D. 1984. "A Positive Model of Private Charity and Public Transfers." *Journal of Political Economy* 92 (1): 136–148. doi:10.1086/261212.

Strohmetz, David B., Bruce Rind, Reed Fisher, and Michael Lynn. 2002. "Sweetening the Till: The Use of Candy to Increase Restaurant Tipping." *Journal of Applied Social Psychology* 32 (2): 300–309. doi:10.1111/j.1559-1816.2002.tb00216.x.

Veblen, Thorstein. 1899. *The Theory of the Leisure Class: An Economic Study of Institutions.* New York: Macmillan.

Weber, Max. 1949. "Objectivity in Social Science and Policy." In *Max Weber on the Methodology of the Social Sciences,* edited by Edward A. Shils and Henry A. Finch, 1–188. Glencoe, IL: Free Press.

Yu, Daniela, and Amy Adkins. 2016. "Charitable Giving: Donors Focus on One or Two Organizations." *Gallup,* June 14, 2016. https://news.gallup.com/businessjournal/192689/charitable-giving-donors-focus-one-two-organizations.aspx.

15   Market & Policy Responses to Social Preferences

Learning Objectives

★ Consider employer strategies to motivate workers with social preferences.

★ Understand how persistent unemployment can be explained by fairness concerns.

★ Appreciate the impact of social preferences on the design of optimal tax policies.

★ Evaluate the effectiveness of social pressure as a policy tool.

When consumers, workers, and citizens exhibit the kinds of social preferences documented in the previous chapter, businesses and governments have at their disposal a broader range of levers to influence behavior. And policies that optimize profits or welfare with standard self-interested individuals may no longer be optimal in a world characterized by altruism, envy, reciprocity, and social image concerns.

Take the case of a restaurant seeking to increase tip income for its servers. With standard customers who are predicted to offer minimal tips for service, the only option for the restaurant would be to introduce an automatic gratuity fee to all bills. But with social preferences, the restaurant could leverage positive reciprocity by gifting customers a piece of chocolate just before delivering the bill. Or to extract higher tips from customers concerned with maintaining a generous social image, the server could increase the visibility of tipping by asking customers paying with a credit card to announce how much they want to tip (instead of allowing the tip to be discreetly written on the bill). Analogous strategies apply for a non-profit organization seeking to increase charitable donations: delivering small gifts to potential donors or publicly announcing donations.

This chapter explores both the evidence and theory for the impact of social preferences on markets and public policy. We begin with employer practices to promote worker motivation and satisfaction. The reciprocal gift-exchange relationship between workers and firms can also help to explain the persistence of unemployment. And in the second half of the chapter we turn to the implications for public policy, including traditional tax policy as well as nudges that shape social pressure.

DOI: 10.4324/9780367854072-20

15.1 Employers   [Labor]

Employers face a complex set of personnel decisions. But no matter the industry or objective (e.g., profit, market share, social impact), firms benefit, all else equal, from workers who are productive and satisfied. This section explores how the social preferences of workers can inform employer strategies for promoting such productivity and satisfaction.

15.1.1 Worker Effort under Pressure

A classic problem in personnel economics is how to encourage high effort from workers. Employers make use of promotions, raises, bonuses, prizes, and of course, the threat of firing (Lazear and Shaw 2007). But for workers with nonstandard preferences, firms may also be able to induce greater worker effort without increasing their own payroll expenditures. Recall that loss averse teachers and factory workers are responsive to the framing of a productivity incentive (Sections 10.3 and 10.4). Incentives structured as lotteries can increase effort for individuals with non-expected utility preferences (Section 12.3.2). And a surprise bonus induces more effort when it takes the form of a non-monetary gift rather than the gift's cash equivalence (Exercise 14.8).

Social image concerns provide another channel through which workers may be motivated. Suppose that workers value being perceived as high-achieving performers by their colleagues. By increasing the observability of worker performance, employers can then intensify social pressure for high effort, without providing any additional compensation. Let's consider two ways in which one's effort can be observable: working in the line-of-sight of co-workers and receiving public recognition for excellence.

A common setting where worker effort can be directly observed by colleagues is in a supermarket. The architecture of most supermarkets is that cashiers work at registers lined up in a row at the front of the store. The productivity of a cashier, measured by the speed at which they scan customer items, is therefore observable only to the cashiers at their back. Mas and Moretti (2009) find that when a high-productivity cashier joins a shift, it causes a productivity increase only for the cashiers in their line-of-sight, with no effect on those behind them. This effect is substantial: a one-percent-higher-productivity worker increases the productivity of co-workers they can observe by a quarter percent, with an even larger impact for physically closer co-workers.

Social pressure provides a compelling explanation for this evidence. The increase in effort when observable by a high-productivity co-worker suggests that cashiers are concerned with how the quality of their work is perceived by their hard-working peers. The fact that high-productivity workers do not influence the efforts of those they do not observe further suggests that workers are responding to social pressure, and not another motivation to work harder as an act of solidarity or cooperation, even if no one is watching.

The implication for employers aiming to induce greater effort is therefore to organize employees in such a way that their work is visible to those with the highest productivity. Of course, the effectiveness of this strategy depends on high-productivity workers maintaining their own motivations for high effort. Employers might further leverage social image concerns to encourage high effort by offering public recognition of excellence. The following field experiment identifies the effectiveness of such recognition.

Field Experiment — Symbolic Awards (Kosfeld and Neckermann 2011)

In Spring 2008 university students in Zurich, Switzerland were offered the opportunity to work a one-time data entry job for two hours, paying the typical student hourly wage for the region. While all students were paid the same fixed wage, no matter their productivity, students were randomly assigned to one of two groups:

1   Award Treatment: A purely symbolic award (congratulatory card signed by the president and managing director of the organization) with no financial benefits would be presented to the two students who put forth the most effort.
2   Control: No award was offered.

Because all students were compensated with the same fixed wage, standard preferences predict students to exert the same level of effort in both groups. Due to random assignment, any differences in productivity between the award treatment and control groups must be due to the presence of the symbolic award.

Kosfeld and Neckermann (2011) find that, on average, students in the award treatment are 12% more productive than students in the control, without any reduction in work quality.

The significant increase in work effort induced by the presentation of a purely symbolic award is consistent with social image concerns. The short-term nature of the job in the above experiment rules out the possibility that students were motivated by future benefits for award-winners. We therefore conclude that at least some people are motivated to work harder simply because doing so can improve their perceived social status as a high achiever. Note that this finding is not specific to student workers or rich countries. Ashraf, Bandiera, and Lee (2014) similarly find in a field experiment with Zambian health care workers that recognition by employers increases performance. In sum, recognition can be a cheap and effective means by which employers motivate workers.

15.1.2   Pay Transparency

Suppose you are working your first job after college. Think about whether you would want to know how much your colleagues earn. Now think about whether you would want your colleagues to know how much you earn. Although it is generally considered impolite to ask someone their salary, many US companies explicitly forbid employees from discussing their salary with co-workers. And even without such a ban, employers rarely provide information on worker salaries internally, let alone to the general public.

What can explain why companies so often want to keep salary information secret?[1] After all, if workers are purely self-interested and have already decided that their salary is high enough for them to show up to work, knowing the salaries of others doesn't change the private costs and benefits of working. Worker satisfaction and behavior should therefore be unaffected, unless learning how much others are paid provides *new* information about one's own expected salary trajectory. That is, workers may interpret the average earnings of others as a signal of their own future earnings potential. In this case, learning that you are paid less than others counts as good news — you now expect to earn more in the future. Similarly, high earners would be disappointed to learn that they are in fact high earners who have little room for salary growth (Card et al. 2010).

But suppose companies suspect their employees have social preferences, concerned with how their pay compares to that of their peers. When individuals value their economic status relative to others, as evidenced in the previous chapter, pay transparency would impact worker satisfaction. While higher-paid workers would benefit from the observability of their higher status, lower-paid workers would suffer a decline in satisfaction. These are the opposite predictions from the self-interested scenario above. In addition, workers may be inequality averse. And if transparency reveals more pay inequality than workers had imagined, everyone's satisfaction is diminished, dampening the social status benefits for high earners and exacerbating the decline for low earners. Overall satisfaction could then fall and less satisfied workers may exert lower effort or look for another job. These consequences provide an incentive for managers to keep salaries secret.

The following field experiment identifies the actual effects of pay transparency on worker satisfaction.

Field Experiment — Salary Reveal (Card et al. 2012)

In March 2008 a searchable database of California public employee salaries was published online. These salaries included employees at University of California (UC) campuses. Just after the launch of the website, employees at three UC campuses were randomly assigned to one of two groups:

1   Treatment: Emailed about the existence of the salary database.
2   Control: Not emailed.

After employees in the treatment group were notified, all employees at the three UC campuses were surveyed about their pay, job satisfaction, and intention to look for a new job. Any difference in responses for employees in the same occupation across these two groups can be attributed to the information revealed by the email notification.

Card et al. (2012) estimate the impact of the pay information, taking into account the fact that not all employees in the treatment group looked at the website and not all employees in the control group were unaware of the website. They find that the pay information reduced job satisfaction among workers with below-median pay and increased their intention to look for a new job. There was no impact on satisfaction or job search intentions for employees with above-median pay.

The findings of this field experiment are exactly what we would expect for employees with relative income concerns (see Exercise 15.3). Pay transparency reduces job satisfaction for lower-paid employees, with no offsetting gains for the higher-paid. The effect on job search is also corroborated by evidence from Norway, where the public disclosure of tax records increased the probability for lower-paid workers to quit (Rege and Solli 2013). And consistent with this evidence is a growing body of work showing that workers typically exert less effort after learning that they earn less than others (see e.g., Bracha, Gneezy, and Loewenstein 2015; Breza, Kaur, and Shamdasani 2018; Cohn et al. 2014; Dube, Giuliano, and Leonard 2019). Taken together, it is not such a puzzle as to why managers resist pay transparency.

Governments are pushing back against complete pay secrecy, with over a dozen US states and ten European countries requiring some degree of pay transparency. The policies are typically motivated by a desire to reduce the wage gap between men and women (Trotter, Zacur, and Stickney 2017). In exposing pay differences, companies may be less inclined to discriminate in the first place (so as to avoid a lawsuit) and those experiencing pay discrimination may have greater bargaining power to increase their earnings. In the United Kingdom and Denmark, for example, organizations must publish data on average wages by gender (ILO 2018). Such disclosure policies are indeed effective at reducing the gender wage gap (Bennedsen et al. 2019).

More complete non-anonymous pay transparency risks exacerbating satisfaction inequality. In fact, when Norway made everyone's income publicly available, the gap in happiness between richer and poorer individuals increased by almost 30% (Perez-Truglia 2020). Choosing the degree of wage transparency is therefore a policy decision with substantial social welfare implications.

15.2   Unemployment   [Labor]

How employers respond to the social preferences of their employees matters not only for a single company's bottom line, but also in aggregate for the entire labor market. A salient characteristic of labor markets is involuntary unemployment. That is, at any moment in time, there are always unemployed people who would prefer to be employed. This section shows how understanding labor supply as part of a reciprocal gift-exchange relationship between worker and employer can explain the otherwise puzzling persistence of unemployment.[2]

But why is unemployment a puzzle in the first place? Imagine a standard competitive labor market. There are a large number of firms with demand for labor and a large number of people willing to supply labor, as illustrated by the demand and supply curves in Figure 15.1. In most competitive markets — e.g., rice, textiles, foreign currency — the price adjusts so that in equilibrium supply equals demand. Applying this logic to the labor market, the price of labor, or the wage, should equate worker supply and firm demand in equilibrium. This equilibrium is labeled as point (L_0, w_0). There is then no involuntary unemployment. The only people who are not working do so voluntarily because the equilibrium wage w_0 is less than what they require to work.

Consider what would happen in this standard framework if there were unemployment. Unemployment corresponds to an excess supply of labor from a wage w^* above w_0, as in Figure 15.1. At this wage, labor supply $\hat{L}$ exceeds labor demand L^*. According to the logic of competitive markets, there are unemployed workers who would offer to work for less than the going wage. This lower wage would increase firm demand for workers and reduce the supply of workers willing to work. And this process of lower

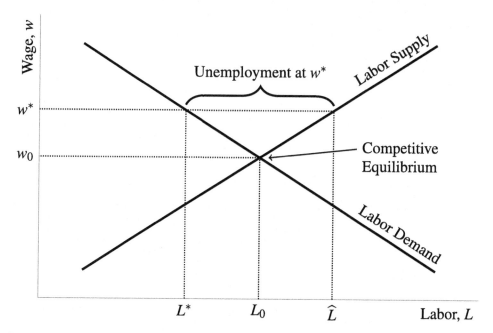

Figure 15.1 A Competitive Labor Market

and lower wage offers would continue until the market wage fell to w_0, eliminating unemployment.

The persistence of unemployment in market economies around the world suggests that something is interrupting this downward process of wage adjustment. Think about the actual decision faced by a firm that is approached by an unemployed worker offering their labor for slightly less than what the firm is currently paying an otherwise identical worker. Why might a firm not accept this offer to pay less for the same work? Perhaps the firm is locked into a long-term contract with current workers and cannot legally replace them or lower their wage. Or it could be that no worker is actually identical to any other, and replacing the current worker would require a long and costly search or training process. A third reason, which is most relevant for our purposes, concerns the reduction in worker effort from paying a lower wage.

Recall the evidence of reciprocity in the workplace (Section 14.4.2). Workers respond to the "gift" of a fair wage above what is minimally required with the "gift" of high effort. Symmetrically, paying a wage that is just barely high enough for a worker to find it worthwhile to show up to work is likely to be reciprocated with the minimal effort not to be fired. Akerlof and Yellen (1990) propose the following mathematical relationship between worker effort e and actual wage w, given a fair wage w^*:

$$e(w) = \min\{w/w^*, 1\}$$

where $e = 1$ corresponds to full effort. This function, graphed in Figure 15.2, captures the logic of reciprocal gift exchange. When the wage falls below what is perceived as fair compensation, workers feel underpaid and reduce effort in kind. Workers who are paid at least the fair wage supply full effort, but overpaying does not induce even greater

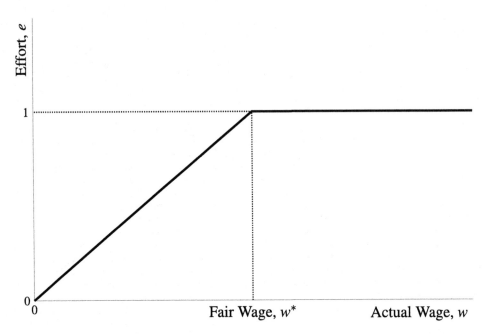

Figure 15.2 A Fair Wage–Effort Relationship

effort. This assumption is reasonable if there are physical, cognitive, or technological constraints that bound maximal effort.

The proposed relationship between effort and wages provides a compelling rationale for the failure of labor markets to eliminate unemployment. Even if a firm is able to offer workers lower wages in the presence of unemployment, doing so may invite a sufficiently large reduction in effort that the fair wage–full effort outcome is preferred. That is, profits may be greater with more highly paid productive workers than with lower paid workers who exert less than full effort. Note that I have yet to clarify how the fair wage is determined. But it is reasonable that the fair wage would be higher when others earn more and lower when finding a job is more difficult. See Exercise 15.6 to work out the implications for the labor market equilibrium in such a setting.

15.3   Optimal Taxation   [Public Finance]

Beyond the effects on employer behavior and market outcomes, social preferences also matter for public policy. In this section we consider the socially optimal design of three different tax policies, each corresponding to a particular model of social preferences. Warm-glow giving influences the optimal tax treatment of charitable giving. Relative income concerns are relevant for optimal income tax rates. And the desire to signal one's social status through conspicuous consumption justifies luxury taxes.

15.3.1   *Welfare Interpretations of Social Preferences*

Before turning to the specific tax policies, it is important to reflect on what it means for a policy to be optimal. Optimal policies are those that maximize the sum of each person's individual welfare, at least when social welfare is utilitarian. And individual welfare is given by *experienced* utility. The nonstandard social preferences explored in the previous chapter are models of *decision* utility (see Section 3.2 for this distinction). That is, the predicted behaviors implied by maximizing these decision utility functions align well with observed behaviors across a variety of settings.

The policy-relevant question, then, is whether our social preference models of decision utility also capture experienced utility. If so, when individuals make decisions motivated by altruism, warm-glow, or envy, the experience of these concerns is relevant for their own individual welfare, and therefore social welfare. An alternative interpretation argues that in spite of the wide range of social motivations for decision making, what matters for individual welfare is only the standard utility from the final private outcome. Under this interpretation there exists a gap between what determines behavior (according to decision utility) and what is relevant for individual welfare (according to experienced utility). In light of these two interpretations, researchers often consider the optimal policy implications for each.

Although reasonable people can disagree on the matter, I adopt a particular convention for individual welfare when characterizing the optimal tax policies in this section. I assume that utility derived from a final outcome, no matter whether the outcome is one's own or someone else's, is included in experienced utility/individual welfare. So purely altruistic and distributional preferences are part of an individual's welfare. But utility derived from the *process* by which an outcome is achieved, like warm-glow, is not included in individual welfare.

A rationale for excluding warm-glow from welfare considerations is that changes in the decision environment can significantly change warm-glow, without any plausible change in well-being. Warm-glow feelings may be influenced, for example, by shifting social norms of obligations to give, the observability of your gift, how much information you have about what you are giving to, whether you are directly asked to give (and by whom), and whether you perceive your generosity towards a common good as an act of giving or as an act of not taking away. But what matters for welfare is presumably how resources are actually allocated between people, charities, and public goods — and not individual perceptions of how these allocations came to be. Moreover, with warm-glow counted in individual welfare, we would be led to the policy implication that scarce resources should be spent on giving people warm-glow feelings. This is a peculiar public policy priority.[3]

15.3.2   Three Tax Policies

Charitable Giving Tax Breaks

A classic failure of private markets is the underprovision of public goods. Such underprovision is a result of the free rider problem: individuals have less incentive to spend on public goods because the cost is private, while the benefits are publicly shared (Section 13.2.3). This means that voluntary charitable giving to support public goods is likely to fall short of what is socially optimal. How might a government address this problem?

One option is for the government to simply fund public goods directly with tax revenue. In fact, the US spends around 18% of national income on public goods, including education, police, and defense (Piketty, Saez, and Zucman 2018). A drawback to government spending on public goods is that it may discourage, or crowd out, private giving. The government's decision of what to fund may also not reflect the preferences of its citizens.

Instead of taxing and spending directly, the government could simply allow citizens to make their own choices of which public goods to privately support. And to help mitigate underprovision, the government could subsidize — reduce the cost of — private charitable giving. The US does exactly this. In particular, taxpayers have the option to deduct their contributions to charities from taxable income. So if taxpayer Jada gives $100 to a charity this year, she does not have to pay income taxes on that $100. And if her income tax rate is 20%, she owes $20 less in income taxes this year. In effect, giving $100 to the charity costs her only $80. And if Jada faced an even higher tax rate of 37%, giving $100 to a charity costs her only $63. Notice that spending $100 on personal clothing, food, or entertainment cannot be deducted, so there is no subsidy and the cost to Jada is the full $100.

Because the US also has a progressive income tax system, with higher tax rates on higher incomes, the charitable giving tax deduction provides a bigger giving subsidy to the rich than the non-rich. But is this the optimal way to encourage private giving? Should everyone instead get the same subsidy for giving, no matter their income? Or should the rich get a lower subsidy for giving than everyone else?

It turns out that if individuals exhibit warm-glow motivations for giving, then the current US system can indeed be the optimal policy (Diamond 2006). To understand the intuition for this result, we must first think through the logic of the tax system. Progressive income taxes redistribute income, reducing inequality, and improving utilitarian social welfare. But progressive income taxes also incentivize the rich to work less.[4] And if the rich earn less, there is less money available to transfer to the non-rich. These are the key benefits and costs that must be balanced in determining optimal tax rates. Now suppose that citizens enjoy the act of giving to a charity. Then a larger charitable giving subsidy for the rich reduces their incentive to work less — by earning less they would receive a less generous subsidy for giving, which they enjoy doing. This subsidy policy therefore diminishes the work disincentive costs of progressive taxation. And as a consequence, a larger giving subsidy for the rich allows the tax system to achieve greater redistribution and higher social welfare.

Warm-glow preferences are essential for the preceding logic. Without them, it can be optimal for charitable giving subsidy rates to be the same for all, or even more generous for the non-rich. In sum, warm-glow giving provides us with a justification for the current US system of allowing charitable giving deductions from taxable income.

Income Taxes

Setting aside the issue of charitable giving, let's focus on the structure of federal income taxes. The federal income tax in the US is a major source of revenue for the government. But not everyone pays the same tax rate. Single earners pay 10 cents in income taxes on each of the first $10,000 in taxable income they earn in a year.[5] The tax increases to 12 cents on each of the next $30,000. And the tax rate continues to rise with income until it maxes out at 37%, as illustrated in Figure 15.3. But to pay this top tax rate a single earner needs to make over $500,000 in taxable income, and even then, only pays 37 cents on each dollar above $500,000 (not on all of their earnings).

Income tax rates, and the income ranges over which they apply, have changed significantly over time, reflecting the sitting government's idea of what is socially desirable. But independent of what is politically feasible, economists have estimated optimal tax

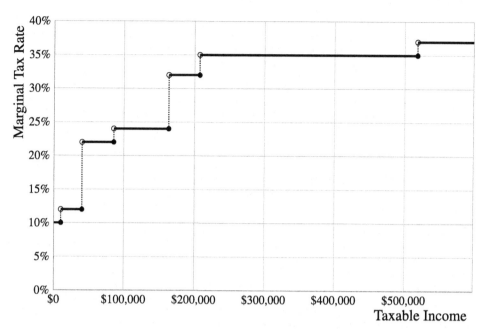

Figure 15.3 US Federal Income Tax System for Single Individuals, 2020
Data Source: IRS (2020).

rates over the income distribution. As noted in the discussion of charitable giving tax breaks, the optimal income tax system must balance the benefit of reducing inequality through redistribution against the cost of discouraging work.[6] Most all optimal tax analyses, however, assume that citizens have standard self-interested preferences.[7]

Motivated by the evidence in the previous chapter, individuals may instead be concerned with relative consumption (or income). That is, they care not strictly about their own consumption, but also how much others are consuming. We can represent such distributional preferences for an individual s, who spends x_s on consumption, with a utility function of the form

$$U_s(x_s, \bar{x}) = u(x_s) + v(\bar{x})$$

where $\bar{x}$ is the average level of consumption spending in society. While $u(\cdot)$ is a standard utility function over the self's own consumption, $v(\cdot)$ captures the impact of others' consumption on the self's well-being. If $v(\cdot)$ is an increasing function, the self is altruistic, valuing the economic success of others. Conversely, if $v(\cdot)$ is a decreasing function, we can interpret the self as envious of others.

Relative consumption concerns are relevant for the design of optimal income taxes because a gain for one person impacts the well-being of another.[8] Suppose first that individuals are primarily altruistic. In this case greater private consumption generates a benefit for others: if I consume more, then I increase average consumption, which you enjoy. To promote the external benefits of consumption, the government should encourage greater consumption by lowering income tax rates relative to the case with standard preferences. The empirical evidence suggests, however, that most individuals are envious of others (Luttmer 2005). That is, if I consume more and push up the average, you are made worse off. The previous result is now flipped. To mitigate the negative spillover effects of consumption, income tax rates should be higher than in the standard case so as to discourage consumption (Oswald 1983). And the more envious individuals are of each other, the more the tax system should redistribute from rich to poor, reducing consumption inequality (Kanbur and Tuomala 2013). Understanding the nature of consumer preferences is therefore essential for determining what makes for an optimal income tax system.

Luxury Taxes

For our third and final tax policy consider the phenomenon of conspicuous consumption, in which individuals consume visible luxury goods to signal their wealth and status to others (Section 14.5.2). People buy expensive cars, watches, and clothing, even though there are functionally identical substitutes available at much lower prices. This is a puzzle for standard preferences: why buy the more expensive version of a car when there is another car with the same engine, quality, and reliability, selling for less? But with social image concerns, the expensive car is valuable precisely because it is expensive (and everyone knows it is expensive). Driving an expensive car signals to others that you are rich enough to afford it. Driving the cheaper version saves you money, but costs you the opportunity to convince others of your high economic status.

From a social welfare perspective, such conspicuous consumption can be wasteful. This is because each person's consumption of a luxury good to improve their own status imposes a negative impact on everyone else who now finds themselves at a lower relative status (Frank 1985). And to prevent falling behind in the perceived social ranking, individuals may respond to the conspicuous consumption of others with their own conspicuous consumption. Producers can subsequently profit from consumers' status concerns by creating ever-changing fashions that induce overspending on status goods (Pesendorfer 1995).

One possible policy response to the high profits earned by manufacturers of luxury goods is to implement a luxury tax, i.e., a tax that applies only to expensive luxury goods. Although such taxes are uncommon, there are examples in recent US history. In the early 1990s the US imposed a short-lived 10% luxury tax on the share of prices above $10,000 for jewelry and furs, above $30,000 for cars, above $100,000 for boats and yachts, and above $250,000 for aircraft. Regardless of their political appeal, are such luxury taxes a socially desirable way to raise government revenue?

From an efficiency perspective, governments should raise revenue with taxes on goods that induce the smallest changes in consumer and producer behavior (Ramsey 1927). A tax on a good with few substitutes, like gasoline, is therefore better than a tax on a good with many alternatives, like tea. Consumers will still buy more expensive gas, but can switch to many other beverages if tea is more expensive. This logic appears to suggest that luxury goods should not be taxed, since there are many alternatives to an expensive car (like a modestly priced car). But when individuals buy luxury goods to signal their social status, paying a high price is the point. If the rich want to spend $200,000 on a car to demonstrate their wealth, then a $15,000 luxury tax on the car does not change anything about the desire to spend $200,000 on a car — it just means that the consumer is now willing to give $15,000 to the government and $185,000 to the car maker. Assuming the car costs less than $185,000 to make, the luxury tax has no impact on consumer or producer behavior because the car still sells. It simply acts as a lump-sum transfer that redistributes money from the manufacturer to the government. The government can therefore efficiently raise money by taxing luxury instead of budget brands (Bagwell and Bernheim 1996). Once again, we observe the sensitivity of optimal tax policy to the underlying motivations and preferences of consumers.

15.4   Social Pressure and Norms as Policy

Tax policy is one way by which a benevolent social planner can impact individual behaviors so as to improve social welfare. Other standard tools include regulations, mandates, and bans. But when people are concerned with their social or self-image, the social planner's toolkit expands. By shaping social pressure or emphasizing social norms, a social planner can incentivize particular behaviors without changing prices or limiting the set of options.

A social planner can influence the degree to which people are subject to social pressure by changing the observability of individual actions. For instance, a school principal may want to encourage academic success, but is aware that many students seek to avoid a studious social image. Then by not publicly announcing honor roll students, the principal can help students to be privately studious without any cost to their social image. Or a state government may want to encourage more low-income families to sign up for public nutritional assistance or health care for which they are eligible. If eligible families are not taking up benefits because of the social stigma associated with being dependent on public support, the government could reduce the observability of such public services. This could be facilitated by allowing families to apply for and receive benefits without showing up in person at a government office for others to see.

A social planner may alternatively nudge behaviors by emphasizing social norms. When individuals aim to act in accordance with social expectations, a change in their understanding of the social norm is relevant for behavior. For example, a school principal might emphasize that the overwhelming majority of students graduate on time, establishing diligent schoolwork as a social norm from which deviation is socially undesirable. Or a state government could mitigate the perceived stigma of welfare support by communicating to low-income families the widespread use of public assistance in the community.

The remainder of this section reviews two field experiments that evaluate such nonstandard public policies in the context of voter participation and tax compliance.

15.4.1   *Voting Pressure*   *[Politics & Law]*

A classic puzzle in political science is the paradox of voting (Downs 1957). In an election with many voters, any single vote is unlikely to matter. Why then do so many people still vote? By abstaining, an individual can save the cost of voting (in terms of time and effort), without impacting the outcome. One possible explanation is that voting enhances one's social image as an engaged member of civic society, fulfilling one's obligation to support the democratic process. Habit formation provides another explanation (Section 6.3.1).

In order for voting to be motivated by social image concerns, it must be publicly observable. Otherwise, it does nothing to change one's social image. Voting is indeed observable when individuals show up to vote in-person at their local polling venue.

Voters can also make their civic act observable, if not verifiable, by talking about voting with friends, posting pictures of voting on social media, or wearing an "I voted" sticker.

A key implication of the social image hypothesis is that voting should be more likely when it is more observable, holding fixed all other costs and benefits of voting. Note that it is not actually necessary for voting to be more observable, as long as people believe it is more observable. The following field experiment tests the social image hypothesis in just this way, by changing voters' beliefs about the observability of their voting behavior.

Field Experiment — Revealing Voters (Gerber, Green, and Larimer 2008)

Prior to the August 2006 primary election in Michigan, 20,000 randomly selected households were mailed a letter that began with the question, "WHAT IF YOUR NEIGHBORS KNEW WHETHER YOU VOTED?" It then went on to display a list of neighbors, along with an indication as to whether or not they voted in the past two elections. The letter concluded by noting that an updated list of the neighbors' voting record would be mailed out after the upcoming primary election. Another 100,000 households were not sent any such letter.

Any difference in the voting activity between households that received the letter and those that did not must be due to the letter.

Gerber, Green, and Larimer (2008) find that the voter turnout rate increased from 29.7% for those who did not receive a letter to 37.8% for those who did receive the letter. This is almost a 30% increase in the turnout rate.

This field experiment provides strong support for the role of social image concerns in voting. In effect, the letter serves to convince people that their voting behavior will be observable to their friends and neighbors. It does not make voting more or less convenient, nor does it change the likelihood that an individual's participation will be the deciding factor in the election. And yet, the letter has a significant impact on voter turnout. Many individuals must care that their neighbors not see them as shirking a civic duty.

Recall that another way to shape social pressure is to emphasize what most people already do. In the context of voting, this could come in the form of a letter, email, or other reminder that "most people vote." Such a message may be effective at encouraging voting for those who aim to comply with prevailing social norms. We now turn to an experiment that examines a social norm nudge in a different setting.

15.4.2 *Tax Collection*   *[Public Finance]*

The collection of taxes owed is important for the financial operations of any government. But it is unsurprising that where there are taxes, there is tax avoidance and evasion. Some individuals may find it worthwhile to move to another state or country to avoid high taxation (Kleven et al. 2020). A less disruptive response is to underreport income or simply delay payment (Slemrod 2007). Governments typically enforce such tax noncompliance with costly audits. But the following field experiment reveals how cheaper social norm messaging can be an effective policy alternative.

Field Experiment — Nudging Tax Compliance (Hallsworth et al. 2017)

In August 2011, just over 100,000 taxpayers in the United Kingdom (UK) had filed a tax return, but not yet made their full tax payment by the July 31 deadline. The tax authority normally sends letters to these taxpayers encouraging payment, before exercising their power to seize goods and assets. By random assignment, noncompliant taxpayers received letters that differed only in the inclusion of a short phrase, typed in standard font, after the first sentence of the letter. The phrases were as follows:

1   Control: No short phrase
2   Basic Treatment: "Nine out of ten people pay their tax on time."
3   Country Treatment: "Nine out of ten people in the UK pay their tax on time."
4   Minority Treatment: "Nine out of ten people in the UK pay their tax on time. You are currently in the very small minority of people who have not paid us yet."

Because of randomization, any differences in making full tax payments across the groups must be due to the particular short phrase included in the letter.

Hallsworth et al. (2017) estimate the impact of each treatment on the likelihood that taxpayers have paid their balance in full within 23 days of the letter. They find that relative to the control, compliance increased by 1.2% with the basic treatment, 1.7% with the country treatment, and 4.9% with the minority treatment.

If the minority treatment had been applied to every late taxpayer, an additional £11.3 million in tax revenue would have been collected in the 23 days after the letter. Including the additional sentence costs £0.

The differences in tax payment behavior due to a single sentence, that communicates no change in the costs or benefits of payment, are unexpected in a world with standard decision makers. The sentence serves to emphasize, clarify, and/or remind taxpayers of the fact that most people pay their taxes on time. And the shift towards this social norm reveals that at least some individuals are motivated to align their behavior with that of their fellow citizens. In conforming to the social norm, individuals can perhaps avoid the moral cost to their self-image of avoiding payment.[9]

The preceding field experiments reveal the effectiveness of nonstandard policies for nonstandard decision makers. But the evidence does not imply that social planners must abandon more traditional tax and regulatory policies to achieve their goals. Instead, the consideration of an expanded range of tools may lead to better and less politically divisive policy.

15.5   Summary

1   Recognition and symbolic awards can motivate effort for workers with social image concerns.

2   Relative income concerns can explain why employers are reluctant to provide pay transparency to workers.

3   Unemployment is predicted to persist if workers and firms are in a reciprocal gift-exchange relationship, exchanging high effort for high wages.

4   Warm-glow giving justifies the current US policy of subsidizing charitable giving more for high-income individuals.

5   Envy of others' consumption justifies higher and more progressive income taxes than is optimal with standard preferences.

6   Luxury taxes can be an efficient means of raising government revenue if individuals buy luxury goods to signal their social status.

7   For individuals concerned with their social or self-image, policy makers can encourage particular behaviors by changing the observability of actions or communicating social norms of what most others are doing.

15.6   Exercises[10]

Exercise 15.1 — Awarding Efforts. Provide a specific example of public recognition or a symbolic award in the workplace. Discuss whether you think such recognition is likely to be effective at motivating effort in your example.

Exercise 15.2 — Star Sellers. [Development] Ashraf, Bandiera, and Jack (2014) run a field experiment with a public health organization in Zambia that recruits hairstylists to sell condoms in their shops, while also training the stylists to provide information about HIV prevention. Incentives to sell condoms were randomly assigned to stylists, as follows:

1   Control: No incentives.
2   Small Financial Treatment: Earn 10% of condom sales.
3   Large Financial Treatment: Earn 90% of condom sales.
4   Non-Financial Treatment: Each condom pack sale is rewarded with a star stamp on a thermometer image that is labeled to indicate the stylist's contribution to community health. Individuals who sell more than 216 packs in a year are also awarded a certificate at a ceremony.

a   Assuming standard preferences without social image concerns, provide a predicted ranking for condom sales across the three treatment incentives.

b   The authors find no difference in sales between the control and either financial treatment. But the non-financial rewards increased condom sales by more than double relative to the control. What does this imply about the preferences of the stylists?

c   If there is social pressure for individuals not to buy condoms, how might shopkeepers encourage condom demand?

Exercise 15.3 — Modeling Transparency (Card et al. 2012). This exercise models the impact of pay transparency. Assume that workers care about their own self's wage w_s and the median wage of others in a similar role w_o, with distributional preferences represented by the following utility function:

$$U_s(w_s, w_o) = \begin{cases} (1 - \rho)w_s + \rho w_o & \text{if } w_s \geq w_o \\ (1 - \sigma)w_s + \sigma w_o & \text{if } w_s < w_o \end{cases}$$

where $1 > \rho \geq \sigma$. Suppose further that with pay secrecy, workers believe (perhaps naively) that they earn the median wage of their peers: $w_o = w_s$. But if pay were transparent for everyone to see, most workers would learn that $w_o \neq w_s$.

a What is the utility change from pay transparency for a high-paid worker who learns that the median is $M less than what she earns: $w_o = w_s - M$?

b Repeat part (a) for a low-paid worker who learns that the median is $M more than what she earns: $w_o = w_s + M$?

c The theoretical predictions in parts (a) and (b) are consistent with the evidence from the Salary Reveal Field Experiment for what values of ρ and σ? Interpret.

Exercise 15.4 — Fairly Unequal Pay. [Labor] Jim and Tim are equally educated and experienced accountants who live in the same city. Jim works at an oil company and Tim works for a clothing retailer. In a standard competitive labor market model, Jim and Tim should make the same wage. To see why, imagine that Jim makes more than Tim. Then Tim could offer to work at the oil company for less than Jim, while still increasing his own wage. In equilibrium, wages must therefore be the same across companies for workers with the same skills and productivity. And yet, there is widespread evidence that more profitable firms pay higher wages to apparently identical workers (see Card et al. (2018) for a review of this evidence). Explain how worker concerns with being paid a fair wage could explain this empirical puzzle.[11]

Exercise 15.5 — Sticky Salaries. [Labor] A recession is a period of significant and widespread decline in a country's economic activity.

a Suppose that a country has a competitive labor market. In normal (non-recession) periods labor supply and demand are as pictured in Figure 15.1, resulting in the equilibrium (L_0, w_0). Now suppose that the country has entered a recession in which the labor demand curve shifts to the left. How do the new equilibrium wage and labor in the recession compare to their pre-recession levels?

b There is widespread empirical evidence that wages do not fall during recessions, even with high unemployment and fierce competition for jobs (Fallick, Lettau, and Wascher 2016). Explain how reciprocity and inequality aversion can help to make sense of why employers are reluctant to cut wages during a recession.[12]

Exercise 15.6 – Faring Well with Labor Market Fairness (Akerlof and Yellen 1990). This exercise explores the consequences of gift exchange for labor market equilibrium. Suppose there are a large number of firms, N, each with profit given by $1000\sqrt{eL} - wL$. L is the number of identical workers the firm hires, w is the wage it pays to each worker, and e is each worker's costly effort. Note that firm revenue depends on *effective labor, eL*, the product of effort and the number of workers. Assume that there are $\bar{L} > 0$ identical workers, each of whom will work at any positive wage.

a In the standard competitive model of the labor market, workers are first offered a given wage and then decide how much effort to exert. Assume that $0.25 \leq e \leq 1$.

i Explain why workers in this simple standard model have no incentive to supply more than minimal effort, $e = 0.25$.

ii **[Calculus Required]** Given that firms recognize the previous observation, determine a firm's labor demand curve, $w(L)$. *Note: In a competitive market the firms take the wage as given.*

iii Sketch a picture of labor supply and labor demand in this competitive market and label the equilibrium wage, w_0. Is there unemployment? *Note: Market demand for labor is the horizontal sum of each firm's labor demand curve.*

For the rest of the problem assume that worker effort is given by $e(w) = \min\{w/w^*, 1\}$, where w^* is the *fair wage*.

b Interpret the above effort function. In particular, provide some intuitive psychological reasoning for the functional form.

c In the presence of unemployment firms can hire workers at any positive wage and will choose to pay a wage that minimizes the total labor cost per unit of effective labor, $wL/(eL)$, which simplifies to w/e.

   i Take the fair wage w^* as given and carefully plot w/e as a function of the wage relative to the fair wage, w/w^*.

   ii Use your plot to determine the range of wages w that minimize the cost of effective labor.

   iii Assume that if firms are indifferent over a range of possible wages, they pay the highest value in this range. With this assumption, what wage do firms pay?

d Suppose that the fair wage is given by $w^* = \bar{w} + a - bu$, where u is the unemployment rate and $\bar{w}$ is the average wage paid by the firms in the economy. Assume $0 \leq a < b$.

   i How do increases in the average wage and unemployment rate impact the fair wage? Provide intuition.

   ii Suppose that all firms choose the cost-minimizing wage from part (c.iii). In this case, solve for the unemployment rate in terms of a and b.

   iii How does the unemployment rate from part (d.ii) vary with the parameters a and b? When is there no unemployment? Provide intuition.

Exercise 15.7 — The Warmth of Friendship. Andreoni (2006, 1225) suggests the following thought experiment. Alice and Anna meet each week for lunch at the local diner. So do Ben and Bill. Everyone always orders the same meal week after week. Alice and Anna ask for separate checks each week, paying only for what they order. But Ben and Bill alternate paying the total bill.

a Suppose that all four diners get warm-glow from giving gifts to others. Which pair of friends is likely to be better off?

b How might the role of reciprocity change your answer in part (a)?

c Do your answers to parts (a) and (b) suggest that warm-glow feelings should be counted in social welfare? Explain.

Exercise 15.8 — Governing over Warm Glow. [Calculus Required] Jay (J) and Kate (K) are the two residents of Hotsville, each with $450 of wealth. They have preferences represented by the following utility functions:

$$U_J = \ln(450 - F_J) + \ln(F) + w \ln(F_J)$$
$$U_K = \ln(450 - F_K) + \ln(F) + w \ln(F_K)$$

where F_i is the charitable contribution to fire management by resident i. F is *total* contributions to fire management. And $w \geq 0$ captures the intensity of warm-glow.

a   Define Hotsville's social welfare as the sum of resident utilities, $U_J + U_K$, as if $w = 0$. Provide a reason for excluding warm-glow from social welfare.

b   Determine the socially optimal funding level for fire management in Hotsville. That is, find the level of $F = F_J + F_K$ that maximizes $U_J + U_K$ (with $w = 0$).

c   Let's now determine what Jay and Kate choose to contribute to fire management. Assume for the rest of the problem that they have warm-glow parameter $w = 0.3$.

   i   Jay observes Kate's contribution fixed at F_K and chooses his own contribution F_J. Determine Jay's first order condition for his utility-maximization problem.

   ii Because Kate faces a symmetric problem, we know that they will both make the same contribution: $F_J = F_K$. Use this insight with your answer in part (c.i) to determine how much each resident contributes to fire management.

   iii How does the outcome in part (c.ii) compare to the socially optimal level in part (b)?

d   The government of Hotsville decides to intervene to achieve the socially optimal level of fire management spending in part (b). In particular, the government imposes a tax of $\$T$ on each resident and spends the $\$2T$ in tax revenue on fire management. The utility functions are now:

$$U_J = \ln(450 - T - F_J) + \ln(F) + 0.3 \ln(F_J)$$
$$U_K = \ln(450 - T - F_K) + \ln(F) + 0.3 \ln(F_K)$$

where total fire management spending is $F = F_J + F_K + 2T$. Determine the per-person tax T that achieves the social optimum. *Hint: Start with the same steps as in parts (c.i) and (c.ii).*

Exercise 15.9 — Sartorial Status. Some schools implement strict dress codes or require students to wear a school uniform. Discuss how such restrictions could improve social welfare if students are concerned with social status.

Exercise 15.10 — Visible Voters. [Politics & Law] Sofia lives in a small Swiss town where she knows most of her neighbors and they know her. Liam lives in a larger Swiss city where it is uncommon to bump into someone he knows. Switzerland introduces the option for everyone to vote by mail, as opposed to only in person. Assume, for simplicity, that voting by mail and voting in person have the same private cost in terms of time and effort.

a   Suppose that Sofia and Liam have standard preferences without social image concerns. How does introducing the option to vote by mail change their likelihood of voting? Explain.

b   Now suppose that Sofia and Liam are concerned with maintaining a social image as a civically-engaged member of the community. In this case, how does adding the option to vote by mail change their likelihood of voting? Explain.

c   Funk (2010) studies this policy change in Switzerland and finds a substantial reduction in voter participation in smaller communities, with little change in larger communities. What does this suggest about motivations for why people vote?

Exercise 15.11 — Nudging with Norms. One way to encourage a particular behavior *B* is to communicate a social norm that "Most people do behavior *B*."

a   Provide an example of such a social norm nudge not discussed in the chapter.
b   Explain why your social norm nudge in part (a) is unlikely to change behavior for a standard decision maker. If the norm actually changes behavior, what can we infer about individual preferences?

Exercise 15.12 — Adding Value to Tax Payments. [Development] Bangladesh struggles to collect tax revenue from businesses. For instance, less than 10% of firms in one region of the capital paid their value-added taxes in 2012. Instead of using audits or fines to enforce tax compliance, Chetty, Mobarak, and Singhal (2014) examine the effectiveness of social norms and social pressure as policy tools. To do so, they conduct a field experiment in which firms are randomly sent different types of informational letters, as follows:

1   Control: No letter.
2   Social Norm Treatment: Letter documents the average tax compliance behavior for nearby firms in the prior year.
3   Social Pressure Treatment: Letter explains that the firm's tax compliance behavior would be shared with nearby firms in a follow-up letter.

Discuss the following results from the experiment, in turn.[13] Be sure to note how the results are similar to or different from the field experiments discussed in the chapter.

a   Result 1: There is no difference in tax compliance between the control and social norm treatment.
b   Result 2: Relative to the control, firms in the social pressure treatment were over twice as likely to make a payment.

Notes

1   See Lawler (1965) for an early analysis of pay secrecy. Danziger and Katz (1997) argue that pay secrecy can increase firm profits by reducing worker mobility. But in more recent work Cullen and Pakzad-Hurson (2019) show that greater pay transparency can increase firm bargaining power and profits in equilibrium.
2   Akerlof (1980) argues that social norms can also provide an explanation for unemployment.
3   See Diamond (2006) and Andreoni (2006) for further justification for excluding warm-glow from welfare. Kaplow (1995, 1998) offers a competing view.
4   Income taxes can reduce reported incomes not only through reductions in labor supply, but because of increased tax avoidance or tax evasion.
5   The income tax rates apply to taxable income, which equals gross income less deductions.

6 Piketty and Saez (2013) provide an excellent review of the optimal labor income taxation literature.

7 Recent exceptions include optimal taxation when individuals exhibit general internalities (Farhi and Gabaix 2020) and more specifically present bias (Lockwood 2020).

8 The effects of relative consumption concerns on optimal nonlinear income taxes can be quite complicated. The qualitative results described here are only valid if the utility function takes a sufficiently simple form.

9 Levitt and List (2007) consider a model of utility with morality.

10 Exercise 15.6 is adapted from Romer (2005, 490-491).

11 See Benjamin (2015) for a model of fairness concerns in labor markets that explains a number of empirical regularities.

12 Bewley (1998) surveys managers, consultants, and labor leaders during the US recession of the early 1990s to understand motivations for wage adjustments.

13 The reported results from Chetty, Mobarak, and Singhal (2014) refer only to those firms that did not pay their value-added tax in the prior year and where at least 15% of their neighboring business did pay.

References

Akerlof, George A. 1980. "A Theory of Social Custom, of which Unemployment may be One Consequence." *The Quarterly Journal of Economics* 94 (4): 749–775. doi:10.2307/1885667.

Akerlof, George A., and Janet L. Yellen. 1990. "The Fair Wage–Effort Hypothesis and Unemployment." *The Quarterly Journal of Economics* 105 (2): 255–283. doi:10.2307/2937787.

Andreoni, James. 2006. "Philanthropy." In *Handbook of the Economics of Giving, Altruism and Reciprocity*, edited by Serge-Christophe Kolm and Jean Mercier Ythier, 2:1201–1269. Elsevier. doi:10.1016/S1574-0714(06)02018-5.

Ashraf, Nava, Oriana Bandiera, and B. Kelsey Jack, 2014. "No Margin, No Mission? A Field Experiment on Incentives for Public Service Delivery." *Journal of Public Economics* 120:1–17. doi:10.1016/j.jpubeco.2014.06.014.

Ashraf, Nava, Oriana Bandiera, and Scott S. Lee. 2014. "Awards Unbundled: Evidence from a Natural Field Experiment." *Journal of Economic Behavior & Organization* 100: 44–63. doi:10.1016/j.jebo.2014.01.001.

Bagwell, Laurie Simon, and B. Douglas Bernheim. 1996. "Veblen Effects in a Theory of Conspicuous Consumption." *American Economic Review* 86 (3): 349–373. https://www.jstor.org/stable/2118201.

Benjamin, Daniel J. 2015. "A Theory of Fairness in Labour Markets." *The Japanese Economic Review* 66 (2): 182–225. doi:10.1111/jere.12069.

Bennedsen, Morten, Elena Simintzi, Margarita Tsoutsoura, and Daniel Wolfenzon. 2019. "Do Firms Respond to Gender Pay Gap Transparency?" NBER Working Paper 25435. Cambridge, MA: National Bureau of Economic Research. doi:10.3386/w25435.

Bewley, Truman F. 1998. "Why Not Cut Pay?" *European Economic Review* 42 (3–5): 459–490. doi:10.1016/s0014-2921(98)00002-6.

Bracha, Anat, Uri Gneezy, and George Loewenstein. 2015. "Relative Pay and Labor Supply." *Journal of Labor Economics* 33 (2): 297–315. doi:10.1086/678494.

Breza, Emily, Supreet Kaur, and Yogita Shamdasani. 2018. "The Morale Effects of Pay Inequality." *The Quarterly Journal of Economics* 133 (2): 611–663. doi:10.1093/qje/qjx041.

Card, David, Ana Rute Cardoso, Joerg Heining, and Patrick Kline. 2018. "Firms and Labor Market Inequality: Evidence and Some Theory." *Journal of Labor Economics* 36 (S1): S13–S70. doi:10.1086/694153.

Card, David, Alexandre Mas, Enrico Moretti, and Emmanuel Saez. 2010. "Inequality at Work: The Effect of Peer Salaries on Job Satisfaction." NBER Working Paper 16396. Cambridge, MA: National Bureau of Economic Research. doi:10.3386/w16396.

———. 2012. "Inequality at Work: The Effect of Peer Salaries on Job Satisfaction." *American Economic Review* 102 (6): 2981–3003. doi:http://0-dx.doi.org.oasys.lib.oxy.edu/10.1257/aer.102.6.2981.

Chetty, Raj, Mushfiq Mobarak, and Monica Singhal. 2014. "Increasing Tax Compliance through Social Recognition." Policy Brief 12/0658. London: International Growth Centre.

Cohn, Alain, Ernst Fehr, Benedikt Herrmann, and Frédéric Schneider. 2014. "Social Comparison and Effort Provision: Evidence from a Field Experiment." *Journal of the European Economic Association* 12 (4): 877–898. doi:10.1111/jeea.12079.

Cullen, Zoë B., and Bobak Pakzad-Hurson. 2019. "Equilibrium Effects of Pay Transparency in a Simple Labor Market." Unpublished.

Danziger, Leif, and Eliakim Katz. 1997. "Wage Secrecy as a Social Convention." *Economic Inquiry* 35 (1): 59–69. doi:10.1111/j.1465-7295.1997.tb01894.x.

Diamond, Peter. 2006. "Optimal Tax Treatment of Private Contributions for Public Goods with and without Warm Glow Preferences." *Journal of Public Economics* 90 (4): 897–919. doi:10.1016/j.jpubeco.2005.06.001.

Downs, Anthony. 1957. *An Economic Theory of Democracy.* New York: Harper Collins.

Dube, Arindrajit, Laura Giuliano, and Jonathan Leonard. 2019. "Fairness and Frictions: The Impact of Unequal Raises on Quit Behavior." *American Economic Review* 109 (2): 620–663. doi:10.1257/aer.20160232.

Fallick, Bruce C., Michael Lettau, and William L. Wascher. 2016. "Downward Nominal Wage Rigidity in the United States During and After the Great Recession." Finance and Economics Discussion Series 2016-001. Washington: Board of Governors of the Federal Reserve System.

Farhi, Emmanuel, and Xavier Gabaix. 2020. "Optimal Taxation with Behavioral Agents." *American Economic Review* 110 (1): 298–336. doi:10.1257/aer.20151079.

Frank, Robert H. 1985. "The Demand for Unobservable and Other Nonpositional Goods." *American Economic Review* 75 (1): 101–116. https://www.jstor.org/stable/1812706.

Funk, Patricia. 2010. "Social Incentives and Voter Turnout: Evidence from the Swiss Mail Ballot System." *Journal of the European Economic Association* 8 (5): 1077–1103. doi:10.1111/j.1542-4774.2010.tb00548.x.

Gerber, Alan S., Donald P. Green, and Christopher W. Larimer. 2008. "Social Pressure and Voter Turnout: Evidence from a Large-Scale Field Experiment." *American Political Science Review* 102 (1): 33–48. Quote from p 46 reproduced with permission, doi:10.1017/S000305540808009X.

Hallsworth, Michael, John A. List, Robert D. Metcalfe, and Ivo Vlaev. 2017. "The Behavioralist as Tax Collector: Using Natural Field Experiments to Enhance Tax Compliance." *Journal of Public Economics* 148: 14–31. Reprinting from p 17, Copyright (2017), with permission from Elsevier, doi:10.1016/j.jpubeco.2017.02.003.

ILO (International Labour Organization). 2018. "Global Wage Report 2018/19: What Lies Behind Gender Pay Gaps." Technical report. ILO. http://www.ilo.org/global/publications/books/WCMS_650553/lang–en/index.htm.

IRS (Internal Revenue Service). 2020. *IRS Provides Tax Inflation Adjustments for Tax Year 2020.* Updated December 17, 2020, https://www.irs.gov/newsroom/irs-provides-tax-inflation-adjustments-for-tax-year-2020.

Kanbur, Ravi, and Matti Tuomala. 2013. "Relativity, Inequality, and Optimal Nonlinear Income Taxation." *International Economic Review* 54 (4): 1199–1217. doi:10.1111/iere.12033.

Kaplow, Louis. 1995. "A Note on Subsidizing Gifts." *Journal of Public Economics* 58 (3): 469–477. doi:10.1016/0047-2727(95)01482-H.

———. 1998. "Tax Policy and Gifts." *American Economic Review* 88 (2): 283–288. https://www.jstor.org/stable/116934.

Kleven, Henrik, Camille Landais, Mathilde Muñoz, and Stefanie Stantcheva. 2020. "Taxation and Migration: Evidence and Policy Implications." *Journal of Economic Perspectives* 34 (2): 119–142. doi:10.1257/jep.34.2.119.

Kosfeld, Michael, and Susanne Neckermann. 2011. "Getting More Work for Nothing? Symbolic Awards and Worker Performance." *American Economic Journal: Microeconomics* 3 (3): 86–99. doi:10.1257/mic.3.3.86.

Lawler, Edward E. 1965. "Managers' Perceptions of their Subordinates' Pay and of Their Superiors' Pay." *Personnel Psychology* 18 (4): 413–422. doi:10.1111/j.1744-6570.1965.tb00296.x.

Lazear, Edward P., and Kathryn L. Shaw. 2007. "Personnel Economics: The Economist's View of Human Resources." *Journal of Economic Perspectives* 21 (4): 91–114. doi:10.1257/jep.21.4.91.

Levitt, Steven D., and John A. List. 2007. "What Do Laboratory Experiments Measuring Social Preferences Reveal about the Real World?" *Journal of Economic Perspectives* 21 (2): 153–174. doi:10.1257/jep.21.2.153.

Lockwood, Benjamin B. 2020. "Optimal Income Taxation with Present Bias." *American Economic Journal: Economic Policy* 12 (4): 298–327. doi:10.1257/pol. 20180762.

Luttmer, Erzo F. P. 2005. "Neighbors as Negatives: Relative Earnings and Well-Being." *The Quarterly Journal of Economics* 120 (3): 963–1002. doi:10.1093/qje/120. 3.963.

Mas, Alexandre, and Enrico Moretti. 2009. "Peers at Work." *American Economic Review* 99 (1): 112–145. doi:10.1257/aer.99.1.112.

Oswald, Andrew J. 1983. "Altruism, Jealousy and the Theory of Optimal Non-linear Taxation." *Journal of Public Economics* 20 (1): 77–87. doi:10.1016/0047-2727(83)90021-X.

Perez-Truglia, Ricardo. 2020. "The Effects of Income Transparency on Well-Being: Evidence from a Natural Experiment." *American Economic Review* 110 (4): 1019–1054. doi:10.1257/aer.20160256.

Pesendorfer, Wolfgang. 1995. "Design Innovation and Fashion Cycles." *American Economic Review* 85 (4): 771–792. https://www.jstor.org/stable/2118231.

Piketty, Thomas, and Emmanuel Saez. 2013. "Optimal Labor Income Taxation." In *Handbook of Public Economics,* edited by Alan J. Auerbach, Raj Chetty, Martin Feldstein, and Emmanuel Saez, 5:391–474. Elsevier. doi:10.1016/B978-0-444-53759-1.00007-8.

Piketty, Thomas, Emmanuel Saez, and Gabriel Zucman. 2018. "Distributional National Accounts: Methods and Estimates for the United States." *The Quarterly Journal of Economics* 133 (2): 553–609. doi:10.1093/qje/qjx043.

Ramsey, Frank P. 1927. "A Contribution to the Theory of Taxation." *The Economic Journal* 37 (145): 47–61. doi:10.2307/2222721.

Rege, Mari, and Ingeborg Solli. 2013. "Lagging behind the Joneses: The Impact of Relative Earnings on Job Separation." Working Paper.

Romer, David. 2005. *Advanced Macroeconomics.* 3rd edition. Boston, MA: McGraw-Hill/Irwin.

Slemrod, Joel. 2007. "Cheating Ourselves: The Economics of Tax Evasion." *Journal of Economic Perspectives* 21 (1): 25–48. doi:10.1257/jep.21.1.25.

Trotter, Richard G., Susan Rawson Zacur, and Lisa T. Stickney. 2017. "The New Age of Pay Transparency." *Business Horizons* 60 (4): 529–539. doi:10.1016/j.bushor.2017.03.011.

Part VI

Beliefs

A standard assumption in the model of individual decision making (Definition 2.9) is that beliefs are accurately calibrated to true probabilities and updated via Bayes' rule. Such standard beliefs p appear in the standard model as an input for calculating expected utility, as highlighted below:

$$\max_{(x_0,x_1,\ldots,x_T)\in X} \sum_{k=0}^{T} \delta^k E[u(x_k) \mid \boxed{p}] \qquad \text{(Standard Model)}$$

The objective of Part VI is to question this assumption and instead consider the implications of allowing for beliefs $\tilde{p} \neq p$ that form in nonstandard ways. Individuals may believe that uncertain outcomes are more or less likely to occur than is actually true. And when receiving new information, they may update their beliefs in ways that deviate from the statistically correct method of applying Bayes' rule. Because beliefs impact reasoning and judgement under uncertainty, with alternative beliefs individuals are predicted to act in ways not anticipated by the standard model. To focus the analysis, we maintain the other standard assumptions that individuals are self-interested discounted expected utility maximizers who evaluate final outcomes. Note that although individual preferences are still represented by an expected utility form, the beliefs used to compute expected utility may not be accurate.

Part VI is organized as follows. Chapter 16 documents evidence of nonstandard beliefs about oneself, in the form of overconfidence, and about uncertain events in the world, like lottery and stock market outcomes. Given this evidence, Chapter 17 shows how such beliefs can be modeled and make sense of otherwise puzzling economic phenomena. Applications include a variety of business and financial decisions. Chapter 18 concludes with an analysis of the implications for profit-maximizing contracts and welfare-maximizing social insurance programs when employees, consumers, and citizens hold nonstandard beliefs.

16 Belief Anomalies

Learning Objectives

★ Understand the multiple ways in which people are overconfident in their self-assessments.

★ Compare the predictions of Bayesian updating with evidence for how beliefs are commonly revised in response to new information.

★ Appreciate how heuristics can make sense of errors in probabilistic reasoning.

The over-weening conceit which the greater part of men have of their own abilities, is an ancient evil remarked by the philosophers and moralists of all ages. (Smith 1776/1827, 44)

The world is rife with uncertainty. In the course of navigating such uncertainty we form beliefs, perhaps unknowingly, over the multitude of possibilities before us. At the individual level, we form beliefs that our efforts will be successful or that our knowledge is accurate. But as noted by Adam Smith in the epigraph, we are inclined towards inflated beliefs of our abilities. Facing outward, we form beliefs about the impact of government policies, the validity of scientific theories, the characteristics of others, and the chance that the near future resembles the recent past. And as we learn new information, these beliefs evolve.

The standard economics approach has simply been to assume that beliefs are "correct." That is, people do not believe outcomes are more or less likely to occur than is true. And when introduced to new information, beliefs are not only revised, but change in the very particular way described by Bayes' rule. These assumptions provide a general and tractable framework for understanding decision making under uncertainty. But if people, at the individual level or in aggregate, do not consistently hold such beliefs, then economists may find themselves modeling a world that is far removed from reality.

This chapter explores evidence for common beliefs that deviate from the standard assumption. We begin with evidence of overconfidence in judgements. Next we explore the phenomenon of confirmation bias, in which individuals tend to perceive new information in ways that confirm what they already believe. The chapter concludes with three well-documented errors in probabilistic reasoning: the gambler's fallacy,

DOI: 10.4324/9780367854072-22

extrapolative beliefs, and base-rate neglect. The organization of topics is intended to highlight the possible psychological motivations underlying actual belief formation.

16.1 Overconfidence

Decisions concerning which college to attend or job to take, what sports or hobbies to pursue, and how much to trust in our own beliefs, depend on assessments of our abilities, skills, and knowledge. But it is difficult to get these self-assessments right. In fact, there is widespread evidence that people are consistently **overconfident**. That is, the confidence individuals have in their judgements exceeds the accuracy of those judgements. The standard assumption that beliefs are accurate rules out such overconfidence — confidence should only be as strong as warranted by reality.

Overconfidence can take a variety of distinct forms (Moore and Healy 2008). The first is **overestimation** of one's ability, performance, or chance of success. A manager, for example, may overestimate her ability to productively lead people. Another form is **overplacement**, in which individuals believe too highly that they are better than others at some task. If an average manager believes that she is the best at her company, then she is overplacing her management skills. Finally, individuals can exhibit excessive certainty that their beliefs are accurate. This inflated confidence in the precision of one's beliefs is **overprecision**. To illustrate, when a manager is overly convinced that she knows what is true, she will be less inclined to solicit other valuable information or perspectives.

It is also useful to distinguish overconfidence from the related concept of **optimism** (Weinstein 1980). Whereas overconfidence concerns one's judgement about a specific skill, task, or belief, optimism describes a more general character trait. An optimist believes that good events are more likely than they are, and bad events are less likely, even if they have no control over the outcome. Optimistic beliefs can similarly impact important life decisions. For instance, optimism is evidenced when individuals are surveyed about their perceived risk for health problems and other hazards, e.g., cancer, ulcer, stroke, high blood pressure, mugging, serious injury. Across age, sex, educational, and occupational groups, respondents typically underestimate their risk (Weinstein 1987). Such optimism could lead to insufficient precaution against, or under-insurance for, life's hazards.

We now turn to empirical evidence of overconfidence in its three different manifestations. Note that relative to other parts of this book, the evidence documented here is weighted towards the work of psychologists more so than economists. And while the evidence is intended to convince you of the robustness of this phenomenon, it is by no means a complete account (see e.g., Hoffrage 2004).

16.1.1 Overestimation

How might we determine whether or not someone is overestimating their abilities, performance, or chance of success? A common and well-established method is to first ask people to predict their performance or success on a future activity. And then by comparing this prediction to the actual outcome of the activity, we can identify the degree to which beliefs are accurately calibrated to reality.

To measure the degree to which students overestimate exam scores, Hacker et al. (2000) ask undergraduates prior to each exam in a course how well they expect to do. High-performing students demonstrated considerable accuracy that improved throughout the course. But low-performing students showed substantial overestimation of their performance, a misjudgement that persisted even after receiving feedback on prior exams.

An implication of overestimating performance is underestimating the time it takes to complete a project. This is known as the **planning fallacy**. Buehler, Griffin, and Ross (1994) survey college seniors to predict when they would finish their thesis under both realistic and worst-case scenarios. On average, students took three weeks longer than their realistic expectation and one week longer than their worst-case expectation. In fact, over half of the students finished their thesis *after* their worst-case prediction. This evidence is also consistent with the procrastination of school work and other investment activities predicted by naive present bias in Chapter 5. Observe that we can interpret naifs as individuals who overestimate their degree of self-control. That is, they believe they have more self-control to follow through with future plans, like working on a thesis, than they actually do.

Students also overestimate the likelihood of pursuing desirable behaviors unrelated to schoolwork. For instance, college students overestimate their future generosity to charities and peers (Epley and Dunning 2000). They also overestimate the chance that their current romantic relationships will last at least 6 more months (Epley and Dunning 2006). And notably, friends are better able to predict romantic relationship longevity than those in the relationship (MacDonald and Ross 1999).

The preceding evidence of overestimation all comes from student participants. But students may not be representative of the general population due to their relative inexperience with managing work and dating. Numerous studies confirm, however, that overestimation extends even to highly educated professionals. For instance, lawyers overestimate their chance of winning an impending case (Loftus and Wagenaar 1988). And managers overestimate their management abilities. Figure 16.1 illustrates the degree to which average manager self-assessments differ from actual management practices, across a range of countries. In no country are beliefs accurately calibrated along the 45-degree line. Overestimation is therefore not simply a quirk of American college students, but a common feature of judgement.

16.1.2   Overplacement

Unlike overestimation, overplacement refers to assessments of skill or performance in comparison to others. A typical instance of overplacement occurs when the majority of people believe themselves to be better than the median. By definition, the median exam score in a class, marathon time in a race, or firm profit in an industry is in the middle of the distribution, with 50% of students, runners, or firms above the median and 50% below. So when the majority (more than 50%) believe themselves to be above the median, at least some have overly positive perceptions of their abilities relative to others.

Note that such overplacement is sometimes referred to as the *better-than-average effect* (Alicke and Govorun 2005), even though the majority can indeed be above average with a skewed distribution. For example, if among four exam-takers the scores are 90%, 80%, 70%, and 0%, the majority are above the average score of 60%. But exactly half the students are above the median score of 75%. In many settings, however, it is reasonable that the distribution of underlying abilities or skills is not

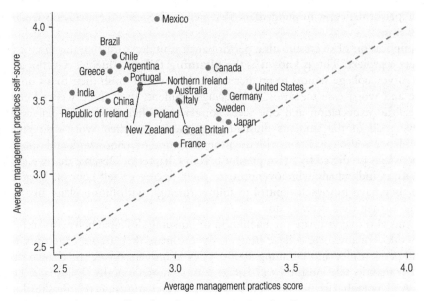

Figure 16.1 Measured versus Self-Evaluated Management Practices Score

Source: Cirera, Xavier; Maloney, William F. 2017. *The Innovation Paradox: Developing-Country Capabilities and the Unrealized Promise of Technological Catch-Up.* ©World Bank. https://openknowledge.worldbank.org/handle/ 10986/28341 License: Creative Commons Attribution (CC BY 3.0 IGO).

particularly skewed. Therefore, while just over 50% of people could indeed be above average, it is highly unlikely that the overwhelming majority can be above average.

And yet, across a multitude of settings most people assess their skills and performance as above the median or average. In a survey of almost one million high school seniors, 70% rated their leadership skills as above average and only 2% rated them below average (College Board 1976). In a survey of University of Oregon college students, 93% rated their driving skills as above the median skill level among those surveyed (Svenson 1981). Men also exhibit stronger overplacement than women. Cooper, Krieg, and Brownell (2018) estimate that the average man in a college physiology course believed himself to be smarter than 66% of the class. Average women students were much better calibrated, believing themselves to be smarter than only 54% of the class. Overplacement is not restricted to youth. Among college professors, 94% rate themselves as above-average teachers, with two-thirds rating themselves in the top quarter (Cross 1977).

Overplacement may be particularly relevant in the context of entrepreneurship. The decision to start a new business, even knowing that most new businesses fail, may be influenced by unrealistic views about one's chance of success relative to others. To test this hypothesis, Camerer and Lovallo (1999) conduct a market game with college students and MBAs. In the game, participants simultaneously decide whether or not to enter an industry. Payoffs are uncertain and depend on one's rank among entrants. In some versions of the game rank is randomly determined, while in other versions, rank is determined by skill, as measured by each player's relative performance on a trivia quiz. More participants enter when rank is determined by skill than luck. This excessive entry in the skill game reduces the average payoffs for entrants below zero. Surprisingly, entrants correctly anticipate the greater entry in the skill-based game. That is, even though they expect average payoffs to be negative, they enter nonetheless. This strongly suggests overplacement — every entrant believes their trivia skills exceed most other entrants and they will therefore be one of the few to make a profit. Of course, many are sorely disappointed to learn that they are not at the top of the skill distribution.

16.1.3 Overprecision

Overconfidence can include not only excessively high beliefs about oneself, but also excessively precise beliefs. Overprecision refers to such excessive confidence that one's beliefs are accurate. The following experiment illustrates a typical research method for identifying the degree of overprecision.

Lab Experiment — Interval Estimates (Russo and Schoemaker 1992)

Russo and Schoemaker (1992, 8) asked over 2,000 managers across multiple industries to each answer 10 confidence interval questions of the following form:

> For each of the following questions, provide a low and high estimate such that you are 90% certain the correct answer will fall within these limits. You should aim to have 90% hits and 10% misses.

1. How many patents did the US Patent and Trademark Office issue in 1990?
2. How many passenger arrivals and departures were there at Chicago's O'Hare airport in 1989?
3. How many German automobiles were sold in Japan in 1989?

While the success rate — the share of correct answers landing within the provided 90% confidence interval — should have been 90% by definition, the actual success rates by industry were as follows:

Manager Industry	Success Rate
Security Analysis	36%
Advertising	39%
Money Management	50%
Petroleum	50%
Data Processing	58%

And fewer than 1% of all surveyed managers provided 90% confidence intervals that contained the right answers at least 90% of the time.

Interpreting the Evidence

What does this evidence reveal? Note that the questions above are designed to be ones in which we would expect it to be unlikely that anyone knows the exact answer with certainty, even for a manager in a related industry. But the standard assumption that beliefs are accurate implies that, regardless of whether someone knows a lot or very little about a topic, they should still know *how much* they don't know. So someone who knows a lot about patent volume in the US should provide a fairly narrow 90% confidence interval, e.g., 200,000 to 500,000 issued patents. Someone who knows close to nothing about patent volume should conversely provide a much wider interval, e.g., 200 to 5 million issued patents. The fact that correct answers land within the 90% confidence intervals only half the time reveals that the intervals are too narrow. Almost everyone believes they know more than they do. This is exactly what to expect with overprecision.

Overprecision when constructing confidence intervals for numerical values is a robust result. It is typical for individuals to provide 90% confidence intervals that contain correct answers less than 50% of the time (Alpert and Raiffa 1982; Klayman et al. 1999). And consistent with the evidence for a gender gap in overplacement, men are more confident in the precision of their knowledge than women. Women provide confidence intervals that are more than 50% wider than those of men (Soll and Klayman 2004).

While constructing confidence intervals may feel like an arbitrary exercise with little connection to reality, it is in fact quite common for professionals to make decisions based on such estimates. An oil company that does not accurately estimate the full range of crude oil prices may regret their decision to build a new oil refinery. A retailer that does not accurately estimate the full range of consumer demand may be unprepared to dispose of unsold product. Physicians who do not accurately estimate the range of underlying causes for a patient's symptoms may prescribe a dangerous course of treatment. And politicians who fail to consider how uncertain world events can be, may pursue diplomatic or military actions with unanticipated consequences.

Anchoring and Adjustment

One hypothesis to explain overprecision is that people reason by **anchoring and adjustment** (Tversky and Kahneman 1974). That is, when asked to estimate an uncertain value, people start from an initial value — the *anchor* — and then generate their final estimate by *adjusting* away from the anchor. The problem is that most people insufficiently adjust, biasing their final estimates towards the anchor. This is particularly problematic when the anchor is completely uninformative but nonetheless impacts estimates. Consider the following famous illustration of anchoring and adjustment with arbitrary anchors.

Lab Experiment — Anchoring Knowledge (Tversky and Kahneman 1974)

A wheel of fortune with numbers from 1 to 100 is rigged to land on only two possible numbers: 10 or 65. After observing a spin of this wheel, subjects who are unaware that it is rigged are asked two questions in the following order:

1 Is the percentage of African countries among United Nations (UN) members bigger or smaller than the number on the wheel?
2 Provide your best estimate for the percentage of African countries among UN members.

It should be obvious that the number selected by the spin of the wheel is irrelevant to answering the second question.

Among those who saw the wheel land on 10, the median answer to the second question was 25%. But for those who saw the wheel land on 65, the median answer to the second question was 45%. The wheel number has the effect of acting as an anchor from which subjects insufficiently adjusted to come up with their estimate.

The implications of this demonstration extend beyond the lab. Randomly increasing the list price of a property significantly increases the property's valuation by a real estate agent, despite the agents' insistence that the list price has no effect on their assessments (Northcraft and Neale 1987). And even experienced trial judges fall victim to an anchoring effect. In a fictitious criminal case, randomly increasing the prosecutor's requested sentencing length from 3 months to 9 months increases the judge's actual sentence from 5 months to 8 months on average (Enough and Mussweiler 2001). Those found guilty therefore face punishments that depend not only on the specific circumstances of the case or sentencing guidelines, but also on the anchors created by prosecutor requests.

While anchoring and adjustment is an important phenomenon in its own right, it could also explain why interval estimates are too narrow. In particular, individuals may construct their intervals by first anchoring on their best guess for the answer and then adjusting outward to account for uncertainty, but insufficiently so. Although reasonable, there is experimental evidence that casts doubt on this hypothesis (Block and Harper 1991; Soll and Klayman 2004). Instead, another important bias may be responsible for generating the observed tendency towards overprecision. We turn to this bias in the next section.

16.2   Confirmation Bias

In addition to holding particular beliefs about our own abilities, performance, or knowledge, we also hold beliefs about the external world. We may form beliefs about the likelihood that a popular diet is healthy, that cannabis is harmful, that someone is smart, that nuclear energy is safe, that gun regulations reduce crime, or that an economic theory is right about the world. These beliefs matter because they influence our behaviors at home, at work, and in the voting booth.

The standard model assumes a particular way for how beliefs about the uncertain state of the world are formed. Starting from an initial belief, as people encounter new evidence or information, they revise their beliefs according to the laws of probability as described by Bayes' rule (Definition 2.5). This process for revising beliefs in light of new evidence is consequently called *Bayesian updating*.

One way in which people may deviate from Bayesian updating is by interpreting or perceiving evidence in ways that support their pre-existing beliefs or hypotheses. This is an example of what psychologists refer to as **confirmation bias** because of the tendency towards confirming what one already believes about the world.[1] Notice that confirmation bias limits the extent to which people are open to having their mind changed. And while a bias in favor of one's current beliefs may feel increasingly relevant in a politically and socially divided America,[2] it is an old observation going back to at least Francis Bacon (1620). Bacon noted over 400 years ago how beliefs in particular superstitions, scientific theories, and philosophical views are strengthened by both accepting the evidence that fits and neglecting that which does not. This can have important practical implications for physicians, generals, juries, and scientists who in the face of new evidence may insufficiently revise their diagnoses, tactics, verdicts, and confidence in prevailing theories (Nickerson 1998).

How do we test whether or not people are actually deviating from Bayesian updating with a confirmation bias? Suppose we find evidence that people with strong beliefs simply stop paying attention to new and freely available evidence. For instance, someone who feels strongly that vaccines cause autism or that climate change is man-made may simply stop reading any new evidence about the issue. Although *ignoring* new evidence has the effect of confirming one's prior hypotheses about the world, it does not necessarily imply that people are *misinterpreting* or *misperceiving* evidence when updating their beliefs. That is, ignoring evidence can be consistent with standard Bayesian updating if there is a cognitive cost associated with processing new information and individuals find it optimal to stop processing once their beliefs are sufficiently strong. For instance, I have strong beliefs that the earth is round, that tobacco contributes to lung cancer, and that the flu vaccine is safe for me. I no longer seek out evidence about these topics because it would take time and effort without doing anything to materially change my mind.

To identify a confirmation bias in the updating of beliefs, we therefore need to examine how beliefs change when people actually interpret new information. Consider the following classic experiment that does just this.

Lab Experiment — Belief Polarization (Lord, Ross, and Lepper 1979)

A group of 151 undergraduates was recruited to answer a survey that included questions about their views on the death penalty. Based on the answers, 48 students were selected to participate in a second round of the experiment. Among the 48, half were selected because they were proponents of the death penalty who believed it to have a deterrent effect on crime. The other half were opposed to the death penalty and doubted its deterrent effect.

The 48 students then read studies with mixed evidence on the deterrence efficacy of the death penalty.

Lord, Ross, and Lepper (1979) asked the students to report how the evidence changed their views about the death penalty. Both groups of students interpreted the evidence as supporting their pre-existing beliefs about the deterrence effect. And consistent with these updated beliefs, the proponents reported more support for the death penalty, while opponents reported less support for the death penalty.

The evidence from this lab experiment demonstrates **belief polarization**. That is, when individuals with different initial beliefs are provided with the same ambiguous information to interpret, their beliefs move further apart. If the goal is to bring people together towards a shared view, more evidence in this case only exacerbates the disagreement. Such belief polarization is impossible if the participants were Bayesian updaters with standard preferences.[3]

But belief polarization is exactly what we would expect with a confirmation bias. In this case, participants focus on the evidence that confirms their views about the deterrence efficacy of the death penalty and neglect the evidence that disconfirms their views. When both proponents and opponents engage in this misinterpreting of the evidence, we end up with the observed polarization of beliefs.[4]

Evidence for belief polarization has been documented in a variety of settings.[5] Subjects given the same information and arguments about the safety of nuclear technology become more convinced of their pro- or anti-nuclear views (Plous 1991). And research summaries about climate change lead to greater polarization for the majority of subjects (Fryer, Harms, and Jackson 2019). In the context of education, a student's performance can polarize beliefs about her academic skill for observers who start with different initial beliefs about her ability (Darley and Gross 1983). A related and pernicious form of confirmation bias occurs when teachers initially believe that a student is smart, consequently grade their work more leniently, and then use the high grades to confirm their belief that the student is indeed very smart. Blind grading practices can serve to protect against such biases.

Finally, observe that confirmation biases provide an explanation for overconfidence (Rabin and Schrag 1999). When people willingly accept information that confirms their views and set aside or neglect information that is disconfirming, they will tend to believe too strongly that the evidence consistently supports their beliefs and hypotheses. This excessive confidence could apply to the chance of success, relative performance, or precision of one's knowledge.

16.3   Representativeness

Assessing the probability of uncertain events in the world is prone to error. Statistical thinking is far from intuitive, as you may know from experience if you have ever taken a probability course. But although individual subjective assessments of probability can often be incorrect, they are not unpredictable. In a classic article, Tversky and Kahneman (1974) argue that people simplify the complex task of accurately assessing probabilities by making use of a few simple procedures. These simple procedures are called **heuristics**, a word derived from the Greek *to find*. That is, a heuristic provides a practical procedure, method, or strategy for finding a solution, even if it is not exactly correct. The procedure of anchoring and adjustment, discussed earlier in the chapter, is an example of one such heuristic.[6]

The heuristic that will help to make sense of the anomalous probabilistic judgements in this section is **representativeness**. According to this heuristic, people evaluate the probability of an uncertain event by the degree to which it reflects the characteristics — i.e., *representative* — of the population from which it is drawn or the process that created it. This is an abstract definition that is best illustrated by examples. For some classic illustrations of representativeness beyond the examples in the remainder of this section, see Exercises 16.13 and 16.14.

16.3.1   *Gambler's Fallacy*   [*Household, Politics & Law, Sports*]

Suppose you are in Las Vegas at a fair roulette wheel and the previous five spins of the wheel have landed on red numbers. For the next spin, would you bet on red or black?

Of course, the chances of landing on a red or black number on the sixth spin are equally likely. But you may be more inclined to bet on a black number, presumably because a black number "is due" after so many red numbers. Croson and Sundali (2005) document such betting behaviors in a casino.

The preceding phenomenon is known as the **gambler's fallacy**. More formally, the gambler's fallacy is the incorrect belief that in a sequence of independent outcomes generated by a single random process, observing one outcome increases the belief that the next outcome will be *different*. It is incorrect because by the assumption of independence, past outcomes have no impact on the likelihood of the next outcome. As a result of the gambler's fallacy, people tend to believe that outcomes will reverse themselves, or alternate, more frequently than predicted by chance.

The gambler's fallacy is consistent with the representativeness heuristic. An implication of this heuristic is that people presume a small random sample must "look like" — be representative of — the population from which it is drawn. While this intuition is true for large random samples, due to the famous *law of large numbers* theorem in probability theory, it is not true for small samples. This mistaken view is referred to as a belief in the tongue-in-cheek moniker **law of small numbers** (Tversky and Kahneman 1971).

In the roulette context, a belief in the law of small numbers means that people expect the share of red numbers in a short sequence of spins to closely approximate the true probability of landing on red, which is about 47.4% (assuming a roulette wheel with two green pockets). Any deviation from this true probability in a sequence of spins "must be corrected" by deviations in the other direction; too many red numbers must be followed by an increase in black numbers in order to obtain a more representative sample. But chance is not a self-correcting process (Tversky and Kahneman 1974).

Not everyone suffers from the gambler's fallacy. When individuals are asked about the chance that the next flip of a fair coin will land on heads after a streak of heads, the majority give the correct answer of 50%. But among those who give incorrect answers, underestimates are more common than overestimates, indicating gambler's fallacy as the dominant form of bias (Dohmen et al. 2009; Benjamin, Moore, and Rabin 2017). Using data from lottery ticket purchases, Suetens and Tyran (2012) also find evidence of the gambler's fallacy among men, but not women. The following experiment illustrates how exactly lottery data can reveal this fallacy.[7]

Quasi-Experiment — Unpopular Lottery Picks (Terrell 1994)

New Jersey offers a daily lottery in which each day bettors buy tickets, guessing the exact three-digit number the state will draw that day. There are 1,000 possible three-digit numbers, from 000 to 999. The state keeps 48% of each day's lottery ticket sales revenue for public expenditure, and divides the remaining 52% equally among all winning tickets. Tickets cost 50 cents each.

Suppose that bettors purchase an equal number of tickets for each possible winning number. With 1,000 tickets, this means that there is a single ticket for each number and therefore a single winner. The state collects $500 in revenue and pays out 52%, or $260 to the winner. If instead 2,000 tickets are sold, there are two tickets for each number and therefore two winners. The state collects $1000 in revenue and divides 52%, or $520, among the two winners. Each winner therefore receives $260 once again. In fact, no matter how many tickets are purchased, as long as they are evenly distributed across all 1,000 possible numbers, winning tickets win $260.

If winning tickets pay out more than $260, then we know that the winnings are divided among fewer people, indicating that the winning number was chosen less frequently than others.

Terrell (1994) groups together winning numbers from 1988 to 1992 based on the duration since the number was previously a winner. He then calculates the average payouts to winning numbers in each group. The results are as follows:

	Count	Average Payout
Winners not repeating within 8 weeks	1622	$260
Winners repeating between 3 and 8 weeks	59	$301
Winners repeating between 2 and 3 weeks	14	$308
Winners repeating between 1 and 2 weeks	8	$349
Winners repeating within 1 week	8	$349

This lottery evidence illustrates the gambler's fallacy. To see why, first note that the vast majority (almost 95%) of all winning numbers are numbers that had not also won in the prior 8 weeks. The average payout for these winning numbers is $260, the exact prediction when each ticket number is being selected with equal frequency. But for winning numbers that had won within the past 8 weeks, the average payouts are higher. The average payout for a number that won within the past 2 weeks is $349, or 34% higher than expected. This high payout implies that recent winners are selected less frequently than other numbers, giving each winner a bigger share of the lottery revenue. And why would recent winning numbers be less popular selections? Because after seeing a recent winner, people likely believe that the chance it is once again selected is less than the true chance of 1 in 1,000. This is the gambler's fallacy in action.

Outside of the gambling context, Chen, Moskowitz, and Shue (2016) document evidence that the gambler's fallacy is also at play for professional baseball umpires and US asylum judges. Baseball umpires are 1.5 percentage points less likely to call a pitch a strike if the previous pitch was called a strike, holding fixed the position of the ball. This effect is even larger when the previous two pitches were called as strikes. But balls in the same position should elicit the same call from the umpire, no matter the previous call(s). The evidence suggests that umpires believe balls near the edge of the strike zone should be strikes with some true probability, and adjust their frequency of strike calls to match this rate in small samples. Streaks of the same call, even if warranted, may feel unrepresentative, and are therefore avoided by excessively alternating calls.

Similarly, US judges reviewing refugee asylum cases are 3.3 percentage points more likely to reject the current case if they approved the previous case. Once again, the decision on the prior case should have no bearing on the decision in the current case, assuming judges are applying equal standards to every case. Rejections should happen on the merits, not as a means to avoid the appearance of an unrepresentative streak of approvals. Given this evidence, one would hope that their case does not fall immediately after an approval. And while it is disappointing that even highly educated and trained judges appear to exhibit the gambler's fallacy, the bias does diminish with greater judicial experience.

16.3.2   *Extrapolative Beliefs*   *[Finance, Sports]*

Suppose you once again find yourself in a casino gambling at a roulette wheel. And after observing recent winning numbers, you become *more* likely to bet on them, presumably because the numbers are "hot" or "lucky."[8] Or after a series of wins, you increase the number of bets you place, thinking that you yourself are "hot" or "on a roll." Evidence of such betting behaviors has been verified empirically (Sundali and Croson 2006). A related phenomenon also exists with lottery ticket sellers. Vendors sell many more tickets if they recently sold a winning ticket with a large prize, presumably because the store is "lucky" (Guryan and Kearney 2008).

The preceding beliefs illustrate a form of **extrapolative beliefs**. That is, people form exaggerated beliefs, or extrapolate, from recent outcomes of one type in a random process that the next outcome will be of the *same* type. As a result, they perceive a streak of outcomes as a trend that will likely continue, and not simply a product of chance. But where a roulette wheel lands or where a winning lottery ticket is sold clearly do not depend on past outcomes.

Notice that extrapolation appears to be the exact opposite of the gambler's fallacy. To extrapolate is to believe in excessive persistence of outcomes, while gambler's fallacy is a belief in excessive reversals. But they are both consistent with a belief in the law of small numbers (Rabin 2002). To see why, consider an individual Cora with such a belief who observes a sequence of coin flips. Suppose the first three outcomes are identical (which happens 25% of the time with a fair coin). Because the small sample does not appear representative of a fair coin, Cora believes too strongly that the streak should end with a different outcome on the 4th coin flip. This is the gambler's fallacy. But if Cora is uncertain about whether or not the coin is actually fair, the streak of three identical outcomes makes her doubt the coin's fairness because it does not appear representative. She therefore believes too strongly that the coin is weighted in favor of one outcome. And given these revised beliefs, she expects the streak to persist. This is extrapolation. The next chapter formalizes this intuition with a nonstandard model of belief formation. For now, we review evidence of extrapolative beliefs outside of casinos and lotteries.

Stock Market Returns

Extrapolative beliefs exist in financial markets. Survey evidence reveals that average investor beliefs about future stock market returns over the next year are positively correlated with the stock market returns of the recent past (Greenwood and Shleifer 2014). The better the past, the better investors expect for the future. If high past stock market returns were actually predictive of high future returns, then such investor beliefs could be accurate. In other words, stock market returns might be like the weather — hot days are indeed more likely to be followed by another hot day than a cold day. But the stock market is not the weather. Average investor beliefs for future returns are in fact negatively correlated with actual future returns. Investors therefore report exaggerated beliefs that future returns will look like recent past returns.

Sport Performance

Another setting where extrapolative beliefs have been explored is in professional sports, and in particular, basketball. When a basketball player has a streak of successful shots, people (spectators, coaches, and players alike) may believe that the player has a hot hand and is more likely to make his next shot. Such beliefs can be rationalized by attributing the psychological benefits of a player's success to increased confidence and focus, which in turn breeds more success. Or people may talk informally about a player getting into the "zone" or "groove."

But in a classic study, Gilovich, Vallone, and Tversky (1985) provide evidence that there is no hot hand in basketball: outcomes of consecutive shots are approximately independent. So when a player has a streak of successful shots, it is not due to increased confidence, but just what is predicted by chance. To illustrate, suppose that a player has a history of making 40% of his shots, but has made 7 of his last 10 shots. Belief in the hot hand would lead someone to think that the player is on a hot streak and will make his next shot with more than a 40% chance. But even if the player always has a 40% chance of making any shot, there is more than a 5% chance that he will make at least 7 out of any 10 shots. So what looks like a hot hand is just randomness in action, and he still has only a 40% chance of making his next shot. Beliefs in a hot hand are therefore incorrect and reflect extrapolation.

More recent analyses, however, have overturned this previously accepted result. There is a true hot hand in basketball: outcomes of consecutive shots are positively correlated (Miller and Sanjurjo 2014, 2017). Hot hands have also been identified among baseball players (Green and Zwiebel 2017) and dart throwers (Jin 2018). But just because there is a hot hand does not rule out the possibility that people still extrapolate too excessively from the recent past. In fact, these studies reveal that baseball pitchers and dart throwers form beliefs about future success that still exceed what is warranted by their true hot hand.

16.3.3   Base-Rate Neglect

This chapter concludes with one more well-known error in probabilistic reasoning.

Lab Experiment — Identifying Jack (Kahneman and Tversky 1973)

A group of 171 University of Oregon students were provided with the following brief personality description of an individual (allegedly) selected at random from a population of 100 professionals who are either engineers or lawyers.

Jack is a 45-year-old man. He is married and has four children. He is generally conservative, careful, and ambitious. He shows no interest in political and social issues and spends most of his free time on his many hobbies which include home carpentry, sailing, and mathematical puzzles. (241)

Each subject was asked to assign a probability that Jack is an engineer. Prior to this task, the students were randomly assigned to one of two groups that differed only in what they were told about the distribution of engineers and lawyers in the population:

1   High Engineer: 70 engineers and 30 lawyers in the population.

2   Low Engineer: 30 engineers and 70 lawyers in the population.

The average reported probabilities by group were:

1   High Engineer: Jack is an engineer with probability 55% and a lawyer with probability 45%.
2   Low Engineer: Jack is an engineer with probability 50% and a lawyer with probability 50%.

To see what is so puzzling about the responses in this experiment, suppose that the probability assessments are consistent with the standard assumption of accurate beliefs updated by Bayes' rule (Definition 2.5). Then the posterior beliefs that Jack is an engineer (E) or lawyer (L) given his personality description (D), are determined as follows:

$$p(E \mid D) = \frac{p(D \mid E)p(E)}{p(D \mid E)p(E) + p(D \mid L)p(L)}$$
$$p(L \mid D) = \frac{p(D \mid L)p(L)}{p(D \mid E)p(E) + p(D \mid L)p(L)} \tag{16.1}$$

The ratio of these two posterior beliefs, known as the *posterior odds*, admits a useful form:

$$\underbrace{\frac{p(E \mid D)}{p(L \mid D)}}_{\text{Posterior Odds}} = \underbrace{\frac{p(D \mid E)}{p(D \mid L)}}_{\text{Likelihood Ratio}} \times \underbrace{\frac{p(E)}{p(L)}}_{\text{Prior Odds}} \tag{16.2}$$

Observe that with Bayesian updating the posterior odds is equal to the product of the *likelihood ratio* and the *prior odds*. The likelihood ratio is the likelihood that an engineer has a description like Jack relative to the likelihood that a lawyer has description like Jack. And the prior odds is the share of engineers relative to lawyers in the population.

The participants in the high and low engineer groups were given different prior beliefs and subsequently reported different posterior beliefs. Let's convert these beliefs into odds ratios for each group and compare the reported posterior odds with the Bayesian prediction in equation (16.2).

The high engineer group, given prior beliefs of $p(E) = 0.7$ and $p(L) = 0.3$, reported posterior beliefs of $p(E|D) = 0.55$ and $p(L|D) = 0.45$. The reported posterior odds is therefore 0.55/0.45, while the predicted posterior odds equals the likelihood ratio times the prior odds 0.7/0.3. This is summarized in the first row of Table 16.1.

Similarly, the low engineer group, given prior beliefs of $p(E) = 0.3$ and $p(L) = 0.7$, reported posterior beliefs of $p(E|D) = p(L|D) = 0.5$. The reported posterior odds is

Table 16.1 Posterior Odds Calculations from Identifying Jack Lab Experiment

Posterior Odds $\frac{p(E\|D)}{p(L\|D)}$	Experimental Reports	Bayesian Predictions via (16.2)
High Engineer	$\frac{0.55}{0.45}$	$\frac{p(D\|E)}{p(D\|L)} \times \frac{0.7}{0.3}$
Low Engineer	$\frac{0.5}{0.5}$	$\frac{p(D\|E)}{p(D\|L)} \times \frac{0.3}{0.7}$
High Engineer / Low Engineer	$\frac{0.55/0.45}{0.5/0.5} \approx 1.2$	$\frac{0.7/0.3}{0.3/0.7} \approx 5.4$

therefore 0.5/0.5, while the predicted posterior odds equals the likelihood ratio times the prior odds 0.3/0.7. This is summarized in the second row of Table 16.1.

Unfortunately we know neither the likelihood that participants believe an engineer has a description like Jack, $p(D|E)$, nor the likelihood that participants believe a lawyer has a description like Jack, $p(D|L)$. But no matter these perceived likelihoods, there is no reason for them to differ on average across the two groups of participants. All participants likely share similar views about the characteristics of engineers and lawyers. Given that these likelihoods are the same across both groups, they cancel out in the ratio of the two groups' posterior odds. This ratio is calculated in the third row of Table 16.1.

The ratio of posterior odds reported by the subjects is 1.2. But this is nowhere close to 5.4, the ratio of posterior odds implied by Bayesian updating. The probability assessments in the experiment are therefore inconsistent with Bayesian updating. In order for the ratio of the posterior odds to equal 5.4, as predicted by Bayes' rule, the high engineer group should have believed that Jack was an engineer with probability closer to 85% (not 55%), holding fixed the low engineer group's 50–50 belief in Jack's profession.

Why do participant beliefs deviate so much from Bayesian updating? As revealed by the complexity of equation (16.1), the seemingly simple question about the likelihood that Jack is an engineer, $p(E|D)$, is actually quite difficult to answer. Suppose that participants instead adopted the simpler representativeness heuristic. In this case, they would have assessed the likelihood that Jack is similar to, or representative of, a typical engineer. But this assessment is closer to the belief that an engineer has a personality like the one describing Jack, $p(D|E)$. Notice this subtle, but important, difference. In particular, judging representativeness does not require knowing anything about the underlying distribution of engineers and lawyers in the population. The extent to which Jack's description is similar to that of an engineer doesn't depend on how many engineers are in the population. But more engineers in the population clearly implies that it is more likely for a randomly selected person, such as Jack, to be an engineer.

The representativeness heuristic can therefore make sense of the experimental results. In answering a question about similarity, the participants largely ignored the prior information about the distribution of engineers and lawyers in the population. And as a result, both the high engineer and low engineer groups reported almost identical beliefs that Jack is an engineer. Such underuse of prior information is known as **base-rate neglect**, where *base rates* are another term for prior beliefs or information (Kahneman and Tversky 1973). In terms of the posterior odds expression (16.2), base-rate neglect means that people answer the original question about Jack's profession by assessing the likelihood ratio, while neglecting the prior odds.

Base-rate neglect is a robust phenomenon. Evidence from numerous variations on the preceding lab experiment consistently find that even when base rates are not completely ignored, they are still underused relative to the predictions of Bayes' rule (Koehler 1996; Barbey and Sloman 2007) Outside of the lab, there is also evidence that base-rate neglect impacts the judgements of doctors, psychologists, and court trials (Meehl and Rosen 1955; Tribe 1971; Eddy 1982). The following chapter explores further implications of base-rate neglect, and the other forms of nonstandard beliefs, particularly in the context of financial markets.

16.4   Summary

1   With **overconfidence**, individuals have more confidence in their judgements than is accurate. This is related to, but distinct from, the characteristic of **optimism** in which people hold a general belief that good events are likely.

2   There is evidence for each of the three forms of overconfidence:

    a   **overestimation:** overconfidence in one's ability, performance, chance of success, or time to complete a task;

    b   **overplacement:** overconfidence in one's abilities relative to others; and

    c   **overprecision:** overconfidence in the precision of one's beliefs.

3   **Anchoring and adjustment** is a **heuristic** that can help to explain overprecision.

4   **Confirmation bias** includes the non-Bayesian tendency of individuals to interpret or perceive new information in ways that confirm their pre-existing beliefs. This bias can generate **belief polarization**, as well as overconfidence.

5   According to the **representativeness heuristic**, people evaluate the probability of an uncertain event by the degree to which it is representative of the population from which it is drawn or the process that generated it. This heuristic provides a psychological explanation for:

    a   the **law of small numbers:** belief that a small random sample must "look like" the population from which it is drawn, when this is only true for large samples; and

    b   **base-rate neglect:** in forming posterior beliefs, prior information is underused, leading to a focus on similarity.

6   With the **gambler's fallacy** recent outcomes of one type excessively increase the belief that the next outcome will be different.

7   With **extrapolative beliefs** recent outcomes of one type excessively increase the belief that the next outcome will be the same.

8   Although the gambler's fallacy and extrapolative beliefs appear contradictory, they are both consistent with a belief in the law of small numbers.

16.5   Exercises

Exercise 16.1 — Identifying Overconfidence. Identify each of the real-world beliefs described below as an instance of optimism, overestimation, overplacement, or overprecision.

a   A law school offers financial aid only for students who earn at least a B-average during the first two years of classes. Every student who accepts the offer believes they will receive financial aid (Segal 2011).

b Among individuals at high risk of Huntington disease, many believe they have only a moderate risk and some believe they have no chance of the disease (Oster, Shoulson, and Dorsey 2013).

c Taxpayers owed an income tax refund believe they will submit their tax returns almost two weeks earlier than they actually do (Buehler, Griffin, and MacDonald 1997).

Exercise 16.2 — Entangled Overconfidence. A common method of identifying overconfidence in the psychology literature is to first ask a general knowledge question with two answers, one of which is correct. Participants are then asked to estimate the probability (from 50% to 100%) that their choice is correct. For example, to the question "Who was born first, Toni Morrison or Maya Angelou?", a respondent might say "Maya Angelou — 80% sure." Many participants are overconfident that their answer is correct. Explain how this evidence can be consistent with two of the three forms of overconfidence.

Exercise 16.3 — Accurate Accounting. Public accountants and weather forecasters are two professional groups that do *not* exhibit overconfidence (Russo and Schoemaker 1992). Experienced accountants estimate confidence ranges for account balances, that if anything, are too wide rather than too narrow. And US Weather Service forecasters are incredibly accurate about the chance of rain the next day. Discuss what this evidence suggests about possible factors that promote accurately calibrated beliefs.

Exercise 16.4 — Dropping Anchor. Subjects are asked to estimate the length of the Mississippi River. But before answering, half of the subjects are first asked if the river is longer than 2,000 miles while the other half are asked if the river is shorter than 30,000 miles.

a For standard decision makers, how would you expect the average estimates of the river's length in each group to compare?

b Mussweiler and Strack (2000) find an average estimate of 3,768 miles for the first group, but 12,144 miles for the second group. (The Mississippi River is actually 2,320 miles long.) What heuristic could explain this evidence? Explain.

Exercise 16.5 — Confirmatory Cases. Explain how confirmation bias may impact belief updating in the following situations.[9]

a Members of a hiring committee form different initial beliefs about the quality of a job applicant based on her resume. The applicant is invited for an interview, at which she answers some questions well and others not so well. This new information is used by the hiring committee members to update their beliefs about the quality of the match between the applicant and the job vacancy.

b Darius believes that cold rainy weather increases his arthritis pain. Suppose that over the next year he experiences arthritis pain on 10% of days, no matter the weather. He uses this experience to update his belief about the connection between weather and pain.

Exercise 16.6 — Double Strike. There is an old saying that "lightning never strikes the same place twice." Identify the error in probabilistic reasoning suggested by the saying.

Exercise 16.7 — Double Up. [Household] Winning lottery tickets are often redeemed for more lottery tickets instead of cash (Clotfelter and Cook 1993). Interpret this behavior using a concept from the chapter.

Exercise 16.8 — Revolutionary Insights. The French mathematician Pierre-Simon Laplace provided an early account of how people incorrectly assess probabilities. Identify the error in probabilistic reasoning described by Laplace (1825/1995, 93) in each of the following passages:

a   I have seen men, ardently longing for a son, learning only with anxiety of the births of boys in the month in which they expected to become fathers. Thinking that the ratio of these births to those of girls ought to be the same at the end of each month, they fancied that the boys already born made it more probable that girls would be born next.

b   In a long series of events of the same kind, the very capriciousness of chance ought sometimes to produce those singular runs of good or bad luck that most players do not fail to attribute to a kind of fate.

Exercise 16.9 — Courting Randomness. [Sports] In an analysis of half a million professional tennis serves, Gauriot, Page, and Wooders (2016) find that players switch the direction of their tennis serves too frequently to be consistent with randomness. For instance, serving to the left increases the likelihood that the next serve is to the right. Suppose that players intend to randomize each serve so opponents cannot predict the direction of the next serve. Explain which error in probabilistic reasoning this evidence suggests.

Exercise 16.10 — Hot and Cold Numbers. [Household] Suetens, Galbo-Jørgensen, and Tyran (2016) analyze data from a weekly Danish lottery in 2005. Interpret the following findings from their analysis as indicative of gambler's fallacy or extrapolative beliefs.

a   After a lottery number wins once, players bet less on it in the following week.

b   For a lottery number that has won at least twice in the recent past, players bet more money on it the more often it was won.

Exercise 16.11 — Reading Readers. Consider the follow scenario (adapted from Kahneman 2011, 151): The person sitting next to you at a New York coffee shop is reading *The New Yorker* magazine. Do you think it is more likely that she has a PhD or no college degree? The most reasonable answer is that she is more likely to not have a college degree than to hold a PhD. Why might you have been tempted to answer otherwise? Explain the error in probabilistic reasoning you would have been making.

Exercise 16.12 — Bayesian Biases. Consider the following two problems from Bar-Hillel (1980, 211-12, 222).
    The Cab Problem:[10]

> Two cab companies operate in a given city, the Blue and the Green (according to the color of cab they run). Eighty-five percent of the cabs in the city are Blue, and the remaining 15% are Green. A cab was involved in a hit-and-run accident at night. A witness later identified the cab as a Green cab. The court tested the witness' ability to distinguish between Blue and Green cabs under nighttime visibility conditions. It found that the witness was able to identify each color correctly about 80% of the time, but confused it with the other color about 20% of the time. What do you think are the chances that the errant cab was indeed Green, as the witness claimed?

The Suicide Problem:

> A study was done on causes of suicide among young adults (aged 25 to 35). It was found that the percentage of suicides is three times larger among single people than among married people. In this age group, 80% are married and 20% are single. Of 100 cases of suicide among people aged 25 to 35, how many would you estimate were single?

a   Use Bayes' rule to compute the correct answers to the above two problems.
b   The most common (and median) response to the first question is 80% and to the second question is 75%. What error in probabilistic reasoning do these common answers indicate?

Exercise 16.13 — Stork Statistics. Consider the following question from Tversky and Kahneman (1974, 1125):

> A certain town is served by two hospitals. In the larger hospital about 45 babies are born each day, and in the smaller hospital about 15 babies are born each day. As you know, about 50 percent of all babies are boys. However, the exact percentage varies from day to day. Sometimes it may be higher than 50 percent, sometimes lower.

> For a period of 1 year, each hospital recorded the days on which more than 60 percent of the babies born were boys. Which hospital do you think recorded more such days?

a   The smaller hospital should expect to record 55 days with more than 60% boys, while the larger hospital should expect to record only 25 such days. Try to provide intuition for this statistical fact.
b   The distribution of answers provided by a sample of 95 undergraduates was:

- The larger hospital (22%)
- The smaller hospital (22%)
- About the same (56%)

The most popular answer suggests that many respondents neglected the size of the hospital when answering the question. Explain how the representativeness heuristic could explain such sample-size neglect.

Exercise 16.14 — Jazzing up Accounting. Consider the following question from Tversky and Kahneman (1983, 297):

> Bill is 34 years old. He is intelligent, but unimaginative, compulsive, and generally life-less. In school, he was strong in mathematics but weak in social studies and humanities.

> Which of the following statements is more probable?

- Bill plays jazz for a hobby.
- Bill is an accountant who plays jazz for a hobby.

a The first statement is more probable than the second. Try to provide intuition for this statistical fact.

b Among a sample of 88 undergraduates, 87% reported that the second statement was more probable. Explain how the representativeness heuristic could explain this error (known generally as the conjunction fallacy).

Notes

1 Confirmation bias more generally can also include seeking out evidence and generating arguments to support current beliefs. See Nickerson (1998) for a review of confirmation bias in the psychology literature.

2 Sunstein (2017) considers the connections between political fragmentation, democracy, and social media.

3 Baliga, Hanany, and Klibanoff (2013) prove that belief polarization is inconsistent with standard preferences. If individuals are ambiguity averse, they show that the result need not hold.

4 Benjamin (2019, Section 8.2) reviews outcomes other than belief polarization that provide evidence of a confirmation bias in Bayesian updating.

5 Gerber and Green (1999) provide a critical review of the belief polarization evidence.

6 Tversky and Kahneman (1974) also identify the availability heuristic, in which people tend to assess probabilities by the ease with which they can bring instances to mind. This concept is related to inattention, the topic of Chapter 20.

7 For further evidence on gambler's fallacy in lottery ticket purchases, see Clotfelter and Cook (1993) and Suetens, Galbo-Jørgensen, and Tyran (2016).

8 The belief that a random process can enter a "hot" state more often than it does is typically referred to as the *hot-hand fallacy* or *hot-hand bias*. Benjamin (2019, Section 2.2) reviews the evidence and theory for this fallacy/bias.

9 Dougherty, Turban, and Callender (1994) and Macan and Dipboye (1994) study confirmation bias in the interviewing process and Redelmeier and Tversky (1996) consider the believed relationship between arthritis and weather.

10 The Cab Problem is originally from Kahneman and Tversky (1972).

References

Alicke, Mark D., and Olesya Govorun. 2005. "The Better-Than-Average Effect." In *The Self in Social Judgment,* 85–106. Studies in self and identity. New York: Psychology Press.

Alpert, Marc, and Howard Raiffa. 1982. "A Progress Report on the Training of Probability Assessors." In *Judgment under Uncertainty: Heuristics and Biases,* edited by Daniel Kahneman, Paul Slovic, and Amos Tversky, 294–305. Cambridge: Cambridge University Press.

Bacon, Francis. 1620. *The New Organon and Related Writings.* New York: Liberal Arts Press.

Baliga, Sandeep, Eran Hanany, and Peter Klibanoff. 2013. "Polarization and Ambiguity." *American Economic Review* 103 (7): 3071–3083. doi:10.1257/aer.103.7. 3071.

Barbey, Aron K., and Steven A. Sloman. 2007. "Base-Rate Respect: From Ecological Rationality to Dual Processes." *Behavioral and Brain Sciences* 30 (3): 241–254. doi:10.1017/S0140525X07001653.

Bar-Hillel, Maya. 1980. "The Base-Rate Fallacy in Probability Judgments." *Acta Psychologica* 44 (3): 211–233. Reprinting from pp 211-212, 222, Copyright (1980), with permission from Elsevier.

Benjamin, Daniel J. 2019. "Errors in Probabilistic Reasoning and Judgment Biases." In *Handbook of Behavioral Economics: Foundations and Applications,* edited by B. Douglas Bernheim, Stefano Della-Vigna, and David Laibson, 2:69–186. North-Holland. doi:10.1016/bs.hesbe.2018.11.002.

Benjamin, Daniel J., Don A. Moore, and Matthew Rabin. 2017. "Biased Beliefs About Random Samples: Evidence from Two Integrated Experiments." NBER Working Paper 23927. Cambridge, MA: National Bureau of Economic Research. doi:10.3386/w23927.

Block, Richard A., and David R. Harper. 1991. "Overconfidence in Estimation: Testing the Anchoring-and-Adjustment Hypothesis." *Organizational Behavior and Human Decision Processes* 49 (2): 188–207. doi:10.1016/0749-5978(91)90048-X.

Buehler, Roger, Dale Griffin, and Heather MacDonald. 1997. "The Role of Motivated Reasoning in Optimistic Time Predictions." *Personality and Social Psychology Bulletin* 23 (3): 238–247. doi:10.1177/0146167297233003.

Buehler, Roger, Dale Griffin, and Michael Ross. 1994. "Exploring the '"Planning Fallacy"': Why People Underestimate Their Task Completion Times." *Journal of Personality and Social Psychology* 67 (3): 366.

Camerer, Colin F., and Dan Lovallo. 1999. "Overconfidence and Excess Entry: An Experimental Approach." *American Economic Review* 89 (1): 306–318. doi:10.1257/aer.89.1.306.

Chen, Daniel L., Tobias J. Moskowitz, and Kelly Shue. 2016. "Decision Making Under the Gambler's Fallacy: Evidence from Asylum Judges, Loan Officers, and Baseball Umpires." *The Quarterly Journal of Economics* 131 (3): 1181–1242. doi:10.1093/qje/qjw017.

Clotfelter, Charles T., and Philip J. Cook. 1993. "The 'Gambler's Fallacy' in Lottery Play." *Management Science* 39 (12): 1521–1525. doi:10.1287/mnsc.39.12.1521.

College Board. 1976. "Student Descriptive Questionnaire." Report. Princeton, NJ: Educational Testing Service.

Cooper, Katelyn M., Anna Krieg, and Sara E. Brownell. 2018. "Who Perceives They are Smarter? Exploring the Influence of Student Characteristics on Student Academic Self-Concept in Physiology." *Advances in Physiology Education* 42 (2): 200–208. doi:10.1152/advan.00085.2017.

Croson, Rachel, and James Sundali. 2005. "The Gambler's Fallacy and the Hot Hand: Empirical Data from Casinos." *Journal of Risk and Uncertainty* 30 (3): 195–209. doi:10.1007/s11166-005-1153-2.

Cross, K. Patricia. 1977. "Not Can, but Will College Teaching Be Improved?" *New Directions for Higher Education* 1977 (17): 1–15. doi:10.1002/he.36919771703.

Darley, John M., and Paget H. Gross. 1983. "A Hypothesis-Confirming Bias in Labeling Effects." *Journal of Personality and Social Psychology* 44 (1): 20–33. doi:10.1037/0022-3514.44.1.20.

Dohmen, Thomas, Armin Falk, David Huffman, Felix Marklein, and Uwe Sunde. 2009. "Biased Probability Judgment: Evidence of Incidence and Relationship to Economic Outcomes from a Representative Sample." *Journal of Economic Behavior & Organization* 72 (3): 903–915. doi:10.1016/j.jebo.2009.07.014.

Dougherty, Thomas W., Daniel B. Turban, and John C. Callender. 1994. "Confirming First Impressions in the Employment Interview: A Field Study of Interviewer Behavior." *Journal of Applied Psychology* 79 (5): 659–665. doi:10.1037/0021-9010.79.5.659.

Eddy, David M. 1982. "Probabilistic Reasoning in Clinical Medicine: Problems and Opportunities." In *Judgment under Uncertainty: Heuristics and Biases,* edited by Daniel Kahneman, Amos Tversky, and Paul Slovic, 249–267. New York: Cambridge University Press.

Enough, Birte, and Thomas Mussweiler. 2001. "Sentencing Under Uncertainty: Anchoring Effects in the Courtroom." *Journal of Applied Social Psychology* 31 (7): 1535–1551. doi:10.1111/j.1559-1816.2001.tb02687.x.

Epley, Nicholas, and David Dunning. 2000. "Feeling '"Holier than Thou"': Are Self-Serving Assessments Produced by Errors in Self- or Social Prediction?" *Journal of Personality and Social Psychology* 79 (6): 861. doi:10.1037/0022-3514.79.6.861.

———. 2006. "The Mixed Blessings of Self-Knowledge in Behavioral Prediction: Enhanced Discrimination but Exacerbated Bias." *Personality and Social Psychology Bulletin* 32 (5): 641–655. doi:10.1177/0146167205284007.

Fryer, Roland G., Philipp Harms, and Matthew O. Jackson. 2019. "Updating Beliefs when Evidence is Open to Interpretation: Implications for Bias and Polarization." *Journal of the European Economic Association* 17 (5): 1470–1501. doi:10.1093/jeea/jvy025.

Gauriot, Romain, Lionel Page, and John Wooders. 2016. "Nash at Wimbledon: Evidence from Half a Million Serves." SSRN Scholarly Paper ID 2850919. Rochester, NY: Social Science Research Network. doi:10.2139/ssrn.2850919.

Gerber, Alan S., and Donald P. Green. 1999. "Misperceptions about Perceptual Bias." *Annual Review of Political Science* 2 (1): 189–210. doi:10.1146/annurev.polisci.2.1.189.

Gilovich, Thomas, Robert Vallone, and Amos Tversky. 1985. "The Hot Hand in Basketball: On the Misperception of Random Sequences." *Cognitive Psychology* 17 (3): 295–314. doi:10.1016/0010-0285(85)90010-6.

Green, Brett, and Jeffrey Zwiebel. 2017. "The Hot-Hand Fallacy: Cognitive Mistakes or Equilibrium Adjustments? Evidence from Major League Baseball." *Management Science* 64 (11): 5315–5348. doi:10.1287/mnsc.2017.2804.

Greenwood, Robin, and Andrei Shleifer. 2014. "Expectations of Returns and Expected Returns." *The Review of Financial Studies* 27 (3): 714–746. doi:10.1093/rfs/hht082.

Guryan, Jonathan, and Melissa S. Kearney. 2008. "Gambling at Lucky Stores: Empirical Evidence from State Lottery Sales." *American Economic Review* 98 (1): 458–473. doi:10.1257/aer.98.1.458.

Hacker, Douglas J., Linda Bol, Dianne D. Horgan, and Ernest A. Rakow. 2000. "Test Prediction and Performance in a classroom Context." *Journal of Educational Psychology* 92 (1): 160–170. doi:10.1037/0022-0663.92.1.160.

Hoffrage, Ulrich. 2004. "Overconfidence." In *Cognitive Illusions: A Handbook on Fallacies and Biases in Thinking, Judgement and Memory*, edited by Rüdiger F. Pohl, 450. London: Psychology Press.

Jin, Lawrence. 2018. "Evidence of Hot-Hand Behavior in Sports and Medicine." In *7th Annual Conference of the American Society of Health Economists*.

Kahneman, Daniel. 2011. *Thinking, Fast and Slow*. New York: Farrar, Straus and Giroux.

Kahneman, Daniel, and Amos Tversky. 1972. "On Prediction and Judgement." *Oregon Research Institute Bulletin* 12 (4).

———. 1973. "On the Psychology of Prediction." *Psychological Review* 80 (4): 237–251. Copyright © 1973 by American Psychological Association. Reproduced with permission, doi:10.1037/h0034747.

Klayman, Joshua, Jack B. Soll, Claudia González-Vallejo, and Sema Barlas. 1999. "Over-confidence: It Depends on How, What, and Whom You Ask." *Organizational Behavior and Human Decision Processes* 79 (3): 216–247. doi:10.1006/obhd.1999. 2847.

Koehler, Jonathan J. 1996. "The Base Rate Fallacy Reconsidered: Descriptive, Normative, and Methodological Challenges." *Behavioral and Brain Sciences* 19 (1): 1–17. doi:10.1017/S0140525X00041157.

Laplace, Pierre-Simon. 1995. *Pierre-Simon Laplace Philosophical Essay on Probabilities*. 1st edition. Translated by Andrew I. Dale. Sources in the History of Mathematics and Physical Sciences 13. New York: Springer-Verlag. Translated from the fifth French edition of 1825. Reprinted by permission from Springer Nature © 1995.

Loftus, Elizabeth F., and Willem A. Wagenaar. 1988. "Lawyers' Predictions of Success." *Jurimetrics* 28 (4): 437–453. https://www.jstor.org/stable/29762095.

Lord, Charles G., Lee Ross, and Mark R. Lepper. 1979. "Biased Assimilation and Attitude Polarization: The Effects of Prior Theories on Subsequently Considered Evidence." *Journal of Personality and Social Psychology* 37 (11): 2098–2109. doi:10.1037/0022-3514.37.11.2098.

Macan, Therese Hoff, and Robert L. Dipboye. 1994. "The Effects of the Application on Processing of Information from the Employment Interview." *Journal of Applied Social Psychology* 24 (14): 1291–1314. doi:https://doi.org/10.1111/j.1559-1816.1994.tb00559.x.

MacDonald, Tara K., and Michael Ross. 1999. "Assessing the Accuracy of Predictions about Dating Relationships: How and Why Do Lovers' Predictions Differ from those Made by Observers?" *Personality and Social Psychology Bulletin* 25 (11): 1417–1429. doi:10.1177/0146167299259007.

Meehl, Paul E., and Albert Rosen. 1955. "Antecedent Probability and the Efficiency of Psychometric Signs, Patterns, or Cutting Scores." *Psychological Bulletin* 52 (3): 194–216. doi:10.1037/h0048070.

Miller, Joshua B., and Adam Sanjurjo. 2014. "A Cold Shower for the Hot Hand Fallacy." Technical report 518. Bocconi University, Milan: IGIER Working Paper.

———. 2017. "A Visible (Hot) Hand? Expert Players Bet on the Hot Hand and Win." SSRN Scholarly Paper ID 3032826. Rochester, NY: Social Science Research Network. doi:10.2139/ssrn.3032826.

Moore, Don A., and Paul J. Healy. 2008. "The Trouble with Overconfidence." *Psychological Review* 115 (2): 502. doi:10.1037/0033-295x.115.2.502.

Mussweiler, Thomas, and Fritz Strack. 2000. "The Use of Category and Exemplar Knowledge in the Solution of Anchoring Tasks." *Journal of Personality and Social Psychology* 78 (6): 1038–1052. doi:10.1037/0022-3514.78.6.1038.

Nickerson, Raymond S. 1998. "Confirmation Bias: A Ubiquitous Phenomenon in Many Guises." *Review of General Psychology* 2 (2): 175–220. doi:10.1037/1089-2680.2.2.175.

Northcraft, Gregory B, and Margaret A Neale. 1987. "Experts, Amateurs, and Real Estate: An Anchoring-and-Adjustment Perspective on Property Pricing Decisions." *Organizational Behavior and Human Decision Processes* 39 (1): 84–97. doi:10.1016/0749-5978(87)90046-X.

Oster, Emily, Ira Shoulson, and E. Ray Dorsey. 2013. "Optimal Expectations and Limited Medical Testing: Evidence from Huntington Disease." *American Economic Review* 103 (2): 804–830. doi:10.1257/aer.103.2.804.

Plous, S. 1991. "Biases in the Assimilation of Technological Breakdowns: Do Accidents Make Us Safer?" *Journal of Applied Social Psychology* 21 (13): 1058–1082. doi:10.1111/j.1559-1816.1991.tb00459.x.

Rabin, Matthew. 2002. "Inference by Believers in the Law of Small Numbers." *The Quarterly Journal of Economics* 117 (3): 775–816. doi:10.1162/003355302760193896.

Rabin, Matthew, and Joel L. Schrag. 1999. "First Impressions Matter: A Model of Confirmatory Bias." *The Quarterly Journal of Economics* 114 (1): 37–82. doi:10.1162/003355399555945.

Redelmeier, Donald A., and Amos Tversky. 1996. "On the Belief that Arthritis Pain is Related to the Weather." *Proceedings of the National Academy of Sciences* 93 (7): 2895–2896. doi:10.1073/pnas.93.7.2895.

Russo, J. Edward, and Paul J.H. Schoemaker. 1992. "Managing Overconfidence." *Sloan Management Review* 33 (2): 7–17. (c) 1992 from MIT Sloan Management Review/Massachusetts Institute of Technology. All rights reserved. Distributed by Tribune Content Agency, LLC.

Segal, David. 2011. "Law Students Lose the Grant Game as Schools Win." *The New York Times*, April 30, 2011. https://www.nytimes.com/2011/05/01/business/law-school-grants.html.

Smith, Adam. 1827. *An Inquiry into the Nature and Causes of the Wealth of Nations*. Printed at the University Press for T. Nelson / P. Brown.

Soll, Jack B., and Joshua Klayman. 2004. "Overconfidence in Interval Estimates." *Journal of Experimental Psychology: Learning, Memory, and Cognition* 30 (2): 299–314. doi:10.1037/0278-7393.30.2.299.

Suetens, Sigrid, Claus B. Galbo-Jørgensen, and Jean-Robert Tyran. 2016. "Predicting Lotto Numbers: A Natural Experiment on the Gambler's Fallacy and the Hot-Hand Fallacy." *Journal of the European Economic Association* 14 (3): 584–607. doi:10.1111/jeea.12147.

Suetens, Sigrid, and Jean-Robert Tyran. 2012. "The Gambler's Fallacy and Gender." *Journal of Economic Behavior & Organization*, Gender Differences in Risk Aversion and Competition, 83 (1): 118–124. doi:10.1016/j.jebo.2011.06.017.

Sundali, James, and Rachel Croson. 2006. "Biases in Casino Betting: The Hot Hand and the Gambler's Fallacy." *Judgement and Decision Making*: 1–12. https://repository.upenn.edu/oid_papers/252.

Sunstein, Cass R. 2017. *#Republic*. Princeton, NJ: Princeton University Press. https://press.princeton.edu/books/hardcover/9780691175515/republic.

Svenson, Ola. 1981. "Are We All Less Risky and More Skillful than Our Fellow Drivers?" *Acta Psychologica* 47 (2): 143–148. doi:10.1016/0001-6918(81)90005-6.

Terrell, Dek. 1994. "A Test of the Gambler's Fallacy: Evidence from Pari-mutuel Games." *Journal of Risk and Uncertainty* 8 (3): 309–317. doi:10.1007/bf01064047.

Tribe, Laurence H. 1971. "Trial by Mathematics: Precision and Ritual in the Legal Process." *Harvard Law Review* 84 (6): 1329–1393. doi:10.2307/1339610.

Tversky, Amos, and Daniel Kahneman. 1971. "Belief in the Law of Small Numbers." *Psychological Bulletin* 76 (2): 105–110. doi:10.1037/h0031322.

———. 1974. "Judgment under Uncertainty: Heuristics and Biases." *Science* 185 (4157): 1124–1131. Reprinting from p 1125 with permission from AAAS, doi:10.1126/science.185.4157.1124.

————. 1983. "Extensional versus Intuitive Reasoning: The Conjunction Fallacy in Probability Judgment." *Psychological Review* 90 (4): 293–315. Copyright © 1983 by American Psychological Association. Reproduced with permission, doi:10.1037/0033-295.X.90.4.293.

Weinstein, Neil D. 1980. "Unrealistic Optimism about Future Life Events." *Journal of Personality and Social Psychology* 39 (5): 806–820. doi:10.1037/0022-3514. 39.5.806.

————. 1987. "Unrealistic Optimism about Susceptibility to Health Problems: Conclusions from a Community-Wide Sample." *Journal of Behavioral Medicine* 10 (5): 481–500. doi:10.1007/BF00846146.

17　Nonstandard Beliefs

Learning Objectives

★　Appreciate how overconfidence can make sense of otherwise puzzling business and finance decisions.

★　Understand modeling of non-Bayesian beliefs.

★　Develop intuition for how extrapolative beliefs can reconcile empirical facts about asset prices.

The evidence from the previous chapter identifies settings in which beliefs systematically deviate from the standard assumptions. Overconfidence reveals that beliefs and judgements are not always accurate. While the gambler's fallacy, extrapolation, and base-rate neglect suggest that new information does not change beliefs according to Bayes' rule.

How do we modify our theoretical framework to better describe actual belief formation? There is no single model unifying the diversity of nonstandard beliefs. Instead, for each belief anomaly there are typically multiple behavioral economics models that can predict it. The goal of this chapter is not to survey all such models, but to demonstrate *how* deviations from Bayesian beliefs can be modeled.[1]

This chapter is organized as follows. We begin with three puzzling behaviors from business and finance — entrepreneurship, mergers, and investor trading — each of which is consistent with overconfidence. In the following section we introduce two non-Bayesian models of belief updating: a belief in the law of small numbers and base-rate neglect. These models can make sense of the beliefs in the previous chapter. And while they make different assumptions about how exactly individuals update beliefs, they both generate extrapolation. The chapter concludes with an application of extrapolation to explain asset price movements in financial markets.

17.1　Overconfidence in Business and Finance Decisions

Taking overconfidence as given, the present objective is to understand how its existence matters in economic settings. In particular, we explore the theoretical predictions and empirical evidence for overconfidence among entrepreneurs, managers, and investors. Conspicuously absent from this list are overconfident employees and consumers. Because they can be exploited by standard profit-maximizing firms, I defer the discussion of employees and consumers to the next chapter's investigation of market responses.

DOI: 10.4324/9780367854072-23

Recall that overconfidence can exist in a variety of forms: overestimation, overplacement, overprecision, or optimism. It is therefore not surprising that there is no one single model of overconfidence. There are multiple mechanisms that may contribute to and strengthen overconfidence. For instance, the previous chapter discusses how the anchoring and adjustment heuristic, as well as confirmation bias, can generate overconfidence. Other biases documented in the psychology literature can also generate overconfidence. Consider *hindsight bias*, the belief that an event in the past was more predictable than it truly was before it happened (Fischhoff 1975; Roese and Vohs 2012). That is, with hindsight people feel that they "knew it all along," failing to recall how much uncertainty existed in the past. And when one feels that they have always been right in the past, they are prone to be overconfident about the future. Alternatively, overconfidence is supported by the *self-attribution bias*, in which people take personal credit for past successes, but blame failures on bad luck (Langer and Roth 1975; Miller and Ross 1975). For our purposes, it is not necessary to choose a specific model of overconfidence. Instead, I will focus on how overconfidence, no matter its source, influences economic behavior.

17.1.1   *Entrepreneurial Entry*   *[Business]*

Approximately 500,000 new businesses are started each year in the US[2] And while some become wildly profitable, they are outliers. Among US startups founded in 1996, 6 years later less than 10% had annual sales in excess of $1 million and only 0.7% earned more than $10 million annually in sales (Shane 2009). Figure 17.1 depicts this distribution, along with the most common outcome for a startup: failure. Typically 50% of all startups shut down within the first four years (Kerr and Nanda 2010).

A Puzzle

These facts are a puzzle for the standard model of decision making. Think of starting a new business as a lottery of uncertain returns. With standard risk averse preferences,

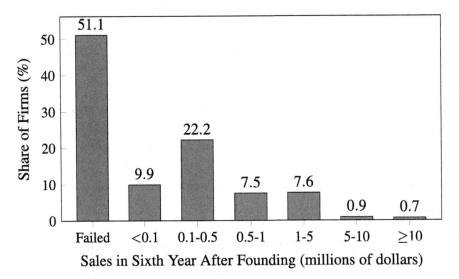

Figure 17.1 Distribution of Sales in 2002 Among US Firms Founded in 1996

Data Source: Shane (2009, Table 4.1).

lotteries are appealing when they offer high expected payoffs and little variability. But entrepreneurship offers neither. Because half of all new business ventures shut down within a few years, the median return to entrepreneurship is very low. And the positive returns are highly variable, ranging from the often modest to the rarely astronomical. Entrepreneurship is therefore sufficiently unappealing to a standard decision maker that no one should want to start a new business (Hall and Woodward 2010). And yet on average, over 1,000 new businesses are started each day.

Why is the standard model failing to predict the high level of entry into entrepreneurial activity?[3] One hypothesis is that entrepreneurs are just not as averse to risk as the rest of us (Kihlstrom and Laffont 1979). In this case, they may not be discouraged by the high risk of starting a company — in fact, they may seek out such risk. But there is little conclusive evidence that entrepreneurs have different risk preferences than the general population. And even if they do, such differences are likely to be too small to fully explain their pursuit of such a high-risk venture.

Predictions and Evidence of Overconfidence

An alternative hypothesis is that entrepreneurs are overconfident. If individuals hold unrealistically high beliefs about their chance of success, their inflated perception of expected returns may motivate entry into entrepreneurship. This is not simply conjecture. In a survey of 3,000 entrepreneurs, a third expected to succeed with 100% chance, while simultaneously rating the chance of success of similar businesses much lower (Cooper, Woo, and Dunkelberg 1988). Such inaccurate beliefs could be due to overplacement, overestimation, or general optimism. (See Exercise 17.2 to consider the implications of overprecision.)

There is evidence for each of these manifestations of overconfidence among entrepreneurs. Recall that we have already seen lab evidence for overplacement in the context of market entry (Camerer and Lovallo (1999) in Section 16.1). That is, when a market is highly competitive and can only support a few firms, market entrants believe too highly that they can beat the competition.

More generally, if potential entrepreneurs overestimate their own abilities and skills, they will tend to form excessively high beliefs for success. One way to identify overestimation is to compare an individual's prediction of their performance on a general knowledge test with their actual performance. Among a sample of Canadians asked to make such a self-assessment, the entrepreneurs in the sample exhibited greater overestimation than the non-entrepreneurs (Astebro, Jeffrey, and Adomdza 2007).

Another important source of overconfidence among entrepreneurs stems from an optimistic disposition.[4] Optimists believe that good events, largely outside one's control, are more likely to occur than they do. Survey evidence reveals that entrepreneurs are indeed more optimistic than non-entrepreneurs about their life expectancy (Puri and Robinson 2007) and the future state of the economy (Bengtsson and Ekeblom 2014). Even among entrepreneurs, those with greater optimism are more likely to persevere in the pursuit of an idea even after being told to quit (Astebro, Jeffrey, and Adomdza 2007).

In sum, overconfidence in the form of overplacement, overestimation, and optimism can help to resolve, at least partially, the puzzle of entrepreneurial entry. But this explanation raises a new question: what factors shape such inflated beliefs of entrepreneurial success? Exposure to entrepreneurs in one's life, for instance, may influence an individual's belief that they could successfully run their own company. People may reason, "If they can do it, so can I." This hypothesis is consistent with evidence that the children and co-workers of entrepreneurs are more likely to be entrepreneurs themselves (Lindquist, Sol, and Van Praag 2015; Nanda and Sørensen 2010).

And finally, even if overconfidence leads to excessive business formation from an individual's perspective, it might still be socially optimal (Bernardo and Welch 2001). After all, without the churn of new business ideas emerging and failing, society could miss out on creative innovations that generate benefits far beyond the entrepreneur's profit.

17.1.2   Managerial Mergers   [Business]

A company can change over time by joining with, or taking over, another company. Such mergers and acquisitions (henceforth, mergers) are big business. Over the past two decades in the United States, there are typically over 10,000 merger transactions announced annually, with total valuations in excess of $1.6 trillion (IMAA 2020).

A Puzzle

According to traditional corporate finance theory, mergers serve to enhance efficiency in a changing industry. And assuming that top managers, like CEOs, act in the interest of their shareholders, we would expect the shareholders of the acquiring company to benefit. But acquiring shareholders have suffered substantial losses at the announcement of merger bids (Moeller, Schlingemann, and Stulz 2005).

Can such low-value mergers be explained by overconfident CEOs? This hypothesis is at least suggested by accounts in the popular press. According to industry expert Dan Tiemann, mergers are "all about optimism and confidence ... You have to keep making bets and they have to pay off" (La Monica 2018).

Predictions of Overconfidence

Economic theory indeed predicts that overconfident CEOs are more likely to conduct mergers (and other investments), particularly when they have plenty of cash on hand (Malmendier and Tate 2008). For intuition, assume there is an overconfident CEO who overestimates the value she can create for her company. This overconfidence has two implications. First, she overestimates the value of a potential merger, making her more eager to acquire another firm. But this eagerness is offset by a second implication of her overconfidence: she believes that her company's prospects are better than what the market perceives. That is, she believes the market is undervaluing her company relative to what it is really worth. As a consequence, she is hesitant to sell shares of the company stock as a means to fund a potential merger — why sell a share for the market price of $10 when you think it is worth $12? For this reason, the less that an overconfident CEO needs to rely on equity financing (i.e., selling of stocks) and can instead use cash on hand, the more likely she is to pursue mergers. Note that if the financing constraints are sufficiently large, overconfidence can in theory reduce merger activity.

The misperceptions by overconfident CEOs are also predicted to generate lower merger returns on average than those earned by CEOs with well-calibrated beliefs.[5] This prediction follows from the two effects of overconfidence noted above. Overconfident CEOs will tend to pursue low value mergers, and additionally forgo high value mergers that require equity financing.

Evidence of Overconfidence

In order to empirically test the impact of overconfidence on mergers, we first need a method for measuring CEO overconfidence. A common approach is to classify as overconfident those CEOs who hold company stock options until the year of expiration (Malmendier and Tate 2005, 2008). The reason for defining overconfidence in this way follows from the standard prediction that individuals will diversify their investments. Investing all of your wealth in only one asset, like your house or your company's stock, is very risky. If something goes wrong — a natural disaster destroys your house or an economic crisis destroys your company — you could lose everything at once. Whereas, if you diversify your investments across many assets, you are better insured against one group of assets doing poorly. A CEO is already heavily invested in the company they lead by virtue of it being their source of employment and compensation. To insure against the risk of company decline and job loss, they should invest heavily in other assets that are unlikely to collapse at the same time as their company. When CEOs receive stock options as a form of compensation, we therefore expect them to sell the company stock as soon as they have the option to do so. But overconfident CEOs, who overestimate the future value of their company, will be less willing to sell their company stock early. Holding on to stock options therefore provides a proxy of CEO overconfidence. According to this measure, about 40% of CEOs in 2010 were classified as overconfident (Malmendier and Tate 2015).[6]

Malmendier and Tate (2008), in making use of the above proxy for overconfidence, find strong evidence for the role of managerial overconfidence in merger activity. In particular, they find that the odds of a merger are 65% higher if the CEO is overconfident. And consistent with the theoretical predictions above, this effect is largest for companies that do not require equity financing to fund the merger. The greater merger activity by overconfident CEOs is also *excessive*, in the sense that their merger announcements generate larger stock price declines than the merger announcements by other CEOs.

While our focus has been on *external* investments in the form of mergers, there is no reason to suspect that overconfidence would not similarly lead to excessive low-value *internal* investments. In fact, companies with abundant cash on hand may prefer to hire overconfident CEOs precisely because they want a leader who will initiate new investments and innovate (Banerjee et al. 2020; Hirshleifer, Low, and Teoh 2012).

17.1.3   Investor Trading Volume   [Finance]

Investors in the US stock market trade a lot. That is, instead of adopting a passive strategy of holding a fixed set of investments over time, many investors actively trade stocks, presumably in search of higher gains. The volume of trading is so large that in each year since 1998, the value of traded shares has exceeded the total value of the stock market (French 2008).

A Puzzle

Such high trading volume in financial markets is a puzzle for the standard model of decision making. To understand why, let's begin with the following key insight from finance. A primary motivation for people to trade a financial asset is disagreement about its value. Suppose the price of an asset is $50, reflecting how much it is valued by market participants. But you disagree and value the asset at $60. There are then gains to trading — the market will sell you the asset for $50 and you are made better off by getting an asset for less than you think it is worth. Whereas if you also valued it at $50, there is no disagreement and therefore no motivation to exchange $50 in cash for an asset that is also worth $50.

But it is hard for standard decision makers, who know that everyone else is a standard decision maker, to disagree about an asset's value. To see why, suppose once again that after careful independent research about the underlying value of an asset, you determine it is worth $60. You then look up the asset's market price to see it is only $50. The implication for a standard investor is *not* to hoard shares of what appears to be a bargain-priced asset. Instead, as a standard investor you should use the $50 market price as new information to update your beliefs about the asset's value. In particular, you should think through the logic of why someone else would be willing to sell you an asset for only $50 if it were actually worth more. Taking this into account, you should revise your beliefs about the asset's value down closer to $50. And as a result, you will be less inclined to trade. In the extreme case, you fully revise your valuation down to the market price — trusting the market's information more than your own — and trade is never predicted to occur (Milgrom and Stokey 1982). Even if this thought experiment appears absurd, the main takeaway is that trading volume is expected to be quite low in markets populated by standard investors, contrary to the trading volume evidence.

Predictions of Overconfidence

A market with overconfident investors, however, will experience much higher trading volume (Odean 1998).[7] Suppose that overconfidence manifests as overprecision, i.e., investors overestimate the precision of their information about the value of an asset. As a result, they hold overly confident beliefs in the accuracy of their asset value judgements relative to others.[8] So market prices that reflect the beliefs of other investors have little effect on shifting the beliefs of an overconfident investor. Applying this logic to the prior example, an overconfident investor who initially believes an asset is worth $60 discounts the information contained in the $50 market price and maintains their higher valuation. Investors can therefore persist with substantial disagreement about asset values that deviate from market prices. And as noted, this disagreement promotes trading.

Evidence of Overconfidence

Just because overconfidence *can* predict high trading volume, does not mean it *is* a primary reason for this phenomenon.[9] To verify the overconfidence hypothesis, we would like to show that overconfident individuals — as determined in settings outside of financial trading — do indeed trade significantly more than non-overconfident folks. The following two studies do exactly this.

Recall the evidence in the previous chapter that men are more overconfident than women (see also Lundeberg, Fox, and Punćcohaŕ 1994). If overconfidence motivates trading, we would therefore expect men to trade more than women on average. Barber and Odean (2001) examine the stock investments of 78,000 individuals between 1991 and 1997 and verify that indeed men trade 45% more than women. The active trading by men also has the effect of increasing the transaction costs that they pay relative to women.

Further evidence comes from the trading behavior of young Finnish men, for whom military service is mandatory. At the time of induction, each man completes a standard psychological assessment in which they rate their self-confidence. Grinblatt and

Keloharju (2009) construct a measure of each man's overconfidence by taking the difference between his self-assessed confidence and actual competence on intellectual ability exams. The researchers find that those who display more overconfidence around age 20 also trade stocks more frequently many years later.

Together, these studies lend support to the overconfidence hypothesis for trading volume. And more generally, they underscore the relevance of overconfidence in shaping real-world, high-stakes decisions.

17.2 Nonstandard Belief Updating

Beyond the inaccuracy of overconfident beliefs, individuals also fail to update their beliefs according to Bayes' rule in light of new information. The gambler's fallacy, extrapolative beliefs, and base-rate neglect, introduced in Section 16.3, are all instances of deviations from Bayesian updating. This section models such beliefs by assuming that individuals use the basic framework of Bayes' rule, but make a particular error in the process.

Before turning to specific errors, let's first review what is prescribed by standard Bayesian updating. Consider two possible states of the world, A and B: either A is true or B is true, but not both. An individual holds prior beliefs before receiving new information, $p(A)$ and $p(B)$, about the chance that each state is true, with $p(A) + p(B) = 1$. Bayes' rule (Definition 2.5) requires that after receiving new information or data D, individuals form updated posterior beliefs about the true state of the world as follows:

$$
\begin{aligned}
p(A \mid D) &= \frac{p(D \mid A)p(A)}{p(D \mid A)p(A) + p(D \mid B)p(B)} \\
p(B \mid D) &= \frac{p(D \mid B)p(B)}{p(D \mid A)p(A) + p(D \mid B)p(B)}
\end{aligned}
\tag{17.1}
$$

where $p(D \mid A)$ is the likelihood of observing D given A, and $p(D \mid B)$ is the likelihood of observing D given B.

In what follows we consider two departures from Bayesian updating. First, we model a belief in the law of small numbers and show how such beliefs generate both the gambler's fallacy and extrapolation. Next, we model base-rate neglect, highlighting how this too can generate extrapolative beliefs.[10] Each model captures a different error in applying Bayes' rule. No matter the error, I denote an individual's incorrect posterior beliefs by $\tilde{p}(A \mid D)$ and $\tilde{p}(B \mid D)$, to distinguish them from the Bayesian posterior beliefs $p(A \mid D)$ and $p(B \mid D)$ as determined by equations (17.1).

17.2.1 Law of Small Numbers

A belief in the law of small numbers (LSN) refers to the mistaken view that a small random sample must "look like" the population from which it is drawn (Tversky and Kahneman 1971). It is mistaken because according to the true law of *large* numbers in probability theory, only large random samples are guaranteed to "look like" the underlying population. Rabin (2002) proposes the following model of the LSN.

Definition 17.1 There is a random process with two possible outcomes:

- x occurs with probability $\theta \in [0, 1]$, and
- y occurs with probability $1-\theta$.

An individual observes a sequence of independent outcomes generated by this process. As a **believer in the law of small numbers**, this individual believes that the outcomes are generated as draws *without replacement* from an urn containing $N < \infty$ balls, of which

- θN balls denote outcome x, and
- $(1 - \theta)N$ balls denote outcome y.

Note: Assume that θN is an integer to rule out fractional balls.

It may not be immediately obvious why this abstract model of drawing balls without replacement from an urn captures the intuition for a belief in the LSN. But imagine an urn with 10 balls, some of which denote outcome x and some of which denote outcome y. Then as an individual randomly draws balls from this urn without replacing before the next draw, the urn grows emptier and the distribution of outcomes in the small sample increasingly looks like the distribution of outcomes in the original urn. This is precisely the idea of a belief in the LSN. Taken to the extreme, after 10 draws, the urn is empty and the small sample *is* the population.[11]

A believer in the LSN is making a mistake. A more accurate mental model for the independent outcomes generated by the random process is that balls are drawn from the urn *with* replacement. When each ball is placed back in the urn before the next draw, it now becomes possible to withdraw the same ball multiple times. In this case, a small sample provides less information about the true population of balls in the urn. Once again considering an extreme case, it is possible to draw the same ball every time, revealing little about the contents of the urn.

We now turn to exploring the implications of this model, particularly its ability to generate both the gambler's fallacy and extrapolative beliefs. And for the sake of concision, I will refer to a believer in the LSN simply as Larry.

Application: Gambler's Fallacy with Certainty about θ

Assume that Larry knows θ with certainty. That is, he knows the distribution of x and y balls in an urn of size N. This certainty about the distribution induces the gambler's fallacy. The following example illustrates how so.[12]

▪ **Example 17.1 — Mutual Fund Returns**. The annual return to a mutual fund is either High (H) or Low (L), each of which is equally likely and independent of prior returns. Translating to the notation in Definition 17.1, $x = H$, $y = L$, and $\theta = 0.5$.

Assume Larry believes that mutual fund returns are drawn without replacement from an urn of size $N = 10$ containing 5 H balls and 5 L balls. Then his belief that the next draw will be H after observing:

- one draw of H is $\frac{5-1}{10-1} = \frac{4}{9} \approx 44\%$, because after the first draw of H there are only 4 H balls among the remaining 9.
- two draws of H is $\frac{5-2}{10-2} = \frac{3}{8} \approx 38\%$, because after two draws of H there are only 3 H balls among the remaining 8.

For Larry, the chance of seeing another High return decreases as more High returns are observed in the past. But the actual chance of a High return is 50%, independent of the past. ∎

In this example Larry exhibits the gambler's fallacy: outcomes of one type decrease his belief that the next outcome will be of the same type. More generally, this model of beliefs can make sense of the gambler's fallacy behaviors documented in the previous chapter. In particular, when the distribution of outcomes is known with certainty, as with a coin flip, roulette wheel spin, or lottery number draw, Larrys will act in accordance with their expectation that random outcomes alternate more frequently than is true.

How does the size of the urn impact Larry's beliefs? Consider the general case with an urn of size N that contains $\theta N \geq 1$ balls denoting outcome x. Then after observing a single draw of x from the urn, Larry's belief that the next draw is once again x is:

$$\tilde{p}(x \mid x) = \frac{x \text{ Balls in Urn After Drawing an } x \text{ Ball}}{\text{Total Balls in Urn After Drawing an } x \text{ Ball}} = \frac{\theta N - 1}{N - 1} \qquad (17.2)$$

The numerator and denominator in this expression are both reduced by one because the first draw of x is not replaced prior to the next draw.

Figure 17.2 plots this belief as a function of urn size N separately for $\theta = 0.2$, 0.5, and 0.8. From this figure, we observe the following:

1. Larry's belief $\tilde{p}(x \mid x)$ about seeing a second x outcome is less than the correct probability $p(x \mid x) = \theta$, no matter the urn size. This is the gambler's fallacy discussed above.
2. No matter the true probability θ of seeing another x outcome, Larry's belief $\tilde{p}(x \mid x)$ is increasing in the size of the urn N.

As a consequence of these two observations, Larry's beliefs are most severely incorrect when the urn is small. For illustration, imagine that the urn size in Example 17.1 were only $N = 2$, with one H and one L ball. Then after observing a single draw of H, Larry would believe it impossible for the second draw to also be H, even though there is truly a 50% chance. But with a very large urn, it makes little difference whether a small random sample is drawn with or without replacement. So Larry would hold approximately correct beliefs. This insight is depicted in Figure 17.2 by the convergence of Larry's belief with the corresponding correct belief for large values of N.

Application: Extrapolative Beliefs with Uncertainty about θ

Now assume that Larry is uncertain about θ. In particular, let there be two possible values of θ, each of which corresponds to a state of the world, A or B. Larry holds prior beliefs $p(A)$ and $p(B)$, before observing any outcomes, about the chance that each state is true.

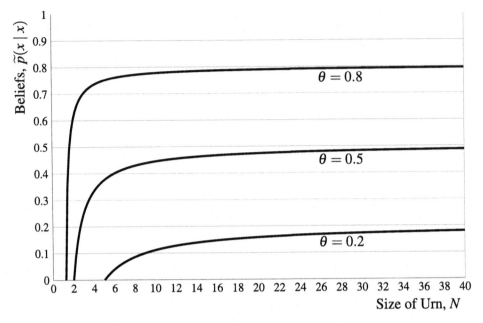

Figure 17.2 Law of Small Numbers Belief for a Repeat of Outcome *x*, per Equation (17.2)

We are interested in computing Larry's posterior beliefs about the state of the world after observing a sequence of outcomes. To do so, assume that Larry updates with Bayes' rule, but uses his incorrect beliefs about the likelihood of observing a sequence of outcomes D in state of the world A, which we denote by $\tilde{p}(D \mid A)$. This perceived likelihood differs from the true likelihood $p(D \mid A)$. Larry makes an analogous error for state of the world B. It is these errors that make Larry's use of Bayes' rule non-Bayesian. The following definition summarizes.

Definition 17.2 Given priors $p(A)$ and $p(B)$ that states of the world A and B are true, a **believer in the law of small numbers forms posterior beliefs** after observing information or data D as follows:

$$\tilde{p}(A \mid D) = \frac{\tilde{p}(D \mid A)p(A)}{\tilde{p}(D \mid A)p(A) + \tilde{p}(D \mid B)p(B)}$$

$$\tilde{p}(B \mid D) = \frac{\tilde{p}(D \mid B)p(B)}{\tilde{p}(D \mid A)p(A) + \tilde{p}(D \mid B)p(B)}$$

where likelihoods $\tilde{p}(D \mid A)$ and $\tilde{p}(D \mid B)$ are those of a believer in the law of small numbers, per Definition 17.1.

Once again, the abstraction of this model is best understood through an example.

■ **Example 17.2 — Mutual Fund Management.**

The Setting: There are two kinds of mutual funds that are equally likely, but differ in the rate at which their annual returns are either High (*H*) or Low (*L*):

- Well-managed funds generate High returns in 70% of years.
- Poorly-managed funds generate High returns in 30% of years.

Translating to the notation in Definition 17.1, $x = H$, $y = L$, $\theta = 0.7$ in the *Well* state of the world, and $\theta = 0.3$ in the *Poorly* state. And with accurate priors about the state of the world, $p(Well) = p(Poorly) = 0.5$.

The Questions: What is an individual's posterior belief that the fund is well-managed after observing three consecutive high returns, *HHH*? And given this, what is their belief that the next outcome is again *H*?

Bayesian Answers: A Bayesian correctly believes that the likelihoods of observing *HHH* in each of the states are $p(HHH \mid Well) = 0.7^3$ and $p(HHH \mid Poorly) = 0.3^3$. This follows from noting that each *H* outcome occurs independently with probability θ. Then according to Bayes' rule in equation (17.1), the posterior belief is:

$$p(Well \mid HHH) = \frac{p(HHH \mid Well)p(Well)}{p(HHH \mid Well)p(Well) + p(HHH \mid Poorly)p(Poorly)}$$

$$= \frac{0.7^3 \cdot 0.5}{0.7^3 \cdot 0.5 + 0.3^3 \cdot 0.5} \approx 93\%$$

The Bayesian believes with probability 93% that the fund is well managed and with probability 7% that it is poorly managed. Because well-managed funds are High with probability 0.7 and poorly-managed funds are High with probability 0.3, she therefore expects next year's return to be High with probability:

$$p(Well \mid HHH) \cdot 0.7 + p(Poorly \mid HHH) \cdot 0.3 \approx 93\% \cdot 0.7 + 7\% \cdot 0.3 \approx 67\%$$

Belief in LSN Answers: Assume Larry believes that mutual fund returns are drawn without replacement from an urn of size $N = 10$, in which a well-managed fund has 7 *H* balls and 3 *L* balls, while a poorly-managed fund has 3 *H* balls and 7 *L* balls. As a consequence, he holds the following incorrect beliefs about the likelihoods of observing *HHH* in each of the states:

$$\tilde{p}(HHH \mid Well) = \frac{7}{10} \times \frac{6}{9} \times \frac{5}{8} = \frac{7}{24}$$

$$\tilde{p}(HHH \mid Poorly) = \frac{3}{10} \times \frac{2}{9} \times \frac{1}{8} = \frac{1}{120}$$

Observe that these likelihoods are calculated by successively removing an *H* ball from the urn. Then according to Definition 17.2, his posterior belief is:

$$\tilde{p}(Well \mid HHH) = \frac{\tilde{p}(HHH \mid Well)p(Well)}{\tilde{p}(HHH \mid Well)p(Well) + \tilde{p}(HHH \mid Poorly)p(Poorly)}$$

$$= \frac{7/24 \cdot 0.5}{7/24 \cdot 0.5 + 1/120 \cdot 0.5} \approx 97\%$$

Relative to a Bayesian, Larry believes too strongly that the mutual fund is well managed (97% > 93%) after observing three consecutive high returns. Intuitively, he underappreciates that a poorly managed firm can get lucky and also generate a short sequence of high returns.

When Larry forms beliefs about the return in year four, assume that like a Bayesian he believes a well-managed firm has a 7/10 chance of generating a high return and a poorly-managed firm has only a 3/10 chance. That is, Larry's mental urns are replenished back to their original states after the first three draws. He therefore expects next year's return to be High with probability:

$$\tilde{p}(Well \mid HHH) \cdot 0.7 + \tilde{p}(Poorly \mid HHH) \cdot 0.3 \approx 97\% \cdot 0.7 + 3\% \cdot 0.3 \approx 69\%$$

Relative to a Bayesian, Larry believes too strongly that the mutual fund will generate another high return (69%>67%) after observing three consecutive high returns. This is a result of his overconfidence that the fund is well managed.   ∎

This fairly long example illustrates a general insight: when uncertainty exists about the population from which a small random sample is drawn, the Larrys of the world believe too strongly that the population looks like the small sample. And this erroneous belief promotes exaggerated expectations that a future draw from the population must then also look like previous small sample. In the mutual fund example, a sequence of high returns makes Larry overconfident that the fund is well managed. And because well-managed funds generate high returns more often than poorly-managed funds, he forecasts future high returns as more likely than is warranted.

Observe that the preceding logic describes a mechanism for extrapolative beliefs: outcomes of one type lead to an exaggerated belief that the next outcome will be of the same type. The evidence for betting on recent winners in casinos, the stock market, and sports can therefore be understood as a consequence of believing in the law of small numbers when there is uncertainty about the underlying random process. That is, the success of a lottery number, financial asset, or athlete may excessively inflate an individual's belief about its true success rate, which in turn increases the belief about future success.

Extrapolative beliefs are particularly important for making sense of financial markets. We cover such applications in the last section of this chapter. But first, let's consider another deviation from Bayesian beliefs that similarly generates extrapolation.

17.2.2 Base-Rate Neglect

Base-rate neglect refers to the tendency for individuals, when updating their beliefs, to underuse their prior information relative to what is required by Bayes' rule. Benjamin, Bodoh-Creed, and Rabin (2019) propose the following nonstandard model of updating to capture such underweighting of prior beliefs.

Definition 17.3 Given priors $p(A)$ and $p(B)$ that states of the world A and B are true, an **individual who suffers from base-rate neglect (BRN) forms**

posterior beliefs after observing information or data D as follows:

$$\tilde{p}(A \mid D) = \frac{p(D \mid A)p(A)^c}{p(D \mid A)p(A)^c + p(D \mid B)p(B)^c}$$

$$\tilde{p}(B \mid D) = \frac{p(D \mid B)p(B)^c}{p(D \mid A)p(A)^c + p(D \mid B)p(B)^c}$$

$$(17.3)$$

where $0 \leq c < 1$.

The expressions above share the same basic structure as Bayes' rule, with one important difference: each instance of a prior belief $p(\cdot)$ is raised to the power of $c \neq 1$. This is the error that makes a sufferer of BRN a non-Bayesian. Interpret c as an individual's weighting of prior information when revising their beliefs. When $c = 0$ the individual completely ignores prior information. Larger values of c correspond to less severe underweighting of prior information. And in the limit as c approaches 1, the individual approximates the inferences made by a standard Bayesian updater.

To translate the model of BRN into a convenient odds form, take the ratio of the two equations in (17.3) to obtain:

$$\underbrace{\frac{\tilde{p}(A \mid D)}{\tilde{p}(B \mid D)}}_{\text{BRN Posterior Odds}} = \underbrace{\frac{p(D \mid A)}{p(D \mid B)}}_{\text{Likelihood Ratio}} \times \left(\underbrace{\frac{p(A)}{p(B)}}_{\text{Prior Odds}} \right)^c \qquad (17.4)$$

This expression is useful in highlighting how values of $c < 1$ diminish the relative weight of prior beliefs in the formation of posterior beliefs, and consequently magnify the relative importance of likelihood assessments. While the underweighting of base rates can potentially lead to dramatic deviations from Bayesian beliefs, this need not always be the case. In particular, when states A and B are each true with close to equal probability ($p(A) \approx 0.5 \approx p(B)$) so that the prior odds is close to 1, the Bayesian posterior odds is well-approximated by the likelihood ratio alone. Because base rates are largely irrelevant for updating beliefs in this case, so too is their neglect. The impact of base-rate neglect will be stronger in settings where one state of the world is much more likely to be true than another. We consider two such settings in the remainder of this section.

Application: Calibrating Base-Rate Neglect with Lab Evidence

Let's apply the model of BRN to the evidence from the Identifying Jack Lab Experiment (Section 16.3.3). To recap, two groups of subjects were given different prior information about the distribution of engineers and lawyers in a population before reading the same description (D) of a randomly selected person named Jack. They then reported their posterior beliefs that Jack is an engineer (state A) or lawyer (state B). By plugging the given prior beliefs and reported posterior beliefs into equation (17.4) for each group, we obtain:

$$\frac{0.55}{0.45} = \frac{p(D \mid Engineer)}{p(D \mid Lawyer)} \times \left(\frac{0.7}{0.3}\right)^c \tag{17.5}$$

$$\frac{0.5}{0.5} = \frac{p(D \mid Engineer)}{p(D \mid Lawyer)} \times \left(\frac{0.3}{0.7}\right)^c \tag{17.6}$$

This is a system of two equations with two unknowns: parameter c and the likelihood ratio $\frac{p(D \mid Engineer)}{p(D \mid Lawyer)}$. We can therefore solve for c by standard algebraic methods, as follows:

$$\frac{0.55/0.45}{0.5/0.5} = \left(\frac{0.7/0.3}{0.3/0.7}\right)^c \qquad \text{by dividing (17.5) by (17.6)}$$

$$\Rightarrow 11/9 = (0.7^2/0.3^2)^c = (7/3)^{2c} \qquad \text{by algebraic manipulation}$$

$$\Rightarrow \ln(11/9) = \ln\left((7/3)^{2c}\right) = 2c \ln(7/3) \qquad \text{by taking logs, and log power rule}$$

$$\Rightarrow c = \frac{\ln(11/9)}{2 \ln(7/3)} \approx 0.12 \qquad \text{by division}$$

The model of BRN can therefore make sense of the otherwise puzzling underuse of prior information. And in particular, the low value of $c \approx 0.12$ that is consistent with the evidence reveals strong base-rate neglect by the subjects.[13]

Application: Base-Rate Neglect as a Source of Extrapolative Beliefs

The following numerical example applies the model of BRN to a mutual fund context.

▪ **Example 17.3 — Mutual Fund Excellence**
The Setting: There are two kinds of mutual funds that differ in the rate at which their annual returns are either High (H) or Low (L):

- Excellent funds generate High returns in 80% of years, i.e., $p(H \mid Excellent) = 0.8$.
- Average funds generate High returns in 50% of years, i.e., $p(H \mid Average) = 0.5$.

Assume that excellent funds are uncommon, accounting for only 10% of funds. Therefore, prior beliefs are $p(Excellent) = 0.1$ and $p(Average) = 0.9$.
The Questions: What is an individual's posterior belief that the fund is excellent after observing a high return H? And given this, what is their belief that the next outcome is H?
Bayesian Answers: Applying Bayes' rule as in equation (17.1) the posterior belief is:

$$p(Excellent \mid H) = \frac{p(H \mid Excellent)p(Excellent)}{p(H \mid Excellent)p(Excellent) + p(H \mid Average)p(Average)}$$

$$= \frac{0.8 \cdot 0.1}{0.8 \cdot 0.1 + 0.5 \cdot 0.9} \approx 15\%$$

The Bayesian believes with probability 15% that the fund is excellent and with probability 85% that it is average. She therefore expects next year's return to be H with probability:

$$p(Excellent \mid H) \cdot 0.8 + p(Average \mid H) \cdot 0.5 \approx 15\% \cdot 0.8 + 85\% \cdot 0.5 \approx 55\%$$

BRN Answers: Assume Nelson suffers from BRN with $c = 0.2$. Then by applying equation (17.3), his posterior belief is:

$$\tilde{p}(Excellent \mid H) = \frac{p(H \mid Excellent)p(Excellent)^{0.2}}{p(H \mid Excellent)p(Excellent)^{0.2} + p(H \mid Average)p(Average)^{0.2}}$$

$$= \frac{0.8 \cdot 0.1^{0.2}}{0.8 \cdot 0.1^{0.2} + 0.5 \cdot 0.9^{0.2}} \approx 51\%$$

Relative to a Bayesian, Nelson believes too strongly that the mutual fund is excellent (51%>15%) after observing a high return. Intuitively, he underappreciates that excellent funds are rare and that a high return likely comes from one of the many average funds.

Given these beliefs, Nelson expects next year's return to be H with probability:

$$\tilde{p}(Excellent \mid H) \cdot 0.8 + \tilde{p}(Average \mid H) \cdot 0.5 \approx 51\% \cdot 0.8 + 49\% \cdot 0.5 \approx 65\%$$

Relative to a Bayesian, Nelson believes too strongly that the mutual fund will generate another high return (65%>55%) after observing one high return. This is a result of his inflated belief that the fund is excellent. ∎

This example illustrates how base-rate neglect, like a belief in the law of small numbers, can provide a psychological mechanism for extrapolative beliefs (Barberis, Shleifer, and Vishny 1998). Note that a critical assumption for the emergence of such incorrect beliefs in the example was the rarity of excellent mutual funds. Because the vast majority of funds are assumed to be average, a Bayesian believes that even a fund with a recent string of high returns is still likely to be average. But for those who underweight base rates, their posterior beliefs are determined primarily by likelihood assessments — high returns are more likely with an excellent fund, so a fund with a few high returns must be excellent. This incorrect judgement leads to an exaggerated belief that future returns will continue to be high. The role of extrapolative beliefs in financial markets, where excellent returns are indeed uncommon, is our next topic.

17.3 Extrapolative Beliefs in Financial Markets [Finance]

Extrapolative beliefs provide an intuitive and powerful explanation for understanding a variety of empirical facts about asset prices in financial markets.

Before introducing the empirical evidence, I first briefly outline the traditional logic of asset pricing. An asset, like a share in a company, has value because it generates some uncertain future stream of cash flows (e.g., dividends) to the investor. The asset's **fundamental value** at any moment in time is the expected present value, given all available information, of these future cash flows. A foundation of modern finance is the hypothesis that if a market is largely populated by investors who make decisions according to the standard model, then the price of an asset at any point in time must equal its fundamental value. To appreciate this logic, suppose that for some reason there exists a *mispricing* in which the price of an asset deviates from its fundamental value. Then standard investors — who are also referred to as *fundamental traders* — will recognize a profit opportunity and trade aggressively to correct the mispricing, causing it to disappear.[14] Investor demand for an underpriced asset will increase the price back to its fundamental value. And the selling of an overpriced asset will decrease the price back to its fundamental value. In effect, self-interested traders have the effect of keeping prices in line with accurate valuations.

17.3.1 *Empirical Facts and Evidence*

This section provides evidence for four empirical facts about stock prices, each of which contradicts the hypothesis that asset prices always equal their fundamental values.

Our first two facts refer to differences in stock price returns, or changes, across the stock market. A glance at the financial section of a newspaper reveals that while some stocks have earned high returns in the past, others have not. But can a stock's past returns predict its future returns? According to the logic of fundamental traders instantly moving prices to reflect all available information at every moment, the answer is no.[15] Any information about future returns would already be priced into the stock: a stock with good cash flow prospects would be more expensive than one with poor prospects. Future movements in the stock price therefore depend on new information about future cash flows that is yet to be learned — not past information. And yet, future stock returns are indeed predictable based on past returns in the following ways.

- **Medium-term momentum** refers to the fact that a stock's return over the past 6 to 12 months (the medium-term) predicts the stock's future return with a *positive* sign. Jegadeesh and Titman (1993) examine the returns of high performing "winner" and low performing "loser" stocks over the past 6 months. They find that past winners generate 10% higher returns than losers over the next 6 months.
- **Long-term reversal** refers to the fact that a stock's return over the past 3 to 5 years (the long term) predicts the stock's future return with a *negative* sign. For instance, De Bondt and Thaler (1985) examine the returns of winner and loser stocks over the prior 3 years. They find that the past winners underperform the past losers by about 25 percentage points over the next 3 years.

A third important observation about the aggregate stock market is its **excess volatility** (Shiller 1981; LeRoy and Porter 1981). Figure 17.3 plots the S&P 500 stock price index over 140 years of US history. It is clearly volatile in its fluctuations over time, but what do we mean by *excessive* volatility? The excess is relative to what we would expect if the stock price index truly reflected its fundamental value. Suppose this were the case. Then the stock price index, as a forecast of the present value of future dividends, should be *less* volatile than the actual present value of future dividends. But Figure 17.3 reveals that stock market index is *much more* volatile than the actual present value of future dividends. If fundamental traders were indeed keeping asset prices in line with the largely stable fundamentals, the stock market would be characterized by tranquility, not turbulence.

Our final fact is the occasional emergence of **bubbles** in asset prices (Shiller 2003). Informally, a bubble refers to a sustained period of time during which an asset is substantially priced over its fundamental value. Oft-cited bubbles include the Dutch Tulip

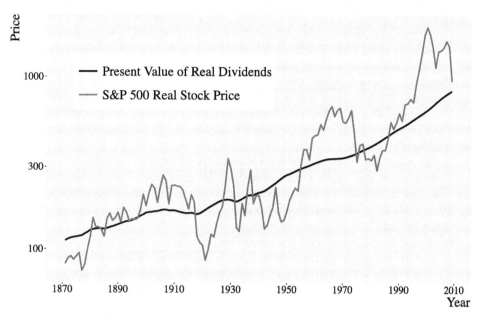

Figure 17.3 Annual Stock Prices and Present Values of Dividends

Data Source: Shiller (2016). Real dividends accruing to the S&P 500 Index are discounted by the constant geometric average real return from 1871 to 2012 of 6.53%.

Mania (1634–7), the British South Sea Company Stock Bubble (1720), the Dot-Com Bubble (1995–2000), and more recently Bitcoin (2017–18). But because the fundamental value of an asset can be difficult to estimate, it is useful to define a bubble as an episode characterized by more directly observable evidence, such as:[16]

i   a sharp increase in the asset price followed by a collapse;
ii early in the episode there is good news about the asset's future cash flows;
iii throughout the episode many investors expect the asset's future return to be strongly positively related to its recent return; and
iv as the asset price approaches its peak there is very high trading volume.

Although we observe episodes with the above characteristics in reality, they are inconsistent with the standard framework.

17.3.2 *Asset Prices with Extrapolative Beliefs*

To make sense of the preceding four empirical facts, this section considers the theoretical implications of introducing investors with extrapolative beliefs. In particular, assume that there are two types of investors: extrapolators and standard fundamental traders. Regardless of the source for extrapolative beliefs — e.g., from a belief in the law of small numbers or base-rate neglect — extrapolators expect future asset returns to be positively related to the asset's recent past returns. Fundamental traders instead form Bayesian beliefs about future asset returns.

Consider the following market setting populated by the two types of traders (see Barberis (2018) for details). There exists a fixed supply of shares in a risky asset that pays a single uncertain cash flow at a future date. At an initial period $t = 0$, everyone expects the future cash flow to be $100. But in each period $t = 1, 2, 3 \ldots$ leading up to the cash flow delivery date, traders observe any new information about the magnitude of the future cash flow. For instance, there may be good news that the future cash flow will be higher than $100, bad news that it will be lower, or no news at all. Traders demand shares based on the available information and the prevailing asset price. The asset price in turn adjusts each period to clear the market so that total trader demand equals the fixed supply of shares.

Let's see what this model predicts for the evolution of the asset price in response to good news about the asset's future cash flow. In particular, assume that there is no new information about the cash flow except in period 2, when investors learn that the future cash flow will be $6 higher. Figure 17.4 plots the market price of this risky asset from periods 1 to 12 with and without extrapolators.

The dashed line segments plot the asset price over time in a market with only fundamental traders. Interpret this price as the fundamental value of the asset. To understand the dynamics of the fundamental value, consider first the counterfactual in which no new information ever arrives. In this case, the asset price would have moved along the dotted line in Figure 17.4. It is increasing because as the investors approach the future cash flow payout date, there are fewer opportunities for information surprises, and therefore less risk about how big the cash flow will actually be. And with less risk, the asset is more desirable to risk averse investors, increasing demand and the market price. Relative to this baseline, the good news in period 2 that the future cash flow will be $6 higher shifts the asset price up by exactly $6 in period 2, and in every subsequent period.

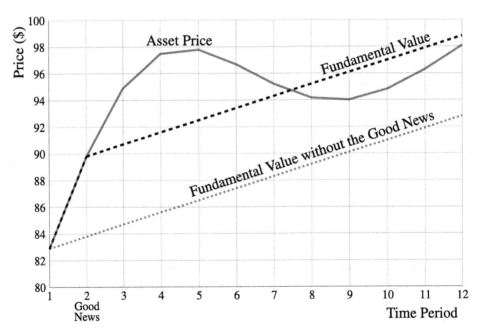

Figure 17.4 Asset Price Movement with Extrapolators

Source: Barberis (2018) develops the asset price model that is plotted here.

More generally, this upward shift demonstrates how a market of exclusively fundamental traders immediately incorporates new information into asset prices.

We are now ready for the main event: the solid line segments track the asset price in a market with 70% extrapolators and 30% fundamental traders. It is immediately clear that the presence of fundamental traders does *not* keep the asset price equal to its fundamental value. This contradicts the traditional hypothesis that fundamental traders will eliminate any mispricings through their buying and selling. Moreover, the particular movements of the asset price are consistent with our four empirical facts.

- *Medium-term momentum* is evidenced by the way the positive return from period 1 to 2 is followed by another positive return from period 2 to 3. Intuitively, the positive return in period 2 caused by the good news leads extrapolators to expect another positive return in the next period. Extrapolators therefore increase their demand for the asset, increasing the asset price in period 3. This self-fulfilling process in which the expectation of high returns creates high returns continues in periods 4 and 5.
- *Long-term reversal* is evidenced by the way the positive return from period 1 to 5 is followed by a negative return from period 5 to 9. The long-term past return is high because the asset price has been pushed up above fundamentals by strong demand from extrapolators. But as extrapolators lose enthusiasm for future returns given the more modest returns in the recent past, the price drops, generating low returns for those who purchased the asset at its peak.
- *Excess volatility* is apparent from the oscillation of the solid line around the dashed line. Although fundamental traders prevent asset prices from deviating too wildly from fundamentals, they do not eliminate excessive volatility.
- Finally, the episode satisfies the four characteristics of a *bubble*. That is, (i) there is a sharp increase in the asset price from period 1 to 5, followed by a collapse; (ii) good cash flow news is announced in period 2; (iii) many investors have extrapolative beliefs about asset returns; and (iv) trading volume increases during the asset price rise, in the sense that extrapolators steadily increase their asset holdings.[17]

As promised, we have demonstrated the intuition for how extrapolative beliefs can reconcile a variety of distinct empirical facts in financial markets. This is not to suggest that extrapolation is the only way by which investors deviate from the standard model. After all, there are finance applications throughout this book. But from a theoretical modeling perspective, it is satisfying to appreciate the instances in which a relatively simple nonstandard assumption can so dramatically enrich our understanding of real-world markets.

17.4 Summary

1 Theory predicts, and evidence supports, the role of overconfidence in explaining:

   a   the high rate of entrepreneurial entry;
   b   the high rate of mergers and acquisitions; and
   c   the high trading volume of stocks.

2 A **believer in the law of small numbers** is modeled as believing that a sequence of random outcomes is generated as draws without replacement from an urn, when it is in fact draws with replacement. This model of beliefs generates:

    a   the gambler's fallacy when there is certainty about the random process; and

    b   extrapolative beliefs when there is uncertainty about the random process.

3   An **individual who suffers from base-rate neglect forms posterior beliefs** by underweighting prior beliefs in the application of Bayes' rule.

4   A foundational hypothesis of modern finance is that an asset price equals its **fundamental value**, i.e., the expected present value, given all available information, of future cash flows. This hypothesis is contradicted by the following empirical facts: **medium-term momentum, long-term reversal, excess volatility**, and **bubbles**.

5   Many empirical facts about asset prices are predicted by a model of trading in which some investors extrapolate future asset returns from recent past returns.

17.5   Exercises[18]

Exercise 17.1 — Start-Up Overconfidence. Jia is employed at an established company that pays her a good salary. But she believes that she has a great business idea and is considering starting her own company. She is aware that in doing so, there are three possible outcomes: she could fail (F), achieve modest success (M), or potentially become hugely successful (H). Jia makes her decision by comparing the utility of keeping her job with the expected utility of entrepreneurship as follows:

$$U(\text{keep job}) = 300$$
$$U(\text{entrepreneurship}) = \tilde{p}_F \cdot 100 + \tilde{p}_M \cdot 250 + \tilde{p}_H \cdot 1{,}000$$

where $\tilde{p}_s$ is her (possibly inaccurate) belief about the probability of outcome $s \in \{F, M, H\}$, with $\tilde{p}_F + \tilde{p}_M + \tilde{p}_H = 1$. The true probabilities are $p_F = 0.5$, $p_M = 0.49$, and $p_H = 0.01$.

    a   Suppose that Jia does careful research and forms accurate beliefs, with $\tilde{p}_s = p_s$ for each outcome s. Compute $U(\text{entrepreneurship})$. Does she become an entrepreneur?

    b   Now suppose that you observe Jia starting her own business. In talking with her you learn that she believes that she has a 70% chance of modest success ($\tilde{p}_M = 0.7$). What then must be Jia's minimal belief $\tilde{p}_H$ about achieving huge success? How does it compare to the true probability of huge success p_H?

Exercise 17.2 — Management of Overprecision. [Business] Herz, Schunk, and Zehnder (2014) conduct a lab experiment in which participants play the role of an ice cream stand manager. In this role, participants can stick with a default business strategy, fine-tune the strategy, or explore radically new strategies that could potentially lead to much larger profits. They find that participants who exhibit greater degrees of overprecision (as measured in a separate experiment) are less likely to explore new strategies.

    a   Interpret the result. That is, provide intuition for why overprecision could cause less exploration and experimentation.

    b   Discuss how this evidence fits, or doesn't fit, with the evidence in the chapter concerning the impact of overconfidence on entrepreneurial activity.

Exercise 17.3 — Money Isn't Everything. An alternative nonstandard motivation for entrepreneurial entry — beyond overconfidence — is the non-monetary benefit of entrepreneurship. That is, even if being an entrepreneur generates less money and more risk than working as an employee for someone else, there are other benefits that might make entrepreneurship preferable. Discuss two non-monetary benefits that may motivate individuals to start their own business.

Exercise 17.4 — Peering into Entrepreneurship. [Business] Lerner and Malmendier (2013) study the entrepreneurial activity of Harvard Business School students after earning their MBA. In the first year of the MBA program students are randomly assigned to different sections that study and work together. The rate of post-MBA entrepreneurship is *lower* among students in sections that had *more* peers with pre-MBA entrepreneurial experience. What does this evidence reveal about the factors that influence beliefs about entrepreneurial success?

Exercise 17.5 — Equity Financing. [Business] Malmendier, Tate, and Yan (2011) show that overconfident managers use less equity financing than their peers. Provide intuition for this finding.

Exercise 17.6 — Overconfident Voters. [Politics & Law] Ortoleva and Snowberg (2015) document the following evidence about overconfidence and political behavior in the U.S.

a   More overconfident citizens are more ideologically extreme. Is this likely due to overestimation, overplacement, or overprecision? Explain.

b   More overconfident citizens are more likely to vote (even after controlling for ideological extremism). Overconfidence is a stronger predictor of voter turnout than income, education, race, gender, or church attendance. Suppose that citizens vote only for the satisfaction of doing so — and not because they think their vote will change the election outcome. Discuss how overconfidence can increase the satisfaction from voting, and therefore voter turnout.

Exercise 17.7 — Hot Hands, Cold Statistics. Suppose that during any given game, basketball players are in one of the following two states: Hot (make 75% of their shots, independent of past success) or Normal (make 50% of their shots, independent of past success).

a   What is the probability that NBA player Paul will make three baskets in a row in the case that he is Hot? What if he is Normal?

b   If Paul is equally likely to be in either state before the game, what is the probability that he is Hot after he makes his first three baskets in a row?

Your friend believes in the law of small numbers. He thinks (erroneously) that if Paul is Hot, he always makes three out of every four shots he takes. Similarly, when Paul is Normal, he makes exactly two out of every four shots.

c   If Paul is Hot, with what probability does your friend believe that Paul will make his first basket? After making his first basket, what does your friend believe about the probability that Paul will make his next basket? Explain why these probabilities are not the same.

d   If your friend believes that each state is equally likely before the game, what would he believe about the chance that Paul is Hot after he makes his first three baskets in a row? Explain intuitively why your friend's belief differs from the correct probability that you calculated in part (b).

Exercise 17.8 — Flooded with Beliefs. Jessica just bought a house in a new town and is considering whether or not to purchase flood insurance. Jessica knows that 50% of towns are prone to flood and 50% are unlikely to flood. The flood-prone towns have a 60% chance of flooding each year. The towns that are unlikely to flood have a 20% chance of flooding each year. Jessica will purchase flood insurance if she believes that the likelihood of living in a flood-prone town is at least 15%. Finally, she knows that in the past two years there has not been a flood in her new hometown.

a   Given the above information, if Jessica has Bayesian beliefs, what is her belief that she lives in a flood-prone town? Will she buy flood insurance?
b   Now suppose that Jessica is a believer in the law of small numbers. That is, she believes (erroneously) that a flood-prone (unlikely to flood) town will flood exactly 3 (1) out of every 5 years. What is her belief in this case that the town is prone to flood? With these beliefs would she buy flood insurance?
c   Finally, suppose that instead of believing in the law of small numbers, Jessica suffers from confirmation bias (Section 16.2). She begins researching the history of floods in her town and talking to her friends and neighbors about the value of flood insurance. If she is initially predisposed not to buy flood insurance, explain how confirmation bias impacts how she processes new information. Does this bias induce her to overestimate or underestimate the value of flood insurance relative to a Bayesian updater without confirmation bias?

Exercise 17.9 — Promoting Beliefs with Law of Small Numbers. A manager has hired a new investment analyst. The manager accurately knows that 20% of analysts are high ability and 80% are low ability. High-ability analysts make investment decisions that yield a positive quarterly return 60% of the time, whereas low-ability analysts make investment decisions that yield a positive quarterly return 40% of the time.

   At the end of the analyst's first year, the manager reviews the analyst's performance over the previous 4 quarters and promotes the analyst if she believes that there is at least a 75% chance that the analyst is high ability. Suppose the analyst has a successful first year, with positive quarterly returns in each of the previous 4 quarters.

a   Given the above information, if the manager has Bayesian beliefs, what is her belief that the analyst is high ability at the end of the first year? Will she promote the analyst?
b   Now suppose that the manager is a believer in the law of small numbers. That is, she believes (erroneously) that across 1 consecutive quarters, a high (low) ability analyst will earn positive quarterly returns exactly 6 (4) times. What is her belief in this case that the analyst is high ability at the end of the first year? Will the manager promote the analyst?
c   Provide intuition for your answers in parts (a) and (b). In addition, explain whether the manager's thinking in part (b) illustrates the gambler's fallacy or extrapolation.

Exercise 17.10 — Promoting Beliefs with Base-Rate Neglect. Suppose that the manager in Exercise 17.9 suffers from base-rate neglect with $c = 0.1$.

a   What is her belief that the analyst is high ability at the end of the first year? Will the manager promote the analyst?
b   Is the manager over- or under-confident about the analyst's ability? Provide intuition.

Exercise 17.11 — Measuring Base-Rate Neglect. Refer back to the Cab Problem introduced in Exercise 16.12. Suppose that in answering the question about the chance that cab was Green, Kara, Lara, and Mara reported beliefs of 70%, 75%, and 80%, respectively. Assuming that they all suffer from base-rate neglect, apply Definition 7.3 to find the value of c for each respondent that would predict their answer.

Exercise 17.12 — Anomalous Asset Prices. [Finance] Explain why the following evidence contradicts the hypothesis that asset prices always equal their fundamental values.

a   *No-News Reactions:* For many of the 50 largest one-day price changes in the stock market from 1946 to 1987, there is no accompanying news about changes in future cash flows (Cutler, Poterba, and Summers 1989).
b   *January Effect:* From 1904 to 1974, the average stock market returns in January were eight times larger than average monthly returns in the other 11 months of the year (Rozeff and Kinney 1976).

Exercise 17.13 — Extrapolator Impact (Barberis 2018). Recall the risky asset described in Section 17.3.2, where good news arrives in period 2 about future cash flows.

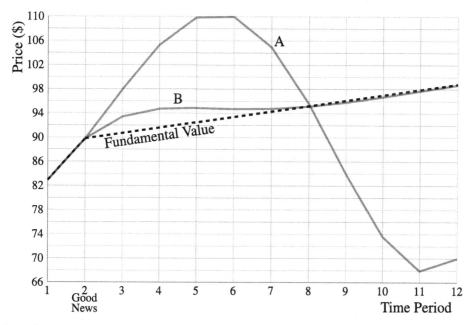

Figure 17.5 Asset Price Movement with Extrapolators in Exercise 17.13
Source: Barberis (2018) develops the asset price model that is plotted here.

When there are no extrapolators in the market, the asset price reflects the fundamental value of the asset, as depicted in Figure 17.5. The introduction of extrapolators to the market changes the dynamics of the asset price. Curves A and B in Figure 17.5 model the asset price for different shares of extrapolators among the investor population.

a   Which curve, A or B, corresponds to a greater share of extrapolators?

b   Compare and contrast the asset price movements with different shares of extrapolators.

Notes

1 See Benjamin (2019) for an excellent review of the evidence and theory for nonstandard beliefs.
2 For more information about the characteristics of business establishments by age and sector, see the US Census Bureau (2020) Business Dynamics Statistics (BDS) Data Tables.
3 See Astebro et al. (2014) for a comprehensive overview of the evidence for entrepreneurship.
4 Rigotti, Ryan, and Vaithianathan (2011) model firm formation in a society populated by people with different degrees of optimism.
5 The prediction — that merger returns are lower for overconfident CEOs — is true as long as over-confident CEOs conduct more mergers than non-overconfident CEOs (Malmendier and Tate 2008).
6 See Malmendier and Tate (2015) for further details on measuring overconfidence using stock options, as well as other metrics.
7 High trading volume is not the only puzzle in finance that can be explained by overconfidence. Excess volatility and momentum, for example, are predicted by overconfidence coupled with the self-attribution bias (Daniel, Hirshleifer, and Subrahmanyam 1998) and by overconfidence from confirmation bias (Pouget, Sauvagnat, and Villeneuve 2017). See Daniel and Hirshleifer (2015) for an excellent review of financial markets with overconfident investors.
8 Similar implications for trading volume can be generated by dismissiveness, i.e., underestimating the precision of others' information (Banerjee and Kremer 2010; Banerjee 2011).
9 Alternative theories of excessive trading volume include disagreement in prior beliefs among standard investors (Morris 1996) and cursed thinking (Eyster, Rabin, and Vayanos 2019).
10 Given that the law of small numbers and base-rate neglect can be understood as consequences of the representativeness heuristic, an alternative modeling approach is to model representativeness directly. Examples of this approach include Gennaioli and Shleifer (2010), Bordalo et al. (2016), and Zhao (2018).
11 An obvious shortcoming of the model in Definition 17.1 is that the sample size must not exceed the urn size. To address this problem Rabin (2002) assumes that the urn is replenished at regular intervals. I largely ignore such replenishing for pedagogical clarity.
12 Examples 17.1 and 17.2 are from DellaVigna (2009).
13 Benjamin (2019) provides an excellent review of the literature estimating base-rate neglect.
14 We set aside frictions, constraints, and risks that may dampen a fundamental trader's willingness or capacity to correct a mispricing. Fundamental traders are also typically referred to as arbitrageurs.
15 This is known as the weak-form efficient market hypothesis.
16 Barberis (2018) proposes a set of bubble episode characteristics that includes those listed in the text plus two more: during the price rise many sophisticated investors report that the asset is overvalued and some sophisticated investors increase their holdings of the asset.
17 The simple asset price model cannot fully capture the idea that trading volume increases given that it assumes a fixed supply of shares.
18 Exercise 17.7 is adapted from an exercise by Olga Shurchkov.

References

Astebro, Thomas, Holger Herz, Ramana Nanda, and Roberto A. Weber. 2014. "Seeking the Roots of Entrepreneurship: Insights from Behavioral Economics." *Journal of Economic Perspectives* 28 (3): 49–70. doi:10.1257/jep.28.3.49.

Astebro, Thomas, Scott A. Jeffrey, and Gordon K. Adomdza. 2007. "Inventor Perseverance after Being Told to Quit: The Role of Cognitive Biases." *Journal of Behavioral Decision Making* 20 (3): 253–272. doi:10.1002/bdm.554.

Banerjee, Snehal. 2011. "Learning from Prices and the Dispersion in Beliefs." *The Review of Financial Studies* 24 (9): 3025–3068. doi:10.1093/rfs/hhr050.

Banerjee, Snehal, and Ilan Kremer. 2010. "Disagreement and Learning: Dynamic Patterns of Trade." *The Journal of Finance* 65 (4): 1269–1302. doi:10.1111/j.1540-6261.2010.01570.x.

Banerjee, Suman, Lili Dai, Mark Humphery-Jenner, and Vikram Nanda. 2020. "Governance, Board Inattention, and the Appointment of Overconfident CEOs." *Journal of Banking & Finance* 113: 105733. doi:10.1016/j.jbankfin.2019.105733.

Barber, Brad M., and Terrance Odean. 2001. "Boys will be Boys: Gender, Overconfidence, and Common Stock Investment." *The Quarterly Journal of Economics* 116 (1): 261–292. doi:10.1162/003355301556400.

Barberis, Nicholas. 2018. "Psychology-Based Models of Asset Prices and Trading Volume." In *Handbook of Behavioral Economics: Foundations and Applications,* edited by B. Douglas Bernheim, Stefano DellaVigna, and David Laibson, 1:79–175. North-Holland. doi:10.1016/bs.hesbe.2018.07.001.

Barberis, Nicholas, Andrei Shleifer, and Robert Vishny. 1998. "A Model of Investor Sentiment." *Journal of Financial Economics* 49 (3): 307–343. doi:10.1016/S0304-405X(98)00027-0.

Bengtsson, Ola, and Daniel Ekeblom. 2014. "The Bright but Right View? A New Type of Evidence on Entrepreneurial Optimism." SSRN Scholarly Paper ID 2398954. Rochester, NY: Social Science Research Network. https://papers.ssrn.com/abstract=2398954.

Benjamin, Daniel J. 2019. "Errors in Probabilistic Reasoning and Judgment Biases." In *Handbook of Behavioral Economics: Foundations and Applications,* edited by B. Douglas Bernheim, Stefano Della-Vigna, and David Laibson, 2:69–186. North-Holland. doi:10.1016/bs.hesbe.2018.11.002.

Benjamin, Daniel J., A. L. Bodoh-Creed, and Matthew Rabin. 2019. "Base-Rate Neglect: Foundations and Implications." Working Paper.

Bernardo, Antonio E., and Ivo Welch. 2001. "On the Evolution of Overconfidence and Entrepreneurs." *Journal of Economics & Management Strategy* 10 (3): 301–330. doi:10.1111/j.1430-9134.2001.00301.x.

Bordalo, Pedro, Katherine Coffman, Nicola Gennaioli, and Andrei Shleifer. 2016. "Stereotypes." *The Quarterly Journal of Economics* 131 (4): 1753–1794. doi:10.1093/qje/qjw029.

Camerer, Colin F., and Dan Lovallo. 1999. "Overconfidence and Excess Entry: An Experimental Approach." *American Economic Review* 89 (1): 306–318. doi:10.1257/aer.89.1.306.

Cooper, Arnold C., Carolyn Y. Woo, and William C. Dunkelberg. 1988. "Entrepreneurs' Perceived Chances for Success." *Journal of Business Venturing* 3 (2): 97–108. doi:10.1016/0883-9026(88)90020-1.

Cutler, David M., James M. Poterba, and Lawrence H. Summers. 1989. "What Moves the Stock Market." *Journal of Portfolio Management* 15 (3): 4–11.

Daniel, Kent, and David Hirshleifer. 2015. "Overconfident Investors, Predictable Returns, and Excessive Trading." *Journal of Economic Perspectives* 29 (4): 61–88. doi:10.1257/jep.29.4.61.

Daniel, Kent, David Hirshleifer, and Avanidhar Subrahmanyam. 1998. "Investor Psychology and Security Market Under- and Overreactions." *The Journal of Finance* 53 (6): 1839–1885. doi:10.1111/0022-1082.00077.

De Bondt, Werner F. M., and Richard H. Thaler. 1985. "Does the Stock Market Overreact?" *The Journal of Finance:* 793–805.

DellaVigna, Stefano. 2009. "Psychology and Economics: Evidence from the Field." *Journal of Economic Literature* 47 (2): 315–372. doi:10.1257/jel.47.2.315.

Eyster, Erik, Matthew Rabin, and Dimitri Vayanos. 2019. "Financial Markets Where Traders Neglect the Informational Content of Prices." *The Journal of Finance* 74 (1): 371–399. doi:10.1111/jofi.12729.

Fischhoff, Baruch. 1975. "Hindsight is not Equal to Foresight: The Effect of Outcome Knowledge on Judgment under Uncertainty." *Journal of Experimental Psychology: Human Perception and Performance* 1 (3): 288–299. doi:10.1037/0096-1523.1.3.288.

French, Kenneth R. 2008. "Presidential Address: The Cost of Active Investing." *The Journal of Finance* 63 (4): 1537–1573. doi:10.1111/j.1540-6261.2008.01368.x.

Gennaioli, Nicola, and Andrei Shleifer. 2010. "What Comes to Mind." *The Quarterly Journal of Economics* 125 (4): 1399–1433. doi:10.1162/qjec.2010.125.4.1399.

Grinblatt, Mark, and Matti Keloharju. 2009. "Sensation Seeking, Overconfidence, and Trading Activity." *The Journal of Finance* 64 (2): 549–578. doi:10.1111/j.1540-6261.2009.01443.x.

Hall, Robert E., and Susan E. Woodward. 2010. "The Burden of the Nondiversifiable Risk of Entrepreneurship." *American Economic Review* 100 (3): 1163–1194. doi:10.1257/aer.100.3.1163.

Herz, Holger, Daniel Schunk, and Christian Zehnder. 2014. "How Do Judgmental Overconfidence and Overoptimism Shape Innovative Activity?" *Games and Economic Behavior* 83:1–23. doi:10.1016/j.geb.2013.11.001.

Hirshleifer, David, Angie Low, and Siew Hong Teoh. 2012. "Are Overconfident CEOs Better Innovators?" *The Journal of Finance* 67 (4): 1457–1498. doi:10.1111/j.1540-6261.2012.01753.x.

IMAA. 2020. "Mergers & Acquisitions in the United States." Technical report. The Institute for Mergers, Acquisitions and Alliances. https://imaa-institute.org/mand-a-us-united-states/.

Jegadeesh, Narasimhan, and Sheridan Titman. 1993. "Returns to Buying Winners and Selling Losers: Implications for Stock Market Efficiency." *The Journal of Finance* 48 (1): 65–91. doi:10.2307/2328882.

Kerr, William R., and Ramana Nanda. 2010. "Banking Deregulations, Financing Constraints, and Firm Entry Size." *Journal of the European Economic Association* 8 (2–3): 582–593. doi:10.1111/j.1542-4774.2010.tb00528.x.

Kihlstrom, Richard E., and Jean-Jacques Laffont. 1979. "A General Equilibrium Entrepreneurial Theory of Firm Formation Based on Risk Aversion." *Journal of Political Economy* 87 (4): 719–748. doi:10.1086/260790.

La Monica, Paul R. 2018. "Companies Have Spent a Stunning $2 Trillion on Mergers so far this Year." *CNNMoney,* May 24, 2018. https://money.cnn.com/2018/05/24/investing/merger-boom/index.html.

Langer, Ellen J., and Jane Roth. 1975. "Heads I Win, Tails It's Chance: The Illusion of Control as a Function of the Sequence of Outcomes in a Purely Chance Task." *Journal of Personality and Social Psychology* 32 (6): 951–955. doi:10.1037/0022-3514.32.6.951.

Lerner, Josh, and Ulrike Malmendier. 2013. "With a Little Help from My (Random) Friends: Success and Failure in Post-Business School Entrepreneurship." *The Review of Financial Studies* 26 (10): 2411–2452. doi:10.1093/rfs/hht024.

LeRoy, Stephen F., and Richard D. Porter. 1981. "The Present-Value Relation: Tests Based on Implied Variance Bounds." *Econometrica* 49 (3): 555–574. doi:10.2307/1911512.

Lindquist, Matthew J., Joeri Sol, and Mirjam Van Praag. 2015. "Why Do Entrepreneurial Parents Have Entrepreneurial Children?" *Journal of Labor Economics* 33 (2): 269–296. doi:10.1086/678493.

Lundeberg, Mary A., Paul W. Fox, and Judith Punćcohař. 1994. "Highly Confident but Wrong: Gender Differences and Similarities in Confidence Judgments." *Journal of Educational Psychology* 86 (1): 114–121. doi:10.1037/0022-0663.86.1.114.

Malmendier, Ulrike, and Geoffrey Tate. 2005. "CEO Overconfidence and Corporate Investment." *The Journal of Finance* 60 (6): 2661–2700. doi:10.1111/j.1540-6261.2005.00813.x.

———. 2008. "Who Makes Acquisitions? CEO Overconfidence and the Market's Reaction." *Journal of Financial Economics* 89 (1): 20–43. doi:10.1016/j.jfineco.2007.07.002.

———. 2015. "Behavioral CEOs: The Role of Managerial Overconfidence." *Journal of Economic Perspectives* 29 (4): 37–60. doi:10.1257/jep.29.4.37.

Malmendier, Ulrike, Geoffrey Tate, and Jon Yan. 2011. "Overconfidence and Early-Life Experiences: The Effect of Managerial Traits on Corporate Financial Policies." *The Journal of Finance* 66 (5): 1687–1733. doi:10.1111/j.1540-6261.2011.01685.x.

Milgrom, Paul R., and Nancy Stokey. 1982. "Information, Trade and Common Knowledge." *Journal of Economic Theory* 26 (1): 17–27. doi:10.1016/0022-0531(82)90046-1.

Miller, Dale T., and Michael Ross. 1975. "Self-Serving Biases in the Attribution of Causality: Fact or Fiction?" *Psychological Bulletin* 82 (2): 213–225. doi:10.1037/h0076486.

Moeller, Sara B., Frederik P. Schlingemann, and René M. Stulz. 2005. "Wealth Destruction on a Massive Scale? A Study of Acquiring-Firm Returns in the Recent Merger Wave." *The Journal of Finance* 60 (2): 757–782. doi:10.1111/j.1540-6261.2005.00745.x.

Morris, Stephen. 1996. "Speculative Investor Behavior and Learning." *The Quarterly Journal of Economics* 111 (4): 1111–1133. doi:10.2307/2946709.

Nanda, Ramana, and Jesper B. Sørensen. 2010. "Workplace Peers and Entrepreneurship." *Management Science* 56 (7): 1116–1126. doi:10.1287/mnsc.1100.1179.

Odean, Terrance. 1998. "Volume, Volatility, Price, and Profit When All Traders Are Above Average." *The Journal of Finance* 53 (6): 1887–1934. doi:10.1111/0022-1082.00078.

Ortoleva, Pietro, and Erik Snowberg. 2015. "Overconfidence in Political Behavior." *American Economic Review* 105 (2): 504–535. doi:10.1257/aer.20130921.

Pouget, Sebastien, Julien Sauvagnat, and Stephane Villeneuve. 2017. "A Mind Is a Terrible Thing to Change: Confirmatory Bias in Financial Markets." *The Review of Financial Studies* 30 (6): 2066–2109. doi:10.1093/rfs/hhw100.

Puri, Manju, and David T. Robinson. 2007. "Optimism and Economic Choice." *Journal of Financial Economics* 86 (1): 71–99. doi:10.1016/j.jfineco.2006.09.003.

Rabin, Matthew. 2002. "Inference By Believers in the Law of Small Numbers." *The Quarterly Journal of Economics* 117 (3): 775–816. doi:10.1162/003355302760193896.

Rigotti, Luca, Matthew Ryan, and Rhema Vaithianathan. 2011. "Optimism and Firm Formation." *Economic Theory* 46 (1): 1–38. doi:10.1007/s00199-009-0501-x.

Roese, Neal J., and Kathleen D. Vohs. 2012. "Hindsight Bias." *Perspectives on Psychological Science* 7 (5): 411–426. doi:10.1177/1745691612454303.

Rozeff, Michael S., and William R. Kinney. 1976. "Capital Market Seasonality: The Case of Stock Returns." *Journal of Financial Economics* 3 (4): 379–402. doi:10.1016/0304-405X(76)90028-3.

Shane, Scott. 2009. *Fool's Gold?: The Truth Behind Angel Investing in America.* Oxford: Oxford University Press.

Shiller, Robert J. 1981. "Do Stock Prices Move Too Much to be Justified by Subsequent Changes in Dividends?" *American Economic Review* 71 (3): 421–436. https://www.jstor.org/stable/1802789.

———. 2003. "From Efficient Markets Theory to Behavioral Finance." *Journal of Economic Perspectives* 17 (1): 83–104. doi:10.1257/089533003321164967.

———. 2016. *U.S. Stock Price Data, Annual, with Consumption, both Short and Long Rates, and Present Value Calculations.* Accessed December 15, 2020, http://www.econ.yale.edu/~shiller/data/chapt26.xlsx.

Tversky, Amos, and Daniel Kahneman. 1971. "Belief in the Law of Small Numbers." *Psychological Bulletin* 76 (2): 105–110. doi:10.1037/h0031322.

US Census Bureau. 2020. *Business Dynamics Statistics (BDS).* Section: Government, https://www.census.gov/programs-surveys/bds.html.

Zhao, Chen. 2018. "Representativeness and Similarity." Technical report. Working Paper.

18 Market & Policy Responses to Nonstandard Beliefs

Learning Objectives

★ Evaluate the impact of nonstandard beliefs on individual welfare.

★ Understand how firms can use complex contracts to exploit the overconfidence of employees and consumers for profit.

★ Consider the implications of nonstandard beliefs for designing social insurance programs.

Workers form beliefs about the chance that their employer's stock price will increase. Cell phone consumers choose service plans based on their beliefs about how much data they will use. The unemployed decide how hard to search for a new job given their beliefs about the effectiveness of job hunting. And beliefs about the benefits of medical treatments impact the decision to seek out health care when sick. It is standard to assume that all of these beliefs are accurately calibrated to reality. But if actual beliefs deviate from this standard assumption, then profit-maximizing firms and welfare-maximizing governments may find it advantageous to adjust their contracts and policies.

Regardless of the particular setting, firms can exploit the nonstandard beliefs of employees and consumers for profit by complicating contracts. Relative to a world in which beliefs are standard, such exploitative contracting increases firm profits, while making employees and consumers worse off. Public policies designed to mitigate individual welfare losses must take into account both actual beliefs and firm responses.

This chapter explores the impact of nonstandard beliefs on market contracts and public policy. We begin with a short review of the distinction between decision utility and experienced utility when beliefs are nonstandard. Our first application concerns overconfident employees. In this case, overconfidence can help to explain the practice of paying stock options to rank-and-file workers. We then turn to exploitative contracting by firms selling goods and services to overconfident consumers. Finally, we explore the design of social insurance, with applications to unemployment and health insurance.

18.1 Welfare with Nonstandard Beliefs

How do we evaluate the welfare of individuals who hold nonstandard beliefs? Although there are alternative approaches, I adopt the following welfare framework introduced in Chapter 3.

DOI: 10.4324/9780367854072-24

The previous two chapters illustrate some of the ways in which people form beliefs $\tilde{p}$ about themselves and the world around them. Regardless of the context or underlying psychological mechanisms that shape one's beliefs, these beliefs matter for decision making. Two people who are identical in every way except for their beliefs will form different expectations, and as a result tend to make different decisions. An expected utility function U that represents preferences in terms of beliefs $\tilde{p}$, no matter their accuracy, therefore reflects decision utility: what an individual maximizes when making their decisions. We can express U compactly as follows:

Decision utility: $U = E(u \mid \tilde{p})$

where u is a standard utility function over uncertain outcomes or states of the world.

Although individual beliefs $\tilde{p}$ impact decisions, the chance of actually experiencing each possible outcome is determined by correct beliefs p that accurately reflect true probabilities and are updated via Bayes' rule. For example, just because someone believes their startup will be a huge success does not make the likely chance of failure any less real. An individual's experienced utility, no matter the degree to which their beliefs are mistaken, is therefore the expected utility of their decisions given correct beliefs p. And because we define individual welfare as equal to experienced utility, we can express individual welfare W compactly as follows:

Individual welfare: $W = E(u \mid p)$

This definition of individual welfare implies that the best an individual can do for their own welfare is to behave as if they have correct beliefs. To act otherwise makes one worse off. Finally, recall that the gap between decision and experienced utilities generates an internality, and a subsequent rationale for paternalistic interventions. We turn to such public policy interventions later in this chapter. But first, we consider how profit-maximizing firms can exploit individuals' nonstandard beliefs for private gain.

18.2   Overconfident Employees   [Labor]

There is more to employee compensation than simply a wage or salary. Many employers offer full-time employees health coverage and retirement benefits. And some companies offer employees stock options. A stock option gives the employee the *option*, after a few years, to purchase company stock at a discounted price. For instance, consider an employee with the option to purchase shares in their company for $50 each when the market price is $60. By buying at $50 and selling at $60, the employee can make $10 on each stock option they exercise. This $10 benefit to the employee is a cost to the firm.

Although stock options are a common form of compensation for executives, they are also offered to rank-and-file employees. Oyer and Schaefer (2005) estimate that non-executives who make annual salaries over $75,000 receive over 60% of the total value of stock options granted. Stock options are also paid, if only modestly, to lower-paid employees. The total value of stock options can account for a large part of a firm's total spending on workers. Among firms that issue some stock options, the value of the options is 25% of all wages (Oyer and Schaefer 2005).

18.2.1 A Compensation Puzzle

According to standard economic theory, a primary motivation for compensating a worker with stock options instead of cash is to incentivize high effort. In the absence of stock options, workers may be motivated to exert effort for a variety of reasons, e.g., to avoid being fired, earn a promotion, public recognition, or personal pride. But because a company's success — as measured by the market price of its shares — increases the value of stock options, an employee compensated with stock options will have an additional incentive to work hard in the company's interest.

The preceding logic of options-as-incentives surely makes sense for executives. Executives make decisions that directly impact the profits and market valuation of a company. So stock option compensation helps to align the private interests of executives with the collective interests of the company; when the company earns higher profits, executives earn more money. But the individual efforts of rank-and-file employees at a large company — from administrative assistants to janitors and middle-level managers — are unlikely to have a material effect on the stock price. And for workers who realize this, the incentive effects of stock options become very small.

18.2.2 Exploitation via Stock Options

What can explain why firms would then choose to compensate rank-and-file employees with stock options instead of higher wages? One compelling answer is overconfidence.[1] That is, if employees are overconfident about the future value of company stock, then firms can profit from this overconfidence by substituting stock options for wages (Bergman and Jenter 2007).

Let's illustrate this insight with a simple model. Oliver is offered a job as a middle-manager at a large publicly traded company. In particular, Oliver is offered an annual wage \$$w$ and s stock options. For simplicity, assume that with probability p the company stock price increases this year and each stock option can be redeemed for \$1. Otherwise, the stock options have no value. Oliver believes that the stock price will increase with probability $\tilde{p} \geq p$. Putting this together, we express Oliver's (risk-neutral) expected decision utility U from working at the firm as:

$$U = w + \tilde{p}s + (1 - \tilde{p})0 = w + \tilde{p}s$$

If he doesn't accept the new job, Oliver can keep his current job in which he obtains utility U^0. Therefore, he will only take the new job if $U \geq U^0$. Finally, because individual welfare W depends on the true probability with which Oliver experiences the benefits of redeeming his stock options, welfare from accepting the job is:

$$W = w + ps + (1 - p)0 = w + ps$$

Now consider compensation from the firm's perspective. Its expected cost C of paying a certain wage \$$w$, and with probability p paying stock options valued at \$$s$, is:

$$C = w + ps + (1 - p)0 = w + ps$$

Note that the expected cost does not depend on employee beliefs $\tilde{p}$ about company performance, but actual company performance. Moreover, the company's cost C has the same form as Oliver's welfare W because his well-being in this model is determined only by what the firm pays.

To see how overconfidence can be exploited by the firm, consider the following numerical examples with $U^0 = 65,000$ and $p = 0.5$.

1 Oliver is accurate: $\tilde{p} = 0.5$. If the firm pays $w = \$60,000$ and $s = 10,000$, then

$$U = 60,000 + 0.5 \cdot 10,000 = 65,000 \geq U^0 \qquad \text{so Oliver accepts, and}$$
$$W = C = 60,000 + 0.5 \cdot 10,000 = 65,000$$

2 Oliver is overconfident: $\tilde{p} = 0.75$. If the firm pays $w = \$50,000$ and $s = 20,000$, then

$$U = 50,000 + 0.75 \cdot 20,000 = 65,000 \geq U^0 \qquad \text{so Oliver accepts, and}$$
$$W = C = 50,000 + 0.5 \cdot 20,000 = 60,000$$

In sum, when Oliver is overconfident, the firm can induce him to accept the job offer at a lower cost. The firm reduces its expected cost from \$65,000 to \$60,000. With less spending on Oliver, his welfare is also lower when he is overconfident. In fact, overconfident Oliver would have achieved higher welfare from rejecting the offer and keeping his current job. See Exercise 18.3 for a more general analysis of compensation in this setting.

Intuitively, employees who are overconfident about the future prospects of a company will believe that stock options are more valuable than they truly are. Profit-maximizing firms can exploit this inaccurate belief by substituting stock options for wages. In doing so, they keep employees feeling sufficiently well compensated, while simultaneously reducing their own costs. It is only later and with regret that overconfident employees may realize that they should have been less willing to forego cash for an uncertain future benefit. The widespread practice of granting stock options to rank-and-file employees whose efforts have little effect on share prices can therefore be rationalized as the outcome of firms reacting to the overconfidence of their employees. In fact, employers have an incentive to inflate worker overconfidence about firm performance so as to justify stock options in lieu of cash compensation.

18.3 Overconfident Consumers   [Industrial Organization]

Just as overconfident workers can inaccurately value a compensation package from an employer, overconfident consumers in the marketplace can misvalue contracts for goods and services. Such overconfidence introduces new profit opportunities for firms, as well as consumer protection motivations for policy makers. This section explores these issues.[2]

We begin by distinguishing between two general ways in which overconfident consumers can misvalue the contracts they are offered. First, overconfident consumers may *misforecast their future consumption*. Such misforecasting arises when consumers overestimate their self-control, or ability to follow through with intended consumption (see Chapter 5). It is not uncommon, for example, to overestimate gym attendance and underestimate credit card borrowing. Another source of misforecasting is overprecision.

That is, even if consumers accurately forecast their median future use, they may overestimate the precision of their forecast, and therefore underappreciate the variability of their future use. For instance, there is significant overprecision among cell phone customers forecasting their own future demand for making calls (Grubb and Osborne 2015).

Second, overconfident consumers may overvalue contracts by *overestimating their ability to navigate the terms of the contract.* For example, by overestimating the probability of mailing in a rebate or cancelling a free trial before billing begins, an overconfident consumer will perceive a contract with such features as more valuable than it is. Experimental evidence confirms that consumers do indeed overestimate their likelihood of redeeming mail-in rebates (Silk 2004).

18.3.1 *Exploitation via Complex Pricing*

Consider a standard profit-maximizing firm that realizes its customers are overconfident and systematically misvalue pricing contracts. How does this realization change the incentives for the firm? Consumers who overvalue contracts will be willing to pay more, allowing for higher prices and profits. The reverse is true for consumers who undervalue contracts. Therefore, the firm will find it profitable to design contracts that exacerbate consumer overvaluations and minimize consumer undervaluations. In other words, the firm wants to create the perception for consumers that they are getting more value from the firm than it is actually giving. Let's apply this general insight to make sense of two features of real-world contracts: three-part tariffs and contact hurdles.

Three-Part Tariffs

What do the following contracts have in common?

- *Car Lease:* Fixed monthly payment for 36 months and 36,000-mile total allowance, plus 15 cents per additional mile.
- *Smart Phone Service:* Fixed monthly payment for unlimited talk and text and 5 gigabytes (GB) of data, plus $15 per additional 1 GB of data each month.
- *Balance-Transfer Credit Card:* In transferring existing credit card debt to a new credit card, the new credit card charges a one-time fee equal to 3% of the transfer amount and zero interest for the first year, but a high interest rate thereafter.

These examples each illustrate a type of pricing contract known as a **three-part tariff**. In particular, the tariff (or price) includes the following three parts:

1   a fixed access fee;
2   an included allowance of units at no additional cost; and
3   a constant marginal price per unit for consumption beyond the allowance.

Take the car lease contract. Over the 3-year horizon of the lease, the sum of monthly payments is the fixed access fee that permits the lessee to drive the car at all. The first 36,000 miles of driving during this period are charged a marginal price of zero. But any driving in excess of the 36,000-mile allowance is charged the marginal price of 15 cents per mile. The same structure applies in the other examples, for the pricing of smart phone data usage and credit card debt. Observe that the simplest pricing contract you see in economics has only part #3 (e.g., gas is $2 per gallon). The two–part tariffs in Section 7.1 consist of parts #1 and #3 (e.g., a county fair charges $15 to access and $1 per ride).

Although three-part tariffs are relatively complicated, it turns out that they (approximately) maximize profits for firms with customers who misforecast future usage due to overprecision (Grubb 2009). To understand the intuition for why this is true, we proceed in a series of logical steps. Assume for now that overconfident consumers face a service contract with only two parts: an access fee and a marginal price per unit.

The first step is to consider the implications for pricing when consumers overestimate their future usage. In this case, they overestimate the likelihood of paying the marginal price for each unit of use. For instance, suppose you overestimate your gym attendance this week, believing you will go with a 100% chance, when in fact you only go with a 50% chance. Then if the gym reduces the per–visit price by $2 and increases the weekly access fee by $2, you would perceive no change in value. But the gym increases its expected profits by $1: it collects the extra $2 access fee from you, and only loses the $2 visit price reduction with a 50% chance. This example illustrates the more general insight that a profit-maximizing firm aiming to increase perceptions of value is incentivized to decrease the marginal price.

The reverse logic applies if consumers underestimate their future usage. In this case consumers underestimate the likelihood of paying the marginal price for each unit and therefore value contracts with high marginal prices more than is warranted. A profit-maximizing firm is now incentivized to increase the marginal price. Let's once again illustrate with an example. Consider the case of a credit card that charges a monthly access fee and an interest rate on the unpaid balance. Suppose you underestimate your credit card spending this month, believing there is only a 50% chance that you will have a $100 unpaid balance (and 50% chance of no unpaid balance), when in fact you will have a $100 unpaid balance with certainty. If the credit card company were to increase the interest rate by 2 percentage points and decrease the access fee by $1, it would make an extra $1 in profit. But you would perceive no change in value: you gain $1 from the reduced access fee and expect to pay an extra $2 in interest with only a 50% chance. The credit card company is profiting from your misforecast.

The logic of the preceding two steps is summarized at the top of Figure 18.1.[3] Our third step is to determine whether overprecise consumers overestimate or underestimate future usage. Suppose that overprecise consumers accurately forecast their median usage Q^M, but overestimate the precision of their estimate. For instance, if true future usage is equally likely to be any amount between $\underline{Q}$ and $\bar{Q}$, an overprecise consumer will believe future usage will fall within a much narrower interval around Q^M, as indicated by the shaded region at the bottom of Figure 18.1. Because this consumer is too confident that her usage will be close to the median, she overestimates the likelihood of consuming at least a below-median amount like Q^{Below} and underestimates the likelihood of consuming an above-median amount like Q^{Above}. The dashed curves in Figure 18.1 point to this asymmetry in misforecasting.

It then follows from the preceding three steps that firms facing overprecise consumers have an incentive to decrease marginal price for units below median consumption and increase marginal price for units above the median. A three-part tariff reflects exactly these incentives. In the car lease example, for instance, 36,000 miles over 3 years indicates the median usage at which the marginal price jumps from the low price of zero to

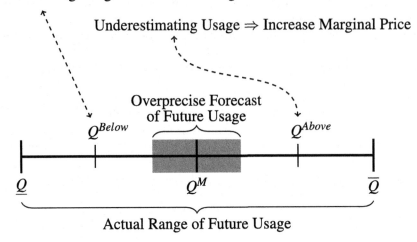

Figure 18.1 Schematic of Logic for Overprecision as Motivation for Three-Part Tariffs

the high price of 15 cents per mile. The real-world existence of three-part tariffs therefore provides suggestive evidence that consumers are indeed overprecise — and firms know it.[4]

Contract Hurdles

It can be challenging to navigate the various terms of a contract. Such terms can take the form of **memory hurdles**, i.e., tasks that consumers must remember to complete in order to reap a future benefit or avoid a future cost (Holman and Zaidi 2010). For instance, the benefits of a rebate or a free trial are only realized by those who remember to follow-through with actually mailing in the rebate at a future date or cancelling a service once the free trial expires.

Contracts can also feature surprise penalty fees. A bank may charge an overdraft fee when the balance of a checking account drops below zero — and keep charging the fee for each transaction before the balance is positive. For example, if a balance drops to −$1 and then the customer goes on to buy a $1 pack of gum and pay a $1 parking meter before realizing they have a negative balance, they could be charged a $35 overdraft fee three times over, turning a −$3 balance into −$108. Or a credit card company may charge a fee when the credit card balance reaches a pre-specified limit. These penalty fees constitute a "surprise" if the bank or credit card company does not notify customers in advance of triggering the penalty. In fact, most people who overdraw their checking accounts do not realize they are doing so (Stango and Zinman 2014). Instead, companies could provide advance warning, in which case the fees would only accrue to those who are willing to accept the penalty in exchange for the benefit of their next purchase. More generally, a surprise penalty fee acts as an **attention hurdle**, requiring consumers to pay close attention to their consumption behavior (Grubb 2015a).

Suppose that consumer overconfidence manifests as overestimating one's ability to navigate the terms, or *clear the hurdles*, of a pricing contract. Then profit-seeking firms have an incentive to include exactly such hurdles. When consumers overestimate the likelihood of cancelling a free trial before billing begins, firms will add free trials and profit from those who forget to cancel. Or when consumers overestimate their attention to monitoring account balances, firms will add surprise penalty fees and profit from the actual inattention.

18.3.2   *Protection via Public Policy*

Overconfidence can reduce consumer welfare. For instance, overvaluation encourages consumers to sign contracts they would be better off rejecting, while undervaluation encourages consumers to reject contracts they would be better off accepting. Consumer welfare can also be extracted for profit by firms that exploit consumer overconfidence with complex pricing contracts. And even if overconfidence makes firms better off while making consumers worse off, the net effect is unambiguously lower social welfare in a competitive market (Grubb 2015b).

What types of policies could help protect consumers from the costs of their overconfidence? One approach would be to ban or limit exploitative contracts, like three-part tariffs and attention or memory hurdles. The US 2009 Credit Card Accountability Responsibility and Disclosure Act, for instance, restricted over-limit and late payment fees on credit cards, saving US credit card users $11.9 billion annually (Agarwal et al. 2015).

Another policy approach would require firms to nudge customers with improved information disclosure or alerts (Section 3.4). Because nudges do not change consumer options or economic incentives, they should not change the behavior of consumers with accurate beliefs. But they could help improve the welfare for those who are overconfident.

To help an overconfident consumer make better contract choices for himself, it is not enough to provide the contract terms in clear, simple language. Consider the case of choosing a smart phone data service contract. Just because he is fully aware of the prices for data usage beyond some threshold does not prevent him from misforecasting his future usage. It would be more useful to understand what his actual total costs are likely to be under various contracts (Bar-Gill 2012). This could be achieved with greater information disclosure. At a minimum, firms could be required to disclose the average monthly bill across all customers in each plan. This would reveal the typical cost of each plan, which may significantly exceed the basic access fee. Even better, firms could offer individual-specific estimates of costs under each plan based on a customer's actual data use history (Kamenica, Mullainathan, and Thaler 2011). Or third party consultants could make use of such information to comparison shop across a broad spectrum of plans and make a personalized recommendation (Thaler and Sunstein 2009). But regardless of the specifics, such information can help an overconfident consumer more accurately forecast the future experience of each contract when making a decision.

Once consumers have selected a contract, attention hurdles can be reduced with required alerts that eliminate the surprise aspect of penalty fees. For consumers who already pay close attention to fee thresholds, alerts will have no effect. But as suggested earlier, welfare for somewhat inattentive consumers could be improved if banks were required to disclose an overdraft fee *before* customers overdraw their account (Armstrong and Vickers 2012; Grubb 2015a). Alerts of this form were introduced in 2011 for US cell phone service customers who face additional charges for exceeding usage allowances or for traveling abroad (FCC 2012). And while many banks and credit card companies offer customers the opportunity to opt-in to alerts about balances, requiring alerts as the default policy could benefit those who are perhaps too overconfident to recognize the value of signing up for notification warnings.

When evaluating a policy proposal designed to improve consumer welfare, it is important to also take into account the behavior of firms in the market. Consider once again the alerts for US cell phone customers who approach or exceed their usage allowance. Grubb and Osborne (2015) estimate that in the absence of any price changes, the introduction of alerts would have benefited the average customer $100 each year. But prices did not stay fixed. In response to the lost revenue from overuse fees, firms increased their monthly access fees, eliminating the consumer benefit. The key lesson is that policy consequences, intended or not, must be part of any analysis.

18.4   Social Insurance   [Public Finance]

A major function of modern welfare states is to provide **social insurance** that insures citizens against adverse events. Consider the types of outcomes for which the US government provides some form of social insurance. For job loss there is unemployment insurance. For illness in old age there is health insurance (called Medicare). For income loss in retirement there is Social Security. There is also disability insurance for career-ending disabilities and workers' compensation for accidents at work. Together these social insurance programs account for over half of all spending by the US federal government.[5]

More generally, insurance — whether it is provided by the government or a private company — works as follows. Insured individuals pay a fixed price, called the **insurance premium**. And in return for paying the insurance premium, the insurer promises to make a payment to cover some or all of the expenses associated with particular outcomes. An unemployment insurance contract pays supplemental wages for those who are laid off from their job and looking for another. A health insurance contract may instead cover the costs of a physical examination, diagnostic test, emergency room visit, or pharmaceuticals.

But why does the government provide insurance instead of just letting the market supply insurance privately? One motivation is to correct market failures. For instance, private insurance markets are prone to experience the phenomenon of adverse selection. That is, if only the highest risk people choose to buy insurance, insurance companies may lose money, leading to the collapse of the private market. There are also positive externalities from insurance — e.g., your health insurance improves your health and reduces contagious spread of disease to others — in which case the private market underprovides insurance. Even without market failures, governments may provide social insurance to achieve redistribution by setting higher premiums for the rich than the poor. Finally, governments may be motivated by a paternalistic concern that individuals mistakenly underinsure themselves against significant risks. When people save less for retirement than they desire, for example, Social Security helps to correct this mistake by forcing individuals to save more.

Regardless of the motivation for providing social insurance, this section explores its optimal design in the contexts of unemployment and health. We start by developing intuition for the key tradeoffs in determining optimal social insurance. And because insurance-related decisions require individuals to form beliefs about uncertain outcomes, we then assess how nonstandard beliefs impact features of optimal insurance design.

18.4.1   Optimal Social Insurance

Consider an individual, Sita, who faces the risk of some adverse event like unemployment or illness. With probability p the adverse event occurs and she experiences a low level of consumption c_L. Otherwise, with probability $1-p$ she achieves high consumption $c_H > c_L$. Sita's welfare W is then equal to her expected utility:

$$W = (1 - p) \times u(c_H) + p \times u(c_L)$$

where $u(\cdot)$ is an increasing and concave utility function over consumption spending.

Note the assumptions on the shape of Sita's utility function. The utility she gains from each additional dollar of consumption is diminishing. That is, an extra dollar of consumption is always valuable, but is more valuable when consumption is low than high. She would therefore achieve greater welfare by shifting consumption in good times — when it is already high and valued less — to bad times when consumption is low and valued more. Such shifting is known as **consumption smoothing**. In the same way that individuals are better off smoothing consumption over time (Section 4.5.4), they also benefit from smoothing consumption across uncertain states of the world.

Now introduce a social insurance program in which Sita always pays an insurance premium, and in return receives a benefit from the government in the adverse state. Assume the government fully funds the benefit with revenue from the premium so that larger benefits require larger premiums. The insurance program reduces c_H because of the premium, but increases c_L because of the government benefit.[6] That is, insurance smooths her consumption across her high and low states. The government essentially takes money from Sita when she is doing well and gives it back to her when she is experiencing a loss, improving her welfare. *Consumption smoothing is the key benefit of social insurance.*

But social insurance is not costless if Sita's behavior changes in response to being insured. For instance, unemployment insurance reduces the incentive to quickly look for another job. But the longer people stay unemployed, the more it costs the government to fund unemployment benefits. In a similar way, health insurance increases the incentive to utilize medical care, increasing total government spending on medical services. These examples illustrate the phenomenon of **moral hazard**, whereby insurance incentivizes the insured to change their behavior in ways that increase the cost of providing insurance. *Moral hazard is the key cost of social insurance.*

Optimal social insurance is the insurance benefit level that maximizes welfare W, taking into account that individuals respond to insurance by choosing behaviors that maximize their decision utility U. For intuition, consider a small increase in the benefit level. This increase provides a welfare gain from increased consumption smoothing, but also creates a moral hazard cost from the behavioral response to more generous insurance. The optimal social insurance benefit level is therefore determined by balancing the consumption smoothing benefit (CS) against the moral hazard cost (MH).

The remainder of this section considers optimal social insurance for two cases. In the first case, individuals make decisions that maximize individual welfare. That is, decision utility U equals welfare W. In the second case, nonstandard beliefs introduce an internality so that decision utility U does *not* equal welfare W. Such a gap could arise because individuals hold a belief about the likelihood of an adverse event that differs from the true probability. Or individuals may form inaccurate beliefs about outcomes in the adverse state. In each case, the optimal level of social insurance balances the consumption smoothing benefit against moral hazard. But with nonstandard beliefs, the social planner must also take into account the ways in which behavior fails to maximize individual welfare.

18.4.2   *Optimal Unemployment Insurance Benefits*

Unemployment insurance (UI) is a major social insurance program in the US, with benefits of approximately $30 billion annually in good economic times, but much more during recessions (BEA 2020b). When an eligible worker becomes unemployed, she receives a benefit equal to about 50% of her previous wages for a maximum of 6 months. These benefits are funded by an insurance premium that takes the form of a small tax on employers. Although firms pay the tax, they can shift the cost of the tax to workers in the form of lower wages.

The primary decision for the unemployed is how much effort to exert searching for a new job. Greater search effort decreases the probability of remaining in the adverse unemployment state. The corresponding moral hazard cost of UI is that more generous benefits reduce the incentive for the unemployed to search for a new job. In other words, higher UI benefits increase the probability that an individual remains unemployed, increasing the cost of insurance.

Standard Beliefs

What is the optimal UI benefit when the unemployed make job search decisions that maximize their own welfare ($U = W$)? A UI benefit increase generates a consumption smoothing benefit by shifting more consumption to the unemployed state. It also generates a moral hazard cost by reducing search efforts. At the optimal UI benefit level, these two effects are exactly equal (Baily 1978; Chetty 2006):

$$\text{Standard Optimal UI: } CS = MH \tag{18.1}$$

If the consumption smoothing benefit were to exceed the moral hazard cost ($CS > MH$), then UI benefits should be increased. And benefits should be reduced in the opposite case. Empirical estimates of actual consumption smoothing and moral hazard typically imply that a benefit equal to 50% of previous wages is approximately optimal (Chetty 2008; Gruber 1997).

Nonstandard Beliefs

The standard analysis of optimal UI benefits assumes that the unemployed hold accurate beliefs about both the likelihood of finding a job and the effectiveness of their job search efforts. But Spinnewijn (2015) documents evidence that neither of these beliefs are accurate. First, job seekers are *optimistic* about the chance of finding a job, expecting to remain unemployed for another 7 weeks, when in fact their unemployment spells last another 23 weeks. In contrast to this optimism about securing employment, job seekers also appear to *underestimate* the effectiveness of their job search efforts. They understand that searching hard for a job increases the chance of re-employment, but do not realize just how large the impact of search effort is.

When individuals make job search decisions based on inaccurate beliefs, then decision utility U does not equal welfare W. In this case, the optimal UI benefit satisfies a condition of the following form (Spinnewijn 2015):[7]

$$\text{Nonstandard Optimal UI}: CS = MH \times (1 + \text{Search Underestimation}) \qquad (18.2)$$

This expression is a modification of the standard optimality condition in (18.1). Consumption smoothing must still be balanced against moral hazard, but the optimal level of UI now depends on the degree to which individuals underestimate the effectiveness of their search effort. This underestimation matters because workers search less than what would maximize their own welfare. Why work hard to find a new job when you don't think it makes much of a difference? And because a more generous UI benefit disincentivizes search effort, it further exacerbates the already insufficient efforts by the unemployed. A social planner who sets the UI benefit according to the standard condition in (18.1) will therefore underestimate the actual social cost and set the benefit too high.

More generally, the preceding analysis demonstrates the sensitivity of optimal policy prescriptions to assumptions about actual individual decision making. It is not without consequence to assume that individuals always maximize their own welfare. Note also that this observation does not imply that every deviation from the standard model of decision making is relevant for the design of optimal policy. The condition for the optimal level of UI in (18.2), for instance, does *not* depend on the optimism of the unemployed about finding a job. A careful understanding of the relevant features of actual decision making in each context is essential for improving the quality of policy recommendations. We turn to the health care context next.

18.4.3 Optimal Health Insurance Copays

The US health care system is massive, accounting for almost 20% of GDP. And although the federal government is less involved in health care relative to most other rich countries, health expenditures are still 30% of all federal spending. That is twice what the US government spends on national defense.[8] The two major health insurance programs provided by the government are Medicare (for those over age 65 or disabled) and Medicaid (for the poor). The government also provides health insurance for the military and veterans.

Health insurance is incredibly complicated in the real world and difficult for the typical consumer to understand (Loewenstein et al. 2013). But a simple health insurance plan can be characterized as follows.[9] The insured pay a premium to the insurer whether they are healthy or sick. In return, the insurer provides the benefit of paying for medical treatment when individuals are sick. But the generosity of the insurance benefit is reduced by a **copay**: the additional price the insured pay to the insurer when they obtain treatment. For instance, you may pay an insurance premium of $300 per month, regardless of your medical care use. And each time you visit the doctor, instead of paying the full price of $100 for the visit, you only pay a copay of $25. Assume that the insurer takes all of the revenue from premiums and copays to reimburse health care providers for their services. So that if the copay is low, the premium will need to be higher to cover the treatment costs. And with a higher copay, the premium can be reduced.

The primary decision for an insured individual is whether or not to obtain medical treatment when sick. This decision depends on the treatment benefit, as well as the copay. For example, with a very low copay I am likely to seek medical care even if the benefit is small. A minor rash, sore throat, or muscle pain may be enough for me to visit the doctor since I pay almost nothing for each visit. But even if the benefit of treatment is small to me, the cost for the doctor or hospital to provide care could be quite high. This is the moral hazard cost of health insurance: a lower copay incentivizes the sick to seek treatment, increasing the total medical costs for the government insurer. These higher costs then get passed back to the insured citizens in the form of higher premiums.

Standard Beliefs

What is the optimal copay for treatment when the insured make medical care decisions that maximize their own welfare ($U = W$)? A lower copay generates a consumption smoothing benefit by reducing the treatment cost when sick. This benefit must be balanced against the moral hazard cost of increased treatment demand. The optimal copay with standard beliefs, P^S, is determined as follows:

$$\text{Standard Optimal Copay: } P^S = \frac{T}{1 + CS/MH} \qquad (18.3)$$

where T is the treatment cost to society, in terms of the resources required.

The optimal copay P^S is determined by three factors. First, it is increasing in the cost of treatment T. More expensive treatments, like surgery, should have higher copays than relatively low-cost blood tests or vaccines. Second, it is decreasing in the consumption smoothing benefit. When the insured value the consumption smoothing benefit of health insurance coverage highly (CS large), it is optimal to provide more consumption smoothing with a lower copay. Finally, when the moral hazard cost MH is high — because patients respond to a lower copay with much higher treatment demand — it is optimal to mitigate excessive health care utilization with a higher copay.

To generate additional intuition for the optimal copay, suppose there is no consumption smoothing benefit at all ($CS = 0$).[10] Then the optimal copay simply equals the treatment cost: $P^S = T$. This is optimal because a lower copay would have no consumption smoothing benefit, by assumption, but would still create a moral hazard cost.

This special case is illustrated in Figure 18.2. The social cost of each treatment unit is indicated by the horizontal line at T. The welfare benefit of each treatment unit is given by the marginal experienced utility curve. And the optimal treatment quantity is then where these two curves intersect, at Q^*. The insured choose to obtain treatment as long as marginal decision utility exceeds the copay. But since experienced utility/welfare W equals decision utility U for standard decision makers, the marginal decision and experienced utility curves are one and the same (Section 3.2). Therefore, at a copay of T, consumers choose to consume the optimal quantity of treatment Q^*. If instead the copay were lowered to $P_1 < T$, the insured would increase treatment to $Q_1 > Q^*$. Because the social cost of each additional treatment exceeds the welfare benefit, there exists a welfare loss, indicated by triangle A. This area is the moral hazard cost of lowering the copay.

Intuitively, when insuring standard consumers, the optimal copay is determined by starting at the treatment cost and then adjusting the copay down, depending on how large the consumption smoothing benefit is relative to the moral hazard cost.

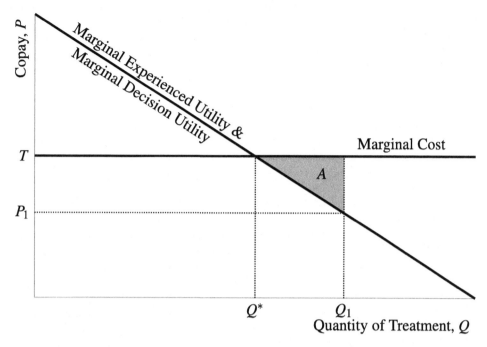

Figure 18.2 Standard Beliefs: Optimal Copay without Consumption Smoothing Benefit

Nonstandard Beliefs

The standard analysis of optimal copays assumes that the insured hold accurate beliefs about the benefits they will experience from various treatments.[11] This is a tall order for the typical individual. Medical care is enormously complex and although doctors, friends, and the internet are sources of health information, individuals may form inaccurate beliefs about treatment benefits (Pauly and Blavin 2008).

With such inaccurate beliefs, individuals can make treatment decisions that fail to maximize their own welfare ($U \neq W$). For instance, those who underestimate benefits are likely to underutilize care. Benefit underestimation may exist with high value interventions like vaccines and screenings, or consistent medication adherence for diabetics and heart attack survivors. Overestimating the benefits of treatments that have little known efficacy, like antibiotics for viral infections or MRIs for back pain, can instead lead to overutilization. See Section 3.5 for a discussion of health care misutilization without insurance.

The gap between what a consumer perceives as the benefit of treatment and the actual experienced benefit of treatment is the internality. A negative internality corresponds to an underestimation of treatment benefits, while a positive internality reflects overestimation. This internality plays a role in determining the optimal copay for nonstandard individuals, P^N, as follows (Baicker, Mullainathan, and Schwartzstein 2015):

$$\text{Nonstandard Optimal Copay: } P^N = \frac{T + \text{Internality}}{1 + CS/MH} \tag{18.4}$$

This new expression for the optimal copay modifies the standard expression in (18.3).[12] Just as before, the copay is increasing in the treatment and moral hazard

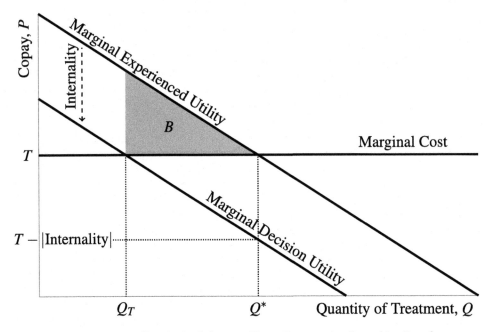

Figure 18.3 Negative Internality: Optimal Copay without Consumption Smoothing Benefit

costs, and decreasing in the consumption smoothing benefit. But now it also depends on the existence and sign of the internality. A negative internality warrants a lower copay, while the copay should be increased with a positive internality.

Consider first a negative internality. In this case consumers underestimate benefits and therefore seek less treatment than they would with accurate beliefs. A lower copay now provides an additional benefit beyond consumption smoothing. It also helps to correct the underutilization of health care by encouraging more treatment.

This insight is illustrated in Figure 18.3 for the case without a consumption smoothing benefit ($CS = 0$). The underestimation of treatment benefits implies that marginal decision utility falls below marginal experienced utility by the magnitude of the internality. From a welfare perspective, treatment should be consumed as long as the welfare benefit, measured by marginal experienced utility, exceeds the cost to society, T. That is, up to Q^*. But the insured make decisions based on marginal decision utility. So if the copay were set at T, as is optimal with standard consumers, treatment demand would be only $Q_T < Q^*$. A welfare loss, given by triangle B, would obtain because treatments with welfare benefits that exceed the cost of provision are not consumed. What copay would induce consumers to choose Q^* instead? Observe that reducing the copay by the magnitude of the internality will do just that. And the nonstandard optimal copay in expression (18.4) is indeed $P^N = T - |\text{Internality}|$ when $CS = 0$ and the internality has a negative sign.

The same intuition works in reverse for a positive internality. When consumers overestimate benefits and subsequently overutilize treatment, it is optimal to increase the copay. The higher copay helps to correct overutilization and improve welfare. And if there is no consumption smoothing benefit from insurance, it is optimal for the copay to increase by the magnitude of the positive internality: $P^N = T +$ Internality. See Exercise 18.11 for the corresponding graphical analysis.

The policy implications of internalities in treatment decisions are significant. For instance, suppose the insured have internalities, but the social planner sets the copay for a treatment with cost $T = \$100$ as if the internalities did not exist. Under a set of assumptions, Baicker, Mullainathan, and Schwartzstein (2015) show that by neglecting negative internalities, the social planner would set a copay of \$99.98, when the optimal copay is only \$0.02. The social planner fails to appreciate the benefits of correcting underutilization with a lower copay. At the other extreme, by neglecting positive internalities, the social planner would set a copay of \$0, when it is in fact optimal to charge almost \$200 for treatment. Once again, the social planner does not consider how a higher copay could help individuals reduce their own excessive use of relatively ineffective care.

In sum, this analysis reveals the role of copays as not only balancing the consumption smoothing benefit against moral hazard, but helping the insured make better decisions for their own welfare. The approach of using copays to encourage high-value care and discourage low-value care is known as value-based insurance design (Chernew, Rosen, and Fendrick 2007). Understanding the value of health interventions is therefore important for improving insurance design.

18.5 Summary

1 Nonstandard beliefs can generate an internality, with individuals making decisions that fail to maximize their own individual welfare.

2 Profit-maximizing firms can exploit employee overconfidence by compensating workers with stock options instead of cash.

3 Profit-maximizing firms can exploit consumer misforecasting of future usage by:

    a Decreasing marginal price when consumers overestimate usage;

    b Increasing marginal price when consumers underestimate usage; and

    c Designing a **three-part tariff** when consumers are overprecise in their usage forecasting.

4 Profit-maximizing firms can exploit consumer overestimation of ability to navigate particular contract terms by including such terms. These can take the form of:

    a **memory hurdles** that require consumers to remember a task to complete; or

    b **attention hurdles** that require consumers to play close attention to their consumption.

5 Overconfident consumers may (or may not) benefit from policies that require greater information disclosure or alerts.

6 **Social insurance** is government-provided insurance that insures citizens against adverse events.

    a An **insurance premium** is the price the insured pay for insurance, whether they are in an adverse state or not.

    b A **copay** is the price the insured pay for benefits in the adverse state.

7 The key benefit of social insurance is **consumption smoothing**: the shifting of consumption from periods when it is high to periods when it is low.

8   The key cost of social insurance is **moral hazard**: the behavioral responses to more generous insurance benefits that increase the cost of providing insurance.

9   **Optimal social insurance** balances the consumption smoothing benefit against the moral hazard cost. And when the insured hold nonstandard beliefs, optimal social insurance must also account for the impact of insurance on changing behaviors that do not maximize an individual's own welfare.

  a   Optimal unemployment insurance benefits depend on the beliefs of the unemployed about the effectiveness of their job search efforts.

  b   Optimal health insurance copays depend on the beliefs of the sick about the benefits from treatment.

18.6   Exercises[13]

Exercise 18.1 — Benefits for Hire. You are a hiring manager whose objective is to hire the best people at the lowest cost for your company. Through survey research you learn that most workers overestimate the likelihood that they will make use of in-office benefits like a fitness center, child care, and complementary beverages and snacks. How does this information impact the benefits and wages you offer? Explain.

Exercise 18.2 — CEO: Chief Executive Overconfidence. [Business] CEOs are hired and compensated by a company's board of directors. Otto (2014) finds that over-confident CEOs (based on overestimation of their firm's future market value) receive fewer bonus payments and less total compensation than their non-overconfident peers. Explain how this finding suggests that boards of directors are aware of CEO over-confidence when designing compensation contracts.

Exercise 18.3 — Options for Overconfidence. Recall the model in Section 18.2 of worker compensation by wage $\$w$ and stock options worth $\$s$ with probability p. The welfare of the worker W, and the expected cost to the firm C, are both $w + ps$. The objective of the firm is to minimize the cost of worker compensation. But for the worker to accept the job, his decision utility $U = w + \tilde{p}s$ must be at least the utility U^0 at his current job. That is, the firm chooses values w^* and s^* that solve the following problem:

$$\min_{w,s} \quad w + ps$$
$$\text{such that} \quad w + \tilde{p}s \geq U^0 \tag{18.5}$$

Hint: To solve this problem throughout this exercise, you do not need to use calculus. Instead, use the insight that the firm minimizes cost by setting $w + \tilde{p}s = U^0$.

  a   Suppose the worker holds accurate beliefs that the stock options will be valuable: $\tilde{p} = p$. In this case there is not a unique solution to problem (18.5). Instead, there is a continuum of cost-minimizing combinations of w^* and s^*. Therefore, for a given wage w^*, determine how many stock options the firm will issue to the worker. In addition, determine the firm's cost C and the worker welfare W evaluated at a cost-minimizing compensation package.

  b   Assume now that the worker is overconfident about the future prospects of the firm and believes that the stock price will increase with probability $\tilde{p} > p$. The firm knows the worker is overconfident. Find the choices of w^* and s^* that solve (18.5).

Determine firm cost C and worker welfare W evaluated at the cost-minimizing compensation package. Compare your answers to part (a) and interpret.

c Assume now that the worker is still overconfident about the value of the firm ($\tilde{p} > p$ and the firm knows this), but the CEO of the firm is even more overconfident. The CEO believes the probability of an increase in value is $\hat{p} > \tilde{p} > p$, and hence chooses compensation that minimizes her *perceived* cost $w + \hat{p}s$. Find the choices of w^* and s^* that solve the CEO's problem. Determine the (actual) firm cost C and worker welfare W evaluated at the cost-minimizing compensation package. Compare your answers to part (a) and interpret.

d In light of your findings in parts (a)–(c), which beliefs are consistent with the assignment of stock options to rank-and-file workers? Interpret.

Exercise 18.4 — Learning Limitations The mistakes of overconfident consumers can be exploited by firms for profit, leaving consumers worse off. Such exploitation could be mitigated if overconfidence diminishes as consumers learn about their actual usage and ability to navigate contract terms. Suggest two reasons why such learning might be modest or slow.[14]

Exercise 18.5 — Complex Contracts in Competition (Grubb 2009). The cost for a cell phone service company to provide a customer with q gigabytes (GB) of data each month is $C(q) = 25 + 2q$. For a given cell phone contract, denote the total customer price for consuming q GB of data in a month by $P(q)$. This total price can include access fees, the marginal price for each q, and surcharges for use beyond a threshold.

Overconfident Olivia values each GB of data at $15. But she is overprecise in estimating her data usage. While there is an equal probability that she uses 3 GB, 5 GB, or 7 GB of data each month, she believes that there is a 100% chance of using 5 GB. Olivia's welfare W and decision utility U, both measured in dollars, are therefore:

$$W = \frac{1}{3}(\$15 \times 3 - P(3)) + \frac{1}{3}(\$15 \times 5 - P(5)) + \frac{1}{3}(\$15 \times 7 - P(7))$$
$$U = \$15 \times 5 - P(5)$$

Note that $U \neq W$ because of her overprecise belief that she will use 5 GB with certainty.

a Company A offers the following two-part tariff contract for a month of data service: fixed access fee of $25 plus $2 for each GB of data used. Determine W, U, and the firm's (true) expected monthly profit from this contract.

b Company B offers the following three-part tariff contract for a month of data service: fixed access fee of $30, an allowance of 5 GB included data, and $15 per GB for additional usage. Determine W, U, and the firm's (true) expected monthly profit from this contract.

c If Olivia is offered the two contracts from companies A and B, which does she choose? For which does she achieve higher welfare? Explain your answers.

d Does the firm that Olivia did *not* choose in part (c) have an incentive to change their pricing contract? Explain.

Exercise 18.6 — Cellular Sales (Grubb 2015b). Firms find it profitable to design contracts that increase consumer overvaluation and therefore willingness to pay. Let's apply this insight to the context of a cellular service company choosing quality of download speed, measured in megabits per second (Mbps).

a   If a customer overestimates usage, should the company offer a faster or slower download speed? Explain.

b   If a customer underestimates usage, should the company offer a faster or slower download speed? Explain.

c   If a customer accurately forecasts their median usage, but is overprecise, should the company increase or decrease download speeds at the median usage threshold? Explain.

d   To your knowledge, is the prediction in part (c) consistent with real-world cellular service contracts?

Exercise 18.7 — Pricing Perks. Businesses sometimes offer surprise loyalty discounts or perks to customers who cross some usage threshold: spend enough with a retail store-issued credit card and you earn a gift card or fly enough airline miles and you are upgraded to elite status. Explain why companies are incentivized to offer such benefits when consumers overestimate their ability to navigate contract terms.

Exercise 18.8 — End of Life Insurance. [Finance] Life insurance provides financial protection for loved ones at the time of one's own death. A typical life insurance policy is structured as follows: the insured individual pays regular installments of an insurance premium until they die, at which point the insurer pays a beneficiary (e.g., spouse) a sum of money. If a policyholder stops making their premium payments (perhaps because they want the money for other immediate consumption), then the policy is typically terminated and the death benefit will not be paid.

An insurer can charge a constant premium over the length of the policy, or shift premiums to be higher early in the policy (front-loaded) or later in the policy (back-loaded). Suppose the insurer learns that most consumers are overconfident and underestimate the chance that they will stop paying their premiums (Gottlieb and Smetters 2019). Does this information incentivize a profit-maximizing insurer to front-load or back-load the premiums? Explain.

Exercise 18.9 — Unemployment Reform. Unemployment insurance (UI) benefits differ across states in the US. Oregon and California are considering changing their UI benefit generosity. Economists in each state have estimated the consumption smoothing benefit (CS) and moral hazard cost (MH) associated with a small increase in the UI benefit relative to current levels. The estimates are as follows:

	Oregon	*California*
CS	0.3	0.5
MH	0.6	0.4

a   Suppose that the unemployed in both states have standard beliefs. Should each state increase or decrease the generosity of its UI benefit?

b   Now assume that the unemployed in both states are optimistic about the chance of finding a new job, but underestimate the effectiveness of their job search efforts. After estimating the magnitude of these deviations from standard beliefs, you

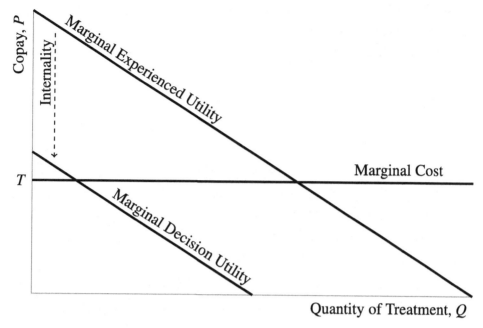

Figure 18.4 Large Negative Internality in Exercise 18.10

determine that one of the two states is already setting its UI benefit at the optimal level. Which state is it? Explain.

Exercise 18.10 — Negative Internalities at Large. Figure 18.4 depicts the marginal experienced and decision utilities over units of a medical treatment with marginal cost to society T. The insured consumers are assumed to achieve no consumption smoothing benefit from insurance.

a   Label Q^* as the socially optimal treatment quantity.
b   Label Q_T as the treatment quantity used if the copay equals T. Explain why $Q_T \neq Q^*$ and give a real-world treatment example where this may be the case.
c   Label the welfare loss associated with setting a copay equal to T.
d   How would you determine the optimal copay in this example? Is it greater or less than T? And if it less than T, is it positive, zero, or negative? Interpret your answer.

Exercise 18.11 — The Price of Positive Internalities. Figure 18.5 depicts the marginal experienced and decision utilities over units of a medical treatment with marginal cost to society T. The insured consumers are assumed to achieve no consumption smoothing benefit from insurance.

a   Label Q^* as the socially optimal treatment quantity.
b   Label Q_T as the treatment quantity used if the copay equals T. Explain why $Q_T \neq Q^*$ and give a real-world treatment example where this may be the case.
c   Label the welfare loss associated with setting a copay equal to T.
d   How would you determine the optimal copay in this example? Is it greater or less than T? And if it less than T, is it positive, zero, or negative? Interpret your answer.

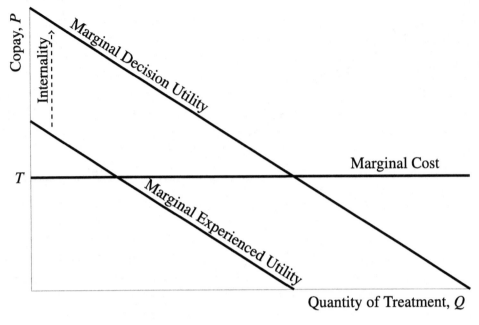

Figure 18.5 Positive Internality in Exercise 18.11

Notes

1 Oyer and Schaefer (2005) also consider employee sorting and retention as justifications for the practice of paying stock options to rank-and-file employees.

2 Grubb (2015b) is an excellent review of consumer overconfidence, from which Section 18.3 is adapted.

3 The analysis of two-part tariffs for present-biased consumers in Section 7.1 aligns with the present logic: the marginal price is profitably reduced for investment goods (which consumers overestimate usage of) and increased for leisure goods (which consumers underestimate usage of).

4 Grubb (2009) shows that while one cannot conclude that all three-part tariff contracts are a response to overprecise consumers, there is convincing evidence that overprecision explains three-part tariffs in the US cell phone service market.

5 For a detailed breakdown of federal expenditures, see the US Bureau of Economic Analysis National Income and Personal Account (BEA 2020a) Table 3.16.

6 The benefit received in the adverse state must exceed the premium paid in the adverse state because the benefit is partially funded by premium payments in the high state when no benefit is paid.

7 Spinnewijn (2015) provides a more general characterization of optimal UI that assumes individuals make a savings decision in addition to their job search effort decision.

8 For a detailed breakdown of federal expenditures, see the US Bureau of Economic Analysis National Income and Personal Account (BEA 2020a) Table 3.16.

9 Section 18.4.3 is adapted from the analysis by Baicker, Mullainathan, and Schwartzstein (2015).

10 No consumption smoothing benefit would exist if the insured were risk neutral and did not value consumption increases in the low state more than in the high state.

11 It is also standard to assume that individuals hold accurate beliefs about the probability of needing treatment at all. This is relevant for the insurance purchase decision, but the focus in this section is on the treatment decisions of the already insured.

12 The characterization of the nonstandard optimal copay applies not only for inaccurate beliefs, but for any behavior that generates an internality in the treatment decision (Baicker, Mullainathan, and Schwartzstein 2015).

13 Exercise 18.3 is adapted from an exercise by Stefano DellaVigna.

14 For research on learning from past mistakes, see Bolger and Önkal-Atay (2004), Agarwal et al. (2009), Agarwal et al. (2013), and Grubb and Osborne (2015).

References

Agarwal, Sumit, Souphala Chomsisengphet, Neale Mahoney, and Johannes Stroebel. 2015. "Regulating Consumer Financial Products: Evidence from Credit Cards." *The Quarterly Journal of Economics* 130 (1): 111–164. doi:10.1093/qje/qju037.

Agarwal, Sumit, John C. Driscoll, Xavier Gabaix, and David Laibson. 2009. "The Age of Reason: Financial Decisions over the Life Cycle and Implications for Regulation." *Brookings Papers on Economic Activity* 2009 (2): 51–117. doi:10.1353/eca.0.0067.

———. 2013. "Learning in the Credit Card Market." SSRN Scholarly Paper ID 1091623. Rochester, NY: Social Science Research Network. doi:10.2139/ssrn.1091623.

Armstrong, Mark, and John Vickers. 2012. "Consumer Protection and Contingent Charges." *Journal of Economic Literature* 50 (2): 477–493. doi:10.1257/jel.50.2.477.

Baicker, Katherine, Sendhil Mullainathan, and Joshua Schwartzstein. 2015. "Behavioral Hazard in Health Insurance." *The Quarterly Journal of Economics* 130 (4): 1623–1667. doi:10.1093/qje/qjv029.

Baily, Martin Neil. 1978. "Some Aspects of Optimal Unemployment Insurance." *Journal of Public Economics* 10 (3): 379–402. doi:10.1016/0047-2727(78)90053-1.

Bar-Gill, Oren. 2012. *Seduction by Contract: Law, Economics, and Psychology in Consumer Markets.* Oxford: Oxford University Press.

BEA (US Bureau of Economic Analysis). 2020a. *GDP & Personal Income.* https://apps.bea.gov/iTable/index_nipa.cfm.

———. 2020b. *Personal Current Transfer Receipts: Government Social Benefits to Persons: Unemployment Insurance [W825RC1].* Accessed July 2, 2020, https://fred.stlouisfed.org/series/W825RC1.

Bergman, Nittai K., and Dirk Jenter. 2007. "Employee Sentiment and Stock Option Compensation." *Journal of Financial Economics* 84 (3): 667–712. doi:10.1016/j.jfineco.2006.01.008.

Bolger, Fergus, and Dilek Önkal-Atay. 2004. "The Effects of Feedback on Judgmental Interval Predictions." *International Journal of Forecasting* 20 (1): 29–39. doi:10.1016/S0169-2070(03)00009-8.

Chernew, Michael E., Allison B. Rosen, and A. Mark Fendrick. 2007. "Value-Based Insurance Design." *Health Affairs* 26 (Supplement 2): w195–w203. doi:10.1377/hlthaff.26.2.w195.

Chetty, Raj. 2006. "A General Formula for the Optimal Level of Social Insurance." *Journal of Public Economics* 90 (10): 1879–1901. doi:10.1016/j.jpubeco.2006.01.004.

———. 2008. "Moral Hazard versus Liquidity and Optimal Unemployment Insurance." *Journal of Political Economy* 116 (2): 173–234. doi:10.1086/588585.

FCC (Federal Communications Commission). 2012. *Bill Shock: Wireless Usage Alerts for Consumers.* Updated April 3, 2020, https://www.fcc.gov/general/bill-shock-wireless-usage-alerts-consumers.

Gottlieb, Daniel, and Kent Smetters. 2019. "Lapse-Based Insurance." Unpublished.

Grubb, Michael D. 2009. "Selling to Overconfident Consumers." *American Economic Review* 99 (5): 1770–1807. doi:10.1257/aer.99.5.1770.

———. 2015a. "Consumer Inattention and Bill-Shock Regulation." *The Review of Economic Studies* 82 (1): 219–257. doi:10.1093/restud/rdu024.

———. 2015b. "Overconfident Consumers in the Marketplace." *Journal of Economic Perspectives* 29 (4): 9–36. doi:10.1257/jep.29.4.9.

Grubb, Michael D., and Matthew Osborne. 2015. "Cellular Service Demand: Biased Beliefs, Learning, and Bill Shock." *American Economic Review* 105 (1): 234–271. doi:10.1257/aer.20120283.

Gruber, Jonathan. 1997. "The Consumption Smoothing Benefits of Unemployment Insurance." *American Economic Review* 87 (1): 192–205. https://www.jstor.org/stable/2950862.

Holman, Jeff, and Farhan Zaidi. 2010. "The Economics of Prospective Memory." SSRN Scholarly Paper ID 1662183. Rochester, NY: Social Science Research Network. doi:10.2139/ssrn.1662183.

Kamenica, Emir, Sendhil Mullainathan, and Richard H. Thaler. 2011. "Helping Consumers Know Themselves." *American Economic Review* 101 (3): 417–422. doi:10.1257/aer.101.3.417.

Loewenstein, George, Joelle Y. Friedman, Barbara McGill, Sarah Ahmad, Suzanne Linck, Stacey Sinkula, John Beshears, et al. 2013. "Consumers' Misunderstanding of Health Insurance." *Journal of Health Economics* 32 (5): 850–862. doi:10.1016/j.jhealeco.2013.04.004.

Otto, Clemens A. 2014. "CEO Optimism and Incentive Compensation." *Journal of Financial Economics* 114 (2): 366–404. doi:10.1016/j.jfineco.2014.06.006.

Oyer, Paul, and Scott Schaefer. 2005. "Why Do Some Firms Give Stock Options to all Employees? An Empirical Examination of Alternative Theories." *Journal of Financial Economics* 76 (1): 99–133. doi:10.1016/j.jfineco.2004.03.004.

Pauly, Mark V., and Fredric E. Blavin. 2008. "Moral Hazard in Insurance, Value-Based Cost Sharing, and the Benefits of Blissful Ignorance." *Journal of Health Economics* 27 (6): 1407–1417. doi:10.1016/j.jhealeco.2008.07.003.

Silk, Timothy Guy. 2004. "Examining Purchase and Non-redemption of Mail-in Rebates: The Impact of Offer Variables on Consumers' Subjective and Objective Probability of Redeeming." PHD Thesis, University of Florida.

Spinnewijn, Johannes. 2015. "Unemployed but Optimistic: Optimal Insurance Design with Biased Beliefs." *Journal of the European Economic Association* 13 (1): 130–167. doi:10.1111/jeea.12099.

Stango, Victor, and Jonathan Zinman. 2014. "Limited and Varying Consumer Attention: Evidence from Shocks to the Salience of Bank Overdraft Fees." *The Review of Financial Studies* 27 (4): 990–1030. doi:10.1093/rfs/hhu008.

Thaler, Richard H., and Cass R. Sunstein. 2009. *Nudge: Improving Decisions about Health, Wealth, and Happiness*. Revised and Expanded. New York: Penguin Books.

Part VII

Decision Processes

A foundational assumption in the standard model of individual decision making (Definition 2.9) is utility maximization. Individuals do not choose any option that is simply good enough. They choose that which generates the maximal utility, as clearly indicated by the "max" operator at the start of the decision problem:

$$\max_{(x_0, x_1, \ldots, x_T) \in X} \sum_{k=0}^{T} \delta^k E[u(x_k) \mid p] \qquad \text{(Standard Model)}$$

In the following chapters we explore two broad ways by which actual decision making fails to conform with this standard assumption. The first deviation concerns how individuals mentally account for money. Implicit in the standard model is the assumption that people treat money as unlabeled. For instance, it is irrelevant whether a dollar arrives from hard work, luck, or as a gift. In each case, the dollar is the same. But when individuals mentally categorize, code, and evaluate economic transactions as if there were distinctions that do not actually exist, the consequent behavior need not maximize utility. This is the subject of Chapter 19.

The utility maximization assumption also presumes that people make use of *all* available information when making decisions. Otherwise, they would not know if their choices truly maximize utility. How can one guarantee that they are choosing their most preferred items from a four-page dinner menu if the last two pages are never viewed? Chapter 20 explores the evidence of inattention to available information across multiple settings. The chapter ends by considering inattention to the incentives of persuaders, which can lead to decisions by the persuaded that are inconsistent with the standard model.

Chapter 21 concludes Part VII with a wide range of evidence — from business, industrial organization, public finance, development, and politics — that reveals how profit-maximizing firms and welfare-motivated policy makers can leverage consumer mental accounting and inattention to achieve their respective objectives. Throughout, the consideration of nonstandard preferences and beliefs is suppressed.

19 Mental Accounting

Learning Objectives

★ Understand how mental accounting differs from standard decision making.

★ Evaluate the evidence for mental accounting across a range of consumption, savings, and investment decisions.

Whether you like it or whether you do not, money is money and that is all there is about it. (Stein 1936)

While economists would tend to agree with novelist Gertrude Stein that money is money, people often behave in ways that suggest this is not quite true. People appear to organize, evaluate, and keep track of their financial activities according to a set of cognitive operations that treat money differently in different contexts. These decision processes are collectively known as **mental accounting** (Thaler 1999). When individuals are motivated to act according to mental accounting principles, they do not necessarily choose the most preferred available option, as assumed in the standard model of decision making.

19.1 An Introduction to Mental Accounting

The foregoing brief introduction is abstract. To concretize mental accounting, we begin with some illustrative examples. A further discussion of mental accounting and a chapter outline conclude this section.

19.1.1 Examples of Mental Accounting

As you read the following examples, reflect on why they constitute puzzles for the standard model of decision making. We begin with two anecdotes from Thaler (1999, 183–184):

• **Example 19.1** A few years ago I gave a talk to a group of executives in Switzerland. After the conference my wife and I spent a week visiting the area. At that time the Swiss franc was at an all-time high relative to the US dollar, so the usual high prices of Switzerland were astronomical. My wife and I comforted ourselves that I had received a fee for the talk that would easily cover the outrageous prices for hotels and meals. Had I

DOI: 10.4324/9780367854072-26

received the same fee a week earlier for a talk in New York though, the vacation would have been much less enjoyable.   ▪

▪ **Example 19.2** A former colleague of mine, a professor of finance, prides himself on being a thoroughly rational man. Long ago he adopted a clever strategy to deal with life's misfortunes. At the beginning of each year he establishes a target donation to the local United Way charity. Then, if anything untoward happens to him during the year, for example an undeserved speeding ticket, he simply deducts this loss from the United Way account. He thinks of it as an insurance policy against small annoyances.   ▪

Lab Experiment — Playing with Budgets (Heath and Soll 1996)

A group of MBA students is asked at the beginning of the week whether they would purchase a theater ticket later in the week, after a certain mid-week event. The students are randomized into two groups that differ in the hypothetical mid-week event:

A   Spending $50 on a sports ticket.
B   Receiving a $50 parking ticket.

Participants in Group *A* report that they are less likely to purchase the theater ticket later in the week than participants in Group *B*.

Lab Experiment — Income Identity (O'Curry 1997)

One group of subjects is asked to judge both the source and use of income on a scale from serious to frivolous, e.g.,

- the winnings from a sports bet with friends is frivolous, whereas an income tax refund is serious; and
- dining at a restaurant is frivolous, but paying utility bills is serious.

A different group of subjects is asked how they would spend a particular income source, such as winnings from a sports bet or income tax refund.

Subjects in the second group have a tendency to spend serious (frivolous) income sources on serious (frivolous) expenditures, as judged by the first group.

19.1.2   *Features of Mental Accounts*

Like an accountant who organizes and documents the financial activities of an organization, individuals similarly account for their personal finances. They may keep track of money coming in, money going out, and money saved to build wealth. The standard approach when modeling such personal financial accounting is to assume that individuals make decisions as if money has no labels, or is **fungible**. That is, every dollar that arrives as income is part of a single income account. There is no difference between a dollar earned from work, a dollar gifted from a friend, or a dollar found on the sidewalk. The same logic applies for dollars that are spent on different goods or saved in different ways.

But evidence suggests that individuals assign activities to specific categories, or *mental accounts*. With such a system:

1   money is no longer fungible — or interchangeable — across mental accounts; and
2   individuals seek to avoid debts within each mental account.

We see these features of mental accounting in our motivating examples:

- Example 19.1: The Thalers create a Swiss mental account that includes only income and spending related to the talk in Switzerland. If the Thalers perceived money as fungible, their enjoyment from spending time in Switzerland would have been the same regardless of the additional income source. But because the income was perceived as a "deposit" to the Swiss mental account, spending money on Swiss hotels and meals is "withdrawn" from that account, avoiding losses in their non-Swiss mental accounts. If the same lecture fee had been paid for work in New York, there would be no deposit to a Swiss mental account and the Thalers would have perceived spending while traveling in high-priced Switzerland as creating undesirable debts in their Swiss mental account.
- Example 19.2: The finance professor has a mental account for unexpected expenses. He credits the mental account each year with an amount of money that he plans to give away in the form of charitable contributions. Then, when the costly unexpected misfortunes of life happen, he withdraws from his pre-designated mental account. This cognitive strategy has the advantage of making unexpected expenses less painful: the mental account balance stays positive and avoids debt (as long as his intended charity is sufficiently high).
- Playing with Budgets Lab Experiment: The participants have a mental account for entertainment expenses. For those in Group *A* who have already spent out of this mental account on a $50 sports ticket, there is less money available for additional entertainment expenses, like going to the theatre. They are therefore less likely to buy a theater ticket than those in Group *B* who paid a $50 parking ticket out of a different mental account and still have money in their entertainment account. If individuals perceived money to be fungible, we would have expected no difference in the willingness to buy a theater ticket since both groups face the same $50 reduction in their budget. But the nature of this $50 expense clearly matters.
- Income Identity Lab Experiment: The participants appear to have separate mental accounts based on the perceived seriousness or frivolity associated with the money. A mental account for serious activities is credited with income from a tax return, which can then be allocated to spending on serious expenses like bills. Whereas a mental account for fun activities is credited with winnings from a slot machine, which can then be spent on frivolous expenditures like drinks at a bar. Spending serious income on frivolous expenses may generate a perceived debt in the frivolous account, which individuals aim to avoid.

19.1.3   *Mental Accounting in this Chapter*

The primary focus of this chapter is understanding how the assignment of activities to different mental accounts can make sense of otherwise puzzling behaviors.[1] We begin with the effects of sunk costs, before turning to consumption and savings decisions over the life cycle. The chapter concludes with the tendency for people to diversify excessively when offered multiple options, each of which can be chosen.

But mental accounting is more general than the applications in this chapter suggest. It "describe[s] the entire process of coding, categorizing, and evaluating events" (Thaler 1999, 186), some of which is discussed elsewhere in this book. For example, one form of mental accounting is how framing decision problems in different but equivalent ways — e.g., as gains vs. losses — affects choices (Section 8.2). Narrow bracketing of decisions is another form of mental accounting that is explored in the context of labor supply and the equity premium puzzle (Chapter 9). Prospect theory (Section 12.1) provides a useful framework for modeling such forms of mental accounting. See Exercise 19.12 for an application of prospect theory to a well-known mental accounting problem.

19.2   Sunk Costs

A **sunk cost** is a cost that has been incurred and cannot be recovered. For instance, the time and effort you invested in a school project last week, the money you spent on filling up your car with gas, or the nonrefundable airplane ticket you bought are all examples of sunk costs. You cannot do anything to get your effort or money back. Therefore, according to standard economic decision making, such sunk costs are irrelevant for your current and future behaviors. This is not an obvious insight. It is perhaps not surprising then that empirical evidence indicates sunk costs do indeed influence behaviors, a puzzle known as the **sunk cost effect**, or **fallacy** (Arkes and Blumer 1985). To see how mental accounting can make sense of this effect, let's begin with an example adapted from Thaler (1980, 47).

▪ **Example 19.3** Suppose you purchased a $100 ticket for a basketball game an hour's drive from home. There is a massive snowstorm on the game day. Assuming that you cannot resell the ticket to someone else, the $100 is a sunk cost. Your decision whether or not to venture out in relatively unsafe driving conditions should therefore be independent of what you paid for your ticket. The risk of driving in a snowstorm to see a basketball game is either worth it or not. But you may be less willing to attend the game if the ticket had been given to you rather than purchasing it yourself. If so, the sunk cost from purchasing the ticket increases the likelihood of you going to the game.   ▪

How does mental accounting explain the influence of sunk costs on decision making? In Example 19.3, the initial purchase of the ticket opens a basketball game mental account, with a $100 deficit. This account can be closed with a zero balance after attending the game and experiencing the benefit of sport spectatorship. A ticket purchaser who misses the game is forced to close this mental account at a loss, which is undesirable. She is therefore more motivated to attend the game than if the ticket had been gifted, in which case no mental accounting debt would be incurred from missing the game.

Kahneman and Tversky (1984) provide evidence from a related context in which subjects were asked if they would be willing to buy a $10 theater ticket after one of two possible events. Subjects are less willing to buy the ticket after losing a previously purchased theater ticket than after losing an equivalent sum of money. In both cases, subjects have incurred the same monetary loss and do not hold a ticket. Their decision about now buying a ticket should therefore be the same. Instead, the evidence suggests that the subjects have a theater-outing mental account and losing a ticket induces a debit from this account, while losing the same amount in cash has no impact on the account.

Consider now the following experimental evidence from the field for ticket purchases.

Field Experiment — Theater Time (Arkes and Blumer 1985)
The first 60 people who approached the ticket window to purchase season tickets to the Ohio University Theater's 1982–1983 season were randomly offered one of the following promotional discounts:

1   No Discount (Full Price)
2   Small Discount (13% off)
3   Large Discount (47% off)

The experimenters tracked how often the subjects attended plays throughout the season.

In the first half of the season, the no-discount group used significantly more tickets than the discount groups. But there were no differences in play attendance between the groups in the second half of the season.

This evidence reveals two insights. First, there is a sunk cost effect: when season tickets incur a larger sunk cost (from no discount), individuals are more inclined to use their previously purchased tickets. But secondly, this is only true in the first half of the season. It appears that the sunk cost effect wears off over time, a phenomenon known as **payment depreciation** (Gourville and Soman 1998).

The diminishing effect of advance purchases is similarly illustrated by evidence from oenophiles (i.e., wine lovers) who buy wine with the intention of storing for consumption many years later.

Lab Experiment — Uncorking Costs (Shafir and Thaler 2006)
Subscribers to the wine newsletter *Liquid Assets* — a population that skews towards economists and business leaders — were surveyed with the following question:

> Suppose you bought a case of a good 1982 Bordeaux in the futures market for $20 a bottle. The wine now sells at auction for about $75 a bottle. You have decided to drink a bottle of this wine with dinner. Which of the following best captures your feeling of the cost to you of drinking this bottle: $0, $20, $20 plus interest, $75, or −$55? (697)

The distribution of answers was: $0 (30%), $20 (18%), $20 plus interest (7%), $75 (20%), and −$55 (25%).

A student of economics recognizes that the above question is asking for the opportunity cost of drinking a bottle. The true opportunity cost is $75: by drinking the bottle an individual foregoes the opportunity to sell it at auction for $75. While this is intuitive for economists, only 20% of respondents reported this answer. Over half said that drinking the bottle was either free or saved them money (drinking a bottle worth $75 that was purchased for only $20 generates the perception of saving $55). And in a follow-up survey, respondents reported that they feel as though advance wine purchases are an investment to be gradually consumed over many years.

The interpretation of this evidence is succinctly expressed in the title of Shafir and Thaler's paper: "Invest Now, Drink Later, Spend Never." The typical wine connoisseur apparently performs the following mental accounting exercise. The initial purchase is perceived as an "investment," and not spending, to avoid the feeling of having spent money. The cost is mentally shifted to the future. But much later, when the wine is actually consumed, it is perceived as costless. As a result, the expensive hobby of drinking wine is seen as "free," or even a way to save money. In Chapter 21 we explore how profit-maximizing firms may exploit such mental accounting by decoupling purchases from consumption (Gourville and Soman 1998; Prelec and Loewenstein 1998).

19.3   Mental Accounting over the Life Cycle   [Household]

The standard life-cycle model of consumption and savings over one's life, introduced in Section 4.5, is a powerful and elegant theory of behavior, making it a cornerstone of modern economics. A key implication of this model is that individuals smooth their consumption over time, saving when income is high (e.g., in middle-age) and borrowing or dissaving when income is low (e.g., when young and old). This strategy allows consumption to be stable, even when income is not.

But there is empirical evidence that is inconsistent with the life-cycle model (Section 4.5.5). We have previously explored how present bias (Section 5.4.3) and reference-dependent preferences (Section 9.5.3) can each help to make sense of this evidence. In this section I focus instead on the role of mental accounting.[2]

19.3.1   A Mental Accounting Life-Cycle Model

Money is assumed to be fungible in the standard life-cycle model. An additional $1000 of wealth, no matter its source, is predicted to have the same effect on behavior. Gaining $1000 from a winning lottery ticket, a bonus at work, or an increase in home value all increase wealth by the same amount (ignoring tax differences).

Suppose instead that individuals create a system of mental accounts to keep track of their wealth. While empirical evidence suggests these mental accounts can be quite detailed, for simplicity let's assume that wealth is disaggregated into three broad accounts (Thaler 1990; Shefrin and Thaler 2004):

I: current income account;
A: current asset account; and
F: future income account.

With this mental accounting system, labor income from work would likely accrue to the *I* account, whereas capital income from asset holdings would be placed in the *A* account. Dividend income, however, may be treated as current income (Shefrin and Statman 1984). Anticipated inheritances, Social Security benefits, and retirement savings would be treated as part of the *F* account. Some sources of wealth, like windfalls or home equity, are more complex to categorize, as we explore in the remainder of this section.

The three mental accounts differ not only in their labels, but also in how tempting individuals find them to spend from. It is most tempting to spend from *I*, more difficult to spend from *A*, and least tempting to withdraw from *F*. This insight suggests that an additional $1 in each account increases consumption by a different amount. That is, each account has its own **marginal propensity to consume (MPC)** (Shefrin and Thaler 2004; Holbrook and Stafford 1971; Levin 1998). The MPC from *I* is close to 1: current income is spent in full. The MPC from *F* is close to 0: increases in future income have effectively no impact on current consumption. And the MPC from *A* is somewhere in between. In contrast, the assumed fungibility of money in the standard life-cycle model implies that the MPC is the same across all types of wealth.

We now turn to implications and evidence of mental accounting within the life-cycle model.

19.3.2   *Income Accounts*

There are sources of income beyond a fixed salary from work and dividends from investments. For instance, some may receive additional cash payments in the form of bonuses or windfalls. Many governments also provide transfers to support families with children and those with low incomes. These transfers can take the form of direct cash payments, or non-cash **in-kind** benefits like coupons for nutritious food. Let's explore the mental accounting of these various income sources.

Bonuses

For present purposes, define a bonus as a fully anticipated, but lumpy payment. How does receiving part of your compensation each year as a bonus change your behavior? Consider the following example adapted from Thaler (1990, 198).

▪ Example 19.4 John and Joan are professors who are identical in every way, except for the path of their incomes. John earns $110,000 this year, paid in equal monthly installments. Joan is a paid a base salary of $100,000, also in equal monthly installments. But she also receives a guaranteed $10,000 summer salary "bonus" on July 1.

According to the standard life-cycle model, John and Joan are predicted to save the same amount, as they earn the same annual income.

But suppose that John and Joan have a system of mental accounts, treating their base salary as current income *I* and any bonus as an asset *A*. Because the MPC out of *I* is close to 1, John and Joan are predicted to spend almost all of their base salaries. This leaves

John with almost no savings. And because the MPC out of A is less than 1, Joan saves some of her bonus. She therefore ends the year with more savings than John, despite their identical incomes.   •

This example illustrates an answer to our question above: with mental accounting, bonuses increase individual savings. Empirical evidence from Japan finds that indeed the MPC from bonuses is less than from regular income, supporting the mental accounting model (Ishikawa and Ueda 1984). Therefore, if you are trying to increase your own savings and aware of your own mental accounts, you may want to seek out employment opportunities that offer a lower base salary in exchange for a predictable bonus.

Windfalls

Unlike a bonus, a **windfall** is typically a sudden and unexpected income gain. According to the mental accounting model, windfalls of different magnitudes are coded into different accounts and therefore spent to different degrees.

Windfalls that are large relative to annual income are coded as an increase in the current asset account A. The MPC to consume from such large windfalls should therefore be moderate, with a share of the windfall consumed and the remainder saved. As evidence, Landsberger (1966) estimates the MPC for Israeli recipients of German restitution payments after World War II. He finds that those who received the largest windfalls — equal to about two-thirds of a family's annual income — had a MPC from the windfall of 0.23. That is, they spent only 23% of the payment, and saved the remaining 77%.

But small windfalls are coded as part of the current income account I, and are therefore predicted to be fully spent. In fact, for the Israeli families that received relatively small restitution payments — equal to about 7% of annual income — the MPC from the small windfall was not only high, it was 2.0. The small windfall was spent twice over, leading to a reduction in wealth. You may have experienced a related phenomenon after winning \$20 in a lottery and then justifying multiple \$20 purchases as "paid for" by your winnings.

More recent evidence for mental accounting comes from small windfalls that take the form of coupons or promotions for shoppers. In the standard life-cycle model with fungible money, a coupon for \$10 off groceries has no meaningful effect on the single account of lifetime wealth. The coupon should therefore have a negligible effect on spending decisions. But the evidence indicates that grocery coupons increase shopper spending, particularly on unplanned items (Heilman, Nakamoto, and Rao 2002) and items that are not typically purchased (Milkman and Beshears 2009). While anomalous for the standard model, this evidence points to consumers treating such small gains as part of their current income account, where the temptation to spend is high.

Government Transfers

With additional children, family resources are split between more people. To help support families with children, many governments provide benefits in the form of cash transfers or tax credits. If money were treated as fungible, these child benefits would have the same impact on behavior as an equivalent increase in income from another source.

In a test of this hypothesis, Kooreman (2000) studies the spending behavior of Dutch families with one child. Every three months these families received a child benefit deposited to their bank account. He estimates that the marginal propensity to consume children's clothing out of the child benefit is much larger than the marginal propensity to consume children's clothing out of other income sources. For example, among two-parent households, 11% of the child benefit was spent on child clothing, while only 1% of an equivalent income increase from another source was similarly allocated to child clothing. This evidence clearly contradicts the hypothesis that families view money as fungible. Instead, they may treat the child benefits as income accruing to a childcare mental account, and therefore direct this income towards childcare expenditures.[3] The Income Identity Lab Experiment at the start of the chapter — where serious income is allocated to serious expenses — reveals a similar income accounting phenomenon.

Mental accounting of government transfers may also arise in the context of the Supplemental Nutrition Assistance Program (SNAP) in the US. This program, also referred to as food stamps, provides low-income families with money — in the form of coupons — that can be spent on groceries from authorized stores. Why are such benefits provided in kind, as opposed to in cash? After all, with cash people have more flexibility to allocate their spending as they desire. The following example and evidence provide a possible justification.

▪ **Example 19.5** Consider a SNAP-eligible household that always spends at least $200 on groceries each month. How would a $200 SNAP benefit change the household's grocery spending relative to a cash benefit of $200 that could be spent on anything?

If the household treated money as fungible, both benefits should have the same impact on grocery spending. To see why, observe that because the household spends at least $200 on groceries, the SNAP benefit frees up $200 of cash — previously spent on groceries — for spending on anything, making the two policies equivalent.

Now suppose that the household has a mental account for groceries. In this case, if the household sees the SNAP money as earmarked explicitly to grocery consumption, then it will increase spending on groceries more with the SNAP benefit than with an equivalent cash benefit that can be spread out across a large number of expense categories.

Hastings and Shapiro (2018) collect 6 years of data from a grocery retail chain (500 million transactions) and find that a $200 SNAP benefit increases grocery spending by $110. A $200 cash benefit, however, only increases grocery spending by about $20. This evidence is inconsistent with the standard model, but aligns with the prediction of mental accounting.   ▪

In sum, if the social objective of nutritional support policy is motivated by paternalism — to encourage low-income families to spend more on groceries than they would freely choose for themselves — and mental accounting is widespread, then the government can use in-kind benefits over cash to better achieve the intended goal. We return to the policy implications of mental accounting in Chapter 21.

19.3.3 Wealth Accounts

A household's wealth typically consists of future income, retirement wealth, and housing wealth. High-income households may also hold substantial wealth in easily accessible savings accounts. But regardless of the source of wealth, the standard life-cycle model assumes that wealth is fungible: all forms of wealth are substitutable for each other. There is strong empirical evidence, however, that different forms of wealth are not close substitutes. Instead, people appear to assign wealth to separate mental accounts. Let's turn to such evidence for retirement and housing wealth.

Retirement Wealth

Pensions are one form of retirement wealth. In a typical pension plan an employer and employee make contributions to an investment portfolio. Then, upon retirement, the employer pays the former employee a specific monthly income for life.

To test the hypothesis that individuals treat pension savings as a substitute for other savings, consider an individual who saves 10% of her salary for retirement. These savings are split between a 5% required contribution to her employer's pension plan and a 5% voluntary allocation to a private savings account. Now suppose that her employer requires that she increase her pension contribution from 5% to 6% of her salary. According to the standard life-cycle model, this change does not impact her desired total savings. She still wants to save 10% of her salary for retirement. Therefore, she is expected to respond by reducing her private savings rate from 5% to 4%. In sum, the prediction of the life-cycle model is that an increase in pension savings by $1 should decrease other savings by $1.

Evidence across multiple decades and countries consistently fails to find such a 1-to-1 negative relationship between pension savings and other savings (Shefrin and Thaler 2004). In fact, some studies find that an increase in pension savings by $1 leads to an *increase* in other savings. And even among studies that find pension savings reduce other savings, the estimated magnitudes of this effect are too small to be consistent with the life-cycle model.

Although the pension savings evidence is anomalous for the life-cycle model, it is consistent with mental accounting. Let Molly be a mental accounter who consumes everything in her current income account I and nothing out of her future income account F. If Molly's employer increases her required pension contribution by $1, assume that she treats the dollar as a flow out of I and into F (see also Exercise 19.9). The outflow from I reduces her current consumption by $1 and has no impact on her non-pension savings. But her total savings increases by $1 because she treats her pension wealth as off-limits for current consumption. In sum, Molly responds to the increase in pension savings not by reducing any other savings, but by adjusting her current consumption downward. This prediction fits well with the evidence noted above.

While pensions are still somewhat common for government jobs, most employers in the private sector no longer provide pension benefits. Instead, employers may offer a 401(k) retirement account. Like a pension, both the employee and employer contribute to a savings account. But unlike a pension, this account is managed by the individual employee who decides upon reaching retirement how they want to withdraw income from this account. Consistent with mental accounting, Choi, Laibson, and Madrian (2009) document evidence that individuals make investments account by account, failing to consider the full scope of investment decisions they are making across multiple accounts.

Mental accounting of retirement wealth is also supported by evidence for individual retirement accounts (Venti and Wise 1990b; Feenberg and Skinner 1989) and Social Security benefits (Barro 1978).

Housing Wealth

For many American homeowners, their primary source of wealth is the equity in their home. **Home equity** is the difference between the market value of a home and the outstanding balance owed on debts incurred to purchase the home. As a home price increases and mortgage debt is paid off, home equity therefore grows.

According to the standard life-cycle model, an increase in home equity should have the same impact on consumption as an equivalent increase in any other form of wealth. This may seem like a surprising prediction, as it is easier to spend wealth sitting in a checking account than wealth in one's home. But note that it is possible to borrow against housing wealth to finance current consumption.

In the mental accounting model, housing wealth is likely its own category, with a marginal propensity to consume between that of the current asset account A and the future income account F. The MPC out of housing wealth is therefore predicted to be quite low. Consistent with this prediction, Skinner (1989) estimates that the MPC out of housing wealth is not significantly different from zero. As a consequence, rising home prices do not increase current consumption. Housing wealth stays within the house and is not typically spent on expenditures in other mental accounts, as would be expected for individuals who perceive wealth as fungible.

The reluctance to spend out of home equity is particularly surprising for older homeowners. This is a population that typically has zero mortgage debt on their home and therefore substantial home equity. Such wealth could be spent to supplement retirement income from pensions or Social Security benefits. The life-cycle model predicts that the elderly will indeed choose to dissave, spending down their housing wealth throughout the end of life. Venti and Wise (1990a) provide evidence to the contrary in an article titled "But They Don't Want to Reduce Housing Equity." Perhaps elderly homeowners maintain their home equity so as to leave wealth for their children when they die. But Hurd (1987) finds that behavior does not differ between those with and without living children. The psychology of mental accounting therefore remains a compelling explanation for such otherwise puzzling consumption and savings decisions.

19.4   Excess Diversification   [Finance]

Some decision problems do not require you to make a single choice. Instead, there may be a menu of many options, each of which can be simultaneously chosen. For instance, you can sign up for multiple classes in a given semester. Or donate to multiple charities this year. Or choose multiple stocks in which to invest your savings. In such settings there is evidence that individuals **diversify excessively**, choosing more variety than they would actually like for themselves (Read and Loewenstein 1995). The following lab experiment provides an illustration.

> **Lab Experiment — Sequential Snacking (Simonson 1990)**
>
> Almost 300 undergraduate students enrolled across nine business classes (all scheduled at the same time of day) made selections from a menu of six snacks at the beginning of a class meeting and received their selection at the end of class. The classes were randomly assigned to one of two groups:
>
> 1   Sequential Choice: Students selected one snack each week for 3 weeks.

> 2   Simultaneous Choice: Students selected all three snacks at once, but received only one each week.
>
> Any difference in the variety of snack selections across these two groups must be due to the timing of the decisions.
>
> ───────────────────────────────────────
>
> Among students in classes assigned to the sequential-choice group, 9% chose three different snacks. But 64% of students in the simultaneous-choice group chose three different snacks.

This evidence of snack selections reveals that participants diversify their simultaneous choices more than they would if faced with each selection sequentially. For instance, a student whose favorite snack on the menu is peanuts is likely to choose peanuts each week if asked sequentially. But when that same student chooses all three snacks in advance, she avoids choosing peanuts for every week and instead diversifies: perhaps peanuts one week, tortilla chips another, and a candy bar for the last week. This diversification is excessive because she is likely disappointed each week that she does not receive her most preferred peanut snack. More generally, this phenomenon reflects how choices depend on whether individuals mentally account for a series of decisions as generating separate outcomes or a collective set of outcomes.

Excessive diversification has important implications for investment behavior. Given how complex investing can be, it is not entirely surprising that individuals may adopt simpler strategies, or heuristics, for decision making. One such heuristic is an extreme form of excess diversification: given a menu of investment options, split your money evenly among each option. This is the **1/n heuristic**, where n is the number of options and $1/n$ is the share allocated to each (Benartzi and Thaler 2001). Although the moniker is modern, the idea is not. Around "the fourth century, a Rabbi Issac bar Aha gave the following asset allocation advice: 'A man should always place his money, a third into land, a third into merchandise, and keep a third at hand.' There is anecdotal evidence that this rule is still in use" (Benartzi and Thaler 2001, 79).

For more recent evidence of the $1/n$ heuristic, consider the decision problem of choosing how to invest in a 401(k) retirement plan. Typically, an employee offered a 401(k) by their employer can choose to direct their savings across a menu of possible investment funds. The key decision is how much retirement savings to invest in high risk/high return stock funds and how much to invest in low risk/low return bond funds. Each individual will make a different decision, depending on their aversion to risk, retirement savings goals, and age. What is not expected to matter for this decision is how many stock funds and bond funds are on the 401(k) menu. But the funds on the 401(k) menu will matter for someone adopting the $1/n$ heuristic. The following example illustrates why.

▪ **Example 19.6** Suri is a standard decision maker who wants to invest 50% of her savings in stocks and 50% in bonds. Nelson is overwhelmed by the investment choices in front of him and therefore adopts the $1/n$ heuristic. What happens to the investment allocations for Suri and Nelson if their 401(k) plan goes from offering two funds (one stock and one bond) to four funds (three stock and one bond)?

For Suri, the menu change does not impact her asset allocation. She keeps 50% of her savings in the single bond fund and allocates the remaining 50% across the stock funds, no matter how many stock funds are available.

The menu change does impact Nelson. With only two funds, Nelson splits his savings evenly: 50% in stocks and 50% in bonds. Following the introduction of two new stock funds, Nelson again divides his savings evenly between all four funds, leading to 75% invested in stocks and 25% in bonds. The simple menu change has induced him to naively increase the share of savings invested in stocks.   •

In sum, for people who adopt the $1/n$ heuristic, a greater share of stock funds offered in a 401(k) plan increases the share of savings invested in stocks. Making use of data from over half a million individual investors, Huberman and Jiang (2006) document evidence for this prediction, as long as there are fewer than 10 funds from which to choose. That is, while the $1/n$ heuristic may describe decision making when options are limited, there is *not* evidence that an individual faced with 25 fund choices allocates 4% of their savings equally across all 25 funds. Instead, when the number of offered funds is large, many people appear to follow a two-step *conditional* $1/n$ heuristic. First, they select only a few funds. And second, they allocate their savings evenly between the selected funds. As evidence, Huberman and Jiang (2006) find that among investors who choose only two funds, 64% allocate their savings evenly between them. Similarly, 37% of those choosing four funds, and 53% of those choosing 10 funds, split their savings evenly. It is worth noting that although this conditional $1/n$ heuristic is a different decision rule than maximizing discounted expected utility, it remains possible that the two decision methods generate the same choices. The topic of nonstandard financial decision making continues in the next chapter on limited attention.

19.5 Summary

1   **Mental accounting** refers to the set of cognitive operations used by individuals to organize, evaluate, and keep track of their financial activities.

2   The standard model of decision making assumes that individuals treat money as if it is **fungible**.

3   Evidence suggests that people often assign activities to **mental accounts** for which:

   a   money is not treated as fungible across mental accounts; and
   b   debts within each mental account are avoided.

4   The **sunk cost effect** or **fallacy** refers to the tendency of individuals to be influenced by **sunk costs** that cannot be recovered.

5   **Payment depreciation** refers to the diminishing effect of sunk costs on decision making over time.

6   In a mental accounting life-cycle model, individuals assign wealth to one of three mental accounts: current income, current assets, and future income. The **marginal propensity to consume (MPC)** is decreasing across these three accounts, respectively. In the standard life-cycle model, the MPC is the same for all forms of wealth.

7   Evidence from bonuses, **windfalls**, government transfers (in cash and **in kind**), **pensions**, and **home equity** confirms the mental accounting hypothesis that the MPC differs based on how wealth is categorized.

8   When faced with a menu of options, each of which can be simultaneously chosen, individuals tend to **diversify excessively**, i.e., more than they would if faced with the same options sequentially.

9   An extreme form of excess diversification is the **1/n heuristic**, by which an individual allocates money equally across *n* possible options. In the context of retirement accounts some appear to adopt a related *conditional* 1/n heuristic.

19.6   Exercises

Exercise 19.1 — Closing Time. [Finance] The disposition effect refers to the documented tendency for investors to sell their "winner" stocks (i.e., those with positive returns) and hold on to "losers" (Odean 1998; Ivković, Poterba, and Weisbenner 2005). This is the opposite prediction of standard economic theory because selling losers reduces taxes, while selling winners increases taxes. Suppose that investors have a mental account for each stock's return that is "closed" upon selling. Explain how such mental accounting could lead to the disposition effect.

Exercise 19.2 — Sunk Costs in Action. Provide an example of a sunk cost that has influenced a decision in your own life. Explain why this constitutes a fallacy.

Exercise 19.3 — If the Shoe Fits. Consider the following thought experiment: "You buy a pair of shoes. They feel perfectly comfortable in the store, but the first day you wear them they hurt. A few days later you try them again, but they hurt even more than the first time" (Thaler 1999, 191).

a   Assume you are a standard decision maker. How does the price you paid for the shoes influence the frequency with which you will try to wear the shoes? And once you stop wearing the shoes, how does the price influence the likelihood of throwing them away? Explain.

b   Now assume that you fall prey to the sunk cost fallacy. How do your answers in part (a) change, if at all? Explain.

Exercise 19.4 — Jumping for the Gym. [Health] Gourville and Soman (1998) obtain monthly attendance data from a Colorado athletic facility that charges membership dues twice per year. They find that attendance is highest in the month when the dues are paid. Attendance declines over the next five months before jumping again when the next bill is due. What does this evidence suggest about the impact of sunk costs on decision making?

Exercise 19.5 — Coffee on the Cheap. Shafir and Thaler (2006, 704) propose the following scenario: "Suppose that you are a devoted coffee drinker and that every morning, on your way to class, you used to go to your favorite café and purchase a large latté for $3.00. Eventually, you decided to purchase a first-rate, $500 espresso maker instead, so that you could make your own latté each morning, saving the repeated trip and expense. Every morning you now make your own latté at home, which is every bit as good as the one you used to get at the café." When prompted with this scenario, the majority of respondents feel that the machine is an investment — not spending — and the coffee it produces is essentially free or even a money saver. Explain how such feelings demonstrate a form of mental accounting.

Exercise 19.6 — Mental Accounting for Savings. Daniela and Camila treat dividends as current income and capital gains as current assets. Daniela receives dividend income worth $500 this year (and no capital gains). Camila receives capital gains income worth $500 this year (and no dividends). Assuming that they are otherwise identical, is Daniela or Camila expected to save more of their total income this year? Explain.

Exercise 19.7 — Drink Up. [Household] Abeler and Marklein (2017) conduct the following field experiment in a restaurant. Guests are randomly assigned to receive either a €8 cash coupon off their bill or a €8 coupon to be applied only to their beverage consumption. Almost every guest at the restaurant consumes at least €8 worth of beverages.

a   Suppose that guests treat money as fungible. In this case, would you expect the two coupons to have the same effect on beverage spending? Why or why not?

b   Now suppose that guests do not treat money as fungible and have a mental account for restaurant beverages. How does your answer to part (a) change, if at all? Explain.

c   The researchers find that beverage spending is €3.45 higher for those who receive the beverage-specific coupon relative to the cash coupon. This difference in spending is due to more expensive beverage purchases, not a greater volume of beverage purchases. What does this evidence suggest about decision making?

Exercise 19.8 — Fuel Fungibility. [Household] Consider a household that purchases a fixed quantity of 1200 gallons of gasoline each year, no matter the price. But the household can choose between two gasoline varieties: regular and more expensive premium gasoline.

a   Assume that the household is a standard economic decision maker that views money as fungible. Should a $1 increase in the per-gallon price of both gasoline varieties increase the household's annual spending on regular gasoline by more, the same, or less than if the household experienced a $1200 income loss? Explain.

b   Now assume that the household has a mental account for gasoline separate from other expenditures. Re-answer the question in part (a).

c   Hastings and Shapiro (2013) collect 4 years of data on household gas purchases and find that a $1 increase in the per-gallon price of gasoline increases households' propensity to purchase regular gas by 1.4 percentage points. A $1200 income loss, however, only increases the propensity to buy regular gas by less than 0.1 percentage points. Given your answers above, what does this evidence suggest about household decision making?

Exercise 19.9 — A Penchant for Savings. [Household] Millie is a mental accounter with a marginal propensity to consume (MPC) out of her current asset account A of 0.3. Her MPC out of her future income account F is zero. Suppose that Millie's employer increases her required pension contribution by $10 and that she treats this change as a transfer out of A and into F.

a   What is the effect of this transfer on Millie's non-pension savings?

b   What is the effect of this transfer on Millie's total (pension plus non-pension) savings?

c   How would the answers to parts (a) and (b) change if Millie instead behaved according to the standard life-cycle model?
d   Green (1981) finds that pension savings increase other savings. Is this evidence consistent with mental accounting or the standard life-cycle model?

Exercise 19.10 — Sweet Variety. [Household] Read and Loewenstein (1995) conduct a field experiment on Halloween night with trick-or-treaters who approach two adjacent houses offering three Musketeers and Milky Way candy bars. Children faced one of the following randomly assigned decision problems:

1   Sequential Choice: At each house, choose one of the two candy bars.
2   Simultaneous Choice: At the first house that is reached, choose two candy bars.

In the sequential-choice treatment, 48% of the children selected different candy bars. But in the simultaneous–choice treatment, 100% of the children selected one of each candy bar. Provide an interpretation of this evidence. In particular, why is it so surprising from the perspective of standard decision making?

Exercise 19.11 — Menu Matters. [Finance] Companies B and S each offer a 401(k) plan with five fund options to their employees (who share similar preferences and characteristics). Company B offers four bond funds and one stock fund. Company S offers four stock funds and one bond fund.

a   Suppose that the employees at both companies are all standard decision makers. Would you expect the average share of 401(k) savings invested in stocks to be the same or different between the two companies? Explain.
b   Benartzi and Thaler (2001) document evidence that 401(k) savings are more heavily invested in stocks at a company like S than like B. Provide an explanation for this finding.

Exercise 19.12 — Bargain Hunting. Tversky and Kahneman (1981, 457) present two versions of the following decision problem to different groups of subjects, assigned at random. One group was given the numbers in parentheses, and the other was given the numbers in brackets.

> Imagine that you are about to purchase a jacket for ($125) [$15], and a calculator for ($15) [$125]. The calculator salesman informs you that the calculator you wish to buy is on sale for ($10) [$120] at the other branch of the store, located 20 minutes drive away. Would you make the trip to the other store?

Over two-thirds of respondents are willing to travel to save $5 off a $15 calculator. But less than a third are willing to travel to save $5 off a $125 calculator.

a   Explain why the evidence is inconsistent with the standard model of decision making.
b   To make sense of the evidence, suppose that respondents mentally account for the benefit of saving $5 at the other store as the difference between paying the lower sale price and the higher regular price:

Utility Benefit of $5 Off Price $P = v(-(P-5)) - v(-P)$

where $v(\cdot)$ is the prospect theory value function (as in Figure 12.1) given by

$$v(x) = \begin{cases} x^{0.7} & \text{if } x \geq 0 \\ -2.25(-x)^{0.7} & \text{if } x < 0 \end{cases}$$

 i   What is the utility benefit of $5 off $15?
 ii What is the utility benefit of $5 off $125?
 iii Suppose that individuals are willing to travel as long as the utility benefit of saving $5 exceeds the utility cost of traveling (in terms of time and effort). Provide a single numerical value of the utility cost such that this model predicts the majority preference for each group of subjects.

Notes

1 This chapter is largely adapted from Thaler (1999) and Thaler (1990).
2 Shefrin and Thaler (2004) consider the implications of a behavioral life-cycle model with both self-control problems and mental accounting.
3 The effect of labeled government transfers on behavior is similarly explored by Benhassine et al. (2015), as described in Exercise 3.11.

References

Abeler, Johannes, and Felix Marklein. 2017. "Fungibility, Labels, and Consumption." *Journal of the European Economic Association* 15 (1): 99–127. doi:10.1093/jeea/jvw007.

Arkes, Hal R., and Catherine Blumer. 1985. "The Psychology of Sunk Cost." *Organizational Behavior and Human Decision Processes* 35 (1): 124–140. doi:10.1016/0749-5978(85)90049-4.

Barro, Robert J. 1978. *The Impact of Social Security on Private Saving, Washington.* Washington, DC: American Enterprise Institute.

Benartzi, Shlomo, and Richard H. Thaler. 2001. "Naive Diversification Strategies in Defined Contribution Saving Plans." *American Economic Review* 91 (1): 79–98. doi:10.1257/aer.91.1.79.

Benhassine, Najy, Florencia Devoto, Esther Duflo, Pascaline Dupas, and Victor Pouliquen. 2015. "Turning a Shove into a Nudge? A 'Labeled Cash Transfer' for Education." *American Economic Journal: Economic Policy* 7 (3): 86–125. doi:10.1257/pol.20130225.

Choi, James J., David Laibson, and Brigitte C. Madrian. 2009. "Mental Accounting in Portfolio Choice: Evidence from a Flypaper Effect." *American Economic Review* 99 (5): 2085–2095. doi:10.1257/aer.99.5.2085.

Feenberg, Daniel, and Jonathan Skinner. 1989. "Sources of IRA Saving." *Tax Policy and the Economy* 3: 25–46. doi:10.1086/tpe.3.20061782.

Gourville, John T., and Dilip Soman. 1998. "Payment Depreciation: The Behavioral Effects of Temporally Separating Payments from Consumption." *Journal of Consumer Research* 25 (2): 160–174. doi:10.1086/209533.

Green, Francis. 1981. "The Effect of Occupational Pension Schemes on Saving in the United Kingdom: A Test of the Life Cycle Hypothesis." *The Economic Journal* 91 (361): 136–144. doi:10.2307/2231703.

Hastings, Justine S., and Jesse M. Shapiro. 2013. "Fungibility and Consumer Choice: Evidence from Commodity Price Shocks." *The Quarterly Journal of Economics* 128 (4): 1449–1498. doi:10.1093/qje/qjt018.

———. 2018. "How Are SNAP Benefits Spent? Evidence from a Retail Panel." *American Economic Review* 108 (12): 3493–3540. doi:10.1257/aer.20170866.

Heath, Chip, and Jack B. Soll. 1996. "Mental Accounting and Consumer Decisions." *Journal of Consumer Research* 23 (1): 40–52. doi:10.1086/209465.

Heilman, Carrie M., Kent Nakamoto, and Ambar G. Rao. 2002. "Pleasant Surprises: Consumer Response to Unexpected In-Store Coupons." *Journal of Marketing Research* 39 (2): 242–252. doi:10.1509/jmkr.39.2.242.19081.

Holbrook, Robert, and Frank Stafford. 1971. "The Propensity to Consume Separate Types of Income: A Generalized Permanent Income Hypothesis." *Econometrica* 39 (1): 1–21. doi:10.2307/1909136.

Huberman, Gur, and Wei Jiang. 2006. "Offering versus Choice in 401(k) Plans: Equity Exposure and Number of Funds." *The Journal of Finance* 61 (2): 763–801. doi:10.1111/j.1540-6261.2006.00854.x.

Hurd, Michael D. 1987. "Savings of the Elderly and Desired Bequests." *American Economic Review* 77 (3): 298–312. https://www.jstor.org/stable/1804096.

Ishikawa, Tsuneo, and Kazuo Ueda. 1984. "The Bonus Payment System and Japanese Personal Savings." In *The Economic Analysis of the Japanese Firm,* edited by Masahiko Aoki, 133–192. Amsterdam: North Holland.

Ivković, Zoran, James Poterba, and Scott Weisbenner. 2005. "Tax-Motivated Trading by Individual Investors." *American Economic Review* 95 (5): 1605–1630. doi:10.1257/000282805775014461.

Kahneman, Daniel, and Amos Tversky. 1984. "Choices, Values, and Frames." *American Psychologist* 39 (4): 341–350. doi:10.1037/0003-066x.39.4.341.

Kooreman, Peter. 2000. "The Labeling Effect of a Child Benefit System." *American Economic Review* 90 (3): 571–583. doi:10.1257/aer.90.3.571.

Landsberger, Michael. 1966. "Windfall Income and Consumption: Comment." *American Economic Review* 56 (3): 534–540. https://www.jstor.org/stable/1823790.

Levin, Laurence. 1998. "Are Assets Fungible?: Testing the Behavioral Theory of Life-Cycle Savings." *Journal of Economic Behavior & Organization* 36 (1): 59–83. doi:10.1016/S0167-2681(98)00070-5.

Milkman, Katherine L., and John Beshears. 2009. "Mental Accounting and Small Windfalls: Evidence from an Online Grocer." *Journal of Economic Behavior & Organization* 71 (2): 384–394. doi:10.1016/j.jebo.2009.04.007.

O'Curry, Suzanne. 1997. "Income Source Effects." DePaul University. Unpublished.

Odean, Terrance. 1998. "Are Investors Reluctant to Realize Their Losses?" *The Journal of Finance* 53 (5): 1775–1798. doi:10.1111/0022-1082.00072.

Prelec, Drazen, and George Loewenstein. 1998. "The Red and the Black: Mental Accounting of Savings and Debt." *Marketing Science* 17 (1): 4–28. doi:10.1287/mksc. 17.1.4.

Read, Daniel, and George Loewenstein. 1995. "Diversification Bias: Explaining the Discrepancy in Variety Seeking between Combined and Separated Choices." *Journal of Experimental Psychology: Applied* 1 (1): 34–49. doi:10.1037/1076-898X.1.1.34.

Shafir, Eldar, and Richard H. Thaler. 2006. "Invest Now, Drink Later, Spend Never: On the Mental Accounting of Delayed Consumption." *Journal of Economic Psychology*, Special Issue: Research Inspired by Thomas C. Schelling, 27 (5): 694–712. Reprinting from pp 697, 704, Copyright (2006), with permission from Elsevier, doi:10.1016/j.joep.2006.05.008.

Shefrin, Hersh M., and Meir Statman. 1984. "Explaining Investor Preference for Cash Dividends." *Journal of Financial Economics* 13 (2): 253–282. doi:10.1016/0304-405X(84)90025-4.

Shefrin, Hersh M., and Richard H. Thaler. 2004. "Mental Accounting, Saving, and Self-Control." In *Advances in Behavioral Economics,* edited by Colin F. Camerer, 395–428. Princeton, NJ: Princeton University Press.

Simonson, Itamar. 1990. "The Effect of Purchase Quantity and Timing on Variety-Seeking Behavior." *Journal of Marketing Research* 27 (2): 150–162. doi:10.1177/002224379002700203.

Skinner, Jonathan. 1989. "Housing Wealth and Aggregate Saving." *Regional Science and Urban Economics* 19 (2): 305–324. doi:10.1016/0166-0462(89)90008-2.

Stein, Gertrude. 1936. "Money." *Saturday Evening Post,* July 13, 1936.

Thaler, Richard H. 1980. "Toward a Positive Theory of Consumer Choice." *Journal of Economic Behavior & Organization* 1 (1): 39–60. Reprinting from pp 43-44, Copyright (1980), with permission from Elsevier, doi:10.1016/0167-2681(80)90051-7.

————. 1990. "Anomalies: Saving, Fungibility, and Mental Accounts." *Journal of Economic Perspectives* 4 (1): 193–205. doi:10.1257/jep.4.1.193.

————. 1999. "Mental Accounting Matters." *Journal of Behavioral Decision Making* 12: 183–206. Copyright © 1999 John Wiley & Sons, Ltd., doi:10.1002/(sici)1099-0771(199909)12:3<183::aid-bdm318>3.0.co;2-f.

Tversky, Amos, and Daniel Kahneman. 1981. "The Framing of Decisions and the Psychology of Choice." *Science* 211 (4481): 453–458. Reprinting from p 457 with permission from AAAS, doi:10.1126/science.7455683.

Venti, Steven F., and David A. Wise. 1990a. "But They Don't Want to Reduce Housing Equity." In *Issues in the Economics of Aging,* edited by David A. Wise, 13–32. Chicago, IL: University of Chicago Press.

————. 1990b. "Have IRAs Increased US Saving?: Evidence from Consumer Expenditure Surveys." *The Quarterly Journal of Economics* 105 (3): 661. doi:10.2307/2937894.

20 Inattention

Learning Objectives

★ Understand a framework for modeling inattention.

★ Estimate the magnitude of attention across a variety of economic settings.

★ Appreciate the factors that influence more or less attention.

★ Identify excessive responses to persuasion.

We live in an information age. Thanks to Wikipedia, we can learn about almost any topic with a few keystrokes. Consumers can quickly find product reviews and medical advice online. Easily accessible financial records of companies and legislative records of politicians inform investment and voting behaviors. The standard economic model assumes that people make use of *all* available information when making decisions. New information about a good, an asset, or a politician may change the relative tradeoffs for a decision, leading to potentially different choices. And by ignoring information, we can choose options that fail to maximize our own well-being.

But with access to so much information, individuals may pay attention to only some of it. As Herbert A. Simon elegantly noted, "a wealth of information creates a poverty of attention" (Simon 1971, 40). People may be inattentive to available information due to the cognitive costs of acquiring or processing information. It is costly to explore every possible major in college, every possible health insurance plan, and every possible retirement savings strategy. If the cost of full attention exceeds the benefit from making a better-informed choice, then inattention can be in an individual's best interest (see e.g., Sims 2003; Caplin and Dean 2015). However, when individuals are inattentive to information that is freely available, requiring little cognitive effort to process, it is more difficult to rationalize their behaviors.

This chapter explores evidence that freely available information is indeed neglected. We begin with a simple framework for modeling inattention. This framework extends the standard model by introducing the possibility that some information receives only partial attention. The following section estimates the magnitude of this partial attention, using evidence from auctions, taxes, and finance. Inattention can also manifest as neglecting the incentives of persuaders. Evidence of such inattention concludes the chapter.

DOI: 10.4324/9780367854072-27

20.1   A Framework for Inattention

We begin with a purposefully simple and abstract framework for modeling inattention to available information (DellaVigna 2009, 349). Consider a good with value V that equals the sum of two components:

$$V = v + o$$

where v is the *visible* component and o is the *opaque* component. For instance, when shopping online, the shipping costs and sales taxes may be opaque relative to the more visible retail prices. While a standard decision maker accurately perceives the value of the good to be V, assume that an inattentive consumer does not fully perceive the opaque component. The following definition formalizes this idea.

> **Definition 20.1** An **inattentive consumer** perceives a good with value $V = v + o$ to have value
>
> $$\hat{V} = v + \alpha o$$
>
> where $0 \leq \alpha \leq 1$ denotes the consumer's attention to the opaque component o.

The standard model of decision making assumes that $\alpha = 1$. That is, attention is *full* and consumers are not inattentive. But what does it mean if $\alpha < 1$, with attention effectively less than full? One interpretation is that consumers fully observe the opaque information o, but cognitively process it only partially. Alternatively, we can understand α as the probability that a consumer observes the opaque information. Regardless of the interpretation, our objective is to make use of the preceding framework to estimate the attention parameter α in real-world decisions.

Figure 20.1 plots empirical estimates of α from a variety of studies, many of which are discussed in the next section. In particular, each estimate of α is plotted against the corresponding good's ratio of opaque to visible attributes. It is clear that attention is not always full, with an average value of $\alpha = 0.44$ across the 11 estimates. And a best-fit curve through the data suggests that with greater relative opaqueness, there is greater attention. Intuitively, when a good's value depends more on opaque information, there is a greater incentive for consumers to pay attention. So they do. Returning to the online shopping example, one is more likely to pay attention to opaque shipping costs when they are large than when they are small. We should therefore not expect attention to be a universal parameter that is constant across every setting. It is responsive to the particulars of the decision environment.

From a high-level perspective, we can also think of many anomalies throughout this book as reflecting a form of inattention (Gabaix 2019). For instance:

- Present bias reflects inattention to the future.
- Overweighting of unlikely events reflects inattention to true probabilities.
- Overconfidence reflects inattention to one's true ability.
- Extrapolative beliefs reflect inattention to actual randomness.
- Base-rate neglect reflects inattention to base rates.

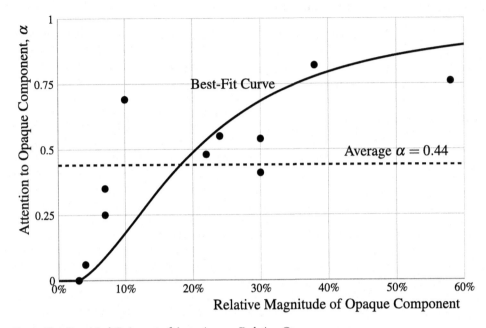

Figure 20.1 Empirical Estimates of Attention vs. Relative Opaqueness

Source: Gabaix (2019) reports the data and calibrates a best-fit attention function that are plotted here.

This list suggests that inattention holds promise as a unifying concept for much of behavioral economics.

20.2 Evidence of Inattention

This section applies the framework in Definition 20.1 to estimate consumer attention across four settings: auctions, taxes, non-leading digits, and finance. In each, the visible and opaque components of a particular good's value are clearly distinguishable from each other. And the opaque information is typically available for free, or at a low cost. The evidence that consumers are not fully attentive to such information is therefore inconsistent with the standard model of decision making.

20.2.1 *Inattention to Prices in Auctions* [Household]

eBay is an online marketplace where consumers and business can buy and sell items either via auction or at fixed prices. The following evidence identifies two forms of bidder inattention in eBay auctions.

Inattention to Shipping Costs

In an eBay auction, an item's price is clearly visible at the top of the webpage. The shipping cost, while still available on the same page, is listed lower, making it a relatively more opaque piece of information. Therefore, define v as a consumer's value of an item up for auction and let o be the negative of the shipping cost c: $o = -c$. An inattentive consumer perceives the item's total value to be:

$$\hat{V} = v + \alpha o = v - \alpha c \tag{20.1}$$

It turns out that in an eBay auction the best strategy — no matter how others bid — is to bid your valuation of the item. An inattentive consumer will then choose to bid their perceived valuation $\hat{V}$.

The seller of the item receives two sources of revenue: the winning bid $b = \hat{V}$ and the shipping cost c. From expression (20.1), we therefore have:

$$\text{Seller Revenue} = b + c = \hat{V} + c = v + (1 - \alpha)c \tag{20.2}$$

This expression is the key to estimating attention α. Observe that an increase in the shipping cost by \$1 increases seller revenue by $\$(1 - \alpha)$:

$$\Delta\text{Seller Revenue} = (1 - \alpha)\Delta c \tag{20.3}$$

With full attention, $\alpha = 1$ and shipping cost has no impact on seller revenue. This is because standard consumers react to a \$1 increase in the shipping cost by reducing their bid by \$1. The seller gains the extra \$1 in shipping costs, but loses \$1 from the reduced bid, leaving revenue unchanged. But seller revenue increases if consumers are inattentive. In this case, a \$1 increase in the shipping cost reduces the bid by $\$\alpha <$ \$1. The seller therefore gains more from the shipping cost increase than is lost from a lower bid. The following field experiment provides data to identify the magnitude of α.

Field Experiment — Shipping Costs (Hossain and Morgan 2006)

Compact discs (CDs) are auctioned on eBay with one of two pricing schemes:

1 No Shipping Cost: free shipping and \$4 minimum bid
2 Shipping Cost: \$3.99 shipping and \$0.01 minimum bid

For a fully attentive bidder these two auctions are equivalent: in each, the minimum cost of acquiring a CD is \$4. If the CD value is $v = \$9$ to a fully attentive consumer, she would bid \$9 with free shipping and \$5.01 with the \$3.99 shipping cost. In both cases, she pays \$9 for the CD and the seller receives \$9 in revenue.

Hossain and Morgan (2006) find that the average seller revenue is \$8.37 with free shipping and \$10.16 with the \$3.99 shipping cost.

The evidence that a higher shipping cost increases seller revenue implies that consumers are not fully attentive. To determine the magnitude of attention α, we combine the experimental data with expression (20.3):

$$\$10.16 - \$8.37 = \Delta \text{Seller Revenue} = (1-\alpha)\Delta c = (1-\alpha)\$3.99$$

$$\Rightarrow 1-\alpha = \frac{\$1.79}{\$3.99} \approx 0.45$$

$$\Rightarrow \alpha \approx 0.55$$

This estimate is far from 1 and reflects substantial inattention.

Equipped with the preceding evidence, a seller is incentivized to increase opaque shipping costs as a means of increasing profit. But there may be limits to this strategy. As discussed in the context of Figure 20.1, the greater is the relative magnitude of the opaque information, the more likely individuals are to attend to that information. Hossain and Morgan (2006) confirm this prediction in a second set of auctions with higher shipping costs. See Exercise 20.2 for details.

Inattention to Fixed Prices

The **bidder's curse** refers to the phenomenon of overbidding in auctions (Malmendier and Lee 2011). That is, bidders may find themselves paying more for an item than they would be willing to pay outside of an auction. Economists have examined possible overbidding in both formal auctions and the auction-like environments of sports, real estate, and corporate finance. Even legal scholars of ancient Rome were concerned with auctions in which the winner was infected by *calor licitantis*, i.e., "bidder's heat" (Malmendier 2002).

But how does one actually know that the bidder's curse is real? Perhaps auction bids, even if seemingly high, truly reflect how much individuals value an item. One strategy is to make use of the fact that on eBay, an item can be offered for sale at a fixed ("buy-it-now") price for immediate purchase from one seller, and simultaneously be offered in an auction from another seller. If auction bidders were fully attentive to the fixed price of the same item on eBay, they would never bid above the fixed price.

Malmendier and Lee (2011) test this hypothesis with two retailers simultaneously selling the same popular board game, Cashflow 101. Any eBay search for Cashflow 101 would show both the fixed-price and the auction listings. Incredibly, 42% of auction sales exceed the fixed price. If shipping costs, which tend to be higher in auctions, are included in the total price of the board game, then 73% of auctions are overbid. The magnitude of overbidding is also significant; almost a third of the auctions are overbid by at least $10, on a $130 game. And overbidding is common among bidders with and without auction experience.

To understand what might be leading to such overbidding, Malmendier and Lee (2011) examine the possibility that bidders are inattentive to the fixed price. That is, they may not fully perceive the fixed price as an alternative price for the item. If true, then auction overbidding should be less likely when the fixed price is more salient, or visible. The fixed price is more salient when it shows up close to the auction listing in the default eBay search results for the board game. The authors compute the "distance" between auction and fixed-price listings as the number of search result rows between them. Consistent with the inattention hypothesis, a smaller distance to fixed-price listings reduces the probability that an auction receives an overbid. In sum, the evidence suggests that overbidding is the result of bidders' inattention to outside purchase options once they start bidding and begin to feel the "heat."

20.2.2 Inattention to Taxes [Public Finance]

Standard models of taxation in public finance assume that individuals are fully attentive to the taxes they pay. But are you fully attentive to income tax rates when you decide how much to work or which job to take? Or are you fully attentive to sales tax rates when shopping or dining? Although these tax rates are freely available public information, people may behave as if they are not paying full attention. And if so, standard predictions about the distributional and efficiency effects of taxes no longer hold (Chetty, Looney, and Kroft 2009; Taubinsky and Rees-Jones 2018).

Chetty, Looney, and Kroft (2009) test the assumption of full attention by studying the impact of sales tax salience on consumer demand. Sales taxes are not typically included in posted prices — they are instead added to the total bill upon payment. In this way, sales taxes are opaque relative to the more visible posted pre-tax prices. Suppose instead that price tags included both the pre-tax and post-tax prices. This would make sales taxes salient to shoppers.

Let's model the effect of such a change in sales tax salience using the framework from the previous section. Define v as a consumer's value of an item, after paying the pre-tax price p. For a consumer who values a (pre-tax) \$10 bottle of shampoo at \$14, $v = \$4$. But with a sales tax rate of t, the consumer must also pay tp in sales taxes at the point of purchase. For instance, a sales tax rate of 7% ($t = 0.07$) creates a tax bill of \$0.70 on the \$10 shampoo. Let o be the negative of this sales tax bill: $o = -tp$. Demand D depends on the consumer's perceived value of the item, $\hat{V}$. Therefore, the quantity demanded by an inattentive consumer facing opaque sales taxes is:

$$D^{\text{Opaque}} = D(\hat{V}) = D(v + \alpha o) = D(v - \alpha tp)$$

If sales taxes were included on price tags, consumers would become fully attentive to the tax bill: $\alpha = 1$. In this case, the item's perceived value $\hat{V}$ is its true value V. And the quantity demanded is now:

$$D^{\text{Salient}} = D(V) = D(v + o) = D(v - tp)$$

It follows from these two expressions — with some additional math[1] — that:

$$\frac{D^{\text{Salient}} - D^{\text{Opaque}}}{\text{Average Demand}} = (1 - \alpha) \times t \times E \tag{20.4}$$

where $E < 0$ is the price elasticity of demand, i.e., the responsiveness of demand to an increase in the pre-tax price p.

Observe the relationship between attention and demand implied by equation (20.4). If consumers were fully attentive to opaque sales taxes not included on price tags, with $\alpha = 1$, then it follows that $D^{\text{Salient}} = D^{\text{Opaque}}$. In words, fully attentive consumers would not change their behavior in response to the posting of sales taxes on price tags. They already account for sales taxes in their shopping decisions, regardless of *how* sales taxes are displayed.

But if consumers are instead somewhat inattentive to opaque sales taxes, with $\alpha < 1$, then $D^{\text{Salient}} < D^{\text{Opaque}}$ (if this is not obvious, recall that $E < 0$). Greater tax salience now increases attention to the true tax-inclusive cost of purchases, reducing demand. And the less attentive people are (smaller α), the more dramatic is the impact of tax salience on behavior. The following field experiment provides empirical evidence to estimate α.

Field Experiment — Tax Salience (Chetty, Looney, and Kroft 2009)

All products in a supermarket were initially labeled with standard pre-tax prices. The 7.375% sales tax rate ($t = 0.07375$) was applied to bills at the point of purchase. Then, price tags on a subset of products were changed as follows:

1   Control Products: No change in price tags.
2   Treatment Products: Price tags changed to show both the pre-tax price and the total tax-inclusive price.

Any demand change for treatment products relative to control products after the price tag intervention reflects the impact of making sales taxes salient for shoppers. The authors also use product demand at two nearby stores as an additional control.

Chetty, Looney, and Kroft (2009) estimate that posting sales taxes on price tags reduced demand by 2.2 units, relative to average product demand of 29 units across all stores. They also estimate the price elasticity of demand to be $E = -1.59$: a 1% increase in price reduces demand by 1.59%.

The negative impact of sales tax salience on demand, evidenced in the foregoing field experiment, reveals that consumers are indeed inattentive to opaque sales taxes. Otherwise, their shopping behavior would have been unaffected by the alteration of the price tags. To estimate the attention parameter α, we plug the experimental evidence into equation (20.4) and rearrange as follows:

$$\frac{-2.2}{29} = \frac{D^{\text{Salient}} - D^{\text{Opaque}}}{\text{Average Demand}} = (1 - \alpha) \times t \times E = (1 - \alpha) \times 0.07375 \times -1.59$$

$$\Rightarrow 1 - \alpha = \frac{-2.2/29}{0.07375 \times -1.59} \approx 0.65$$

$$\Rightarrow \alpha \approx 1 - 0.65 = 0.35$$

This estimate reflects significant inattention, and even less attention than was estimated in the context of the Shipping Costs Field Experiment (where $\alpha \approx 0.55$).

In a second quasi-experimental study, Chetty, Looney, and Kroft (2009) make use of tax differences across US states and over time to estimate the separate effects of two taxes on beer consumption: excise taxes and sales taxes. A key difference between these two taxes is that excise taxes are included in posted prices for beer, whereas sales taxes are only added later at the point of purchase. Inattentive consumers would therefore be more responsive to changes in excise taxes (that change posted prices) than to changes in sales taxes (that do not impact posted prices). Of course, both taxes equally impact the total cost of beer. The evidence is consistent with the inattention hypothesis, implying an attention estimate of $\alpha = 0.06$. Beer consumers pay even less attention to sales taxes than the supermarket shoppers in the field experiment above. But given that the average alcohol sales tax rate in the US (4.3%) is less than the supermarket sales tax rate (7.375%), it is unsurprising that attention is higher when the magnitude of the opaque tax is larger. If alcohol were subject to higher sales taxes, beer consumers would likely be more attentive.

The magnitude of sales taxes is not the only factor that influences consumer attention. For instance, Goldin and Homonoff (2013) find that low-income cigarette consumers are more attentive to sales taxes levied at the register than high-income consumers. Understanding the connection between income and attention to taxes is relevant for the design of optimal tax policy.

20.2.3   *Inattention to Non-Leading Digits*   [Household]

Retail prices often end in nines. It is not uncommon to see fast food french fries priced at $1.39, a burger at $6.99, a pair of shoes at $29.99, and a home at $349,999. What can explain the prevalence of such pricing? While "pricing in nines" can be consistent with standard models of decision making (Basu 1997, 2006), it might also reflect sellers' beliefs that consumers have a **left-digit bias**. That is, consumers may be fully attentive to the left-most leading digit in a multi-digit number, but at least somewhat inattentive to the other non-leading digits. In this case, a $6.99 burger will be perceived as much cheaper than a $7.00 burger. By charging $6.99 instead of $7.00, the seller can therefore increase sales without any material reduction in the price. This intuition is developed further in Exercise 20.6.

The left-digit bias need not be restricted to prices. Lacetera, Pope, and Sydnor (2012) explore buyers' left digit bias when evaluating the mileage of used cars sold at auction. Mileage information is freely available to potential used car buyers and is an important factor in evaluating a car's value. The standard model predicts that consumers would be fully attentive to every digit in a car's odometer reading. Buying a car is, after all, a significant financial decision.

Consider the following model of left-digit bias for inattentive car buyers. We begin by writing mileage $m < 100,000$ as the sum of two components: $m = l \times 10,000 + r$, where $l \in \{0, 1, \ldots, 9\}$ is the leading left-hand digit and r is the remainder. For instance, if $m = 24,768$, then $l = 2$ and $r = 4,768$. A consumer who is inattentive to non-leading digits instead perceives actual mileage m as $\hat{m}$, where:

$$\hat{m} = l \times 10,000 + \alpha r \tag{20.5}$$

Such a consumer therefore perceives an odometer reading of $m = 24,768$ as $\hat{m} = 20,000 + 4,768\alpha$. If attention is less than full, then $\alpha < 1$ and $\hat{m} < m$; perceived mileage is less than actual mileage.

Suppose that the true value of a car with mileage m is $V = c - dm$, where c is the value of the car if it were new with zero mileage, and d is the rate at which the car value depreciates with each additional mile. An inattentive consumer, who misperceives the mileage as $\hat{m}$, therefore perceives the car's value to be:

$$\hat{V} = c - d\hat{m} = c - d(l \times 10,000) - \alpha dr \tag{20.6}$$

where the second equality follows from equation (20.5). Within the framework of Definition 20.1, the visible component of $\hat{V}$ accounts for depreciation only at each 10,000-

mile increment: $v = c - d(l \times 10,000)$. The opaque component is the additional depreciation for each mile that increases the remainder r between 10,000-mile increments: $o = -dr$.

Figure 20.2 plots both V and $\hat{V}$ as functions of actual mileage m. The true car value V is a straight line with slope $-d$, as each additional mile reduces the car's value by d. But perceived value $\hat{V}$ takes the form of downward-sloping steps. From equation (20.6) we can measure both the slope of, and drop between, each step.

- *Slope of each step:* Each step has slope $-\alpha d$ because only α share of each additional mile is perceived by the buyer. This slope corresponds mathematically to the coefficient on the remainder mileage r in equation (20.6). In the extreme case with zero attention to remainder mileage, $\alpha = 0$ and the steps would no longer be sloping, but flat. A car with 20,000 miles and another with 29,999 miles would both be perceived as having the same mileage.

- *Drop between each step:* At each 10,000-mile interval, $\hat{V}$ drops by $d(1 - \alpha)10,000$. To see why, consider the change in $\hat{V}$ between 49,999 and 50,000 miles:

$$\hat{V}(50,000) = c - d(50,000)$$

$$\hat{V}(49,999) = c - d(40,000) - \alpha d(9,999)$$

$$\Rightarrow \hat{V}(50,000) - \hat{V}(49,999) = -d(10,000) + \alpha d(9,999)$$

$$\approx -d(10,000) + \alpha d(10,000)$$

$$= -d(1 - \alpha)10,000$$

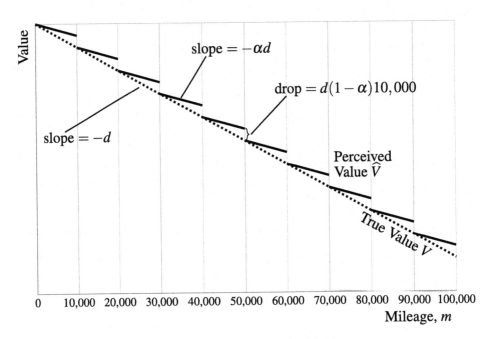

Figure 20.2 Predicted Used Car Value by Mileage with Left-Digit Bias

Intuitively, when an additional mile changes the leading digit, the inattentive consumer becomes fully attentive to the car's true mileage: $\hat{V} = V$ at the 10,000-mile intervals. This requires the consumer to mentally depreciate the $1 - \alpha$ share of the last 10,000 miles that was not previously attended to, leading to a big drop.

To test the theoretical prediction of left-digit bias, Lacetera, Pope, and Sydnor (2012) collect data from over 22 million cars sold at auction from 2002 to 2008. The observed auction sales prices reflect the buyers' perceived valuations. To visualize the empirical relationship between perceived value and mileage, the authors group cars into 500-mile bins, so that cars with 0–499 miles are in the same bin, cars with 500–999 miles are in the same bin, and so on. For each bin they then calculate the average *residual* sales price, i.e., the sales price after removing the effects of make, model, model year, and body of each car. Each point in Figure 20.3 represents one 500-mile bin. The empirical data follow almost exactly the pattern modeled in Figure 20.2. Prices decline with greater mileage, but drop discontinuously at every 10,000-mile interval up to 100,000 miles. Of course, actual car depreciation is continuous. But buyers perceive cars to suddenly become much less valuable each time the first digit in the odometer reading increases. The evidence clearly reveals buyer inattention to non-leading odometer digits.

Let's apply the model to estimate the magnitude of buyer attention in the used car market. In particular, the ratio of the drop at each 10,000-mile interval to the true

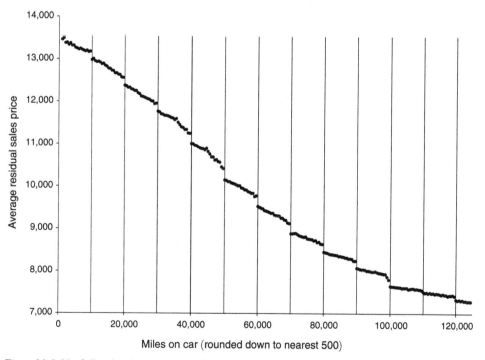

Figure 20.3 Used Car Auction Price Residuals and Mileage

Source: Lacetera, Pope, and Sydnor (2012). Copyright American Economic Association; reproduced with permission of the *American Economic Review*.

depreciation rate is:

$$\frac{\text{Drop Between Steps}}{\text{True Depreciation Rate}} = \frac{d(1-\alpha)10,000}{d} = (1-\alpha)10,000 \tag{20.7}$$

Lacetera, Pope, and Sydnor (2012) estimate an average drop of \$165 at 10,000-mile intervals and a true depreciation rate of 0.0535. Plugging these values into equation (20.7), we obtain:

$$\frac{165}{0.0535} = (1-\alpha)10,000$$

$$\Rightarrow 1 - \alpha = \frac{165/0.0535}{10,000} \approx 0.31$$

$$\Rightarrow \alpha \approx 0.69$$

This relatively high level of attention — although still less than full — is likely due to the high-stakes nature of buying a car. But the attention estimate obscures differences based on car age and consumer characteristics. For instance, Busse et al. (2013) find that attention is greater for newer more expensive cars and lower for lower-income buyers in the retail used car market. Outside of the car market, Strulov-Shlain (2019) examines retail scanner data across thousands of products and finds evidence of a left-digit bias in prices, with an attention parameter of $\alpha = 0.74$. Together, these studies suggest that the magnitude of attention to non-leading digits is relatively stable across different market settings.

20.2.4   Inattention in Finance   *[Finance]*

A striking illustration of inattention in finance emerges from examining news announcements about the small biotechnology company EntreMed (Huberman and Regev 2001). Figure 20.4 plots the price (and trading volume) of EntreMed stock over a 15-month period. The circumstances of the three key dates labeled in the figure are as follows.

- November 28, 1997: On the previous day, the scientific journal *Nature* published an article about a major breakthrough in EntreMed's efforts to commercialize a possible cancer-curing process. On that same day, *The New York Times* reported on the *Nature* article, publishing their article on page A28, i.e., on the 28th page of the first section. This is not a particularly salient page of the newspaper. Similar news was also reported by CNN and CNBC. In response, the stock price jumps by 28% on November 28.
- May 4, 1998: On the previous day, the *The New York Times* published another article about EntreMed's process with no new information relative to what had been reported five months earlier. But this article was placed in the top left corner of the front page of the Sunday edition, a very salient position. Despite no new information, the stock price jumps 330% over the weekend. In addition, all biotech companies experience a 7.5% one-day return. The EntreMed stock price comes down after the spike, but remains elevated relative to its level prior to the May 3rd *Times* article.
- November 12, 1998: A front-page article in *The Wall Street Journal* announces that other labs cannot replicate the results as previously reported. The stock price drops by 24%. But its closing price is still double what it was just before the May 3rd *Times* article.

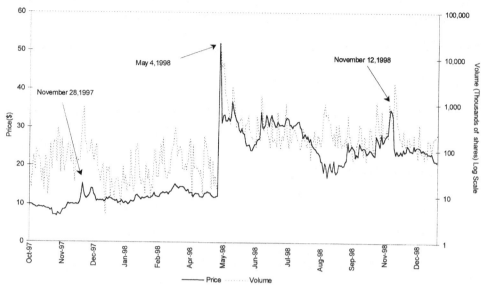

Figure 20.4 EntreMed Prices and Trading Volume

Source: Reprinted from Gur Huberman and Tomer Regev. 2001. "Contagious Speculation and a Cure for Cancer: A Nonevent that Made Stock Prices Soar." *The Journal of Finance* 56, (1): 387–396. Copyright ©2001 The American Finance Association, with permission from John Wiley and Sons.

The case of EntreMed suggests that many investors are not paying full attention to all available information. If they were, the stock price would respond quickly to new information as investors make buying and selling decisions based on what they have learned. Instead, the EntreMed stock price is more responsive to the information's salience than its availability. Related evidence comes from the positioning of news on the Bloomberg terminal, a primary source of information for professional investors. Fedyk (2018) finds that salient news on the front page impacts stock prices quickly (within a few minutes), while prices adjust slowly (over days and sometimes weeks) to non-front-page news.

Quarterly earnings reports are an important source of financial news. These reports provide investors with information about a company's value, and therefore impact stock market prices. If investors are inattentive to earnings announcements, they will only partially process the new information upon its release. Stock prices will therefore adjust based on this partial attention. Over time, as the information becomes more salient to investors, through media reports or other channels, stock prices will fully adjust to reflect all of the information released in the prior quarterly report. The inattention framework is applied to this context in Exercise 20.7.

An implication of the preceding logic is that with greater inattention, prices will adjust to earnings news more slowly. One possible source of inattention is the weekend. Investors are likely to be more distracted on Fridays when they are thinking about weekend activities and therefore less attentive to news. Consistent with the inattention hypothesis, DellaVigna and Pollet (2009) find that the immediate impact on prices is lower when companies release their earnings news on Fridays. Inattention is also likely to be greater on days when more companies are releasing earnings news. It is more difficult to pay attention to 20 new reports than five. Indeed, the immediate responsiveness of stock prices to news is lower on days with more announcements (Hirshleifer, Lim, and Teoh 2009). Once again the evidence points to investor inattention.

The decision for an individual investor about which stocks to buy — among thousands of options — is similarly plagued by information overload. Instead of systematically processing all available information in order to make a buying decision, investors may choose to buy stocks that have caught their attention (Odean 1999). Stocks could be *attention-grabbing* for a variety of reasons: recent media coverage, abnormally high trading volume, or extreme returns (high or low) in the past day. But such attention-grabbing characteristics are likely to matter less for an investor's decision about which stocks to sell. The selling decision is simpler because an individual only has to be attentive to the handful of stocks they already own. Barber and Odean (2008) confirm that individual investors are more likely to be buyers of attention-grabbing stocks than sellers. In sum, limited attention matters for understanding investor behavior and asset price movements.

20.3   Persuasion

We regularly encounter information about products, assets, and politicians. We might learn, for instance, that car X gets 40 miles per gallon of gas, mutual fund Y earned a 7% return last year, and senator Z voted for gun control legislation. But not all information is simply an observable fact of the matter. Many economic and political decisions are instead shaped by information that is provided by people who have an interest in the outcome. Companies and political parties use a variety a marketing and advertising strategies to convince others to act in ways that increase their own profits or political power.

Define **persuasion** as a message — in words or images — that attempts to convince others to take a particular action. This definition excludes attempts to influence others with money, threats, or physical force. Think of persuasion as a billboard, not a bill or a bully. And while persuasion is less direct than monetary incentives or coercion, it is more direct than social pressure. With social pressure an individual is influenced to take an action, not because of someone's message, but simply because that someone is present (Section 14.5). For instance, a persuasive message is your friends encouraging you to vote, while social pressure can arise when your friends simply observe your voting behavior.

To be influenced by a persuasive message is not necessarily bad or irrational. In fact, within the standard model of decision making, persuasion cannot make people worse off. Persuasive messages increase the supply of information, leading to better-informed decisions and higher welfare. This logic, however, assumes that individuals take into account the quality of the information and the incentives of those who are sending the messages. If instead individuals are inattentive to, or neglect, such features, they will tend to be overly influenced by messages (e.g., Eyster and Rabin 2010; DeMarzo, Vayanos, and Zwiebel 2003).

Consider, for example, the role of a message sender's credibility. If I were to write equally glowing letters of recommendation for every student that applies to graduate school, admissions committees should discount the value of my messages. I would not be a very credible source for communicating differences in student preparedness and potential. They should value a strong letter more if it were rare for me to write one. But if an admissions committee gives similar weight to a strong letter from me in both cases, they are insufficiently adjusting for the credibility of my recommendation.

The remainder of this section documents evidence that persuasion influences investing and voting behaviors. Moreover, the evidence reveals that people can be excessively influenced, neglecting the incentives of persuaders. I omit the effects of persuasion on consumer purchases (for which the evidence is mixed) and on charitable donations (a topic of Part V).[2]

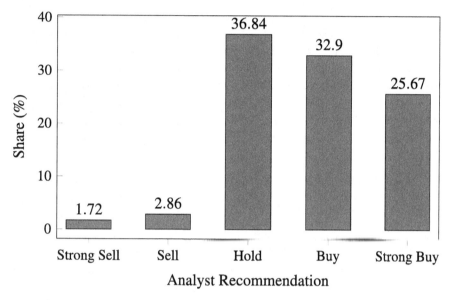

Figure 20.5 Distribution of Analyst Recommendations

Data Source: Malmendier and Shanthikumar (2007).

20.3.1   *Persuading Investors*   *[Finance]*

It is challenging for investors to fully attend to the massive flow of available financial data. To help guide investors, analysts specialize in covering a handful of stocks within an industry. They communicate their analyses to investors, who can make use of this summary information in their own investment decisions. Analysts therefore serve as an information intermediary between the companies that release data and the investors that consume it.

One part of an analyst's communication is advice to buy or sell. In particular, an analyst will make one of the following recommendations for a traded stock: strong buy, buy, hold, sell, or strong sell. But there is a significant upward bias in these recommendations. As pictured in Figure 20.5, only 4.6% of recommendations are in the sell or strong sell categories (Malmendier and Shanthikumar 2007). Analyst recommendations are far too enthusiastic about future profitability to be credibly taken at face value. This upward bias is even more pronounced for affiliated analysts, i.e., those who are employed at a bank that has a relationship with the companies they cover. Affiliated analysts have a conflict of interest given that they are in a position to benefit financially from recommending a stock for which they are supposed to be an impartial judge. This conflict of interest provides a plausible motivation for the relatively larger upward bias.

Malmendier and Shanthikumar (2007) document how large and small investors, as determined by the size of their trades, respond to analyst recommendations. Large investors account for analysts' upward bias by discounting the recommendation. That is, they respond to a buy recommendation by holding the stock. And they respond to a hold recommendation by selling. So while large investors make use of *relative* information to inform their trading decisions, they do not take the recommendations literally. In addition, they do not respond to buy and strong buy recommendations from affiliated analysts. They apparently understand that affiliated analysts have a conflict of interest, and as a result neglect their advice. These behaviors are consistent with a sophisticated response to persuasive messaging, as predicted by the standard model.

In contrast, small investors follow analyst recommendations literally. If analysts recommend a buy, they buy. They also exhibit no differential response based on analyst affiliation. Together, these observations suggest that small investors are excessively influenced by persuasion, failing to account for analyst credibility and conflicts of interest. Franco, Lu, and Vasvari (2007) confirm similar results in a related analysis.

20.3.2 *Persuading Voters*   *[Politics & Law]*

Persuasion is big business in the arena of politics. In the lead up to an election, voters often receive persuasive messages from individual campaigns, get-out-the-vote groups, and the news media. Are such messages effective at changing behavior? Kalla and Broockman (2018) review evidence from 49 field experiments and estimate *zero* effect of persuasive campaign messages — via mail, phone calls, or canvassing — on Americans' candidate choices in general elections. But there are contexts in which campaigns matter. For instance, in less partisan settings, like elections for ballot measures or primary candidates, campaign messaging can have meaningful effects. And get-out-the-vote messages are effective at increasing turnout (Gerber and Green 2000, 2017). These findings provide insight into why campaigns increasingly focus on mobilizing their current supporters to vote, rather than trying to persuade undecided or swing voters (Panagopoulos 2016).

If campaigns are not persuading voters, perhaps the news media is. Identifying the causal impact of television reporting on voting behavior is difficult. It would be unsurprising to find that the political orientation of TV news messages are correlated with the voting behaviors of its viewers. This correlation could arise because conservative news persuades its viewers to vote for conservative candidates. Or there could be zero persuasive effect and conservative voters just choose to watch TV messages that align with their views. The following quasi-experiment cleverly addresses this identification problem.

Quasi-Experiment — The Fox News Effect (DellaVigna and Kaplan 2007)

Fox News, a conservative cable news channel relative to other US networks (Groseclose and Milyo 2005), was introduced in October 1996. While some cable systems added Fox News right away, others did not. Towns with and without access to Fox News between 1996 and 2000 shared similar demographics and voting histories (conditional on a set of control variables). Therefore, access to Fox News prior to the 2000 presidential election was largely determined at random, creating two groups:

1 Control Towns: No access to Fox News.
2 Treatment Towns: Access to Fox News.

Any differences in voting behavior between the control and treatment towns can be plausibly attributed to the availability of Fox News.

DellaVigna and Kaplan (2007) find that the Republican (conservative party) vote share in the 2000 presidential race was 0.5 percentage points higher in treatment towns relative to control towns. This effect implies that Fox News persuaded up to 30% of its non-Republican audience to vote Republican.

The above evidence reveals that the news media can persuade voters. But is being persuaded by Fox News consistent with the standard model? While the answer may be yes in the short run, it is likely no in the longer run (DellaVigna and Kaplan 2006). Consider a viewer who watches Fox News for the first time in the late 1990s. A Fox News endorsement for the Republican candidate George Bush is new information that leads her to update beliefs in favor of Bush. This is a reasonable response. But if after continued viewing she sees that Fox News reports favorably on every Republican and critically on every Democrat, she should update her beliefs once again to account for the channel's conservative bias. A Fox News endorsement for Bush should be discounted relative to a Bush endorsement from a source that is not exclusively pro-Republican. Those who fail to account for the credibility of the news source will be excessively persuaded relative to the predictions of the standard model.

Evidence for the persuasive effects of TV extends beyond the US. During the 1999 Russian parliamentary elections only one national TV station was independent. All other major networks supported the government party. The signal availability of independent TV across the country was incomplete and largely random. Enikolopov, Petrova, and Zhuravskaya (2011) leverage this randomness as a quasi-experiment and estimate that independent TV decreased the aggregate vote for the government party by 8.9 percentage points, while increasing the vote for opposition parties by 6.3 percentage points. Similarly, Barone, D'Acunto, and Narciso (2015) find that the introduction of digital TV channels in Italy — which unlike state TV, were not slanted towards Prime Minister Silvio Berlusconi — reduced the vote share of Berlusconi's coalition by 5.5–7.5 percentage points. This is a sizable effect given Berlusconi's overall vote share of 52% at the time. The researchers conclude that voters underestimate media slant. Because news media has the power to shape voting, incumbent governments have an incentive to consolidate and shape the news in their favor. The next chapter explores ways in which governments use information and propaganda to shape national outcomes.

20.4   Summary

1   The standard model of decision making assumes that individuals pay attention to all available information. It can be in an individual's best interest to ignore information that is costly to acquire or process.

2   An **inattentive consumer** is modeled as being fully attentive to *visible* information, but only partially attentive to *opaque* information.

3   Attention tends to be greater when the opaque information is relatively larger.

4   In auction settings bidders are inattentive to shipping costs and fixed prices, which can explain the phenomenon of overbidding, i.e., the **bidder's curse**.

5   Consumers are inattentive to sales taxes that are applied at the point of purchase.

6   Inattention to non-leading digits generates a **left-digit bias**, which is documented in the used car market.

7   Investors respond quickly to salient or attention-grabbing information, but react with a delay to less salient publicly available information.

8   **Persuasion** is a message — in words or images — that attempts to convince others to take a particular action.

9   If individuals neglect the incentives of those intending to persuade, they will tend to be excessively influenced by persuasive messages. Supporting evidence for this hypothesis comes from financial analysts persuading small investors and the media persuading voters.

20.5   Exercises[3]

Exercise 20.1 — Measuring Opaqueness. Recall the Shipping Costs Field Experiment. The evidence implies an attention parameter of $\alpha \approx 0.55$. Define the relative magnitude of the opaque shipping cost as the ratio of i) the average shipping cost across the two auction pricing schemes (with and without shipping costs) to ii) the visible component v implied by equation (20.2). Compute this relative magnitude. Can you identify the point corresponding to this field experiment in Figure 20.1?

Exercise 20.2 — More Shipping Costs. [Household] Hossain and Morgan (2006) conduct a second eBay CD auction experiment, similar to the Shipping Costs Field Experiment. In it, the two pricing schemes are:

1   Low Shipping Cost: $2 shipping and $6 minimum bid.
2   High Shipping Cost: $6 shipping and $2 minimum bid.

a   If bidders are fully attentive to shipping costs, how should the average seller revenue compare across these two treatments? Explain.

b   Hossain and Morgan (2006) find that average seller revenue is $12.15 with low shipping costs and $12.87 with high shipping costs. Estimate the magnitude of attention α implied by these data.

c   How does your answer in part (b) compare to the attention estimate of 0.55 for the first field experiment? Provide intuition for the difference in attention.

Exercise 20.3 — Degrees of Tax Attention. [Public Finance] Taubinsky and Rees-Jones (2018) estimate consumer attention to sales taxes in an online shopping experiment.

When sales taxes are 7.3%, the implied attention parameter is $\alpha = 0.25$. When sales taxes are tripled to 22%, do you expect attention to be larger or smaller? Explain.

Exercise 20.4 — Attention Takes a Toll. [Public Finance] Some toll roads in the US have electronic toll collection (ETC) systems that automatically charge tolls as a car drives through the toll plaza, as opposed to exchanging cash in person.

a Do you expect drivers to be more attentive to tolls paid electronically or with cash?
b Finkelstein (2009) estimates that toll rates are higher with ETC than they would have been with a fully manual cash toll system. In light of your answer in part (a), propose an explanation for why politicians would set higher tolls with ETC systems than cash tolls.
c What does your answer in part (b) suggest more generally about the connection between inattention and the size of government?

Exercise 20.5 — Modeling Tax Attention (Chetty, Looney, and Kroft 2009). Consider the following model for a local beer market. Market demand D and market supply S for six-packs of beer are: $D(P) = 1200-50P$ and $S(P) = 100P$, where P is the price of a six-pack.

a Determine the price P^* that equates demand and supply. What is the total market quantity Q^* that is supplied at price P^*?
b Suppose that a tax of $1 is imposed on each six-pack of beer that is purchased. If sellers receive price P, then the price paid by consumers is now $P + 1$. Therefore, market demand is.

$$D(P + 1) = 1200 - 50(P + 1)$$

Determine the price that equates demand with supply. This is the new seller price P^S. Determine the new buyer price $P^B = P^S + 1$. And determine the new market quantity $Q^{**} = S(P^S)$.
c Now assume that consumers are partially inattentive to the tax in part (b), with attention parameter $\alpha = 0.2$. That is, if the seller receives price P, the consumers pay $P + 1$, but only perceive their price to be $P + \alpha \times 1 = P + 0.2$. As a result, market demand is now

$$D(P + 0.2) = 1200 - 50(P + 0.2)$$

Repeat the analysis in part (b) with this new demand.
d Use your answers in parts (b) and (c) to discuss how inattention to taxes impacts the market effects of taxation.

Exercise 20.6 — Pricing to the Nines. The sale price p of a good can be written as the sum of d dollars and c cents, so that $p = d + 0.01c$ where $c \in \{0, 1, \ldots, 99\}$. For instance, if $p = 4.39$, then $d = 4$ and $c = 39$. Assume that buyers are fully attentive to the dollars, but inattentive to the cents. That is, buyers perceive the price to be $\hat{p} = d + 0.01\alpha c$ where α is the attention parameter.

a Plot the perceived price $\hat{p}$ as a function of the true price p, for $p \in [0, 5]$ and $\alpha = 0$.

b   Suppose that consumers will buy the good as long as the perceived price $\hat{p}$ is no higher than \$3.80. And assume that the seller wants to set the highest price such that consumers actually buy the good. If $\alpha = 0$, what price would the seller set? What if consumers only buy when $\hat{p} \leq \$3.20$? Do your answers match the real-world pricing you typically see?

c   Repeat parts (a) and (b) in a case with intermediate attention to cents: $\alpha = 0.5$.

Exercise 20.7 — Gradual News. [Finance] This exercise applies the inattention framework to understand the impact of quarterly earnings news on asset prices. Let v denote the known information about expected cash flows of a company and o denote the new information about expected cash flows contained in the earnings announcement. Assume that the true company value is equal to its expected cash flows and that:

*   On the day before the announcement, the company price is $P = v$.
*   The short-run company price (2 days after the announcement) is $P_{SR} = v + \alpha o$.
*   The long-run company price (75 days after the announcement) is $P_{LR} = v + o$.

a   According to this model, how does the earnings announcement impact the company price in the short run and in the long run? Provide intuition for your answers, along with an interpretation of what α represents.

b   DellaVigna and Pollet (2009) apply this model to data on US quarterly earnings announcements between 1984 and 2006. They estimate the stock price returns, r, following earnings announcements in the short run (r_{SR}) and long run (r_{LR}):

$$r_{SR} = \frac{P_{SR} - P}{P} = 6.59\% \qquad r_{LR} = \frac{P_{LR} - P}{P} = 12.18\%$$

Use these returns and the above model to estimate α.

c   When restricting the analysis to earnings announcements that occur on Fridays, DellaVigna and Pollet (2009) estimate $\alpha = 0.41$. How does this attention estimate compare to the estimate in part (b)? Given this observation, when would companies want to release bad earnings news?

Exercise 20.8 — News on the Links. [Finance] Consider the following example from Cohen and Frazzini (2008, 1978–79):

In 2001, Coastcast Corporation was a leading manufacturer of golf club heads. Since 1993 Coastcast's major customer had been Callaway Golf Corporation, a retail company that specialized in golf equipment ... In a press release on June 8 Callaway lowered second-quarter revenue projections to \$250 million, down from a previous projection of \$300 million ... By market close on June 8, Callaway shares were down by \$6.23 to close at \$15.03, a 30% drop since June 6 ... [T]he negative news in early June about Callaway's future earnings did not impact Coastcast's share price at all ... Ultimately ... on July 19 [Coastcast] ... experienced negative returns over the subsequent 2 months.

Explain what about this scenario is surprising for the standard model of decision making. Provide an interpretation of investor behavior that could explain this otherwise puzzling example.

Exercise 20.9 — Media Markets. [Finance] Consider the following two empirical findings:

1 Stock recommendations on the popular TV show *Mad Money*, hosted by Jim Cramer, lead to large overnight returns. These returns are largest when viewership is high (Engelberg, Sasseville, and Williams 2011).
2 Local media coverage of a stock's public earnings announcement increases trading of that stock by local investors (Engelberg and Parsons 2011).

Discuss what this evidence reveals about investor decision-making.

Exercise 20.10 — Ranks Rule. [Education] *US News and World Report* rates colleges with a quality score from 0 to 100. These scores are then used to rank colleges. A school with the same score in two consecutive years can shift ranks as the scores of other colleges change. Pope (2006) finds that, holding constant the quality score, improvements in rank decrease the acceptance rate and increase standardized test scores of incoming students. What does this evidence suggest about student attention?

Exercise 20.11 — Paying a Premium. [Health] A health insurance policy typically charges two types of prices: the premium that is paid regardless of health status, and out-of-pocket costs that are paid upon receiving health care services (see Section 18.4). According to the standard model of decision making, a $1 increase in the health insurance premium is equivalent to a $1 increase in expected out-of-pocket costs. But Abaluck and Gruber (2011) find that Medicare recipients are much less likely to choose a prescription drug plan if the premium is increased by $1 than if expected out-of-pocket costs are increased by $1. Based on this evidence, which price is likely more salient to consumers? Explain why this would be the case.

Exercise 20.12 — Disclosure Deficiency. Cain, Loewenstein, and Moore (2005) conduct a lab experiment with a group of undergraduate students, each of whom is randomly assigned a role as an estimator or an advisor. The estimation task was to estimate the value of coins in a jar. Estimators were paid for the accuracy of their estimate. But estimators saw the jar from a distance of 3 feet and only for about 10 seconds. To help with their estimation, they relied on advice from students acting as advisors who were allowed to closely examine the jar. Advisors were randomized into two payment schemes as follows:

1 Accurate Treatment: Advisor paid for estimator's estimate being accurate.
2 High Treatment: Advisor paid for estimator's estimate being high.

Estimators were made aware of how their advisor was being paid.

a Suppose that estimators fully account for the incentives of their advisor when forming their estimate. In this case, would you expect the average estimates to be similar or different across the two treatments? Explain.
b Estimates in the high treatment are 28% higher than those in the accurate treatment. What does this evidence suggest about the effectiveness of persuasion?

Exercise 20.13 — Surprise Endorsements. [Politics & Law] Newspapers endorse candidates for election. While some newspapers are politically neutral, others lean towards one end of the political spectrum, almost always endorsing candidates from a single party.

a   Suppose that voters account for the credibility of newspaper endorsements. In this case, should an endorsement for a Democratic candidate be more influential on voter views if it comes from a left-leaning newspaper or a right-leaning newspaper? Explain. *Note: Democrats are the major left-leaning party in the US.*

b   Chiang and Knight (2011) find that newspaper endorsements have a large effect on voter attitudes only when the endorsement is a departure from the usual political orientation of the newspaper. Is this evidence consistent with your prediction in part (a)? Interpret.

Exercise 20.14 — Papal Persuasion. [Health] Pope John Paul II visited Brazil in October 1991. Papal speeches during this visit condemned contraception and highlighted the importance of marriage and procreation. These persuasive messages were consistent with mainstream Catholic doctrine and therefore not new information. Bassi and Rasul (2017) estimate that the Papal visit i) reduced intentions to use contraception by more than 40%; ii) increased the frequency of unprotected sex by 30%; and iii) increased births 9 months later by 1.6%. Do you find this evidence surprising? Why or why not? What does it suggest about how information influences behavior?

Notes

1 To derive equation 20.4, we first write the difference in demands as the slope of the demand function, D', multiplied by the corresponding difference in values:

$$
\begin{aligned}
D^{\text{Salient}} - D^{\text{Opaque}} &= D' \times (v - tp - (v - \alpha tp)) \\
&= D' \times (1 - \alpha) \times (-tp) \\
&= (1 - \alpha) \times t \times \left[\frac{-pD'}{\text{Average Demand}} \right] \times \text{Average Demand}
\end{aligned}
$$

Define elasticity $E = \frac{-pD'}{\text{Average Demand}}$ and divide both sides of the above expression by Average Demand to complete the derivation.

2 DellaVigna and Gentzkow (2010) provide an excellent overview of the empirical evidence for persuasion.

3 Exercise 20.6 is adapted from an exercise by Stefano DellaVigna.

References

Abaluck, Jason, and Jonathan Gruber. 2011. "Heterogeneity in Choice Inconsistencies among the Elderly: Evidence from Prescription Drug Plan Choice." *American Economic Review* 101 (3): 377–381. doi:10.1257/aer.101.3.377.

Barber, Brad M., and Terrance Odean. 2008. "All that Glitters: The Effect of Attention and News on the Buying Behavior of Individual and Institutional Investors." *The Review of Financial Studies* 21 (2): 785–818. doi:10.1093/rfs/hhm079.

Barone, Guglielmo, Francesco D'Acunto, and Gaia Narciso. 2015. "Telecracy: Testing for Channels of Persuasion." *American Economic Journal: Economic Policy* 7 (2): 30–60. doi:10.1257/pol.20130318.

Bassi, Vittorio, and Imran Rasul. 2017. "Persuasion: A Case Study of Papal Influences on Fertility-Related Beliefs and Behavior." *American Economic Journal: Applied Economics* 9 (4): 250–302. doi:10.1257/app.20150540.

Basu, Kaushik. 1997. "Why Are so Many Goods Priced to End in Nine? And Why this Practice Hurts the Producers." *Economics Letters* 54 (1): 41–44. doi:10.1016/S0165-1765(97)00009-8.

———. 2006. "Consumer Cognition and Pricing in the Nines in Oligopolistic Markets." *Journal of Economics & Management Strategy* 15 (1): 125–141. doi:10.1111/j.1530-9134.2006.00094.x.

Busse, Meghan R., Nicola Lacetera, Devin G. Pope, Jorge Silva-Risso, and Justin R. Sydnor. 2013. "Estimating the Effect of Salience in Wholesale and Retail Car Markets." *American Economic Review* 103 (3): 575–579. doi:10.1257/aer.103.3.575.

Cain, Daylian M., George Loewenstein, and Don A. Moore. 2005. "The Dirt on Coming Clean: Perverse Effects of Disclosing Conflicts of Interest." *The Journal of Legal Studies* 34 (1): 1–25. doi:10.1086/426699.

Caplin, Andrew, and Mark Dean. 2015. "Revealed Preference, Rational Inattention, and Costly Information Acquisition." *American Economic Review* 105 (7): 2183–2203. doi:10.1257/aer.20140117.

Chetty, Raj, Adam Looney, and Kory Kroft. 2009. "Salience and Taxation: Theory and Evidence." *American Economic Review* 99 (4): 1145–1177. doi:10.1257/aer.99.4.1145.

Chiang, Chun-Fang, and Brian Knight. 2011. "Media Bias and Influence: Evidence from Newspaper Endorsements." *The Review of Economic Studies* 78 (3): 795–820. doi:10.1093/restud/rdq037.

Cohen, Lauren, and Andrea Frazzini. 2008. "Economic Links and Predictable Returns." *The Journal of Finance* 63 (4): 1977–2011. © 2008 The American Finance Association, doi:10.1111/j.1540-6261.2008.01379.x

DellaVigna, Stefano. 2009. "Psychology and Economics: Evidence from the Field." *Journal of Economic Literature* 47 (2): 315–372. doi:10.1257/jel.47.2.315.

DellaVigna, Stefano, and Matthew Gentzkow. 2010. "Persuasion: Empirical Evidence." *Annual Review of Economics* 2 (1): 643–669. doi:10.1146/annurev.economics. 102308.124309.

DellaVigna, Stefano, and Ethan Kaplan. 2006. "The Fox News Effect: Media Bias and Voting." NBER Working Paper 12169. Cambridge, MA: National Bureau of Economic Research. doi:10.3386/w12169.

———. 2007. "The Fox News Effect: Media Bias and Voting." *The Quarterly Journal of Economics* 122 (3): 1187–1234, doi:10.1162/qjec.122.3.1187.

DellaVigna, Stefano, and Joshua M. Pollet. 2009. "Investor Inattention and Friday Earnings Announcements." *The Journal of Finance* 64 (2): 709–749. doi:10.1111/j.1540-6261.2009.01447.x.

DeMarzo, Peter M., Dimitri Vayanos, and Jeffrey Zwiebel. 2003. "Persuasion Bias, Social Influence, and Unidimensional Opinions." *The Quarterly Journal of Economics* 118 (3): 909–968. doi:10.1162/00335530360698469.

Engelberg, Joseph E., and Christopher A. Parsons. 2011. "The Causal Impact of Media in Financial Markets." *The Journal of Finance* 66 (1): 67–97. doi:10.1111/j.1540-6261.2010.01626.x.

Engelberg, Joseph, Caroline Sasseville, and Jared Williams. 2011. "Market Madness? The Case of Mad Money." *Management Science* 58 (2): 351–364. doi:10.1287/mnsc.1100.1290.

Enikolopov, Ruben, Maria Petrova, and Ekaterina Zhuravskaya. 2011. "Media and Political Persuasion: Evidence from Russia." *American Economic Review* 101 (7): 3253–3285. doi:10.1257/aer.101.7.3253.

Eyster, Erik, and Matthew Rabin. 2010. "Naïve Herding in Rich-Information Settings." *American Economic Journal: Microeconomics* 2 (4): 221–243. doi:10.1257/mic.2.4.221.

Fedyk, Anastassia. 2018. "Front Page News: The Effect of News Positioning on Financial Markets." Unpublished.

Finkelstein, Amy. 2009. "E-ztax: Tax Salience and Tax Rates." *The Quarterly Journal of Economics* 124 (3): 969–1010. doi:10.1162/qjec.2009.124.3.969.

Franco, Gus De, Hai Lu, and Florin P. Vasvari. 2007. "Wealth Transfer Effects of Analysts' Misleading Behavior." *Journal of Accounting Research* 45 (1): 71–110. doi:10.1111/j.1475-679X.2006.00228.x.

Gabaix, Xavier. 2019. "Behavioral Inattention." In *Handbook of Behavioral Economics: Foundations and Applications,* edited by B. Douglas Bernheim, Stefano DellaVigna, and David Laibson, 2:261–343. North-Holland. doi:10.1016/bs.hesbe.2018.11.001.

Gerber, Alan S., and Donald P. Green. 2000. "The Effects of Canvassing, Telephone Calls, and Direct Mail on Voter Turnout: A Field Experiment." *American Political Science Review* 94 (3): 653–663. doi:10.2307/2585837.

———. 2017. "Field Experiments on Voter Mobilization: An Overview of a Burgeoning Literature." In *Handbook of Economic Field Experiments,* edited by Abhijit V. Banerjee and Esther Duflo, 1:395–438. North-Holland. doi:10.1016/bs.hefe.2016.09.002.

Goldin, Jacob, and Tatiana Homonoff. 2013. "Smoke Gets in Your Eyes: Cigarette Tax Salience and Regressivity." *American Economic Journal: Economic Policy* 5 (1): 302–336. doi:10.1257/pol.5.1.302.

Groseclose, Tim, and Jeffrey Milyo. 2005. "A Measure of Media Bias." *The Quarterly Journal of Economics* 120 (4): 1191–1237. doi:10.1162/003355305775097542.

Hirshleifer, David, Sonya Seongyeon Lim, and Siew Hong Teoh. 2009. "Driven to Distraction: Extraneous Events and Underreaction to Earnings News." *The Journal of Finance* 64 (5): 2289–2325. doi:10.1111/j.1540-6261.2009.01501.x.

Hossain, Tanjim, and John Morgan. 2006. "... Plus Shipping and Handling: Revenue (Non) Equivalence in Field Experiments on eBay." *The B.E. Journal of Economic Analysis & Policy* 6 (2). doi:10.2202/1538-0637.1429.

Huberman, Gur, and Tomer Regev. 2001. "Contagious Speculation and a Cure for Cancer: A Nonevent that Made Stock Prices Soar." *The Journal of Finance* 56 (1): 387–396. doi:10.1111/0022-1082.00330.

Kalla, Joshua L., and David E. Broockman. 2018. "The Minimal Persuasive Effects of Campaign Contact in General Elections: Evidence from 49 Field Experiments." *American Political Science Review* 112 (1): 148–166. doi:10.1017/S0003055417000363.

Lacetera, Nicola, Devin G. Pope, and Justin R. Sydnor. 2012. "Heuristic Thinking and Limited Attention in the Car Market." *American Economic Review* 102 (5): 2206–2236. doi:10.1257/aer.102.5.2206.

Malmendier, Ulrike. 2002. *Societas Publicanorum: Staatliche Wirtschaftsaktivitäten in den Händen Privater Unternehmer.* Cologne, Germany: Verlag Böhlau.

Malmendier, Ulrike, and Young Han Lee. 2011. "The Bidder's Curse." *American Economic Review* 101 (2): 749–787. doi:10.1257/aer.101.2.749.

Malmendier, Ulrike, and Devin Shanthikumar. 2007. "Are Small Investors Naive about Incentives?" *Journal of Financial Economics* 85 (2): 457–489. doi:10.1016/j.jfineco.2007.02.001.

Odean, Terrance. 1999. "Do Investors Trade Too Much?" *American Economic Review* 89 (5): 1279–1298. doi:10.1257/aer.89.5.1279.

Panagopoulos, Costas. 2016. "All about that Base: Changing Campaign Strategies in U.S. Presidential Elections." *Party Politics* 22 (2): 179–190. doi:10.1177/1354068815605676.

Pope, Devin G. 2006. "Reacting to Rankings: Evidence from 'America's Best Hospitals and Colleges'." Working Paper. UC Berkeley Economics Department.

Simon, Herbert A. 1971. "Designing Organizations for an Information-Rich World." In *Computers, Communications, and the Public Interest,* edited by Martin Greenberger, 37–52. Baltimore, MD: Johns Hopkins University Press.

Sims, Christopher A. 2003. "Implications of Rational Inattention." *Journal of Monetary Economics,* Swiss National Bank/Study Center Gerzensee Conference on Monetary Policy under Incomplete Information, 50 (3): 665–690. doi:10.1016/S0304-3932(03)00029-1.

Strulov-Shlain, Avner. 2019. "More than a Penny's Worth: Left-Digit Bias and Firm Pricing." SSRN Scholarly Paper ID 3413019. Rochester, NY: Social Science Research Network. doi:10.2139/ssrn.3413019.

Taubinsky, Dmitry, and Alex Rees-Jones. 2018. "Attention Variation and Welfare: Theory and Evidence from a Tax Salience Experiment." *The Review of Economic Studies* 85 (4): 2462–2496. doi:10.1093/restud/rdx069.

21 Market & Policy Responses to Mental Accounting & Inattention

Learning Objectives

★ Understand various selling strategies by firms as profitable responses to the mental accounting and inattention of consumers.

★ Consider how mental accounting and inattention can be leveraged by policy makers to promote welfare.

★ Evaluate the effects of government persuasion on social attitudes and behaviors.

The compelling evidence of mental accounting and inattention in the preceding chapters undermines the standard assumption that individuals maximize utility using all available information. This evidence matters not only for economists. It is relevant for firms seeking to exploit consumer decisions for profit. Policy makers can similarly leverage the insights of mental accounting and inattention to design interventions that promote individual welfare. Such policy interventions, by adjusting the decision environment or clarifying the relevant tradeoffs, have the potential to generate substantial benefits at little cost.

This chapter begins with the implications of mental accounting for selling strategies. In particular, we interpret a variety of otherwise puzzling phenomena — perpetual discounts, sold-out concerts, all-inclusive vacation packages, the marketing of certain goods as gifts — as consistent with firms profitably responding to the mental accounting of customers. Next, we consider the relevance of mental accounting for the design of policies to improve savings rates. In the second half of the chapter we turn to the implications of inattention: first, for the incentives of firms to shroud information from consumers, and second, for policies that nudge attention to promote better-informed decisions. The impacts of nudging interventions for health, education, and income decisions are discussed in turn. The chapter concludes with empirical evidence that reveals the power of a government's persuasive messaging to shape cultural attitudes and individual behaviors.

21.1 Mental Accounting: Selling Strategies [Business]

Let's examine the implications of mental accounting for the incentives and strategies of sellers. See Thaler (1999, 2008) for further development of these insights.

DOI: 10.4324/9780367854072-28

21.1.1   *Transaction Utility*

People love the experience of getting a great deal, like buying a coat on sale, or snagging concert tickets before they sell out and are only available at much higher prices on a secondary market. And yet, standard economic theory ignores the mental accounting of such deals. By taking into account the perceived value of a deal, however, we can make sense of some common consumer behaviors and marketing strategies.

Modeling Transaction Utility

To introduce a preference for a deal, Thaler (2008) proposes that consumers obtain two kinds of utility from a purchase: **acquisition utility** and **transaction utility**. Acquisition utility corresponds to the standard consumer surplus from purchasing a good: the difference between valuation and price. For a good that a consumer values at v, selling at price p, the acquisition utility U_A (from actually acquiring the good) is therefore

$$U_A = v - p$$

Transaction utility U_T instead captures the value of getting a deal: the difference between a *reference price* p^* and the actual price p. That is,

$$U_T = p^* - p$$

The reference price is the price that the consumer expects to pay, which is influenced by their perception of what is fair or just. Total utility can be expressed as the sum of acquisition and transaction utility: $U = U_A + U_T$.

Transaction utility changes the predictions for consumer behavior. Without it, consumers make a purchase as long as $U_A \geq 0$, or equivalently when the value v exceeds the price p. But when consumers also account for the value of the transaction, they make a purchase if $U_A + U_T \geq 0$. As a result, greater transaction utility — from a higher reference price p^* — increases the likelihood of a purchase, without any change in the good's value v or its price p. The following lab experiment illustrates the role of transaction utility in a simple purchase decision.

Lab Experiment — Transaction Utility on the Beach (Thaler 2008)

The following scenario was given to participants in an executive development program who reported themselves to be regular beer drinkers. One subset of the participants received the scenario with the phrases in brackets omitted, while the phrases in parentheses were omitted for the remaining participants.

You are lying on the beach on a hot day. All you have to drink is ice water. For the last hour you have been thinking about how much you would enjoy a nice cold bottle of your favorite brand of beer. A companion gets up to go make a phone call and offers to bring back a beer from the only nearby place where beer is sold (a fancy resort hotel) [a small, run-down grocery store]. He says that the beer might be expensive and so asks how much you are willing to pay for the beer. He says that he will buy the beer if it costs as much or less than the price you state. But if it costs more than the price you state he will not buy it. You trust your friend, and there is no possibility of bargaining with (the bartender) [store owner]. What price do you tell him? (20)

The median reported prices in the fancy resort hotel and small run-down grocery store versions were $2.65 and $1.50 (in 1984 prices), respectively.

The results of this lab experiment are striking. Participants are willing to pay almost double for the beer based only on the characteristics of the seller. In both scenarios the acquisition utility from buying a bottle of beer for $2 would be the same, as the value v of drinking beer on the beach is the same no matter who sells it. The greater willingness to pay for a beer from a fancy resort can be explained with the concept of transaction utility. In particular, participants likely assign a higher reference price p^* to a beer from a fancy resort — perhaps because fancy resorts have higher costs and are therefore justified in charging larger markups — than from a grocery store. As a result, total utility $U_A + U_T$ is higher at the fancy resort, and consumers are willing to pay a higher actual price p. Intuitively, a $2 beer ($5 in 2020 dollars) may be an annoyance at a resort, but an unacceptable rip-off at a grocery store.

Increasing Reference Prices

The introduction of transaction utility to the decision making of consumers generates a clear incentive for sellers: increase the perceived reference price. With a higher reference price consumers are willing to pay more and buy more, thereby increasing seller profits. But how exactly could a seller increase the perceived reference price?

One strategy, suggested by the above lab experiment, is to increase the perceived costs of the product. If the small run-down grocery store created the perception of a luxury experience — e.g., by offering some select high-end products in a clean, freshly painted environment — consumers would tend to expect higher prices, increasing transaction utility and demand for beer. This is despite no change in the actual quality of the beer.

A more direct strategy is to explicitly provide a high reference price in addition to the actual posted price. For example, apparel, furniture, and home-goods sellers that perpetually offer almost everything "on sale" are using the non-sale prices as suggested reference prices. The lower posted prices therefore generate transaction utility for consumers who enjoy the experience of getting a good deal. But this strategy may be limited if consumers are sufficiently familiar with the products and learn to ignore suggested reference prices.

Underpricing and Sellouts

The widespread phenomenon of sold-out concerts, sporting events, and restaurant reservations is puzzling for standard economics. After all, if more people want to see a concert than there are tickets available, why wouldn't the concert organizers set a higher ticket price? As long as the concert venue remains full, a higher price increases profit. By underpricing high-demand concerts, some consumers end up paying high prices for tickets on the secondary market — money that instead could have gone directly to the performer.

Let's see how transaction utility can make sense of such underpricing. The reference price for a particular concert, sporting event, or restaurant is shaped by the typical prices for other concerts, season tickets, or restaurants. As a consequence, a seller who anticipates a sold-out event risks creating substantial transaction *disutility* ($U_T < 0$) by setting a price that far exceeds the reference price. This transaction disutility only matters to the seller insofar as the seller is engaged in an ongoing economic relationship with the buyers. For a one-time event, the seller would not care about the potential transaction disutility from setting an abnormally high price that maximizes profit. But concert goers, sports fans, and diners are often repeat customers. These businesses must therefore trade off the short-term gains of high prices against the longer-term costs of losing customers who feel offended by the perceived price gouging. So while underpricing appears to be a mistake within the standard economic framework, it is consistent with businesses responding to consumers motivated, at least in part, by transaction utility.

21.1.2 *Payment Decoupling*

In using a system of mental accounts for organizing economic activities, individuals may think about the costs of an activity while experiencing its benefits. That is, costs and benefits are mentally *coupled* within the corresponding mental account (Prelec and Loewenstein 1998). But this link can be weakened. Recall, for instance, the discussion of wine collectors in Section 19.2. The evidence revealed that in prepaying for wine far in advance, many individuals enjoyed the later wine consumption experience as if it were costless. This example reveals a more general insight: to make products more attractive to potential consumers, sellers will find it profitable to *decouple* payments from consumption benefits. Many real-world pricing strategies have the effect of decoupling, which suggests that sellers are responding to the mental accounting of their customers.

A fixed-fee price, like a flat rate for unlimited cell phone data or unlimited gym visits, reflects a form of payment decoupling. Relative to a per-unit price, a monthly fixed fee allows customers to enjoy the benefits of use without thinking about the cost of each additional data gigabyte or gym visit. Even when per-unit prices can save money relative to the fixed fee, many customers still prefer the latter (Prelec and Loewenstein 1998). It is no surprise then why sellers would offer fixed fees.

A similar logic applies for urban car owners who would save money by relying on taxis. Buying or leasing a car generates a monthly payment that is decoupled from each car trip. But paying for a taxi each time you go to the grocery store makes the cost of transportation highly salient, reducing the perceived value of taxis. Rideshare companies may therefore find it profitable to offer membership-based pricing in which customers pay a monthly fee for a fixed number of taxi rides each month. Prix fixe menus for expensive multi-course meals also serve to decouple the price of each course from what may be a relatively modest quantity of food.

Alternatively, payments can be decoupled from consumption by bundling the costs of multiple activities together. All-inclusive vacation packages do exactly this (Thaler 1980). When travel, meals, lodging, and recreation are priced as a single fee, vacationers can enjoy their trip without thinking about the accumulating cost of each dinner, drink, and guided tour. This pricing strategy is particularly beneficial given the transaction disutility that travelers would experience from paying — in real time — the high prices typical of resorts and tourist locales.

Paying with a credit card instead of cash similarly weakens the link between payment and consumption. It does so in two key ways. First, it delays the time at which payment is due. For a credit card billing cycle that restarts on the first of each month, a $50 purchase on May 1st will not be due until a few weeks after the closing of the current month. So instead of paying in cash on May 1st, a credit card may not require a payment until the middle of June. This payment decoupling increases the enjoyment of consumption. Second, by paying for the $50 purchase as part of a larger credit card bill, it appears as a smaller cost than if it were an isolated payment. This, too, diminishes the perceived costs of consumption. Credit cards should therefore induce customers to spend more than if paying in cash were the only option. This prediction is consistent with the fact that many retailers are willing to pay high fees to credit card companies in order to provide consumers with the option of paying by credit.

21.1.3   Gift Giving

Mental accounting provides a framework to understand gift giving. Suppose that individuals set budget limits for different goods, but intentionally set low limits on items for which they are worried about excessive consumption. For instance, a wine drinker might limit their mental account for a bottle of wine at $20. This limit helps to manage the temptation to spend more than intended. So a special bottle of wine priced at $30 that the individual values at $40 will not be purchased, as it would exceed the mental budget. But an implication of this logic is that the individual would appreciate receiving the $30 bottle of wine as a gift *more* than receiving a $30 cash gift. An additional $30 in cash does not change the budget limit on wine, whereas the wine gift permits the individual to indulge in the luxury of drinking a special bottle.

The preceding example is consistent with the advice (from non-economists) that the best gift is something an individual would not typically buy for themself. Such gifts allow receivers to enjoy occasional luxuries without violating their mental accounts. Standard economic theory instead implies that the best gift is either cash — which people can spend as they desire — or an item that the recipient would have bought for themself. The reluctance of many people to give cash or everyday items as gifts suggests that mental accounting is a more compelling model of actual decision making.

Given that luxurious gifts can be preferred to cash, sellers have an incentive to market goods as potential gifts. Flowers, boxed chocolates, watches, and jewelry — goods for which most people would set low budget limits — are often marketed as great gift ideas. In fact, entire gift shops exist to sell items that people would never buy for themselves. A similar logic applies when marketing campaigns encourage consumers to indulge themselves. If people are inclined to exceed their normal budget limits while on vacation or for special occasions, it is in the interest of advertisers to suggest that consumption of their product is itself a special occasion.

This analysis extends to employers as well. Employers may find that an in-kind gift is more highly valued by employees than an equivalent cash gift. For instance, a nice $50 bottle of wine that an individual would never buy for themself is perceived as special and thoughtful, whereas a $50 cash bonus might be sufficiently small relative to one's salary that its value is largely discounted. At a more extravagant scale, Thaler (1999) notes that the National Football League was able to induce players to attend the annual Pro Bowl not with cash, but by locating the game in Hawaii and providing roundtrip airfare and accommodations.

Finally, consider the implications for the packaging of addictive goods. Individuals who set low budget limits on particularly tempting goods, like cigarettes and alcohol, do so to help regulate their consumption. But as a consequence, they will pay a premium to purchase small quantities (Wertenbroch 1998). With a daily mental budget of $6 for beer, an individual would not buy a six-pack for $12, but would purchase two cans priced at $3 each. These individual can prices are 50% higher than the per-can price in the six-pack. This behavior incentives sellers to offer single bottles of beer, mini travel-sized bottles of hard alcohol, and half-packs of cigarettes at high markups.

21.2   Mental Accounting: Savings Policy   [Development]

Without sufficient savings, households are vulnerable to negative income shocks that include job loss or medical emergencies. How can public policy help promote individual savings behaviors? Defaults and commitment strategies offer one approach (Section 7.2.3).

The mental accounting life-cycle model (Section 19.3) provides further insights for the design of policy aimed at increasing savings. Recall that the marginal propensity to consume out of wealth that is mentally categorized as future income is approximately zero. So while people spend almost all money that is perceived as current income, they save almost all money that is perceived as future income. Policies that encourage people to categorize money as belonging to a future income account are therefore predicted to increase total savings. This section reviews experimental evidence from such policies.

For households in developing countries with limited savings, it is difficult to invest in preventative health measures like mosquito nets (Tarozzi et al. 2014). This underinvestment has serious consequences. Jones et al. (2003) estimate that 63% of mortality for children under five years of age could be averted if households invested in available preventative health products. The following field experiment tests the effectiveness of a savings policy in Kenya designed to influence the mental accounting of money.

Field Experiment — Labeling Savings (Dupas and Robinson 2013)

Over 200 individuals in rural Kenya were encouraged to set a specific health savings goal for themselves. They were randomly assigned to one of the following groups:

1   Control: No new method of savings provided.
2   Treatment: Participants were provided with a lockable metal box (with a slot for contributing money), a padlock, and its key. A passbook was also provided in which to record deposits without opening the box. Finally, participants were asked to indicate on the first page of the passbook the name of the health product they were saving for.

Because the control group is not prevented from saving, and the treatment group can unlock their savings box at any time, the standard model of decision making predicts no difference in savings behavior between the two groups. Any difference in savings rates and health investments between the groups must therefore be due to the labeling of a physical storage space for savings.

Dupas and Robinson (2013) estimate that relative to the control group, the lockbox treatment increased preventative health investments by 66%–75%, and increased the likelihood that people reach their health savings goals by 14 percentage points. In follow-up surveys the participants in the treatment group reported that by placing money in the lockbox, they found it easier to save small change, limit luxury spending (like packaged chips at the market), and decline money requests from friends and relatives.

This experimental evidence reveals the relevance of mental accounting for household saving decisions. By shifting money out of the current income account and into a health savings mental account, facilitated by the labeled box, the deposited money became less fungible. The propensity to spend the labeled money was lower than it would have been in the absence of the lockable box. This experiment highlights a low-cost intervention to promote savings that can improve health and even save lives. The following field experiment highlights the effectiveness of an alternative labeling intervention.

Field Experiment — Partitioning Savings (Soman and Cheema 2011)

One hundred and forty-six workers at a construction project in rural India were recruited to receive savings advice from a social worker. Participants were given a target savings amount, much higher than their current low savings rate. The participants were then randomly assigned to receive their weekly salaries in one of two ways:

1   Control: Salary placed in a single envelope.
2   Treatment: Salary partitioned into two separate envelopes: one labeled for consumption and the other labeled for saving.

Because the treatment group is not restricted from opening and spending the money in the envelope labeled for saving, the standard model predicts no difference in savings behavior between the two groups. Any difference in savings must therefore be due to the labeling of money in a separate envelope.

Soman and Cheema (2011) find that average savings is 241 rupees in the control group and 414 rupees in the treatment group. The partitioning of money into two envelopes increased savings by over 70%.

In addition to labeling, simple text message reminders to save are effective. Across a set of field experiments in Bolivia, Peru, and the Philippines, Karlan et al. (2016) show that reminders increase savings by 6% and the likelihood of reaching a savings goal by

3%. Reminders that highlighted an individual's specific savings goal — like school fees — were twice as effective as generic reminders. The importance of emphasizing specific savings goals is consistent with mental accounting: people are more motivated to allocate savings to a mental account with a particular purpose than to a general savings account that can be used for any future consumption. The effectiveness of reminders also suggests inattention, with reminders serving to increase the salience of savings goals. We explore market and policy responses to inattentive consumers in the remainder of this chapter.

A general insight emerges from the preceding evidence. Policy interventions informed by the actual features of consumer decision making — and not simply the assumed utility maximization framework of the standard economic model — hold potential to generate significant welfare gains. Such interventions can also be inexpensive, adaptable across regions, and complementary to pre-existing institutions and policies.

21.3   Shrouding Add-on Prices   [Industrial Organization]

From the previous chapter we know that consumers are inattentive to opaque components of prices, like shipping costs (Hossain and Morgan 2006) and sales taxes (Chetty, Looney, and Kroft 2009). In light of such inattention, this section explores the incentives for profit-maximizing firms to *shroud* — i.e., make opaque, or less visible — product attributes. Shrouding could be accomplished by burying information in the fine print of a contract or in a hard-to-find section of a website, or by simply omitting public information from advertising materials. (Section 18.3.1 discusses a related practice by which firms design contract hurdles to profitably exploit consumer overconfidence.)

Consider the case of **add-ons**. The total cost of many products consists of a base price, plus the costs of complementary add-on goods. For example, to print documents at home, one needs to buy not only the actual printer, but the add-on ink cartridges. Hotel room prices exclude the add-ons of parking, dry cleaning, and minibar consumption. Airlines charge a base price for a ticket, plus add-ons for stowed baggage and seat selection. A laptop may be advertised at a low base price, with upgraded memory or hard drive capacity available as add-ons. Such add-on prices tend to be quite high relative to the base price (e.g., Hall 1997; Ellison and Ellison 2009).[1] And because of their secondary nature, it is feasible for add-on prices to be shrouded while the base price is advertised clearly.

21.3.1   Unshrouding in the Standard Model

Shrouding add-on prices, at first glance, might appear to be an obvious strategy for profit-maximizing firms. But if consumers are standard decision makers, firms should in fact unshroud — make visible — all of their prices (Jovanovic 1982; Milgrom 1981). The key insight to understanding this prediction is that standard consumers will expect the worst of a company that shrouds information. They will reason that companies shroud only the information that is unfavorable for consumers, as companies have a clear incentive to make favorable information visible. Therefore, any company that shrouds its add-on prices will lose customers to competitors that are transparent about all prices. The result is no shrouding in the market.

21.3.2   Shrouding with Inattention

The preceding logic fails if some consumers are inattentive to shrouded add-on prices. In this case, shrouding is sustained in the market. The following example provides intuition.

- **Example 21.1 — Gabaix and Laibson (2006).** Consider two hotel chains, Hilton and Transparent, each of which incurs a $100 cost for supplying a hotel room.

- Hilton guests typically spend $20 per night on add-ons (like parking), which cost Hilton nothing to supply. In the competitive equilibrium with zero profits, Hilton advertises a nightly hotel stay at $80, knowing that it will collect another $20 from add-on purchases, exactly covering its costs.
- Transparent instead provides add-ons for free. Because they are not charging for add-ons, they charge $100 to cover their costs in the competitive equilibrium.

Suppose that there are two types of consumers: *myopes* who are inattentive to add-on prices when booking a hotel room, and *sophisticates* who are attentive to add-on prices. Consider their reactions to the hotel pricing schemes.

- Myopes, ignoring the add-on prices associated with parking, phone calls, etc. at Hilton, perceive the $80 Hilton price as a bargain relative to the $100 Transparent price. They book a room at the Hilton.
- Sophisticates anticipate the high-priced add-ons at Hilton, but might still prefer to stay at the Hilton. By substituting away from Hilton-provided add-ons (e.g., taking a taxi to avoid parking fees, buying snacks at a corner shop to avoid minibar prices), sophisticates can pay Hilton only $80 for their stay. If the cost of the add-on substitutes is less than $20, it is cheaper to stay at Hilton than Transparent.

In sum, all consumers are choosing Hilton, with its shrouded add-on prices.

Suppose that Transparent, in an attempt to attract some customers away from Hilton, advertises the high-priced add-ons at Hilton. This education campaign has the effect of turning myopes into sophisticates. But everyone still chooses Hilton over Transparent. Although this truth-telling does not benefit Transparent, it reduces Hilton's profits and improves consumer welfare as educated myopes learn to save money by substituting away from expensive Hilton add-ons. Therefore, neither Transparent nor Hilton profit by educating consumers about shrouded prices.   ∎

The key lessons from the preceding example are threefold. First, firms can exploit inattentive consumers by shrouding high add-on prices. Second, when consumers are attentive to add-on prices, they can in turn exploit firms by paying the low base price while finding ways to avoid the high add-on prices. And finally, no firm is incentivized to educate inattentive consumers. It is therefore not surprising to observe shrouded add-on prices in practice.

21.3.3   Regulation

Social welfare is not maximized in the market equilibrium with shrouded add-on prices (Gabaix and Laibson 2006). Although add-ons are socially valuable (recall that Hilton's add-ons cost Hilton nothing to supply in Example 21.1, but still provide benefits to hotel guests), attentive consumers exert effort to avoid buying the add-ons. This substitution away from add-ons is the source of the social welfare loss.

Can policy interventions help mitigate such a welfare loss? The government could require greater transparency, warn consumers about shrouded costs, or explicitly impose markup caps on shrouded attributes. The tradeoffs of such policies are complex, with sometimes unintended consequences.[2] For instance, because the social welfare loss with shrouded prices stems from the behavior of attentive consumers, policies that increase attentiveness in the population can actually reduce social welfare (Kosfeld and Schüwer 2011). And from a political economy perspective, even if a welfare-improving regulation exists, consumers may not vote in favor of it if they under-appreciate their own inattention (Warren and Wood 2010).

21.4　Nudging Attention　　　　　　　　　　　　　　　[Public Finance]

Consumer inattention motivates policy interventions to simplify and make visible information that is complex, opaque, or otherwise cognitively costly to acquire and process.[3] The simplification and targeted provision of publicly available information are examples of nudges (Section 3.4). They change neither the available options nor the underlying incentives. For fully attentive consumers who process all readily available information, any such communication is unlikely to impact behavior. After all, they learn nothing from an email, letter, or phone call that simply repeats or reframes public information. But in settings where attention is less than full, the clear presentation of relevant public information can promote better-informed decision making and generate welfare gains.

The impact of an informational nudge on behavior and individual welfare is depicted in Figure 21.1 (Handel and Schwartzstein 2018). For concreteness, suppose an

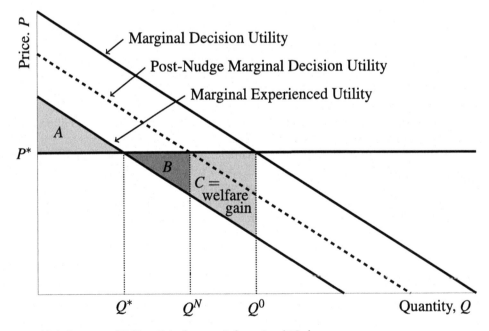

Figure 21.1 Consumer Welfare Gain from an Informational Nudge

inattentive consumer is choosing the quantity of a branded drug for which a cheaper generic counterpart is also available. Although the active ingredients are the same in each, and clearly printed on the packaging, people still buy brand-name options (Bronnenberg et al. 2015). In the figure the consumer chooses Q^0 units of the branded drug, as that is the point at which marginal decision utility no longer exceeds the market price P^* of the branded drug.

The consumer would maximize their welfare by choosing only Q^* units, where price equals marginal experienced utility (Section 3.2). We can interpret marginal experienced utility as the valuation made by a standard fully attentive consumer, like a medical expert in the drug choice context. Instead of achieving maximal consumer surplus equal to area A at Q^*, consumer surplus at Q^0 is given by area A less $B + C$. Perhaps the consumer is overbuying branded drugs because they find it burdensome to seek out the generic option at the store or to examine the ingredient labels. But a nudge that provides clear information relevant for the decision — like the equivalence of branded and generic drugs — has the effect of moving marginal decision utility closer to marginal experienced utility. The gap between the perceived value and actual experienced value of consumption is reduced. With the nudge, the consumer now chooses Q^N, increasing consumer surplus by area C (from $A - B - C$ to $A - B$). An analogous logic follows for the case in which an individual underconsumes. For example, inattention may be a factor in underutilization of valuable treatments for chronic diseases (Section 3.5) and energy-efficient lightbulbs (Section 3.6).

Inattention is likely to be more severe, and informational nudges consequently more impactful, when the cognitive costs of acquiring and processing information are high. For instance, some information may be particularly difficult to access or require financial literacy to understand. Or if the set of available options is large, individuals may not exert the effort to fully attend to all options. Inattention can also be exacerbated by poverty. When money is scarce, individuals may shift their attention to pressing matters like putting food on the table each day, leading to attentional neglect in other domains (Shah, Mullainathan, and Shafir 2012; Mullainathan and Shafir 2013). Limited attention to longer-term financial matters can then have the perverse effect of reinforcing poverty (Banerjee and Mullainathan 2008).

This section reviews evidence for how drawing attention to relevant information affects a variety of decisions related to health, education, and income support. Of course, there remain more direct policy tools — taxes, subsidies, mandates, bans, and defaults — that can guide inattentive consumers towards improved decisions. Evaluating which type of policy is best given the underlying cause for information neglect is an important research question (Handel and Schwartzstein 2018).

21.4.1 *Health*

We begin by exploring the role of clear information about food and health insurance plans.

Calorie Labels

A major public health concern is the rising rate of obesity in many parts of the world. Obesity is associated with diabetes, heart disease, stroke, and some cancers (CDC 2020). Policy interventions to reduce obesity could include bans on certain foods or taxes on sugar (Section 7.3.3). But if people are simply inattentive to the nutritional content of their consumption, then requiring salient calorie labels may be an alternative means of helping consumers make decisions that align with their own personal health goals.

As of May 2018, all US chain restaurants must post nutritional labels on standard menu items. This labeling does not constitute new information for attentive consumers, as the information was typically available on restaurant websites and/or in-store brochures. Therefore, any change in consumption patterns due to mandatory labeling on menus would suggest that consumers are somewhat inattentive to relevant health information. The following quasi-experiment estimates the impact of such labeling at New York Starbucks locations.

Quasi-Experiment — Calorie Concerns (Bollinger, Leslie, and Sorensen 2011)

In 2008 New York City implemented a calorie labeling law for items sold at chain restaurants. Because chains like Starbucks operate stores both in and out of New York City, this law created a quasi-experiment in which some, but not all, Starbucks stores posted calorie information on their menus. Starbucks locations in New York City were treated with the new law, while otherwise similar Starbucks locations outside New York City (e.g., Boston and Philadelphia) continued to not post calorie information, serving as controls. By comparing consumer behavior at treated and control locations, it is possible to identify the causal impact of the calorie labels, controlling for other regional trends in Starbucks shopping behavior unrelated to the calorie labels.

The impact of the calorie labels on shopping behavior at Starbucks is illustrated graphically in Figure 21.2. Following the introduction of calorie labels on April 1, 2008 in New York City, average food calories per transaction dropped at New York City locations (solid line), but remained relatively flat at the control city locations (dashed line). Using these data, Bollinger, Leslie, and Sorensen (2011) estimate that the mandatory calorie labeling led to a 14% decline in average food calories per transaction at Starbucks, with no substantial change in beverage consumption.

This evidence shows how information salience can change behavior. Moving beyond the existence of nutritional information on menus, one could also consider the impact of *how* the information is communicated. Are calories posted next to each menu item in a small font? Or are they posted clearly in a large font together with the item's relative caloric share of a recommended daily diet? Perhaps there are even warnings next to high-calorie foods about the risks of obesity. In Exercise 21.10 you are asked to evaluate the welfare implications for varying *intensities* of calorie labels.

The above findings are also consistent with evidence in the previous chapter that even when information is publicly available, people do not always act as if they are paying attention to it. Otherwise, the calorie labels alone would not have changed behavior. It is perhaps surprising that even when consuming goods with which we are presumably very familiar (most Starbucks customers have plenty of experience shopping at

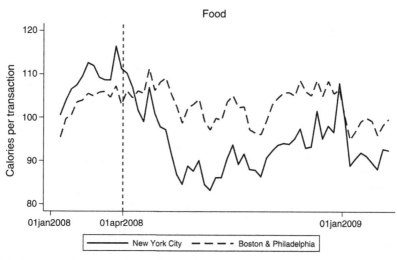

Figure 21.2 Food Calories per Starbucks Transaction

Source: Bollinger, Leslie, and Sorensen (2011). Copyright American Economic Association; reproduced with permission of the *American Economic Journal: Economic Policy.*

Starbucks), there is still inattention to the characteristics of what we are buying. This does not bode well for more complex decisions that are made infrequently and for which available information is not so easily accessible.

Health Insurance Plans

Medicare is the public health insurance program in the US for those over the age of 65. Although Medicare has been around since 1966, starting in 2006 seniors gained access to a new prescription drug benefit known as Medicare Part D. This program is designed as a marketplace where consumers are offered a variety of prescription drug insurance plans from which to choose. But this can be a complex choice to make, with seniors often facing a menu of 40 to 60 plans that differ in their premiums, coinsurance, and coverage of particular drugs. A majority of seniors report difficulty understanding how Medicare Part D works (Heiss, McFadden, and Winter 2006) and most do not choose the plan predicted by the standard model of decision making (Abaluck and Gruber 2011).

Medicare's Plan Finder website helps seniors navigate their Part D plan options. For instance, by inputting one's personal prescription drug use into the Plan Finder, individuals can compare their current plan to the costs and benefits of other plans. This information is easily accessible, and standard consumers are therefore expected to make use of the Plan Finder to inform their decision. After all, this is a decision of serious consequence for many seniors who face high medical costs with limited resources. The following field experiment examines the extent to which seniors are in fact making use of this information.

Field Experiment — Comparison Shopping Help (Kling et al. 2012)

Over 400 seniors completed a baseline survey in November 2006 about their prescription drug use and current Medicare Part D drug plan. The following month, each participant received, at random, one of two types of letters in the mail:

1   Control: Letter includes website address for Medicare's Plan Finder.
2   Treatment: Letter includes personalized price information generated by entering personal drug use information into Medicare's Plan Finder website. The letter shows how much an individual would save by switching from their their current plan to the lowest-cost plan.

Follow-up surveys in 2007 and 2008 were conducted to determine actual plan choices.

Because the personalized information in the treatment letter was also easily accessible to those who received the control letter, any difference in plan choice behavior between the two groups can be attributed to the effect of directly providing information instead of directing individuals to access it themselves.

Kling et al. (2012) find that 17% of individuals in the control group switched drug plans, while 28% of the treatment group switched. The treatment reduced average annual costs by about $100 (including switchers and nonswitchers).

This field experiment points to the relevance of not only making information available and easily accessible, but directly providing it. And given the substantial savings for the treatment group, the government may find it in the public interest to mail personalized drug plan information to all seniors. Alternatively, the government could adopt other strategies that simplify the decision process, like defaulting everyone into the lowest cost option each year, or banning unreasonably costly plans.

21.4.2   Education

The value of easily accessible and clear information is also evidenced by the educational choices of students and parents.

Student College Choices

For college-bound students, the decisions about where to apply, which school to attend, and how to pay can shape opportunities and outcomes, both professional and personal, throughout one's life. Although college websites provide details about costs, financial aid, and program attributes, this is a complex set of information. It is therefore not an unreasonable hypothesis that without the help of savvy parents or school counselors, many students make college application decisions with only partial information. In fact, high-achieving students from low-income families apply to far more "safety" and non-selective schools than other high-achieving students (Hoxby and Avery 2012). As a result, talented low-income students can end up paying more for college than they would at a more selective institution with better academic outcomes and generous financial aid.

To address the potential informational problem, the Expanding College Opportunities (ECO) project is a policy intervention designed to examine the impacts of providing clear, personalized information about college characteristics. The results of this intervention are outlined in the following field experiment.

Field Experiment — College Counseling (Hoxby and Turner 2015)

Almost 6,000 students in the 2011–12 cohort of high school seniors, with the following characteristics, were targeted:

- high achieving: top 10% of SAT or ACT scores; and
- low income: bottom third of income distribution for families with a 12th grader.

The ECO project randomly assigned the targeted students to one of two groups:

1 Control: No additional information is provided.
2 Treatment: Mailing is sent with information about applying to colleges, college characteristics, what families might actually pay (after financial aid), and no-paperwork fee waivers to apply to selective colleges.

Hoxby and Turner (2015) report that relative to the control, the treated students submitted 48% more applications and were admitted to 31% more colleges. Treated students enrolled in colleges with higher median SAT/ACT scores, higher graduation rates, and higher instructional spending.

   When surveyed, treated students were about 40% more likely (than control students) to say that they were much more likely to apply to a college if they knew they would get enough financial aid to attend, if the college had a high graduation rate, or if the college's average student had a test score and GPA like their own.

The fact that the ECO field experiment significantly changed college application choices and enrollment outcomes for high-achieving low-income students suggests that attention to complex information was indeed a barrier. The survey results confirm that students in the control group relied on incomplete information about net prices and college characteristics. The low-cost informational mailing helps students to make better-informed educational investment decisions.

Parent Public School Choices

School choices also exist prior to college. Following the No Child Left Behind Act of 2001, a number of US urban public school districts implemented school choice plans in which students can choose to attend higher-performing schools outside their neighborhood. Such a policy can have the effect of incentivizing low-performing schools to improve academic achievement, so as to prevent losing local students to non-local schools (Hastings, Kane, and Staiger 2005). This logic hinges on the premise that parents will indeed send their children to higher-performing schools when given the opportunity. But when school quality information is opaque and hard to find, parents may not be fully attentive to academic differences between schools, dampening the degree to which low-performing schools lose students.

Hastings and Weinstein (2008) study public school choices in the Charlotte-Mecklenburg Public School District of North Carolina. To learn about school quality in 2002, a family could consult a school choice guide with positive aspects of each school (written by the schools themselves) filling over 100 pages. Objective information was only available by searching the school district website. But starting in 2004, the district made school-by-school comparison information more salient by sending families a three-page spreadsheet with test scores for every school. This simplified information had an effect. Parents were more likely to choose higher-scoring schools for their children, and as a consequence, increased their children's test scores.

Once again, we see that policy makers must consider not only the formal rules of a policy, but also the degree to which individuals can reasonably be attentive to opaque information, even if it is technically available to the public.

21.4.3 Government Income Support Programs

The complexity of government programs that provide income support, like Social Security for the aged and the Earned Income Tax Credit (EITC) for the poor, can pose a barrier to well-informed decision making.

Social Security

Social Security is a mandated public retirement savings program in the US. Workers make contributions during their working years and then upon retirement, collect benefits until death. While much of the program is automatic, there are two key decisions: when to stop working and when to start receiving benefits. These decisions can lead to different benefit levels for the rest of one's life. And even if one is perfectly informed about how benefit levels are adjusted based on the timing of retirement and the benefit start date, the tradeoffs are challenging to assess. An individual must form expectations about future earnings from work and life expectancy for both themself and their spouse.

Liebman and Luttmer (2015) implement a field experiment by mailing informational brochures with key provisions of Social Security to workers approaching retirement age. This simple intervention increased the probability of working by 4.2 percentage points, with a particularly strong effect for women. There was no significant effect on the probability that individuals start claiming their Social Security benefits. The evidence suggests that with some simple facts about Social Security, individuals better understand the benefits of delaying retirement.

Earned Income Tax Credit (EITC)

The EITC is the largest means-tested cash transfer program in the US, providing $66 billion in income support to 27 million low-income families in 2017 (CRS 2020). But EITC benefits are not automatically paid to recipients, and a quarter of all who are eligible fail to fully claim their benefits (Plueger 2009). In doing so, a typical non-claimant gives up over $1,000, or 33 days of income (Bhargava and Manoli 2015).

Given the low cost in terms of time and effort to file a claim, coupled with the large and private nature of EITC benefits, incomplete take-up constitutes a puzzle for standard economics (Currie 2006).

Working with the Internal Revenue Service, Bhargava and Manoli (2015) mailed reminders, with program eligibility details, to over 35,000 individuals who collectively failed to claim $26 million in EITC benefits. In response, an additional $4 million was claimed. This field experiment, coupled with responses in a follow-up survey, lead the researchers to conclude that it is limited awareness about a complex program that contributes to the phenomenon of low EITC take-up. Extrapolating to the general population, they estimate that simplified information and reminders could increase take-up from 75% to 78%, with a corresponding $500 million increase in total benefits received.

Not all informational interventions change behavior. As discussed above, the Social Security brochure did not impact when individuals begin claiming benefits. In addition, information about the work incentives created by the EITC program — and the earnings levels for which EITC benefits are maximized — does not systematically impact how much people choose to work (Chetty and Saez 2013). This non-effect is not entirely surprising given that work hours are often fixed by an employer and not so easily adjusted.

21.5   Government Persuasion   [Politics & Law]

Persuasive messaging, as reviewed in the previous chapter, can shape a variety of individual behaviors. This evidence motivates persuasion as a policy tool for governments. Public service announcements — on the radio, TV, or billboards — about health and safety are examples of such messaging that aims to change attitudes and behaviors. A particularly successful public health campaign in Egypt during the 1980s encouraged oral rehydration therapy for dehydrated infants, leading to a 70% reduction in the infant mortality rate (Abdulla 2004). In this section we highlight quasi-experimental evidence of the effects from governments using persuasion, via education and radio, to achieve their national aims.

21.5.1   Education Curriculum

One means by which a government may seek to communicate persuasive messages is through the national curriculum taught in schools. But is this effective? The following studies suggest that the answer is yes.

Miguel (2004) considers the case study of two nearby rural districts in Africa: one in Tanzania and one in Kenya. These two regions share a common culture, geography, and history of colonialism. But since their independence from the British in the early 1960s, these two countries have differed in their nation-building policies. For instance, the public school curriculum in Tanzania emphasized common national values, culture, and history. Teachers were even required to serve for a period in the national service organization, further aligning the nation's interests with those who educate the youth. In contrast, the Kenyan government made little attempt to build national identity through the schooling curriculum. Miguel (2004) finds that ethnically diverse communities in Tanzania achieve greater cooperation — as measured by funding for local public goods, like the maintenance of schools and water wells — than similarly diverse communities in Kenya. This difference suggests that education can mitigate interethnic conflict, leading to improved social outcomes.

In a related effort, between 2004 and 2010 the Chinese Communist Party implemented a major college textbook reform with the aim, among others, to promote a common national identity across ethnic groups. Cantoni et al. (2017) estimate from survey evidence that the curricular reform shifted students' attitudes in favor of China's governance and against free markets, as intended. But the researchers do not find significant evidence that the reform promoted a stronger sense of a multiethnic Chinese national identity, an attitude that may only evolve over a longer period. Whether teaching a shared ideology in school is harmful or beneficial for social welfare depends, in part, on the extent to which it could diminish worker productivity, while simultaneously promoting cooperation.

21.5.2   *Radio Communication*

The media serves as another channel through which governments communicate persuasive messaging. Given the evidence that independent TV can diminish support for incumbent political parties (Section 20.3.2), governments have an interest in controlling political communication. The following evidence shows how radio communication can be used by those in power to bring people together, or drive them apart.

Following the Rwandan genocide of the Tutsi population by Hutu extremists in 1994, the Rwandan government has made it a top priority to foster an inclusive multiethnic national identity. Textbooks have been rewritten and the mention of ethnicity in public discourse has been banned. The government has also sought to shape attitudes through its ownership of Radio Rwanda, a primary source of news and information for the population. To identify the impact of political messaging via state radio, Blouin and Mukand (2019) leverage the quasi-experiment created by the country's mountainous topography: some areas receive radio signals, while others do not. Differences in interethnic attitudes across areas that differ only in radio signal coverage can then be plausibly attributed to the state radio. The researchers find that radio exposure not only increases interethnic trust and cooperation, but also decreases the likelihood of using ethnicity to categorize people. This is compelling evidence for the power of media to shape citizen identities.

Not all radio serves benevolent ends. Although the Rwandan government has used the persuasive power of radio for ethnic reconciliation, during the Rwandan genocide a hate-filled radio station that encouraged violence against the Tutsi population increased participation in killings (Yanagizawa-Drott 2014). Nazi radio propaganda similarly had the effect of inciting anti-Semitic actions (Adena et al. 2015). Public radio can also generate unintended effects when it is accessible beyond national borders. DellaVigna et al. (2014) show that Croatians with access to nationalistic Serbian radio signals became more anti-Serbian and more likely to vote for extreme nationalist parties.

In sum, radio has proven to be a powerful tool in shaping not only beliefs, but actions. And while radio, television, and print media can be monopolized by the state in obvious ways, the emergence of social media generates both challenges and opportunities for governments that seek to exploit psychology for political gain. Such gains may or may not align with social welfare improvements.

21.6   Summary

1   To model the perceived value of getting a good deal, individuals derive not only standard **acquisition utility** from acquiring an object, but also **transaction utility** from the value of the transaction itself.

2   Given consumer decisions that depend on transaction utility, sellers have an incentive to create the perception that transactions generate great value.

3   Mental accounting motivates sellers to decouple payments from consumption benefits, market speciality goods as gifts for others, and sell addictive goods in small portions.

4   Policies that encourage people to mentally categorize money as savings are effective at increasing savings rates.

5   In contrast to evidence, the standard model of decision making predicts that **add-on** prices will be made transparent by firms. But shrouding add-on prices is predicted when some consumers are inattentive.

6   Policy interventions that serve to nudge inattentive individuals by simplifying and making salient information that is otherwise complex and opaque can benefit individual welfare. There is empirical evidence that such nudges impact decisions related to health, education, and navigating public programs.

7   Governments are a source of persuasive messaging that shapes the attitudes and behaviors of citizens.

21.7   Exercises[4]

Exercise 21.1 — Deal Ordeals. Explain how transaction utility can explain why you may sometimes buy something on sale that you later do not find particularly useful.

Exercise 21.2 — Blanket Accounting. Consider the following anecdote: "A friend of mine was once shopping for a quilted bedspread. She went to a department store and was pleased to find a model she liked on sale. The spreads came in three sizes: double, queen and king. The usual prices for these quilts were $200, $250 and $300 respectively, but during the sale they were all priced at only $150. My friend bought the king-size quilt and was quite pleased with her purchase, though the quilt did hang a bit over the sides of her double bed" (Thaler 1999, 184).

Model this economic choice, where v is the valuation of the king-size quilt, p is its actual price, and the reference price p^* is the regular non-sale price for the king-size quilt. For what range of v would an individual *not* buy the king-size quilt if they cared only about acquisition utility ($U_A < 0$), but would buy the king-size quilt if they cared about both acquisition and transaction utility ($U_A + U_T \geq 0$)? Interpret your answers.

Exercise 21.3 — Welfare Acquisition. Zoe's valuation for a bottle of water is $v = \$3$ (no matter where she buys it). She will purchase the bottle of water as long as the sum of her acquisition and transaction utilities are non-negative: $U_A + U_T \geq 0$.

a   Zoe reports that she is willing to pay at most $2 for a bottle of water from a grocery store. What does this imply about the reference price p^* at the grocery store?

b   Zoe reports that she is willing to pay at most $4 for a bottle of water from a fancy resort. What does this imply about the reference price p^* at the fancy resort?

c   Suppose a bottle of water is $2.50 at a grocery store. Will Zoe buy it? If her individual welfare from a purchase is equal to her acquisition utility alone, would she be better off acting otherwise? Explain.

Exercise 21.4 — Pennies-A-Day. A common selling and fund-raising strategy is to frame an annual fee or donation as costing only a few pennies each day (Gourville

1998). What does this strategy suggest about how consumers and donors mentally account for small costs?

Exercise 21.5 — Present Accounts. Consider the following anecdote: "Mr. S admires a $125 cashmere sweater at the department store. He declines to buy it, feeling that it is too extravagant. Later that month he receives the same sweater from his wife for a birthday present. He is very happy. Mr. and Mrs. S have only joint bank accounts" (Thaler 2008, 15).

a What is odd about this anecdote from the perspective of standard decision making?
b Explain how this anecdote is consistent with Mr. S having a mental account for clothing spending that is capped at $50 per month (perhaps to prevent himself from overspending on clothing). In particular, why is he so happy with the gift?

Exercise 21.6 — Auto Options. Use the concept of inattention to explain why, in buying a new car, there is such a long list of optional and expensive add-ons from which to choose.

Exercise 21.7 — The Fine Print. Pedro is a sophisticated shopper who is fully attentive to the add-on costs associated with buying a home printer. What are some ways in which Pedro could partially substitute away from expensive ink cartridges? Do these behaviors make Pedro more or less likely to purchase a printer with low base price and high add-on costs (relative to higher base price printer with lower add-on costs)?

Exercise 21.8 — Payday Prices. [Finance] Payday loans are designed to provide short-term financial support to borrowers until their next payday. But the interest rates associated with such loans can be very high. In a field experiment, Bertrand and Morse (2011) provide information about the costs of payday loans to customers entering a random subset of payday lending offices.

a The customers in the control group who wish to take out a payday loan are informed of the loan's interest rate before consenting. Customers in treated stores are additionally provided the loan cost in dollar terms. For example, paying back a $300 loan in 3 months costs $270, while paying back $300 of credit card spending in 3 months typically costs $15. Explain how the information treatment is expected to affect the borrowing behavior for a standard consumer.
b The information treatment reduces the likelihood of borrowing by 11%. Interpret.
c Suggest a public policy intervention designed to improve consumer welfare motivated by this evidence.

Exercise 21.9 — Agricultural Attention. [Development] Seaweed is farmed by attaching strands (pods) of seaweed to lines submerged in the ocean. But this description belies a large number of complex decisions: the length of lines, distance between lines, distance between pods on each line, etc. In surveying experienced seaweed farmers in Indonesia, Hanna, Mullainathan, and Schwartzstein (2014) find that most fail to notice the importance of pod length for productivity.

The farmers participated in an experiment on their seaweed plots, varying pod length and measuring the resulting yields. But they still did not change their methods. Farmers only began to change their methods after receiving summary data from the experiment on their plots and having the relationship between pod length and yields highlighted.

Discuss some lessons from this evidence about the scope of inattention and how to correct it.

Exercise 21.10 — Nudging Nutritional Knowledge. Jared is choosing consumption of *excess* calories (i.e., calories beyond what is needed for survival) denoted by $x \geq 0$. For simplicity, assume that the excess calories don't cost any money. His (decision) utility is:

$$U(x \mid L) = (1 - L) \cdot 6,750\sqrt{x} - L \cdot \frac{x^2}{2}$$

where we interpret $L \in (0, 1)$ as the degree to which the calories are clearly labeled. The first term in the utility function reflects the pleasure from eating the calories. The second term captures the perceived future health cost from consuming x. While the actual health costs are $x^2/2$, Jared's partial inattention causes him to discount these costs.

a   How do increases in x and L impact both the pleasure and perceived cost of excess calories? Interpret.

b   **[Calculus Required]** Derive Jared's utility-maximizing choice of x. How does this choice depend on L? Provide intuition.

Jared's experienced utility from consuming x is:

$$U^{exp}(x \mid L) = (1 - L) \cdot 6,750\sqrt{x} - \frac{x^2}{2}$$

c   How does Jared's experienced utility differ from his decision utility? Interpret.

d   Jared's welfare is determined by his experienced utility. Suppose that $L_0 = 0.25$. Use part (b) to compute Jared's calorie choice in this no-label environment, as well as his experienced utility. Repeat the same calculations with two different levels of calorie labeling: small font labels ($L_1 = 0.5$) and large font labels ($L_2 = 0.75$). Which labeling policy yields the highest welfare for Jared? Use your results to briefly comment on the benefits and costs of calorie label nudges.

Exercise 21.11 — School Quality Moves. [Public Finance] GreatSchool is a non-profit that provides free US school quality ratings on its website. Bergman, Chan, and Kapor (2020) conduct a field experiment with low-income families eligible for public housing support. When eligible families click on a rental listing using the government's online housing search platform they all see the property profile. But some families are randomly treated with additional information: they see the GreatSchool quality ratings of nearby schools.

a   What is the predicted effect of this experimental treatment for standard decision makers?

b   The researchers find that the treatment causes families to choose neighborhoods with higher performing and less segregated schools. What does this evidence suggest about individual decision making?

c   Discuss the social costs and benefits for this type of treatment.

Exercise 21.12 — Schooling Limits. [Education] Bettinger et al. (2012) conduct a field experiment with low-income parents of high school seniors upon receiving tax help. Families were randomized into a control group and two treatment groups:

- Information Treatment: Families receive college aid information about tuition costs at nearby colleges.
- Information and Assistance Treatment: In addition to the information treatment, families also receive assistance completing the Free Application for Federal Student Aid (FAFSA).

The information treatment alone does not impact outcomes, but when combined with FAFSA assistance, college attendance, persistence, and aid all increase. Discuss what this evidence suggests about the barriers that can prevent individuals from maximizing their own welfare.

Exercise 21.13 — A Lack of Energy. [Energy and Environment] Starting in 2002, residential electricity customers in Texas had the option to switch away from the incumbent electricity provider to new lower-priced electricity retailers. A website provided households with the ability to comparison shop and switch to a new provider. The process of switching retailers takes about 15 minutes and would save the average customer $100 in the first year. But the majority of households did not switch (Hortaçsu, Madanizadeh, and Puller 2017). Discuss at least two reasons that could explain this inertia in consumer choice. What policies might you recommend to improve consumer welfare?

Exercise 21.14 — Minding Nudges. [Public Finance] You recently donated to a charity — an act that you enjoyed doing. The charity now has your email address and sends you a request to donate again. But because of limited attention you missed or forgot this email solicitation. The charity, aware that such inattention is common, nudges you a week later with a reminder email to donate.

a   In what ways could the reminder email improve your welfare?
b   In what ways could the reminder email decrease your welfare?
c   Damgaard and Gravert (2018) study the effects of such a reminder in a field experiment and find that it significantly increases both donations to the charity and unsubscriptions from the charity's mailing list. Is this evidence consistent with a net gain in consumer welfare, a net loss, or is the effect of the reminder on welfare ambiguous? Explain.

Exercise 21.15 — Creditworthy Concerns. A FICO score is a summary measure of an American's creditworthiness. It is improved by paying bills on time and not carrying too much debt, among other factors. This score is important for individuals seeking to borrow money to finance a car, house, or business venture. Most Americans have free access to their FICO scores, but may not act as if they do. Suggest a field experiment that aims to estimate whether or not people are attentive to their freely available FICO score. In particular, what is your treatment? What is your observable outcome variable that you will compare between the control and treatment groups? And how would you interpret the absence or presence of a treatment effect?[5]

Notes

1   The phenomenon of high markups for add-ons has been explained within a variety of standard economic frameworks. See, for example Lal and Matutes (1994), Farrell and Klemperer (2007), and Ellison (2005).
2   See Köszegi (2014) for a discussion of the challenges with regulating exploitative contracts.

3 Handel and Schwartzstein (2018) provide an excellent and accessible review of consumer welfare issues when individuals do not use all available information.

4 Exercise 21.10 is adapted from an example by Jimenez-Gomez (2018).

5 Homonoff, O'Brien, and Sussman (2019) conduct a field experiment on FICO score knowledge among student loan borrowers.

References

Abaluck, Jason, and Jonathan Gruber. 2011. "Choice Inconsistencies among the Elderly: Evidence from Plan Choice in the Medicare Part D Program." *American Economic Review* 101 (4): 1180–1210. doi:10.1257/aer.101.4.1180.

Abdulla, Rasha A. 2004. "Entertainment-Education in the Middle East: Lessons from the Egyptian Oral Rehydration Therapy Campaign." In *Entertainment-Education and Social Change: History, Research, and Practice,* edited by Arvind Singhal, Michael J. Cody, Everett M. Rogers, and Miguel Sabido. Mahwah, NJ: Lawrence Erlbaum Associates.

Adena, Maja, Ruben Enikolopov, Maria Petrova, Veronica Santarosa, and Ekaterina Zhuravskaya. 2015. "Radio and the Rise of the Nazis in Prewar Germany." *The Quarterly Journal of Economics* 130 (4): 1885–1939. doi:10.1093/qje/qjv030.

Banerjee, Abhijit V., and Sendhil Mullainathan. 2008. "Limited Attention and Income Distribution." *American Economic Review* 98 (2): 489–493. doi:10.1257/aer.98.2.489.

Bergman, Peter, Eric W Chan, and Adam Kapor. 2020. "Housing Search Frictions: Evidence from Detailed Search Data and a Field Experiment." NBER Working Paper 27209. Cambridge, MA: National Bureau of Economic Research. doi:10.3386/w27209.

Bertrand, Marianne, and Adair Morse. 2011. "Information Disclosure, Cognitive Biases, and Payday Borrowing." *The Journal of Finance* 66 (6): 1865–1893. doi:10.1111/j.1540-6261.2011.01698.x.

Bettinger, Eric P., Bridget Terry Long, Philip Oreopoulos, and Lisa Sanbonmatsu. 2012. "The Role of Application Assistance and Information in College Decisions: Results from the H&R Block FAFSA Experiment." *The Quarterly Journal of Economics* 127 (3): 1205–1242. doi:10.1093/qje/qjs017.

Bhargava, Saurabh, and Dayanand Manoli. 2015. "Psychological Frictions and the Incomplete Take-Up of Social Benefits: Evidence from an IRS Field Experiment." *American Economic Review* 105 (11): 3489–3529. doi:10.1257/aer.20121493.

Blouin, Arthur, and Sharun W. Mukand. 2019. "Erasing Ethnicity? Propaganda, Nation Building, and Identity in Rwanda." *Journal of Political Economy* 127 (3): 1008–1062. doi:10.1086/701441.

Bollinger, Bryan, Phillip Leslie, and Alan Sorensen. 2011. "Calorie Posting in Chain Restaurants." *American Economic Journal: Economic Policy* 3 (1): 91–128. doi:10.1257/pol.3.1.91.

Bronnenberg, Bart J., Jean-Pierre Dubé, Matthew Gentzkow, and Jesse M. Shapiro. 2015. "Do Pharmacists Buy Bayer? Informed Shoppers and the Brand Premium." *The Quarterly Journal of Economics* 130 (4): 1669–1726. doi:10.1093/qje/qjv024.

Cantoni, Davide, Yuyu Chen, David Y. Yang, Noam Yuchtman, and Y. Jane Zhang. 2017. "Curriculum and Ideology." *Journal of Political Economy* 125 (2): 338–392. doi:10.1086/690951.

CDC (Centers for Disease Control and Prevention). 2020. *Obesity is a Common, Serious, and Costly Disease.* Accessed June 29, 2020, https://www.cdc.gov/obesity/data/adult.html.

Chetty, Raj, Adam Looney, and Kory Kroft. 2009. "Salience and Taxation: Theory and Evidence." *American Economic Review* 99 (4): 1145–1177. doi:10.1257/aer.99.4.1145.

Chetty, Raj, and Emmanuel Saez. 2013. "Teaching the Tax Code: Earnings Responses to an Experiment with EITC Recipients." *American Economic Journal: Applied Economics* 5 (1): 1–31. doi:10.1257/app.5.1.1.

CRS (Congressional Research Service). 2020. "The Earned Income Tax Credit (EITC): How It Works and Who Receives It." Report R43805. United States Congress. https://fas.org/sgp/crs/misc/R43805.pdf.

Currie, Janet. 2006. "The Take-Up of Social Benefits." In *Public Policy and the Income Distribution,* edited by David Card, John M. Quiggin, and Alan J. Auerbach, 80–148. New York: Russell Sage Foundation.

Damgaard, Mette Trier, and Christina Gravert. 2018. "The Hidden Costs of Nudging: Experimental Evidence from Reminders in Fundraising." *Journal of Public Economics* 157: 15–26. doi:10.1016/j.jpubeco.2017.11.005.

DellaVigna, Stefano, Ruben Enikolopov, Vera Mironova, Maria Petrova, and Ekaterina Zhuravskaya. 2014. "Cross-Border Media and Nationalism: Evidence from Serbian Radio in Croatia." *American Economic Journal: Applied Economics* 6 (3): 103–132. doi:10.1257/app.6.3.103.

Dupas, Pascaline, and Jonathan Robinson. 2013. "Why Don't the Poor Save More? Evidence from Health Savings Experiments." *American Economic Review* 103 (4): 1138–1171. doi:10.1257/aer.103.4.1138.

Ellison, Glenn. 2005. "A Model of Add-On Pricing." *The Quarterly Journal of Economics* 120 (2): 585–637. doi:10.1093/qje/120.2.585.

Ellison, Glenn, and Sara Fisher Ellison. 2009. "Search, Obfuscation, and Price Elasticities on the Internet." *Econometrica* 77 (2): 427–452. doi:10.3982/ECTA5708.

Farrell, Joseph, and Paul Klemperer. 2007. "Coordination and Lock-In: Competition with Switching Costs and Network Effects." In *Handbook of Industrial Organization*, edited by Mark Armstrong and Robert H. Porter, 3:1967–2072. Elsevier. doi:10.1016/S1573-448X(06)03031-7.

Gabaix, Xavier, and David Laibson. 2006. "Shrouded Attributes, Consumer Myopia, and Information Suppression in Competitive Markets." *The Quarterly Journal of Economics* 121 (2): 505–540. doi:10.1162/qjec.2006.121.2.505.

Gourville, John T. 1998. "Pennies-a-Day: The Effect of Temporal Reframing on Transaction Evaluation." *Journal of Consumer Research* 24 (4): 395–408. doi:10.1086/209517.

Hall, Robert E. 1997. "The Inkjet Aftermarket: An Economic Analysis." Stanford University. Unpublished.

Handel, Benjamin, and Joshua Schwartzstein. 2018. "Frictions or Mental Gaps: What's Behind the Information We (Don't) Use and When Do We Care?" *Journal of Economic Perspectives* 32 (1): 155–178. doi:10.1257/jep.32.1.155.

Hanna, Rema, Sendhil Mullainathan, and Joshua Schwartzstein. 2014. "Learning through Noticing: Theory and Evidence from a Field Experiment." *The Quarterly Journal of Economics* 129 (3): 1311–1353. doi:10.1093/qje/qju015.

Hastings, Justine S., Thomas J. Kane, and Douglas O. Staiger. 2005. "Parental Preferences and School Competition: Evidence from a Public School Choice Program." NBER Working Paper 11805. Cambridge, MA: National Bureau of Economic Research. doi:10.3386/w11805.

Hastings, Justine S., and Jeffrey M. Weinstein. 2008. "Information, School Choice, and Academic Achievement: Evidence from Two Experiments." *The Quarterly Journal of Economics* 123 (4): 1373–1414. doi:10.1162/qjec.2008.123.4.1373.

Heiss, Florian, Daniel McFadden, and Joachim Winter. 2006. "Who Failed to Enroll in Medicare Part D, and Why? Early Results." *Health Affairs* 25 (Supplement 1): W344–W354. doi:10.1377/hlthaff.25.w344.

Homonoff, Tatiana, Rourke O'Brien, and Abigail B. Sussman. 2019. "Does Knowing Your FICO Score Change Financial Behavior? Evidence from a Field Experiment with Student Loan Borrowers." *The Review of Economics and Statistics*: 1–45. doi:10.1162/rest_a_00888.

Hortaçsu, Ali, Seyed Ali Madanizadeh, and Steven L. Puller. 2017. "Power to Choose? An Analysis of Consumer Inertia in the Residential Electricity Market." *American Economic Journal: Economic Policy* 9 (4): 192–226. doi:10.1257/pol.20150235.

Hossain, Tanjim, and John Morgan. 2006. "... Plus Shipping and Handling: Revenue (Non) Equivalence in Field Experiments on eBay." *The B.E. Journal of Economic Analysis & Policy* 6 (2). doi:10.2202/1538-0637.1429.

Hoxby, Caroline M., and Christopher Avery. 2012. "The Missing 'One-Offs': The Hidden Supply of High-Achieving, Low Income Students." NBER Working Paper 18586. Cambridge, MA: National Bureau of Economic Research. doi:10.3386/w18586.

Hoxby, Caroline M., and Sarah Turner. 2015. "What High-Achieving Low-Income Students Know about College." *American Economic Review* 105 (5): 514–517. doi:10.1257/aer.p20151027.

Jimenez-Gomez, David. 2018. "Nudging and Phishing: A Theory of Behavioral Welfare Economics." SSRN Scholarly Paper ID 3248503. Rochester, NY: Social Science Research Network. https://papers.ssrn.com/abstract=3248503.

Jones, Gareth, Richard W. Steketee, Robert E. Black, Zulfiqar A. Bhutta, and Saul S. Morris. 2003. "How Many Child Deaths Can We Prevent this Year?" *The Lancet* 362 (9377): 65–71. doi:10.1016/S0140-6736(03)13811-1.

Jovanovic, Boyan. 1982. "Truthful Disclosure of Information." *The Bell Journal of Economics* 13 (1): 36–44. doi:10.2307/3003428.

Karlan, Dean, Margaret McConnell, Sendhil Mullainathan, and Jonathan Zinman. 2016. "Getting to the Top of Mind: How Reminders Increase Saving." *Management Science* 62 (12): 3393–3411. doi:10.1287/mnsc.2015.2296.

Kling, Jeffrey R., Sendhil Mullainathan, Eldar Shafir, Lee C. Vermeulen, and Marian V. Wrobel. 2012. "Comparison Friction: Experimental Evidence from Medicare Drug Plans." *The Quarterly Journal of Economics* 127 (1): 199–235. doi:10.1093/qje/qjr055.

Kosfeld, Michael, and Ulrich Schüwer. 2011. "Add-On Pricing, Naive Consumers, and the Hidden Welfare Costs of Education." SSRN Scholarly Paper ID 1955401. Rochester, NY: Social Science Research Network. https://papers.ssrn.com/abstract=1955401.

Köszegi, Botond. 2014. "Behavioral Contract Theory." *Journal of Economic Literature* 52 (4): 1075–1118. doi:10.1257/jel.52.4.1075.

Lal, Rajiv, and Carmen Matutes. 1994. "Retail Pricing and Advertising Strategies." *The Journal of Business* 67 (3): 345–370. doi:10.1086/296637.

Liebman, Jeffrey B., and Erzo F. P. Luttmer. 2015. "Would People Behave Differently If They Better Understood Social Security? Evidence from a Field Experiment." *American Economic Journal: Economic Policy* 7 (1): 275–299. doi:10.1257/pol.20120081.

Miguel, Edward. 2004. "Tribe or Nation: Nation Building and Public Goods in Kenya versus Tanzania." *World Politics* 56: 327–362. doi:10.1353/wp.2004.0018.

Milgrom, Paul R. 1981. "Good News and Bad News: Representation Theorems and Applications." *The Bell Journal of Economics* 12 (2): 380–391. doi:10.2307/3003562.

Mullainathan, Sendhil, and Eldar Shafir. 2013. *Scarcity: Why Having Too Little Means So Much.* New York: Henry Holt / Company.

Plueger, Dean. 2009. "Earned Income Tax Credit Participation Rate for Tax Year 2005." Research Bulletin. Internal Revenue Service. https://www.irs.gov/pub/irs-soi/09resconeitcpart.pdf.

Prelec, Drazen, and George Loewenstein. 1998. "The Red and the Black: Mental Accounting of Savings and Debt." *Marketing Science* 17 (1): 4–28. doi:10.1287/mksc.17.1.4.

Shah, Anuj K., Sendhil Mullainathan, and Eldar Shafir. 2012. "Some Consequences of Having Too Little." *Science* 338 (6107): 682–685. doi:10.1126/science.1222426.

Soman, Dilip, and Amar Cheema. 2011. "Earmarking and Partitioning: Increasing Saving by Low-Income Households." *Journal of Marketing Research* 48 (SPL): S14–S22. doi:10.1509/jmkr.48.SPL.S14.

Tarozzi, Alessandro, Aprajit Mahajan, Brian Blackburn, Dan Kopf, Lakshmi Krishnan, and Joanne Yoong. 2014. "Micro-loans, Insecticide-Treated Bednets, and Malaria: Evidence from a Randomized Controlled Trial in Orissa, India." *American Economic Review* 104 (7): 1909–1941. doi:10.1257/aer.104.7.1909.

Thaler, Richard H. 1980. "Toward a Positive Theory of Consumer Choice." *Journal of Economic Behavior & Organization* 1 (1): 39–60. Reprinting from pp 43-44, Copyright (1980), with permission from Elsevier, doi:10.1016/0167-2681(80)90051-7.

———. 1999. "Mental Accounting Matters." *Journal of Behavioral Decision Making* 12: 183–206. Copyright © 1999 John Wiley & Sons, Ltd., doi:10.1002/(sici)1099-0771(199909)12:3<183::aid-bdm318>3.0.co;2-f.

———. 2008. "Mental Accounting and Consumer Choice." *Marketing Science* 27 (1): 15–25. Republished with permission of INFORMS; permission conveyed through Copyright Clearance Center, Inc., doi:10.1287/mksc.1070.0330.

Warren, Patrick L., and Daniel H. Wood. 2010. "Will Governments Fix What Markets Cannot? The Positive Political Economy of Regulation in Markets with Overconfident Consumers." SSRN Scholarly Paper ID 1605146. Rochester, NY: Social Science Research Network. doi:10.2139/ssrn.1605146.

Wertenbroch, Klaus. 1998. "Consumption Self-Control by Rationing Purchase Quantities of Virtue and Vice." *Marketing Science* 17 (4): 317–337. doi:10.1287/mksc.17.4.317.

Yanagizawa-Drott, David. 2014. "Propaganda and Conflict: Evidence from the Rwandan Genocide." *The Quarterly Journal of Economics* 129 (4): 1947–1994. doi:10.1093/qje/qju020.

Index

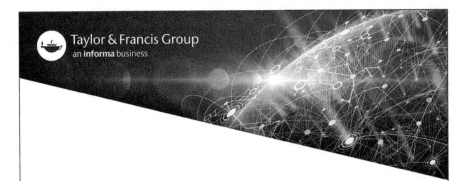

Printed in the United States
by Baker & Taylor Publisher Services